ILLUSTRATION INDEX VI: 1982-1986

by

Marsha C. Appel

The Scarecrow Press, Inc.
Metuchen, N.J., & London
1988

PREVIOUS VOLUMES:

Illustration Index, by Lucile E. Vance. New York: Scarecrow Press, 1957. Covers 1950 through June 1956.

Illustration Index, First Supplement, by Lucile E. Vance.
New York: Scarecrow Press, 1961. Covers July 1956
through 1959.

Illustration Index, Second Edition, by Lucile E. Vance and
Esther M. Tracey. New York and London: Scarecrow
Press, 1966. Covers 1950 through June 1963.

Illustration Index, Third Edition, by Roger C. Greer.
Metuchen, N.J.: Scarecrow Press, 1973. Covers July
1963 through December 1971.

Illustration Index IV, by Marsha C. Appel. Metuchen,
N.J., and London: Scarecrow Press, 1980. Covers
1972 through 1976.

Illustration Index V, by Marsha C. Appel. Metuchen, N.J.,
& London: Scarecrow Press, 1984. Covers 1977 through
1981.

British Library Cataloguing-in-Publication data available.

Library of Congress Cataloging-in-Publication Data

Appel, Marsha C., 1953-
    Illustration index VI, 1982-1986.

    1. Pictures--Indexes. I. Title.
N7525.A66 1988   011'.37   88-18207
ISBN 0-8108-2146-X

Dedicated to the three generations
in my little family.
To "my guys":
Al, Mark, and Sam.

PREFACE

This sixth volume of the Illustration Index is entirely new and covers the years 1982-1986. It follows the patterns of scope, style, and arrangement set in the fourth and fifth volumes. The depth of indexing is attested to by the existence of over 17,000 individual subject headings, encompassing about 35,000 entries.

Though not claiming to be totally comprehensive, the only illustrations methodically excluded are ads. Individual personalities are included, provided that the personality is considered of sufficient historical significance to warrant a separate article in the World Book Encyclopedia. The rationale for this criterion is the fact that photos of people enjoying ephemeral fame abound and can easily be located through the periodical indexes.

Each illustration within each journal article is treated separately, rather than indexing a few illustrations from an article to represent its major theme. This system of handling each picture individually allows better access to more obscure subject matter.

There is an extensive system of cross-references. It should be easy for a user unfamiliar with the volume to be steered to the proper entry by following related-term "see also's" and primary "see" references. In the interest of easy and multiple access to each citation, there are frequently three or more entries for one illustration, or several cross-references. Using the format and cross-reference structure of the World Book Encyclopedia, entries tend toward the specific. The Hudson, Amazon, Rio Grande, and Danube rivers can be found under their respective names, but there are "see also" references from RIVERS and from the states or countries in which they are located.

Several main listings operate as key locators to identify every example of a given category to be found alphabetically within the book. The following are the key listings:

Amusements	Indians of North America
Animals	Industries
Architectural Structures	Insects
Arms	Minerals
Art Forms	Mountains
Art Works (for art works	Musical Instruments
listed under individual	National Parks
artists' names)	Occupations
Arts & Crafts	Peoples
Birds	Plants
Boats	Rivers
Fish	Rulers & Monarchs
Flowering Plants	Sports
Geological Phenomena	Transportation
Housewares	Trees
Housing	Water Formations
	Weather Phenomena

Publications were selected for their richness of illustration and for the availability of back issues in libraries. All the periodicals indexed in the previous volume have been continued here.

A user desiring anything and everything on a specific country will go to the geographical entry. Here will be found general citations to illustrations of the country, perhaps some photographs of doctors or policemen there, maybe a farm or food market. But suppose the user wants pictures of policemen of various nationalities, or would like to see how farmers do their plowing in different parts of the world. The subject breakdowns are geared to yield just this sort of cross-cultural information. There is a major emphasis on historical and sociocultural phenomena, and a quick glance at the entries and cross-references under FESTIVALS, OCCUPATIONS, and RELIGIOUS RITES AND FESTIVALS will show just how extensive this coverage is. MILITARY COSTUME, for example, is indexed not only by different societies, but also by different centuries as well, introducing a valuable historical perspective.

Marsha C. Appel
Auburndale, New York

USER'S GUIDE

The following is an example of a typical citation under a
subject entry:

Nat Geog 170:124-5 (drawing,c,1) Jl '86

Most journal titles are abbreviated; "Nat Geog" refers to
National Geographic. A complete list of journal abbrevia-
tions used follows below in the list of periodicals indexed.
The journal designation is followed by the volume number
of the publication. After the colon comes inclusive pagina-
tion.

Most illustrations in the book are photographs. If the
text has identified an illustration as a painting, drawing,
or lithograph, etc., this additional information will appear
as the first item inside the parentheses. If the illustrations
are all photographs or a combination of photographs and
other pictorial forms, no special notation will be made.
There is one exception: if a map accompanies a set of
photographs, "map" will appear in the parentheses. If,
however, a map is the only illustration, the word "map" will
appear in the subject heading (e.g., GREAT BRITAIN--
MAPS).

The next item in the sample citation above is a "c,"
which indicates that the illustration is in color. Lack of a
"c" denotes black and white.

Size of illustration is the last item indicated within
the parentheses. There will always be a number from 1 to
4 present:

1   Full page or larger
2   ½ page or larger, but less than a full page

3   Larger than ¼ page, but less than ½ page
4   ¼ page or smaller

In the case of numerous illustrations in a single citation, the size of the largest one is indicated.

The date is the final item cited, with months in abbreviated form:

Ja	January	Jl	July
F	February	Ag	August
Mr	March	S	September
Ap	April	O	October
My	May	N	November
Je	June	D	December

PERIODICALS INDEXED

Here are the addresses for each publication where you
may write regarding reproduction rights to illustrations indexed in this volume. Please note that both National Geographic and Ebony state that their pictures are not generally
available to the public for reproduction purposes.

American Heritage
Rights and Permissions Dept.
60 Fifth Ave.
New York, N.Y. 10011

Smithsonian
Picture Editor
900 Jefferson Drive, S.W.
Washington, D.C. 20560

Life Picture Service
Room 2858
Time & Life Building
Rockefeller Center
New York, N.Y. 10020

Sports Illustrated
Editorial Rights Bureau
Room 1919
Time & Life Building
Rockefeller Center
New York, N.Y. 10020

National Wildlife Magazine
National Wildlife Federation
1412 16th Street, N.W.
Washington, D.C. 20036

Travel/Holiday
Reprints Department
51 Atlantic Avenue
Floral Park, N.Y. 11001

Natural History
Picture Editor
American Museum of Natural
    History
Central Park West at 79th
    Street
New York, N.Y. 10024

ILLUSTRATION INDEX

1

ACROBATIC STUNTS (cont.)
  Smithsonian 16:44-7 (c,3)
    Je '85
--Pie in the face
  Sports Illus 57:32 (c,3) N
    29 '82
--Qalandar people (Pakistan)
  Natur Hist 92:50-8 (c,1)
    My '83
--Raising woman on man's legs
  Life 5:73 (c,4) S '82
--Teenagers (Chicago, Illinois)
  Ebony 40:76-80 (2) S '85
--3 person pyramid
  Sports Illus 58:46 (c,4) My
    30 '83
--Tumbling at 1980 Olympics
    (Moscow, U.S.S.R.)
  Life 9:390-1 (c,1) Fall '86
--See also
    ATHLETIC STUNTS
    GYMNASTICS
ACROPOLIS, ATHENS, GREECE
  Smithsonian 12:44-53 (c,1)
    Mr '82
  Trav/Holiday 165:45 (c,2) Mr
    '86
--See also
    PARTHENON
ACTORS
--1920s actresses
  Life 7:8-13 (1) D '84
--1930s Hollywood stars
  Smithsonian 13:100-5 (2) F '83
--1943 M-G-M stars
  Life 9:20-1 (c,1) Fall '86
--Black entertainers
  Ebony 41:89-98, 124-34 (c,2)
    N '85
--Charles Macready
  Smithsonian 16:168-86 (c,4)
    O '85
--Movie stars in bathtubs
  Life 9:159-67 (c,2) My '86
--Patriotic activities during
    World War II
  Life 8:88-90 (c,2) Spring '85
--Recycled clothing from Holly-
    wood stars
  Life 9:125-9 (c,2) My '86
--Therapists working on Hollywood
    stars
  Life 9:63-72 (c,1) My '86
--See also
    ADAMS, MAUDE
    ASTAIRE, FRED
    BALL, LUCILLE

BARRYMORE, JOHN
BENCHLEY, ROBERT
BERGMAN, INGRID
BOGART, HUMPHREY
BOW, CLARA
BRANDO, MARLON
CAGNEY, JAMES
DAVIS, BETTE
DIETRICH, MARLENE
DUSE, ELEONORA
ENTERTAINERS
FAIRBANKS, DOUGLAS, JR.
FLYNN, ERROL
FONDA, HENRY
FORREST, EDWIN
GABLE, CLARK
GARBO, GRETA
GARLAND, JUDY
GISH, LILLIAN
GRABLE, BETTY
HARLOW, JEAN
HAYES, HELEN
HEPBURN, KATHARINE
LOMBARD, CAROLE
MONROE, MARILYN
OLIVIER, SIR LAURENCE
PICKFORD, MARY
ROBESON, PAUL
ROBINSON, EDWARD G.
ROGERS, GINGER
RUSSELL, LILLIAN
STEWART, JAMES
STRASBERG, LEE
SWANSON, GLORIA
TAYLOR, ELIZABETH
TEMPLE, SHIRLEY
THEATER
VON STROHEIM, ERICH
WAYNE, JOHN
WELLES, ORSON
ADAMS, HENRY BROOKS
  Am Heritage 38:27 (4) D '86
--1891 tomb of wife Clover (Wash-
    ington, D.C.)
  Am Heritage 36:52 (c,2) Je '85
ADAMS, JOHN
  Smithsonian 14:56 (painting,c,3)
    S '83
  Am Heritage 36:14 (drawing,4)
    F '85
  Am Heritage 38:27 (4) D '86
--The Adams family
  Am Heritage 38:27 (4) D '86
ADAMS, JOHN QUINCY
  Am Heritage 33:17 (4) Je '82
  Am Heritage 38:27 (4) D '86

ADAMS, MAUDE
  Am Heritage 33:64 (4) F '82
ADAMS, SAMUEL
  Smithsonian 16:124 (engrav-
    ing,4) Ap '85
  Am Heritage 38:27 (4) D '86
ADDERS
--Sidewinders
  Nat Wildlife 20:13 (c,3) O '82
  Nat Geog 164:364-5, 372-3
    (c,1) S '83
ADDIS ABABA, ETHIOPIA
  Nat Geog 163:624-5 (c,1) My
    '83
ADIRONDACK MOUNTAINS, NEW
    YORK
--The Flume
  Sports Illus 65:89 (c,3) O
    20 '86
ADOBE HOUSES
--Pueblos (New Mexico)
  Sports Illus 60:66 (c,2) Mr
    26 '84
ADVERTISING
--1820 ad for men's beaver hats
  Smithsonian 15:168 (4) N '84
--1872 ad for fireworks
  Am Heritage 34:4 (c,1) Je
    '83
--Late 19th cent. chocolate ads
  Smithsonian 16:55 (c,2) F
    '86
--1880s ads for cable cars
  Am Heritage 36:95, 114 (c,2)
    Ap '85
--1881 greeting card company ad
  Smithsonian 13:158 (c,4) D
    '82
--1883 first Metropolitan Opera
    ad, New York
  Am Heritage 34:6 (4) O '83
--1887 New Year ad for almanac
  Am Heritage 34:15 (c,4) D
    '82
--1890s ad for newspaper
  Am Heritage 33:64 (draw-
    ing,c,4) O '82
--1894 soda ad
  Smithsonian 17:122 (c,4) Jl '86
--20th cent. Wheaties cereal ads
  Sports Illus 56:70-80 (c,3)
    Ap 5 '82
--Early 20th cent. ads with
    Statue of Liberty theme
  Life 9:76-7 (c,3) Jl '86
--Early 20th cent. Coca-Cola ad
  Smithsonian 17:120 (c,3) Jl '86

--Early 20th cent. patent medicine
    ads
  Smithsonian 15:116-18 (4) Jl '84
--1905 ad for Borax
  Smithsonian 14:104 (c,4) N '83
--1913 Arrow shirt ad
  Am Heritage 36:cov. (c,1) Ap
    '85
--1920 billboard ad for laundry
    (Texas)
  Am Heritage 37:52 (4) F '86
--1920s-1930s (U.S.)
  Am Heritage 36:cov., 75-89
    (c,1) Ap '85
--1920s Fuller Brush ad
  Am Heritage 37:29 (c,3) Ag '86
--1920s posters advertising Chicago
    attractions
  Am Heritage 37:33-9, 114 (c,2)
    D '85
--1929 brick housing ad
  Am Heritage 35:29 (2) F '84
--1929 Cord automobile
  Nat Geog 164:24 (3) Jl '83
--1929 Franklin automobile
  Am Heritage 37:8 (painting,c,4)
    Ap '86
--1930s cereal ad
  Smithsonian 14:146 (4) D '83
--1930s supermarket ad
  Am Heritage 36:24 (4) O '85
--1935 cigarette ad starring Buster
    Crabbe
  Sports Illus 61:159 (c,3) Jl 18
    '84
--1936 magazine ads
  Life 9:50-6 (4) Fall '86
--Mid 20th cent. billboards
  Life 6:74-5 (c,4) Je '83
--1953 ad for air conditioner
  Am Heritage 35:20-1 (painting,c,1)
    Ag '84
--Appliance posters (China)
  Nat Geog 168:292-3 (c,1) S '85
--Baseball players in margarine
    commercial (1980)
  Sports Illus 62:84 (c,4) Mr 25 '85
--Catfish farm ad (Alabama)
  Natur Hist 91:76-7 (3) Jl '82
--Fifteen-foot tall beer can (Florida)
  Nat Geog 162:202 (c,3) Ag '82
--Filming an auto commercial
  Nat Geog 164:8-9 (c,1) Jl '83
--Reagan in beer poster (Great
    Britain)
  Sports Illus 65:2-3 (c,1) Jl 7 '86
--Reagan in Chesterfield cigarette ad

ADVERTISING (cont.)
  Sports Illus 64:76 (4) Mr 17
    '86
--Reagan in shirt ad (1949)
  Life 9:95 (4) My '86
--Tobacco ads painted on barns
    (Midwest)
  Smithsonian 13:112-13 (c,3)
    Ag '82
--Writing pen sign (India)
  Natur Hist 94:66 (c,4) F '85
--Using black celebrities
  Ebony 39:81-6 (c,3) Jl '84
--Using football player as en-
    dorser
  Sports Illus 64:40-1 (c,4)
    Mr 17 '86
--See also
    POSTERS
ADVERTISING--HUMOR
--Athletes endorsing sneakers
  Sports Illus 60:56-68 (draw-
    ing,c,1) Ja 23 '84
AFFENPINSCHERS (DOGS)
--Posing as acrobat
  Smithsonian 15:117 (2) S '84
AFGHANISTAN
--See also
    HINDU KUSH MOUNTAINS
    KABUL
AFGHANISTAN--COSTUME
  Nat Geog 167:497-505 (c,1)
    Ap '85
--Refugees (Pakistan)
  Life 7:16 (c,3) N '84
  Nat Geog 167:cov., 772-97
    (c,1) Je '85
AFGHANISTAN--HISTORY
--Mongol occupation of Afghani-
    stan
  Nat Geog 167:498 (c,4) Ap '85
AFGHANISTAN--POLITICS AND
    GOVERNMENT
--Refugees from Soviet warfare
    (Pakistan)
  Nat Geog 167:cov., 772-97
    (c,1) Je '85
--War with U.S.S.R.
  Life 7:22-8 (c,1) F '84
AFRICA
--Hot springs at Rift (Kenya)
  Nat Geog 168:560-1 (c,1) N '85
--See also
    AFRICAN TRIBES
    LAKE VICTORIA
    NILE RIVER
    SAHARA DESERT

    individual countries
AFRICA--MAPS
--Black nations
  Ebony 41:78 (2) N '85
--Tsetse fly areas
  Nat Geog 170:824 (c,2) D '86
AFRICA--SCULPTURE
  Smithsonian 16:212 (c,4) Ap '85
  Ebony 40:31-4, 38 (c,2) Jl '85
--Ancient Benin head
  Smithsonian 13:89 (c,1) F '83
--Funerary sculpture
  Smithsonian 12:144 (c,4) Ja '82
--Primitive sculpture
  Smithsonian 12:40-1 (c,4) F '82
AFRICAN TRIBES
  Nat Geog 166:600-33 (c,1) N '84
--Afars (Ethiopia)
  Nat Geog 163:620-1 (c,1) My '83
--Amhara (Ethiopia)
  Nat Geog 163:640-3 (c,1) My '83
--Ayt Brahim women (Morocco)
  Natur Hist 92:72 (c,2) Je '83
--Bamileke people (Cameroon)
  Nat Geog 166:614-15 (c,1) N '84
--Bozo people (Mali)
  Nat Geog 162:416-17 (c,1) S '82
--Dan (Ivory Coast)
  Nat Geog 162:106-7, 113 (c,1)
    Jl '82
--Dinka (Sudan)
  Life 5:156-9 (c,1) D '82
  Nat Geog 166:606-7 (c,2) N '84
--Diola people manhood rites (Sene-
    gal)
  Nat Geog 168:240-1 (c,1) Ag '85
--Kung people (Namibia)
  Nat Geog 161:770-1 (c,1) Je '82
--Makere man (Zaire)
  Natur Hist 91:76-7 (3) Mr '82
--Masai people (Kenya)
  Nat Geog 170:816-19 (c,1) D '86
--Masai warriors (Kenya)
  Nat Geog 166:608-9 (c,2) N '84
--Mondari (Sudan)
  Nat Geog 161:366 (c,2) Mr '82
--Murle people hunting (Sudan)
  Sports Illus 59:52-3 (c,1) S 5
    '83
--Mursi big-lipped woman (Ethiopia)
  Nat Geog 163:636-7 (c,1) My '83
--Ndebele people (South Africa)
  Nat Geog 169:cov., 261-82 (c,1)
    F '86
--Nuba man (Sudan)
  Sports Illus 65:63 (c,4) Ag 4
    '86

AFRICAN TRIBES (cont.)
--Nuba wrestling match (Sudan)
   Nat Geog 161:368-9 (c,1) Mr
      '82
--Nuers (Sudan)
   Nat Geog 161:350-1 (c,1) Mr
      '82
   Life 5:162 (c,2) D '82
   Nat Geog 167:618-21 (c,1)
      My '85
--Pokot people (Kenya)
   Nat Geog 161:121-39 (c,1) Ja
      '82
--Rendille people (Kenya)
   Nat Geog 166:610-11 (c,2) N
      '84
--Shilluk tribe (Sudan)
   Nat Geog 167:614-15 (c,1) My
      '85
--Surma (Sudan)
   Life 5:160 (c,2) D '82
--We tribe (Ivory Coast)
   Nat Geog 162:109, 112 (c,2)
      Jl '82
--Wodaabe people (Niger)
   Nat Geog 164:cov., 482-508
      (c,1) O '83
   Nat Geog 166:633 (c,1) N '84
--Yorba headdress (Nigeria)
   Trav/Holiday 157:44 (4) F
      '82
--See also
      ASANTE CIVILIZATION
      BERBER PEOPLE
      PYGMIES
AFRICAN VIOLETS
   Natur Hist 94:42 (c,1) F '85
AGASSIZ, ALEXANDER
   Am Heritage 34:99 (3) Ap '83
AGASSIZ, LOUIS
   Am Heritage 37:101 (2) Ag
      '86
   Smithsonian 17:146 (4) S '86
Agave plants. See
      CENTURY PLANTS
AGED
--1931 (France)
   Smithsonian 16:65 (1) S '85
--Australia
   Nat Geog 168:272 (c,1) Ag
      '85
--Celebrating birthday in nurs-
      ing home (California)
   Life 7:34 (3) F '84
--Centenarians (U.S.S.R.)
   Nat Wildlife 22:44 (c,4) D '83
--Couple married 81 years

   (Alabama)
   Life 9:34 (c,2) Jl '86
--Idaho
   Nat Geog 161:810-11 (c,1) Je
      '82
--Old woman (Poland)
   Nat Geog 170:366-7 (c,1) S '86
--Old woman born as slave
   Nat Geog 166:36-7 (c,1) Jl '84
--103 year old Indian (Washington)
   Life 6:78-9 (c,1) F '83
--103 year old Russian man (New
      York)
   Life 6:170 (c,2) D '83
--South Carolina
   Nat Geog 163:460-3 (c,1) Ap '83
--Wrinkled hands
   Ebony 39:30 (4) F '84
Agra, India. See
      TAJ MAHAL
AIDS. See
      DISEASES
AILANTHUS TREES
   Am Heritage 35:44-7 (c,1) Ap
      '84
   Am Heritage 35:14 (4) Ag '84
AIR CONDITIONERS
--1889 refrigerating company
      (Colorado)
   Am Heritage 36:110 (3) F '85
--1939
   Am Heritage 35:26 (4) Ag '84
--1950s air-conditioned bus (Texas)
   Am Heritage 36:13 (3) D '84
--1953 ad for air conditioner
   Am Heritage 35:20-1 (paint-
      ing,c,1) Ag '84
--History of air conditioning
   Am Heritage 35:cov., 20-33
      (c,1) Ag '84
Air Force. See
      U.S. AIR FORCE
AIR POLLUTION
--Acid rain
   Life 7:62-70 (c,1) N '84
--"American Gothic" figures wearing
      oxygen masks
   Life 6:59 (c,2) S '83
--Athens, Greece
   Smithsonian 12:47 (c,3) Mr '82
--Automobile catalytic converter
   Nat Geog 164:688-9 (c,1) N '83
--Mexico City, Mexico
   Nat Geog 166:154 (c,3) Ag '84
--New England
   Natur Hist 95:62-5 (c,2) Jl '86
--Poisonous gas sign (Wyoming)

AIR POLLUTION (cont.)
  Sports Illus 56:86 (4) My 17
    '82
--Smoke from chimneys (Alaska)
  Nat Wildlife 24:34 (c,4) Ap
    '86
--Smokestacks (Linz, Austria)
  Nat Geog 167:429 (c,4) Ap
    '85
--Steubenville, Ohio
  Life 5:84-90 (1) N '82
--Weather maps tracking pollu-
    tion paths
  Natur Hist 95:64-5 (c,3) Jl
    '86
AIRPLANE FLYING
--Aiming straight down in air
    show
  Sports Illus 60:90 (c,4) Je
    25 '84
--Blue Angels precision flying
  Ebony 41:27-34 (c,2) Je '86
--French flying team
  Life 9:8 (c,1) Jl '86
--Simulated flight in ultralight
    plane
  Nat Geog 164:200-1 (c,1)
    Ag '83
--Sitting in cockpit
  Sports Illus 61:88 (c,3) Jl 18
    '84
--Small plane
  Sports Illus 60:94-5 (c,1) Ja
    16 '84
--Stunt flying (Florida)
  Trav/Holiday 162:20 (c,3) D
    '84
--Stunt flying (Texas)
  Life 8:58-9 (1) My '85
--Stunt flying accident (New York)
  Life 8:68-9 (1) S '85
--Test pilots
  Life 7:50-1 (c,1) Ap '84
--Training on flight simulators
  Smithsonian 17:78-87 (c,2)
    Je '86
AIRPLANE PILOTS
  Ebony 39:46 (3) D '83
  Ebony 41:75, 78, 82 (c,3) F
    '86
--Early 20th cent. woman pilot
  Smithsonian 14:112-26 (c,1)
    Ja '84
--1910
  Am Heritage 36:107 (4) Je '85
--1920s air mail carriers
  Smithsonian 13:84-91 (1)

  My '82
--1930s
  Smithsonian 17:144 (1) N '86
--1943 Air Force pilot
  Smithsonian 13:149 (4) S '82
--Mongolia
  Nat Geog 167:248 (c,4) F '85
--Test pilots
  Life 7:47-56 (c,1) Ap '84
--Woman Air Force pilot
  Ebony 38:46-8 (3) Ja '83
--World War I pilot (U.S.)
  Smithsonian 15:113 (1) Ja '85
--See also
    CURTISS, GLENN
    EARHART, AMELIA
    LINDBERGH, CHARLES
    WRIGHT, WILBUR AND OR-
      VILLE
AIRPLANES
  Smithsonian 15:168 (4) My '84
--1906 box-kite plane
  Smithsonian 16:36-7 (c,4) My
    '85
--1908
  Smithsonian 15:27 (4) D '84
--1909 ultralight plane
  Nat Geog 164:200 (3) Ag '83
--1910 Blériot
  Smithsonian 16:148-9, 158 (1)
    S '85
--1910s Fokker
  Smithsonian 15:105 (4) Ja '85
--1912 Blériot XI monoplane
  Smithsonian 14:114, 121, 126
    (c,3) Ja '84
--1914 hydroplane
  Smithsonian 16:36-7 (c,4) My
    '85
--1919 Curtiss NC Flying Boat
  Am Heritage 37:66-7 (draw-
    ing,c,2) O '86
--1930s small private planes
  Smithsonian 17:153 (4) N '86
--1931 autogyro
  Am Heritage 34:110 (3) F '83
--1935 "China Clipper"
  Am Heritage 36:110-11 (4) O '85
  Smithsonian 16:184-204 (c,1) N
    '85
--1935 small private planes
  Am Heritage 36:110 (4) Ag '85
--1940s Curtis C-35 commando
  Am Heritage 37:112 (3) Je '86
--1940s Douglas SBD-2 Dauntless
  Am Heritage 37:69 (drawing,c,4)
    O '86

AIRPLANES (cont.)
    Nat Geog 161:440-1 (c,1) Ap
        '82
--Vietnam War plane wreckage
        (Laos)
    Nat Geog 170:692-6 (c,1) N
        '86
--"Voyager" lightweight aircraft
    Smithsonian 15:72-7 (c,1) F
        '85
--World War II German Stuka
    Smithsonian 13:174 (4) N '82
--World War II German war
        planes
    Smithsonian 14:36-7 (c,1) Ag
        '83
--World War II hospital plane
        (Italy)
    Smithsonian 12:122 (4) Ja '82
--World War II planes (U.S.)
    Ebony 38:45 (2) N '82
    Am Heritage 36:49 (2) O '85
--See also
        AIRPORTS
        AIRSHIPS
        AVIATION
        CRASHES
        CROP DUSTER PLANES
        HELICOPTERS
        ROCKETS
        SPACECRAFT
AIRPORTS
    Ebony 37:80 (4) Ap '82
--1985 Frankfurt Airport bomb-
        ing (West Germany)
    Life 8:50-1 (1) Ag '85
--Aerial view of runway (La-
        Guardia, New York)
    Smithsonian 17:81 (c,4) Je '86
--Airstrip (California)
    Sports Illus 62:86 (c,2) Ja
        14 '85
--Grenada
    Nat Geog 166:696-7 (c,1) N
        '84
--JFK, New York City, New York
    Ebony 40:136-42 (c,2) Je '85
--Los Angeles, California
    Ebony 42:152 (4) N '86
--Ticket counter
    Sports Illus 58:24 (c,4) F
        28 '83
AIRSHIPS
--Blimp race (New York)
    Sports Illus 65:2-3 (c,1) Jl
        14 '86
--World War II blimps

Am Heritage 33:34-5 (paint-
        ing,c,1) F '82
    Life 5:80-4 (c,1) Jl '82
ALABAMA
--Greene County historical plaque
    Ebony 37:147 (4) My '82
--Pickens County
    Ebony 37:144-6 (3) My '82
--Rural lifestyle
    Nat Geog 169:384-7 (c,1) Mr
        '86
--Tuskegee
    Ebony 37:52-9 (3) Jl '82
--See also
        BIRMINGHAM
        HUNTSVILLE
        MOBILE
        MONTGOMERY
ALAMO, TEXAS
    Smithsonian 16:54-67 (c,1) Mr
        '86
    Am Heritage 37:102 (4) Je '86
--1836 battle scenes
    Smithsonian 16:54-67 (c,1) Mr
        '86
--Alamo souvenirs
    Am Heritage 37:102-5 (c,2) Je
        '86
ALASKA
--1899 Harriman Alaska expedition
    Am Heritage 33:75-82 (c,2) Je
        '82
    Natur Hist 91:60 (4) Ag '82
--Arctic region
    Nat Geog 163:146-73, 222-3
        (map,c,1) F '83
--Brooks Range
    Nat Geog 163:170-1 (c,1) F '83
--Chilkat Mountains
    Life 8:16 (c,2) F '85
--Copper River
    Life 5:96-7 (c,1) N '82
--Countryside
    Nat Wildlife 22:10 (c,4) Je '84
--Frozen Innoko River
    Nat Geog 163:412-13 (c,1) Mr
        '83
--Glacier Bay
    Nat Wildlife 24:38-9 (c,1) D '85
--Glaciers
    Smithsonian 13:80-7 (c,1) Ja '83
    Trav/Holiday 161:57 (c,3) F '84
    Trav/Holiday 163:51-2 (c,1) F
        '85
    Nat Wildlife 24:38-45 (c,1) D '85
--Iditarod Trail Sled Dog Race
    Nat Geog 163:410-21 (c,1) Mr '83

ALASKA (cont.)
  Sports Illus 62:28-9 (c,1)
    Ap 1 '85
  Sports Illus 64:2-4, 90-107
    (map,c,1) F 17 '86
  Nat Wildlife 24:40-5 (c,1) F '86
--Kenai Peninsula
  Trav/Holiday 163:48-51 (c,1)
    Je '85
--Marshlands
  Nat Geog 168:552-3 (c,1) O
    '85
--Mount Veniaminof
  Smithsonian 14:161 (c,2) Mr
    '84
--Oil industry
  Natur Hist 91:8-18 (map,c,2)
    O '82
  Nat Geog 163:154 (c,1) F '83
--Postage stamp commemorating
    statehood
  Am Heritage 34:56 (c,4) D
    '82
  Nat Geog 164:554 (c,4) N '83
--Scenes along the Alaska Marine
    Highway
  Trav/Holiday 157:47-51 (c,1)
    My '82
--Skagway
  Trav/Holiday 161:57 (c,2) F
    '84
--Southeastern region
  Nat Geog 165:50-87 (map,c,1)
    Ja '84
--Thunder Bay
  Trav/Holiday 161:57 (c,3) F
    '84
--See also
    ALASKA PIPELINE
    ALASKA RANGE
    ALEUT PEOPLE
    ALEUTIAN ISLANDS
    ATTU ISLAND
    BERING SEA
    DENALI NATIONAL PARK
    ESKIMOS
    GOLD RUSH
    JUNEAU
    KATMAI NATIONAL PARK
    KETCHIKAN
    LAKE CLARK NATIONAL
      PARK
    MOUNT McKINLEY
    PRIBILOF ISLANDS
    SITKA
    TONGASS NATIONAL
      FOREST

ALASKA PIPELINE, ALASKA
  Nat Wildlife 24:34-5 (c,1) Ap '86
ALASKA RANGE, ALASKA
  Nat Geog 168:166-7 (c,1) Ag '85
  Nat Wildlife 24:44-5 (c,1) F '86
--See also
    MOUNT McKINLEY
ALASKAN MALAMUTES
  Ebony 38:92 (3) Mr '83
ALBATROSSES
  Nat Wildlife 23:4-11 (c,1) F '85
ALBERTA
--Chateau Lake Louise
  Trav/Holiday 162:27 (c,3) D '84
--See also
    BANFF NATIONAL PARK
    CALGARY
    EDMONTON
    LAKE LOUISE
ALBUQUERQUE, NEW MEXICO
  Trav/Holiday 161:62 (c,2) Ja '84
  Smithsonian 16:134 (c,4) My '85
ALCOHOLISM
--Drunk Eskimo on street (Alaska)
  Nat Geog 163:167 (c,3) F '83
--Man arrested for drunkenness
    (1933)
  Am Heritage 35:16 (4) D '83
--Ojibwa Indian drinking beer
    (Ontario)
  Natur Hist 94:66 (4) Jl '85
ALCOTT, LOUISA MAY
  Am Heritage 35:78 (drawing,4) F '84
--Bronson Alcott and family
  Am Heritage 37:73 (4) F '86
ALEUT PEOPLE (ALASKA)
--Costume and lifestyle
  Nat Geog 164:346-57 (c,1) S '83
ALEUTIAN ISLANDS, ALASKA
  Nat Geog 164:336-63 (map,c,1)
    S '83
--See also
    ALEUT PEOPLE
    ATTU ISLAND
ALEXANDER I (RUSSIA)
  Smithsonian 17:62, 67 (paint-
    ing,c,2) S '86
ALEXANDER THE GREAT
--Ancient stone bust
  Trav/Holiday 164:66 (c,4) Ag '85
ALEXANDRIA, EGYPT
--3rd cent. B.C. Pharos lighthouse
  Smithsonian 14:59 (drawing,4)
    Mr '84
ALEXANDRIA, VIRGINIA
--Flounder house
  Trav/Holiday 166:12 (c,4) N '86

ALFALFA
  Smithsonian 17:71 (c,2) S '86
ALFALFA INDUSTRY--
    HARVESTING
--Minnesota
  Smithsonian 17:68-79 (c,1) S
    '86
Algeria. See
    SAHARA DESERT
ALI, MUHAMMAD
  Ebony 41:60, 300 (3) N '85
--Clay-Liston fight (1964)
  Life 9:14-15 (c,1) Fall '86
--Training underwater (1961)
  Life 9:273-4 (2) Fall '86
ALLEGHENY NATIONAL FOREST,
    PENNSYLVANIA
--Tionesta Forest
  Natur Hist 95:74-8 (map,c,2)
    N '86
ALLEGHENY RIVER, PITTS-
    BURGH, PENNSYLVANIA
  Trav/Holiday 163:52-3 (c,1)
    My '85
ALLEN, FRED
  Am Heritage 37:46 (4) Ag '86
ALLIGATORS
  Smithsonian 15:73 (c,2) My
    '84
  Nat Wildlife 23:27 (c,4) D '84
  Nat Wildlife 23:58-9 (c,1) Ap
    '85
  Nat Wildlife 23:52-3 (c,1) O
    '85
  Nat Geog 169:58-9 (c,1) Ja
    '86
  Natur Hist 95:52-3 (c,1) Ja
    '86
  Trav/Holiday 165:46 (c,4) Ja
    '86
  Nat Wildlife 24:13 (c,4) Ap '86
--Baby alligators
  Nat Wildlife 24:2 (c,2) F '86
--Caymans
  Nat Geog 168:350-1 (c,1) S
    '85
  Natur Hist 95:42 (c,4) Mr '86
--Man wrestling alligator (Florida)
  Life 9:52-3 (c,1) Ag '86
ALMOND TREES
  Life 5:69 (c,3) Ap '82
  Nat Geog 166:55 (c,1) O '84
ALPHABETS
--Burma
  Nat Geog 166:119 (c,4) Jl '84
--Russian characters
  Nat Geog 163:210 (c,4) F '83

  Am Heritage 36:119 (4) D '84
--Viking alphabet
  Nat Geog 167:291 (c,4) Mr '85
--See also
    HIEROGLYPHICS
    ROSETTA STONE
    WRITING
ALPS, AUSTRIA
--Tyrol
  Nat Geog 167:436-7 (c,1) Ap '85
ALPS, FRANCE
  Trav/Holiday 164:56-9 (map,c,3)
    N '85
ALPS, ITALY
--Bormio
  Sports Illus 62:16-17 (c,1) F 18
    '85
ALPS, SWITZERLAND
  Nat Geog 169:98-9 (c,1) Ja '86
--Great St. Bernard Pass
  Nat Geog 161:154-5 (c,1) F '82
--See also
    MATTERHORN
AMARANTH (PLANT)
  Natur Hist 95:102-3 (c,1) Ap '86
AMAZON RIVER, BRAZIL
  Nat Geog 92:60-7 (c,1) Jl '83
--Dam sites
  Natur Hist 92:60-3 (map,c,1) Jl
    '83
AMBER
--Amber ornament (Latvia)
  Nat Geog 167:300 (c,4) Mr '85
--Insects trapped in amber
  Natur Hist 91:26-32 (c,1) Je '82
AMBULANCES
--Civil War
  Am Heritage 35:66-7 (1) O '84
--World War II
  Am Heritage 36:35 (4) F '85
AMERICA--DISCOVERY AND EX-
    PLORATION
--1519 Mexican conquest by Cortés
  Nat Geog 166:420-59 (map,c,1)
    O '84
--1523 painting of America's con-
    quest (Netherlands)
  Natur Hist 95:76 (c,4) D '86
--Late 16th cent. drawings from
    Drake's voyages
  Am Heritage 36:81-96 (c,1) Ag
    '85
--1585 map of Roanoke Island
  Am Heritage 34:34 (c,4) Ag '83
--1656 French map of New World
  Smithsonian 15:126 (c,3) My '84
--18th cent. travels of Daniel Boone

AMERICA--DISCOVERY AND
EXPLORATION (cont.)
--18th cent. travels of Daniel
Boone
Nat Geog 168:812-41
(map,c,1) D '85
--1899 Harriman Alaska expedition
Am Heritage 33:75-82 (c,2)
Je '82
Natur Hist 91:60 (4) Ag '82
--Drama about Roanoke settle-
ment (North Carolina)
Trav/Holiday 157:53 (c,3)
My '82
--La Salle claiming Mississippi
River for France (1682)
Am Heritage 33:6 (4) Ap '82
--Maps of possible Columbus
routes
Nat Geog 170:584-5, 588-9,
596 (c,1) N '86
--Retracing journeys of Columbus
Nat Geog 170:cov., 563-99
(map,c,1) N '86
--See also
EXPLORERS
AMERICAN SAMOA
Life 6:32-40 (c,1) My '83
Nat Geog 168:455-63
(map,c,1) O '85
--Pago Pago
Nat Geog 168:458-9 (c,1) O
'85
AMERICAN SAMOA--COSTUME
Life 6:32-40 (c,1) My '83
Nat Geog 168:455-63 (c,1) O
'85
--1920s
Smithsonian 14:66-72 (1) Ap
'83
AMISH PEOPLE
--Making buggy (Kansas)
Nat Geog 168:380 (c,4) S '85
--Ohio
Nat Wildlife 20:44-51 (c,1)
Ag '82
--Pennsylvania
Nat Geog 165:492-519 (c,1)
Ap '84
AMMAN, JORDAN
Nat Geog 165:252-5 (c,1) F
'84
Ammunition. See
ARMS
AMOS 'N ANDY
Am Heritage 37:46 (4) Ag '86
Am Heritage 37:8 (4) O '86

Amphibians. See
FROGS
SALAMANDERS
TOADS
AMSTERDAM, NETHERLANDS
Trav/Holiday 163:28-9 (4) Ja '85
--Anne Frank house
Trav/Holiday 163:29 (4) Ja '85
--Dam Square
Trav/Holiday 161:94 (4) Mr '84
--Houses
Trav/Holiday 163:48 (c,3) Mr
'85
--Red light district
Nat Geog 170:512-13 (c,2) O '86
AMUSEMENT PARKS
--Captain Hook's ship (Disneyland,
California)
Ebony 38:120 (c,4) Ja '83
--Cedar Point, Sandusky, Ohio
Life 8:33-8 (c,1) Ag '85
--Disney World, Orlando, Florida
Life 9:111 (c,3) Fall '86
--Epcot, Orlando, Florida
Trav/Holiday 158:28 (4) O '82
Life 5:138-9 (c,1) O '82
Life 5:I-XXIII (c,1) D '82
Ebony 38:122 (c,4) Ja '83
Am Heritage 35:70, 75, 79 (c,1)
D '83
--Geosphere (Epcot, Orlando,
Florida)
Nat Geog 162:176-7 (c,1) Ag '82
--Million-balloon salute to Disney-
land, California
Life 9:8-9 (c,1) F '86
--Ride at state fair (Missouri)
Trav/Holiday 162:40 (c,2) Ag '84
--Water slide (Israel)
Nat Geog 168:17 (c,3) Jl '85
--Water slide (Ontario)
Trav/Holiday 160:34 (4) N '83
--West Edmonton Mall, Alberta
Smithsonian 17:34-5, 42-3 (c,1)
D '86
--Willow Grove Park, Philadelphia,
Pennsylvania (1929)
Am Heritage 36:116-17 (1) D '84
--See also
CONEY ISLAND
FERRIS WHEELS
MERRY-GO-ROUNDS
PINBALL MACHINES
ROLLER COASTERS
Amusements. See
AMUSEMENT PARKS
ART GALLERIES

AMUSEMENTS (cont.)
    AUCTIONS
    AUDIENCES
    BATHING
    BEAUTY CONTESTS
    BILLIARD PLAYING
    BIRD WATCHING
    BULLFIGHTING
    CARD PLAYING
    CAVE EXPLORATION
    CIGAR SMOKING
    CIGARETTE SMOKING
    CIRCUSES
    CLUBS
    CONCERTS
    CONTESTS
    CROQUET PLAYING
    DANCES
    DANCING
    DOG SHOWS
    FAIRS
    FASHION SHOWS
    FERRIS WHEELS
    FESTIVALS
    FIREWORKS
    FLEA MARKETS
    FOLK DANCING
    GAMBLING
    GAME PLAYING
    GARDENING
    GUM CHEWING
    HAND SHAKING
    HEALTH CLUBS
    KISSING
    MAGIC ACTS
    MASSAGES
    MERRY-GO-ROUNDS
    MOTION PICTURES
    MUSEUMS
    MUSIC
    NIGHT CLUBS
    PARADES
    PARTIES
    PHOTOGRAPHY
    PICNICS
    PINBALL MACHINES
    PIPE SMOKING
    READING
    RESTAURANTS
    RODEOS
    ROLLER COASTERS
    ROMANCE
    ROPE JUMPING
    SAUNAS
    SEWING
    SPECTATORS
    SPORTS
    SUNBATHING
    TATTOOING
    TELEVISION WATCHING
    THEATER
    TOYS
    TREE CLIMBING
    WHISTLING
    ZOOS

ANATOMY
--15th cent. diagram of nervous
    system (Iran)
    Smithsonian 14:64 (c,4) Je '83
--Diagram of injured knee
    Sports Illus 63:41 (c,4) Jl 29
    '85
--Diagram of olfactory sense
    Nat Geog 170:336-7 (c,1) S '86
--Glands located in brain
    Natur Hist 92:20 (drawing,c,4)
    Je '83
--Human immune system
    Nat Geog 169:702-32 (c,1) Je
    '86
--Ovaries
    Life 5:46 (c,4) N '82
--Seen through medical scanning
    equipment
    Smithsonian 14:64-70 (c,1) Ja
    '84
--Smelling armpits for deodorant
    research
    Nat Geog 170:330-1 (c,1) S '86
--See also
    ANTLERS
    BLOOD
    BRAIN
    EYES
    FEET
    HANDS
    HEARTS
    SKIN
    TEETH
    TONGUES

ANCHORS
--18th cent. British ship
    Nat Geog 164:515 (c,4) O '83
--19th cent. "Monitor" ship
    Smithsonian 14:87 (c,4) O '83

ANCIENT WORLD
--Nabataean mausoleum (Saudi
    Arabia)
    Nat Geog 168:480-1 (c,1) O '85
--Nabataean ruins (Petra, Jordan)
    Nat Geog 165:236, 246-7 (c,1)
    F '84
    Trav/Holiday 163:29 (c,4) Je '85
    Nat Geog 168:513 (c,1) O '85

ANCIENT WORLD (cont.)
--Wonders of the Ancient World
   Smithsonian 14:59 (drawing,4)
     Mr '84
--See also
     ALEXANDER THE GREAT
     ARCHAEOLOGICAL SITES
     BABYLON
     EGYPT, ANCIENT
     GREECE, ANCIENT
     MAN, PREHISTORIC
     MESOPOTAMIA
     PERSIAN EMPIRE
     ROMAN EMPIRE
     ROSETTA STONE
ANCIENT WORLD--RELICS
--Bactrian gold sculpture and
   jewelry
   Natur Hist 94:68-70 (c,3) D
     '85
--Etruscan civilization (Italy)
   Smithsonian 15:cov., 48-57
     (c,1) F '85
ANDERSEN, HANS CHRISTIAN
--Andersen Museum, Odense,
   Denmark
   Trav/Holiday 157:55 (c,4) Je
     '82
--Sites related to him (Denmark)
   Trav/Holiday 157:cov., 50-5
     (c,1) Je '82
ANDERSON, MARIAN
   Smithsonian 14:136 (paint-
     ing,c,4) Je '83
   Ebony 40:122 (4) D '84
   Ebony 41:60, 272 (3) N '85
ANDES MOUNTAINS, ECUADOR
--Chimborazo
   Natur Hist 95:40-1 (c,1) F '86
ANDES MOUNTAINS, PERU
   Nat Geog 161:286-7, 308-9
     (c,1) Mr '82
ANGELES NATIONAL FOREST,
   CALIFORNIA
   Nat Geog 328-9, 338 (c,1) S
     '82
ANGELFISH
   Nat Wildlife 24:24 (sculp-
     ture,c,4) Ag '86
Angelico, Fra. See
     FRA ANGELICO
ANGELS
--15th cent. Fra Angelico
   painting
   Smithsonian 17:57 (c,3) D '86
--Decorating church
   Nat Geog 163:641 (paint-

     ing,c,1) My '83
ANGOLA--SOCIAL LIFE AND CUS-
   TOMS
--Traditional dance
   Ebony 42:132 (c,4) D '86
Animal sacrifice. See
     RELIGIOUS RITES AND
     FESTIVALS
ANIMAL SKINS
--Preparing caribou skins (Canada)
   Nat Geog 161:388 (c,1) Mr '82
--Snow leopard
   Nat Geog 169:806-7 (c,1) Je '86
--See also
     LEATHER INDUSTRY
ANIMAL TRACKS
   Nat Wildlife 20:12-16 (c,1) O '82
--Dinosaur trackways (Texas)
   Natur Hist 95:4-11 (3) Ag '86
--Grizzly bear print
   Nat Geog 167:683 (c,4) My '85
--Namib Desert, Namibia
   Nat Geog 164:364-5, 376-7 (c,1)
     S '83
ANIMAL TRAINERS
--1930s
   Am Heritage 34:61-2 (paint-
     ing,c,2) Ag '83
--Taming tigers
   Sports Illus 65:34-6, 41, 44
     (c,1) Jl 21 '86
ANIMALS
--Animal shelters
   Smithsonian 13:41-9 (1) S '82
--Animals of cretaceous and tertiary
   periods
   Nat Geog 170:408 (drawing,c,1)
     S '86
--Baby animals
   Nat Wildlife 21:50-9 (c,1) Ap '83
--Chart of animal lifespans
   Nat Wildlife 22:42 (c,2) D '83
--Endangered marbled cat
   Life 5:17 (4) Ag '82
--Endangered species
   Nat Wildlife 23:8-15 (c,1) Ap '85
   Nat Wildlife 24:6-13 (c,1) D '85
--Forest residents (Northwest)
   Nat Wildlife 24:8-9 (painting,c,1)
     F '86
--Jaguarundis
   Nat Wildlife 21:14, 17 (c,3) O
     '83
--Java wildlife, Indonesia
   Nat Geog 167:750-71 (c,1) Je '85
--Life in rain forests
   Nat Geog 163:12-19 (painting,c,1)

ANIMALS (cont.)
Ja '83
--Mythical creatures
Sports Illus 64:54-64 (draw-
ing,c,1) Ja 6 '86
--Paintings of wildlife
Nat Wildlife 24:14-19 (c,1) D
'85
--Serengeti National Park, Tan-
zania
Nat Geog 169:560-601 (c,1)
My '86
--Taxidermists' works
Nat Wildlife 23:22-4 (c,1) Ag
'85
--Under medical treatment
Smithsonian 15:76-85 (c,1)
Je '84
--Wildlife stamps
Nat Wildlife 24:16 (c,4) D '85
--Zoo babies
Life 5:cov., 42-8 (c,1) Je '82
--See also
AARDVARKS
AARDWOLVES
ALLIGATORS
ANTEATERS
ANTELOPES
ARMADILLOS
BADGERS
BATS
BEARS
BISON
BOARS, WILD
BOBCATS
BUFFALOES
BURROS
CAMELS
CARIBOU
CATS
CATTLE
CHEETAHS
CIVETS
COATIS
CONIES
COYOTES
DEER
DOGS
DOLPHINS
DONKEYS
DUGONGS
ECHIDNAS
ELEPHANTS
ELKS
FOXES
GIBBONS
GIRAFFES
GOATS
GUANACOS
HEDGEHOGS
HIPPOPOTAMI
HORSES
HYENAS
IBEXES
JACKALS
JAGUARS
KANGAROOS
LEOPARDS
LLAMAS
LYNXES
MARTENS
MINKS
MONGOOSES
MONKEYS
MOOSE
MOUNTAIN LIONS
MULES
MUSK OXEN
MUSKRATS
OCELOTS
OTTERS
PANDAS
PANGOLINS
PANTHERS
PIGS
PIKAS
PLATYPUSES
PORCUPINES
PRAIRIE DOGS
PRONGHORNS
RABBITS
RACCOONS
REINDEER
RHINOCERI
ROCKY MOUNTAIN GOATS
SEA COWS
SEALS
SHEEP
SHREWS
SLOTHS
SPONGES
SURICATES
TARSIERS
TASMANIAN DEVILS
TASMANIAN TIGERS
TIGERS
TREE SHREWS
WALRUSES
WATER BUFFALOES
WEASELS
WILDEBEESTS
WOLVERINES
WOLVES
WOODCHUCKS

ANIMALS (cont.)
>WORMS
>YAKS
>ZEBRAS
Animals--types. See
>AMPHIBIANS
>APES
>ARACHNIDS
>ARTHROPODS
>BIRDS
>CETACEANS
>COELENTERATES
>CRUSTACEANS
>ECHINODERMS
>FISH
>INSECTS
>MARINE LIFE
>MARSUPIALS
>MOLLUSKS
>POND LIFE
>REPTILES
>RODENTS
>WORMS
ANIMALS, EXTINCT
--Ancient animals (Australia)
>Nat Geog 169:38-9 (draw-
>ing,c,1) Ja '86
--Extinct animals of Mediter-
>ranean islands
>Natur Hist 95:52-7 (map,c,1)
>S '86
--Great Irish deer
>Natur Hist 91:60-1 (paint-
>ing,c,2) F '82
>Natur Hist 95:54 (drawing,4)
>Mr '86
--Sketches of prehistoric mammals
>Smithsonian 15:102-4 (c,3) Jl
>'84
--See also
>BIRDS, EXTINCT
>DINOSAURS
>MASTODONS
>SABER-TOOTHED CATS
>TRILOBITES
ANN ARBOR, MICHIGAN
>Trav/Holiday 163:68-71 (c,2)
>F '85
ANNAPOLIS, MARYLAND
>Trav/Holiday 161:39-40, 75
>(c,1) Ja '84
--1750 tavern
>Smithsonian 17:28 (c,4) S '86
--William Paca house and gardens
>Am Heritage 37:18 (c,4) O '86
ANTARCTIC EXPEDITIONS
>Nat Geog 163:544-61 (c,1)

>Ap '83
--1838 Wilkes expedition
>Smithsonian 16:48-63 (c,1) N '85
--Bipolar expedition
>Nat Geog 164:464-81 (c,1) O '83
ANTARCTICA
>Trav/Holiday 158:cov., 55, 57
>(c,1) N '82
>Smithsonian 13:44-9 (c,1) D '82
>Nat Geog 163:544-61 (c,1) Ap
>'83
>Nat Geog 164:472-9 (c,1) O '83
>Nat Wildlife 22:10-11 (c,1) D '83
>Smithsonian 15:cov., 48-61
>(map,c,1) O '84
>Nat Geog 166:634-59 (map,c,1)
>N '84
>Smithsonian 15:46-59 (c,1) N '84
>Life 8:32-7 (c,1) F '85
>Trav/Holiday 164:8-10 (c,2) N
>'85
--Marine life
>Nat Geog 169:494-511 (c,1) Ap
>'86
--Research expedition
>Smithsonian 17:116-27 (c,1) N
>'86
--See also
>SOUTH POLE
ANTARCTICA--MAPS
--Seymour Island
>Natur Hist 95:61-3 (c,4) My '86
ANTEATERS
>Smithsonian 14:74-80 (c,2) Ag
>'83
>Natur Hist 92:54-9 (c,1) O '83
--See also
>AARDVARKS
>ECHIDNAS
>PANGOLINS
ANTELOPES
>Am Heritage 33:34 (c,4) Je '82
>Sports Illus 65:cov., 56-63 (c,1)
>S 8 '86
--Bamana people sculpture (Mali)
>Ebony 40:31 (c,2) Jl '85
--Bongos
>Natur Hist 94:84 (painting,c,4)
>N '85
--Impalas
>Natur Hist 91:57 (c,4) My '82
>Nat Geog 169:570-1 (c,1) My '86
--Klipspringers
>Natur Hist 94:40-7 (c,1) N '85
--Lechwes
>Sports Illus 65:59 (c,4) S 8 '86
--Oryxes

ANTELOPES (cont.)
   Nat Wildlife 24:8-9 (c,1) D
      '85
   Sports Illus 65:58 (c,2) S 8
      '86
--See also
   BLACK BUCKS
   DIK-DIKS
   ELANDS
   KUDUS
   GAZELLES
   GEMSBOKS
   ROCKY MOUNTAIN GOATS
   SPRINGBOKS
ANTENNAS
--Microwave antennas
   Smithsonian 17:78 (c,2) N '86
--Satellite dishes
   Nat Geog 164:292-5 (c,1) S
      '83
ANTHONY, SUSAN B.
   Nat Geog 166:12 (painting,c,4)
      Jl '84
   Am Heritage 37:24, 29 (paint-
      ing,c,1) D '85
--Depicted on postage stamp
   Am Heritage 34:59 (c,4) D '82
Anthropologists. See
   LEAKEY, LOUIS S. B.
   MEAD, MARGARET
Antigua. See
   LEEWARD ISLANDS
Antilles. See
   list under WEST INDIES
ANTLERS
   Nat Wildlife 23:10-17 (c,1) O
      '85
   Natur Hist 95:cov., 54-65
      (c,1) Mr '86
   Smithsonian 17:98-108 (c,1)
      Jl '86
   Nat Geog 170:538-9, 555 (c,1)
      O '86
Antoinette, Marie. See
   MARIE ANTOINETTE
ANTS
   Nat Geog 163:52-6 (c,1) Ja
      '83
   Natur Hist 92:58 (c,4) O '83
   Nat Geog 165:774-813 (c,1)
      Je '84
   Natur Hist 93:78-84 (c,1) O
      '84
   Natur Hist 94:62-8 (c,1) S '85
   Natur Hist 94:48-52 (c,1) N
      '85
   Nat Geog 170:282-6 (c,1) Ag '86

--Acacia ants
   Smithsonian 17:113 (c,4) D '86
--Anthills
   Smithsonian 15:101 (c,3) Jl '84
--Fire ants
   Nat Wildlife 22:46-8 (drawing,c,1)
      Ap '84
--Harvester ants
   Smithsonian 15:99 (c,3) Jl '84
--Honey
   Nat Wildlife 21:2 (c,1) F '83
   Natur Hist 95:24-5 (c,4) Mr '86
--Larvae
   Nat Geog 163:53 (c,4) Ja '83
--Leafcutter ants
   Smithsonian 15:92-101 (c,1) O
      '84
--Marauder ants
   Nat Geog 170:272-86 (c,1) Ag
      '86
--Preserved in amber
   Natur Hist 91:28 (c,1) Je '82
--Weaver ants
   Nat Wildlife 23:27 (c,1) F '85
APACHE INDIANS (ARIZONA)
--Coming-of-age pollen powder rite
   Nat Geog 166:518 (c,4) O '84
APARTMENT BUILDINGS
--1930s (New York City)
   Am Heritage 35:23 (1) Ag '84
--1960s public housing (Paris,
      France)
   Smithsonian 17:99 (c,4) D '86
--Abandoned (Scotland)
   Nat Geog 166:57 (c,3) Jl '84
--Baghdad, Iraq
   Nat Geog 167:91 (c,3) Ja '85
--Beirut, Lebanon
   Nat Geog 163:268-9 (c,1) F '83
   Life 7:30-1 (1) Ag '84
--Cambridge, Massachusetts
   Life 9:59 (c,2) N '86
--The Dakota, New York City,
      New York
   Life 7:91-8 (c,1) D '84
--Lima, Peru
   Trav/Holiday 157:49 (c,2) Ja '82
--Miami Beach, Florida
   Nat Geog 162:175 (c,3) Ag '82
--New Delhi, India
   Nat Geog 167:520-1 (c,1) Ap '85
--New York City, New York
   Nat Wildlife 22:34 (c,2) O '84
--Rotterdam, Netherlands
   Nat Geog 170:500-1 (c,1) O '86
--Tokyo, Japan
   Nat Geog 170:634-5 (c,1) N '86

APES
--Bush babies
   Nat Geog 163:370 (c,4) Mr
      '83
--Museum specimens
   Life 6:92-3 (c,1) D '83
--See also
   BABOONS
   CHIMPANZEES
   GIBBONS
   GORILLAS
   MONKEYS
   ORANGUTANS
APHIDS
   Nat Wildlife 20:22 (c,4) Ag '82
   Nat Wildlife 21:45-9 (c,1) Je
      '83
   Smithsonian 16:68-74 (c,1) Jl
      '85
APPALACHIAN MOUNTAINS,
      KENTUCKY
   Nat Geog 168:822-3 (c,1) D
      '85
APPALACHIAN MOUNTAINS,
      VIRGINIA
--Satellite photo
   Nat Geog 168:168-9 (c,1) Ag
      '85
APPALACHIAN TRAIL, EASTERN
      U.S.
--Autumn scenes
   Life 9:38-48 (c,1) O '86
APPLE INDUSTRY--HARVESTING
--New Hampshire
   Life 9:125 (c,4) Ja '86
APPLE TREES
   Nat Wildlife 20:4, 10-11 (c,4)
      O '82
   Smithsonian 17:122-33 (c,1)
      S '86
--Dwarf trees
   Smithsonian 12:57 (c,4) Mr '82
APPLES
   Ebony 40:118 (c,4) O '85
   Smithsonian 17:123, 130, 132
      (c,4) S '86
--As food for wildlife
   Nat Wildlife 20:5-11 (c,1) O
      '82
--See also
   CRAB APPLES
Appliances. See
   AIR CONDITIONERS
   FANS
   HAIR DRYERS
   HEATERS
   SEWING MACHINES

STOVES
APRICOT INDUSTRY
--Drying apricots (California)
   Nat Geog 162:473 (c,3) O '82
AQUARIUMS
--Baltimore, Maryland
   Trav/Holiday 163:670-1 (c,1) Je
      '85
--Home aquarium
   Sports Illus 59:62 (c,4) S 12 '83
--Miniature kitchen in fish tank
   Life 7:80 (c,2) F '84
--Monterey Bay Aquarium, California
   Smithsonian 16:94-100 (c,1) Je
      '85
   Trav/Holiday 166:18 (c,3) Ag '86
ARABIAN DESERT, SAUDI ARABIA
--Archaeological finds
   Smithsonian 14:cov., 42-53 (c,1)
      S '83
ARABS--COSTUME
   Natur Hist 92:52-9 (c,1) Jl '83
--Dubai
   Sports Illus 65:80-1, 90-2 (c,1)
      D 1 '86
Arachnids. See
   DADDY LONGLEGS
   KING CRABS
   MITES
   SPIDERS
   TICKS
ARAPAHO INDIANS--RELICS
--19th cent. buckskin shield
   Am Heritage 37:22 (c,3) Ag '86
ARC DE TRIOMPHE, PARIS,
      FRANCE
   Sports Illus 65:12-13 (c,1) Ag
      4 '86
ARCHAEOLOGICAL SITES
--15th cent. Columbus sites (Samana
      Cay, Bahamas)
   Nat Geog 170:578-9 (c,1) N '86
--16th cent. Basque whaling port
      (Labrador, Newfoundland)
   Nat Geog 168:cov., 40-71
      (map,c,1) Jl '85
--Alexandria, Virginia
   Am Heritage 34:42-3 (c,3) Ag
      '83
--Arago, France
   Nat Geog 168:608 (c,2) N '85
--Burgess Shale, British Columbia
   Natur Hist 94:30, 34-9 (c,1) D
      '85
--Dakhla basin Egypt
   Nat Geog 161:219 (c,3) F '82
--Ephesus, Turkey

ARCHAEOLOGY (cont.)
    everyday artifacts
    Am Heritage 34:2 (c,2) Ag '83
--Sorting pottery shards (Bahamas)
    Nat Geog 170:580-1 (c,1) N
      '86
--Underwater archaeology (Florida)
    Smithsonian 17:72-83 (c,1) D
      '86
ARCHERFISH
    Nat Geog 167:764 (c,2) Je '85
ARCHERY
    Sports Illus 59:36-8 (c,2) O
      10 '83
    Sports Illus 60:78 (c,4) Mr 5
      '84
    Life 7:126-7 (c,1) Je '84
    Sports Illus 61:26-7 (c,1) S
      5 '84
--16th cent. archer (Great Britain)
    Nat Geog 163:664 (painting,c,2)
      My '83
--16th cent. longbows and arrows
    (Great Britain)
    Nat Geog 163:664-5 (c,2) My
      '83
--Late 19th cent. child
    Smithsonian 12:44 (4) Ja '82
--Agta people hunting (Philippines)
    Natur Hist 95:36-41 (c,1) My
      '86
--Japanese kyudo
    Nat Geog 169:534 (c,4) Ap '86
--Karuk Indian (1926)
    Smithsonian 15:161 (4) Ap '84
--Ultramodern bow
    Smithsonian 17:36-7 (c,4) Ap
      '86
ARCHITECTS
    Smithsonian 15:59 (c,4) Je '84
    Ebony 39:52-60 (c,2) Je '84
    Ebony 42:148-50 (3) N '86
--1884 drafting room
    Am Heritage 34:94 (drawing,c,1) D '82
--See also
      BLUEPRINTS
      OLMSTEAD, FREDERICK
        LAW
      WRIGHT, FRANK LLOYD
ARCHITECTURAL FEATURES
--Firemen's pole in house (Texas)
    Sports Illus 63:63 (c,2) N
      11 '85
--See also

    BATHROOMS
    BEDROOMS
    BENCHES
    CHIMNEYS
    DINING ROOMS
    DOORS
    ESCALATORS
    FENCES
    FIREPLACES
    FOUNTAINS
    GATES
    KITCHENS
    LIVING ROOMS
    OUTHOUSES
    PARKING LOTS
    PARLORS
    STAIRCASES
    STUDIES
    SWINGS
    WALLS
    WINDOWS
Architectural structures. See
    AIRPORTS
    APARTMENT BUILDINGS
    ART GALLERIES
    BARBERSHOPS
    BANKS
    BARNS
    BOATHOUSES
    BRIDGES
    CAPITOL BUILDINGS
    CAR WASHES
    CASTLES
    CHATEAUS
    CHURCHES
    CITADELS
    CITY HALLS
    COURTHOUSES
    DAMS
    EMBASSIES
    FACTORIES
    FARMHOUSES
    FIREHOUSES
    FORTRESSES
    FORTS
    GAMBLING CASINOS
    GASOLINE STATIONS
    GOVERNMENT BUILDINGS
    GREENHOUSES
    HOSPITALS
    HOTELS
    HOUSES
    HOUSING
    LABORATORIES
    LABYRINTHS
    LIBRARIES
    LIGHTHOUSES

ARCTIC, NORWAY
  Nat Geog 163:148-9, 194-7
    (map,c,1) F '83
ARCTIC, U.S.S.R.
  Nat Geog 163:207-23 (c,1) F
    '83
ARCTIC EXPEDITIONS
  Nat Geog 164:100-26 (c,1) Jl
    '83
--Early 19th cent. Franklin ex-
    peditions
  Smithsonian 16:116-30
    (map,c,1) Je '85
  Nat Geog 169:128-40
    (map,c,1) Ja '86
--Early 20th cent.
  Ebony 39:80-4 (4) N '83
--1909 Peary expedition
  Nat Geog 170:295 (4) S '86
--1909 North Pole explorer
  Ebony 40:114 (4) S '85
--Bipolar expedition
  Nat Geog 164:464-81 (c,1) O
    '83
--Dogsled expedition to North
    Pole
  Nat Geog 170:cov., 288-323
    (map,c,1) S '86
  Sports Illus 65:122-3 (c,1) D
    22 '86
--Ill-fated 1897 balloon trip
  Smithsonian 14:122-36 (c,3)
    My '83
--Peary commemorative stamp
    (1961)
  Am Heritage 34:52 (c,4) D '82
--U.S. flag sent to the North Pole
    (1909)
  Nat Geog 165:280 (c,4) Mr
    '84
ARGENTINA
  Nat Geog 170:226-55 (map,c,1)
    Ag '86
--Desert land
  Life 7:64-5 (c,1) Ap '84
--Patagonia
  Smithsonian 16:72-84 (map,c,1)
    O '85
--See also
    BUENOS AIRES
    IGUAÇU FALLS
    TIERRA DEL FUEGO
ARGENTINA--COSTUME
  Nat Geog 170:226-55 (c,1) Ag
    '86
Argentina--History. See
    PERON, JUAN
ARGENTINA--HOUSING
--Ranch house
  Nat Geog 170:234-5 (c,1) Ag '86
ARGENTINA--POLITICS AND GOV-
    ERNMENT
--Crowds listening to president
  Nat Geog 170:230-1 (c,1) Ag '86
--Victims of 1970s military dictator-
    ship
  Life 7:34-42 (c,1) My '84
ARIZONA
--Aerial view of Scottsdale housing
    development
  Nat Wildlife 24:22-3 (c,1) Ap '86
--Bradshaw Mountains
  Natur Hist 95:30-2 (map,c,1) Jl
    '86
--Canyon de Chelly
  Nat Geog 162:72-3 (c,1) Jl '82
--Desert
  Sports Illus 59:28-9 (c,1) D 5
    '83
--Glen Canyon Dam, Colorado River
  Nat Wildlife 23:44-5 (c,1) O '85
--Lake Powell
  Natur Hist 91:80-1 (c,1) Ja '82
--Landscape
  Natur Hist 92:80 (c,4) F '83
--Little Colorado River
  Life 5:125 (c,1) O '82
--Meteor Crater
  Nat Geog 170:392-3 (c,1) S '86
--Oak Creek Canyon
  Natur Hist 94:34-6 (c,1) Ja '85
--Peralta Canyon
  Natur Hist 95:28-32 (map,c,1)
    D '86
--Postage stamp commemorating
    statehood (1961)
  Am Heritage 34:52 (c,4) D '82
--Sonoran Desert
  Smithsonian 13:48 (c,4) F '83
  Natur Hist 93:47 (c,1) Ja '84
  Natur Hist 95:74-5 (c,1) Ap '86
--Southeast Arizona desert
  Natur Hist 93:85 (c,1) O '84
--Superstition Mountains
  Trav/Holiday 160:40-3 (c,2) O
    '83
  Natur Hist 95:28-9, 31 (c,1)
    D '86
--Sycamore Canyon
  Natur Hist 93:cov., 86-9
    (map,c,1) N '84
--Use of Colorado River water

ARMS (cont.)
    CAMOUFLAGE
    CANNONS
    DAGGERS
    DUELS
    EXPLOSIONS
    GUNS
    HARPOONS
    HOWITZERS
    KNIVES
    MILITARY COSTUME
    MINES, EXPLODING
    MISSILES
    RIFLES
    SUBMARINES
    SWORDS
    TANKS, ARMORED
    TOOLS
ARMSTRONG, LOUIS
  Ebony 40:122 (4) D '84
  Ebony 41:131 (4) F '86
--Statue (New Orleans, Louisiana)
  Ebony 38:34 (4) Mr '83
Army. See
    MILITARY COSTUME
    U.S. ARMY
ARNO, PETER
--Cartoon about the Automat
  Smithsonian 16:51 (4) Ja '86
ART EDUCATION
--1907 painting class
  Smithsonian 13:121 (3) Mr '83
Art forms. See
    CARTOONS
    CAVE PAINTINGS
    COLLAGES
    COMIC STRIPS
    DESIGN, DECORATIVE
    FIGUREHEADS
    FRESCOES
    GRAFFITI
    HOLOGRAPHY
    KALEIDOSCOPES
    METALWORK
    MOSAICS
    MURALS
    NEEDLEWORK
    PAINTINGS
    PHOTOGRAPHY
    POSTERS
    POTTERY
    RESTORATION OF ART
      WORKS
    ROCK CARVINGS
    ROCK PAINTINGS
    SCULPTURE
    SILHOUETTES

    SNOW SCULPTURES
    STAINED GLASS
    TAPESTRIES
    TOTEM POLES
    WOOD CARVINGS
ART GALLERIES
--Huntington, San Marino, California
  Smithsonian 12:64-73 (c,1) F '82
ART WORKS
--1920s-1930s
  Smithsonian 17:156-67 (c,1) N '86
--Aerial views of patterned farms
  Nat Geog 166:390-9 (c,1) S '84
  Nat Wildlife 24:53-9 (c,1) O '86
--Art forgeries
  Smithsonian 16:60-9 (c,1) O '85
--Art glass
  Life 5:78-82 (c,1) F '82
  Smithsonian 15:140-7 (c,1) O '84
--Artistic paper snowflakes
  Sports Illus 65:26 (c,4) D 22 '86
--Buffalo nickels recarved by hoboes
  Am Heritage 34:81-3, 114 (c,2) Ag '83
--Cigar box art
  Sports Illus 57:74-81 (c,1) D 27 '82
--Contemporary works by black Americans
  Ebony 41:46-54 (c,3) My '86
--Emerging artists
  Smithsonian 13:128-33 (c,2) My '82
--Fabergé jeweled eggs (U.S.S.R.)
  Smithsonian 14:cov., 46-53 (c,1) Ap '83
  Smithsonian 14:12 (c,4) Je '83
--Farmland portrait of Will Rogers (Kansas)
  Nat Geog 168:370-1 (c,1) S '85
--Folk art (Shelbourne Museum, Vermont)
  Am Heritage 33:17-29 (c,1) Ap '82
--Graphics by Milton Glaser
  Smithsonian 15:117-21 (c,2) F '85
--Michael Heizer's land sculpture
  Smithsonian 17:68-77 (c,1) Ap '86
--Human formation of Statue of Liberty (1918)
  Life 9:80 (2) Jl '86
--Illustrated house facades (Switzerland)

ART WORKS (cont.)
  Trav/Holiday 166:38 (c,4)
    N '86
--International folk art
  Life 5:103-8 (c,1) N '82
--Made from trash
  Smithsonian 14:82-91 (c,1)
    Ag '83
--Modern art
  Life 5:83-6 (c,2) My '82
  Lie 8:46-52 (c,1) My '85
--Pennsylvania Dutch hex signs
    (Pennsylvania)
  Trav/Holiday 165:79 (c,4) My
    '86
--Pont Neuf wrapped in nylon
    by Christo, Paris, France
  Life 8:74-5 (1) N '85
--Sidewalk chalk "Mona Lisa"
    (Madrid, Spain)
  Nat Geog 169:161 (c,2) F '86
--Street art at Vienna Festival,
    Austria
  Nat Geog 167:411 (c,1) Ap '85
--Studio glass art works
  Smithsonian 15:192 (c,4) Ap
    '84
--Treasures of Ashmolean Museum,
    Oxford, England
  Smithsonian 14:114-25 (c,1)
    S '83
--Treasures of Fitzwilliam Mu-
    seum, Cambridge, England
  Smithsonian 14:115-25 (c,1) S
    '83
--Vatican treasures
  Smithsonian 13:120-31 (c,1) D
    '82
  Life 5:58-70 (c,1) D '82
  Nat Geog 168:764-77 (c,1) D
    '85
--Video sculpture
  Life 6:74 (c,1) Ja '83
--Works by Friedensreicht Hun-
    dertwasser
  Smithsonian 16:74-85 (c,1)
    Ja '86
--See also
      ABBOTT, BERENICE
      ARNO, PETER
      AUDUBON, JOHN JAMES
      BARTHOLDI, FREDERIC
        AUGUSTE
      BEERBOHM, SIR MAX
      BELLINI, GENTILE
      BIERSTADT, ALBERT
      BINGHAM, GEORGE CALEB

BLAKE, WILLIAM
BOSCH, HIERONYMUS
BOTTICELLI, SANDRO
BOUCHER, FRANCOIS
BOURKE-WHITE, MARGARET
BREUGHEL, JAN THE ELDER
BREUGHEL, PIETER THE
  ELDER
CALDER, ALEXANDER
CARAVAGGIO
CASSATT, MARY
CATLIN, GEORGE
CEZANNE, PAUL
CHAGALL, MARC
CONSTABLE, JOHN
COPLEY, JOHN SINGLETON
CRANACH, LUCAS THE
  ELDER
CURRIER & IVES
DALI, SALVADOR
DAUMIER, HONORE
DAVID, JACQUES LOUIS
DEGAS, EDGAR
DELACROIX, FERDINAND
DÜRER, ALBRECHT
EAKINS, THOMAS
EL GRECO
FABERGE, CARL
FRA ANGELICO
GAINESBOROUGH, THOMAS
GAUGUIN, PAUL
GHIRLANDAIO, DOMENICO
GIOTTO
GOYA, FRANCISCO
HALS, FRANS
HELD, JOHN, JR.
HENRI, ROBERT
HOMER, WINSLOW
HOPPER, EDWARD
INNESS, GEORGE
KANDINSKY, VASILY
LEAR, EDWARD
LEGER, FERNAND
LEONARDO DA VINCI
LICHTENSTEIN, ROY
MAGRITTE, RENE
MANET, EDOUARD
MARSH, REGINALD
MATISSE, HENRI
MICHELANGELO
MILLAIS, SIR JOHN EVERETT
MIRO, JOAN
MODIGLIANI, AMADEO
MONDRIAN, PIET
MONET, CLAUDE
MOORE, HENRY
MORSE, SAMUEL F. B.

ART WORKS (cont.)
    NAST, THOMAS
    O'KEEFFE, GEORGIA
    PEALE, CHARLES WILLSON
    PHIDIAS
    PICASSO, PABLO
    POLLAIUIOLO, ANTONIO
    POLLOCK, JACKSON
    RAPHAEL
    REMBRANDT
    REMINGTON, FREDERIC
    RENOIR, PIERRE AUGUSTE
    REYNOLDS, SIR JOSHUA
    RIVERA, DIEGO
    ROCKWELL, NORMAN
    RODIN, AUGUSTE
    ROGERS, RANDOLPH
    ROSSETTI, DANTE GABRIEL
    ROUSSEAU, HENRI
    RUBENS, PETER PAUL
    RUISDAEL, JACOB VAN
    RUSSELL, CHARLES
      MARION
    ST. GAUDENS, AUGUSTUS
    SARGENT, JOHN SINGER
    SLOAN, JOHN
    STIEGLITZ, ALFRED
    STUART, GILBERT
    TITIAN
    TOULOUSE-LAUTREC,
      HENRI DE
    UCCELLO, PAOLO
    VAN GOGH, VINCENT
    VELASQUEZ, DIEGO
    VERMEER, JOHANNES
    WATTEAU, ANTOINE
    WEST, BENJAMIN
    WHISTLER, JAMES McNEILL
    WOOD, GRANT
    WYETH, ANDREW
ARTESIAN WELLS
--California
  Smithsonian 13:50 (c,1) Mr
  '83
Arthropods. See
    ARACHNIDS
    CRUSTACEANS
    INSECTS
    MILLIPEDES
    TRILOBITES
ARTISTS
  Nat Wildlife 21:43 (4) F '83
  Am Heritage 34:4, 81-9
    (painting,c,1) F '83
--19th-20th cent. studios
  Am Heritage 34:4, 81-9
    (painting,c,1) F '83

--Early 20th cent.
  Smithsonian 13:124 (4) Mr '83
--Henry Alexander self-portrait
  Smithsonian 12:116 (painting,4)
  Mr '82
--Ethiopia
  Nat Geog 163:624 (c,4) My '83
--Henri Fantin-Latour self-portrait
  Smithsonian 14:73 (painting,c,4)
  Jl '83
--Fantin-Latour's painting of French
  impressionists
  Smithsonian 14:75 (painting,c,3)
  Jl '83
--John F. Kensett
  Smithsonian 16:58 (4) Jl '85
--Joan Miro's studio (Spain)
  Life 7:75 (c,2) F '84
--Mondrian studio (1930)
  Smithsonian 12:116 (4) F '82
--Painting of Mark Rothko by Milton
  Avery
  Smithsonian 13:112 (c,4) O '82
--Renoir's studio (France)
  Life 8:54 (c,2) O '85
--Charles Russell's studio (Montana)
  Nat Geog 169:78-9 (c,1) Ja '86
--Sculptors' studio (New Jersey)
  Smithsonian 13:111 (c,4) Ap '82
--Everett Shinn
  Am Heritage 37:67 (4) D '85
--Sidewalk artists (Italy)
  Smithsonian 13:58 (c,3) N '82
--Studios (New York)
  Smithsonian 14:98-9 (c,3) D '83
--James Tissot portrait by Edgar
  Degas (1868)
  Smithsonian 15:134 (painting,c,3)
  D '84
--See also
    AUDUBON, JOHN JAMES
    CARTOONISTS
    CHAGALL, MARC
    CONSTABLE, JOHN
    DALI, SALVADOR
    EAKINS, THOMAS
    EL GRECO
    ERNST, MAX
    FABERGE, CARL
    GIACOMETTI, ALBERTO
    GROSZ, GEORGE
    HELD, JOHN, JR.
    HENRI, ROBERT
    KANDINSKY, VASILY
    LEGER, FERNAND
    LICHTENSTEIN, ROY
    LIPSCHITZ, JACQUES

ARTISTS (cont.)
    MANET, EDOUARD
    MATISSE, HENRI
    MIRO, JOAN
    MONDRIAN, PIET
    MONET, CLAUDE
    MOORE, HENRY
    MORSE, SAMUEL F. B.
    O'KEEFFE, GEORGIA
    PAINTING
    PICASSO, PABLO
    REMBRANDT
    RENOIR, PIERRE AUGUSTE
    RIVERA, DIEGO
    RODIN, AUGUSTE
    ROUSSEAU, HENRI
    RUSSELL, CHARLES MARION
    ST. GAUDENS, AUGUSTUS
    SARGENT, JOHN SINGER
    SCULPTING
    STUART, GILBERT
    TOULOUSE-LAUTREC,
        HENRI DE
    VAN GOGH, VINCENT
    WARHOL, ANDY
    WEST, BENJAMIN
    WHISTLER, JAMES McNEILL
    WOOD, GRANT
    WYETH, ANDREW
ARTS AND CRAFTS
--Black folk crafts (South)
    Life 6:52-8 (c,1) Ag '83
--Making plastic food (Japan)
    Smithsonian 14:129-37 (c,1)
        Mr '84
--Origami cat
    Natur Hist 92:70 (3) D '83
--Sandblasted glass panels
    Smithsonian 14:112-17 (c,1)
        F '84
--Straw plaiting (Bahamas)
    Nat Geog 162:388-9 (c,1) S '82
--U.S. crafts
    Life 9:83-6 (c,1) Jl '86
--See also
    BARRELL MAKING
    BASKET WEAVING
    BLACKSMITHS
    CANDLE MAKING
    CARPENTRY
    COLLAGES
    DESIGN, DECORATIVE
    HOLOGRAPHY
    METALWORKING
    NEEDLEWORK
    PAINTING
    POTTERY MAKING

    QUILTING
    SCULPTING
    SEWING
    SILHOUETTES
    WEAVING
    WOOD CARVING
    WOOD WORKING
    YARN SPINNING
ARUBA, NETHERLANDS ANTILLES
    Trav/Holiday 161:74 (c,3) F '84
ARUBA, NETHERLANDS ANTILLES
    --COSTUME
--Mardi Gras
    Trav/Holiday 161:73-4, 108
        (c,2) F '84
ASANTE CIVILIZATION (GHANA)
--19th cent.
    Natur Hist 93:64-5 (map,c,3)
        O '84
ASANTE CIVILIZATION--COSTUME
--Dancer
    Nat Geog 166:620-1 (c,1) N '84
ASANTE CIVILIZATION--RELICS
--19th cent.
    Natur Hist 93:62-73, 106 (c,1)
        O '84
Ashanti civilization. See
    ASANTE CIVILIZATION
ASHE, ARTHUR
    Ebony 38:79-82 (2) Jl '83
    Sports Illus 59:46, 53-5 (c,4)
        Ag 22 '83
ASHEVILLE, NORTH CAROLINA
    Trav/Holiday 166:36-9 (c,1) S
        '86
Asia. See
    HIMALAYAN MOUNTAINS
    individual countries
ASIA--MAPS
--Route of Sinbad's 13th cent.
        voyages
    Nat Geog 162:12-13 (c,2) Jl '82
--World War II map of Himalayas
    Am Heritage 37:66-7 (c,1) Ag
        '86
ASIAN TRIBES
--Gologs (China)
    Nat Geog 161:244-63 (c,1) F '82
--Minority groups (China)
    Nat Geog 165:282-334, 424 (c,1)
        Mr '84
--Sherpa people (Nepal)
    Nat Geog 161:704-23 (c,1) Je '82
ASIAN TRIBES--RELICS
--Yukagir pictographic love letter
        (Siberia, U.S.S.R.)
    Nat Geog 94:86 (c,3) Je '85

ASIMOV, ISAAC
  Life 6:46-7 (c,1) Jl '83
ASPEN, COLORADO
  Trav/Holiday 159:32-7 (c,1)
    Je '83
ASPEN TREES
  Nat Geog 161:338-9 (c,1)
    Mr '82
  Nat Wildlife 21:54-8 (c,1)
    O '83
  Nat Geog 167:538-9 (c,1) Ap
    '85
  Nat Geog 167:666-7 (c,1) My
    '85
  Trav/Holiday 164:55 (c,4) O
    '85
--Leaves
  Nat Wildlife 21:58, 60 (c,1)
    O '83
--Scarred by elk
  Nat Wildlife 20:12 (c,4) O '82
ASTAIRE, FRED
  Life 9:178 (c,2) My '86
  Life 9:360 (2) Fall '86
ASTEROIDS
  Smithsonian 13:70, 75-7
    (painting,c,1) S '82
ASTERS
  Nat Wildlife 24:52 (c,1) Je
    '86
ASTROLABES
--1304 (Middle East)
  Smithsonian 14:61 (c,4) Je '83
ASTRONAUTS
  Smithsonian 13:72 (paint-
    ing,c,4) S '82
  Ebony 38:176 (3) Ag '83
  Ebony 39:163-4 (c,2) N '83
  Ebony 40:62 (c,2) Ag '85
  Life 9:8-15 (c,1) Mr '86
--1960 desert survival training
  Life 9:368 (c,3) Fall '86
--Astronaut entering spacecraft
    (1961)
  Life 9:244 (4) Fall '86
--Challenger shuttle tragedy
    victims
  Ebony 41:82-3, 90, 94 (c,2)
    My '86
--Clothing for altitude simulation
    chamber
  Life 8:62 (2) Mr '85
--Cosmonauts at splash-down
  Life 5:140-1 (c,1) O '82
--Crew of Apollo I that died in
    fire (1967)
  Life 9:15 (4) Mr '86

--Film of space travel
  Smithsonian 16:132-7 (c,1) Je
    '85
--History of space suit
  Smithsonian 14:107-14 (c,2) Ap
    '83
--In training
  Life 8:34-40 (c,2) D '85
--Man walking on moon (1969)
  Life 9:344 (c,2) Fall '86
--Russian cosmonauts
  Nat Geog 170:cov., 420-57 (c,1)
    O '86
  Life 9:67-8 (4) D '86
--Space clothing
  Life 7:64-78 (c,1) O '84
Astronomy. See
    HALLEY, EDMUND
    LOWELL, PERCIVAL
    OBSERVATORIES
    PLANETARIUMS
    TELESCOPES
    UNIVERSE
ASUNCION, PARAGUAY
  Nat Geog 162:242-4 (c,1) Ag '82
ATHENA
--5th cent. B.C. Greek vase
  Nat Geog 168:409 (c,4) S '85
ATHENS, GREECE
  Smithsonian 12:47 (c,3) Mr '82
--See also
    ACROPOLIS
    PARTHENON
ATHLETES
--20th cent. female Olympic athletes
  Life 7:38-45 (c,1) Summer '84
--20th cent. Olympic athletes
  Life 7:entire issue (c,1) Summer
    '84
--1910s sporting cards of swimmers
  Sports Illus 63:104-5 (c,1) D
    23 '85
--1932 Olympics
  Am Heritage 33:71 (1) Ag '82
--Athletes' movements
  Life 6:82-92 (1) S '83
--China
  Life 6:54-60 (c,1) D '83
--Retarded athletes
  Life 6:121-4 (c,1) Jl '83
--Women
  Ebony 37:116-22 (2) Ag '82
--See also
    ALI, MUHAMMAD
    ASHE, ARTHUR
    BASEBALL PLAYERS
    BASKETBALL PLAYERS

ATHLETES (cont.)
> BERRA, YOGI
> BODYBUILDERS
> BOXERS
> BUDGE, DONALD
> CHAMBERLAIN, WILT
> COBB, TY
> CRABBE, BUSTER
> DEMPSEY, JACK
> DIDRIKSON, BABE
> DIMAGGIO, JOE
> FENCERS
> FOOTBALL PLAYERS
> GIPP, GEORGE
> GOLFERS
> GRANGE, RED
> HENIE, SONJA
> HOGAN, BEN
> JOHNSON, JACK
> JONES, BOBBY
> LACROSSE PLAYERS
> LOUIS, JOE
> MANTLE, MICKEY
> MAYS, WILLIE
> OWENS, JESSE
> PAIGE, SATCHEL
> PALMER, ARNOLD
> ROBINSON, JACKIE
> ROCKNE, KNUTE
> RUTH, GEORGE HERMAN
>   (BABE)
> SKIERS
> SULLIVAN, JOHN L.
> TENNIS PLAYERS
> THORPE, JIM
> TILDEN, WILLIAM
> WILLIAMS, TED
> WILLS, HELEN
> WRESTLERS

ATHLETIC STUNTS
--1876 crossing of Niagara Falls
   on high wire
   Smithsonian 14:109 (4) Ja
   '84
--1967 motorcycle jump over
   fountain (Nevada)
   Sports Illus 56:94 (4) Je 7
   '82
--Aerial stunt outside airplane
   Smithsonian 13:160-1 (c,4)
   D '82
--Balancing hockey stick on nose
   Sports Illus 58:54 (c,4) F
   21 '83
--Bicycle stunt (California)
   Smithsonian 13:68 (c,4) S '82
--Bicycling across river hanging

from wire (China)
   Nat Geog 165:315 (c,4) Mr '84
--Bicycling out of airborne plane
   Life 7:124 (c,2) Jl '84
--Bicycling over people (Illinois)
   Life 8:96-7 (1) D '85
--Driving into stacked cars (France)
   Life 5:98-9 (c,1) Ag '82
--Motorcycle jumping over trucks
   Sports Illus 64:10 (c,3) Mr 17
   '86
--Riding cycle on high wire (Spain)
   Nat Geog 169:142-3 (c,1) F '86
--Supercross motorcycle jumps
   (California)
   Sports Illus 61:2-3, 32-9 (c,1)
   N 12 '84
--Walking on hot coals (California)
   Life 7:119 (c,2) Jl '84
   Life 8:42-3, 48 (c,2) Mr '85
--See also
   ACROBATIC STUNTS
ATLANTA, GEORGIA
   Trav/Holiday 161:41 (c,2) Mr
   '84
   Trav/Holiday 164:12-14 (c,1) D
   '85
--Mid 19th cent. stores
   Nat Geog 166:8-9 (1) Jl '84
--Downtown plaza
   Ebony 40:43 (c,2) N '84
--High art museum
   Sports Illus 14:38-47 (c,1) Ja
   '84
   Trav/Holiday 164:13 (c,4) D '85
--King Center for Nonviolent Social
   Change
   Ebony 38:120-7 (c,2) F '83
ATLANTIC CITY, NEW JERSEY
   Trav/Holiday 158:39-43 (c,2)
   Ag '82
--Early 20th cent. amusements
   Smithsonian 13:61-5 (c,3) S '82
--1930s aerial view
   Am Heritage 36:111 (1) D '84
   Am Heritage 36:11 (4) Ap '85
ATLANTIC OCEAN
--1888 chart of abandoned ships
   Natur Hist 94:44-5 (1) Je '85
--Atlantic Ocean currents
   Natur Hist 94:48-9 (c,1) Je '85
   Natur Hist 95:90 (c,4) N '86
ATLANTIC OCEAN--MAPS
--Mid-Atlantic Ridge
   Natur Hist 95:52-62 (c,1) O '86
ATOMIC BOMBS
--1945 bombing of Nagasaki, Japan

ATOMIC BOMBS (cont.)
Am Heritage 35:79 (4) O '84
Life 8:14 (4) Spring '85
--1945 first atomic bomb ex-
plosion (New Mexico)
Am Heritage 37:67 (4) Ap '86
Life 9:192 (4) Fall '86
--1946 explosion (Bikini)
Smithsonian 14:150 (2) Mr '84
--1954 hydrogen bomb explosion
(Bikini)
Nat Geog 169:810-12 (c,1)
Je '86
--Bikini testing sites
Nat Geog 169:815-34 (map,c,1)
Je '86
--Cleaning ship decks after 1946
blast (Bikini)
Nat Geog 169:819 (3) Je '86
--Site where 1945 A-bomb was
loaded (Tinian, Marianas)
Life 8:102 (c,2) Spring '85
--Watching 1951 explosion (Bikini)
Nat Geog 169:818-19 (2) Je
'86
Atomic energy. See
NUCLEAR ENERGY
ATOMS
Smithsonian 14:34-5 (draw-
ing,c,4) My '83
--Atomic research
Nat Geog 167:635-61 (c,1) My
'85
--Uranium atom
Life 9:243 (c,4) Fall '86
ATTU ISLAND, ALEUTIANS,
ALASKA
--World War II battlefield
Nat Geog 164:342-3 (c,1) S
'83
AUCKLAND, NEW ZEALAND
Trav/Holiday 164:52, 56 (c,2)
S '85
--Albert Park
Trav/Holiday 166:52 (c,2) Ag
'86
AUCTIONS
--Mid 19th cent. slave auction
(Virginia)
Nat Geog 166:8 (drawing,4)
Jl '84
--Deer (New Zealand)
Nat Geog 170:554 (c,1) O '86
--Horses
Sports Illus 59:26-7 (c,1) Ag
1 '83
--Horses (Kentucky)

Smithsonian 17:116-29 (c,1) Ap
'86
--Pearl auction (Japan)
Nat Geog 168:204-5 (c,1) Ag '85
AUDIENCES
--1960s Beatles concerts
Life 7:58-9 (c,1) F '84
--1969 Woodstock concert, New York
Life 9:344-5 (c,1) Fall '86
--Concert (New York)
Ebony 37:49 (c,3) My '82
--Gospel concert (Israel)
Ebony 39:36-7 (c,2) D '83
--Opera (Argentina)
Nat Geog 170:242-3 (c,2) Ag '86
--Opera (New York)
Smithsonian 14:83, 86 (3) S '83
--Outdoor ballet (Tulsa, Oklahoma)
Nat Geog 164:396-7 (c,1) S '83
--Outdoor rock concert (Hungary)
Nat Geog 163:232-3 (c,1) F '83
--Pop music concert (Netherlands)
Ebony 41:156 (c,3) My '86
--Television show
Ebony 38:46 (c,3) Ap '83
--See also
SPECTATORS
AUDUBON, JOHN JAMES
Natur Hist 94:cov., 98 (c,1)
Ap '85
Sports Illus 63:126, 135-40
(painting,c,1) D 23 '85
--Home (Pennsylvania)
Natur Hist 94:104 (painting,c,4)
Ap '85
--Painting of great egret
Natur Hist 92:66-7 (c,1) S '83
--Paintings of birds
Natur Hist 94:89-114 (c,1) Ap
'85
--Paintings of wildlife
Sports Illus 63:128-9, 142 (c,4)
D 23 '85
AUGUSTA, GEORGIA
--Capitol Building
Trav/Holiday 162:18 (c,4) Jl '84
AUKS
--Parakeet auklets
Nat Geog 162:547 (c,4) O '82
--See also
MURRES
AURORA BOREALIS
Nat Geog 161:405 (c,1) Mr '82
Life 6:88 (c,4) Mr '83
Nat Wildlife 23:63 (c,4) D '84
Nat Wildlife 23:50-3 (c,1) F '85

AUSTERLITZ, BATTLE OF (1805)
--Reenactment
    Nat Geog 161:166-7 (c,1) F
        '82
AUSTIN, TEXAS
    Trav/Holiday 166:cov., 46,
        66 (c,1) Jl '86
--Austin's sesquicentennial cele-
        bration
    Trav/Holiday 166:cov. (c,1)
        Jl '86
AUSTRALIA
    Nat Geog 164:600-7 (c,1) N
        '83
    Sports Illus 62:84-156 (c,1)
        F 11 '85
--Ayres Rock
    Life 6:132 (c,2) My '83
    Trav/Holiday 166:6-8 (c,2) Jl
        '86
--Cairns
    Trav/Holiday 165:40-5
        (map,c,1) F '86
--Central Desert
    Natur Hist 93:62-71
        (map,c,1) Mr '84
--Effects of drought
    Nat Geog 165:150-2, 172-7
        (c,1) F '84
--Endeavor River (18th cent.)
    Smithsonian 13:78-9 (engrav-
        ing,4) Mr '83
--Freemantle
    Sports Illus 62:84-5, 98-100
        (c,1) F 11 '85
--Freemantle Harbor
    Trav/Holiday 166:43 (c,1) Ag
        '86
--Gosses Bluff
    Nat Geog 167:47 (c,3) Ja '85
--Iron mine
    Nat Geog 168:174-5 (c,1) Ag
        '85
--Murray River area
    Nat Geog 168:252-77 (map,c,1)
        Ag '85
--Nullarbor Plain
    Nat Geog 169:736-57 (map,c,1)
        Je '86
    Smithsonian 17:100-13
        (map,c,1) Je '86
--Outback
    Trav/Holiday 159:53-4 (c,2)
        My '83
    Nat Geog 169:736-57 (map,c,1)
        Je '86
    Smithsonian 17:100-13

(map,c,1) Je '86
    Trav/Holiday 166:68-70 (map,c,1)
        O '86
--Pinnacles desert
    Sports Illus 62:104-5, 128-9
        (c,1) F 11 '85
--Queensland
    Nat Geog 169:2-37 (map,c,1) Ja
        '86
    Trav/Holiday 165:40-5 (map,c,1)
        F '86
--Sinkhole areas
    Nat Geog 165:128-42 (c,1) Ja '84
--Western Australia
    Trav/Holiday 160:44 (c,3) O '83
--See also
        ABORIGINES
        BRISBANE
        MELBOURNE
        MURRAY RIVER
        NORFOLK ISLAND
        PERTH
        SYDNEY
        TASMANIA
AUSTRALIA--ART
--Ricketts sculptures (Pitchi Richi)
    Trav/Holiday 166:cov., 84 (c,1)
        Ag '86
AUSTRALIA--COSTUME
    Trav/Holiday 162:55-7 (c,2) Ag
        '84
--Lifeguards
    Sports Illus 62:130-56 (c,1) F
        11 '85
--Outback
    Nat Geog 169:736-55 (c,1) Je '86
    Smithsonian 17:102-13 (c,1) Je
        '86
--Outback residents (Daly River)
    Life 8:64-5 (1) S '85
--Perth
    Nat Geog 161:638-67 (c,1) My
        '82
--Queensland
    Nat Geog 169:2-37 (c,1) Ja '86
--Southeastern Australia
    Nat Geog 168:252-75 (c,1) Ag
        '85
AUSTRALIA--MAPS
--Revised world map with Australia
        on top
    Smithsonian 15:123 (c,4) My '84
AUSTRALIA--SOCIAL LIFE AND
        CUSTOMS
--Surf Life Saving competition
    Sports Illus 62:132-56 (c,1) F
        11 '85

AUSTRIA
    Nat Geog 167:411-49 (map,c,1)
      Ap '85
    Trav/Holiday 164:4, 50-3 (c,1)
      Ag '85
--Alpbach
    Nat Geog 167:440-1 (c,1) Ap
      '85
--Belvedere Palace
    Smithsonian 15:61-2 (c,2) Ja
      '85
--Tyrol in summer
    Trav/Holiday 157:78-83 (c,1)
      Ap '82
--See also
      ALPS
      DANUBE RIVER
      GRAZ
      INNSBRUCK
      SALZBURG
      VIENNA
AUSTRIA--ART
--Early 20th cent. works
    Smithsonian 17:70-81 (paint-
      ing,c,1) Ag '86
AUSTRIA--COSTUME
    Nat Geog 167:411-49 (c,1) Ap
      '85
--Traditional (Linz)
    Nat Geog 167:445 (c,2) Ap '85
AUSTRIA--HISTORY
--1936 soup line
    Am Heritage 37:94 (3) Ag '86
--Turkish siege of Vienna (1683)
    Smithsonian 15:56-7 (paint-
      ing,c,1) Ja '85
--Viennese crowds watching Ger-
      mans approaching (1938)
    Am Heritage 35:71 (2) Je '84
--See also
      AUSTERLITZ, BATTLE OF
      CHARLEMAGNE
      HOLY ROMAN EMPIRE
AUSTRIA--HOUSING
--Chalets (Tyrol)
    Trav/Holiday 157:78-9, 83
      (c,1) Ap '82
    Nat Geog 167:446-7 (c,1) Ap
      '85
AUSTRIA--RITES AND FESTIVALS
--Schemenlauf Festival (Imst)
    Nat Geog 167:449 (c,1) Ap
      '85
--Vienna Festival
    Nat Geog 167:411 (c,1) Ap
      '85

AUSTRIA--SOCIAL LIFE AND CUS-
    TOMS
--Waitress carrying beer mugs
    Trav/Holiday 164:cov. (c,1) Ag
      '85
AUTOGRAPH SIGNING
--Actors
    Ebony 39:61 (c,4) F '84
--Baseball players
    Sports Illus 56:88 (c,4) My 24
      '82
    Sports Illus 58:58 (c,4) Ap 4
      '83
    Sports Illus 58:39 (c,4) My 16
      '83
    Sports Illus 60:43 (c,3) Ap 2
      '84
    Ebony 41:111 (c,4) Jl '86
--Country singer kissing fan
      (Tennessee)
    Nat Geog 169:618-19 (c,1) My
      '86
--Football players
    Sports Illus 57:15 (c,4) Ag 30
      '82
--Hockey players
    Sports Illus 56:14-15 (c,1) F 15
      '82
--Skiers
    Sports Illus 62:36 (c,4) Ja 28
      '85
--Tennis players
    Sports Illus 62:82 (c,4) Je 24
      '85
--Track stars
    Nat Geog 161:23 (c,4) Ja '82
AUTOGRAPH SIGNING--HUMOR
--Baseball players
    Sports Illus 56:94-106 (draw-
      ing,c,1) Ap 12 '82
AUTOGRAPHS
--Adolph Hitler
    Life 6:19-22 (4) Je '83
AUTOMOBILE INDUSTRY
--1918 blueprint of Ford plant
      production line (Michigan)
    Am Heritage 37:54 (2) O '86
--1937 General Motors strike
    Am Heritage 33:49-63 (2) Ap '82
--Auto manufacturing mural by
      Diego Rivera (Michigan)
    Smithsonian 16:43-5 (c,1) F '86
--Catalytic converter
    Nat Geog 164:688-9 (c,1) N '83
--Crash tests
    Nat Geog 164:26-7 (c,1) Jl '83

AUTOMOBILE INDUSTRY (cont.)
--Designing cars
    Ebony 39:80-4 (c,2) Ja '84
--Hand-made Rolls Royce (Great
        Britain)
    Nat Geog 164:10-11 (c,2) Jl
        '83
--History
    Nat Geog 164:2-35 (c,1) Jl
        '83
    Life 6:66-74 (c,1) S '83
--India
    Nat Geog 167:518 (c,4) Ap '85
--Robots in plant (Delaware)
    Nat Geog 162:454-5 (c,1) O
        '82
--Tennessee
    Nat Geog 169:610-11 (c,1)
        My '86
--Testing Mercedes at factory
        (West Germany)
    Nat Geog 164:5-7, 26-7 (c,1)
        Jl '83
--Use of lasers
    Nat Geog 165:348-9 (c,1) Mr
        '84
--See also
    FORD, HENRY
AUTOMOBILE MECHANICS
--Repair shop (Mexico City,
        Mexico)
    Nat Geog 166:170-1 (c,1) Ag
        '84
--Restoring old cars (California)
    Smithsonian 15:52-62 (c,1)
        Mr '85
--Servicing racing car
    Sports Illus 56:32-3 (c,4) Je
        7 '82
--Training
    Ebony 37:93 (4) Mr '82
AUTOMOBILE RACING
    Sports Illus 59:83 (c,4) O 17
        '83
    Sports Illus 63:12-15 (c,1)
        S 9 '85
    Sports Illus 63:13 (c,4) N 11
        '85
--1938 ERA racing car
    Sports Illus 57:35 (c,4) D 20
        '82
--1950s racing cars
    Sports Illus 57:34-43 (c,2) D
        20 '82
--1955 tragic racing car accident
        (Le Mans, France)
    Sports Illus 64:80-96

    (painting,c,1) My 12 '86
--California
    Sports Illus 60:75 (c,3) Ap 9
        '84
    Sports Illus 62:70, 74 (c,3) Ap
        22 '85
--Crashes
    Sports Illus 60:68 (c,4) F 8 '84
    Sports Illus 60:52-3 (c,4) F 27
        '84
    Life 8:86-7 (1) Ap '85
    Sports Illus 62:31 (c,3) My 20
        '85
    Sports Illus 63:14-15 (c,3) S 9
        '85
    Sports Illus 64:90-2 (c,2) F 10
        '86
    Sports Illus 64:12-13 (c,1) F 24
        '86
--Daytona 500
    Sports Illus 60:92-4 (c,3) F 13
        '84
--Daytona 500 (1982)
    Sports Illus 57:32 (c,4) S 13 '82
--Daytona 500 (1983)
    Sports Illus 58:20-1 (c,4) F 28
        '83
--Daytona 500 (1984)
    Sports Illus 60:50-3 (c,4) F 27
        '84
--Daytona 500 (1985)
    Sports Illus 62:20-3 (c,2) F 25
        '85
--Daytona 500 (1986)
    Sports Illus 64:12-15 (c,1) F 24
        '86
--Demolition Derby (New York)
    Nat Geog 164:20-1 (c,1) Jl '83
--Detroit Grand Prix
    Sports Illus 56:58-65 (c,4) Je
        14 '82
--Drivers
    Sports Illus 56:68-9 (c,3) Ja 11
        '82
    Sports Illus 56:58 (c,4) My 24
        '82
    Sports Illus 57:31-2 (c,2) S 13
        '82
--Fatal crash
    Sports Illus 56:61 (c,4) My 24
        '82
--Festivities surrounding Indianap-
        olis 500
    Sports Illus 60:54-9 (drawing,c,1)
        My 28 '84
--Grand Prix 1986 (Miami, Florida)
    Sports Illus 62:60-1 (c,3) Mr 4 '85

AUTOMOBILES (cont.)

--1929 Duesenberg Dual Cowl
  Phaeton
  Am Heritage 37:cov., 3, 114
    (c,1) F '86
--1929 Franklin
  Am Heritage 37:8 (painting,c,4)
    Ap '86
--1930 Cadillac
  Life 6:68-9 (c,1) S '83
  Am Heritage 37:38 (c,4) F '86
--1930 Coupé Napoléon
  Smithsonian 14:91 (c,2) D '83
--1930s
  Natur Hist 92:6-7 (1) Mr '83
--1930s best cars
  Am Heritage 37:32-40 (c,4)
    F '86
--1930s Cords
  Nat Geog 164:24-5 (c,1) Jl '83
--1930s to 1980s
  Life 9:88-94 (c,2) Mr '86
--Early 1930s Dodge
  Life 5:43 (3) Mr '82
--1931 Marmon
  Am Heritage 37:38 (c,4) F '86
--1932 Duesenberg
  Am Heritage 37:33 (c,4) F '86
--1932 Lincoln
  Am Heritage 37:35 (c,4) F '86
--1932 Packard
  Am Heritage 37:112 (2) D '85
  Am Heritage 37:39 (c,4) F '86
--1932 Stutz
  Am Heritage 37:32, 34 (c,4) F
    '86
--1933 Pierce-Arrow
  Am Heritage 37:37 (c,4) F '86
--1934
  Am Heritage 35:105 (3) D '83
--1936 Cord 810 Westchester sedan
  Smithsonian 17:164 (c,4) N
    '86
--1936 Lincoln Zephyr
  Life 6:10 (4) N '83
--1937
  Am Heritage 33:cov. (paint-
    ing,c,1) Ap '82
--1937 Cord
  Am Heritage 37:40 (c,4) F
    '86
--1938 models
  Life 9:90 (3) Mr '86
--1939 Ford coupe
  Sports Illus 65:51 (c,4) S 29
    '86
--1940 La Salle

Life 6:10 (4) N '83
--1942
  Am Heritage 35:66-7 (1) D '83
  Nat Geog 169:519 (2) Ap '86
--1947 Triumph
  Sports Illus 58:34 (c,4) Mr 28
    '83
--1949 Ford
  Life 6:10 (4) N '83
--1950 Buick
  Nat Geog 164:17 (c,3) Jl '83
--1953 Studebaker
  Life 6:10 (4) N '83
--1955 Chevrolet
  Sports Illus 57:67 (c,4) Jl 12
    '82
  Am Heritage 37;41 (c,4) F '86
  Ebony 41:106 (c,4) Jl '86
--1955 Thunderbird
  Life 6:10 (4) N '83
--1956 Bentley once owned by John
  Lennon
  Nat Geog 164:32-3 (c,2) Jl '83
--1958 Nash
  Life 8:80-1 (c,1) Ag '85
--1959 Cadillac
  Smithsonian 15:cov. (c,1) Mr
    '85
--1959 Cadillac impaled with a spike
  Nat Geog 164:34-5 (c,1) Jl
    '83
--1960s Morgan
  Sports Illus 62:12 (c,4) Je 24 '85
--1963 Avanti
  Life 6:10 (4) N '83
--1973 Jaguar XKE
  Life 5:107 (c,4) Ap '82
--1987 models
  Ebony 42:84-94 (c,3) N '86
--Abandoned station wagon
  Sports Illus 56:77 (c,4) My 17
    '82
--Abandoned stripped car (New York)
  Nat Geog 166:805 (c,2) D '84
--Aerial view of new cars in lot
  (California)
  Life 8:84-5 (1) O '85
--Alfa Romeos
  Smithsonian 14:86-7 (c,2) D '83
--Amphibious car (New Jersey)
  Nat Wildlife 24:10-11 (c,1) O '86
--Antique European cars
  Smithsonian 14:86-91 (c,1) D '83
--Eva Braun's roadster (1940s)
  Life 6:84-5 (c,1) Jl '83
--Bugatti
  Sports Illus 64:67 (painting,c,3)

AUTOMOBILES (cont.)
My 5 '86
--Cadillacs half-buried to form
   sculpture (Texas)
   Smithsonian 15:58-9 (c,2) Mr
   '85
--Child's car
   Sports Illus 62:80-1 (c,1) Ja
   28 '85
--Cord Phaeton
   Smithsonian 14:73 (c,3) F '84
--Cruising the boulevard (Los
   Angeles, California)
   Nat Geog 164:2-3 (c,1) Jl '83
--Designs for future vehicles
   Smithsonian 14:78-85 (c,1)
   F '84
   Ebony 40:133-8 (c,3) Ag '85
--Driving car
   Sports Illus 60:64-5 (c,1) Ja
   30 '84
   Ebony 41:152 (2) Mr '86
   Sports Illus 65:80-1 (c,1) D
   8 '86
--Dune buggies
   Sports Illus 56:78 (c,4) Ja
   11 '82
--Early Model T Ford
   Am Heritage 34:7 (c,3) O '83
--Early Rolls Royces
   Smithsonian 14:89 (c,4) D '83
--Electric car (Channel Islands)
   Smithsonian 17:96 (4) My '86
--Farmans
   Smithsonian 14:89 (c,4) D
   '83
--Go-karts
   Sports Illus 61:78 (4) O 8
   '84
--Gordinis
   Smithsonian 14:86-7 (c,2) D
   '83
--History
   Nat Geog 164:2-35 (c,1) Jl '83
   Life 6:66-74 (c,1) S '83
--Junkyard (California)
   Smithsonian 15:cov., 52-63
   (c,1) Mr '85
--Junkyard (Michigan)
   LIfe 5:38-9 (c,1) Ag '82
--Low riders (California)
   Natur Hist 91:28-39 (c,1)
   Ap '82
   Nat Geog 164:22-3 (c,1) Jl '83
--Mercedes Benzes
   Smithsonian 14:88 (c,4) D '83
--Model A Ford

   Nat Geog 161:47 (c,3) Ja '82
--Model A Porter
   Sports Illus 64:46 (c,4) Mr 17
   '86
--Model T Ford
   Am Heritage 37:36 (c,4) F '86
--Painted low-rider car (New
   Mexico)
   Nat Geog 161:334-5 (c,1) Mr
   '82
--Parts of old cars
   Smithsonian 15:54-63 (c,1) Mr
   '85
--People pushing stalled car
   Life 5:16 (4) Ap '82
--Pink Cadillacs
   Nat Geog 166:284-5 (c,1) S '84
--Police car (New York)
   Smithsonian 14:98 (c,4) Je '83
--Porsches
   Sports Illus 58:36 (c,3) Ja 17
   '83
--Role of cars in 20th cent. Amer-
   ican life
   Life 9:88-94 (c,2) Mr '86
--Rolls Royce
   Ebony 37:28-9 (c,2) Jl '82
   Smithsonian 13:87 (c,2) N '82
   Life 9:10-11 (c,1) F '86
   Ebony 41:104-6 (c,3) Jl '86
--Sculpture of cars embedded in
   concrete
   Life 6:152 (c,2) O '83
   Smithsonian 16:18 (c,4) My '85
--Stripped stolen cars (New York)
   Nat Geog 163:602 (c,1) My
   '83
--Washing antique car (California)
   Sports Illus 57:59 (c,4) N 15 '82
--With bullhorn figurehead (Texas)
   Trav/Holiday 166:41 (c,4) Jl '86
--Zimmer roadster
   Ebony 40:100-1 (c,1) S '85
--See also
   ACCIDENTS
   AUTOMOBILE INDUSTRY
   AUTOMOBILES--TRAFFIC
   CAR WASHES
   CRASHES
   GASOLINE STATIONS
   JEEPS
   LICENSE PLATES
   TIRES
   TRAFFIC LIGHTS
AUTOMOBILES--HUMOR
--1920s humorous map of rural traffic
   Smithsonian 17:102 (c,2) S '86

AUTOMOBILES--TRAFFIC
--1920s humorous map of rural
    traffic
    Smithsonian 17:102 (c,2) S '86
--Amman, Jordan
    Nat Geog 165:254 (c,3) F '84
--Analyzing urban traffic con-
    gestion
    Smithsonian 17:42-51 (c,1)
        Ap '84
--Bangkok, Thailand
    Nat Geog 162:510-11 (c,1)
        O '82
--Beirut, Lebanon
    Nat Geog 163:273 (c,3) F '83
--Budapest, Hungary
    Nat Geog 163:234-5 (c,1)
        F '83
--Crowded street (New Delhi,
    India)
    Nat Geog 167:506-7 (c,1) Ap
        '85
--Indonesia
    Natur Hist 93:22 (c,3) Mr '84
--New York City, New York
    Smithsonian 17:44 (c,3) Ap
        '86
--Rangoon, Burma
    Nat Geog 166:96-7 (c,1) Jl '84
--Taipei, Taiwan
    Nat Geog 161:96-7 (c,1) Ja
        '82
AUTUMN
    Nat Wildlife 24:4-9 (c,1) O
        '86
--Adirondack Mountains, New York
    Trav/Holiday 162:49-51 (c,1)
        Ag '84
--Appalachian Trail
    Life 9:38-48 (c,1) O '86
--Aspen tree forest (New Mexico)
    Nat Geog 161:338-9 (c,1) Mr
        '82
--Autumn leaves
    Natur Hist 95:82 (c,4) O '86
--California forest
    Natur Hist 94:79 (c,1) S '85
--Cascade Range, Washington
    Nat Wildlife 22:4-7 (c,1) O
        '84
--Closeups of decaying leaves
    Natur Hist 95:54-7 (c,1)
        Ag '86
--Colorado
    Nat Geog 166:190, 216 (c,1)
        Ag '84
--Kentucky mountains

Nat Geog 168:820 (c,2) D '85
--Maine
    Nat Geog 166:790-1 (c,1) D '84
--Michigan
    Nat Wildlife 22:53 (c,4) O '84
    Nat Geog 167:538-9 (c,1) Ap
        '85
--New England
    Trav/Holiday 162:52-5 (c,1) S
        '84
--Oak leaves
    Nat Wildlife 23:60 (c,1) O '85
--Pennsylvania street
    Nat Geog 167:354-5 (c,1) Mr '85
--Raking leaves (Kansas)
    Nat Geog 168:354-5 (c,1) S '85
--Trees (Georgia)
    Nat Geog 163:466-7 (c,1) Ap '83
--Trees (Idaho)
    Nat Geog 161:808-9 (c,1) Je '82
--Trees (Louisiana)
    Nat Wildlife 20:37, 40 (c,1) O
        '82
AVALANCHES
    Sports Illus 56:76-90 (c,1) Ap
        19 '82
    Nat Geog 162:277, 280-304
        (map,c,1) S '82
--Avalanche control techniques
    Nat Geog 162:290-303 (c,1) S
        '82
--U.S.S.R.
    Nat Geog 170:263 (c,4) Ag '86
AVIATION
--1953 airplane construction
    (Georgia)
    Ebony 41:220 (2) N '85
--Aircraft manufacturing (Israel)
    Nat Geog 168:34 (c,1) Jl '85
--Performing safety check on jet-
    liner (California)
    Smithsonian 17:48-59 (c,1) O '86
--Use of wind tunnels in flying
    Smithsonian 12:76-85 (c,1) Ja
        '82
--See also
        AIRPLANE FLYING
        AIRPLANE PILOTS
        AIRPLANES
        AIRPORTS
        CRASHES
        U.S. AIR FORCE
AVIATION--HISTORY
--1903 first flight by Wright Broth-
    ers (North Carolina)
    Nat Geog 164:217 (3) Ag '83
--1908 Orville Wright flights

AVIATION--HISTORY (cont.)
Smithsonian 15:27-8 (4) D
'84
--1910 barnstorming (Washington,
D.C.)
Smithsonian 16:86 (4) Mr '86
--1910 Folkstone air show (Great
Britain)
Smithsonian 16:148-9 (1) S
'85
--Career of John Moisant
Smithsonian 16:148-70 (2) S
'85
--Commemorated on postage stamp
Am Heritage 34:55 (c,4) D
'82
--World War I air battles
Smithsonian 15:102-13 (1) Ja
'85
AVON RIVER, ENGLAND
--Bath
Trav/Holiday 164:6 (c,4) D
'85
AWARDS
--Academy Awards Oscar
Ebony 38:168 (4) Ag '83
Life 9:173 (c,2) My '86
--Emmy Award
Ebony 39:62 (4) F '84
Ebony 42:43 (4) D '86
--Gold records
Ebony 37:58-60 (3) S '82
Ebony 39:38 (c,4) Je '84
Ebony 40:30 (4) Ja '85
Life 8:25 (c,4) Ag '85
--Marconi International Fellow-
ship Award
Smithsonian 12:145 (c,4) Mr
'82
--Platinum records
Ebony 41:160 (c,3) My '86
--See also
MEDALS
NOBEL PRIZE
TROPHIES
AXES
--Prehistoric stone ax
Natur Hist 93:22-4 (c,4) Jl
'84
--Maori tribe adze (New Zealand)
Natur Hist 93:58 (c,3) S '84
AZALEAS
Smithsonian 14:106 (c,4) My
'83
Life 8:55 (c,4) Je '85
AZTEC CIVILIZATION (MEXICO)
--1519 conquest by Cortes

Nat Geog 166:420-59 (map,c,1)
O '84
--Tenochtitlan
Nat Geog 166:456-7 (painting,c,1)
O '84
AZTEC CIVILIZATION--ARCHITEC-
TURE
--Model of the Great Temple area,
Mexico City, Mexico
Natur Hist 91:50-1 (c,1) Jl '82
--Monte Alban temple, Oaxaca,
Mexico
Trav/Holiday 166:10 (c,4) O '86
AZTEC CIVILIZATION--RELICS
--Artifacts from the Great Temple,
Mexico City, Mexico
Natur Hist 91:48-56 (c,1) Jl '82
--Stone calendar (Mexico)
Trav/Holiday 162:58 (c,2) Jl '84

- B -

BABIES
Sports Illus 56:32 (c,4) Ap 5
'82
Ebony 38:36 (3) Mr '83
Life 6:42-3 (c,1) Ap '83
Life 6:78 (c,2) N '83
Life 6:110-11 (1) D '83
Sports Illus 59:23 (c,2) D 19 '83
Nat Geog 165:442 (c,3) Ap '84
Sports Illus 60:53 (c,4) My 28
'84
Life 7:96-104 (c,1) Je '84
Life 8:37-40 (c,1) Ja '85
Life 8:82, 118-19 (c,1) My '85
Life 8:100 (c,1) Jl '85
Life 8:103-8 (c,1) S '85
Ebony 41:cov., 132-4, 140 (c,1)
Mr '86
Life 9:8-9 (c,1) Ap '86
Ebony 41:78-84 (4) S '86
--13th cent. American Indian nurs-
ing mother
Natur Hist 94:72-3 (sculpture,c,1)
S '85
--1900
Am Heritage 34:28 (3) F '83
--Early 20th cent. Kiowa Indian
cradleboard
Smithsonian 15:136 (c,4) Ag '84
--At parents' offices
Life 5:112-17 (1) O '82
--Babies playing underwater
Life 8:11-14 (c,1) Je '85
--Bedouin (North Yemen)

BABIES (cont.)
   Nat Geog 168:504 (c,1) O '85
--Being fed by mother
   Ebony 41:156 (c,4) Je '86
--Being hugged
   Sports Illus 57:68-9 (c,1) D
      27 '82
--Conceived in vitro
   Life 5:cov., 44-52 (c,1) N '82
   Life 8:100 (c,1) Jl '85
--Diapering baby
   Ebony 40:90 (c,4) Jl '85
--Diapering baby (Australia)
   Sports Illus 61:369 (c,4) Jl
      18 '84
--Dressed in baseball uniform
   Sports Illus 63:36-7, 68
      (c,2) Ag 19 '85
--Dressed in feathers and ribbons
   Life 7:8-12 (c,1) F '84
--Eskimo (Alaska)
   Nat Geog 165:818 (2) Je '84
--Eskimo carried on mother's
      back (Northwest Terri-
      tories)
   Nat Geog 163:184 (c,3) F '83
--Face
   Smithsonian 16:39 (c,4) Je '85
--Father feeding baby in high
      chair
   Life 9:148 (c,4) My '86
--Father feeding toddler
   Sports Illus 60:28-9 (c,4) Ap
      23 '84
--Hopi Indian baby (Arizona)
   Nat Geog 162:624-5 (c,1) N
      '82
--Houseboat playpen
   Nat Geog 161:495 (c,3) Ap '82
--Imitating facial expressions
   Smithsonian 16:118 (4) Mr '86
--In backpack
   Trav/Holiday 165:30 (c,4) F
      '86
--In backpack (Japan)
   Smithsonian 16:238 (4) N '85
--In bassinet (Maryland)
   Smithsonian 14:69 (c,1) Jl '83
--In playpen (Florida)
   Sports Illus 56:62-3 (c,1) Ap
      26 '82
--In playpen (Israel)
   Nat Geog 161:445 (c,1) Ap '82
--Infant
   Sports Illus 59:35 (c,4) Jl 4
      '83
   Am Heritage 35:79 (2) Je '84

--Japan
   Sports Illus 61:428 (4) Jl 18 '84
--Medical treatment of embryos
   Life 6:38-44 (c,1) Ap '83
--Nannies (U.S.)
   Life 8:103-8 (c,1) S '85
--Nanny school (Colorado)
   Life 8:104-5 (c,1) S '85
--Navajo papoose
   Natur Hist 95:80 (4) S '86
--Newborn held by doctor
   Life 9:93 (2) Fall '86
--Newborn infant
   Life 8:55 (2) My '85
   Sports Illus 63:59 (c,4) S 23 '85
   Sports Illus 63:80, 94 (c,1) N
      11 '85
   Life 9:32 (c,1) Mr '86
--Newborn infant (Cambodia)
   Life 8:78 (2) Ap '85
--Niger
   Nat Geog 164:489 (c,1) O '83
--Nude toddler on beach (Australia)
   Nat Geog 169:8-9 (c,1) Ja '86
--Nursing baby (Philippines)
   Nat Geog 170:92 (c,3) Jl '86
--One-year old quadruplets
   Ebony 40:114 (4) S '85
--Prince Harry (Great Britain)
   Life 8:104 (c,2) F '85
--Prince William (Great Britain)
   Life 5:98-9 (c,1) S '82
   Life 6:97 (c,2) F '83
--Quadruplets
   Life 8:58-9 (1) F '85
--Quintuplets
   Life 7:cov., 71-8 (c,1) Jl '84
   Ebony 41:cov., 31-40 (c,1) D
      '85
--Rear view
   Life 7:166 (c,2) Ja '84
--Sextuplets (Great Britain)
   Life 8:166 (c,2) D '85
--Sleeping in hammock (Quebec)
   Nat Geog 161:416-17 (c,1) Mr
      '82
--Teaching parents to bathe babies
   Ebony 40:78 (4) Mr '85
--Toddlers (Great Britain)
   Ebony 39:42-8 (3) Ap '84
--Tossed in the air
   Sports Illus 63:72-3 (c,2) Jl 22
      '85
--28-week-old human fetus
   Life 9:100-1 (c,1) Fall '86
--Wrapped in blankets (Mongolia)
   Nat Geog 167:252-3 (c,2) F '85

BABIES (cont.)
--Young child on skis (St. Moritz, Switzerland)
Life 9:82 (c,4) Ap '86
--See also
BABY CARRIAGES
BABY CRIBS
BABY STROLLERS
CHILDBIRTH
CHILDREN
DAY CARE CENTERS
FAMILIES
PREGNANCY
BABOONS
Natur Hist 91:30-9 (c,1) S '82
Nat Geog 163:639 (c,4) My '83
Natur Hist 93:54-5, 60-1
(c,1) F '84
Smithsonian 16:105 (c,4) D '85
Nat Geog 169:581 (c,4) My
'86
BABY CARRIAGES
Nat Geog 163:584 (c,3) My '83
--1880s pram (Florida)
Sports Illus 57:36 (c,4) D
13 '82
--1921 (New York)
Am Heritage 34:68 (3) Ag '83
--Great Britain
Life 5:54-5 (c,1) D '82
Smithsonian 14:98, 102-3 (c,2)
Ja '84
Life 7:94 (c,2) Ja '84
--Greenland
Nat Geog 163:192-3 (c,2) F
'83
--West Germany
Natur Hist 92:42-3 (c,1) Je '83
--1st cent. A.D. (Italy)
Nat Geog 165:565 (c,1) My '84
BABY STROLLERS
Ebony 37:101 (4) F '82
Ebony 37:64 (4) Jl '82
--For quintuplets
Ebony 41:33 (c,1) D '85
--For twins
Life 7:74-5 (c,1) Jl '84
--For twins (Great Britain)
Ebony 39:46 (3) Ap '84
BABYLON
--6th cent. B.C. Hanging Gardens
of Babylon
Smithsonian 14:59 (drawing,4)
Mr '84
BABYLON--RELICS
--164 B.C. Babylonian cuneiform
tablet

Life 8:33 (c,1) O '85
Natur Hist 94:16 (3) D '85
BACHELOR'S-BUTTONS (PLANTS)
--Made of glass
Smithsonian 13:103 (c,4) O '82
BACTERIA
Smithsonian 14:127-34 (c,3) S
'83
Smithsonian 15:48 (4) Je '84
Nat Geog 169:717-19 (c,1) Je
'86
BADEN-BADEN, WEST GERMANY
--Casino room
Trav/Holiday 157:45 (c,4) Je
'82
BADEN-POWELL, ROBERT
Am Heritage 36:71 (2) F '85
Smithsonian 16:35 (4) Jl '85
BADGERS
Life 5:108 (c,4) D '82
Nat Wildlife 21:29-32 (c,1) F
'83
Natur Hist 95:50-7 (c,1) D '86
BADGERS
--Honey badger
Nat Geog 163:380 (c,4) Mr '83
BADLANDS, NORTH DAKOTA
Nat Geog 162:348-9 (c,1) S '82
Trav/Holiday 164:54-5 (c,1) Jl
'85
BAGHDAD, IRAQ
Nat Geog 167:80-109 (map,c,1)
Ja '85
--1258 siege of Baghdad by Genghis
Khan's grandson
Smithsonian 17:162 (painting,c,3)
O '86
--See also
TIGRIS RIVER
BAGPIPE PLAYING
--Washington, D.C.
Smithsonian 12:30 (c,4) Ja '82
BAGPIPES
Smithsonian 13:116 (c,3) Jl '82
BAHAMAS
Nat Geog 162:cov., 364-95
(map,c,1) S '82
Ebony 38:117-20 (c,2) Ap '83
Trav/Holiday 166:33-40 (map,c,1)
Ag '86
--Beach
Ebony 41:74 (c,3) My '86
--Fortune Island
Nat Geog 170:595 (c,4) N '86
--Long Island
Nat Geog 170:590-2, 596-7
(map,c,2) N '86

BAHAMAS (cont.)
--Samana Cay
  Nat Geog 170:466-89 (map,c,1)
    N '86
--See also
  NASSAU
BAHAMAS--COSTUME
  Nat Geog 162:366-95 (c,1) S
    '82
  Nat Geog 170:566-7, 578-81,
    594-5 (c,1) N '86
BAHAMAS--MAPS
  Natur Hist 92:10 (c,3) Ap '83
BAHAMAS--RITES AND FESTI-
    VALS
--Junkanoo Parade
  Ebony 38:120 (c,4) Ap '83
BAKERS
--Early 20th cent. carving of
    baker
  Am Heritage 37:40-1 (c,1) Ag
    '86
--Bakery (Alaska)
  Nat Geog 163:162-3 (c,1) F
    '83
--Connecticut
  Nat Geog 166:796 (c,2) D '84
Baking. See
  BREAD MAKING
  COOKING
BALANCHINE, GEORGE
  Life 7:171 (4) Ja '84
  Life 9:352 (2) Fall '86
BALDNESS
  Ebony 38:54-8 (3) Je '83
  Sports Illus 59:50 (c,4) Ag
    29 '83
BALDWIN, JAMES
  Ebony 41:61 (4) N '85
BALL, LUCILLE
  Life 9:82-3 (c,1) O '86
BALLET DANCING
  Trav/Holiday 157:18, 42 (4)
    My '82
  Life 6:34-9 (c,1) F '83
  Trav/Holiday 159:8 (c,4) Ap
    '83
  Smithsonian 15:91, 96 (c,3)
    Je '84
  Trav/Holiday 163:59 (c,4) My
    '85
  Life 8:34-5 (c,1) S '85
  Sports Illus 65:2-3 (c,1) O 13
    '86
--1908 painting of ballet
  Am Heritage 37:72-3 (c,1) D
    '85

--Cambodia
  Nat Geog 161:595 (c,1) My '82
--Pas de deux
  Sports Illus 65:88 (c,3) N 24 '86
--Practice
  Nat Geog 161:815 (c,2) Je '82
--Practice (New York City)
  Smithsonian 13:64 (4) My '82
--Slow motion photo
  Life 9:97 (1) Fall '86
--Toe shoes
  Smithsonian 15:88-99 (c,1) Je
    '84
  Trav/Holiday 163:58 (c,1) My
    '85
--See also
  BALANCHINE, GEORGE
  NIJINSKY
BALLET DANCING--EDUCATION
  Life 7;138-44 (c,1) My '84
--Alabama
  Ebony 37:59 (4) Jl '82
--Alberta
  Nat Geog 165:388-9 (c,1) Mr '84
--Children's class (Monaco)
  Life 9:80-1 (c,1) Ap '86
BALLOONING
--1783 (Paris, France)
  Smithsonian 14:63 (drawing,c,3)
    S '83
  Nat Geog 164:780 (drawing,c,4)
    D '83
--1907 (Pennsylvania)
  Am Heritage 35:97-101 (1) O '84
--Alaska
  Life 8:90 (c,2) Jl '85
--Colorado
  Trav/Holiday 159:32 (c,1) Je
    '83
--Cross-Pacific flight
  Nat Geog 161:512-21 (map,c,1)
    Ap '82
--France
  Trav/Holiday 165:42-4, 75 (c,1)
    Je '86
--Ill-fated 1897 Arctic expedition
  Smithsonian 14:122-36 (c,3) My
    '83
--In lawn chair (California)
  Life 6:171 (c,2) Ja '83
--Kenya
  Trav/Holiday 160:cov. (c,1) S
    '83
--Paris, France
  Life 6:148-9 (c,1) O '83
  Nat Geog 164:778-97 (c,1) D '83
--Tennessee

BALLOONING (cont.)
Nat Geog 169:624-5 (c,1) My
'86
--Transatlantic flight
Nat Geog 167:270-6 (c,1) F
'85
--Vermont
Natur Hist 91:96 (3) F '82
BALLONS
Trav/Holiday 162:42 (c,4)
Ag '84
--Balloon shaped like motorcycle
Life 9:11 (c,1) O '86
--Brazil
Trav/Holiday 164:122 (4) O
'85
--Displayed as art against U.S.
landscapes
Life 5:8-15 (c,2) Mr '82
--Mickey Mouse balloon
Life 9:35 (c,4) D '86
--Shaped like elephant
Sports Illus 63:7 (c,4) O 14
'85
--Used as World War II weapon
by Japan
Am Heritage 33:88-92 (paint-
ing,c,1) Ap '82
BALLONS, TOY
Nat Geog 161:34-5 (c,1) Ja
'82
--Balloon vendor (Mexico)
Trav/Holiday 157:57 (c,3) F
'82
--Million-balloon salute to Disney-
land, California
Life 9:8-9 (c,1) F '86
--Released at football stadium
Sports Illus 60:78 (c,4) My
14 '84
BALTIMORE, MARYLAND
Trav/Holiday 163:67-71 (c,1)
Je '85
--Fort McHenry (1874 painting)
Am Heritage 33:22-3 (c,2) Je
'82
--Row houses
Life 9:119 (c,4) Ja '86
BAMBOO PLANTS
Nat Geog 169:298-9 (c,1) Mr
'86
BANANA INDUSTRY--HARVESTING
--Florida
Smithsonian 16:40-1 (c,3) D
'85
BANANA PLANTS
Natur Hist 93:50-1 (c,1) D '84

BANDELIER NATIONAL MONUMENT,
NEW MEXICO
--Anasazi caves
Nat Geog 162:578 (c,3) N '82
BANDS
--Big band sound (Mongolia)
Nat Geog 167:250-1 (c,1) F '85
--Civil War musicians
Am Heritage 33:76 (3) F '82
--Country-western
Sports Illus 60:54 (c,4) F 6 '84
--Jazz
Ebony 39:130-1 (c,1) F '84
--Jazz (Missouri)
Trav/Holiday 157:33 (c,1) Je
'82
BANDS, MARCHING
--Early 20th cent. family band
(Iowa)
Am Heritage 35:11 (2) F '84
--College
Ebony 40:25, 30 (c,3) D '84
Sports Illus 65:4-5 (c,3) D 1 '86
--College football game
Sports Illus 57:44-51 (c,1) D 6
'82
Sports Illus 59:57 (c,4) N 7 '83
Sports Illus 59:96-7 (c,3) N 28
'83
Smithsonian 14:151 (c,2) N '83
--Colorado winter carnival
Trav/Holiday 157:55 (c,3) Ja '82
--High school band (Ohio)
Sports Illus 59:48 (c,4) S 5 '83
--Scottish band (North Carolina)
Smithsonian 13:110 (c,4) Jl '82
--U.S. Naval Academy, Annapolis,
Maryland
Trav/Holiday 161:40 (c,2) Ja '84
BANFF NATIONAL PARK, ALBERTA
Natur Hist 93:26-7 (c,1) Jl '84
Trav/Holiday 163:52-5 (c,1) Ja
'85
--Banff Springs Hotel, Alberta
Trav/Holiday 162:26-7 (c,4) D
'84
Trav/Holiday 163:55 (c,1) Ja '85
--See also
LAKE LOUISE
BANGKOK, THAILAND
Smithsonian 13:34-43 (c,1) Je
'82
Nat Geog 162:500-25 (c,1) O '82
Trav/Holiday 163:58-63 (c,1)
Ap '85
BANGLADESH
--Flooded land

BANGLADESH (cont.)
    Nat Geog 165:738-41 (c,1)
    Je '84
BANGLADESH--COSTUME
    Nat Geog 165:738-43 (c,1)
    Je '84
BANJO PLAYING
--Kentucky
    Nat Geog 163:818-19 (c,2) Je
    '83
BANJUL, GAMBIA
    Nat Geog 168:228-9 (c,2) Ag
    '85
BANK OF ENGLAND, LONDON,
    ENGLAND
    Smithsonian 13:72-5 (c,2) N
    '82
BANKS
--1st cent. Roman money box
    Nat Geog 162:687 (c,4) D '82
--16th cent. usurer
    Smithsonian 13:102 (paint-
    ing,c,4) Mr '83
--19th-20th cents.
    Am Heritage 35:27-35, 114 (1)
    Ap '84
--Mid-19th cent. (Conway, Mas-
    sachusetts)
    Am Heritage 35:27 (1) Ap '84
--1900 (Detroit, Michigan)
    Am Heritage 35:28-9 (2) Ap
    '84
--1920s (Johnstown, Pennsyl-
    vania)
    Am Heritage 35:114 (litho-
    graph,c,4) Ap '84
--Banking activities (Switzerland)
    Nat Geog 169:106-7 (c,1) Ja
    '86
--Teller machine (California)
    Am Heritage 35:35 (3) Ap '84
--Toy bank shaped like Flatiron
    Building
    Smithsonian 14:168 (c,4) S
    '83
--See also
        CHECKS, BANKING
        CREDIT CARDS
BANNERS
--Baseball
    Sports Illus 61:29 (c,2) D 10
    '84
--Basketball "Champion" banners
    Ebony 40:59 (c,4) Ap '85
--Carp banners (Japan)
    Natur Hist 93:51 (c,1) S '84
--Football pennants

    Sports Illus 57:22 (c,4) S 6 '82
BAPTISMS
--9th cent. (Russia)
    Nat Geog 167:284-5 (painting,c,1)
    Mr '85
--1930 blacks (Alabama)
    Am Heritage 34:36 (painting,c,3)
    Je '83
--1955 baptism by fire hose (New
    York)
    Ebony 41:220 (4) N '85
--Adult (Arizona)
    Sports Illus 64:42 (c,2) Mr 3
    '86
--Adult (Kentucky)
    Nat Geog 163:815 (c,2) Je '83
--Australian outback
    Nat Geog 169:32-3 (c,2) Ja '86
--Germany
    Nat Geog 164:452-3 (c,1) O '83
--Great Britain
    Nat Geog 170:751 (c,1) D '86
--Mexico
    Life 5:108 (sculpture,c,1) N '82
--Mormons (Bolivia)
    Sports Illus 63:85 (c,1) S 4 '85
--Royal christening (Great Britain)
    Life 8:104 (c,2) F '85
--U.S.S.R.
    Nat Geog 164:760 (c,2) D '83
BAPTISMS--COSTUME
--Christening outfit (Great Britain)
    Life 5:104 (c,4) Ap '82
--Hungary
    Nat Geog 163:258 (c,4) F '83
--Spain
    Nat Geog 169:176-7 (c,1) F '86
BARBADOS
    Trav/Holiday 162:44-7 (c,1) Ag
    '84
BARBADOS--HOUSING
    Natur Hist 94:38-44 (c,4) O '85
Barbecues. See
    COOKING
BARBERSHOPS
    Ebony 39:34 (3) Je '84
--1896 (New York)
    Smithsonian 13:114 (4) Mr '83
--Colorado
    Life 8:112 (c,2) Mr '85
--Kentucky
    Nat Geog 163:814 (c,2) Je '83
--New York
    Life 7:78 (c,4) N '84
--Shaving man in railroad station
    (Pakistan)
    Nat Geog 165:709 (c,1) Je '84

BARBERSHOPS (cont.)
--Steelton, Pennsylvania
  Nat Geog 167:376-7 (c,1) Mr
    '85
--Virginia
  Nat Geog 168:86-7 (c,1) Jl '85
--See also
    BEAUTY PARLORS
    HAIRDRESSING
    HAIRSTYLES
BARCELONA, SPAIN
  Nat Geog 165:102-9 (c,1) Ja
    '84
--Gaudi sculpture in Parque
    Güell
  Trav/Holiday 157:48 (c,2) F
    '82
--Sagrada Familia Church
  Trav/Holiday 157:47 (c,2) F
    '82
  Nat Geog 165:104-5 (c,1) Ja
    '84
BARGES
--Great Britain
  Nat Geog 163:758-9 (c,1) Je
    '83
--Oxford college clubhouse, Eng-
    land
  Nat Geog 163:768-9 (c,1) Je
    '83
--Royal barge (Thailand)
  Smithsonian 13:34 (c,2) Je '82
  Nat Geog 162:488-9 (c,1) O '82
--Vacation barges (Belgium)
  Trav/Holiday 159:75-6 (c,2)
    Mr '83
BARNACLES
  Nat Wildlife 22:20-4 (c,1) Ag
    '84
BARNS
--19th cent. (Ontario)
  Trav/Holiday 163:122 (c,4) Ap
    '85
--1820 stone barn (Pennsylvania)
  Smithsonian 15:163 (c,1) Mr
    '85
--1927 mail-order barn
  Smithsonian 16:98 (c,4) N '85
--Abandoned destroyed barn
    (North Dakota)
  Life 5:152-3 (1) N '82
--British Columbia
  Ebony 38:157 (c,4) My '83
--Octagonal (Wisconsin)
  Am Heritage 34:20 (c,4) Ag '83
--Ontario
  Sports Illus 61:48 (c,3) D

10 '84
--Oregon
  Sports Illus 59:40 (c,3) Jl 18
    '83
--West Virginia
  Trav/Holiday 164:59 (c,2) O '85
--See also
    FARMS
    STABLES
BARNS--CONSTRUCTION
--Barn raising (Pennsylvania)
  Nat Geog 165:516-17 (c,1) Ap
    '84
BARNUM, PHINEAS TAYLOR
--1889 cartoon
  Smithsonian 13:136 (c,4) My '82
BAROMETERS
--17th cent. barometer (Italy)
  Smithsonian 13:92 (engraving,4)
    S '82
BARRACUDAS
  Smithsonian 15:32 (c,4) Ag '84
BARREL MAKING
--Massachusetts
  Am Heritage 33:41 (c,4) Ag '82
BARRELS
--16th cent. whale oil casks (New-
    foundland)
  Nat Geog 168:52-3 (c,2) Jl '85
BARRYMORE, JOHN
--Caricature
  Am Heritage 37:51 (c,4) Je '86
BARTENDERS
--Woman bartender (Connecticut)
  Sports Illus 57:65 (c,4) D 13
    '82
BARTHOLDI, FREDERIC AUGUSTE
  Am Heritage 35:98 (4) Je '84
  Nat Geog 170:10 (4) Jl '86
  Life 9:52 (4) Jl '86
BARTLETT, JOHN
  Am Heritage 35:104 (4) Ag '84
BARTON, CLARA
--Depicted on postage stamp
  Am Heritage 34:59 (c,4) D '82
BARUCH, BERNARD
  Smithsonian 13:117 (painting,4)
    Mr '83
BASEBALL
--Batting practice machine
  Sports Illus 62:40 (c,3) My 6 '85
--Catching
  Nat Geog 161:530 (c,1) Ap '82
--Children playing (Israel)
  Life 6:74-5 (c,1) N '83
--Local teenagers (Delaware)
  Nat Geog 164:182-3 (c,1) Ag '83

BASEBALL (cont.)
--Nicaragua
  Nat Geog 168:780 (c,4) D '85
--Pitching at senior citizens
    game (Florida)
  Nat Geog 162:173 (c,1) Ag '82
--Scenes from the film "The
    Natural"
  Sports Illus 60:92-106 (c,1)
    My 7 '84
  Sports Illus 60:71 (c,4) My
    21 '84
BASEBALL--AMATEUR
--Little League
  Sports Illus 63:42-4 (c,3) Jl
    29 '85
--Little League (Pennsylvania)
  Sports Illus 64:2-3 (c,1) Je
    2 '86
--Little League World Series
  Nat Geog 167:358-9 (c,1) Mr
    '85
BASEBALL--COLLEGE
--Coaches
  Ebony 37:106-14 (4) Mr '82
--Pitching
  Sports Illus 58:64 (c,4) My
    30 '83
--Sliding
  Sports Illus 62:62 (c,3) My
    13 '85
  Sports Illus 62:2-3, 60 (c,1)
    Je 17 '85
BASEBALL--HISTORY
--1840's Elysian Baseball Field,
    Hoboken, New Jersey
  Sports Illus 64:34 (paint-
    ing,c,4) Je 30 '86
--Early 20th cent. baseball song
    illustrations
  Am Heritage 34:76-9, 114 (c,4)
    Je '83
--Baseball Hall of Fame, Coopers-
    town, New York
  Smithsonian 15:129 (c,4) Ap
    '84
--Early history of professional
    baseball
  Am Heritage 34:68-79, 110
    (c,1) Je '83
--See also
        BASEBALL--PROFESSIONAL
        BASEBALL PLAYERS
        BASEBALL TEAMS
        DOUBLEDAY, ABNER
BASEBALL--HUMOR
--Small town game

  Sports Illus 65:124-34 (paint-
    ing,c,1) D 22 '86
BASEBALL--PROFESSIONAL
  Sports Illus 56:40-52 (c,1) F 10
    '82
  Sports Illus 56:16-19 (c,3) Ap
    26 '82
  Sports Illus 57:16-25 (c,2) Ag
    2 '82
  Sports Illus 57:cov., 14-19 (c,1)
    Ag 9 '82
  Sports Illus 57:12-17 (c,1) Ag
    23 '82
  Sports Illus 58:40-54 (c,1) F
    16 '83
  Sports Illus 58:30-9 (c,1) Je 13
    '83
  Sports Illus 59:18-23 (c,2) Jl 18
    '83
  Sports Illus 59:16-21 (c,1) Ag 1
    '83
  Sports Illus 59:cov., 2-3, 20-5
    (c,1) O 3 '83
  Sports Illus 59:2, 28-41 (c,1) O
    17 '83
  Sports Illus 59:20-37 (c,1) O 24
    '83
  Sports Illus 60:38-47 (c,1) F 8
    '84
  Sports Illus 60:32-5 (c,3) My 14
    '84
  Sports Illus 61:2-3, 16-27 (c,1)
    Ag 27 '84
  Sports Illus 61:28-43 (c,1) O 15
    '84
  Sports Illus 62:cov., 22-120 (c,1)
    Ap 15 '85
  Sports Illus 63:36-49 (c,2) O 21
    '85
  Sports Illus 64:entire issue (c,1)
    Ap 14 '86
  Sports Illus 65:cov., 2-3, 18-25
    (c,1) O 20 '86
--1887
  Am Heritage 38:8 (4) D '86
--Early 20th cent.
  Sports Illus 63:54-8 (c,1) Ag 19
    '85
--Early 20th cent. baseball equip-
    ment
  Sports Illus 63:100-1 (c,1) D 23
    '85
--1930s poster
  Natur Hist 91:78 (3) Mr '82
--1969 parade honoring New York
    Mets (New York City)
  Sports Illus 65:80 (2) S 15 '86

BASEBALL--PROFESSIONAL (cont.)
--1974 Hank Aaron hit #715
Ebony 41:330 (4) N '85
--1986 parade honoring New York
Mets (New York City)
Sports Illus 65:2-3 (c,1) N
10 '86
--Arguing with umpire
Sports Illus 57:35 (c,4) O 4
'82
Sports Illus 64:19 (c,4) Mr 10
'86
Sports Illus 64:28 (c,4) Mr 17
'86
--At bat
Sports Illus 56:34 (c,2) Je 21
'82
--Baseball Hall of Fame, Coopers-
town, New York
Trav/Holiday 166:28 (c,4) Ag
'86
--Batting cage
Sports Illus 65:28 (c,3) Jl 7
'86
--Breaking bat while hitting
Sports Illus 57:31 (c,3) O 25
'82
Sports Illus 58:27 (c,2) Je 20
'83
Sports Illus 63:2-3 (c,1) S 2
'85
--Bunting
Sports Illus 56:50 (c,4) Mr 29
'82
Sports Illus 61:2-3 (c,1) O 1
'84
Sports Illus 62:56 (c,4) Ap 15
'85
--Calling runner out at plate
Sports Illus 65:2-3 (c,1) Jl 21
'86
--Calling runner safe
Sports Illus 65:25 (c,2) Ag 18
'86
--Catchers
Sports Illus 56:51 (c,4) My 3
'82
Sports Illus 56:52 (c,4) Je 14
'82
Sports Illus 57:46 (c,4) Ag 30
'82
Sports Illus 59:2, 86 (c,2) O
3 '83
Sports Illus 62:42 (c,4) Ap 15
'85
Sports Illus 63:28-9 (c,1) N 4
'85

--Celebrating
Sports Illus 56:14-15 (c,1) Ap
26 '82
Sports Illus 56:26-7 (c,1) My
17 '82
Sports Illus 59:37 (c,4) O 24 '83
Sports Illus 61:28-9 (c,1) O 15
'84
Sports Illus 61:26-7 (c,3) O 22
'84
Sports Illus 63:17 (c,2) Ag 12
'85
Sports Illus 63:cov., 38 (c,1)
N 4 '85
--Celebrating with champagne
Sports Illus 61:58 (c,4) O 8 '84
Sports Illus 61:43 (c,4) O 15 '84
Sports Illus 61:44 (c,4) O 22 '84
--Coaching catchers
Sports Illus 59:60-1 (c,1) D 26
'83
--Errors
Sports Illus 58:28 (c,3) Je 20
'83
Sports Illus 62:22-3 (c,4) My 27
'85
--Fielding
Sports Illus 56:42-3 (c,2) F 10
'82
Sports Illus 56:94, 96 (c,4) My
10 '82
Sports Illus 56:70 (c,3) My 31
'82
Sports Illus 57:16-17 (c,2) O 4
'82
Sports Illus 57:24-5 (c,1) O 11
'82
Sports Illus 57:38 (c,3) O 25 '82
Sports Illus 58:48 (c,4) Ap 4 '83
Sports Illus 58:38 (c,3) My 16
'83
Sports Illus 58:30-3, 39 (c,1)
Je 13 '83
Sports Illus 59:18-19 (c,2) Ag 1
'83
Sports Illus 59:25, 27 (c,2) Ag
8 '83
Sports Illus 59:12-13, 34 (c,4)
S 12 '83
Sports Illus 59:22-3, 28-31 (c,1)
O 24 '83
Sports Illus 60:42-3 (c,3) F 8 '84
Sports Illus 61:20-1 (c,2) Jl 30
'84
Sports Illus 62:42-3 (c,1) Ap 15
'85
Sports Illus 62:36-7 (c,1) My 6

BASEBALL--PROFESSIONAL (cont.)
'85
    Sports Illus 62:37 (c,3) My
        13 '85
    Sports Illus 63:37 (c,3) O 7
        '85
    Sports Illus 65:24-5 (c,1) O
        27 '86
--Fielding collision
    Sports Illus 64:2-3 (c,2) Je 16
        '86
--Fight
    Sports Illus 62:46-7 (c,1) Ap
        15 '85
    Sports Illus 64:52 (c,4) Je 9
        '86
--Fight over umpire's decision
    Sports Illus 57:18-19 (c,3) Ag
        2 '82
--History of newspaper box
        scores
    Sports Illus 58:89-90 (c,4)
        Ap 4 '83
--Hitting
    Sports Illus 56:90-1 (c,2) My
        10 '82
    Sports Illus 56:64 (c,4) My 24
        '82
    Ebony 37:74 (3) Je '82
    Sports Illus 57:24, 26 (c,3) Jl
        12 '82
    Sports Illus 57:18-21, 26 (c,2)
        Jl 19 '82
    Sports Illus 57:14-16 (c,4) Ag
        23 '82
    Sports Illus 57:18-20 (c,3) O
        4 '82
    Sports Illus 57:31-7 (c,2) O 25
        '82
    Sports Illus 58:58-9 (c,4) F
        21 '83
    Sports Illus 58:38-9, 47 (c,2)
        Mr 21 '83
    Sports Illus 58:54, 114 (c,3)
        Ap 4 '83
    Sports Illus 58:24 (c,2) Ap 25
        '83
    Sports Illus 58:34, 39 (c,2)
        My 30 '83
    Sports Illus 58:76 (c,2) Je
        13 '83
    Sports Illus 59:24-5 (c,1) Jl
        4 '83
    Sports Illus 59:16-17, 54 (c,1)
        Ag 1 '83
    Sports Illus 59:22-3, 58 (c,1)
        Ag 8 '83

Ebony 39:74 (2) Ja '84
Sports Illus 60:18-23 (c,1) Ap
    16 '84
Sports Illus 60:cov., 32-3 (c,1)
    Ap 23 '84
Sports Illus 60:18-19, 22-3 (c,1)
    My 7 '84
Ebony 39:62 (c,4) Je '84
Sports Illus 60:2-3, 28 (c,1) Je
    4 '84
Sports Illus 60:49 (c,4) Je 25
    '84
Sports Illus 61:63 (c,3) Ag 6
    '84
Sports Illus 62:22-4 (c,1) Ap 15
    '85
Sports Illus 63:20-1 (c,4) Ag 12
    '85
Sports Illus 64:cov., 24-42 (c,2)
    Ap 14 '86
Sports Illus 65:26-7 (c,1) Ag 25
    '86
--Hitting home run
    Sports Illus 57:17 (c,4) Ag 2
        '82
    Sports Illus 57:cov. (c,1) Ag 9
        '82
    Sports Illus 57:61 (4) Ag 23 '82
    Sports Illus 57:cov. (c,1) O 11
        '82
    Sports Illus 59:22 (c,3) O 3 '83
--Japan
    Sports Illus 63:2-3, 62-76 (c,1)
        S 9 '85
    Smithsonian 17:108-20 (c,2) S '86
--Japan (1920)
    Smithsonian 17:110-11 (3) S '86
--Japan (1948)
    Smithsonian 17:110 (4) S '86
--Japanese at U.S. spring training
    Sports Illus 56:36-41 (paint-
        ing,c,1) Mr 29 '82
--Roger Maris breaking Babe Ruth's
        home run record (1961)
    Sports Illus 63:26 (4) D 23 '85
--Mascots
    Sports Illus 57:44 (c,3) Jl 26
        '82
    Sports Illus 60:68 (painting,c,4)
        F 27 '84
    Sports Illus 62:86 (c,3) Ja 28 '85
--Missing pop-up
    Sports Illus 58:59 (c,4) F 21 '83
--Pitching
    Sports Illus 56:46 (c,1) F 10 '82
    Sports Illus 56:28 (c,4) My 17
        '82

BASEBALL--PROFESSIONAL (cont.)
   Sports Illus 56:46 (c,4) Je
      28 '82
   Sports Illus 57:24 (c,4) Ag
      30 '82
   Sports Illus 57:26 (c,4) S 13
      '82
   Sports Illus 57:26 (c,2) O 11
      '82
   Sports Illus 58:28 (c,2) Ja 24
      '83
   Sports Illus 58:cov., 39, 88-
      94 (c,1) Ap 18 '83
   Sports Illus 58:36 (c,4) My 9
      '83
   Sports Illus 59:48 (c,4) Jl 4
      '83
   Sports Illus 59:74-5 (c,1) Jl
      11 '83
   Sports Illus 59:22 (c,3) Jl 18
      '83
   Sports Illus 59:46 (c,4) Jl 25
      '83
   Sports Illus 59:74-80, 86 (c,1)
      Ag 22 '83
   Sports Illus 59:43 (c,4) Ag
      29 '83
   Sports Illus 59:cov. (c,1) O 3
      '83
   Sports Illus 59:20-22, 30 (c,1)
      O 24 '83
   Sports Illus 60:24-5 (c,2) Ap
      30 '84
   Sports Illus 60:40 (c,4) My 28
      '84
   Sports Illus 60:33, 92-3 (c,4)
      Je 4 '84
   Sports Illus 61:26-9, 35 (c,2)
      S 24 '84
   Sports Illus 62:cov., 26-7,
      38-9 (c,1) Ap 15 '85
   Ebony 40:75 (c,2) Je '85
   Sports Illus 63:14-15 (c,1) Ag
      12 '85
   Sports Illus 63:cov., 14-18
      (c,1) S 2 '85
   Sports Illus 64:92, 95 (c,3)
      F 3 '86
   Sports Illus 65:cov., 12-14
      (c,1) Ag 25 '86
--Pitching practice
   Life 5:86 (c,2) F '82
--Pitching spitballs
   Life 7:91-4 (c,3) Ag '84
--Pitching split-fingered ball
   Sports Illus 64:66-78 (c,1) Je
      9 '86

--Pete Rose breaking Ty Cobb's
      hitting record
   Sports Illus 63:2, 60-5 (c,2) S
      23 '85
   Life 9:95 (c,2) Ja '86
--Running
   Sports Illus 56:52 (c,4) Ap 12
      '82
   Sports Illus 56:92 (c,4) My 10
      '82
   Sports Illus 58:44 (c,3) Ap 4
      '83
--Scoring run
   Sports Illus 59:27, 32 (c,3) O
      24 '83
--Sliding
   Sports Illus 56:22 (c,2) My 3 '82
   Sports Illus 56:34 (c,4) Je 7 '82
   Sports Illus 56:23 (c,4) Je 28
      '82
   Sports Illus 57:24-7, 30-1 (c,1)
      O 18 '82
   Sports Illus 57:28-9 (c,1) O 25
      '82
   Sports Illus 58:42-3 (c,1) Ap 4
      '83
   Sports Illus 59:45 (c,4) Ag 8
      '83
   Sports Illus 59:10-12 (c,1) S
      12 '83
   Sports Illus 59:26-7 (c,3) O 3
      '83
   Sports Illus 60:38-41 (c,1) F 8
      '84
   Sports Illus 60:22-3 (c,2) Mr 12
      '84
   Ebony 39:66 (c,4) Je '84
   Sports Illus 60:26-7 (c,2) Je 4
      '84
   Sports Illus 61:2-3, 20-1 (c,1)
      Ag 27 '84
   Sports Illus 62:14-15 (c,1) Ap
      29 '85
   Sports Illus 62:40-2 (c,2) My
      20 '85
   Sports Illus 62:42-50 (c,1) Je
      17 '85
   Sports Illus 63:18-19 (c,2) Ag 5
      '85
   Sports Illus 64:20-1 (c,1) My 5
      '86
   Sports Illus 65:106-7 (c,2) O 13
      '86
--Sliding (1887)
   Am Heritage 38:8 (4) D '86
--Sliding (1946 World Series)
   Sports Illus 62:14 (3) Mr 18 '85

BASEBALL--PROFESSIONAL (cont.)
Sports Illus 63:79 (c,3) O 14
'85
--World Series 1985 (Kansas City
vs. St. Louis)
Sports Illus 63:cov., 26-35
(c,1) O 28 '85
Sports Illus 63:cov., 2-3, 22-
38 (c,1) N 4 '85
--World Series 1986 (New York
vs. Boston)
Sports Illus 65:cov., 18-28
(c,1) O 27 '86
Sports Illus 65:cov., 16-28
(c,1) N 3 '86
Sports Illus 65:26-8 (c,2) N
10 '86
Sports Illus 65:102-3 (c,1) D
22 '86
--World Series history
Sports Illus 57:53-66 (4) O 4
'82
Sports Illus 61:65-75 (c,3) O
15 '84
Sports Illus 63:59-79 (c,3)
O 14 '85
Sports Illus 65:59-78 (c,2)
O 13 '86
BASEBALL--PROFESSIONAL--
HUMOR
--Depiction of team owner as
pirate
Sports Illus 56:40-1 (draw-
ing,c,1) My 10 '82
--Umpires
Sports Illus 56:54-5 (paint-
ing,c,1) F 22 '82
Sports Illus 56:34-42 (paint-
ing,c,2) Mr 1 '82
--Use of computers
Smithsonian 14:150-70 (draw-
ing,c,1) O '83
BASEBALL BATS
Sports Illus 58:77 (c,3) Je
13 '83
Life 7:147 (c,3) Ja '84
Sports Illus 60:72 (paint-
ing,c,4) F 27 '84
Smithsonian 15:152-76 (c,4)
O '84
Sports Illus 62:82 (c,4) Mr
25 '85
Sports Illus 64:51, 66-80 (c,1)
Ap 14 '86
--1927 bat of Babe Ruth
Smithsonian 15:176 (c,4) O '84
--Unusual bats

Smithsonian 15:152-76 (c,4) O
'84
BASEBALL PLAYERS
Life 5:69 (c,1) Ja '82
Sports Illus 56:cov., 22-3 (c,1)
Mr 15 '82
Sports Illus 56:30-6 (c,2) Mr 22
'82
Sports Illus 56:78 (c,2) Ap 12
'82
Sports Illus 58:cov., 27-33 (c,1)
Mr 14 '83
Sports Illus 60:cov. (c,1) Ap 16
'84
Sports Illus 62:cov. (c,1) Mr 18
'85
--19th cent.
Am Heritage 34:69-74, 110 (c,2)
Je '83
--1880s
Am Heritage 36:102 (painting,c,1)
Ap '85
--1884
Smithsonian 15:174 (4) O '84
--1910s
Sports Illus 56:102 (4) My 10
'82
--1934
Am Heritage 35:16 (4) Je '84
--Catchers
Sports Illus 58:cov. (c,1) Ap 4
'83
--Depicted on church stained glass
(New York)
Am Heritage 35:60 (c,1) F '84
--Dressed in top hats and tails
Life 9:30-1 (c,1) D '86
--Mexico
Life 5:88 (c,4) F '82
--Rear view
Sports Illus 56:22 (c,3) Ap 19
'82
--See also
BERRA, YOGI
COBB, TY
DIMAGGIO, JOE
MANTLE, MICKEY
MAYS, WILLIE
ROBINSON, JACKIE
RUTH, GEORGE HERMAN
(BABE)
PAIGE, SATCHEL
WILLIAMS, TED
BASEBALL TEAMS
Sports Illus 58:86-7, 96 (c,1)
Ap 18 '83
--1867 Troy Haymakers

BASEBALL TEAMS (cont.)
  Am Heritage 34:69 (4) Je '83
--1875 Boston Red Stockings
  Am Heritage 34:70 (2) Je '83
--1882 Cincinnati Reds
  Am Heritage 34:73 (c,3) Je
    '83
--1885 Chicago White Stockings
  Am Heritage 36:66 (4) D '84
--1888 Chicago White Stockings
  Am Heritage 34:72 (3) Je '83
--1891
  Sports Illus 64:E3 (4) Ap 14
    '86
--1975 Boston Red Sox
  Sports Illus 61:53 (3) O 1 '84
--1975 Cincinnati Reds
  Sports Illus 61:54 (c,4) O 1
    '84
BASEBALLS
  Sports Illus 60:90-1 (c,1) Je
    4 '84
  Sports Illus 60:98 (c,4) Je
    25 '84
  Sports Illus 62:83-4 (c,4) Ja
    28 '85
  Sports Illus 64:66-7, 72 (c,1)
    Je 9 '86
--Early 20th cent. autographed
    balls
  Life 6:94-5 (c,1) D '83
--The "Abner Doubleday base-
    ball"
  Am Heritage 34:67 (4) Je '83
BASEL, SWITZERLAND
--Fasnacht carnival
  Natur Hist 91:cov., 28-40
    (c,1) F '82
BASIE, COUNT
  Ebony 39:76, 130-1 (c,1) F
    '84
  Ebony 39:98 (4) S '84
  Ebony 41:346 (4) N '85
  Ebony 41:132 (4) F '86
BASIL
  Nat Geog 163:398 (c,4) Mr '83
BASKET WEAVING
--France
  Smithsonian 14:56 (c,4) Je '83
--Norfolk Island, Australia
  Nat Geog 164:534 (c,3) O
    '83
--Southern U.S.
  Life 6:54-5 (c,1) Ag '83
BASKETBALL
--Aerial view of ball over hoop
  Sports Illus 59:56-7 (c,1)

D 26 '83
--Alabama
  Nat Geog 169:384 (c,4) Mr '86
--Basketball camp (Pennsylvania)
  Sports Illus 61:70-84 (c,1) Ag
    27 '84
--Basketball hoop
  Sports Illus 61:87 (c,4) N 26
    '84
--Harlem Magicians act
  Sports Illus 62:78-90 (c,1) Ap
    22 '85
--Playground basketball
  Sports Illus 59:40-7 (c,1) Jl 4
    '83
--Playground basketball (Indiana)
  Sports Illus 65:93 (c,3) D 22
    '86
--Playground basketball (Massach-
    setts)
  Sports Illus 65:2-3 (c,1) Ag 4
    '86
--Playground basketball (Pakistan)
  Natur Hist 95:28, 32 (c,4) S '86
--Rat playing basketball
  Sports Illus 63:2-3 (c,1) Jl 1
    '85
--Shooting
  Life 7:58-9 (c,1) Summer '84
--Swimming pool basketball game
    (Alaska)
  Nat Geog 163:168 (c,4) F '83
BASKETBALL--AMATEUR
--1984 Olympic trials
  Sports Illus 60:16-21 (c,1) Ap
    30 '84
--1984 Olympics (Los Angeles)
  Sports Illus 61:72-6 (c,2) Ag 20
    '84
--Tournament (Lowell, Michigan)
  Sports Illus 63:62-76 (c,1) Jl 8
    '85
BASKETBALL--COLLEGE
  Sports Illus 56:20-1 (c,2) Ja 25
    '82
  Sports Illus 56:96-110 (c,1) F
    10 '82
  Sports Illus 56:14-17 (c,1) F 22
    '82
  Sports Illus 56:20-5 (c,1) Mr 8
    '82
  Sports Illus 57:54-61 (draw-
    ing,c,1) Ag 2 '82
  Sports Illus 57:cov., 14-21 (c,1)
    D 20 '82
  Sports Illus 58:36-9 (c,2) F 7 '83
  Sports Illus 58:98-108 (c,1) F

BASKETBALL--COLLEGE (cont.)

--Jump ball

Sports Illus 56:20-1 (c,1) Mr
8 '82

Sports Illus 58:48-9 (c,1) Mr
21 '83

Sports Illus 64:3 (c,3) Mr 17
'86

--Mascots

Sports Illus 62:29 (c,4) Ja
7 '85

--NCAA Championships 1957
(North Carolina vs. Kan-
sas)

Sports Illus 56:58-9, 69-75
(2) Mr 29 '82

--NCAA Championships 1982 (North
Carolina vs. Georgetown)

Sports Illus 56:cov., 14-19
(c,1) Ap 5 '82

--NCAA Championships 1983
(North Carolina State
vs. Houston)

Sports Illus 58:cov. 18-23
(c,1) Ap 11 '83

--NCAA Championships 1984
(Georgetown vs. Houston)

Sports Illus 60:cov., 18-23
(c,1) Ap 9 '84

--NCAA Championships 1985 (Vil-
lanova vs. Georgetown)

Sports Illus 62:cov., 14-23
(c,1) Ap 1 '85

Sports Illus 62:cov., 32-5
(c,2) Ap 8 '85

--NCAA Championships 1986
(Louisville vs. Duke)

Sports Illus 64:cov., 28-35
(c,1) Ap 7 '86

--NCAA Playoffs 1982

Sports Illus 56:cov., 16-21
(c,1) Mr 22 '82

Sports Illus 56:cov., 16-23
(c,1) Mr 29 '82

--NCAA Playoffs 1984

Sports Illus 60:18-25 (c,1) Ap
2 '84

--NCAA Women's Championships
1983 (USC vs. La. Tech.)

Sports Illus 58:24-5 (c,2) Ap
11 '83

--NCAA Women's Championships
1984 (USC vs. Tennessee)

Sports Illus 60:46-8 (c,3) Ap 9
'84

--Rebounding

Sports Illus 57:28-9 (c,3) D

27 '82

Sports Illus 58:24-8 (c,1) Ap 4
'83

Sports Illus 60:20-1 (c,1) Mr 5
'84

--Shooting

Sports Illus 56:26-7 (c,2) Ja 18
'82

Sports Illus 56:32 (c,2) F 15 '82

Sports Illus 56:22-3 (c,1) Mr 8
'82

Sports Illus 56:26-9 (c,2) Mr 15
'82

Sports Illus 56:16-19 (c,1) Mr
22 '82

Sports Illus 56:cov., 16-23 (c,1)
Mr 29 '82

Sports Illus 57:103 (c,4) N 29
'82

Sports Illus 57:cov. (c,1) D 20
'82

Sports Illus 58:43-4 (c,2) Ja 17
'83

Sports Illus 58:58 (c,4) Ja 31
'83

Sports Illus 58:24 (c,4) Mr 28
'83

Sports Illus 58:29-32 (c,4) Ap
4 '83

Sports Illus 60:2, 22 (c,2) Ja
16 '84

Sports Illus 60:92-7 (c,1) F 8
'84

Sports Illus 62:16-19 (c,2) Ap 1
'85

Sports Illus 62:22-3 (c,2) My 6
'85

--Sitting on bench

Sports Illus 56:27 (c,4) Mr 15
'82

--Sitting on hoop

Sports Illus 58:27, 33 (c,4) Ap
4 '83

--Standing on hoop

Sports Illus 64:64 (c,2) F 3 '86

--Victor clipping net

Sports Illus 64:33 (c,2) Ap 7 '86

BASKETBALL--COLLEGE--HUMOR

Sports Illus 57:42-3 (drawing,c,1)
N 29 '82

BASKETBALL--HIGH SCHOOL

Sports Illus 56:50-62 (painting,c,1) Mr 1 '82

Sports Illus 62:41-61 (c,2) F
18 '85

--Coaches

Ebony 37:105-6 (2) Ap '82

BASS (FISH)
  Nat Wildlife 20:12-14 (c,1)
    Je '82
--Rockfish
  Sports Illus 15:34 (4) D '84
--Striped bass
  Sports Illus 60:40-2 (c,2) Ap
    23 '84
BASS PLAYING
  Smithsonian 15:155 (2) My
    '84
  Ebony 40:42 (4) S '85
BASSET HOUNDS
  Sports Illus 61:40 (c,4) N 5
    '84
BATH, ENGLAND
  Trav/Holiday 158:29-30 (c,1)
    Ag '82
  Smithsonian 15:122-35 (c,1)
    N '84
  Trav/Holiday 164:6 (c,4) D '85
BATHING
--1800 (Bath spa, England)
  Smithsonian 15:122-3 (draw-
    ing,c,1) N '84
--Early 20th cent. maid drying
    child
  Am Heritage 35:23 (draw-
    ing,c,2) Ap '84
--Athlete in bubble bath
  Sports Illus 65:70 (c,3) Jl
    21 '86
--Athletes in whirlpool
  Sports Illus 64:74 (c,4) Ap
    7 '86
  Sports Illus 64:34 (c,4) Je
    16 '86
  Sports Illus 65:2-3 (c,1) D 8
    '86
--Bathing dog
  Life 9:50-1 (c,1) N '86
--Bathing in icy water (China)
  Life 8:153 (c,3) D '85
--Bathing infant
  Life 8:104-5 (c,1) S '85
--Ceremonial bath (Nepal)
  Nat Geog 166:729 (c,1) D '84
--Children in bathtub (Michigan)
  Life 5:41 (c,2) Ag '82
--Couple in bathtub together
  Life 8:98 (c,2) Ja '85
--Drying child's hair
  Life 6:96 (3) My '83
--Family in tub (Japan)
  Nat Geog 170:638-9 (c,1) N
    '86
--Hosing down runner (North

  Carolina)
  Sports Illus 63:37 (c,4) D 9 '85
--Hot springs (Antarctica)
  Trav/Holiday 158:57 (c,4) N '82
  Trav/Holiday 164:8 (c,4) N '85
--Hot tub (Japan)
  Trav/Holiday 163:50 (c,4) Ja '85
--Hot tub (Washington, D.C. home)
  Sports Illus 58:54 (c,2) Je 6
    '83
--Hot tubs (California)
  Nat Geog 162:475 (c,3) O '82
  Ebony 38:142 (c,2) D '82
  Sports Illus 62:35 (c,4) Ja 28
    '85
--Ice bathing ritual (Japan)
  Life 8:56-7 (1) Mr '85
--In basin (Kalahari Desert, Bots-
    wana)
  Life 7:134-5 (c,3) N '84
--In bathtub
  Sports Illus 56:70-1 (c,1) My 3
    '82
--In mountain stream (Arizona)
  Trav/Holiday 160:43 (c,2) O '83
--In outdoor tub (British Columbia)
  Nat Geog 170:46-7 (c,1) Jl '86
--In volcanic mud (Italy)
  Nat Geog 162:718-19 (c,1) D '82
--In waterfall (Jamaica)
  Nat Geog 167:116-17 (c,1) Ja
    '85
--Jacuzzi (New Mexico)
  Ebony 39:43 (c,2) O '84
--Man drinking wine in bubble bath
  Sports Illus 60:10 (c,4) Ja 9 '84
--Man shampooing hair
  Ebony 38:144 (c,4) Ag '83
--Movie stars in bathtubs
  Life 5:84-5 (c,1) Mr '82
  Life 9:159-67 (c,2) My '86
--Nude in icy water (Antarctica)
  Life 8:37 (c,1) F '85
--Outdoor bath from truck water
    tank (Australia)
  Nat Geog 169:4 (c,4) Ja '86
--Outdoor shower (Society Islands)
  Sports Illus 64:124-5 (c,1) F
    10 '86
--Quintuplets
  Ebony 41:34 (c,4) D '85
--Nancy Reagan bathing dog
  Life 8:70-1 (1) Mr '85
--Ritual Hindu bath in Ganges Riv-
    er, India
  Smithsonian 16:93 (c,1) S '85
--Sand bathing (Japan)

BATHING (cont.)
    Trav/Holiday 158:52 (c,4) N
        '82
--Shampooing elephant (New York)
    Life 6:134 (c,2) Jl '83
--Squirting water at child (Kenya)
    Nat Geog 161:121 (c,2) Ja
        '82
--Steam baths (Alaska)
    Nat Geog 165:830 (2) Je '84
--Tennis player washing face
    Sports Illus 63:2-3 (c,1) S
        16 '85
--Two in a bathtub (Colorado)
    Life 6:78-9 (c,1) Ag '83
--Two in a bathtub (West Ger-
        many)
    Life 5:27 (c,4) Mr '82
--Warm Mineral Springs, Florida
    Smithsonian 17:72-3 (c,1) D
        '86
--Warm springs (Steamboat
        Springs, Colorado)
    Trav/Holiday 164:51 (c,2) N
        '85
--Washing face
    Ebony 39:121 (c,2) Ja '84
--Washing hair in cow urine
        (Sudan)
    Life 5:159 (c,4) D '82
--Washing mud from volcano
        victim (Colombia)
    Nat Geog 169:647 (c,1) My '86
--Wearing formal attire in bathtub
    Life 6:cov., 114-15 (c,1) My
        '83
--Whirlpool
    Sports Illus 56:74 (c,3) Ja
        11 '82
--Whirlpool (California)
    Life 6:89 (c,4) O '83
--Whirlpool bath aboard ship
    Trav/Holiday 165:15 (c,4) Je
        '86
--Woman in bathtub filled with
        soda
    Life 9:34-5 (c,1) D '86
--Woman in bubble bath
    Life 7:96-7 (c,1) Jl '84
--Woman showering
    Ebony 40:114 (c,4) Mr '85
--See also
        BATHS
        BATHTUBS
        BEACHES, BATHING
        SAUNAS
        SWIMMING

        SWIMMING POOLS
BATHING SUITS
    Ebony 37:80-6 (c,1) Ja '82
    Sports Illus 56:cov., 56-71 (c,1)
        F 8 '82
    Life 5:cov., 96-103 (c,1) F '82
    Life 5:cov., 76-7 (c,1) Jl '82
    Sports Illus 57:26-31 (c,1) Ag
        23 '82
    Ebony 38:70-4, 120 (c,1) Ja '83
    Life 6:cov., 84-90 (c,1) F '83
    Sports Illus 58:cov., 4, 54-64
        (c,1) F 14 '83
    Ebony 39:92-6 (c,2) Ja '84
    Sports Illus 60:cov., 4-5, 64-87
        (c,1) F 13 '84
    Life 7:cov., 38-44 (c,1) Mr '84
    Ebony 39:cov., 104-10 (c,1) Jl
        '84
    Ebony 40:100-4 (c,3) Ja '85
    Life 8:cov., 83-8 (c,1) F '85
    Sports Illus 62:cov., 2-3, 102-31
        (c,1) F 11 '85
    Life 8:103 (c,3) D '85
    Sports Illus 64:cov., 2-3, 102-35
        (c,1) F 10 '86
    Life 9:cov., 66-80 (c,1) F '86
    Ebony 41:122-6 (c,2) Mr '86
--1930s-1980s
    Life 9:cov., 66-80 (c,1) F '86
--1931
    Life 5:43 (3) Mr '82
--1940
    Smithsonian 13:64-5 (3) S '82
--1942 children's swimsuits
    Am Heritage 35:34 (4) F '84
--1943
    Life 9:310 (2) Fall '86
--1947
    Life 9:66 (2) Fall '86
--Australia
    Nat Geog 161:643 (c,3) My '82
BATHROOMS
--1850s sink (Wisconsin)
    Am Heritage 34:14 (c,3) Ag '83
--British embassy, Washington, D.C.
    Life 8:55 (c,4) N '85
--French chateau
    Trav/Holiday 163:67 (c,3) Ap '85
--Mansion (Illinois)
    Ebony 41:94 (c,3) S '86
--On yacht
    Ebony 39:104 (c,4) S '84
--Public ladies room (Wisconsin)
    Life 5:62 (4) S '82
--Spacecraft toilet
    Life 7:74 (c,4) O '84

BATHROOMS (cont.)
--See also
    OUTHOUSES
BATHS
--Ancient Roman (Bath, England)
    Trav/Holiday 158:29 (c,1) Ag
      '82
    Smithsonian 15:126 (c,4) N '84
--Ancient Roman (Ostia Antica,
    Italy)
    Nat Geog 170:326 (c,4) S '86
--Bathhouse (Chicago, Illinois)
    Life 9:27 (c,3) O '86
--Public baths (Tokyo, Japan)
    Nat Geog 170:626-7 (c,1) N
      '86
BATHTUBS
--1st cent. A.D. (Italy)
    Nat Geog 165:593 (c,4) My '84
--Mid-19th cent. tin sitz bath
    Am Heritage 37:40 (c,4) Ag
      '86
--Heart-shaped tub (California)
    Life 9:162 (c,2) My '86
--Huge tub (New York)
    Life 7:94-5 (c,1) D '84
--Japan
    Trav/Holiday 157:50 (c,4) Ja
      '82
--Outdoor tub (British Columbia)
    Nat Geog 170:46-7 (c,1) Jl '86
BATS
    Nat Wildlife 20:35-9 (2) Ag
      '82
    Smithsonian 14:74-80 (c,1) Ja
      '84
--Bat tower (Texas)
    Am Heritage 33:110, 112 (4)
      Je '82
--Big-eared
    Natur Hist 94:52-3 (c,1) Je '85
--Catching mouse
    Natur Hist 93:112-13 (c,1) Ap
      '84
--Free-tailed
    Smithsonian 13:75, 80-1 (3) N
      '82
--Frog-eating bats
    Nat Geog 161:78-91 (c,1) Ja
      '82
    Natur Hist 94:58-9 (c,1) Je
      '85
    Natur Hist 95:40-1 (c,2) Je '86
--Fruit bats
    Smithsonian 13:100 (c,4) Je '82
    Life 5:50 (c,2) S '82
    Natur Hist 94:52-9 (c,1) Je '85

--Gray bats
    Natur Hist 95:22 (c,4) Je '86
--Nectar-eating bats
    Smithsonian 14:74-5, 79 (c,1)
      Ja '84
--Poachers killing bats (Thailand)
    Smithsonian 14:76 (c,4) Ja '84
--Tent-making bats
    Smithsonian 17:28 (c,4) Jl '86
--White bats
    Life 5:47 (c,4) S '82
--See also
    FLYING FOXES
Battles. See
    WARFARE
    WARS
    AUSTERLITZ
    BUNKER HILL
    WATERLOO
BATTLESHIPS
--16th cent. warship (Great Britain)
    Nat Geog 163:648-73 (c,1) My
      '83
--Late 19th cent. U.S. Navy ships
    Am Heritage 37:81-96 (1) Je '86
--Early 20th cent. U.S. Navy ship
    Am Heritage 37:94-5 (1) Je '86
--1940s (France)
    Smithsonian 16:122-36 (3) Jl '85
--1940s (Great Britain)
    Smithsonian 16:128 (4) Jl '85
--1940s (Japan)
    Am Heritage 36:30 (4) Ag '85
--1940s (U.S.)
    Smithsonian 15:12 (4) Jl '84
    Am Heritage 36:114-15 (1) D '84
    Am Heritage 36:26-35 (2) F '85
--1969 (U.S.)
    Am Heritage 35:10 (4) D '83
--Damaged in World War II
    Am Heritage 36:26 (2) F '85
--U.S.
    Am Heritage 34:10-25 (c,1) Ap
      '83
    Ebony 39:74 (4) F '84
    Life 7:30-6 (c,1) Mr '84
Bays. See
    CHESAPEAKE BAY
    DELAWARE BAY
    HUDSON BAY
BEACHES
    Smithsonian 16:26 (c,3) Jl '85
--Barbados
    Trav/Holiday 162:44-5 (c,2) Ag
      '84
--Captiva Island, Florida
    Trav/Holiday 163:14 (c,3) Ja '85

BEACHES (cont.)
--Delaware Bay, Delaware/New
    Jersey
    Natur Hist 95:68-71 (c,1)
      My '86
--Florida
    Trav/Holiday 157:54 (c,3)
      F '82
--Hawaii
    Trav/Holiday 163:27, 82 (c,2)
      Mr '85
--Honduras
    Nat Geog 164:616-17 (c,1) N
      '83
--Mexico
    Am Heritage 33:8 (c,1) Ap
      '82
--Olympic Peninsula coast, Wash-
    ington
    Trav/Holiday 159:cov. (c,1)
      My '83
--Pensacola, Florida
    Nat Geog 162:218-19 (c,1)
      Ag '82
--Perth, Australia
    Nat Geog 161:660-1 (c,1) My
      '82
--Pfeiffer Beach, California
    Nat Geog 165:428-9 (c,1) Ap
      '84
--Wales coast
    Nat Geog 164:60-1 (c,1) Jl '83
--Wisconsin
    Trav/Holiday 159:57 (c,1) My
      '83
BEACHES, BATHING
--Antigua
    Ebony 37:105 (c,4) Ja '82
    Trav/Holiday 166:52 (c,3) S
      '86
--Atlantic City, New Jersey
    Trav/Holiday 158:40 (c,2) Ag
      '82
--Bahamas
    Ebony 41:74 (c,3) My '86
--Bahia, Brazil
    Trav/Holiday 162:54 (c,2) N
      '84
--Barry Island, Wales
    Nat Geog 164:44-5 (c,1) Jl
      '83
--Boardwalk (Atlantic City, New
    Jersey)
    Trav/Holiday 158:40 (c,2) Ag
      '82
--Boardwalk (Coney Island, New
    York)

Sports Illus 64:70 (c,3) Mr 24
  '86
--Burma
    Smithsonian 15:98-9 (c,1) My '84
--Cannes, France
    Life 9:10-11 (c,1) N '86
--Caracas, Venezuela
    Trav/Holiday 163:60-1 (c,2) F
      '85
--Cayman Islands
    Trav/Holiday 161:72-3 (c,2) My
      '84
--Child playing in sand
    Trav/Holiday 158:26 (4) Ag '82
--Children playing in sand (Cali-
    fornia)
    Sports Illus 61:44 (c,3) S 24 '84
--Children playing in sand (France)
    Life 7:44 (c,4) Je '84
--Coney Island, New York
    Nat Geog 163:606-7 (c,1) My '83
    Sports Illus 64:70 (c,3) Mr 24
      '86
--Costa Brava, Spain
    Nat Geog 165:96-7 (c,1) Ja '84
--Delaware
    Nat Geog 164:190-1 (c,1) Ag '83
--Galveston, Texas
    Ebony 41:78 (c,3) My '86
--Guadeloupe
    Trav/Holiday 165:82 (c,3) Ap '86
--Huntington Beach, California
    Sports Illus 65:14-15 (c,3) S 8
      '86
--Lake Balaton, Hungary
    Nat Geog 163:254-5 (c,1) F '83
--Lyme Regis, Dorset, England
    Trav/Holiday 160:4 (c,4) S '83
--Mar del Plata, Argentina
    Nat Geog 170:246 (c,3) Ag '86
--Miami Beach, Australia
    Nat Geog 169:6-7 (c,1) Ja '86
--Miami Beach, Florida
    Trav/Holiday 163:54 (c,1) Je '85
--Myrtle Beach, South Carolina
    Trav/Holiday 164:50-1 (c,4) S '85
--Negril, Jamaica
    Ebony 41:76 (c,3) My '86
--New Hampshire
    Nat Geog 162:780-1 (c,1) D '82
--Nice, France
    Trav/Holiday 158:34 (c,4) Jl '82
--North Carolina
    Trav/Holiday 161:34 (4) Mr '84
--Perth, Australia
    Trav/Holiday 166:46 (c,4) Ag
      '86

BEACHES, BATHING (cont.)
--Rimini, Italy
    Nat Geog 162:728-9 (c,1) D
      '82
--St. Maarten
    Trav/Holiday 157:57 (c,4) My
      '82
--Siberia, U.S.S.R.
    Trav/Holiday 165:51 (c,2) My
      '86
--Tijuana, Mexico
    Nat Geog 167:763-7 (c,1) Je
      '85
--Tobago
    Ebony 40:103 (c,2) N '84
--Virginia Beach, Virginia
    Nat Geog 168:98-9 (c,1) Jl
      '85
--Waikiki, Hawaii
    Trav/Holiday 166:58-61 (c,1)
      Ag '86
BEAGLES
    Nat Geog 170:352 (c,4) S '86
BEAN, JUDGE ROY
--Artifacts
    Nat Geog 165:226 (c,4) F '84
BEARDS
    Life 5:27 (2) Ap '82
    Smithsonian 13:114 (c,2) Je
      '82
--1877 mutton-chop whiskers
    Am Heritage 37:106 (paint-
      ing,4) D '85
--1880 (Australia)
    Smithsonian 14:42 (4) Je '83
--1885 side beard
    Am Heritage 36:67 (paint-
      ing,2) D '84
--1901
    Nat Geog 162:272 (2) Ag '82
--Large white beard (Alaska)
    Nat Wildlife 21:43 (c,3) Ag '83
--Yukon
    Trav/Holiday 164:61 (c,1) Ag
      '85
--See also
    MUSTACHES
BEARS
    Trav/Holiday 157:47 (c,4) My
      '82
--Black bear cub
    Nat Wildlife 21:58 (c,4) Ap '83
--Black bears
    Smithsonian 14:86-94 (c,1) Ap
      '83
    Nat Geog 165:67 (c,3) Ja '84
    Nat Wildlife 22:18 (c,4) Ag '84

--Brown bear claws
    Nat Geog 165:66-7 (c,1) Ja '84
--Brown bear eating salmon
    Natur Hist 95:102-3 (c,1) My
      '86
--Brown bear face
    Nat Wildlife 24:7 (c,1) Ap '86
--Brown bears
    Nat Wildlife 21:cov. (c,1) Ap '83
    Natur Hist 94:32 (c,4) My '85
--Kodiak bear trophy
    Am Heritage 33:16 (2) Ap '82
--Man wounded by grizzly bear
    (Yukon)
    Nat Geog 168:644-5 (c,1) N '85
--Smokey the Bear
    Nat Geog 162:332 (drawing,c,4)
      S '82
--See also
    GRIZZLY BEARS
    HONEY BEARS
    POLAR BEARS
BEATLES
    Am Heritage 35:11 (3) F '84
    Life 7:cov., 59-67 (c,1) F '84
    Life 9:359 (4) Fall '86
    Life 9:33 (4) D '86
BEATLES
--1960s fans
    Life 7:58-67 (c,1) F '84
--Football players recreating "Abbey
    Road" cover
    Sports Illus 65:29 (c,3) Ag 11
      '86
--John Lennon's 1956 Bentley car
    Nat Geog 164:32-3 (c,2) Jl '83
--Ringo Starr
    Life 9:50 (c,4) Ja '86
--See also
    LENNON, JOHN
BEAUTY CONTESTS
--1957 "Miss America" contestants
    Life 9:105 (c,2) Fall '86
--1970 "Miss Ohio"
    Ebony 37:119 (3) Ja '82
--1983 "Miss America"
    Ebony 41:344 (4) N '85
--Beauty queens
    Ebony 40:173-4 (4) My '85
--Campus queens
    Ebony 37:140-8 (c,3) Ap '82
    Ebony 38:cov., 40-50 (c,2) My
      '83
    Ebony 40:36-45 (c,3) Ap '85
    Ebony 41:132-43 (c,3) Ap '86
--Crowning "Miss America"
    Ebony 39:44 (3) Je '84

BEAUTY CONTESTS (cont.)
--Fiesta (San Antonio, Texas)
  Smithsonian 16:118 (c,4) D
  '85
--Great River Carnival Queen
  (Memphis, Tennessee)
  Nat Geog 169:621 (c,4) My '86
--High school queen (Kentucky)
  Nat Geog 161:544-5 (c,1) Ap
  '82
--"Miss America"
  Ebony 39:cov., 132-6 (c,1) D
  '83
--"Miss Op" (California)
  Sports Illus 65:14 (c,4) S 8
  '86
--Potato queen (Maine)
  Nat Geog 161:692 (c,1) My '82
--"Sweetest Girl" winner (Florida)
  Life 9:31 (c,2) Jl '86
BEAUTY PARLORS
--Alberta
  Nat Geog 165:401 (c,2) Mr '84
--Ivory Coast
  Nat Geog 162:103 (c,4) Jl '82
--See also
  BARBERSHOPS
  HAIRDRESSING
  HAIRSTYLES
BEAVERS
  Nat Wildlife 20:47 (c,4) Je
  '82
  Sports Illus 56:72 (c,4) Je
  28 '82
  Nat Wildlife 22:8-15 (c,1) Je
  '84
  Smithsonian 15:162-71 (c,1) N
  '84
  Nat Wildlife 23:13 (painting,c,3)
  F '85
  Natur Hist 95:82 (drawing,4)
  N '86
BEDOUINS
--Israel
  Nat Geog 161:422-48 (c,1)
  Ap '82
  Nat Geog 168:32-3 (c,1) Jl '85
--Jordan
  Nat Geog 165:246-7, 257 (c,2)
  F '84
--North Yemen
  Nat Geog 168:504 (c,1) O '85
--Saudi Arabia
  Smithsonian 15:44-57 (c,1) D
  '84
BEDOUINS--RELICS
--Saudi Arabia

Smithsonian 14:148 (c,4) Ap '83
BEDOUINS--SOCIAL LIFE AND
  CUSTOMS
--Eating communal meal (Saudi
  Arabia)
  Smithsonian 15:16 (c,4) F '85
BEDROOMS
  Ebony 38:118 (c,2) O '83
--13th cent. castle (Great Britain)
  Nat Geog 168:680-1 (c,1) N '85
--17th cent. decor (New York)
  Trav/Holiday 166:32 (c,4) Jl '86
--18th cent. (Pennsylvania)
  Smithsonian 14:101 (c,4) My '83
--Aboard the "Titanic" (1912)
  Nat Geog 170:724 (4) D '86
--British embassy, Washington,
  D.C.
  Life 8:54-5 (c,1) N '85
--California
  Ebony 37:32 (c,4) Ap '82
--Country inn (Connecticut)
  Trav/Holiday 160:13 (c,4) D '83
--French chateau
  Smithsonian 14:59 (c,2) Ag '83
--Illinois mansion
  Ebony 37:28 (c,4) F '82
  Ebony 41:94 (c,3) S '86
--On yacht
  Ebony 39:104 (c,4) S '84
--Teenage athlete's room (Indiana)
  Sports Illus 65:86 (c,2) D 22
  '86
--Teenage boys (New York)
  Sports Illus 61:44 (c,3) N 26
  '84
  Sports Illus 62:51 (c,4) Mr 25
  '85
--Teenage girl (Texas)
  Life 9:38-9 (c,1) Mr '86
--Teenager's bedroom
  Sports Illus 60:48 (c,4) Je 18
  '84
BEDS
--1st cent. A.D. (Italy)
  Nat Geog 165:592-3 (c,4) My '84
--17th cent. bedstead (New England)
  Smithsonian 13:111 (c,2) Je '82
--18th cent. Austrian bed (Califor-
  nia)
  Ebony 37:68 (c,4) Je '82
--1899 sailor's bunk
  Am Heritage 37:96 (4) Je '86
--Astronaut's sleep sack aboard
  spacecraft
  Life 7:78 (c,2) O '84
--Bunk beds (Mississippi)

BEDS (cont.)
 Sports Illus 59:71 (c,4) N 14
  '83
--Bunk beds (New York)
 Ebony 38:76 (4) Ag '83
--Child jumping on bed (Illinois)
 Life 8:148-9 (c,1) Je '85
--18 people in one bed
 Life 9:32-3 (c,1) D '86
--Japanese futons
 Trav/Holiday 157:50 (c,4) Ja
  '82
--Man sprawled across bed read-
  ing
 Sports Illus 60:60-1 (c,1) F
  20 '84
--Modern platform bed (New York)
 Life 5:88 (c,2) My '82
--Self-making bed
 Smithsonian 15:114 (c,4) Ag
  '84
--Submarine bunks
 Life 7:56 (c,4) N '84
 Sports Illus 65:29 (c,4) N 19
  '86
--Waterbeds
 Sports Illus 57:38 (c,4) S 6
  '82
--See also
  BABY CRIBS
  HAMMOCKS
BEE KEEPING
 Nat Geog 166:510-11 (c,1) O
  '84
--Vatican City
 Nat Geog 168:746 (c,1) D '85
BEER
--Fifteen-foot tall beer can
  (Florida)
 Nat Geog 162:202 (c,3) Ag '82
BEER INDUSTRY
--Brewery (North Carolina)
 Ebony 38:40-2 (c,2) Je '83
--Brewery exterior (Oslo, Nor-
  way)
 Sports Illus 65:62 (c,4) Jl 7
  '86
--Brewery interior (St. Louis,
  Missouri)
 Trav/Holiday 157:34-5 (c,1) Je
  '82
BEERBOHM, SIR MAX
--Caricature of G. K. Chesterton
 Smithsonian 14:120 (draw-
  ing,c,4) S '83
--Cartoon about Rudyard Kipling
 Smithsonian 16:39 (c,4) Ja '86

BEES
 Nat Wildlife 21:21-4 (c,1) F '83
 Nat Geog 166:510 (c,3) O '84
 Smithsonian 15:71 (c,3) Mr '85
--Bee feces
 Life 7:24 (c,4) Ag '84
--Bee nest
 Life 7:26 (c,4) Ag '84
--Honeybees
 Nat Wildlife 20:23 (c,2) Ag '82
 Nat Wildlife 22:17 (c,2) Ag '84
--See also
  BEE KEEPING
  BUMBLEBEES
BEETLES
 Smithsonian 12:58 (c,3) Mr '82
 Nat Wildlife 20:16 (c,3) O '82
 Nat Wildlife 21:12 (c,4) Ap '83
 Nat Geog 164:368 (c,4) S '83
 Natur Hist 93:56 (c,4) D '84
 Natur Hist 94:98-9 (c,2) S '85
 Natur Hist 95:100-1 (c,1) Mr '86
 Natur Hist 95:75-7 (c,1) Ap '86
 Smithsonian 17:122 (c,1) My '86
 Natur Hist 95:54-61 (c,1) Jl '86
 Smithsonian 17:81, 88 (c,4) S
  '86
 Natur Hist 95:2 (drawing,c,4)
  S '86
--Diving beetles
 Natur Hist 93:48-51 (c,1) F '84
--See also
  LADYBUGS
BEGGAR-TICKS (PLANTS)
 Natur Hist 91:26 (c,4) D '82
BEGGARS
--India
 Nat Geog 169:229 (c,1) F '86
--Morocco
 Nat Geog 169:347 (c,4) Mr '86
BEIJING, CHINA
 Trav/Holiday 164:46-9 (c,1) S
  '85
--Forbidden City
 Natur Hist 95:34-5, 40-3 (c,1)
  S '86
BEIRUT, LEBANON
 Life 7:30-6 (1) Ag '84
--Aftermath of 1982 Israeli invasion
 Nat Geog 163:262-85 (c,1) F '83
--View from the sea
 Life 7:34-5 (c,1) Mr '84
--War damage
 Life 5:4, 22-30 (c,1) Ag '82
 Life 6:24-32 (c,1) Je '83
BELGIUM
 Trav/Holiday 159:cov., 75-7

BELGIUM (cont.)
(c,1) Mr '83
--Ooidonck Castle, Deurle
Trav/Holiday 159:cov. (c,1)
Mr '83
--Waterloo farm
Nat Geog 161:184 (c,1) F '82
--See also
BRUGES
BRUSSELS
BELGIUM--COSTUME
--Mounted policemen
Life 5:112-13 (1) Ap '82
Belgium--History. See
LEOPOLD III
WATERLOO, BATTLE OF
BELIZE
Trav/Holiday 158:58, 85 (c,1)
N '82
Sports Illus 61:66-72 (c,1) D
17 '84
Trav/Holiday 166:23 (c,4) Jl
'86
--Mayan sites (Cuello)
Nat Geog 162:126-40 (c,1) Jl
'82
BELIZE--COSTUME
Sports Illus 61:66-76 (c,1) D
17 '84
BELL, ALEXANDER GRAHAM
Nat Geog 162:272 (2) Ag '82
--Depicted on 1940 postage stamp
Am Heritage 34:51 (c,4) D
'82
BELLINI, GENTILE
--"Procession in Piazza San
Marco" (1496)
Smithsonian 13:102 (paint-
ing,c,4) S '82
BELLOW, SAUL
Life 9:21-7 (c,2) O '86
BELLS
--University of Tulsa, Oklahoma
Sports Illus 57:70 (c,4) D
6 '82
BELUGAS
Nat Geog 161:400-1 (c,1) Mr
'82
Nat Geog 164:112 (sculp-
ture,c,4) Jl '83
Life 8:79 (2) Je '85
BENCHES
--Calgary, Alberta
Nat Geog 165:384 (c,3) Mr '84
BENCHLEY, ROBERT
Smithsonian 12:122-42 (1) F
'82

Am Heritage 37:113 (2) F '86
Am Heritage 37:82-91 (1) Ap '86
BENNY, JACK
Sports Illus 64:84 (4) Ap 21 '86
BERBER PEOPLE (MOROCCO)--
COSTUME
--Berber women
Nat Geog 166:626-7 (c,1) N '84
BERBER PEOPLE (MOROCCO)--
RITES AND FESTIVALS
--Fantasia event (Fez)
Nat Geog 169:348-9 (c,1) Mr '86
BERCHTESGADEN, WEST GERMANY
--Church
Trav/Holiday 158:12 (c,4) D '82
BERGMAN, INGRID
Life 6:147-8 (3) Ja '83
Life 8:136 (c,4) N '85
BERING SEA
Nat Geog 164:338-9 (c,1) S '83
BERLIN, GERMANY
--1936
Life 7:102-3 (1) Summer '84
--American sector sign
Life 5:86 (c,2) My '82
--East Berlin
Nat Geog 161:cov., 3-33
(map,c,1) Ja '82
Trav/Holiday 165:6 (c,4) Ap '86
--Reichstag
Trav/Holiday 165:6 (c,4) Ap '86
--West Berlin
Nat Geog 161:6-13, 34-51
(map,c,1) Ja '82
--See also
BERLIN WALL
BERLIN WALL, GERMANY
Nat Geog 161:4-11 (c,1) Ja '82
Life 9:30-1 (c,1) Mr '86
BERMUDA
Trav/Holiday 157:46, 49, 69 (c,3)
Je '82
Ebony 37:36-42 (c,2) S '82
Trav/Holiday 162:10-11 (c,2) D
'84
Ebony 40:74 (c,3) Ja '85
--See also
HAMILTON
BERMUDA--COSTUME
Ebony 37:36-42 (c,2) S '82
--Policeman
Ebony 39:173 (c,4) My '84
BERMUDA--MAPS
--1609
Am Heritage 34:31 (c,3) Ap '83
BERN, SWITZERLAND
Nat Geog 169:124-5 (c,1) Ja '86

BERRA, YOGI
    Sports Illus 60:cov., 85-98
        (c,1) Ap 2 '84
BERRIES
    Natur Hist 93:42-53 (c,1) Ag
        '84
--Elderberries
    Natur Hist 91:95 (4) My '82
--Greenbrier berries
    Smithsonian 14:78 (c,2) Jl '83
--See also
        BLUEBERRIES
        BUNCHBERRIES
        CRANBERRIES
        MULBERRIES
        STRAWBERRIES
BETHUNE, MARY McLEOD
    Smithsonian 12:141 (4) Ja '82
    Ebony 37:131 (4) Mr '82
    Ebony 38:146 (4) D '82
    Ebony 40:32 (4) F '85
    Ebony 41:62, 172-80, 214 (1)
        N '85
--Monument (Washington, D.C.)
    Ebony 37:61 (2) F '82
    Ebony 38:136 (2) D '82
BHUTAN
--Wong Chu River
    Life 5:80-2 (c,1) N '82
--See also
        HIMALAYAN MOUNTAINS
BHUTAN--COSTUME
--Shepherd
    Smithsonian 14:116 (c,4) O '83
BIBLES
--9th cent. Book of Kells (Ireland)
    Trav/Holiday 163:66 (c,4) F
        '85
--1483 Nuremberg Bible woodcut
        of Noah's ark
    Smithsonian 14:89 (c,4) Je '83
--1529 translation by Martin
        Luther
    Nat Geog 164:444-5 (c,1) O '83
--18th cent. (Great Britain)
    Nat Geog 164:512 (c,4) O '83
--Actress portraying Eve
    Life 8:61 (c,2) O '85
--Field's "Garden of Eden" (1860)
    Smithsonian 15:69 (paint-
        ing,c,2) Ag '84
--Gutenberg page
    Smithsonian 12:68 (c,4) F '82
--Painting of Job by William Blake
    Smithsonian 13:50-1 (c,1) S
        '82
--Reading Bible to children

(1950; Missouri)
    Life 9:282-3 (1) Fall '86
--See also
        ANGELS
        CHRISTIANITY
        JESUS CHRIST
        JUDAISM
        NOAH'S ARK
        SAINTS
BICYCLE RACES
    Sports Illus 59:52, 54 (c,4) Jl
        25 '83
    Sports Illus 59:76 (4) Ag 1 '83
    Sports Illus 62:192 (painting,c,4)
        F 11 '85
--Children's bicycle motocross race
        (Oklahoma)
    Sports Illus 65:28-36 (c,1) D 8
        '86
--Colorado
    Sports Illus 65:30-1 (c,3) S 15
        '86
--Great Britain
    Nat Geog 169:408-9 (c,1) Mr '86
--Speed racing (Utah)
    Sports Illus 63:54-6 (c,3) Jl 29
        '85
--Triathlon (France)
    Sports Illus 59:86-98 (c,2) O 10
        '83
--U.S. Pro Cycling Championship
        1985 (Philadelphia)
    Sports Illus 63:22-9 (c,1) Jl 1
        '85
BICYCLE TOURS
--Colorado
    Sports Illus 63:46-55 (c,1) Ag
        26 '85
--Tour de France 1984
    Sports Illus 61:52-64 (c,3) S 3
        '84
--Tour de France 1985
    Sports Illus 63:2-3, 16-21 (c,1)
        Jl 29 '85
--Tour de France 1986
    Sports Illus 65:56-7 (c,3) Jl 21
        '86
    Sports Illus 65:12-17 (c,1) Ag 4
        '86
    Sports Illus 65:112-13 (c,1) D
        22 '86
BICYCLES
    Nat Geog 164:390 (c,2) S '83
--19th cent.
    Smithsonian 14:126 (c,2) F '84
--19th cent. style Penny Farthing
        high wheel cycle

BICYCLES (cont.)
Sports Illus 64:80 (c,4) Ja
27 '86
--1884
Am Heritage 37:111 (2) Ag '86
--Early 20th cent. (Missouri)
Am Heritage 33:53 (2) Ag '82
--Bicyclists commuting to work
(China)
Life 8:156 (c,2) D '85
--Child on tricycle (Great Britain)
Smithsonian 14:104 (c,4) Ja
'84
--Japan
Life 6:42-3 (c,1) S '83
--Locking bicycle on street (New
York)
Sports Illus 63:31 (c,4) S 23
'85
--Silk tires (France)
Nat Geog 165:37 (c,4) Ja '84
--Unusual human-powered vehicles
Smithsonian 15:90-9 (c,1) Ja
'85
BICYCLING
Ebony 37:128 (4) My '82
Sports Illus 57:30 (c,3) Jl
26 '82
Ebony 38:96, 101 (3) N '82
Sports Illus 57:82 (c,4) N 1
'82
Nat Geog 165:518-19 (c,1)
Ap '84
Sports Illus 62:32-3 (c,1) Ja
14 '85
--19th cent.
Trav/Holiday 160:8 (engrav-
ing,4) Jl '83
--1984 Olympics (Los Angeles)
Sports Illus 61:42-6 (c,3) Ag
6 '84
Sports Illus 61:82-5 (c,3) Ag
13 '84
Sports Illus 62:12-15 (c,2)
Ja 21 '85
--Amish people (Pennsylvania)
Nat Geog 165:518-19 (c,1)
Ap '84
--Arab children (Israel)
Life 6:82 (c,2) N '83
--Bicycling out of airborne plane
Life 7:124 (c,2) Jl '84
--Chicago, Illinois
Sports Illus 63:80 (c,3) S 30
'85
--Child on bicycle
Ebony 39:56 (4) Ap '84

--China
Trav/Holiday 158:49 (c,3) Jl '82
--Denmark
Trav/Holiday 161:63, 67 (c,2)
My '84
--Doing wheelie (Texas)
Smithsonian 16:122 (c,3) D '85
--Family bicycle outing
Sports Illus 64:60 (c,3) Je 2
'86
--Japan
Trav/Holiday 165:65 (c,4) Je '86
--Pennsylvania
Nat Geog 163:342 (c,4) Mr '83
--Stunt biking over people (Illinois)
Life 8:96-7 (1) D '85
--Switzerland
Sports Illus 61:2-3, 50-1 (c,1)
S 3 '84
--Tandem bike
Sports Illus 57:62 (c,4) Jl 19
'82
Sports Illus 65:55 (c,4) Ag 18
'86
--Tot on tricycle (Alabama)
Ebony 38:114 (3) Ag '83
--Touring (Wisconsin)
Trav/Holiday 157:63 (c,4) Ap '82
BICYCLING--HUMOR
--Bike loaded down with gear
Sports Illus 60:112 (drawing,c,4)
My 7 '84
BIERCE, AMBROSE
Smithsonian 16:164 (drawing,4)
My '85
BIERSTADT, ALBERT
--1869 painting of Niagara Falls
Smithsonian 16:128 (c,2) S '85
--"Wind River, Wyoming" (1870)
Natur Hist 94:58-9 (painting,c,1)
N '85
BIG BEN CLOCK TOWER, LONDON,
ENGLAND
Nat Geog 170:741 (c,1) D '86
BIG BEND NATIONAL PARK,
TEXAS
Natur Hist 91:53 (c,4) Je '82
Natur Hist 93:40 (c,2) Ja '84
Trav/Holiday 162:cov., 30-3
(c,1) O '84
Life 9:88-95 (c,1) Jl '86
Life 9:42-3 (c,1) Ag '86
--See also
RIO GRANDE RIVER
BIG THICKET NATIONAL MONU-
MENT, TEXAS
Natur Hist 95:98-100 (map,c,1)
Ap '86

BIKINI ATOLL
  Nat Geog 169:815-34
    (map,c,1) Je '86
--1946 relocation of residents
    to allow atomic testing
  Nat Geog 169:815-17 (map,c,1)
    Je '86
BILLIARD PLAYING
  Life 5:90 (c,3) O '82
  Life 6:59 (c,4) F '83
  Sports Illus 58:51 (c,4) Mr
    14 '83
  Ebony 38:64 (c,4) My '83
  Sports Illus 59:102 (c,4) S
    19 '83
  Sports Illus 62:53 (c,4) F 4
    '85
  Sports Illus 62:62 (c,4) F
    18 '85
  Sports Illus 63:80 (c,3) N 20
    '85
  Life 9:74,76 (c,4) N '86
--Late 18th cent. billiard table
    (Maryland)
  Smithsonian 14:104 (c,4) My
    '83
--1910 Victorian-style pool room
  Am Heritage 34:98 (draw-
    ing,c,3) D '82
--Australia
  Nat Geog 169:751 (c,3) Je '86
--Bumper pool
  Sports Illus 60:72 (c,4) Ap
    23 '84
--Home pool table
  Sports Illus 57:59 (c,4) S 1
    '82
  Sports Illus 57:41 (c,4) D 13
    '82
  Ebony 40:64 (c,3) O '85
--Pool hall (Alaska)
  Nat Geog 163:172-3 (c,1) F
    '83
--Shot-gun pool cue
  Sports Illus 61:16 (c,4) N 5
    '84
--Sleazy pool hall
  Sports Illus 57:74 (4) Jl 5 '82
--Snooker (Great Britain)
  Sports Illus 60:42-8 (c,2) My
    7 '84
--Texas
  Life 8:43 (c,4) Ag '86
--Mark Twain at table (1908)
  Am Heritage 36:105 (4) F '85
BINGHAM, GEORGE CALEB
--"Fur Traders Descending the

Missouri" (1840s)
  Am Heritage 34:17 (painting,c,2)
    O '83
BINOCULARS
  Ebony 41:45 (c,2) D '85
--Mounted on Coast Guard boat
  Smithsonian 13:32 (c,1) Jl '82
Biology. See
    ANATOMY
    CELLS
    GENETICS
    REPRODUCTION
BIORHYTHMS
--Biorhythm charts
  Natur Hist 91:90-3 (4) O '82
BIRCH, JOHN
  Sports Illus 61:76 (4) Ag 6 '84
BIRCH TREES
  Nat Wildlife 21:41 (painting,c,2)
    O '83
  Nat Geog 167:538-9 (c,1) Ap '85
BIRD BATHS
  Nat Wildlife 21:38 (c,4) O '83
BIRD CAGES
  Smithsonian 13:118 (c,1) Jl '82
  Sports Illus 61:87 (c,4) Jl 18
    '84
BIRD FEEDERS
  Natur Hist 92:90 (c,2) S '83
  Sports Illus 60:60 (c,4) Ja 9 '84
BIRD HOUSES
--Construction (New Jersey)
  Nat Wildlife 22:24 (c,4) Ap '84
--Purple martin apartment complex
  Smithsonian 16:40-1 (c,4) O '85
BIRD NESTS
  Natur Hist 91:60-5 (c,1) My '82
--Blue jays
  Natur Hist 95:47 (c,1) O '86
--Caciques
  Natur Hist 95:40-7 (c,1) Mr '86
--Cape penduline tit
  Nat Geog 163:378-9 (c,1) Mr '83
--Chickadees
  Natur Hist 94:44 (c,4) Mr '85
--Collected for Oriental bird nest
    soup
  Smithsonian 14:66-75 (c,1) S '83
--Flycatchers
  Nat Geog 164:266 (c,1) Ag '83
--Great blue herons
  Nat Geog 165:544 (c,1) Ap '84
--Grebes
  Natur Hist 92:69 (c,4) F '83
--Loons
  Nat Geog 166:574 (c,3) N '84
--Masked weaver making nest

BIRD NESTS (cont.)
Nat Geog 163:368 (c,4) Mr
'83
--Orioles
Natur Hist 94:70 (c,4) O '85
--Parrots
Sports Illus 60:54-8, 68 (c,1)
Ja 9 '84
--Pelicans
Nat Geog 162:353 (c,1) S '82
--Social weaver birds
Natur Hist 91:80 (3) S '82
--Swallows
Nat Wildlife 20:50 (c,4) Ag '82
BIRD WATCHING
Nat Wildlife 23:32 (3) D '84
Nat Wildlife 24:40-1 (c,1) Ap
'86
--New Jersey
Smithsonian 13:36 (c,4) D '82
--Pennsylvania
Trav/Holiday 162:37 (c,3) S
'84
--Texas
Trav/Holiday 166:54-5 (c,3)
N '86
BIRD WATCHING--HUMOR
Nat Wildlife 24:46-51 (draw-
ing,c,1) O '86
BIRDS
--Antbirds
Nat Geog 163:45 (c,3) Ja '83
--Banding hawk
Nat Wildlife 21:9 (c,2) Ap '83
--Bee-eaters
Nat Wildlife 21:2 (c,1) D '82
Natur Hist 93:cov., 50-9
(c,1) O '84
Natur Hist 94:83 (c,1) Jl '85
--Bird leg bands
Nat Wildlife 21:12-13 (c,3) O
'83
--Bird skins and feathers
Smithsonian 12:102-5 (c,1) Mr
'82
--Caciques
Natur Hist 95:38-47 (c,1) Mr
'86
--Cape penduline tit
Nat Geog 163:378-9 (c,1) Mr
'83
--Crimson rosellas
Trav/Holiday 16:57 (c,3) Ag
'84
--Eggs
Nat Wildlife 24:4 (c,4) Je '86
Nat Wildlife 25:6-14 (c,1) D '86

--Endangered cranes
Nat Wildlife 21:33-6 (c,1) Ap '83
--Endangered species
Natur Hist 91:28-43 (c,1) Mr '82
Smithsonian 13:95-103 (c,1) Je
'82
Nat Wildlife 23:10-15 (c,1) Ap
'85
--Endangered whooping cranes
Natur Hist 91:70-2 (c,1) F '82
Nat Wildlife 20:7 (c,2) Ap '82
Nat Wildlife 21:35 (4) D '82
Nat Wildlife 21:33 (c,4) Ap '83
Nat Wildlife 22:31 (4) Ap '84
Nat Wildlife 23:10-11 (c,2) Ap
'85
--Flocks
Natur Hist 92:27 (c,4) S '83
--Gull guano
Smithsonian 17:27 (c,4) Ag '86
--Honeycreepers
Natur Hist 91:40-5 (c,1) D '82
--Kauai'o
Nat Wildlife 23:15 (painting,c,4)
Ap '85
--Manakins
Natur Hist 93:54-9 (c,1) Jl '84
--Oilbirds
Smithsonian 13:80 (c,4) N '82
--Oo
Natur Hist 94:85 (painting,c,4)
S '85
--Oxpecker
Nat Geog 169:584-5 (c,1) My '86
--Paintings by Audubon
Natur Hist 94:89-114 (c,1) Ap
'85
--Paintings by Edward Lear
Natur Hist 94:62-5 (c,2) D '85
--Paintings of birds
Natur Hist 92:66-75, 94 (c,1)
S '83
Nat Wildlife 24:23-8 (c,1) O '86
--Quelea
Natur Hist 94:34-5 (c,1) F '85
--Residents of South American
forests
Natur Hist 93:37 (drawing,c,1)
N '84
--Studying bird singing
Smithsonian 13:119-27 (draw-
ing,c,4) Jl '82
--Waterfowl
Nat Geog 166:562-99 (c,1) N '84
Nat Wildlife 23:54-5 (c,1) Ap '85
--Waterfowl in flight
Nat Wildlife 20:50-1 (c,3) Je '82

BIRDS (cont.)
  Nat Wildlife 21:25, 30-1 (c,1)
      D '82
  Natur Hist 91:20-1 (c,1) D
      '82
  Nat Geog 166:564-5, 572-3,
      578-9 (c,1) N '84
--Woodcreeper
  Natur Hist 93:40 (c,4) N '84
--See also
      ALBATROSSES
      AUKS
      BIRDS OF PARADISE
      BITTERNS
      BLACKBIRDS
      BLUE JAYS
      BLUEBIRDS
      BOOBY BIRDS
      BOWERBIRDS
      BROWN THRASHERS
      BULBULS
      BUNTINGS
      BUZZARDS
      CANADA GEESE
      CARACARAS
      CARDINALS
      CATBIRDS
      CHICKADEES
      CHICKENS
      CHICKS
      COCKATOOS
      COCKS-OF-THE-ROCK
      CONDORS
      CORMORANTS
      COWBIRDS
      CRANES
      CROWS
      CURASSOWS
      DARTERS
      DODO BIRDS
      DOVES
      DUCKS
      EAGLES
      EGRETS
      FALCONS
      FEATHERS
      FINCHES
      FLAMINGOS
      FLICKERS
      FLYCATCHERS
      FRIGATE BIRDS
      GALLINULES
      GEESE
      GOLDFINCHES
      GOSHAWKS
      GREBES
      GROSBEAKS

GROUSE
GULLS
HAWKS
HERONS
HORNBILLS
HUMMINGBIRDS
IBISES
JACANAS
JAYS
KESTRELS
KINGBIRDS
KINGFISHERS
KITES
KITTIWAKES
KIWI BIRDS
LOONS
MACAWS
MAGPIES
MALLARDS
MARTINS
MEADOWLARKS
MERGANSERS
MOCKINGBIRDS
MOTMOTS
MOURNING DOVES
MURRES
NUTCRACKERS
ORIOLES
OSTRICHES
OVENBIRDS
OWLS
PARAKEETS
PARROTS
PASSENGER PIGEONS
PEACOCKS
PELICANS
PENGUINS
PETRELS
PHALAROPES
PHEASANTS
PIGEONS
PLOVERS
PRAIRIE CHICKENS
PTARMIGANS
PUFFINS
QUAIL
QUETZALS
RAILS
REDSTARTS
REDWINGED BLACKBIRDS
RHEAS
ROAD RUNNERS
ROBINS
ROOSTERS
SANDERLINGS
SANDPIPERS
SAPSUCKERS

BIRDS (cont.)
>SECRETARY BIRDS
>SHEARWATERS
>SHOEBILLS
>SKIMMERS
>SPARROWS
>SPOONBILLS
>STORKS
>SWALLOWS
>SWANS
>SWIFTS
>TANAGERS
>TERNS
>THRUSHES
>TOUCANS
>TROGONS
>TURKEYS
>VULTURES
>WARBLERS
>WATER OUZELS
>WAXWINGS
>WEAVERBIRDS
>WHOOPING CRANES
>WOOD DUCKS
>WOOD PEWEES
>WOODCOCKS
>WOODPECKERS
>WRENS
>YELLOWLEGS
>YELLOWTHROATS
BIRDS--HUMOR
--House sparrow's spread across
>America
>Smithsonian 17:174-90 (paint-
>ing,c,1) N '86
BIRDS, EXTINCT
--Ivory-billed woodpeckers
>Nat Wildlife 22:4 (c,4) Ag
>'84
>Nat Wildlife 24:4 (c,4) Ap '86
--See also
>DODO BIRDS
>PASSENGER PIGEONS
BIRDS OF PARADISE
>Smithsonian 13:90-7 (c,1) F
>'83
BIRMINGHAM, ALABAMA
--1963 bombed church
>Ebony 41:299 (4) N '85
Birth. See
>CHILDBIRTH
>REPRODUCTION
BIRTHDAY PARTIES
--1955 party for quadruplets
>(Illinois)
>Ebony 41:216 (3) N '85
--1963 children's party

(Washington, D.C.)
>Life 6:70-1 (c,1) N '83
--Austin's sesquicentennial celebra-
>tion, Texas
>Trav/Holiday 166:cov. (c,1) Jl
>'86
--Babies eating cake (Great Britain)
>Ebony 39:46 (3) Ap '84
--Birthday cakes
>Life 9:415 (c,2) Fall '86
--Birthday cake for Pope John
>Paul II
>Life 8:63 (4) Jl '85
--Blowing out birthday candles
>(Missouri)
>Life 6:62 (3) My '83
--Celebration of Houston's 150th
>birthday
>Life 9:14-15 (c,1) Je '86
--Million-balloon salute to Disney-
>land, California
>Life 9:8-9 (c,1) F '86
--Nursing home residents (Califor-
>nia)
>Life 7:34 (3) F '84
--Sardine cake for dolphins
>Life 9:38 (c,2) D '86
--USFL birthday cake
>Sports Illus 60:32-3 (c,1) F 27
>'84
BISON
>Nat Geog 162:343-4, 347 (c,1)
>S '82
>Trav/Holiday 161:12 (c,4) My
>'84
>Nat Geog 168:162-3 (c,1) Ag '85
>Nat Wildlife 23:54-5 (c,1) O '85
>Nat Wildlife 24:30-5 (c,1) Je '86
--Depicted on U.S. Department of
>Interior seal
>Sports Illus 59:66-7 (drawing,c,2)
>S 26 '83
--Drowning
>Natur Hist 93:14 (c,3) Ja '84
--Ramming tree
>Nat Wildlife 20:12 (c,3) O '82
--Walking in snow
>Nat Wildlife 21:6-7 (c,1) D '82
BITTERNS
>Nat Wildlife 22:41 (painting,c,4)
>Je '84
BLACK AMERICANS
--Late 19th cent. middle class black
>Americans
>Ebony 41:126, 140 (3) Ag '86
--1920s life (Columbia, South Caro-
>lina)

BLACK AMERICANS (cont.)
  Am Heritage 37:88-95 (1) O
    '86
--1930 baptism (Alabama)
  Am Heritage 34:36 (paint-
    ing,c,3) Je '83
--1934 black lifestyle (New Or-
    leans, Louisiana)
  Am Heritage 38:60 (paint-
    ing,c,2) D '86
--Black cemetery (Savannah,
    Georgia)
  Nat Geog 164:811 (c,1) D '83
--Black folk crafts (South)
  Life 6:52-8 (c,1) Ag '83
--Black voters at ballot box
    (Mississippi)
  Ebony 39:128 (2) Ag '84
--Brooklyn, New York
  Nat Geog 163:592-7 (c,1) My
    '83
--Children of interracial couples
  Ebony 40:156-62 (c,3) S '85
--Funeral (North Carolina)
  Nat Geog 166:810-11 (c,2) D
    '84
--Life on Daufuskie Island, South
    Carolina
  Smithsonian 13:88-97 (1) O
    '82
--See also
    BLACKS IN AMERICAN
      HISTORY
BLACK BUCK ANTELOPES
  Sports Illus 65:2-3 (c,1) S 8
    '86
BLACK FOREST, WEST GER-
    MANY
--Ailing trees
  Smithsonian 16:211-30 (c,2)
    N '85
BLACK HISTORY
  Ebony 41:entire issue (c,1)
    N '85
--1860s blacks voting
  Ebony 39:114 (etching,4) Ag
    '84
  Ebony 40:120 (engraving,4)
    N '84
--1862 slaves' escape by boat
    (South Carolina)
  Ebony 38:147-50 (woodcut,3)
    O '83
--1872 black governor P.B.S.
    Pinchback (Louisiana)
  Ebony 42:116 (2) N '86
--1920s anti-lynching poster

  Ebony 39:51 (4) Jl '84
--1920s life (Columbia, South Caro-
    lina)
  Am Heritage 37:88-95 (1) O '86
--Africatown, Mobile, Alabama
  Life 9:13-14 (c,4) S '86
--Blacks in Reconstruction govern-
    ments
  Am Heritage 34:13 (4) O '83
--Fate of Loyalist refugees from
    American Revolution
  Am Heritage 34:102-9 (c,1) Je
    '83
--Figures from black history
  Ebony 37:61-6 (2) F '82
--Prominent figures in 20th cent.
    black history
  Ebony 41:60-76, 298-350 (2) N
    '85
--Raised fists at 1968 Olympics
    awards (Mexico City)
  Ebony 39:148 (4) Je '84
  Life 7:106 (c,4) Summer '84
--Underground Railroad
  Nat Geog 166:cov., 2-39 (c,1)
    Jl '84
--See also
    ABOLITIONISTS
    BLACK AMERICANS
    BLACKS IN AMERICAN HIS-
      TORY
    CIVIL RIGHTS
    CIVIL RIGHTS MARCHES
    CIVIL WAR
    KU KLUX KLAN
    NAACP
    SLAVERY--U.S.
Black Mountains, North Carolina.
    See
    MT. MITCHELL
BLACK TUPELO TREES
--Housing raccoons
  Nat Wildlife 20:2 (c,2) O '82
BLACKBIRDS
  Natur Hist 94:39-41 (c,1) F '85
  Nat Wildlife 24:48 (c,4) F '86
  Nat Wildlife 24:40 (c,4) Ag '86
BLACKBOARDS
  Life 5:46-7 (c,1) F '82
  Sports Illus 56:48 (c,4) My 10
    '82
  Nat Geog 163:736, 740 (c,4) Je
    '83
  Ebony 38:158 (c,4) Ag '83
  Smithsonian 16:135 (c,3) Ap '85
  Life 8:82-3 (1) Je '85
  Nat Geog 169:611 (c,4) My '86

BLACKBOARDS (cont.)
--1901
   Smithsonian 16:122-3 (1) Ap
      '85
BLACKFEET INDIANS (MONTANA)
--Burning land
   Natur Hist 92:8 (painting,c,2)
      F '83
BLACKS IN AMERICAN HISTORY
--1870s Louisiana governor
   P.B.S. Pinchback
   Ebony 37:94 (3) O '82
--Black celebrities in ads
   Ebony 39:81-6 (c,3) Jl '84
--Black comedians
   Ebony 37:38-42 (2) Je '82
--Black mayors
   Ebony 39:82-6, 122 (c,3) Ag
      '84
--Black politicians
   Ebony 39:entire issue (c,2)
      Ag '84
--Famous blacks in U.S. history
   Ebony 37:128-33 (4) Mr '82
--Motown celebrities
   Life 6:128-9 (c,1) My '83
--NAACP officers
   Ebony 39:49-52 (3) Jl '84
--Prominent contemporary blacks
   Ebony 37:132-3, 138 (4) Je
      '82
   Ebony 37:80-2 (4) S '82
   Ebony 39:130-8 (c,1) F '84
--See also
      ALI, MUHAMMAD
      ANDERSON, MARIAN
      ARMSTRONG, LOUIS
      ASHE, ARTHUR
      BALDWIN, JAMES
      BASIE, COUNT
      BETHUNE, MARY McLEOD
      BLAKE, EUBIE
      BUNCHE, RALPH
      CARVER, GEORGE WASH-
         INGTON
      CHAMBERLAIN, WILT
      COLE, NAT KING
      DAVIS, MILES
      DOUGLASS, FREDERICK
      DU BOIS, W. E. B.
      DUNBAR, PAUL LAURENCE
      ELLINGTON, DUKE
      EVERS, MEDGAR
      GILLESPIE, JOHN BIRKS
         (DIZZY)
      HAMPTON, LIONEL
      HANDY, W. C.

      HOLIDAY, BILLIE
      HORNE, LENA
      HUGHES, LANGSTON
      JOHNSON, JACK
      KING, MARTIN LUTHER, JR.
      LOUIS, JOE
      MALCOLM X
      MARSHALL, THURGOOD
      MAYS, WILLIE
      OWENS, JESSE
      PAIGE, SATCHEL
      PARKER, CHARLIE
      ROBESON, PAUL
      ROBINSON, JACKIE
      ROBINSON, LUTHER (BILL)
      TRUTH, SOJOURNER
      TUBMAN, HARRIET
      WASHINGTON, BOOKER T.
      WASHINGTON, DINAH
      WILKINS, ROY
      WRIGHT, RICHARD
BLACKSMITHS
   Smithsonian 12:66-7 (c,2) Mr '82
--Channel Islands
   Smithsonian 17:98 (c,4) My '86
--Massachusetts
   Am Heritage 33:40 (c,4) Ag '82
--Statue (Helsinki, Finland)
   Trav/Holiday 166:9 (c,4) D '86
--Utah
   Trav/Holiday 161:76 (c,4) Ap '84
BLADDERWORT PLANTS
   Nat Wildlife 22:4-5 (c,1) Ap '84
   Natur Hist 94:88 (c,4) F '85
   Smithsonian 16:55 (c,3) My '85
BLAINE, JAMES G.
--1884 cartoon
   Am Heritage 33:65 (drawing,3)
      O '82
BLAKE, EUBIE
   Ebony 38:27-32 (c,2) My '83
   Life 7:173 (4) Ja '84
   Ebony 41:343 (4) N '85
BLAKE, WILLIAM
--Illustration from "Paradise Lost"
   Smithsonian 12:68 (c,4) F '82
   Smithsonian 13:59 (painting,c,2)
      S '82
--Paintings by him
   Smithsonian 13:50-9 (c,1) S '82
BLIGH, WILLIAM
   Smithsonian 13:217 (drawing,4)
      N '82
BLINDFISH
   Smithsonian 13:78 (c,4) N '82
BLINDNESS
   Ebony 39:84 (2) Ap '84

BLINDNESS (cont.)
--Israel (1950)
   Smithsonian 16:239 (3) N '85
BLIZZARDS
--1912 (Antarctica)
   Nat Geog 163:554 (4) Ap '83
BLOOD
--Freeze-dried hemoglobin
   Smithsonian 14:92 (c,4) Jl '83
--Human blood cells infected with
    AIDS virus
   Natur Hist 95:78-81 (2) My
    '86
--Magnified red blood cells
   Lie 9:98-9 (c,1) Fall '86
BLOODHOUNDS
   Smithsonian 16:cov., 64-73
    (c,1) Ja '86
   Nat Geog 170:353 (c,1) S '86
BLOWGUNS
--Ecuador
   Natur Hist 93:72-3 (c,3) S '84
BLUE JAYS
   Nat Wildlife 22:59 (paint-
    ing,c,2) F '84
   Natur Hist 93:28 (c,4) Ap '84
   Natur Hist 95:40-7 (c,1) O
    '86
--Chicks
   Nat Wildlife 21:58 (c,4) D '82
   Natur Hist 95:47 (c,1) O '86
BLUE RIDGE MOUNTAINS,
  SOUTHERN U.S.
   Nat Geog 163:466-7, 472-3
    (c,1) Ap '83
BLUEBERRIES
   Life 5:84-5 (c,1) Ag '82
   Natur Hist 93:48-9 (c,1) Ag
    '84
BLUE BIRDS
   Nat Wildlife 20:10-11 (c,1) O
    '82
   Sports Illus 58:82 (c,4) My
    30 '83
   Nat Wildlife 22:24-8 (c,1) Ap
    '84
   Natur Hist 94:8, 12 (c,3) Je
    '85
BLUEBONNETS (FLOWERS)
   Nat Wildlife 21:4-5 (c,1) Ag
    '83
BLUEPRINTS
--1918 blueprint of Ford plant
    production line (Michigan)
   Am Heritage 37:54 (2) O '86
BOA CONSTRICTORS
   Ebony 39:52 (c,4) N '83

   Natur Hist 93:91 (c,4) S '84
   Nat Wildlife 24:24 (c,4) Je '86
--Eating fawn
   Smithsonian 17:114 (c,4) D '86
--Tree boa
   Smithsonian 17:88 (c,4) S '86
BOARS, WILD
--Artificial insemination of boar
    (Minnesota)
   Nat Geog 170:350 (c,2) S '86
BOAT RACES
   Sports Illus 59:60-74 (paint-
    ing, c,2) Jl 4 '83
--Argentina
   Nat Geog 170:238-9 (c,1) Ag '86
--Bol d'Or (Switzerland)
   Nat Geog 169:114-15 (c,1) Ja ' 86
--Canoes (Hawaii)
   Nat Geog 164:590-1 (c,1) N '83
--Canoes (Tahiti)
   Sports Illus 64:136-7 (c,2) F 10
    '86
--Catamarans (Florida)
   Sports Illus 63:42-3 (c,2) N 25
    '86
--Dragon Boat Race, Singapore
   Trav/Holiday 165:132 (4) Ap '86
--Grenada
   Nat Geog 166:706-7 (c,1) N '84
--Henley Royal Regatta, England
   Nat Geog 163:750-1, 770-1 (c,1)
    Je '83
--Hydroplane accident (Washington)
   Sports Illus 57:22-3 (c,3) Ag 9
    '82
--Through Panama Canal
   Nat Geog 169:480-1 (c,1) Ap '86
BOAT RACES. See also
    MOTORBOAT RACES
    SAILBOAT RACES
BOATHOUSES
--Philadelphia boating clubs, Penn-
    sylvania
   Nat Geog 163:335 (c,4) Mr '83
BOATING
--Airboat sightseeing tour (Ever-
    glades, Florida)
   Trav/Holiday 165:44-5 (c,1) Ja
    '86
--Ice boating (Wisconsin)
   Sports Illus 56:146 (c,3) F 10
    '82
--Jet boating (New Zealand)
   Trav/Holiday 160:56 (c,2) S '83
--Lake boat at resort (China)
   Nat Geog 168:314 (c,1) S '85
--Punting (Cambridge, England)

BOATING (cont.)
    Trav/Holiday 161:6,8 (c,4) F
        '84
--See also
        CANOEING
        KAYAKING
        RAFTING
        ROWING
        SAILING
BOATS
--1860s pontoon boat
    Am Heritage 36:55 (3) F '85
--1924 ice boat (New York)
    Am Heritage 34:72 (3) Ag '83
--Airboats (Florida)
    Nat Wildlife 20:50-1 (c,1) O
        '82
--Amphibious car (New Jersey)
    Nat Wildlife 24:10-11 (c,1) O
        '86
--Ancient Rome
    Nat Geog 165:602-3 (c,1) My
        '84
--Bolivia
    Sports Illus 63:84 (c,1) S 4
        '85
--Channel markers (Maryland)
    Nat Wildlife 22:12 (c,4) Ap
        '84
--Coast Guard patrol boats
    Smithsonian 13:cov., 32-42
        (c,1) Jl '82
--Docks (London, England)
    Nat Geog 163:756-7 (c,1) Je '83
--Falling into lake from boat
        (Montana)
    Life 7:152 (c,2) My '84
--Glass-bottom boat (Australia)
    Trav/Holiday 165:40 (c,4) F
        '86
--High-rise storage (Florida)
    Nat Geog 162:193 (c,3) Ag '82
--Ice boats (New York)
    Life 5:164-6 (c,1) D '82
--Inflatable
    Smithsonian 13:50-1 (c,1) D
        '82
--Inflatable (Indonesia)
    Nat Geog 167:758-9 (c,1) Je
        '85
--Longboats (Pitcairn Island)
    Nat Geog 164:521 (c,2) O '83
--Longtail boats (Thailand)
    Trav/Holiday 159:52 (c,2) Ap
        '83
--Mailboat (Oregon)
    Trav/Holiday 166:86 (4) Jl '86

--Oruwas (Sri Lanka)
    Smithsonian 15:72-3 (c,1) D '84
--Pilot launches
    Smithsonian 17:71, 78-9 (c,1) Jl
        '86
--Reed (Peru)
    Natur Hist 91:34-7 (c,1) Ja '82
--Resort watercycle (Hawaii)
    Trav/Holiday 166:61 (c,4) Ag
        '86
--Sailing toy boats in Central Park
        pond, New York City
    Sports Illus 63:101 (c,3) N 11
        '85
    Sports Illus 65:16 (c,4) O 20
        '86
--Sightseeing boat (Paris, France)
    Nat Geog 161:478-9 (c,1) Ap '82
--Sightseeing boats (Georgia)
    Nat Geog 164:809 (c,3) D '83
--Speedboat carried on sled (North-
        west Territories)
    Nat Geog 163:184-5 (c,1) F '83
--Towboat (Illinois)
    Nat Wildlife 23:9 (c,1) Je '85
--Toy canoe (Western Samoa)
    Nat Geog 168:452-3 (c,1) O '85
--Venezuelan bongos
    Smithsonian 16:53 (c,4) My '85
--Windmill boat (Maine)
    Nat Geog 167:224 (c,3) F '85
--See also
        ANCHORS
        BARGES
        BATTLESHIPS
        BOATHOUSES
        CANOES
        CLIPPER SHIPS
        CONSTITUTION
        CRUISE SHIPS
        FERRY BOATS
        FIGUREHEADS
        FISHING BOATS
        FREIGHTERS
        FRIGATES
        FULTON, ROBERT
        GONDOLAS
        HOUSEBOATS
        HYDROPLANES
        JUNKS
        KAYAKS
        MARINAS
        MAURY, MATTHEW FONTAINE
        MOTORBOATS
        NAVIGATION INSTRUMENTS
        OCEAN CRAFT
        RAFTS

BOATS (cont.)
> RIVERBOATS
> ROWBOATS
> SAILBOATS
> SAMPANS
> SHIPS
> STEAMBOATS
> SUBMARINES
> TANKERS
> TITANIC
> TUGBOATS
> TRAWLERS
> UMIAKS
> WHALING SHIPS
> YACHTS

BOATS--CONSTRUCTION
--9th cent. riverboats (U.S.S.R.)
> Nat Geog 167:280-1 (painting,c,1) Mr '85
--Canoe (Australia)
> Nat Geog 166:734 (c,4) D '84
--Canoe (Connecticut)
> Sports Illus 64:102 (c,4) Ap 21 '86
--Canoe (Truk)
> Nat Geog 170:484 (c,3) O '86
--Channel Islands
> Smithsonian 17:98 (c,4) My '86
--Fishing boats (Portugal)
> Nat Geog 166:472 (c,1) O '84
--Kayak (Greenland)
> Nat Geog 165:528-9 (c,1) Ap '84
--Model of 1791 British man-of-war
> Nat Geog 168:435 (c,4) O '85
--Wooden boats (Washington)
> Nat Geog 165:660-1 (c,1) My '84

BOBCATS
> Nat Wildlife 24:2 (c,2) D '85

BOBSLEDDING
> Sports Illus 60:46-7 (c,3) Ja 9 '84
> Sports Illus 60:76 (c,4) F 6 '84
> Sports Illus 64:56 (c,3) Mr 3 '86
--1984 Olympics (Sarajevo)
> Sports Illus 60:17 (c,4) F 20 '84
--Bobsledding shorts
> Sports Illus 65:16 (c,4) D 22 '86
--Luge
> Sports Illus 59:36-7 (c,4) D 5 '83

Sports Illus 60:34-5, 64 (c,1) F 6 '84
--Luge (1984 Olympics)
> Sports Illus 60:20-1 (c,4) F 20 '84

Bobwhites. See
> QUAIL

BODYBUILDERS
> Ebony 42:90 (c,3) D '86
--Iceland
> Smithsonian 16:123 (c,4) Ja '86

BODYBUILDING
> Sports Illus 56:30-7 (c,1) Je 28 '82
> Ebony 38:57-60 (1) Jl '83
> Sports Illus 59:39-41, 51 (c,2) Jl 18 '83
--Women
> Ebony 37:116 (4) Ag '82
> Life 5:cov., 46-52 (c,1) O '82
> Life 5:23 (4) D '82
> Sports Illus 62:10 (c,4) F 4 '85

BOGART, HUMPHREY
> Am Heritage 33:10 (4) Ap '82
> Am Heritage 35:6, 32-6 (c,1) D '83
> Life 9:122 (4) Fall '86
--1945 marriage to Lauren Bacall
> Life 9:104 (4) Je '86

Bogs. See
> MARSHES

BOHR, NIELS
> Life 9:190 (4) Fall '86

BOISE, IDAHO
> Trav/Holiday 161:10 (c,4) Je '84

BOK, EDWARD
> Am Heritage 36:102 (4) D '84

Bolivia. See
> LAKE TITICACA

BOLIVIA--COSTUME
--Siriono Indians
> Natur Hist 95:8, 10 (c,4) Mr '86
--Street vendor
> Natur Hist 92:77 (3) Mr '83

BOLIVIA--MAPS
> Natur Hist 95:6 (c,4) Mr '86

BOLL WEEVILS--HUMOR
> Smithsonian 13:60-8 (drawing,c,2) Ag '82

BOLOGNA, ITALY
> Trav/Holiday 160:56 (c,2) O '83

BOMBAY, INDIA
--Victoria Station
> Trav/Holiday 160:46 (c,4) N '83

BOMBS
--1951 construction of bomb shelter (California)

BOMBS (cont.)
  Am Heritage 37:72 (4) Ap '86
--1952 first hydrogen bomb ex-
    plosion (Eniwetok)
  Am Heritage 34:62-3 (1) Je '83
--1954 hydrogen bomb explosion
    (Bikini)
  Nat Geog 169:810-12 (c,1) Je
    '86
--Aerial view of Korean bridge
    explosion
  Smithsonian 14:157 (4) Mr '84
--Air raid shelter (Nicaragua)
  Life 6:28 (c,2) S '83
--Being dropped on Germany
    (1943)
  Smithsonian 14:38-9 (1) Ag '83
--Explosion (Paris, France)
  Life 5:122-3 (c,1) Je '82
--Explosion (Tikul, Ethiopia)
  Nat Geog 168:392-3 (c,1) S
    '85
--Police bomb squad (Israel)
  Life 7:66-72 (c,1) D '84
--Setting up bomb (Northern Ire-
    land)
  Life 8:42-3 (c,1) O '85
--See also
    ATOMIC BOMBS
    EXPLOSIONS
BOMBS--DAMAGE
--1940 survivors of Coventry
    bombing (Great Britain)
  Life 8:76-7 (1) Spring '85
--1940s bombing of Wimbledon
    tennis club, England
  Sports Illus 56:76 (4) Je 21
    '82
--1940s factory (Germany)
  Smithsonian 14:43 (2) Ag '83
--1943 bombed monastery (Milan,
    Italy)
  Nat Geog 164:676-7 (2) N '83
--Aftermath of U.S. Marine head-
    quarters bombing (Beirut)
  Life 7:46-51 (c,1) Ja '84
--Beirut, Lebanon
  Nat Geog 163:270, 275-83 (c,1)
    F '83
--Blown-up auto (Lebanon)
  Life 5:24 (c,4) Ag '82
--Bomb-damaged airplane interior
  Life 9:16-17 (c,1) Je '86
--Bombed bus (Israel)
  Life 7:66 (c,4) D '84
--Frankfurt Airport, West Ger-
    many (1985)

  Life 8:50-1 (1) Ag '85
--Nagasaki, Japan (1945)
  Life 8:14-15, 83 (1) Spring '85
--Ruins of bombed pharmacy
    (Uganda)
  Nat Geog 167:622-3 (c,1) My
    '85
--Victims of bombing (Great Britain)
  Life 7:192-3 (1) D '84
BOOBY BIRDS
  Natur Hist 91:12 (3) Ja '82
  Nat Wildlife 21:4 (c,4) F '83
  Nat Geog 165:168 (c,3) F '84
  Trav/Holiday 161:77 (c,1) Mr
    '84
  Natur Hist 95:84-5 (c,1) Ag '86
--Covered with flies
  Natur Hist 92:8 (4) Ap '83
BOOKS
--9th cent. Book of Kells (Ireland)
  Trav/Holiday 163:66 (c,4) F '85
--11th cent. Domesday Book (Great
    Britain)
  Smithsonian 17:82-94 (c,1) Jl '86
--15th cent. illustrated manuscript
    (Iceland)
  Smithsonian 16:116-17 (c,3) Ja
    '86
--16th cent. leather book cover
    (Great Britain)
  Nat Geog 163:674-5 (c,2) My '83
--1638 Downame volume
  Life 9:35 (c,4) S '86
--19th cent. dime novels about In-
    dian captives
  Natur Hist 94:54-5 (c,2) D '85
--Mid-19th cent. "Go West" books
  Nat Geog 170:155, 174 (c,1) Ag
    '86
--Late 19th cent. book on the hor-
    rors of the big city
  Am Heritage 35:111 (4) Ag '84
--1905 children's book cover
  Smithsonian 14:173 (c,4) O '83
--1915 researcher for the Oxford
    English Dictionary
  Smithsonian 13:34 (4) Ag '82
--"Alice in Wonderland" illustration
  Nat Geog 163:753 (4) Je '83
--"Alice in Wonderland" on stage
    (London, England)
  Smithsonian 13:92 (c,4) N '82
--"Alice in Wonderland" on stage
    (Minnesota)
  Smithsonian 13:cov., 52-9 (c,1)
    Ag '82
--"Alice in Wonderland" television

BOOKS (cont.)
production
Life 8:162 (c,2) D '85
--Ancient Maya "Madrid Codex"
Nat Geog 169:462-3 (c,2) Ap
'86
--Anna Karenina manuscript
Nat Geog 169:772 (2) Je '86
--"Babar"
Smithsonian 15:90-6 (c,1) Jl
'84
--Bartlett's Quotations
Am Heritage 35:102-3 (c,2)
Ag '84
--Book sale (Washington, D.C.)
Nat Geog 163:122-3 (c,1) Ja
'83
--Bookstore (Budapest, Hungary)
Smithsonian 17:57 (c,4) N '86
--Bookstores (Paris, France)
Trav/Holiday 158:61-2 (c,4)
N '82
--Children dressed as Tom Sawyer
characters (Missouri)
Life 8:156-7 (c,1) N '85
--Children's book illustrations by
Maurice Sendak
Smithsonian 12:90-1 (c,4) Ja
'82
--Diet books
Life 5:52 (c,2) My '82
--Divine Comedy illustration
Smithsonian 13:56-7 (paint-
ing,c,2) S '82
--Early how-to books
Smithsonian 16:149 (c,4) Jl '85
--Gone with the Wind cover
(1936)
Am Heritage 37:111 (4) Je '86
--Illustrations from Grimm's fairy
tales
Smithsonian 17:109-18 (c,4)
My '86
--Illustrations from Huckleberry
Finn
Smithsonian 13:128 (4) Ag '82
Am Heritage 35:81-5 (draw-
ing,4) Je '84
Am Heritage 36:10 (drawing,4)
D '84
Nat Wildlife 23:5 (drawing,4)
Je '85
--Illustrations from Washington
Irving tales
Smithsonian 14:96-8 (paint-
ing,c,2) Ag '83
--Illustrations from Rudyard

Kipling stories
Smithsonian 16:36-44 (c,2) Ja
'86
--Illustrations from old books
Smithsonian 12:68-9 (c,4) F '82
--Samuel Johnson's Dictionary
(1755)
Smithsonian 15:61 (c,4) D '84
--Rudyard Kipling paperbacks
(India)
Smithsonian 16:40 (c,4) Ja '86
--McGuffey Readers
Smithsonian 15:182-208 (c,2) N
'84
--Michelin guidebooks
Smithsonian 17:57-8, 62-4 (c,3)
Je '86
--"Paradise Lost" illustration
Smithsonian 12:69 (c,4) F '82
Smithsonian 13:59 (painting,c,2)
S '82
--Poster advertising Uncle Tom's
Cabin
Am Heritage 34:111 (c,4) F '83
--Solving of puzzle "Masquerade"
Smithsonian 13:154, 160 (3) My
'82
--Stack of law books
Sports Illus 57:134 (c,4) Jl 12
'82
--The Wind in the Willows illustra-
tion
Sports Illus 56:78 (drawing,4)
Je 28 '82
--"Wizard of Oz" on stage (Minne-
sota)
Smithsonian 13:56 (c,2) Ag '82
--See also
BIBLES
DON QUIXOTE
HOLMES, SHERLOCK
LIBRARIES
PRINTING INDUSTRY
READING
SINBAD THE SAILOR
WRITERS
BOOMERANGS
Smithsonian 15:118-25 (c,1) Je
'84
Life 8:61 (3) Ag '85
Trav/Holiday 164:83 (4) Ag '85
BOONE, DANIEL
Nat Geog 168:813, 824, 831
(painting,c,1) D '85
--18th cent. travels of Daniel
Boone
Nat Geog 168:812-41 (map,c,1)

BOONE, DANIEL (cont.)
   D '85
--Home (Kentucky)
   Nat Geog 168:832-3 (c,1) D
      '85
--Home (Missouri)
   Nat Geog 168:812 (4) D '85
--Tombs (Kentucky and Missouri)
   Nat Geog 168:838-9 (c,1) D
      '85
BOOTH, JOHN WILKES
   Am Heritage 38:26 (4) D '86
BORDEAUX, FRANCE
--15th cent. clock tower
   Trav/Holiday 160:60 (c,1) S
      '83
BORDERS
--Oman-South Yemen border
   Nat Geog 168:497 (c,3) O '85
--San Ysidro U.S. Customs Sta-
      tion, California
   Nat Geog 167:726 (c,4) Je '85
--U.S.-Mexican border (Laredo,
      Texas)
   Life 9:4 (c,4) Ag '86
--U.S.-Mexican border patrol
   Nat Geog 167:720-1 (c,1) Je
      '85
BORNEO
--Gomantong Cave
   Smithsonian 14:66-71 (c,1) S
      '83
BOSCH, HIERONYMUS
--16th cent. painting of infant
      Jesus
   Smithsonian 14:22 (4) F '84
BOSTON, MASSACHUSETTS
   Trav/Holiday 158:cov., 29-30,
      62 (c,1) Jl '82
--1919 molasses disaster
   Smithsonian 14:222-9 (4) N '83
--Boston Garden
   Sports Illus 64:2-3, 112-26
      (c,1) My 19 '86
--Copley Place
   Trav/Holiday 163:75 (c,4) Mr
      '85
--Faneuil Hall Marketplace
   Trav/Holiday 162:40 (4) D '84
--Frog Pond, Commons (1920s)
   Smithsonian 14:216 (4) N '83
--Isabella Stewart Gardner Mu-
      seum
   Trav/Holiday 163:70 (c,1) Mr
      '85
--Massachusetts General Hospital
   Am Heritage 35:50-1 (c,1) O '84

--Museum of Fine Arts
   Trav/Holiday 163:72 (c,4) Mr '85
--Museum of Science exhibits
   Trav/Holiday 163:73 (c,2) Mr '85
--Public Garden
   Trav/Holiday 162:77 (4) Jl '84
BOSTON MARATHON
--1983
   Sports Illus 58:54-8 (c,1) My 2
      '83
   Sports Illus 58:102 (c,4) Je 27
      '83
BOSWELL, JAMES
   Smithsonian 15:65 (painting,c,4)
      D '84
BOTSWANA
--Pastureland
   Nat Geog 170:828-9 (c,1) D '86
--Rakops village
   Nat Geog 165:148-9 (c,1) F '84
--See also
      KALAHARI DESERT
BOTTICELLI, SANDRO
--"Primavera"
   Smithsonian 13:cov., 63-4 (paint-
      ing,c,1) N '82
BOTTLES
   Nat Geog 163:401 (c,2) Mr '83
--1628 (Sweden)
   Nat Geog 161:68 (c,4) Ja '82
--1790 (Great Britain)
   Nat Geog 168:432 (c,4) O '85
--Late 19th cent. soda pop bottles
   Life 7:60 (c,2) My '84
--1880s belladonna jar
   Am Heritage 35:30 (c,4) O '84
--1880s camphor jar
   Am Heritage 35:25 (c,4) O '84
--Early Coca-Cola bottles
   Am Heritage 37:98-101 (c,2) Je
      '86
--Handmade perfume bottles (Cali-
      fornia)
   Life 9:84 (c,2) Jl '86
--Olive oil bottles (Italy)
   Smithsonian 15:107 (c,2) Mr '85
--Plastic soda bottles
   Smithsonian 16:82 (c,4) N '85
--See also
      WINE
BOUCHER, FRANÇOIS
--Paintings by him
   Smithsonian 16:cov., 98-109
      (c,1) Mr '86
BOURKE-WHITE, MARGARET
   Life 9:56 (4) Fall '86
--Photograph of George Washington

BOURKE-WHITE, MARGARET
(cont.)
Bridge (1933)
Smithsonian 13:136 (4) N '82
BOW, CLARA
Smithsonian 13:102 (4) F '83
BOWERBIRDS
Natur Hist 92:48-55 (c,1) S '83
BOWIE, JAMES
Smithsonian 16:57 (painting,4)
Mr '86
BOWLING
Sports Illus 56:48 (c,4) Mr 1
'82
Sports Illus 57:76-90 (c,1) N
15 '82
Ebony 39:74 (3) Ja '84
Sports Illus 63:36-8 (c,1) Jl
15 '85
Sports Illus 64:56 (c,3) Ja 20
'86
Ebony 41:157-9, 162 (3) F '86
Sports Illus 64:87 (c,3) Ap 7
'86
--Bowling pins
Sports Illus 63:82 (c,4) N 20
'85
--Children
Ebony 37:44 (4) My '82
--Lawn bowling (Tahiti)
Sports Illus 64:144 (c,3) F 10
'86
--Women
Ebony 37:80-2, 88 (4) F '82
Sports Illus 59:E3 (c,4) N 21
'83
BOXERS
Sports Illus 56:cov. (paint-
ing,c,1) Je 7 '82
Sports Illus 57:cov. (c,1) O
18 '82
Sports Illus 64:cov. (c,1) Ja
6 '86
--1850s (Great Britain)
Nat Geog 170:740 (drawing,4)
D '86
--1873 (Australia)
Smithsonian 14:42 (4) Je '83
--1889
Smithsonian 15:154-6 (3) D '84
--1940s
Sports Illus 62:72 (3) Je 17
'85
--Injured boxers
Sports Illus 57:59 (c,4) Ag 9
'82
Life 8:78 (2) Mr '85

--Panama
Nat Geog 169:484-5 (c,1) Ap '86
--Ten-year-old amateur boxer
(Mexico)
Nat Geog 166:173 (c,1) Ag '84
--See also
ALI, MUHAMMAD
DEMPSEY, JACK
JOHNSON, JACK
LOUIS, JOE
SULLIVAN, JOHN L.
BOXERS (DOGS)
Sports Illus 63:62 (4) Ag 19 '85
Sports Illus 64:91 (c,4) My 19
'86
BOXES
--1871 paper boxes (Pennsylvania)
Am Heritage 36:37 (2) Ag '85
BOXING
Sports Illus 57:50-2 (c,4) D 20
'82
--Ancient Greek Olympics
Smithsonian 15:66 (painting,c,4)
Je '84
--Australia
Nat Geog 169:14-15 (c,1) Ja '86
--Friends exercising
Life 6:44 (c,4) Ag '83
--Practicing on punching bag
Sports Illus 57:30 (c,3) Jl 26
'82
Sports Illus 59:86 (c,4) O 17 '83
Sports Illus 59:74 (c,4) D 19 '83
Sports Illus 61:399 (c,4) Jl 18
'84
--Street boxers (Washington, D.C.)
Nat Geog 163:106-7 (c,1) Ja '83
BOXING--AMATEUR
Sports Illus 60:50 (c,4) Mr 19
'84
Sports Illus 60:66-7 (c,4) Ap 23
'84
Sports Illus 61:18-25 (c,2) Jl 16
'84
BOXING
--1984 Olympics (Los Angeles)
Sports Illus 61:56-69 (c,2) Ag
20 '84
BOXING--PROFESSIONAL
Sports Illus 56:45, 49 (c,4) Ja
25 '82
Sports Illus 56:22-7 (c,1) F 8 '82
Sports Illus 56:112-20 (c,1) F
10 '82
Sports Illus 56:64-5, 74-6 (c,2)
Ap 26 '82
Sports Illus 56:30-3 (c,3) My 17

BOXING--PROFESSIONAL (cont.)
'82
  Sports Illus 56:cov., 42-50,
    86 (painting,c,1) Je 7 '82
  Sports Illus 57:cov., 10-13,
    32 (c,1) Ag 2 '82
  Sports Illus 57:28-31 (c,2) Ag
    16 '82
  Sports Illus 57:82-3 (c,2) O
    18 '82
  Sports Illus 57:32-4 (c,1) N 8
    '82
  Sports Illus 57:36, 45 (c,3) N
    15 '82
  Sports Illus 57:cov., 26-31,
    34-5 (c,1) N 22 '82
  Sports Illus 57:34-5 (c,2) D 6
    '82
  Sports Illus 57:24 (c,2) D 13
    '82
  Sports Illus 58:112-20 (c,1) F
    16 '83
  Sports Illus 58:44-54 (c,4) Ap
    11 '83
  Ebony 38:35 (c,2) My '83
  Sports Illus 58:cov., 22-7 (c,1)
    Je 27 '83
  Sports Illus 59:32-5 (c,2) Jl
    25 '83
  Sports Illus 59:18-19 (c,1) Ag
    15 '83
  Sports Illus 59:32-41 (c,1) S
    19 '83
  Sports Illus 59:36-9 (c,2) O 3
    '83
  Sports Illus 59:cov., 30-9 (c,1)
    N 21 '83
  Sports Illus 59:26-7 (c,2) D 5
    '83
  Sports Illus 59:22-3 (c,3) D
    26 '83
  Sports Illus 60:14-17 (c,1) Ja
    23 '84
  Sports Illus 60:104-12 (c,1) F
    8 '84
  Sports Illus 60:38-9 (c,2) My
    21 '84
  Sports Illus 60:50-4 (c,3) Je
    11 '84
  Sports Illus 60:36-40 (c,2) Je
    25 '84
  Sports Illus 62:14-16 (c,1) F
    25 '85
  Sports Illus 62:16-19 (c,2) Mr
    25 '85
  Sports Illus 62:48-58 (paint-
    ing,c,2) Ap 8 '85

  Sports Illus 62:cov., 20-5 (c,1)
    Ap 22 '85
--1889
  Smithsonian 15:152-62 (1) D '84
--1934
  Sports Illus 58:56 (4) Ap 11 '83
--1940s
  Sports Illus 62:82, 89-90 (4) Je
    17 '85
--Artifacts from boxing history
  Sports Illus 63:106-7 (c,1) D 23
    '85
--Championship belts
  Sports Illus 57:41 (c,4) Ag 2 '82
  Sports Illus 58:20-1 (c,2) Mr 28
    '83
  Sports Illus 58:53 (c,4) Je 6 '83
  Sports Illus 60:32 (c,4) F 18 '85
  Ebony 39:27 (c,2) Mr '84
  Sports Illus 62:32 (c,4) F 18 '85
  Sports Illus 62:80 (c,2) My 20
    '85
  Sports Illus 63:25 (c,4) Ag 19
    '85
  Sports Illus 63:66 (c,4) D 23 '85
--Clay-Liston fight (1964)
  Life 9:14-15 (c,1) Fall '86
--The count
  Sports Illus 59:36-7 (c,2) O 3
    '83
--Decision
  Sports Illus 59:39 (c,4) O 3 '83
--Defeated boxer
  Life 8:78 (2) Mr '85
--Fitzsimmons-Corbett fight (1897)
  Sports Illus 65:30 (2) Jl 21 '86
--Foreman-Frazier fight (1973)
  Ebony 39:33 (4) O '84
--Holmes-Cooney fight (1982)
  Sports Illus 56:cov., 14-29 (c,1)
    Je 21 '82
  Ebony 37:117 (c,2) S '82
--Holmes-Witherspoon fight (1983)
  Sports Illus 58:cov., 24-9 (c,1)
    My 30 '83
--Knock out
  Sports Illus 56:18-19 (c,3) Mr 1
    '82
  Sports Illus 56:70 (c,4) Mr 8 '82
  Sports Illus 58:46-7 (c,3) Je 6
    '83
  Sports Illus 60:66-7 (c,3) Je 18
    '84
  Life 8:74 (4) Je '85
--Leonard-Hearns fight (1981)
  Ebony 37:38 (4) Ja '82
  Life 5:66 (c,3) Ja '82

BOXING--PROFESSIONAL (cont.)
--Louis-Schmeling fight (1938)
  Sports Illus 63:74-5 (c,1) S
    23 '85
--Player on mat
  Sports Illus 62:22-3 (c,1) Ap
    22 '85
--Punch
  Sports Illus 61:51 (c,2) N 19
    '84
  Sports Illus 62:58 (c,3) Mr 4
    '85
--Sitting in corner
  Sports Illus 59:2 (c,1) S 19
    '83
--Spinks-Braxton fight (1983)
  Sports Illus 58:cov., 14-21
    (c,1) Mr 28 '83
--Spinks-Holmes fight (1985)
  Sports Illus 63:cov., 20-7
    (c,1) S 30 '85
  Ebony 41:36 (4) Mr '86
--Sullivan-Kilrain fight (1889)
  Smithsonian 15:152-62 (1) D
    '84
--Training
  Sports Illus 56:20-1 (c,3) Ap
    19 '82
  Sports Illus 58:37 (c,4) Mr 28
    '83
  Sports Illus 60:64-5 (c,2) Je
    18 '84
--Training underwater (1961)
  Life 9:273-4 (2) Fall '86
--Training with punching bag
  Life 6:57 (c,2) F '83
  Sports Illus 58:4 (4) Mr 14 '83
  Sports Illus 59:39 (c,3) Ag 1
    '83
  Sports Illus 59:80 (c,2) N 7
    '83
  Sports Illus 62:87 (c,3) My 20
    '85
  Sports Illus 65:cov., 28 (c,1)
    S 8 '86
--Tyson-Berbick fight (1986)
  Sports Illus 65:cov., 18-21
    (c,1) D 1 '86
--Walcott-Charles fight (1951)
  Ebony 39:56 (4) O '84
BOY SCOUTS
  Life 5:140-1 (2) O '82
  Smithsonian 16:cov., 32-41
    (c,1) Jl '85
--1911 first uniform
  Am Heritage 36:8 (4) Je '85
--1925 Boy Scout uniform

Am Heritage 36:66 (drawing,1)
  F '85
--1925 merit badges
  Am Heritage 36:68 (4) F '85
--1927 badge
  Am Heritage 36:114 (c,2) F '85
--History
  Am Heritage 36:66-71 (c,1) F
    '85
  Smithsonian 16:cov., 34-5 (c,1)
    Jl '85
--See also
  BADEN-POWELL, ROBERT
BRADY, MATHEW
--1860 photograph of Matthew
    Maury
  Smithsonian 14:176 (4) Mr '84
--Tombstone (Washington, D.C.)
  Am Heritage 33:68 (c,4) Je '82
BRAIN
--Diagram of olfactory sense
  Nat Geog 170:336-7 (c,1) S '86
--Diagrams of brain damage from
    boxing
  Sports Illus 58:60-3 (c,4) Ap 11
    '83
BRANDO, MARLON
  Sports Illus 64:42 (4) Je 30 '86
BRAZIL
--Amazon River area
  Natur Hist 92:60-7 (c,1) Jl '83
  Nat Geog 165:674-93 (c,1) My
    '84
--Bahia
  Trav/Holiday 162:52-5, 65 (c,2)
    N '84
--Cattle ranch
  Nat Geog 163:40-1 (c,1) Ja '83
--Gold mines
  Nat Geog 163:6-7 (c,1) Ja '83
  Smithsonian 15:88-93 (c,1) Ap
    '84
--Maranhão
  Natur Hist 94:40-7 (c,1) D '85
--Neblinka Mountain
  Natur Hist 93:89 (c,3) S '84
  Natur Hist 93:16 (c,4) D '84
--Rain forests
  Nat Geog 163:34-7, 40-5 (c,1)
    Ja '83
--See also
  AMAZON RIVER
  IGUAÇU FALLS
  RIO DE JANEIRO
  SAO PAULO
BRAZIL--COSTUME
--Early 20th cent. Indians

BRAZIL--COSTUME (cont.)
Natur Hist 93:32-4, 44-8 (3)
O '84
--Bahia
Trav/Holiday 162:53, 55 (c,4)
N '84
--Farm worker's family
Ebony 40:106 (4) Ag '85
--Kayapo Indians
Nat Geog 165:674-93 (c,1) My
'84
Natur Hist 95:4 (c,4) Ap '86
--Maranhão
Natur Hist 94:40-7 (c,1) D '85
--Mardi Gras (Rio de Janeiro)
Trav/Holiday 161:62-4 (c,1) F
'84
--Miners
Smithsonian 15:88-97 (c,1) Ap
'84
BRAZIL--HOUSING
--Miners' huts
Smithsonian 15:91 (c,4) Ap '84
BRAZIL--MAPS
Natur Hist 93:30 (c,4) O '84
BREAD
Ebony 37:124-8 (c,2) F '82
BREAD MAKING
Sports Illus 59:3 (c,4) D 5
'83
--Easter bread (Greece)
Nat Geog 164:773 (c,2) D '83
--Eskimos (Canada)
Nat Geog 169:694 (c,4) My '86
--France
Smithsonian 14:56 (c,4) Je '83
--Matzohs (Bedouins; Egypt)
Nat Geog 161:432-3 (c,1) Ap
'82
--Sardinia, Italy
Natur Hist 92:cov., 54-63
(c,1) Ja '83
BREADFRUIT
Natur Hist 94:34-41 (c,1) Mr
'85
BREADFRUIT TREES
Natur Hist 94:40 (c,3) Mr '85
BRECKINRIDGE, JOHN C.
--1865 escape to the Caribbean
Smithsonian 13:70-8 (paint-
ing,c,1) D '82
BREMERTON, WASHINGTON
Trav/Holiday 159:42 (c,3) My
'83
BREUGHEL, JAN THE ELDER
--"Hearing" (1716)
Smithsonian 13:30 (painting,c,4)

Ja '83
BREUGHEL, PIETER THE ELDER
--"Children's Games" (1560)
Smithsonian 14:40 (painting,c,2)
D '83
--"The Peasant Dance" (1567)
Smithsonian 14:30 (painting,c,4)
Jl '83
--"Spring" (1565)
Smithsonian 15:66 (drawing,3)
N '84
BREZHNEV, LEONID
Life 6:143 (4) Ja '83
BRIDGES
--1922 Joseph Stella painting
Am Heritage 34:25 (c,2) O '83
--Arched (Mostar, Yugoslavia)
Sports Illus 59:102 (c,3) O 24
'83
--Bosporus bridge, Istanbul, Tur-
key
Nat Geog 167:170-1 (c,1) F '85
Smithsonian 17:130-1 (c,3) N
'86
--Bow Bridge, Old Lyme, Con-
necticut
Smithsonian 12:108 (painting,c,2)
Ja '82
--Charles Bridge, Prague, Czecho-
slovakia
Life 6:120 (c,2) D '83
--Covered (New Brunswick)
Trav/Holiday 163:84 (c,4) Mr '85
--Covered (Vermont)
Am Heritage 33:17 (c,4) Ap '82
--Curaçao
Trav/Holiday 159:57 (c,3) Je '83
--Dangerous wooden span (India)
Smithsonian 15:114 (c,4) O '83
--Delaware Memorial Bridge, Dela-
ware
Nat Geog 164:170-1 (c,1) Ag '83
--Drawbridge (Wisconsin)
Trav/Holiday 159:59 (c,4) My '83
--Family standing on wooden bridge
(Oregon)
Sports Illus 60:46 (c,4) F 6 '84
--Great Stone Bridge, China
Natur Hist 95:38 (4) S '86
--Japanese garden (California)
Smithsonian 12:71 (c,4) F '82
--Lanzhou, Gansu, China
Nat Geog 165:304 (c,2) Mr '84
--Memphis, Tennessee
Nat Geog 169:634-5 (c,1) My '86
--Mittlere, Basel, Switzerland
Natur Hist 91:34-5 (c,2) F '82

BRIDGES (cont.)
--Newport, Rhode Island
   Trav/Holiday 160:42-3 (c,1)
      Jl '83
--Ohio River, Ohio/Kentucky
   Am Heritage 34:96-101 (c,1)
      O '83
--Paris, France
   Nat Geog 161:478-9 (c,1) Ap
      '82
--Pittsburgh, Pennsylvania
   Trav/Holiday 163:52-3 (c,1)
      My '85
--Pont Neuf wrapped in nylon
      by Christo, Paris, France
   Life 8:74-5 (1) N '85
--Ponte Vecchio, Florence, Italy
   Smithsonian 13:60 (c,4) N
      '82
--Princip, Sarajevo, Yugoslavia
   Sports Illus 56:50 (c,3) Mr
      22 '82
--Pulteney, Bath, England
   Trav/Holiday 158:30 (c,3) Ag
      '82
   Smithsonian 15:125 (c,4) N '84
--Railroad bridge (Great Britain)
   Nat Geog 169:392-3 (c,1) Mr
      '86
--Railroad bridge (India)
   Nat Geog 165:710-11, 720-1
      (c,1) Je '84
--Railroad bridge (Mississippi)
   Nat Geog 169:368-9 (c,1) Mr
      '86
--River Kwai, Thailand
   Nat Geog 162:519 (c,3) O '82
--Ryogokubashi, Tokyo, Japan
   Nat Geog 170:613 (paint-
      ing,c,4) N '86
--Seven Mile Bridge, Florida Keys
   Nat Geog 166:816-17 (c,1) D
      '84
--Spokane Street Bridge, Seattle,
      Washington
   Sports Illus 57:66 (4) Jl '82
--Szecheny Chain Bridge, Buda-
      pest, Hungary
   Trav/Holiday 163:cov., (c,1)
      Mr '85
--Thousand Islands, New York/
      Ontario
   Trav/Holiday 162:10 (4) S '84
--Tower Bridge, London, England
   Nat Geog 163:780-1 (c,1) Je '83
--Washed out in flood (Ecuador)
   Nat Geog 165:146-7 (c,1) F '84

--Washington, D.C.
   Nat Geog 163:90-1 (c,1) Ja '83
--"Wind-and-rain bridge" (Guangxi
      region, China)
   Nat Geog 165:332-3 (c,1) Mr '84
--Wooden bridge (New York)
   Smithsonian 15:70-1 (c,3) O '84
--See also
      BROOKLYN BRIDGE
      GEORGE WASHINGTON BRIDGE
      GOLDEN GATE BRIDGE
BRIDGES--CONSTRUCTION
--Brooklyn Bridge, New York City,
      New York (1870s)
   Nat Geog 163:cov., 571-3 (draw-
      ing,c,2) My '83
--Golden Gate, San Francisco,
      California (1930s)
   Smithsonian 13:101-7 (c,1) Jl
      '82
--Ohio River Bridge (1860s)
   Am Heritage 34:96-8 (1) O '83
BRISBANE, AUSTRALIA
   Trav/Holiday 162:10, 28 (c,3)
      O '84
   Nat Geog 169:26-7 (c,1) Ja '86
BRISTLECONE PINE TREES
   Nat Wildlife 23:16 (c,3) D '84
   Natur Hist 94:cov., 38-41 (c,1)
      My '85
   Smithsonian 16:55 (c,1) Jl '85
   Nat Wildlife 24:20 (c,1) D '85
BRITISH COLUMBIA
--Burgess Shale, Mount Wapta
   Natur Hist 94:30 (4) D '85
--Cathedral Crags
   Natur Hist 94:34-5 (c,1) D '85
--Cranberry Marsh
   Nat Geog 166:584-5 (c,1) N '84
--Fraser River areas
   Nat Geog 170:44-75 (map,c,1)
      Jl '86
--See also
      FRASER RIVER
      ROCKY MOUNTAINS
      VANCOUVER
      VICTORIA
      YOHO NATIONAL PARK
BRONX, NEW YORK CITY, NEW
      YORK
--Bronx Zoo groundhog den
   Smithsonian 16:22 (c,4) Ap '85
--Hunts Point Market
   Natur Hist 95:86 (c,4) D '86
--Yankee Stadium
   Sports Illus 60:102-3 (c,1) Je 4
      '84

Bronze Age. See
    MAN, PREHISTORIC
BROOKLYN, NEW YORK CITY,
    NEW YORK
    Trav/Holiday 159:46-51
        (map,c,1) Ap '83
    Nat Geog 163:564-612
        (map,c,1) My '83
--Mid 19th cent.
    Am Heritage 35:45 (paint-
        ing,c,3) Ap '84
--1860s
    Am Heritage 35:6 (4) Ag '84
--Early 20th cent.
    Am Heritage 37:87 (paint-
        ing,c,4) F '86
--Park Slope house
    Trav/Holiday 157:73 (c,4) Ap
        '82
--Slums
    Life 6:48-9 (c,1) Ap '83
--See also
    BROOKLYN BRIDGE
    CONEY ISLAND
BROOKLYN BRIDGE, NEW YORK
    CITY, NEW YORK
    Trav/Holiday 157:73 (c,4) Ap
        '82
    Smithsonian 14:78-85 (c,1) Ap
        '83
    Trav/Holiday 159:cov. (c,1)
        Ap '83
    Nat Geog 163:cov., 564-79
        (c,1) My '83
    Life 6:104-8 (c,1) My '83
    Life 7:10-11 (c,1) Ja '84
    Nat Geog 170:42-3 (c,1) Jl '86
--1900
    Am Heritage 34:101 (3) O '83
--Early 20th cent. depictions by
        Joseph Stella
    Smithsonian 13:136 (paint-
        ing,c,4) N '82
    Am Heritage 38:59 (drawing,c,4)
        D '86
--Fireworks for centennial cele-
        bration
    Life 7:10-11 (c,1) Ja '84
BROOMS
    Sports Illus 57:57 (c,4) Jl 26
        '82
BROUN, HEYWOOD
    Am Heritage 33:66 (4) O '82
BROWN, JOHN
    Nat Geog 166:32 (painting,c,4)
        Jl '84
    Am Heritage 35:14 (painting,4)

O '84
--Home and grave (Lake Placid,
    New York)
    Nat Geog 166:34 (c,1) Jl '84
BROWN THRASHERS
    Natur Hist 94:94 (painting,c,1)
        Ap '85
BRUGES, BELGIUM
    Trav/Holiday 161:95 (4) Mr '84
BRUSHES
--1871 household brushes (Penn-
        sylvania)
    Am Heritage 36:34 (2) Ag '85
BRUSSELS, BELGIUM
    Nat Geog 166:677 (c,1) N '84
--Steelworkers riot
    Life 5:112-13 (1) Ap '82
BRYAN, WILLIAM JENNINGS
    Am Heritage 38:32 (4) D '86
--1908 Presidential campaign
    Am Heritage 35:108 (2) O '84
BRYCE CANYON NATIONAL PARK,
    UTAH
    Sports Illus 59:68 (c,3) S 26 '83
BUCHWALD, ART
    Nat Geog 163:113 (c,4) Ja '83
BUCKINGHAM PALACE, LONDON,
    ENGLAND
--View from palace
    Life 7:8-9 (1) Mr '84
BUDAPEST, HUNGARY
    Nat Geog 163:224-57 (c,1) F '83
    Trav/Holiday 163:cov., 64-9
        (c,1) Mr '85
    Smithsonian 17:52-63 (c,1) N '86
--1956
    Smithsonian 17:52-7 (1) N '86
--Freedom Statue, Gellert Hill
    Smithsonian 17:56 (c,4) N '86
BUDDHA
--5th cent. wooden sculpture
    Smithsonian 13:59 (c,4) Ap '82
--5th cent. statue (Aukana, Sri
        Lanka)
    Trav/Holiday 158:41 (c,1) S '82
--Borobudur statue, Indonesia
    Nat Geog 163:126-7, 142 (c,1)
        Ja '83
--Carved into cliff (Burma)
    Smithsonian 15:107 (c,4) My '84
--Gold sculpture (Thailand)
    Smithsonian 13:42-3 (c,1) Je '82
--Statues (Burma)
    Nat Geog 166:107 (c,4) Jl '84
BUDDHISM--ART
--5th-9th cents.
    Smithsonian 13:56-61 (c,1) Ap '82

BUDDHISM--ART (cont.)
--10th cent. murals (Tibet)
   Natur Hist 95:cov., 38-45
     (c,1) Jl '86
--Depictions of Kingdom of
     Shambhala (Tibet)
   Natur Hist 92:54-63 (c,1) Ap
     '83
--Statues of deities (Tibet)
   Natur Hist 92:cov., 57 (c,1)
     Ap '83
BUDDHISM--COSTUME
--Child novice monks (Burma)
   Smithsonian 15:110 (c,4) My
     '84
--Dalai Lama
   Smithsonian 14:83 (c,4) Mr '84
--Hindu converts to Buddhism
     (India)
   Natur Hist 95:31, 34-5 (4) O
     '86
--Lamas (Tibet)
   Nat Geog 165:308-9 (c,1) Mr
     '84
--Monks (China)
   Nat Geog 161:256 (c,1) F '82
--Monks (Thailand)
   Nat Geog 162:496, 500-1 (c,1)
     O '82
--Novices (Sri Lanka)
   Trav/Holiday 158:43 (c,4) S '82
--Nuns (Burma)
   Nat Geog 166:110-11 (c,1) Jl
     '84
--Tibetan exiles (India)
   Smithsonian 14:82-91 (c,1) Mr
     '84
BUDDHISM--RITES AND FESTI-
    VALS
--Buddha's birthday festival
     (India)
   Smithsonian 14:112 (c,4) O '83
--Carrying prayer books on back
     (Tibet)
   Nat Geog 165:307 (c,2) Mr '84
--Chanting (California)
   Life 8:24 (c,1) Ag '85
--Esala Perahera (Sri Lanka)
   Nat Geog 164:254-5 (c,1) Ag
     '83
--Giving gift scarves to Buddha
     (Tibet)
   Nat Geog 165:306 (c,4) Mr '84
--Initiating novice monk (Burma)
   Nat Geog 166:108-9 (c,1) Jl '84
--Monlam prayer festival (India)
   Smithsonian 14:82-3 (c,1) Mr '84

--Procession (Sri Lanka)
   Nat Geog 162:19 (c,1) Jl '82
--Thai Supreme Patriarch preparing
     blessing
   Smithsonian 13:14 (4) Ja '83
--Thami, Nepal
   Nat Geog 161:708-9 (c,1) Je '82
BUDDHISM--SHRINES AND SYMBOLS
--Borobudur, Java, Indonesia
   Nat Geog 163:126-42 (c,1) Ja '83
--China
   Nat Geog 161:254-5 (c,1) F '82
--Mandala (India)
   Natur Hist 92:54-5 (c,1) Ap '83
   Smithsonian 14:85 (c,4) Mr '84
--Prayer flags (Tibet)
   Natur Hist 91:50-1 (c,3) S '82
--Prayer flags in tree (Nepal)
   Nat Geog 161:724-5 (c,1) Je '82
--Prayer wheel (China)
   Nat Geog 161:257 (c,2) F '82
--Site of Buddha's 6th cent. B.C.
     sermon (Sarnath, India)
   Nat Geog 169:237, 245 (c,4) F
     '86
--Tsaparang, Tibet
   Natur Hist 95:cov., 34-45 (c,1)
     Jl '86
BUDGE, DONALD
   Sports Illus 59:45-6 (c,3) Ag 22
     '83
BUENOS AIRES, ARGENTINA
   Nat Geog 170:238-45 (c,1) Ag '86
--1970s torture center
   Life 7:42 (c,2) My '84
BUFFALOES
   Sports Illus 62:80 (c,4) My 27 '85
   Natur Hist 94:42-3 (painting,c,1)
     Ag '85
   Nat Geog 169:584-5 (c,1) My '86
BUGLES
--1876 U.S. Army bugle
   Nat Geog 170:810 (c,4) D '86
Buildings. See
     APARTMENT BUILDINGS
     HOUSES
     OFFICE BUILDINGS
     lists of structures under
       ARCHITECTURAL STRUC-
       TURES and HOUSING
BUILDINGS--CONSTRUCTION
   Smithsonian 14:43-5 (c,3) O '83
--1924 (New York City, New York)
   Am Heritage 38:56 (painting,c,2)
     D '86
--Carrying mortar (Egypt)
   Nat Geog 161:436-7 (c,2) Ap '82

BUILDINGS--CONSTRUCTION
(cont.)
--Hayden Planetarium, New York
City (1934)
Natur Hist 94:4 (3) O '85
--Miami, Florida
Nat Geog 162:186 (c,1) Ag '82
--Natural History building,
Washington, D.C.
Smithsonian 15:30 (4) Mr '85
--New York City office building
scaffolding
Life 6:110 (c,2) N '83
--Paraguay mansion
Nat Geog 162:244 (c,4) Ag '82
--Urban office buildings
Smithsonian 16:44-53 (c,1) S
'85
BUILDINGS--DEMOLITION
--Boston hotel, Massachusetts
(1983)
Sports Illus 64:124 (c,3) My
19 '86
--Demolishing structures with ex-
plosives
Smithsonian 17:98-104 (c,2) D
'86
--Demolishing floor of Colorado
house
Nat Geog 166:215 (c,4) Ag '84
--New York City theater
Life 6:156 (4) Ja '83
BULBUL BIRDS
Natur Hist 91:41 (c,4) Mr '82
Bulgaria. See
SOFIA
BULLDOGS
Ebony 39:74-6 (4) Jl '84
Sports Illus 61:16 (c,4) O 1 '84
Am Heritage 37:92-3 (1) O '86
BULLDOZERS
Nat Geog 165:457 (c,3) Ap '84
Ebony 41:47 (c,4) Je '86
Bullets. See
ARMS
BULLFIGHTING
Sports Illus 61:104 (paint-
ing,c,4) D 10 '84
--Mexico
Ebony 37:41 (3) Ja '82
Nat Geog 166:466-7 (c,1) O '84
--Spain
Nat Geog 169:166-7 (c,1) F '86
--See also
MATADORS
BULLFROGS
Nat Wildlife 23:54-5 (c,1) D '84

Natur Hist 94:30 (painting,c,4)
Ap '85
BUMBLEBEES
Nat Wildlife 21:21, 24 (c,2) F
'83
BUMPER STICKERS
--Coal mining man (West Virginia)
Nat Geog 163:793 (c,4) Je '83
BUNCHBERRIES
Nat Geog 165:76 (c,4) Ja '84
Natur Hist 95:91 (c,3) Ja '86
BUNCHE, RALPH
Ebony 39:68 (4) Jl '84
Ebony 41:254, 260 (4) N '85
BUNKER HILL, BATTLE OF (1775)
Ebony 39:28 (painting,4) F '84
BUNTINGS (BIRDS)
Nat Wildlife 22:23, 25 (draw-
ing,c,4) D '83
Nat Wildlife 24:17 (painting,c,4)
D '85
BURMA
Nat Geog 166:90-121 (map,c,1)
Jl '84
--1923
Natur Hist 94:26 (c,3) O '85
--Irrawaddy River area
Smithsonian 15:98-111 (c,1) My
'84
--Pondaung Formation
Natur Hist 94:28, 34 (map,c,4)
O '85
--See also
IRRAWADDY RIVER
MANDALAY
RANGOON
BURMA--ART
--Golden sculpture
Nat Geog 166:106-7 (c,1) Jl '84
BURMA--COSTUME
Smithsonian 15:98-110 (c,1)
My '84
Nat Geog 166:90-121 (c,1) Jl '84
--Drug dealers
Nat Geog 167:145 (c,1) F '85
BURMA--HOUSING
--Stilt houses
Smithsonian 15:102 (c,3) My '84
BURMA--POLITICS AND GOVERN-
MENT
--Karen people's war for indepen-
dence
Nat Geog 166:112-15 (c,1) Jl '84
BURR, AARON
Am Heritage 34:19 (drawing,4)
D '82

BURROS
  Nat Geog 166:478-9 (c,1) O
    '84
BURROUGHS, JOHN
  Am Heritage 33:81 (4) Je '82
  Nat Geog 162:346 (4) S '82
BUSES
  Sports Illus 57:45 (c,4) D 6
    '82
--Early 20th cent. tourist bus
    (Montana park)
  Natur Hist 91:20 (3) Je '82
--1928
  Life 6:80 (4) Je '83
--1950s air-conditioned bus
    (Texas)
  Am Heritage 36:13 (3) D '84
--Athletes sleeping on bus
    (Mexico)
  Sports Illus 57:30-1, 37 (c,1)
    Ag 30 '82
--Birmingham, England
  Ebony 38:127 (c,2) Jl '83
--Canada
  Sports Illus 61:394 (c,3) Jl 18
    '84
--Children on bus (Scotland)
  Natur Hist 92:46 (c,3) Je '83
--Double-decker (London, Eng-
    land)
  Trav/Holiday 157:22 (4) Je '82
--High school students on bus
    (Minnesota)
  Sports Illus 63:92 (c,3) N 4
    '85
--Interior of city bus (Chicago,
    Illinois)
  Ebony 37:60 (4) Je '82
--Ken Kesey's Merry Prankster
    bus
  Life 5:99 (c,4) N '82
--Painted buses (Panama City)
  Trav/Holiday 165:92 (4) F '86
--Running on natural gas (China)
  Nat Geog 168:312-13 (c,1)
    S '85
--Spain
  Nat Geog 169:148-9 (c,1) F '86
--Sudan
  Nat Geog 161:370-1 (c,2) Mr
    '82
  Nat Geog 167:613 (c,4) My '85
--See also
    TRANSIT WORKERS
BUSINESSMEN
  Ebony 38:130-4 (c,3) N '82
--Late 19th cent. "Robber Barons"

Am Heritage 38:28 (drawing,c,4)
    D '86
--Black entrepreneurs
  Ebony 38:53-8 (4) My '83
--See also
    AGASSIZ, ALEXANDER
    BARUCH, BERNARD
    CARNEGIE, ANDREW
    FORD, HENRY
    FULLER, ALFRED
    GETTY, J. PAUL
    HARRIMAN, EDWARD HENRY
    HEARST, WILLIAN RAN-
      DOLPH
    LIPTON, SIR THOMAS J.
    LUCE, HENRY
    MEETINGS
    MELLON, ANDREW W.
    OFFICE WORK
    OFFICES
    PULITZER, JOSEPH
    ROCKEFELLER, JOHN D.
    SALESMEN
    VANDERBILT, WILLIAM H.
BUTCHERS
  Sports Illus 56:23 (c,4) Ap 26
    '82
  Sports Illus 57:43 (c,4) Ag 2
    '82
--Budapest, Hungary
  Nat Geog 163:234 (c,3) F '83
--Kosher butcher shop (Poland)
  Nat Geog 170;384-5 (c,1) S '86
--New York shop
  Life 5:22 (c,4) N '82
BUTTE, MONTANA
--Ghost town
  Trav/Holiday 164:16 (c,4) Ag
    '85
BUTTERCUPS
  Nat Geog 165:136-7 (c,1) Ja '84
BUTTERFLIES
  Smithsonian 12:146 (c,4) F '82
  Natur Hist 91:42-9 (c,1) Ap '82
  Nat Wildlife 20:3, 26-32 (c,1)
    Ap '82
  Nat Wildlife 20:52 (c,1) Je '82
  Smithsonian 13:41 (c,3) Ja '83
  Nat Wildlife 21:60 (c,1) Ap '83
  Nat Wildlife 22:64 (c,1) D '83
  Natur Hist 93:46 (c,3) Ja '84
  Nat Wildlife 22:50 (c,4) Je '84
  Nat Wildlife 22:14-15, 52 (c,1)
    O '84
  Nat Wildlife 23:61 (c,4) D '84
  Natur Hist 93:51 (c,4) D '84
  Smithsonian 15:114-21 (c,1) Ja '85

BUTTERFLIES (cont.)
 Nat Wildlife 23:64 (c,1) Ap
 '85
 Smithsonian 16:54 (c,3) My
 '85
 Natur Hist 94:48-9 (c,1) O '85
 Natur Hist 94:52-5 (c,1) N
 '85
 Nat Wildlife 24:62 (c,2) D '85
 Nat Wildlife 24:52 (c,1) Ag
 '86
 Nat Wildlife 25:50-1 (c,1) D
 '86
--Catching with net
 Smithsonian 13:116-17 (c,1)
 My '82
--Fossil
 Natur Hist 93:106 (4) Ap '84
--Mexican sanctuary for monarchs
 Smithsonian 14:174-82 (c,1)
 N '83
--Monarchs
 Natur Hist 91:39 (c,3) Jl '82
 Nat Wildlife 20:22 (c,4) Ag '82
 Nat Wildlife 21:57 (c,2) D '82
 Nat Wildlife 21:30 (4) O '83
 Smithsonian 14:174-82 (c,1) N
 '83
 Nat Wildlife 24:60 (c,1) O '86
--Stages of life
 Smithsonian 17:128-9 (c,4) My
 '86
BUTTONS
--17th cent. (Netherlands)
 Nat Geog 161:59, 76 (c,4) Ja
 '82
--1870s U.S. Army tunic button
 Life 8:118 (c,4) Mr '85
--1932 Hoover campaign button
 Am Heritage 38:25 (4) D '86
--"Remember Pearl Harbor"
 button
 Life 8:21 (c,4) Spring '85
BUZZARDS
 Nat Geog 165:222-3 (c,1) F
 '84
BYRON, LORD
 Smithsonian 13:143 (painting,4)
 F '83
BYZANTINE EMPIRE--ART
 Nat Geog 164:cov., 708-65
 (c,1) D '83
--12th cent. mosaic of Apostles
 (Venice, Italy)
 Smithsonian 15:50-1 (c,2) S
 '84
--Frescoes (Romania)

 Nat Geog 164:730-1, 764-5 (c,1)
 D '83
--Icon (Yugoslavia)
 Nat Geog 164:cov. (c,1) D '83
--Mosaics (Italy)
 Life 7;181-8 (c,1) D '84
BYZANTINE EMPIRE--HISTORY
--1453 fall of Constantinople to
 Turks
 Nat Geog 164:764-5 (fresco,c,1)
 D '83
--Scenes from Byzantine history
 Nat Geog 164:cov., 708-67
 (map,c,1) D '83
--See also
 CONSTANTINE THE GREAT
 JUSTINIAN THE GREAT

- C -

CABBAGE INDUSTRY--HARVESTING
--Texas
 Life 9:45 (c,4) Ag '86
CABINS
--19th cent. slave quarters
 (Louisiana)
 Nat Geog 166:26-9 (c,1) Jl '84
--Summer cabin (Rocky Mountains,
 Colorado)
 Smithsonian 17:44 (c,4) O '86
--See also
 LOG CABINS
CABLE CARS (GONDOLAS)
--Adirondack chairlift, New York
 Trav/Holiday 162:52 (c,2) Ag
 '84
--Grenoble, France
 Trav/Holiday 164:59 (c,3) N '85
--Italian Alps (Bormio)
 Sports Illus 62:16-17 (c,1) F 18
 '85
--Mountain tram (New Mexico)
 Smithsonian 14:69 (c,3) F '84
--Stone Mountain, Georgia
 Ebony 41:80 (c,3) My '86
Cable cars (streetcars). See
 TROLLEY CARS
CACTUS
 Smithsonian 12:71 (c,4) F '82
 Trav/Holiday 158:57 (c,4) N '82
 Trav/Holiday 161:49 (c,3) Je '84
--Barrel cactus
 Trav/Holiday 159:53 (c,4) F '83
--Cactus flowers
 Smithsonian 12:cov. (c,1) F '82
--Caroon cactus

CACTUS (cont.)
    Trav/Holiday 165:57 (c,4) Ja
      '86
--Hedgehog cactus
    Nat Wildlife 22:52 (c,1) Ag '84
--Saguaro
    Sports Illus 56:40 (paint-
      ing,c,3) Mr 29 '82
    Nat Geog 166:516-17 (c,1) O
      '84
    Smithsonian 15:122-6 (c,1) D
      '84
    Nat Wildlife 23:2 (c,2) Ap '85
    Natur Hist 95:31 (c,4) Jl '86
    Natur Hist 95:32 (c,3) D '86
CAGES
--Animal shelter cat cages
    Smithsonian 13:41, 49 (1) S
      '82
CAGNEY, JAMES
    Am Heritage 35:32-9 (c,1) D
      '83
    Life 7:3, 58-70 (c,1) Mr '84
--Caricature
    Am Heritage 37:53 (4) Je '86
Cafes. See
    COFFEEHOUSES
    RESTAURANTS
CAIRO, EGYPT
    Trav/Holiday 157:36-41 (c,1)
      F '82
    Nat Geog 167:576-7, 600-1
      (c,1) My '85
--Garbage dumps
    Nat Geog 163:442-5 (c,1) Ap
      '83
CALCULATORS
--Early macaroni-box comptometer
    Am Heritage 36:8 (4) Ap '85
CALDER, ALEXANDER
--"Five disks: one empty"
    Trav/Holiday 165:47 (sculp-
      ture,c,4) My '86
--"Peau Rouge Indiana" sculpture
    Smithsonian 16:131 (c,4) Ja
      '86
--"Woman with Lamp Shade" (1928)
    Smithsonian 13:118 (sculpture,4)
      Mr '83
CALENDARS
--18th-20th cents.
    Smithsonian 15:184 (c,4) D '84
--Anasazi Indian solar petroglyph
    (New Mexico)
    Nat Geog 162:580-1 (c,2) N '82
--Aztec (Mexico)
    Trav/Holiday 162:58 (c,2) Jl '84

CALGARY, ALBERTA
    Nat Geog 165:378-403 (map,c,1)
      Mr '84
    Trav/Holiday 163:66-9, 81 (c,1)
      My '85
CALIFORNIA
--19th-20th cent. paintings
    Am Heritage 36:86-99 (c,1) D
      '84
--1846 California independence flag
    Am Heritage 37:6 (4) O '86
--All-American Canal, Imperial Val-
    ley
    Nat Wildlife 22:10 (c,1) F '84
--Alpine Meadows avalanche (1982)
    Nat Geog 162:277, 280-9
      (map,c,1) S '82
--Altamont Pass countryside
    Life 6:84-5 (c,1) N '83
--Anza-Borrego Desert State Park
    Natur Hist 94:70-1 (c,1) O '85
--Calistoga
    Trav/Holiday 164:4 (c,4) S '85
--Channel Islands
    Trav/Holiday 157:66-8, 98 (c,1)
      Mr '82
    Smithsonian 17:138 (c,4) Je '86
--Coloma
    Trav/Holiday 163:20 (c,4) Ja '85
--Daly City
    Nat Geog 169:670-1 (c,1) My '86
--Diablo Canyon nuclear power
    plant
    Life 5:36 (c,4) My '82
--Donner Lake
    Nat Geog 170:172-3 (c,1) Ag '86
--Fall River Valley, Shasta
    Trav/Holiday 166:76 (c,2) O '86
--Filoli gardens, Woodside
    Life 8:52-3 (c,1) Je '85
--Fire damage to Southern California
    hillsides
    Smithsonian 13:132-43 (c,1) O
      '82
--Hearst Castle, San Simeon
    Nat Geog 165:450-3 (c,1) Ap '84
    Smithsonian 16:60-71 (c,1) D '85
--Homes of movie stars
    Life 9:132-42 (c,1) My '86
--Huntington Beach
    Smithsonian 13:68-9 (c,1) S '82
--Malibu
    Nat Geog 165:596-7 (c,1) My '84
--Mid-coast area
    Nat Geog 165:424-60 (map,c,1)
      Ap '84
--Mono Lake

CALIFORNIA (cont.)
  Sports Illus 58:76-86 (c,1)
    My 30 '83
--Recreation of Sutter's 1848
    mill
  Smithsonian 13:97 (c,1) D '82
--17-Mile Drive, Monterey Penin-
    sula
  Trav/Holiday 161:70 (c,1) Ap
    '84
--Silicon Valley
  Life 5:32-8 (c,1) Mr '82
  Nat Geog 162:458-77 (map,c,1)
    O '82
--Soda Lake plain
  Sports Illus 65:88 (c,3) O 20
    '86
--Solvang
  Trav/Holiday 159:21, 24 (4)
    Ap '83
--White Mountains
  Natur Hist 94:38-41 (c,1) My
    '85
--Yuba
  Life 9:152 (c,2) Ja '86
--See also
    ANGELES NATIONAL FOREST
    CARMEL
    CASCADE RANGE
    DEATH VALLEY
    FARALLON ISLANDS
    GOLDEN GATE BRIDGE
    GOLDEN GATE NATIONAL
      RECREATION AREA
    HOLLYWOOD
    LAVA BEDS NATIONAL
      MONUMENT
    LONG BEACH
    LOS ANGELES
    MONTEREY
    MOUNT SHASTA
    OAKLAND
    PASADENA
    SACRAMENTO
    SAN ANDREAS FAULT
    SAN DIEGO
    SAN FRANCISCO
    SANTA BARBARA
    SANTA CLARA
    SANTA MONICA
    SEQUOIA NATIONAL PARK
    SIERRA NATIONAL FOREST
    SIERRA NEVADA MOUNTAINS
    YOSEMITE NATIONAL PARK
CALIFORNIA--MAPS
--Changing earth formations near
    San Francisco

  Nat Geog 168:154-5 (c,1) Ag '85
--Hollywood (1887)
  Am Heritage 35:26 (4) D '83
CALISTHENICS
  Ebony 37:118 (4) F '82
  Sports Illus 56:72 (c,4) My 10
    '82
  Life 5:37-9 (c,1) Je '82
  Ebony 37:91 (2) S '82
  Sports Illus 57:96-102 (c,2) O
    4 '82
  Ebony 38:108-12 (c,1) Ja '83
  Ebony 38:80-6 (c,1) F '83
  Sports Illus 58:68, 70, 74 (c,4)
    F 7 '83
  Ebony 39:105-6 (c,2) N '83
  Ebony 41:54 (4) F '86
--1961 class (Oklahoma)
  Sports Illus 58:74 (4) F 7 '83
--At exercise bar
  Ebony 39:70 (4) My '84
--Athletes doing warmup stretches
  Sports Illus 61:62-3 (c,2) Jl 30
    '84
  Sports Illus 64:30 (c,4) Mr 17
    '86
--Back bend
  Sports Illus 61:48 (c,3) O 22
    '84
--Back flip
  Life 9:98 (c,2) Ja '86
--Children doing sit-ups
  Sports Illus 58:62 (c,4) F 7 '83
--Chin-ups
  Sports Illus 59:22 (c,4) Ag 15
    '83
--Class
  Sports Illus 62:45 (c,3) Ap 29
    '85
--Climbing ropes
  Sports Illus 61:40 (c,4) S 3 '84
--Football players doing warmup
    stretches
  Sports Illus 57:18 (c,2) Ag 16
    '82
  Sports Illus 59:35 (c,3) O 10 '83
  Sports Illus 59:64-5 (c,1) D 26
    '83
  Sports Illus 61:68 (c,4) N 19 '84
  Sports Illus 63:2-3 (c,1) Ag 26
    '85
  Sports Illus 65:22 (c,3) Ag 25
    '86
--Hand-stand
  Sports Illus 62:45 (c,1) Ap 15
    '85
--Headstand

CALISTHENICS (cont.)
  Sports Illus 63:64 (c,3) N 11
    '85
--Hockey team
  Sports Illus 57:48 (c,3) O 11
    '82
--Leg lifts
  Sports Illus 57:80-1 (c,1) N 1
    '82
  Sports Illus 58:86 (c,3) Ap 25
    '83
  Ebony 40:104 (3) Mr '85
--Locked arms with partner
  Ebony 39:58 (4) Ja '84
--Mass calisthenics competition
    (Czechoslovakia)
  Life 8:70-1 (1) S '85
--One-armed push-ups
  Nat Geog 166:198-9 (c,1) Ag
    '84
--Push-ups
  Life 5:68 (c,4) Mr '82
--Sit-ups
  Ebony 42:153 (c,2) D '86
--Split
  Ebony 38:86-7 (2) N '82
--Stretching
  Life 5:76-7 (c,1) D '82
  Ebony 39:38 (4) Mr '84
  Sports Illus 65:22-3 (c,4) S
    29 '86
--Taiwan
  Nat Geog 161:106-7 (c,1) Ja
    '82
--Walkers warming up
  Sports Illus 60:62 (c,4) Mr 26
    '84
--Warm-up exercises for dancer
  Ebony 39:33-8 (c,3) Jl '84
--West Germany
  Nat Geog 161:42-3 (c,2) Ja '82
--"Wrestler's bridge"
  Sports Illus 64:27 (c,2) Ja 6
    '86
--Wrestlers doing handstands
  Nat Geog 169:240 (c,4) F '86
--See also
    EXERCISING
    GYMNASTICS
    YOGA
CALLA LILIES
--X-ray photo
  Smithsonian 17:92 (1) O '86
Calligraphy. See
    WRITING
CALVIN, JOHN
  Nat Geog 164:424 (drawing,c,4)

O '83
CAMBODIA
  Nat Geog 161:548-623 (map,c,1)
    My '82
--Children's drawings of refugee
    camps (Thailand)
  Natur Hist 92:64-7 (c,2) Ja '83
--Temples of Angkor
  Nat Geog 161:cov., 548-89 (c,1)
    My '82
--See also
    PHNOM PENH
CAMBODIA--COSTUME
  Nat Geog 161:590-623 (c,1) My
    '82
--Khmer Rouge
  Life 8:78 (2) Ap '85
--Refugees in Thailand
  Nat Geog 170:662-7 (c,1) N '86
CAMBODIA--POLITICS AND GOV-
    ERNMENT
--Victims of Khmer Rouge
  Life 7:14 (c,2) N '84
--Victims of Pol Pot regime
  Nat Geog 161:600-3 (4) My '82
  Nat Geog 167:575 (c,3) My '85
CAMBRIDGE, ENGLAND
--Punting on the Cam River
  Trav/Holiday 161:6, 8 (c,4) F
    '84
CAMBRIDGE, MASSACHUSETTS
--Apartment building
  Life 9:59 (c,2) N '86
--Charles River
  Life 9:24-5 (c,1) S '86
--See also
    HARVARD UNIVERSITY
CAMBRIDGE UNIVERSITY, ENG-
    LAND
--Kings College
  Trav/Holiday 161:8 (c,4) F '84
CAMDEN, NEW JERSEY
--Harbor (1941)
  Am Heritage 36:114-15 (1) D '84
--Slum
  Sports Illus 57:40-1 (c,2) Ag
    2 '82
CAMELS
  Trav/Holiday 157:36 (c,1) F '82
  Natur Hist 92:52-9 (c,1) Jl '83
  Nat Geog 168:402-3 (c,1) S '85
  Nat Geog 168:478-9 (c,1) O '85
  Life 8:153 (c,3) D '85
--Australian safari
  Trav/Holiday 159:53-4, 77 (c,2)
    My '83
--Bedouin camel race (Saudi Arabia)

CAMELS (cont.)
  Smithsonian 15:56-7 (c,1) D
    '84
--Camel race (Florida)
  Sports Illus 62:6-7 (c,1) Mr
    11 '85
--Camel race (Oman)
  Natur Hist 92:56 (c,4) Jl '83
--Head of camel
  Smithsonian 14:cov. (c,1) F '84
--Silhouetted against sunset
    (Dubai)
  Sports Illus 65:94 (c,3) D 1
    '86
--With rider (Israel)
  Ebony 39:42 (c,3) D '83
--See also
    CARAVANS
CAMERAS
--1930s Speed Graphic
  Nat Geog 166:334 (c,4) S '84
--1938 Deardorff
  Life 5:18 (c,4) Jl '82
--1960s home movie camera
  Life 6:4 (4) N '83
--Antique
  Smithsonian 13:122 (4) Mr '83
--Disc
  Life 5:16 (c,2) My '82
--Equipment bag
  Trav/Holiday 161:36 (4) Mr '84
--New amateur equipment
  Life 5:8-16 (c,1) My '82
--Professional camera
  Nat Geog 163:283 (c,4) Mr '83
--Skycam
  Sports Illus 63:29 (c,4) Ag 26
    '85
--Telephoto lens
  Nat Wildlife 21:2 (c,3) Ap '83
--Television
  Sports Illus 56:42 (c,4) Ap 5
    '82
  Sports Illus 57:39 (c,4) D 27
    '82
  Ebony 38:100 (4) Mr '83
  Sports Illus 60:63 (c,4) Ja 30
    '84
  Sports Illus 61:107 (c,4) N 26
    '84
--3-D
  Life 5:10 (c,4) My '82
--Tripod
  Nat Geog 164:275 (c,4) S '83
  Nat Wildlife 22:2 (c,3) Ap '84
--Underwater photography
  Life 6:13 (c,4) Je '83

--Underwater remotely piloted vehi-
    cle
  Nat Geog 163:312-13 (c,3) Mr '83
--See also
    MOTION PICTURE PHOTOG-
      RAPHY
    PHOTOGRAPHY
CAMEROON--ART
--Late 19th cent. stool
  Natur Hist 94:78 (c,4) Jl '85
--Childbirth stool
  Ebony 40:32 (c,4) Jl '85
CAMEROON--COSTUME
--Bamileke people
  Nat Geog 166:614-15 (c,1) N '84
CAMEROON--HOUSING
--Bamileke king's house
  Nat Geog 166:614-15 (c,1) N '84
CAMEROON--SCULPTURE
  Ebony 40:32 (c,2) Jl '85
CAMOUFLAGE
--1940s camouflaged defense plant
    (California)
  Smithsonian 14:154-5 (2) Mr '84
CAMPANULA PLANTS
--X-ray photo
  Smithsonian 17:91-2 (4) O '86
CAMPFIRES
--California
  Nat Geog 165:448-9 (c,2) Ap '84
  Nat Wildlife 24:64-5 (c,1) D '85
--Jumping over fire to celebrate
    "White Night" (Latvia)
  Nat Geog 167:294-5 (c,1) Mr '85
--New Mexico
  Smithsonian 14:75 (c,1) F '84
--Oklahoma
  Trav/Holiday 165:55 (c,4) F '86
--Toasting marshmallows (Alaska)
  Trav/Holiday 163:50 (c,2) Je '85
CAMPING
--California beach
  Nat Geog 166:348-9 (c,1) S '84
--Camp for children with cancer
    (California)
  Life 7:32-40 (c,1) S '84
--Coleman lantern
  Nat Geog 168:372 (c,4) S '85
--Drying socks (Yukon)
  Nat Geog 168:634 (c,4) N '85
--Mexico
  Nat Geog 166:429 (c,4) O '84
--Missouri
  Sports Illus 56:70 (c,3) Je 28
    '82
--Mount Everest, Nepal
  Sports Illus 59:88-9, 96, 100-1

CAMPING (cont.)
    (c,1) N 14 '83
--Pitching tent (Anatarctica)
    Smithsonian 13:48 (c,3) D '82
--Pitching tent (Canada)
    Nat Geog 169:133 (c,3) Ja '86
--Preparing lunch (Yukon)
    Trav/Holiday 164:59 (c,2) Ag
    '85
--Yosemite National Park camp-
    grounds, California
    Nat Geog 167:58-9 (c,1) Ja
    '85
--See also
        CAMPFIRES
        HIKING
        SLEEPING BAGS
        TENTS
CAMPING--HUMOR
    Sports Illus 56:50-1 (paint-
    ing,c,1) F 1 '82
CAMPSITES
    Trav/Holiday 161:31, 34 (4)
    Ap '84
--Trailer camps (1930s)
    Am Heritage 37:99-103 (c,3)
    D '85
CANADA
--Hudson Bay area
    Nat Geog 161:380-418 (map,c,1)
    Mr '82
--Urban scenes
    Trav/Holiday 157:38-44 (c,2)
    My '82
--See also
        ALBERTA
        ARCTIC
        BRITISH COLUMBIA
        HUDSON BAY
        MACKENZIE RIVER
        MANITOBA
        NEW BRUNSWICK
        NORTHWEST TERRITORIES
        NOVA SCOTIA
        ONTARIO
        PRINCE EDWARD ISLAND
        QUEBEC
        ROCKY MOUNTAINS
        ST. LAWRENCE RIVER
        THOUSAND ISLANDS
        YUKON
CANADA--COSTUME
--Alberta
    Nat Geog 165:384-403 (c,1) Mr
    '84
CANADA--HISTORY
--16th cent. Basque whaling

port (Labrador, Newfound-
    land)
    Nat Geog 168:cov., 40-71
    (map,c,1) Jl '85
CANADA--MAPS
--1546 map
    Nat Geog 168:71 (c,3) Jl '85
--Route of cross-country railway
    Trav/Holiday 166:66 (c,4) O '86
CANADA--RITES AND CERE-
    MONIES
--Paying Indian $5 for land (North-
    west Territories)
    Nat Geog 163:174 (c,3) F '83
CANADA--RITES AND FESTIVALS
--Treaty Day Festival (Northwest
    Territories)
    Nat Geog 163:174, 176-7 (c,1)
    F '83
CANADA--SOCIAL LIFE AND CUS-
    TOMS
--Outhouse race (Yukon)
    Trav/Holiday 164:63 (c,2) Ag
    '85
CANADA GEESE
    Life 7:133 (c,4) Ja '84
    Nat Wildlife 22:11 (c,4) Ap '84
    Nat Geog 166:596-9 (c,2) N '84
    Nat Wildlife 23:42-5 (c,1) F '85
    Nat Wildlife 24:6 (c,4) Ap '86
    Nat Wildlife 24:6 (c,4) Je '86
--Goslings
    Smithsonian 15:cov. (c,1) S '84
--In flight
    Nat Wildlife 20:38-9 (c,1) O '82
    Sports Illus 57:52 (painting,c,2)
    N 22 '82
    Nat Wildlife 21:30-1 (c,1) D '82
CANALS
--Ala Wai, Oahu, Hawaii
    Trav/Holiday 160:8 (c,4) S '83
--All-American, California
    Nat Wildlife 22:10 (c,1) F '84
--Bangkok klongs, Thailand
    Trav/Holiday 163:58-61 (c,1) Ap
    '85
--Houston Ship Canal, Texas
    Smithsonian 16:88-99 (c,1) O '85
--Mississippi Delta, Louisiana
    Nat Geog 164:239 (c,4) Ag '83
--See also
        ERIE CANAL
        PANAMA CANAL
        SUEZ CANAL
        VENICE, ITALY
CANALS--CONSTRUCTION
--Sudan

CANALS--CONSTRUCTION
(cont.)
Nat Geog 161:352-3 (c,1) Mr
'82
CANCER
--Cancer cells
Nat Geog 169:724-7 (c,1) Je
'86
--Cancer research
Nat Geog 166:843-5 (draw-
ing,c,2) D '84
--Children with cancer
Life 7:32-40 (c,1) S '84
Nat Geog 169:704-5 (c,1) Je
'86
--Common cancer spots for men
Ebony 38:69 (diagram,4) Mr
'83
--Lesions on bone scan
Life 5:62 (4) Ag '82
CANDLE MAKING
--19th cent. style (Massachusetts)
Am Heritage 33:41 (c,4) Ag
'82
CANDLES
Smithsonian 14:148 (c,3) S '83
--12th cent. candlesticks (Afghan-
istan)
Smithsonian 16:225 (c,4) O '85
CANDY
--History of candy bars
Am Heritage 37:74-80 (c,4) O
'86
Canes. See
WALKING STICKS
CANNONS
--16th cent. (Great Britain)
Nat Geog 163:646, 656-9, 666-7
(c,1) My '83
--17th cent. (Turkey)
Smithsonian 15:58 (c,4) Ja '85
--Early 19th cent. (France)
Nat Geog 161:149-56 (c,4) F
'82
--Early 19th cent. (Trinidad
and Tobago)
Ebony 40:106 (c,4) N '84
--Late 19th cent. U.S. Navy
ship
Am Heritage 37:90 (1) Je '86
--Replicas of Revolutionary War
cannons
Smithsonian 15:150 (c,3) Ap
'84
--War of 1812 (U.S.)
Nat Geog 163:306-7 (c,2) Mr
'83

--See also
HOWITZERS
CANOEING
--Canoe overturning (Texas)
Life 9:90 (c,2) Jl '86
--Ceremonial dugout canoes (Tuvalu)
Life 6:82-3 (c,1) Ja '83
--Dolores River, Colorado
Nat Wildlife 21:10 (c,3) Ap '83
--Down waterfall (Tennessee)
Nat Wildlife 21:56 (c,4) D '82
--Florida marsh
Nat Wildlife 23:27 (c,1) D '84
--Minnesota
Life 6:144-5 (c,1) D '83
--Missouri
Sports Illus 56:64-8 (c,1) Je 28
'82
--North Carolina
Trav/Holiday 166:46-7 (c,1) S
'86
--Texas
Life 9:88-95 (c,1) Jl '86
CANOES
Trav/Holiday 157:64 (c,3) Ap '82
Smithsonian 13:55 (c,2) D '82
Trav/Holiday 162:52 (c,4) Ag '84
--15th cent. Indian paddle (Baha-
mas)
Nat Geog 170:583 (c,4) N '86
--18th cent. Maori canoes (New
Zealand)
Nat Geog 166:546-7 (c,1) O '84
--Construction (Australia)
Nat Geog 166:734 (c,4) D '84
--Construction (Connecticut)
Sports Illus 64:102 (c,4) Ap 21
'86
--Construction (Truk)
Nat Geog 170:484 (c,3) O '86
--Dugout (Peru)
Nat Geog 168:346-7 (c,1) S '85
--Dugout (Venezuela)
Trav/Holiday 157:62 (c,3) Mr '82
Nat Geog 168:331 (c,1) S '85
--Hawaii
Nat Geog 164:590-1 (c,1) N '83
--Mayan (Mexico)
Natur Hist 94:50-1, 58-9 (1) Mr
'85
--Model canoes (Ghana)
Natur Hist 91:44-7 (c,1) Mr '82
CANS
--Cans of household chemicals
Nat Wildlife 24:20-3 (c,1) Ag '86
CANTON, CHINA
--1800

CANTON, CHINA (cont.)
  Natur Hist 93:62-3 (paint-
    ing,c,1) F '84
--1830s port
  Am Heritage 33:40-1, 43
    (painting,c,1) F '82
CANVASBACKS (DUCKS)
  Nat Wildlife 23:50-1 (paint-
    ing,c,2) D '84
CAPE SOUNION, GREECE
  Nat Geog 170:196-7 (c,1) Ag
    '86
CAPE TOWN, SOUTH AFRICA
  Sports Illus 63:92 (c,3) S 4
    '85
CAPITAL PUNISHMENT
--1860s hangings
  Am Heritage 33:89, 93 (2) O
    '82
--1864 military execution
  Am Heritage 36:110 (4) Je '85
--1896 execution of outlaw by
    firing squad (Wyoming)
  Am Heritage 34:108-9 (3) Ag
    '83
--1917 execution of Mata Hari by
    firing squad (France)
  Smithsonian 17:158-9 (2) My
    '86
--Contras executing government
    agent (Nicaragua)
  Life 8:80-1 (2) Je '85
--Germans hanging Russian parti-
    sans (1941)
  Life 8:79 (4) Spring '85
--Man in electric chair getting
    pardon
  Sports Illus 60:74 (drawing,c,3)
    My 7 '84
--See also
    LYNCHINGS
CAPITOL BUILDING, WASHING-
    TON, D.C.
  Trav/Holiday 161:cov., 62-3
    (c,1) Mr '84
  Sports Illus 60:42 (c,4) Ap 23
    '84
  Smithsonian 15:118-19 (c,1) Je
    '84
  Life 7:58-9, 64 (1) Je '84
  Ebony 39:40 (c,1) Ag '84
  Am Heritage 37:cov., 22-3,
    26 (c,1) Ap '86
  Ebony 41:122 (2) My '86
--Night scene
  Smithsonian 16:50 (c,4) S '85

CAPITOL BUILDINGS--STATE
--Augusta, Georgia
  Trav/Holiday 162:18 (c,4) Jl '84
--Montgomery, Alabama
  Ebony 37:146 (4) My '82
  Am Heritage 33:63 (4) Je '82
--Monpelier, Vermont
  Life 5:34-5 (c,1) Jl '82
--St. Paul, Minnesota
  Trav/Holiday 158:51 (c,3) Jl '82
--Salt Lake City, Utah
  Nat Geog 167:706-9 (c,1) Je '85
CAPONE, AL
  Am Heritage 33:7 (4) Ap '82
CAPOTE, TRUMAN
  Life 8:137 (2) Ja '85
CAPUCHIN MONKEYS
  Natur Hist 95:44-53 (c,1) F '86
  Natur Hist 95:42-3 (c,1) Mr '86
--Capuchins trained to help quadri-
    plegiacs
  Smithsonian 17:125-33 (c,1) O
    '86
CAPYBARAS
  Smithsonian 13:41 (c,4) Ja '83
CAR WASHES
--Illinois
  Ebony 37:32 (4) F '82
--Washing car (Virginia)
  Nat Geog 163:810-11 (c,1) Je '83
CARACARAS (BIRDS)
  Nat Wildlife 24:16 (painting,c,4)
    D '85
  Natur Hist 95:54-61 (c,1) F '86
  Trav/Holiday 166:55 (c,4) N '86
CARACAS, VENEZUELA
  Trav/Holiday 163:58-61 (c,1) F
    '85
CARAVAGGIO, MICHELANGELO
    MERISI DA
--"Deposition"
  Smithsonian 13:128 (painting,c,4)
    D '82
CARAVANS
--Camels (China)
  Nat Geog 165:296-7 (c,1) Mr '84
--Yaks (Nepal)
  Smithsonian 13:cov., 50-61 (c,1)
    O '82
--Yaks (Tibet)
  Natur Hist 95:56-7, 62-5 (c,1)
    Ja '86
--See also
    CAMELS
CARCASSONNE, FRANCE
  Life 9:103 (c,2) D '86

CARD PLAYING
    Sports Illus 56:35 (c,3) Je
      14 '82
--16th cent. (Flanders)
    Smithsonian 15:178 (paint-
      ing,c,2) O '84
--Afghanistan
    Nat Geog 167:499 (c,3) Ap '85
--Bridge
    Am Heritage 35:19 (drawing,c,4)
      Ap '84
--Bridge tournament
    Ebony 40:146-52 (2) O '85
--Cribbage (Alaska)
    Nat Geog 165:81 (c,3) Ja '84
--Gambling (Louisiana)
    Nat Geog 164:237 (c,4) Ag '83
--Gin (Texas)
    Sports Illus 56:40 (c,4) F 8
      '82
--Mus (Spain)
    Nat Geog 166:483 (c,4) O '84
--Poker
    Sports Illus 60:80-1 (c,1) My
      28 '84
    Ebony 41:108 (3) Mr '86
--Poker (California)
    Sports Illus 62:92 (c,4) Je 3
      '85
--Watten (Austria)
    Nat Geog 167:438-9 (c,2) Ap
      '85
CARDIFF GIANT
    Smithsonian 15:129 (c,4) Ap '84
CARDINAL FLOWERS
    Nat Geog 163:396 (c,4) Mr '83
    Nat Wildlife 22:40 (paint-
      ing,c,4) Je '84
CARDINALS (BIRDS)
    Nat Wildlife 21:12-16 (c,1) D
      '82
    Natur Hist 92:90 (c,2) S '83
    Nat Wildlife 22:55 (c,4) O '84
    Nat Wildlife 23:14 (c,4) D '84
CARDS
--Playing cards
    Sports Illus 59:80 (drawing,c,4)
      O 24 '83
--See also
    CREDIT CARDS
    GREETING CARDS
Caribbean. See
    WEST INDIES
CARIBOU
    Nat Wildlife 20:41-3 (c,1) Ag
      '82
    Nat Wildlife 22:35 (4) Ap '84

    Sports Illus 61:100-14 (c,1) O
      15 '84
    Nat Wildlife 23:10, 13 (c,1) O
      '85
    Nat Geog 169:134-6 (c,1) Ja '86
    Natur Hist 95:54-5, 60, 64-5
      (c,1) Mr '86
    Nat Wildlife 24:24-5 (c,1) Ap '86
    Nat Geog 169:690-1 (c,2) My '86
CARIBOU
--Antlers
    Natur Hist 95:54-5, 64-5 (c,1)
      Mr '86
CARMEL, CALIFORNIA
    Life 9:98-104 (c,1) Jl '86
CARNEGIE, ANDREW
--Depicted on 1960 postage stamp
    Am Heritage 34:50 (c,4) D '82
Carnivals. See
    FESTIVALS
Carousels. See
    MERRY-GO-ROUNDS
Carnivorous plants. See
    BLADDERWORT PLANTS
    PITCHER PLANTS
    SUNDEW PLANTS
    VENUS FLYTRAPS
CARP
    Natur Hist 93:42-51 (c,1) S '84
CARPENTRY
    Ebony 37:74 (4) Ag '82
--China
    Nat Geog 164:68-9 (c,1) Jl '83
Carriages. See
    BABY CARRIAGES
    BABY STROLLERS
    CARRIAGES AND CARTS--
      HORSE-DRAWN
CARRIAGES AND CARTS--HORSE-
    DRAWN
--19th cent.
    Am Heritage 38:cov. (draw-
      ing,c,1) D '86
--19th cent. (France)
    Smithsonian 15:84-5 (painting,c,2)
      F '85
--1850s (New York City)
    Am Heritage 33:18-19 (paint-
      ing,c,1) Je '82
--1887 (Nebraska)
    Natur Hist 94:50-1 (1) S '85
--Amish people (Ohio)
    Nat Wildlife 20:44, 50-1 (c,1)
      Ag '82
--Amish people (Pennsylvania)
    Nat Geog 165:492-3, 513 (c,1)
      Ap '84

CARRIAGES AND CARTS--
    HORSE-DRAWN (cont.)
--Bermuda
    Ebony 37:37 (c,4) S '82
    Ebony 39:178 (c,4) My '84
    Ebony 40:74 (c,3) Ja '85
--British carriages pulled by
    zebras
    Smithsonian 16;142 (4) Je '85
--British royalty (Great Britain)
    Life 6:62 (c,3) Ja '83
--Carvings of 19th cent. wagons
    (Kentucky)
    Smithsonian 15:148-9 (c,2) D
    '84
--Charleston, South Carolina
    Trav/Holiday 157:75 (c,4) Mr
    '82
--Colorado resort
    Trav/Holiday 164:49 (c,4) N
    '85
--Dominican Republic
    Trav/Holiday 158:20 (4) Ag '82
--Gold replica of Nicholas II's
    coronation coach (U.S.S.R.)
    Smithsonian 14:46 (c,2) Ap '83
--Great Britain
    Nat Geog 168:658, 667 (c,2)
    N '85
--Horse-drawn sled (U.S.S.R.)
    Nat Geog 163:212-13 (c,2) F
    '83
--Idaho ski resort
    Smithsonian 15:114 (c,4) D '84
--Kentucky
    Trav/Holiday 165:58-9 (c,1)
    Ja '86
--Montreal, Quebec
    Trav/Holiday 166:33 (c,4) S
    '86
--New Orleans, Louisiana
    Ebony 38:120 (c,4) Ja '83
--New York City, New York
    Natur Hist 92:36-7 (c,1) Ag
    '83
--Ox-drawn (Paraguay)
    Nat Geog 162:268-9 (c,1) Ag
    '82
--Sark, Channel Islands
    Smithsonian 17:92-3, 100 (c,1)
    My '86
CARROLL, LEWIS
--"Alice in Wonderland" illustration
    Nat Geog 163:753 (4) Je '83
--"Alice in Wonderland" on stage
    Smithsonian 13:cov., 52-9
    (c,1) Ag '82

Smithsonian 14:92 (c,4) N '83
--"Alice in Wonderland" television
    production
    Life 8:162 (c,2) D '85
--Scene from "Hunting of the Snark"
    Smithsonian 13:152-3 (woodcut,4)
    Ap '82
CARROTS
    Life 8:92-3 (c,1) Mr '85
CARSON, RACHEL
    Smithsonian 14:128 (4) Je '83
    Nat Wildlife 24:51 (4) Ap '86
CARTER, JIMMY
    Life 5:138 (c,4) My '82
    Life 8:82-3 (1) Je '85
    Life 9:211, 226-7 (c,1) Fall '86
--Renovating slum (New York City,
    New York)
    Life 8:56 (c,3) Ja '85
--Rosalynn Carter
    Life 9:108-9 (c,1) Jl '86
Cartoon characters. See
    CHARACTER SYMBOLS
    COMIC STRIPS
    DONALD DUCK
    MICKEY MOUSE
CARTOONISTS
    Am Heritage 33:73 (4) Ag '82
--Animation instruction (California)
    Smithsonian 13:48-9 (c,4) Ja '83
--Argentina
    Nat Geog 170:240 (c,3) Ag '86
--Gary Larson
    Smithsonian 15:119 (c,2) Ap '84
--Dick Tracy's Chester Gould
    Nat Geog 164:291 (c,4) S '83
--See also
    DISNEY, WALT
CARTOONS
--By Gary Larson
    Smithsonian 15:113-18 (4) Ap '84
--By Gluyas Williams
    Am Heritage 36:50-7 (1) D '84
--Caricatures by William Auerbach-
    Levy
    Am Heritage 37:50-5 (c,1) Je '86
--Caricatures of 1920s and 1930s
    celebrities
    Smithsonian 15:174-9 (c,2) N '84
    Am Heritage 37:50-5 (c,1) Je '86
--Cartoons about determining safe
    pollutant levels
    Nat Wildlife 22:29-32 (4) Ag '84
--Cartoons about the Automat
    Smithsonian 16:51, 59 (4) Ja '86
--Environmental issues
    Nat Wildlife 21:34-8 (drawing,4)

CARTOONS (cont.)
F '83
--Environmental Protection Agency
problems
Nat Wildlife 20:16, 18 (draw-
ing,3) Ag '82
--Irish potato famine (1880s)
Nat Geog 161:689 (4) My '82
--Mad's "Spy vs. Spy"
Life 9:59 (c,2) S '86
--Robert Osborn works
Smithsonian 13:148, 150 (c,3)
D '82
--Soil erosion
Nat Wildlife 23:23 (draw-
ing,c,4) F '85
--Symbolic use of Statue of Lib-
erty
Smithsonian 15:54-5 (c,4) Jl
'84
--See also
ARNO, PETER
CARTOONISTS
CHARACTER SYMBOLS
COMIC STRIPS
HIRSCHFELD, AL
NAST, THOMAS
POLITICAL CARTOONS
CARUSO, ENRICO
Smithsonian 14:81 (4) S '83
Am Heritage 35:104-10 (2) F
'84
Am Heritage 35:9 (4) Ag '84
CARVER, GEORGE WASHINGTON
Smithsonian 14:136 (paint-
ing,c,4) Je '83
--Tuskegee's Carver museum,
Alabama
Ebony 37:53 (4) Jl '82
CASABLANCA, MOROCCO
--Modern buildings
Trav/Holiday 160:5 (c,4) D
'83
CASCADE RANGE, CALIFORNIA
Trav/Holiday 166:72-7 (map,c,1)
O '86
CASCADE RANGE, NORTHWEST
Nat Geog 162:320 (c,1) S '82
CASCADE RANGE, OREGON
--Proxy Falls
Nat Wildlife 21:52 (c,1) Ag
'83
CASCADE RANGE, WASHINGTON
Nat Wildlife 22:4-7 (c,1) O '84
--Misty forest
Nat Wildlife 24:11 (c,1) F '86
--See also

MOUNT HOOD
MOUNT RAINIER
MOUNT ST. HELENS
MOUNT SHASTA
CASSATT, MARY
--1895 pastel of Mrs. Havemeyer
and daughters
Am Heritage 33:18 (c,4) Ap '82
--"Tea Party" (1891)
Smithsonian 12:100 (painting,c,4)
F '82
--"Young Woman in Black" (1883)
Smithsonian 13:8 (painting,c,4)
Je '82
CASTLES
--13th cent. Schloss Zell, Mosel
area, West Germany
Trav/Holiday 163:73 (c,2) Ap
'85
--Alnwick Castle, England
Smithsonian 15:72-83 (c,1) Ag
'84
--Blarney, Cork, Ireland
Trav/Holiday 164:64 (c,3) S '85
--Burghley House, Lincolnshire,
England
Life 8:33 (c,4) N '85
--Castle of Mey, Scotland
Life 7:14 (3) Mr '84
--Colditz, East Germany
Life 6:9 (4) Ap '83
--Conwy, Wales
Nat Geog 164:36-7 (c,1) Jl '83
--Diósgyör, Miskolc, Hungary
Nat Geog 163:246-7 (c,1) F '83
--Dunvegan, Scotland
Trav/Holiday 162:36-7 (c,1) N
'84
--Egeskov, Denmark
Trav/Holiday 157:52 (c,2) Je '82
--Ehrenpels Castle, West Germany
Trav/Holiday 162:58 (c,3) S '84
--Elaborate sand castles
Smithsonian 17:104-11 (c,1) Ag
'86
--40 foot high sand castle (Califor-
nia)
Life 8:100-1 (1) O '85
--Hartenfels, Torgau on the Elbe,
East Germany
Nat Geog 164:436 (c,3) O '83
--Hearst, San Simeon, California
Nat Geog 165:450-3 (c,1) Ap '84
Smithsonian 16:60-71 (c,1) D '85
--Hochosterwitz, Austria
Nat Geog 167:412-14 (c,1) Ap '85
--Howard, Yorkshire, England

CASTLES (cont.)
  Nat Geog 168:664-7 (c,1) N
    '85
--Howard hallway, Yorkshire,
    England
  Life 8:36 (c,3) N '85
--Ice castle (Minnesota)
  Life 9:6-7 (c,1) Ap '86
--Inverness, Scotland
  Trav/Holiday 159:42-3 (2) Ja
    '83
--Karlstejn, Czechoslovakia
  Trav/Holiday 158:42 (2) Jl '82
--Kolossi, Limassol, Cyprus
  Trav/Holiday 157:72 (c,4) Mr
    '82
--Larnach, New Zealand
  Trav/Holiday 166:48-9 (c,1)
    Ag '86
--Ooidonck, Deurle, Belgium
  Trav/Holiday 159:cov. (c,1)
    Mr '83
--Peñafiel, Spain
  Nat Geog 166:484 (c,1) O '84
--Powis Castle, Wales
  Nat Geog 168:680-1 (c,1) N '85
  Life 8:34-5 (c,1) N '85
--Valdemar, Denmark
  Trav/Holiday 157:55 (c,2) Je
    '82
--Wartburg, Germany
  Nat Geog 164:440-1 (c,1) O
    '83
--See also
    CHATEAUS
CASTRO, FIDEL
  Life 9:364 (4) Fall '86
--Man dressed as Castro at party
  Life 9:61 (4) F '86
CATBIRDS
  Natur Hist 91:63 (c,3) My '82
CATERPILLARS
  Nat Wildlife 20:28 (c,4) Ap '82
  Natur Hist 92:56-63 (c,1) F
    '83
  Smithsonian 15:46-54 (c,1) My
    '84
  Smithsonian 16:51, 56 (c,4) My
    '85
  Natur Hist 94:48-52 (c,1) N '85
  Natur Hist 95:45 (c,3) D '86
--Stages of life
  Smithsonian 17:128-9 (c,4) My
    '86
--See also
    BUTTERFLIES
    COCOONS

    MEASURING WORMS
    MOTHS
    SILKWORMS
CATFISH
  Nat Geog 165:472-3 (c,1) Ap '84
  Smithsonian 15:54-63 (c,1) S
    '84
  Natur Hist 95:94-5 (c,3) Ap '86
--Land sculpture shaped like cat-
    fish (Ottawa)
  Smithsonian 17:77 (c,1) Ap '86
CATFISH INDUSTRY
--Alabama
  Natur Hist 91:76-80 (3) Jl '82
--Mississippi
  Smithsonian 15:56 (c,4) S '84
Cathedrals. See
    CHURCHES
CATHER, WILLA
  Nat Geog 162:71, 75, 84 (4) Jl
    '82
  Am Heritage 34:26, 31 (2) Ag
    '83
--Birthplace (Virginia)
  Nat Geog 162:80-1 (c,1) Jl '82
--Home (Red Cloud, Nebraska)
  Trav/Holiday 164:28 (c,4) Ag '85
Catholic church. See
    CHRISTIANITY
CATLIN, GEORGE
--Paintings of Mandan tribe (1840s)
  Sports Illus 65:98, 104, 106
    (c,3) D 1 '86
CATS
  Life 5:38 (4) O '82
  Nat Geog 162:708-9 (c,1) D '82
  Sports Illus 57:66-7 (c,1) D 27
    '82
  Nat Geog 163:392-3 (c,2) Mr '83
  Smithsonian 15:84-5 (c,1) Je '84
  Nat Geog 167:cov., 111-13 (c,1)
    Ja '85
  Life 9:26-8 (3) My '86
  Natur Hist 95:46-53 (c,1) Jl '86
  Life 9:352 (2) Fall '86
--Abyssinian
  Sports Illus 61:52 (c,4) Jl 23 '84
--At animal shelter
  Smithsonian 13:41-9 (1) S '82
--Kittens
  Life 8:22-8 (c,1) Jl '85
  Smithsonian 16:148 (4) S '85
--Marbled cat
  Lie 5:17 (4) Ag '82
--Ringtail cats
  Natur Hist 95:58-9 (c,1) Je '86
--See also

CATS (cont.)
    BOBCATS
    CHEETAHS
    JAGUARS
    LEOPARDS
    LIONS
    LYNXES
    MOUNTAIN LIONS
    OCELOTS
    PANTHERS
    SABER-TOOTHED CATS
    TIGERS
CATTLE
    Nat Geog 161:372-3 (c,1) Mr
      '82
    Am Heritage 33:29 (c,3) Je '82
    Nat Geog 163:634-5 (c,2) My
      '83
    Nat Geog 163:762 (c,4) Je '83
    Ebony 38:37 (c,3) Jl '83
    Smithsonian 14:48-9 (c,3) Ag
      '83
    Sports Illus 63:42-3 (c,1) Jl
      15 '85
--Cow rummaging through trash
    (India)
    Nat Geog 165:724-5 (c,1) Je
      '84
--Cow washing calf
    Nat Geog 162:82-3 (c,1) Jl '82
--Cows
    Natur Hist 94:51 (c,1) My '85
    Sports Illus 65:112-13 (c,1)
      D 22 '86
--Highland
    Nat Geog 166:66-7 (c,1) Jl '84
    Natur Hist 93:105 (c,3) N '84
--Longhorns
    Sports Illus 60:28-38 (c,1) Je
      18 '84
    Sports Illus 65:67 (c,3) S 8
      '86
    Sports Illus 65:58 (c,3) D 8 '86
--See also
    BISON
    BUFFALOES
    DAIRYING
    GAURS
    MUSK OXEN
    RANCHING
    WATER BUFFALOES
    YAKS
CAVE EXPLORATION
    Nat Wildlife 20:16, 19 (c,1) Ap
      '82
--Bonaire, Netherlands Antilles
    Sports Illus 60:114 (c,3) F 13

      '84
--Missouri
    Sports Illus 56:72-81 (c,1) Mr
      15 '82
CAVE PAINTINGS
--Ancient deer paintings (Lascaux,
    France)
    Nat Geog 170:541 (c,4) O '86
--Namibia
    Nat Geog 161:792-3 (c,1) Je '82
--Paleolithic Age
    Smithsonian 14:36-45 (c,1) Ap
      '83
--Paleolithic Age (France)
    Smithsonian 14:40-5 (c,1) Ap '83
--Paleolithic Age (Spain)
    Smithsonian 14:42 (c,4) Ap '83
    Natur Hist 92:50-1 (c,2) Ag '83
--Spotted horses (France)
    Natur Hist 95:76 (4) S '86
--Stone Age (Tanzania)
    Nat Geog 164:84-99 (c,1) Jl '83
--Stone Age paintings of hunting
    (Spain)
    Natur Hist 95:8, 10 (c,3) Jl '86
CAVES
--Amarnath shrine, Kashmir, India
    Natur Hist 92:50-1 (c,1) Jl '83
--Ancient rock shelters (Pennsyl-
    vania)
    Natur Hist 95:20 (c,3) D '86
--Animal life in caves
    Smithsonian 13:74-82 (c,1) N '82
--Bandelier National Monument,
    New Mexico
    Nat Geog 162:578 (c,3) N '82
--Blanchard Springs Caverns,
    Arkansas
    Natur Hist 95:22-24 (map,c,1) Je
      '86
--Borneo
    Smithsonian 14:66-71 (c,1) S '83
--Cave City, California
    Trav/Holiday 160:24 (c,4) Ag '83
--Clover Hollow, Virginia
    Nat Wildlife 20:16, 19 (c,1) Ap
      '82
--Crete
    Nat Geog 170:210 (c,3) Ag '86
--Grand Canyon, Arizona
    Natur Hist 95:10-14 (c,3) Ap '86
--Ice cave (Yukon)
    Nat Geog 168:649 (c,1) N '85
--Italy
    Life 8:34 (c,3) Mr '85
--Limestone (Great Britain)
    Nat Geog 169:407-8 (c,1) Mr '86

CAVES (cont.)
--Limestone (Tasmania, Aus-
    tralia)
    Nat Geog 163:688-9 (c,1) My
    '83
--Missouri
    Sports Illus 56:72-84 (c,1) Mr
    15 '82
--Orvieto, Italy
    Smithsonian 14:188 (c,4) N '83
--Prehistoric cave dwellings
    (Reignac, France)
    Smithsonian 17:76-7 (c,2) O '86
--Used as middle-class dwellings
    (France)
    Smithsonian 14:50-9 (c,1) Je
    '83
--Vindija, Yugoslavia
    Nat Geog 168:613 (c,2) N '85
--See also
        MAMMOTH CAVE NATIONAL
        PARK
CAVIAR INDUSTRY
--Breeding sturgeon (California)
    Nat Wildlife 24:22-7 (c,1) D
    '85
CAYMAN ISLANDS
    Trav/Holiday 161:72-5 (map,c,2)
    My '84
    Nat Geog 167:798-824 (map,c,1)
    Je '85
CEDAR TREES
    Natur Hist 91:58-9 (c,1) O '82
CELLO PLAYING
    Life 5:91-4 (2) F '82
--At swimming pool
    Sports Illus 56:32-3 (c,1) Mr
    29 '82
CELLS
--Human immune system
    Nat Geog 169:702-32 (c,1) Je
    '86
--Magnified red blood cells
    Life 9:98-9 (c,1) Fall '86
--RNA model
    Smithsonian 15:46 (c,4) Je '84
--Transforming matter into primi-
    tive cells
    Natur Hist 92:40-2 (c,1) F '83
CEMETERIES
--17th cent. Jamestown, Virginia
    Am Heritage 34:36 (c,3) Ag
    '83
--American (Normandy, France)
    Trav/Holiday 161:85 (c,4) My
    '84
    Life 7:44-5 (c,1) Je '84

--Black (Georgia)
    Nat Geog 164:811 (c,1) D '83
--Congressional Cemetery, Washing-
    ton, D.C.
    Am Heritage 33:65-9 (c,1) Je '82
--Georgia
    Ebony 38:37 (c,3) Jl '83
--Iran
    Nat Geog 168:120-1 (c,1) Jl '85
    Life 8:100 (c,3) S '85
--Jewish (Poland)
    Nat Geog 170:370-1, 388-9 (c,1)
    S '86
--Louisiana
    Sports Illus 59:50 (c,4) N 7 '83
--Maryland
    Sports Illus 65:76-7, 92 (c,1) N
    10 '86
--Mass graves (Cambodia)
    Nat Geog 161:602-3 (c,1) My '82
--Mexico
    Nat Geog 166:452-3 (c,1) O '84
--Morocco
    Nat Geog 169:332-3, 352 (c,1)
    Mr '86
--Munich, Germany
    Ebony 37:40 (c,4) My '82
--New Orleans, Louisiana
    Life 6:160 (2) D '83
--Pakistan
    Trav/Holiday 164:38-9 (c,1) Ag
    '85
--Philippines
    Nat Geog 170:112-13 (c,1) Jl '86
--Pre-Columbian burial site (Chile)
    Natur Hist 94:74-5 (c,1) O '85
--Queens, New York
    Life 7:42 (c,4) O '84
--South Yemen
    Nat Geog 168:490-1 (c,1) O '85
--South African blacks
    Life 8:101 (2) Je '85
--Ute Indians (Colorado)
    Am Heritage 33:112 (4) Ap '82
--Viking (Sweden)
    Nat Geog 167:292-3 (c,1) Mr '85
--Withyham church, Great Britain
    Nat Geog 161:59 (c,4) Ja '82
--World War II K-9 dog corps
    (Guam)
    Life 8:101 (c,4) Spring '85
--World War II victims (Leningrad,
    U.S.S.R.)
    Life 8:54-5 (c,1) Spring '85
--See also
        FUNERAL RITES AND CERE-
        MONIES

CHARACTER SYMBOLS
--Bibendum, Michelin tire man
  Smithsonian 17:56, 60, 67
    (c,2) Je '86
--Bob's Big Boy restaurant sym-
    bol
  Life 9:32 (c,4) D '86
--Chaplin's "Little Tramp" char-
    acter
  Smithsonian 17:cov., 51-7 (c,1)
    Jl '86
--Chaplin's "Little Tramp" played
    by little girl
  Life 5:176-7 (c,1) N '82
--E.T.
  Life 5:184 (c,2) D '82
  Ebony 38:cov., 127 (c,1) D
    '82
  Life 6:36-7 (c,1) Ja '83
  Natur Hist 92:45 (c,2) O '83
--Goofy
  Ebony 38:129 (c,4) D '82
--Howdy Doody
  Life 9:205-6 (2) Fall '86
--San Diego Chicken
  Sports Illus 57:44 (c,3) Jl 26
    '82
--See also
    COMIC STRIPS
    DONALD DUCK
    HOLMES, SHERLOCK
    KING KONG
    MICKEY MOUSE
    TARZAN
CHARIOT RACES
--Ancient Greek Olympics
  Smithsonian 15:70 (paint-
    ing,c,3) Je '84
CHARLEMAGNE
--Crown
  Smithsonian 14:131 (c,4) O '83
CHARLES II (GREAT BRITAIN)
--Armor (1644)
  Smithsonian 13:70 (c,4) O '82
CHARLESTON, SOUTH CAROLINA
  Nat Geog 164:798-829
    (map,c,1) D '83
--Charleston Harbor (1863)
  Am Heritage 38:60-1 (paint-
    ing,c,3) D '86
--See also
    FORT SUMTER
CHARLOTTE, NORTH CAROLINA
  Ebony 41:92 (c,3) Ap '86
CHARLOTTE AMALIE, VIRGIN
    ISLANDS
  Trav/Holiday 163:62-5, 76
    (map,c,1) My '85

CHARLOTTESVILLE, VIRGINIA
--University of Virginia
  Ebony 38:54 (4) Mr '83
  Am Heritage 35:49-64, 110 (c,1)
    Je '84
--See also
    MONTICELLO
CHATEAUS
--Banff Springs Hotel, Alberta
  Trav/Holiday 162:26-7 (c,4) D
    '84
  Trav/Holiday 163:55 (c,1) Ja '85
--Chantilly, France
  Smithsonian 14:62-9 (c,1) My '83
--Chateau d'Artigny, Montbazon,
    France
  Trav/Holiday 163:64-6 (c,1) Ap
    '85
--Chateau de la Brède, Graves,
    France
  Trav/Holiday 160:59 (c,2) S '83
--Chateau de Chillon, Montreux,
    Switzerland
  Trav/Holiday 161:69 (c,2) Ap '84
--Chateau de Marçay, Chinon,
    France
  Trav/Holiday 163:64, 67 (c,3)
    Ap '85
--Chateau de Remaisnil, France
  Life 7:78 (c,2) Ap '84
--Chateau Frontenac, Quebec
  Trav/Holiday 157:38 (c,4) My '82
  Trav/Holiday 161:38 (4) My '84
  Trav/Holiday 165:80-1 (c,1) Mr
    '86
--Chateau Rochepot, Burgundy,
    France
  Trav/Holiday 165:42-3 (c,1) Je
    '86
--Lake Louise, Alberta
  Trav/Holiday 162:27 (c,3) D '84
--Laurier, Ottawa, Ontario
  Trav/Holiday 162:26-7 (c,3) D
    '84
--Ruins of Chateau Guillard, France
  Nat Geog 161:499 (c,3) Ap '82
--Vaux-le-Vicomte, France
  Smithsonian 14:56-65 (c,1) Ag
    '83
--Washington winery
  Trav/Holiday 158:14 (c,4) Jl '82
CHAUCER, GEOFFREY
--Illustration of him in his manu-
    script
CHECKS, BANKING
--Social Security check
  Life 8:139 (3) D '85

CHICKS (cont.)
  Nat Wildlife 21:58 (c,4) D '82
  Natur Hist 95:47 (c,1) O '86
--Bluebirds
  Nat Wildlife 22:26-8 (c,2) Ap
    '84
--Cardinals
  Nat Wildlife 21:16 (c,2) D '82
--Condors
  Life 6:58 (c,2) Je '83
  Nat Wildlife 21:28 (4) Ag '83
  Smithsonian 14:79-81 (c,1) D
    '83
--Eaglets
  Nat Wildlife 21:53 (c,1) Ap '83
  Nat Wildlife 24:16 (c,4) Ap '86
--Flycatchers
  Nat Geog 164:266 (c,1) Ag '83
--Goshawks
  Natur Hist 91:cov. (c,1) Ap
    '82
--Great egrets
  Nat Wildlife 21:60 (c,4) D '82
  Natur Hist 94:54-61 (c,1) My
    '85
--Herons
  Nat Wildlife 21:52 (c,4) Ap '83
--Jacanas
  Nat Geog 164:265 (c,4) Ag '83
--Kites
  Nat Wildlife 22:40-3 (c,1) Ag
    '84
--Orioles
  Natur Hist 91:50-1 (c,1) O '82
--Owls
  Nat Geog 166:131 (c,4) Jl '84
--Pelicans
  Nat Wildlife 21:29 (c,4) D '82
--Peregrine falcons
  Life 6:3, 54-6 (c,1) Je '83
  Nat Wildlife 24:10-11 (c,1) Ap
    '86
--Prairie falcons
  Nat Wildlife 23:61 (c,4) D '84
--Red-winged blackbirds
  Smithsonian 14:83 (c,4) Jl '83
--Robins
  Nat Wildlife 22:34-6 (c,1) Je
    '84
  Nat Wildlife 22:54 (c,2) O '84
--Roseate spoonbills
  Nat Wildlife 24:40-1 (c,1) Je
    '86
--Sandhill crane chick and eggs
  Life 9:17-18 (c,4) Jl '86
--Swallows
  Nat Wildlife 20:50 (c,4) Ag '82

--Tanagers
  Nat Wildlife 22:61 (c,3) D '83
--Terns
  Nat Wildlife 21:48 (c,4) Ag '83
--Various species
  Natur Hist 91:60-5 (c,1) My '82
--Warblers
  Natur Hist 91:46-7 (c,1) S '82
--Water ouzels
  Nat Wildlife 21:50-1 (c,1) Ap '83
--Wood ducks
  Nat Wildlife 24:cov. (c,1) Je '86
CHIHUAHUAS
  Natur Hist 95:4 (3) D '86
CHILDBIRTH
  Life 5:68-72 (1) Jl '82
--1938 photos
  Life 9:301 (4) Fall '86
--Childbirth stool (Cameroon)
  Ebony 40:32 (c,4) Jl '85
--Midwife (Texas)
  Life 9:50 (c,2) Ag '86
--Newborn held by doctor
  Life 9:93 (2) Fall '86
--Tennessee
  Nat Geog 169:628-9 (c,3) My '86
--Texas
  Nat Geog 167:730 (c,4) Je '85
--See also
    PREGNANCY
CHILDREN
--1890 pioneer children heading
    west
  Am Heritage 37:90-1 (1) D '85
--1898 pioneer children dancing
    (Montana)
  Am Heritage 37:94-5 (1) D '85
--Early 20th cent. orphans shipped
    to midwestern homes
  Smithsonian 17:94-103 (1) Ag '86
--Early 20th cent. street children
  Natur Hist 94:86-91 (2) O '85
--1905 poetry book cover
  Smithsonian 14:173 (c,4) O '83
--1953 first grade class picture
    (New York City, N.Y.)
  Sports Illus 63:80 (3) D 23 '85
--1955 fifth grader examining re-
    port card (Washington)
  Life 9:295 (1) Fall '86
--Bicycle motocross competition
    (Oklahoma)
  Sports Illus 65:28-36 (c,1) D 8
    '86
--Breughel's "Children's Games"
    (1560)
  Smithsonian 14:40 (painting,c,2)

CHILDREN (cont.)
D '83
--British royal children
Life 9:50, 54 (c,2) S '86
Life 9:61 (2) Fall '86
--Child playing in snow
Nat Wildlife 24:5 (c,1) D '85
--Child prodigies
Smithsonian 14:70-9 (c,1) Mr
'84
--Child sleeping with dolls (West
Virginia)
Life 8:150 (c,4) Je '85
--Children of U.S. Presidents
Life 7:cov., 2, 32-50 (c,1)
N '84
--Doing homework (Japan)
Nat Geog 170:637 (c,4) N '86
--Dressed in mothers' clothes
(Oklahoma)
Nat Geog 164:391 (c,2) S '83
--Nude Wayana Indians playing
with ball (French Guiana)
Nat Geog 163:75 (c,3) Ja '83
--Playing (Taiwan)
Nat Geog 161:112-13 (c,1) Ja
'82
--Playing (Washington, D.C.)
Nat Geog 163:88-9, 100-1
(c,1) Ja '83
--Playing "horsie" on father
Life 6:90-1 (c,1) O '83
--Playing in fountain (Philadel-
phia, Pennsylvania)
Nat Geog 163:342-3 (c,1) Mr
'83
--Playing under lawn sprinkler
(1942)
Am Heritage 35:34 (4) F '84
--Playing with armored tank
(Nicaragua)
Life 7:10-11 (c,1) N '84
--Playing with weapons (Lebanon)
Nat Geog 163:284-5 (c,1) F
'83
--Pretending to be corpses (Italy)
Life 6:95 (1) F '83
--Quintuplets
Ebony 41:cov., 31-40 (c,1) D
'85
--St. Nicholas children's magazine
(early 20th cent.)
Am Heritage 37:41-7 (c,2) D
'85
--School earthquake drill (Cali-
fornia)
Nat Geog 169:668 (c,2) My '86

--Sick children
Life 8:153-60 (1) O '85
--Street life of runaway teens
(Washington)
Life 6;34-42 (1) Jl '83
--Students at professional school
(New York City)
Smithsonian 13:60-9 (1) My '82
--Three-year-old quintuplets (New
Jersey)
Life 9:80 (c,3) N '86
--Toddler being fed by adult
Sports Illus 60:2-3 (c,1) Mr 12
'84
--Toddler in hiker's backpack
(Yukon)
Nat Geog 168:634 (c,4) N '85
--Toddler throwing ball
Sports Illus 65:118-19 (c,1) D
22 '86
--With nannies (Great Britain)
Smithsonian 14:cov., 96-105
(c,1) Ja '84
--See also
BABIES
DAY CARE CENTERS
FAMILIES
FAMILY LIFE
PLAYGROUNDS
TOYS
YOUTH
CHILDREN--COSTUME
--1792 (Great Britain)
Smithsonian 14:172 (painting,c,2)
O '83
--1860s school children
Am Heritage 33:108 (3) O '82
--Late 19th cent.
Smithsonian 12:44 (4) Ja '82
--Late 19th cent. (Texas)
Am Heritage 37:50-1 (1) F '86
--1882 (France)
Am Heritage 37:40-1 (paint-
ing,c,1) O '86
--Early 20th cent. (Missouri)
Am Heritage 33:48-9 (2) Ag '82
--Early 20th cent. (Pennsylvania)
Am Heritage 34:86, 92-3, 96-7
(1) Ag '83
--Early 20th cent. orphans
Smithsonian 17:94-103 (1) Ag '86
--1901 high school students (Massa-
chusetts)
Smithsonian 16:122-3 (1) Ap '85
--1903 twin babies (Ohio)
Am Heritage 34:106 (2) D '82
--1907 (Chile)

CHILDREN--COSTUME (cont.)
  Smithsonian 13:199 (4) O '82
--1907 (France)
  Life 5:115 (4) My '82
--1907 girls' wear
  Am Heritage 36:104 (draw-
    ing,4) D '84
--1912 (Germany)
  Sports Illus 65:52 (4) Ag 4
    '86
--1912 (Massachusetts)
  Natur Hist 94:86-7 (2) O '85
--1913 wealthy children (Penn-
    sylvania)
  Smithsonian 14:100 (4) Ap '83
--1930s campers (Georgia)
  Am Heritage 33:45 (1) Je '82
--China
  Natur Hist 93:72-81 (c,1) N
    '84
--Ghana
  Natur Hist 91:44-7 (c,1) Mr
    '82
  Natur Hist 91:38 (c,3) Jl '82
--Girls at boarding school
    (France)
  Nat Geog 161:160 (c,1) F '82
--School children (Ireland)
  Trav/Holiday 163:67 (c,3) F
    '85
--School uniforms (Korea)
  Trav/Holiday 159:61 (c,4) F
    '83
--School uniforms (Pennsylvania)
  Nat Geog 163:342-3 (c,1) Mr
    '83
--South Korea
  Sports Illus 61:76-7 (c,1) D
    24 '84
--Student (Japan)
  Nat Geog 170:606-7 (c,1) N '86
--Turkey
  Smithsonian 17:140 (c,3) N '86
--Young Pioneers (U.S.S.R.)
  Life 9:8-9 (c,1) Ja '86
--See also
      BOY SCOUTS
      GIRL SCOUTS
      HAIRSTYLES--CHILDREN
CHILE
--Countryside
  Smithsonian 16:82, 85 (c,1)
    O '85
--See also
      EASTER ISLAND
      JUAN FERNANDEZ ARCHI-
        PELAGO

CHILE--COSTUME
--1907 child
  Smithsonian 13:199 (4) O '82
CHILE, ANCIENT--RELICS
--Pre-Columbian artifacts
  Natur Hist 94:74-80 (c,1) O '85
--Pre-Columbian mummies
  Natur Hist 94:74-7 (c,1) O '85
CHIMNEYS
--Smoke from chimneys (Alaska)
  Nat Wildlife 24:34 (c,4) Ap '86
--Smokestacks
  Smithsonian 13:130-1 (c,2) N
    '82
--Smokestacks (New Hampshire)
  Nat Geog 162:776-7 (c,1) D '82
CHIMPANZEES
  Nat Wildlife 20:18 (4) Je '82
  Nat Wildlife 21:10 (c,2) Ag '83
  Nat Wildlife 23:26 (c,4) F '85
  Trav/Holiday 164:46 (c,4) Jl '85
  Nat Wildlife 23:16-17 (c,1) Ag
    '85
  Nat Wildlife 24:24 (c,4) F '86
  Natur Hist 95:88 (c,3) O '86
--17th cent. drawings
  Natur Hist 92:20-2 (4) D '83
--Skull
  Smithsonian 15:57 (c,1) Ag '84
CHINA
  Nat Geog 165:283-333 (map,c,1)
    Mr '84
  Life 8:150-6 (c,1) D '85
--Bezeklik monastery
  Nat Geog 165:20-1 (c,1) Ja '84
--Commune farm
  Nat Geog 165:22-3 (c,1) Ja '84
--Countryside
  Natur Hist 91:72-3 (3) Mr '82
  Nat Geog 165:34-5 (c,1) Ja '84
--Great Stone Bridge Anji
  Natur Hist 95:38 (4) S '86
--Guangzhou mosque
  Nat Geog 162:40 (c,4) Jl '82
--Guilin
  Trav/Holiday 158:14, 20 (c,4) O
    '82
--Min Shan range
  Nat Geog 165:284-5 (c,1) Mr '84
--Mount Huang
  Life 7:48-54 (c,1) Mr '84
--Pearl industry
  Nat Geog 168:214-15 (c,1) Ag
    '85
--Shenzhen Special Economic Zone
  Nat Geog 164:64-81 (map,c,1)
    Jl '83

CHINA (cont.)
--Shiqi
    Trav/Holiday 158:49 (c,3) Jl
        '82
--Sichuan
    Nat Geog 168:cov., 280-317
        (map,c,1) S '85
--Song Yue temple pagoda
    Natur Hist 95:41 (4) S '86
--Summer Palace, Beijing
    Natur Hist 95:40-1 (c,1) S '86
--Wolong area
    Nat Geog 169:298-9, 302-5
        (c,1) Mr '86
--See also
    BEIJING
    CANTON
    CHENGDU
    GREAT WALL OF CHINA
    SHANGHAI
    TIBET
CHINA--ARCHITECTURE
--Old official structures
    Natur Hist 95:34-43 (c,1) S '86
CHINA--COSTUME
    Trav/Holiday 158:49, 57 (c,3)
        Jl '82
    Nat Geog 164:64-83 (c,1) Jl
        '83
    Natur Hist 93:72-81 (c,1) N '84
    Natur Hist 94:52-61 (c,1) F '85
    Life 8:76-86 (c,1) S '85
    Life 8:151-6 (c,1) D '85
--Early 19th cent. wealthy man
    Am Heritage 33:48 (paint-
        ing,c,3) F '82
--1945
    Am Heritage 34:47 (1) O '83
--Merchant seamen
    Nat Geog 162:41 (c,1) Jl '82
--Minority groups
    Nat Geog 165:282-329, 424 (c,1)
        Mr '84
--Protective winter face masks
    Nat Geog 166:737 (c,4) D '84
--Shanghai
    Trav/Holiday 162:cov., 44-7
        (c,1) S '84
--Sichuan
    Nat Geog 168:cov., 280-316
        (c,1) S '85
--Workers
    Nat Geog 165:4-9, 30-1, 34
        (c,1) Ja '84
CHINA--HISTORY
--12th cent. emperor's burial site
    Life 8:150-1 (c,1) D '85

--18th cent. items exported to
    America
    Natur Hist 93:64-76 (c,1) F '84
--Early 19th cent. trade with the
    west
    Am Heritage 33:40-8 (c,1) F '82
--1840 Opium War (Dinghai)
    Nat Geog 167:152-3 (painting,c,1)
        F '85
--1900 Boxer Rebellion
    Smithsonian 15:138 (painting,4)
        Je '84
    Smithsonian 16:156 (cartoon,4)
        My '85
--See also
    CHIANG KAI-SHEK
    MONGOL EMPIRE
    MAO ZEDONG
CHINA--HOUSING
--Housing project (Sichuan)
    Nat Geog 168:296-7 (c,1) S '85
CHINA--MAPS
--Panda reserves
    Nat Geog 169:286-7 (c,1) Mr '86
--Relief satellite photo
    Nat Geog 164:318-21 (1) S '83
CHINA--RITES AND FESTIVALS
--Dragon Boat Festival
    Nat Geog 165:328-9 (c,2) Mr '84
--New Year celebration
    Natur Hist 94:52-61 (c,1) F '85
    Life 8:152 (c,3) D '85
CHINA--SCULPTURE
--Carved jade pieces
    Smithsonian 17:cov., 34-5, 39,
        138 (c,1) Ag '86
--8th cent. Fergana horse
    Natur Hist 93:cov. (c,1) F '84
CHINA--SOCIAL LIFE AND CUS-
    TOMS
--"Dragon dancing" before sporting
    event
    Life 6:54 (c,4) D '83
--Foot-binding victim
    Nat Geog 161:115 (c,4) Ja '82
--Lifestyles
    Life 8:152-6 (c,3) D '85
--Teens learning dance steps
    Life 8:70-1 (1) Je '85
CHINA, ANCIENT--ART
    Smithsonian 13:81-5 (c,1) F '83
--480-222 B.C.
    Smithsonian 13:205 (c,4) O '82
--Bronze horses from Emperor Qin's
    tomb
    Life 5:92-6 (c,1) Mr '82

CHINA, ANCIENT--SCULPTURE
--Han dynasty storyteller
  Nat Geog 168:298 (c,4) S '85
--Qin Dynasty terra cotta sol-
    diers (3rd cent. B.C.)
  Trav/Holiday 164:6 (c,2) N
    '85
  Life 9:10-11 (c,1) D '86
CHINESE AMERICANS
--Life in New York
  Smithsonian 13:70-9 (1) Ja '83
CHINATOWN, NEW YORK CITY,
    NEW YORK
  Trav/Holiday 157:74 (c,4) Ap
    '82
  Smithsonian 13:70-9 (1) Ja
    '83
  Trav/Holiday 159:51 (c,2) Ja
    '83
CHINATOWN, SAN FRANCISCO,
    CALIFORNIA
  Trav/Holiday 159:50-1 (c,4)
    Ja '83
CHINATOWN, WASHINGTON, D.C.
  Trav/Holiday 159:49 (c,2) Ja
    '83
CHINAWARE
--16th cent. pewter dinnerware
    (Great Britain)
  Nat Geog 163:668-9 (c,1) My
    '83
--18th cent. platinum sugar bowl
    (France)
  Nat Geog 164:694-5 (c,1) N
    '83
--1770s porcelain plate (China)
  Natur Hist 93:71 (c,2) F '84
--1796 (China)
  Natur Hist 93:70 (c,4) F '84
--1890 gilded porcelain plate
    (New York)
  Am Heritage 35:114 (c,3) Ag
    '84
CHIPMUNKS
  Nat Wildlife 20:2 (c,1) Je '82
  Smithsonian 13:76-85 (c,1) O
    '82
  Nat Wildlife 22:53 (c,1) Je '84
  Natur Hist 93:46 (c,1) Ag '84
  Nat Wildlife 24:6-7 (c,2) O
    '86
CHIVES
  Nat Geog 163:398, 340 (c,4)
    Mr '83
CHOCOLATE
--38 ft. high chocolate monument
    at 1893 Chicago fair

  Smithsonian 16:56 (c,4) F '86
CHOCOLATE INDUSTRY
  Nat Geog 166:664-87 (c,1) N '84
  Smithsonian 16:54-65 (c,1) F '86
--Late 19th cent. chocolate ads
  Smithsonian 16:55 (c,2) F '86
--Ivory Coast
  Nat Geog 166:664-7 (c,1) N '84
CHRISTCHURCH, NEW ZEALAND
--Cathedral Square
  Trav/Holiday 166:51 (c,2) Ag '86
Christian Science. See
    EDDY, MARY BAKER
CHRISTIANITY
--Carrying mobile cross on beach
    (Florida)
  Nat Geog 162:203 (c,4) Ag '82
--See also
    AMISH PEOPLE
    CHURCHES
    JESUS CHRIST
    MENNONITES
    MORMONS
    SHAKERS
CHRISTIANITY--ART
--12th cent. mosaic of Apostles
    (Venice)
  Smithsonian 15:50-1 (c,2) S '84
--15th cent. works by Fra Angelico
  Smithsonian 17:cov., 46-57 (c,1)
    D '86
--16th cent. Russian icon
  Nat Geog 168:192 (c,1) Ag '85
--"Adoration" by Durer
  Smithsonian 17:148 (painting,c,4)
    D '86
--"Adoration of the Magi" by Giotto
  Life 8:32 (painting,c,4) O '85
--"Journey of the Magi" (19th cent.
    painting)
  Smithsonian 15:137 (painting,c,3)
    D '84
--Treasures of the Vatican
  Smithsonian 13:120-31 (c,1) D
    '82
  Life 5:58-70 (c,1) D '82
  Nat Geog 168:764-77 (c,1) D '85
CHRISTIANITY--COSTUME
--13th cent. Dominican monk (Italy)
  Smithsonian 13:104 (fresco,c,3)
    Mr '83
--16th cent. cardinal (Spain)
  Smithsonian 13:52 (painting,c,4)
    Jl '82
--Anglican bishop (South Africa)
  Ebony 40:81 (2) Ja '85
--Archbishop (Italy)

CHRISTMAS (cont.)
D '82
--Outdoor Christmas mass (San
Francisco, California)
Nat Geog 169:735 (c,2) Je '86
--Radish sculpture nativity
scene (Mexico)
Natur Hist 95:58-9 (c,1) D '86
--Street decorations (Coopers-
town, New York)
Nat Geog 167:358 (c,4) Mr
'85
--U.S. soldiers entertaining Brit-
ish children (1943)
Am Heritage 33:87 (2) Je '82
--See also
CHRISTMAS TREES
JESUS CHRIST
SANTA CLAUS
CHRISTMAS ISLAND
Sports Illus 59:80-92 (map,c,1) D
26 '83
Trav/Holiday 166:22 (c,3) S '86
CHRISTMAS TREES
--1903 (Ohio)
Am Heritage 34:106 (2) D '82
--Cut in Nova Scotia
Sports Illus 61:110-21 (c,1)
D 24 '84
--Louisiana log tower
Trav/Holiday 158:27 (c,4) D
'82
CHRYSANTHEMUMS
Trav/Holiday 164:4 (c,4) O
'85
CHUBS (FISH)
Natur Hist 95:36-7 (c,1) Ag
'86
--Hornyhead chub
Natur Hist 92:54 (c,4) Mr '83
CHUCKWALLAS (LIZARDS)
Natur Hist 91:60 (c,1) S '82
CHURCH SERVICES
--1955 drive-in church (Florida)
Life 9:94 (2) Mr '86
--African Methodist Episcopal
Church (Florida)
Ebony 38:103 (3) S '83
Ebony 40:68 (2) Mr '85
--Baptist church (Dallas, Texas)
Nat Geog 166:293 (c,4) S '84
--Child preacher (Kansas)
Ebony 39:52 (4) Ap '84
--Christmas Eve (Great Britain)
Trav/Holiday 164:7 (c,3) D
'85
--Civil War army camp

Am Heritage 33:71 (3) F '82
--Guadeloupe
Trav/Holiday 165:81 (c,4) Ap
'86
--Mass (Italy)
Nat Geog 165:614-15 (c,1) My
'84
--Mass before auto race (Florida)
Sports Illus 57:35 (c,4) S 13
'82
--Outdoor Christmas mass (San
Francisco, California)
Nat Geog 169:735 (c,2) Je '86
--Tent revival meeting (North
Carolina)
Life 8:10 (4) O '85
--Tent revival meeting (Virginia)
Nat Geog 168:102-3 (c,2) Jl '85
--Villa Malta, Rome, Italy
Smithsonian 12:114 (c,3) Ja '82
--Wittenberg, East Germany
Nat Geog 164:456 (c,1) O '83
--See also
BAPTISMS
COMMUNION
CHURCHES
--12th cent. (Ethiopia)
Nat Geog 163:640 (c,2) My '83
--14th cent. Battle Abbey, Portugal
Trav/Holiday 160:54 (c,3) Ag
'83
--Early 19th cent. (Charleston,
South Carolina)
Am Heritage 34:30-1 (paint-
ing,c,1) Je '83
--Abyssinian Baptist Church inte-
rior, New York City
Ebony 37:152 (2) My '82
--Bahamas
Nat Geog 162:392-3 (c,1) S '82
--Bahia church interior, Brazil
Trav/Holiday 162:55 (c,4) N '84
--Baptist church interior (Los
Angeles, California)
Ebony 40:148 (c,4) D '84
--Basilica of Guadalupe, Mexico
City, Mexico
Trav/Holiday 159:103 (4) Mr '83
--Basilica of Monreale, Sicily, Italy
Life 7:181-8 (c,1) D '84
--Berchtesgaden, West Germany
Trav/Holiday 158:12 (c,4) D '82
--Cape Cod, Massachusetts
Life 9:40-1 (c,1) S '86
--Cathedral of Popayan, Colombia
Smithsonian 15:138 (c,1) Mr '85
--Cathedral of Rouen, France

CHURCHES (cont.)
  Nat Geog 161:304 (c,3) Ap
    '82
--Chiapas, Mexico
  Trav/Holiday 162:40 (c,3) O
    '84
--Church of Reconciliation, Ber-
    lin, Germany
  Nat Geog 161:10-11 (c,1) Ja
    '82
--Cistercian abbey, Wilhering,
    Austria
  Nat Geog 167:415-17 (c,1) Ap
    '85
--Cuzco, Peru
  Trav/Holiday 166:52 (c,3) N
    '86
--Danville, Kansas
  Nat Geog 168:382-3 (c,1) S
    '85
--Dubrovnik, Yugoslavia
  Trav/Holiday 159:44 (c,3) Je
    '83
--Duomo, Florence, Italy
  Trav/Holiday 159:38 (c,4) F
    '83
--East Meon, Hampshire, England
  Smithsonian 17:95 (c,2) Jl '86
--Erfurt, East Germany
  Nat Geog 164:422-3 (c,1) O
    '83
--Ethiopia
  Nat Geog 163:640-1 (c,1) My
    '83
--Gloucester Cathedral, England
  Trav/Holiday 164:43 (c,2) Jl
    '85
--Greek Orthodox (Greenport,
    New York)
  Trav/Holiday 165:86 (c,3) Ap
    '86
--Hawaii
  Trav/Holiday 162:36 (c,4) O
    '84
--Idaho
  Nat Geog 161:798-9 (c,1) Je
    '82
--Interior (Chicago, Illinois)
  Ebony 40:117 (c,3) Ja '85
--Interior (Louisiana)
  Ebony 38:117 (4) D '82
--Kolomenskof, U.S.S.R.
  Smithsonian 14:131 (c,4) Ja '84
--Lima, Peru
  Trav/Holiday 157:46 (c,2) Ja
    '82
--Methodist church's art deco

  interior (Tulsa, Oklahoma)
  Trav/Holiday 163:8 (c,4) Mr '85
--Metropolitan Cathedral, Mexico
    City, Mexico
  Trav/Holiday 159:65 (c,2) Mr '83
--Model of 12th cent. Norwegian
    church (Wisconsin)
  Trav/Holiday 164:60-1 (c,1) O
    '85
--Modern (Chicago, Illinois)
  Ebony 41:74-6 (c,2) D '85
--Nebraska
  Nat Geog 162:76-7 (c,1) Jl '82
--New England
  Nat Geog 164:207 (c,1) Ag '83
--New Hampshire
  Nat Geog 162:770-1 (c,1) D '82
--New Mexico
  Nat Geog 162:92-3 (c,1) Jl '82
--Notre Dame Church interior,
    Montreal, Quebec
  Trav/Holiday 162:4 (c,3) Jl '84
--Orvieto, Italy
  Smithsonian 14:140-1 (c,1) N '83
--Painted exterior (Romania)
  Nat Geog 164:730-1 (c,1) D '83
--Panama
  Nat Geog 169:476 (c,4) Ap '86
--Personal chapel (Vermont)
  Life 5:48 (c,4) F '82
--Pittsburgh, Pennsylvania
  Trav/Holiday 163:54 (c,4) My '85
--Princeton University Chapel, New
    Jersey
  Trav/Holiday 165:49 (c,4) My '86
--Sagrada Familia, Barcelona, Spain
  Trav/Holiday 157:47 (c,2) F '82
  Nat Geog 165:104-5 (c,1) Ja '84
--St. Basil's Cathedral, Moscow,
    U.S.S.R.
  Smithsonian 13:65 (c,2) Mr '83
  Trav/Holiday 163:61 (c,2) My '85
  Sports Illus 65:13 (c,4) Jl 21 '86
--St. David's Cathedral, Wales
  Trav/Holiday 159:64 (c,2) My '83
--St. Fin Barre's, Cork, Ireland
  Trav/Holiday 164:62 (c,1) S '85
--St. Mary's Cathedral interior, San
    Francisco, California
  Smithsonian 13:117 (c,1) F '83
--St. Matthews Cathedral, Budapest,
    Hungary
  Trav/Holiday 163:69 (c,1) Mr '85
--St. Patrick's Cathedral, Dublin,
    Ireland
  Trav/Holiday 163:66 (c,4) F '85
--St. Paul's Cathedral, London,

CHURCHES (cont.)
England
Life 5:86-7 (c,1) Ja '82
Smithsonian 13:88-9 (c,2) N '82
--St. Paul's Cathedral interior,
London, England
Life 8:167 (c,4) O '85
--St. Peter's, Bermuda
Trav/Holiday 162:10-11 (c,2)
D '84
--St. Stephen's Cathedral, Vienna,
Austria
Trav/Holiday 164:53 (c,4) Ag
'85
--Samoa
Life 6:38 (c,2) My '83
Nat Geog 168:468 (c,3) O '85
--San Xavier del Bac, Tucson,
Arizona
Trav/Holiday 159:54 (c,2) F
'83
--São Paulo Cathedral, Brazil
Trav/Holiday 159:cov. (c,1) Ja
'83
--Taxco, Mexico
Trav/Holiday 159:62 (c,4) Mr
'83
--Temppeliaukio Church, Hel-
sinki, Finland
Trav/Holiday 166:9 (c,3) D '86
--Toledo Cathedral, Spain
Nat Geog 161:746-7 (c,1) Je
'82
--U.S.
Smithsonian 13:158-68 (c,1) N
'82
--U.S.S.R.
Smithsonian 13:65-7, 73 (c,1)
Mr '83
--Vermont
Trav/Holiday 157:28 (4) Je '82
Am Heritage 34:cov. (c,1) D
'82
--Washington Cathedral's iron-
work screen, Washington,
D.C.
Smithsonian 13:18 (c,4) My '82
--Washington Cathedral's rose
window, Washington, D.C.
Smithsonian 16:114 (c,4) Jl '85
--Wittenberg Church interior,
East Germany
Nat Geog 164:456 (c,1) O '83
--See also
MISSIONS
MONASTERIES
MOSQUES

NOTRE DAME
ST. JOHN THE DIVINE
ST. MARK'S CATHEDRAL
ST. PATRICK'S CATHEDRAL
ST. PETER'S CHURCH
ST. SOPHIA CATHEDRAL
SYNAGOGUES
TEMPLES
WESTMINSTER ABBEY
CHURCHILL, WINSTON
Life 5:16 (3) F '82
Am Heritage 33:95-6 (1) O '82
Am Heritage 34:85 (2) O '83
Smithsonian 16:124 (4) Jl '85
Life 8:20 (4) Spring '85
Life 8:170 (4) O '85
Am Heritage 37:27 (2) O '86
Life 9:196, 269, 363 (c,2) Fall
'86
Am Heritage 38:112 (3) D '86
--1965 funeral (London, England)
Life 8:167 (c,4) O '85
--Birthplace (Blenheim Palace, Eng-
land)
Trav/Holiday 159:62-3 (c,1) Ap
'83
Nat Geog 168:668-9 (c,1) N '85
--Cabinet War Rooms, London, Eng-
land
Trav/Holiday 165:86 (4) Ja '86
--Statue (London, England)
Nat Geog 170:756 (c,1) D '86
CHURCHILL, MANITOBA
Nat Geog 161:390-1 (c,1) Mr '82
Trav/Holiday 160:cov., 38-9 (c,1)
O '83
Churchill Downs. See
RACE TRACKS
CIGAR INDUSTRY
--Cigar box art
Sports Illus 57:74-81 (c,1) D 27
'82
CIGAR MAKING
--Florida
Nat Geog 162:213 (c,3) Ag '82
Trav/Holiday 166:18 (c,4) D '86
--Nicaragua
Nat Geog 168:794-5 (c,2) D '85
CIGAR SMOKING
Sports Illus 56:53 (c,2) F 15 '82
Sports Illus 59:cov., 66-74 (c,1)
Ag 8 '83
Life 7:82-3 (c,1) O '84
Life 7:38-9 (c,1) N '84
Sports Illus 62:41 (c,4) Ja 14 '85
Life 8:39, 42 (c,2) Je '85
Sports Illus 63:24 (c,4) Ag 5 '85

CITY HALLS (cont.)
　　Trav/Holiday 165:38-43 (c,1)
　　　Ja '86
--Newark City Hall's stairs, New
　　Jersey
　　Ebony 41:128 (3) S '86
--Pasadena, California
　　Ebony 37:113 (c,2) Ag '82
--Philadelphia, Pennsylvania
　　Ebony 39:44-5 (c,1) My '84
--Washington, New Hampshire
　　Nat Geog 162:770-1 (c,1) D
　　　'82
CIVETS
　　Natur Hist 94:66-7 (paint-
　　　ing,c,1) D '85
CIVIL RIGHTS
--1949 integration of University
　　of Arkansas
　　Ebony 41:208 (3) N '85
--1954 Supreme Court desegrega-
　　tion decision
　　Ebony 40:108-16 (4) My '85
--1955 arrest of Rosa Parks (Ala-
　　bama)
　　Ebony 41:274 (2) N '85
--1955 scene of Rosa Parks on
　　bus (Alabama)
　　Life 9:196 (4) Fall '86
--1956 Montgomery bus boycott,
　　Alabama
　　Ebony 41:276 (2) N '85
　　Ebony 41:44 (4) Ja '86
--1957 Little Rock high school
　　desegregation
　　Ebony 37:131 (2) Ap '82
　　Ebony 41:278 (3) N '85
　　Am Heritage 37:52-3 (1) D '85
--1960 lunch counter sit-in
　　(North Carolina)
　　Ebony 39:162 (4) Ag '84
　　Am Heritage 36:16 (4) F '85
　　Ebony 41:284 (4) N '85
--1960s civil rights leaders
　　Ebony 40:108-14 (4) Ap '85
--1963 arrest of M. L. King at
　　store boycott (Alabama)
　　Ebony 41:160-8 (2) N '85
--1963 bombed church (Birming-
　　ham, Alabama)
　　Ebony 41:299 (4) N '85
--Black power salute at 1968
　　Mexico City Olympics
　　Ebony 41:102 (4) N '85
--Blacks' encounters with racists
　　Ebony 40:51-6 (2) N '84
--Blacks registering to vote

　　Ebony 40:122 (4) N '84
--Andrew Goodman
　　Ebony 41:300 (4) N '85
--History of NAACP
　　Ebony 39:49-52 (3) Jl '84
--Hosing down 1963 civil rights
　　demonstrators (Alabama)
　　Life 9:338-9 (1) Fall '86
--Martin Luther King, Jr.'s role in
　　civil rights movement
　　Ebony 41:44-54 (4) Ja '86
--James Meredith integrating U. of
　　Mississippi (1962)
　　Ebony 40:38 (4) D '84
　　Ebony 41:292 (4) N '85
--Prominent figures in 20th cent.
　　civil rights movement
　　Ebony 41:60-76, 248-350 (2) N
　　　'85
--Singing "We Shall Overcome" with
　　linked arms
　　Ebony 41:188 (4) N '85
--George Wallace "standing in school-
　　house door" (Alabama)
　　Ebony 38:44 (3) S '83
--See also
　　　BLACK HISTORY
　　　EVERS, MEDGAR
　　　KING, MARTIN LUTHER, JR.
　　　KU KLUX KLAN
　　　MALCOLM X
　　　NAACP
　　　list under BLACKS IN AMER-
　　　　ICAN HISTORY
CIVIL RIGHTS MARCHES
--1963 (Washington, D.C.)
　　Ebony 39:52 (4) Jl '84
　　Ebony 41:296 (4) N '85
　　Ebony 41:40-2, 50 (1) Ja '86
--1965 (Selma, Alabama)
　　Am Heritage 33:48-63 (c,1) Je
　　　'82
　　Ebony 40:120 (3) N '84
　　Ebony 41:304 (4) N '85
　　Ebony 41:90 (2) Ja '86
--1981 solidarity day (Washington,
　　D.C.)
　　Ebony 37:33 (3) Ja '82
--1983 march on Washington, D.C.
　　Ebony 39:152-60 (c,1) N '83
CIVIL WAR
　　Am Heritage 36:70-84 (painting,1)
　　　D '84
--1861 shelling of Fort Sumter, South
　　Carolina
　　Am Heritage 37:98 (4) Ap '86
--1863 journalists

CIVIL WAR (cont.)
  Am Heritage 36:28-9 (2) Je '85
--1863 Lincoln visit to Gettys-
    burg
  Life 6:96-112 (1) O '83
--1865 Breckinridge escape from
    the South
  Smithsonian 13:70-8 (paint-
    ing,c,1) D '82
--Andersonville Prison, Georgia
  Am Heritage 33:78-91 (draw-
    ing,c,1) O '82
--Army life
  Am Heritage 33:2, 68-79 (c,1)
    F '82
--Battle of Atlanta (1864)
  Smithsonian 16:70-4 (paint-
    ing,c,1) Ag '85
--Battle of Champion Hill, Mis-
    sissippi (1863)
  Trav/Holiday 163:90 (draw-
    ing,4) Je '85
--Battle of Gettysburg (1863)
  Smithsonian 16:75-8 (paint-
    ing,c,1) Ag '85
--Charleston Harbor, South
    Carolina (1863)
  Am Heritage 38:60-1 (paint-
    ing,c,3) D '86
--Confederacy memorial (Alabama)
  Ebony 37:52 (3) Jl '82
--Confederate flag
  Am Heritage 33:48 (c,2) Je '82
  Life 8:63 (c,4) Ap '85
  Nat Geog 169:602-3 (c,1) My
    '86
--Doctor amputating leg
  Am Heritage 35:65-7 (1) O '84
--Sam Houston denying Confederacy
    (1861)
  Nat Geog 169:328 (cartoon,4)
    Mr '86
--Loading cannon
  Trav/Holiday 159:55 (draw-
    ing,4) Ap '83
--Reenactment of Confederate
    camp (Mississippi)
  Trav/Holiday 166:54 (c,1) Jl
    '86
--Union troops storming Fort
    Wagner, Charleston, S.C.
  Ebony 41:156 (painting,4) N '85
--Wisconsin color guard (1863)
  Smithsonian 13:12 (4) Jl '82
--See also
    ABOLITIONISTS
    BRECKINRIDGE, JOHN C.

    FARRAGUT, DAVID GLASGOW
    GRANT, ULYSSES S.
    LEE, ROBERT E.
    LINCOLN, ABRAHAM
    RECONSTRUCTION
    SEWARD, WILLIAM H.
    SHERMAN, WILLIAM TECUM-
      SEH
    SLAVERY--U.S.
    WILKES, CHARLES
Civilizations. See
    PEOPLE AND CIVILIZATIONS
CLAM DIGGING
--Long Island, New York
  Natur Hist 91:78-9 (2) Je '82
--Maine
  Nat Geog 167:210-11 (c,1) F '85
CLAMS
--Giant clams
  Smithsonian 14:30 (c,4) Ag '83
  Trav/Holiday 165:42 (c,4) F '86
CLASSROOMS
--1400 (France)
  Smithsonian 17:38 (painting,c,4)
    Je '86
--1871 one-room school
  Smithsonian 15:182-3 (painting,c,2)
    N '84
--Early 20th cent. American Indian
    boarding schools
  Natur Hist 93:4-12 (c,1) Ag '84
--1901 high school (Massachusetts)
  Smithsonian 16:122-3 (1) Ap '85
--Elementary school
  Ebony 40:77-8 (3) F '85
  Ebony 40:43-50 (2) O '85
  Ebony 42:48 (3) N '86
--Elementary school (Illinois)
  Life 8:82-3 (1) Je '85
--Elementary school (New Jersey)
  Ebony 42:28 (c,4) D '86
--Elementary school (Texas)
  Ebony 39:150 (4) Mr '84
--Ethiopia
  Nat Geog 163:629 (c,3) My '83
--Ethiopian Jews (Israel)
  Nat Geog 168:21 (c,2) Jl '85
--First grade (North Carolina)
  Ebony 39:65 (c,3) Mr '84
--High school
  Ebony 41:144-6 (3) Ap '86
--High school (Massachusetts)
  Smithsonian 16:123-35 (c,3) Ap
    '85
--High school (Minnesota)
  Smithsonian 16:49 (c,4) D '85
--High school (Mississippi)

CLASSROOMS (cont.)
Ebony 37:106 (3) Ap '82
--High school (New York City,
New York)
Smithsonian 16:82-6 (3) My '85
--Italy
Life 8:29 (c,4) Mr '85
--One-room schoolhouses (Ne-
braska)
Smithsonian 16:120-8 (c,1) O
'85
--Outdoors (India)
Nat Geog 167:530-1 (c,1) Ap
'85
--Prison religion class (New York)
Ebony 38:156 (3) Ap '83
--School earthquake drill (Cali-
fornia)
Nat Geog 169:668 (c,2) My '86
--See also
BLACKBOARDS
MEDICAL EDUCATION
SCHOOLS
CLASSROOMS--UNIVERSITIES
Ebony 38:80 (3) Jl '83
Ebony 38:90 (4) O '83
Ebony 39:30 (4) Ja '84
Ebony 40:118 (3) Mr '85
--Computer class
Ebony 40:94 (c,4) Ag '85
--Law school (Wisconsin)
Ebony 37:45 (3) Mr '82
--New Hampshire
Nat Geog 162:788-9 (c,4) D
'82
Clemens, Samuel. See
TWAIN, MARK
CLEOPATRA
--Actress portraying Cleopatra
Life 8:62-3 (c,1) O '85
CLEVELAND, GROVER
--1885 inauguration
Am Heritage 36:62 (2) D '84
--1886 wedding
Am Heritage 37:109 (draw-
ing,4) Je '86
--Wife Frances
Am Heritage 35:92 (paint-
ing,c,4) O '84
CLEVELAND, OHIO
--Ohio Theater interior
Smithsonian 14:98-9 (c,4) Je
'83
CLIFFS
--Cliff dwellings (Cappadocia,
Turkey)
Trav/Holiday 166:cov., 40-2

(c,1) S '86
--Missouri
Nat Wildlife 23:42-5 (c,1) F '85
--Mohegan Bluffs, Block Island,
Rhode Island
Trav/Holiday 158:4 (4) Ag '82
--Pink Cliffs, Dixie National Forest,
Utah
Natur Hist 95:90-2 (map,c,1)
My '86
--Red Rock Cliff, New Mexico
Sports Illus 60:58-9 (c,1) Mr 26
'84
CLIMATE
--Climate changes recorded in cave
sediment (Yugoslavia)
Nat Geog 168:613 (c,2) N '85
CLIPPER SHIPS
--1850s
Smithsonian 14:172 (painting,4)
Mr '84
--1884
Am Heritage 34:70 (drawing,c,4)
Ap '83
CLOCKS
--15th cent. clock tower (Bordeaux,
France)
Trav/Holiday 160:60 (c,1) S '83
--15th cent. clock tower (Venice,
Italy)
Am Heritage 35:39 (painting,c,3)
Je '84
--1588 clock tower (Graz, Austria)
Trav/Holiday 160:6 (c,4) Ag '83
--18th cent. flower clock by Lin-
naeus (Germany)
Natur Hist 91:30 (c,4) O '82
--19th cent. Breguet clocks (France)
Smithsonian 16:cov., 92-101 (c,1)
My '85
--19th cent. silk velvet clock
(France)
Nat Geog 165:40 (c,3) Ja '84
--1810 Hepplewhite clock (Massachu-
setts)
Am Heritage 36:46-7 (c,2) F '85
--Chinese pedestal clock
Sports Illus 58:50 (c,3) My 9 '83
--Railroad station (U.S.S.R.)
Nat Geog 169:789 (c,2) Je '86
--Street clock (St. Louis, Missouri)
Trav/Holiday 157:35 (c,4) Je '82
--U.S. House of Representatives
(1915)
Am Heritage 33:2 (2) Je '82
--Unusual clocks by Wendell Castle
Smithsonian 16:186 (c,4) Mr '86

CLOCKS (cont.)
--See also
    BIG BEN CLOCK TOWER
    SUNDIALS
    WATCHES

CLOTHING
--1940s Eisenhower jacket for
    women
    Life 8:21 (4) Spring '85
--1940s women's fashions
    Ebony 41:222-3 (2) N '85
--1942 zoot suit
    Life 9:65 (4) Ag '86
--1950s women's fashions
    Ebony 41:222-4 (c,2) N '85
--1956 crinoline slips
    Life 9:66 (4) Ag '86
--1960s women's fashions
    Ebony 41:224-32 (c,2) N '85
--1968 Nehru jacket
    Life 9:71 (3) Ag '86
--1970s women's fashions
    Ebony 41:232-4 (c,2) N '85
--Advice to wives on proper way
    to undress (1937)
    Life 9:298 (4) Fall '86
--Black-tie affair (Washington,
    D.C.)
    Nat Geog 163:102-5 (c,1) Ja
    '83
--Child's snowsuit
    Nat Wildlife 24:5 (c,1) D '85
--High school prom attire
    Life 8:85-90 (c,1) Jl '85
--Insulated apparel for Arctic
    expedition
    Nat Geog 170:288-323 (c,1) S
    '86
--Kilts (Scotland)
    Nat Geog 166:45 (c,1) Jl '84
--Kimonos (Japan)
    Trav/Holiday 165:62-4 (c,1) Je
    '86
    Nat Geog 170:610-11 (c,1) N '86
--Leg make-up during 1940s nylon
    shortage
    Life 8:20 (4) Spring '85
--Made of turkey feathers (1948)
    Life 9:109-10 (2) D '86
--Man adjusting tie
    Ebony 38:130 (c,4) Je '83
--Man dressing as woman for
    movie role
    Life 5:55-9 (c,1) S '82
--Man in top hat and tails
    Life 8:148-9 (c,1) Ja '85
--Mini skirts
    Life 5:91-4 (c,1) My '82
--Mary Pickford's bloomers (1930s)
    Life 9:125 (c,4) My '86
--Protective winter face masks
    (China)
    Nat Geog 166:737 (c,4) D '84
--Recycled clothing from Hollywood
    stars
    Life 9:125-9 (c,2) My '86
--Reptile skin accessories and fakes
    Life 9:96-8 (c,1) D '86
--Rubber toxic waste protection
    suits
    Nat Geog 163:437 (c,3) Ap '83
    Nat Wildlife 23:38-41 (c,1) Je
    '83
--Saris (India)
    Nat Geog 169:239 (c,1) F '86
--Survival suit
    Life 5:98 (c,1) N '82
--Long underwear
    Life 5:99 (c,2) N '82
--Tie-tying instructions
    Ebony 40:138 (drawing,c,4) N
    '84
--Trousers for 500 lb. man
    Ebony 38:66-8 (2) Ja '83
--Tuxedo
    Ebony 39:164 (c,2) Je '84
--Well-stocked man's clothes closet
    (Illinois)
    Sports Illus 58:34 (c,4) Ja 10
    '83
--Winter fur apparel (Italy)
    Nat Geog 165:201 (c,3) F '84
--See also
    BATHING SUITS
    BUTTONS
    CHILDREN--COSTUME
    COATS
    EYEGLASSES
    FOOTWEAR
    GLOVES
    GOGGLES
    HATS
    HEADGEAR
    MILITARY COSTUME
    PURSES
    RAINWEAR
    SNOWSHOES
    SPORTSWEAR
    U.S.--COSTUME
    individual countries--COSTUME
    list under OCCUPATIONS

CLOTHING--HUMOR
--Sports clothes worn in cities
    Smithsonian 15:123-37 (draw-
    ing,c,1) Ja '85

CLOUDS
    Smithsonian 14:57 (paint-
        ing,c,4) My '83
--Gathering storm
    Am Heritage 38:55 (paint-
        ing,c,2) D '86
--Honduras
    Nat Geog 164:608-9 (c,1) N '83
--Storm clouds (Midwest)
    Smithsonian 17:76-7 (c,1) S
        '86
CLOWNS
    Trav/Holiday 162:42 (c,4) Ag
        '84
    Trav/Holiday 164:78 (c,4) O '85
--Jester costumes
    Life 5:134-5 (c,1) N '82
CLUBS
--Academie Parmentier (France)
    Nat Geog 161:690-1 (c,1) My
        '82
--Baker Street Irregulars
    Smithsonian 17:61-9 (c,1) D
        '86
--Country club (Mexico City,
        Mexico)
    Nat Geog 166:156-7 (c,1) Ag
        '84
--Fraternity and sorority emblems
    Ebony 39:98 (drawing,c,4)
        D '83
--Fraternity pledge activities
    Ebony 39:96 (2) D '83
--Golf club (South Africa)
    Sports Illus 58:86 (c,4) My 16
        '83
--Men's club exterior (London,
        England)
    Trav/Holiday 165:16 (draw-
        ing,4) Je '86
--Meteorite society (West Germany)
    Nat Geog 170:403 (c,2) S '86
--New York Yacht Club model
        room
    Natur Hist 92:69 (4) My '83
--Oakmont Country Club, Penn-
        sylvania
    Sports Illus 58:30-1 (c,2) Je
        27 '83
--Port wine traders (Portugal)
    Nat Geog 166:467 (c,4) O '84
--Postage stamps commemorating
        clubs
    Am Heritage 34:53 (c,4) D '82
--Shriners
    Ebony 42:130 (4) N '86
--See also

    BOY SCOUTS
    GIRL SCOUTS
    KU KLUX KLAN
    MASONRY
    NIGHT CLUBS
    TENNIS CLUBS
COAL INDUSTRY--TRANSPORTA-
        TION
--Alabama
    Nat Geog 169:382-3 (c,1) Mr '86
COAL MINES
--Denuded strip mine (Ohio)
    Natur Hist 95:30-1 (c,1) Ag '86
COAL MINING
--Appalachia
    Nat Geog 163:798-801 (c,1) Je
        '83
--Coal refuse (Montana)
    Life 6:111 (c,4) Jl '83
--Hungary
    Nat Geog 163:230 (c,4) F '83
--Strip mining
    Sports Illus 59:76 (c,4) S 26 '83
--See also
    MINERS
Coast Guard. See
    U.S. COAST GUARD
COATIS
    Smithsonian 12:86-95 (c,1) F '82
COATS
--1920s raccoon coat
    Sports Illus 63:129 (3) S 4 '85
--Child's fur coat (U.S.S.R.)
    Nat Geog 163:207 (c,1) F '83
--Fur coats
    Ebony 40:140-4 (2) D '84
--Raccoon coat
    Life 6:64 (c,2) Ap '83
Coats of arms. See
    SEALS AND EMBLEMS
COBB, TY
    Smithsonian 15:160 (4) O '84
    Life 8:115, 120 (4) My '85
    Sports Illus 62:60 (sculpture,c,4)
        My 6 '85
    Sports Illus 63:54-63 (c,1) Ag
        19 '85
    Sports Illus 63:131 (4) S 4 '85
COBRAS
    Nat Wildlife 20:45 (3) O '82
    Smithsonian 13:110 (c,4) Mr '83
--Spitting cobra
    Natur Hist 94:78-9 (c,1) Ag '85
--Venom on fangs
    Trav/Holiday 159:56 (c,4) Ja '83
COCKATOOS
    Smithsonian 16:61-7 (c,1) Ap '85

COCKFIGHTING
--Civil War army camp
  Am Heritage 33:77 (3) F '82
COCKROACHES
  Nat Geog 170:350 (c,4) S '86
--Eating a bat
  Natur Hist 93:118-19 (c,1) O
    '84
--Rear view
  Natur Hist 94:96 (c,3) My '85
COCKS-OF-THE-ROCKS (BIRDS)
  Smithsonian 13:38 (c,4) Ja '83
  Nat Geog 164:830-9 (c,1) D
    '83
COCONUTS
  Natur Hist 94:90-2 (c,1) My
    '85
  Nat Geog 169:488-9 (c,1) Ap
    '86
  Nat Geog 170:103 (c,1) Jl '86
COCOONS
  Smithsonian 15:54 (c,4) My '84
CODY, WILLIAM (BUFFALO
      BILL)
  Smithsonian 13:58-67 (c,1) Ja
    '83
--1875 poster
  Am Heritage 34:8 (drawing,c,3)
    Ap '83
--Depicted in films
  Smithsonian 13:64-5 (4) Ja '83
Coelenterates. See
      CORALS
      JELLYFISH
      POLYPS
      PORTUGUESE MAN-OF-WAR
      SEA ANEMONES
COFFEE INDUSTRY
--Beans drying in sun (Nicaragua)
  Nat Geog 168:797 (c,4) D '85
--Warehouse (Ivory Coast)
  Nat Geog 162:120 (c,3) Jl '82
COFFEEHOUSES
--1900 (Vienna, Austria)
  Smithsonian 17:70-1 (paint-
    ing,c,1) Ag '86
--Baghdad, Iraq
  Nat Geog 167:108-9 (c,1) Ja
    '85
--Kansas hardware store hangout
  Nat Geog 168:368-9 (c,1) S
    '85
--Vienna, Austria
  Trav/Holiday 157:62 (c,4) Ja
    '82
COFFINS
  Sports Illus 65:29 (c,3) Jl 14

  '86
  Sports Illus 65:116-17 (c,1) D
    22 '86
--17th cent. (Great Britain)
  Nat Geog 161:62-3 (c,1) Ja '82
--American Vietnam War dead
  Life 9:39-40 (c,2) Jl '86
--Gabled lids (Turkey)
  Nat Geog 161:59 (c,4) Ja '82
--Italy
  Life 8:28-9 (c,1) Mr '85
--Rwanda
  Life 9:70 (c,4) N '86
COINS
--132 A.D. Roman coin depicting
      Hadrian
  Smithsonian 16:72 (c,4) Ap '85
--4th cent. Roman coin
  Nat Geog 164:722 (c,4) D '83
--16th cent. (Great Britain)
  Nat Geog 163:661 (c,3) My '83
--19th cent. private and regional
      coins (U.S.)
  Am Heritage 36:47 (c,4) D '84
--1830 (U.S.S.R.)
  Nat Geog 164:694 (c,4) N '83
--1984 Olympics
  Sports Illus 60:72-3 (c,4) Mr 5
    '84
--Ancient Greece
  Natur Hist 93:69 (c,4) Je '84
--Ancient Rome
  Smithsonian 14:120 (c,4) S '83
--Buffalo nickels recarved by
      hoboes
  Am Heritage 34:81-3, 114 (c,2)
    Ag '83
--Coin production (Denver Mint,
      Colorado)
  Trav/Holiday 165:68 (c,4) Je '86
--Gambia
  Nat Geog 170:826 (c,4) D '86
--Lincoln penny
  Life 6:156 (c,4) Ja '83
--Lincoln penny (1909)
  Am Heritage 35:15 (4) Ag '84
--Medieval Arabic coins
  Nat Geog 167:293 (c,4) Mr '85
--Pennies
  Life 6:3 (c,4) O '83
--Testing British coins (London,
      England)
  Smithsonian 13:89 (c,4) N '82
--U.S. coins
  Sports Illus 58:61 (c,4) Ja 24
    '83
--U.S. gold coins (1787-1984)

COINS (cont.)
  Am Heritage 36:cov., 42-8,
    122 (c,1) D '84
--See also
    CURRENCY
COLE, NAT KING
  Ebony 41:304 (4) N '85
--1948 wedding
  Ebony 40:74 (4) Mr '85
COLERIDGE, SAMUEL TAYLOR
  Smithsonian 16:124 (draw-
    ing,c,4) My '85
COLLAGES
--Depictions of jazz by Romare
    Bearden
  Am Heritage 33:86-95 (c,1) F
    '82
COLLEGE LIFE
--1870s Harvard dorm room
    (Massachusetts)
  Smithsonian 17:152 (4) S '86
--1881 Harvard college students
    (Massachusetts)
  Smithsonian 17:160 (4) S '86
--1961 "Happening" (Florida)
  Am Heritage 37:103 (4) Ap '86
--College student fads (1939-
    1975)
  Life 9:65-71 (4) Ag '86
--Dorm room
  Sports Illus 64:54 (c,2) Mr
    17 '86
--Dorm room (California)
  Sports Illus 60:68 (c,4) Mr 5
    '84
  Ebony 41:150 (c,4) My '86
--Fraternity pledge activities
  Ebony 39:96 (2) D '83
--Harvard dorm room, Massa-
    chusetts
  Life 9:30-1 (c,1) S '86
--Statue of student reading
    (Princeton, New Jersey)
  Trav/Holiday 165:48 (c,4) My
    '86
--Students in class (Kentucky)
  Life 5:69 (c,4) Mr '82
--Students registering for classes
  Ebony 40:125 (3) N '84
--Students vacationing in Fort
    Lauderdale, Florida
  Nat Geog 162:202-3 (c,2) Ag
    '82
--Studying
  Ebony 38:52 (4) Mr '83
  Sports Illus 58:50 (c,4) Mr 7
    '83

--Studying in dorm room
  Sports Illus 58:62 (c,4) Ja 10
    '83
--Studying law books
  Sports Illus 56:60 (c,4) My 17
    '82
--See also
    SCHOLARS
COLLEGES AND UNIVERSITIES
--1949 integration of University of
    Arkansas
  Ebony 41:208 (3) N '85
--Amherst octagonal building, Mas-
    sachusetts
  Am Heritage 34:18-19 (c,1) Ag
    '83
--Bethune-Cookman, Dayton, Florida
  Ebony 38:138 (4) D '82
  Ebony 41:172-3 (1) N '85
--Boston College, Boston, Massachu-
    setts
  Sports Illus 63:52-3 (c,1) D 2
    '85
--UC at Berkeley
  Ebony 41:96 (3) O '86
--UC at Berkeley's Sproul Hall
  Life 7:142-3 (c,1) D '84
--UCLA dorm
  Sports Illus 60:68 (c,4) Mr 5 '84
--Cheyney, Pennsylvania
  Ebony 40:73 (4) D '84
--Cleveland State University science
    building, Ohio
  Ebony 38:64 (c,4) Jl '83
--College library card catalog (Ohio)
  Ebony 40:40 (3) D '84
--U. of Georgia history plaque
  Sports Illus 64:34 (c,4) F 24 '86
--Howard University, Washington,
    D.C.
  Ebony 38:123 (2) S '83
  Ebony 40:140-6 (c,2) S '85
--Indiana University School of Music
  Smithsonian 16:130-48 (1) Ja '86
--University of Kentucky
  Life 5:67-9 (c,1) Mr '82
--Lincoln University, Jefferson City,
    Missouri
  Ebony 41:83 (c,3) O '86
--University of Maryland, College
    Park
  Ebony 39:27-32 (4) Ja '84
--University of Maryland dorm
  Sports Illus 64:22 (c,4) Je 30 '86
--Meharry Medical College, Nash-
    ville, Tennessee
  Ebony 41:42-50 (3) Mr '86

COLLEGES AND UNIVERSITIES
(cont.)
--James Meredith integrating U.
of Mississippi (1962)
Ebony 40:38 (4) D '84
Ebony 41:292 (4) N '85
--Miami University, Oxford, Ohio
Sports Illus 64:48 (c,2) Mr 3
'86
--Morehouse Medical, Atlanta,
Georgia
Ebony 38:74-8 (3) N '82
--Morgan State, Baltimore, Mary-
land
Ebony 38:136 (4) F '83
--U. of North Carolina at Chapel
Hill's Dean Dome
Sports Illus 64:24-5 (c,4) Ja
27 '86
--Notre Dame, South Bend, Indi-
ana
Sports Illus 58:58-70 (c,1) Ja
10 '83
--Notre Dame's Grotto, South
Bend, Indiana
Sports Illus 61:24-5 (c,1) N 5
'84
--Oral Roberts University, Tulsa,
Oklahoma
Nat Geog 164:394-5 (c,1) S '83
--University of Texas, Austin
Smithsonian 14:140-51 (c,1) N
'83
Trav/Holiday 166:46 (c,1) Jl
'86
--Texas Southern University law
school
Ebony 38:63 (c,3) Jl '83
--Tulane, New Orleans, Louisiana
Sports Illus 62:36 (c,2) Ap 8
'85
--USC Swim Stadium, California
Trav/Holiday 160:62 (c,4) N '83
--Villanova University, Pennsyl-
vania
Sports Illus 64:60-1 (c,3) Mr
3 '86
--University of Virginia, Char-
lottesville
Ebony 38:54 (4) Mr '84
Am Heritage 35:49-64, 110
(c,1) Je '84
--Wichita State University, Kansas
Ebony 38:68 (c,4) Jl '83
--Wilberforce, Ohio
Ebony 40:73 (4) D '84
--See also

CAMBRIDGE UNIVERSITY
CLASSROOMS--UNIVERSITIES
COLLEGE LIFE
COLUMBIA UNIVERSITY
COMMENCEMENT
HARVARD UNIVERSITY
OXFORD UNIVERSITY
PRINCETON UNIVERSITY
STANFORD UNIVERSITY
YALE UNIVERSITY
COLLEGES AND UNIVERSITIES--
COSTUME
--Amherst College robe
Smithsonian 13:120 (painting,c,4)
Ap '82
COLLIES
Smithsonian 13:68 (c,3) Ap '82
COLOGNE, WEST GERMANY
--Cathedral stained glass
Trav/Holiday 161:46 (c,4) My '84
COLOMBIA
--1985 volcano damage
Nat Geog 169:640-9, 652-3
(map,c,1) My '86
--Crater Lake Guatavita
Nat Geog 168:341 (c,4) S '85
--Mud volcanoes (Turbaco)
Nat Geog 168:338-9 (c,1) S '85
--See also
ORINOCO RIVER
COLOMBIA--ART
--Church treasures
Smithsonian 15:138-47 (c,1) Mr
'85
COLOMBIA--COSTUME
--Volcano victims
Life 9:12-13, 139 (c,1) Ja '86
COLOMBIA, ANCIENT--ART
--Gold pectoral (400-700 A.D.)
Smithsonian 15:68 (c,4) My '84
--Gold sculpture of royal figure
Nat Geog 168:340-1 (c,1) S '85
COLORADO
Nat Geog 166:186-219 (map,c,1)
Ag '84
--Countryside near Durango
Trav/Holiday 163:4 (c,3) Mr '85
--Durango-Silverton Narrow Gauge
Railroad
Nat Geog 166:190 (c,4) Ag '84
Trav/Holiday 163:4 (c,3) Mr '85
Trav/Holiday 165:cov. (c,1) Je
'86
--Lizard Head Pass
Am Heritage 33:26 (c,1) Je '82
--Rocky Mountain Biological Labora-
tory (Gothic)

COLORADO (cont.)
  Smithsonian 13:116-27 (c,1)
    My '82
--Rocky Mountain meadows
  Natur Hist 93:30-1 (c,1) Jl '84
--San Juan Mountains
  Nat Geog 166:190-1 (c,1) Ag
    '84
--Steamboat Springs Winter
    Carnival
  Trav/Holiday 157:55 (c,3) Ja
    '82
--Taylor River
  Natur Hist 95:58-60 (c,1) Ag
    '86
--Tulleride
  Trav/Holiday 161:18 (4) Ja '84
--See also
    ASPEN
    DENVER
    GARDEN OF THE GODS
    GREAT SAND DUNES NA-
      TIONAL MONUMENT
    GUNNISON NATIONAL
      FOREST
    ROCKY MOUNTAIN NATIONAL
      PARK
    ROCKY MOUNTAINS
    WHITE RIVER NATIONAL
      FOREST
COLORADO RIVER, SOUTHWEST
  Smithsonian 13:44-55 (map,c,1)
    F '83
--1983 flood
  Nat Wildlife 23:42-7 (map,c,1)
    O '85
--Glen Canyon Dam, Arizona
  Nat Wildlife 23:44-5 (c,1) O
    '85
--Grand Canyon, Arizona
  Natur Hist 91:74-82 (c,1) Ja
    '82
  Trav/Holiday 166:16 (c,2) Jl '86
--See also
    HOOVER DAM
COLOSSEUM, ROME, ITALY
  Nat Geog 165:202-3 (c,1) F '84
  Trav/Holiday 64:50 (c,4) O '85
COLUMBIA, SOUTH CAROLINA
  Nat Geog 166:808 (c,4) D '84
Columbia River, Northwest. See
    GRAND COULEE DAM
COLUMBIA UNIVERSITY, NEW
    YORK CITY, NEW YORK
  Sports Illus 65:42, 45, 48
    (c,3) D 1 '86
COLUMBINE PLANTS

--X-ray photo
  Smithsonian 17:91 (4) O '86
COLUMBUS, CHRISTOPHER
  Smithsonian 14:134 (painting,c,4)
    F '84
--15th cent. description of Colum-
    bus' Niña
  Nat Geog 170:600-1 (c,1) N '86
--Columbus' log of his travels
  Nat Geog 170:574 (c,1) N '86
--Maps of possible Columbus routes
  Nat Geog 170:584-5, 588-9, 596
    (c,1) N '86
--Recreation of Columbus' 15th cent.
    Niña
  Nat Geog 170:602-5 (c,1) N '86
--Retracing his journeys to the New
    World
  Nat Geog 170:cov., 563-99
    (map,c,1) N '86
COMBINES
  Nat Geog 161:804-5 (c,1) Je '82
  Smithsonian 15:47 (1) Ag '84
--Great Britain
  Natur Hist 94:48-9 (c,1) My '85
--Spain
  Natur Hist 94:74-5 (c,2) N '85
Comedians. See
    ENTERTAINERS
COMETS
--Depicted in art
  Smithsonian 16:160-5 (c,2) N '85
--See also
    HALLEY'S COMET
COMIC BOOKS
--1943 "Real Heroes"
  Smithsonian 14:156 (2) D '83
COMIC STRIPS
--"Cathy"
  Life 5:90-1 (c,1) S '82
--Comic strip characters in "Hands
    Across America" effort
  Life 9:57-60 (1) Je '86
--"Doonesbury"
  Life 6:156 (c,4) Ja '83
  Life 7:cov., 55-62 (c,1) O '84
--"For Better or For Worse"
  Life 5:92-3 (c,1) S '82
--"Krazy Kat"
  Am Heritage 33:72-7 (c,2) Ag '82
  Am Heritage 34:7 (4) D '82
--"Les Frustres," by Bretecher
  Life 5:94-5 (1) S '82
--"Mutt and Jeff" (1910)
  Life 8:35 (4) O '85
--"Peanuts"
  Sports Illus 63:110-23 (c,2) D

COMIC STRIPS (cont.)
  23 '85
--"Sylvia," by Hollander
  Life 5:96 (c,2) S '82
--See also
  CARTOONS
COMMENCEMENT
--Nanny school (Great Britain)
  Smithsonian 14:101 (c,2) Ja
  '84
COMMENCEMENT--COSTUME
--1968 college graduation (Mis-
  souri)
  Life 9:408 (2) Fall '86
--Arab college graduate (Israel)
  Nat Geog 168:28 (c,4) Jl '85
--College graduation
  Ebony 39:128 (3) Je '84
  Sports Illus 60:44-5, 50
  (c,1) Je 4 '84
  Ebony 40:37, 69 (4) Ag '85
  Ebony 40:141 (c,2) S '85
  Sports Illus 64:64-5 (c,3) Mr
  3 '86
--High school graduation cap
  Ebony 38:31 (4) F '83
--Jordan
  Nat Geog 165:237 (c,1) F '84
--UCLA (1969)
  Sports Illus 63:8-9, 82 (c,1)
  D 23 '85
COMMUNION
--Given to baseball player
  Life 5:104 (4) O '82
--Russian Orthodox (Alaska)
  Nat Geog 165:83 (c,4) Ja '84
COMMUTERS
--Bicyclists commuting to work
  (China)
  Life 8:156 (c,2) D '85
--Commuters on bus (Madrid,
  Spain)
  Nat Geog 169:148-9 (c,1) F '86
--Commuters on Staten Island
  Ferry, New York City
  Nat Geog 170:32-3 (c,1) Jl '86
--See also
  AUTOMOBILES--TRAFFIC
  MASS TRANSIT
  SUBWAYS
COMPASSES
--15th cent.
  Nat Geog 170:575 (c,4) N '86
--World War II U.S. Air Force
  compass
  Smithsonian 17:107 (c,4) Ap
  '86

Composers. See
  COPLAND, AARON
  GERSHWIN, IRA
  GILBERT, SIR WILLIAM
  IVES, CHARLES
  LISZT, FRANZ
  MENDELSSOHN, FELIX
  MOZART, WOLFGANG AMA-
  DEUS
  MUSICAL INSTRUMENTS
  MUSICIANS
  PORTER, COLE
  RACHMANINOFF, SERGEI
  SULLIVAN, SIR ARTHUR
  WAGNER, RICHARD
COMPUTER INDUSTRY
  Nat Geog 162:cov., 420-57 (c,1)
  O '82
--1950s 16K memory bank (Massa-
  chusetts)
  Nat Geog 162:438 (c,1) O '82
--Computer animation techniques
  Smithsonian 13:86-95 (c,1) Jl '82
--Computer tape room (Utah)
  Am Heritage 33:11 (c,4) Ag '82
COMPUTER TERMINALS
  Ebony 37:124 (3) Mr '82
  Life 5:32-3 (c,1) Mr '82
  Sports Illus 57:24 (c,4) S 6 '82
  Life 5:116-17 (1) O '82
  Life 6:76 (c,2) Ja '83
  Sports Illus 58:72 (c,4) Je 6 '83
  Smithsonian 14:47 (c,4) Jl '83
  Ebony 38:62 (2) Ag '83
  Ebony 38:123 (4) S '83
  Smithsonian 14:44-8 (3) F '84
  Life 7:99-102 (1) My '84
  Sports Illus 61:56 (c,4) Jl 30 '84
  Life 9:46 (c,4) N '86
--Aboard boat (Maine)
  Nat Geog 167:215 (c,3) F '85
--Child at terminal
  Smithsonian 17:34 (c,4) N '86
--Sitting at terminal
  Smithsonian 13:116 (painting,c,4)
  Ag '82
  Nat Geog 162:435 (c,3) O '82
  Ebony 39:59-60, 64 (c,4) My '84
  Ebony 41:98, 102 (4) My '86
  Smithsonian 17:50 (c,4) Ag '86
COMPUTERS
--Aboard boat
  Sports Illus 65:44 (c,3) N 10 '86
--Computer-generated fractal ab-
  stract patterns
  Smithsonian 14:cov., 110-17 (c,1)
  D '83

COMPUTERS (cont.)
--Disassembled NASA computer
  Nat Geog 162:436-7 (c,1) O '82
--Hand-held
  Life 5:38 (c,4) Mr '82
--In cars
  Nat Geog 162:452-3 (c,1) O
    '82
--Reading printout
  Sports Illus 59:20 (c,4) S 5
    '83
--Social Security Administration
    (Maryland)
  Life 8:140-1 (1) D '85
--Used in baseball
  Sports Illus 59:73 (c,3) N 28
    '83
--Used in coal mining (Kentucky)
  Nat Geog 163:808 (c,4) Je '83
--Used in sports
  Sports Illus 59:73+ (c,3) N
    28 '83
COMPUTERS--HUMOR
--Used in baseball
  Smithsonian 14:150-70 (draw-
    ing,c,1) O '83
CONCENTRATION CAMPS
--1940s inmate (France)
  Am Heritage 34:88 (4) Je '83
--1940s Zyklon gas cannister
  Am Heritage 35:94 (c,2) Ag '84
--1945 Buchenwald inmates and
    victims
  Life 8:80-1 (1) Spring '85
  Life 9:192 (4) Fall '86
--1945 death list from Mathausen
    camp
  Am Heritage 35:94 (c,2) Ag '84
--Aerial view of Auschwitz
  Smithsonian 14:153 (2) Mr '84
--Drawings by Theresienstadt
    children, Czechoslovakia
  Life 7:88-9 (c,4) N '84
--World War II camps for
    Japanese-Americans (U.S.)
  Nat Geog 169:520-7 (c,1) Ap
    '86
Concert halls. See
    THEATERS
CONCERTS
--Classical (Israel)
  Trav/Holiday 165:52 (c,2) Ja
    '86
--Classical (Maryland)
  Life 6:90 (4) Ap '83
--Classical performers taking bows
    (Washington, D.C.)

Nat Geog 163:86-7 (c,1) Ja '83
--Fundraising telethons
  Life 9:80-5 (c,1) Ja '86
--Gospel singers (Israel)
  Ebony 39:36-40 (c,2) D '83
--Harlem church choir, New York
  Ebony 37:152 (2) My '82
--"Live Aid" (Philadelphia and Lon-
    don)
  Life 8:cov., 39-45 (c,1) S '85
  Life 9:80-1 (c,1) Ja '86
--Rock concerts
  Life 7:87-96 (c,1) S '84
--"We are the World" recording
    session
  Life 8:36-48 (c,1) Ap '85
  Ebony 40:40 (4) O '85
  Ebony 41:350 (3) N '85
  Life 9:82-3 (c,1) Ja '86
--See also
    AUDIENCES
    BANDS
    CONDUCTORS, MUSIC
    MUSICIANS
CONCHES
  Smithsonian 12:119-25 (c,1) Mr
    '82
--Conch shells
  Nat Geog 170:587 (c,4) N '86
--Drying conch meat (Bahamas)
  Nat Geog 170:587 (c,4) N '86
CONDORS
  Nat Wildlife 20:cov. (c,1) Ap '82
  Smithsonian 14:72-81 (c,1) D '83
  Nat Wildlife 23:14, 31 (paint-
    ing,c,4) Ap '85
  Nat Wildlife 24:13 (c,1) Ap '86
--Ancient condor skull
  Natur Hist 95:12-13 (c,4) Ap '86
--Chick
  Life 6:58 (c,2) Je '83
  Nat Wildlife 21:28 (4) Ag '83
  Smithsonian 14:79-81 (c,1) D '83
CONDUCTORS, MUSIC
  Smithsonian 15:88-97 (1) S '84
--Marching band
  Ebony 40:25 (c,4) D '84
--Michigan
  Ebony 40:38 (3) S '85
--Oregon
  Ebony 40:36 (3) S '85
--Rehearsal (Philadelphia, Pennsyl-
    vania)
  Nat Geog 163:329 (c,4) Mr '83
--West Germany
  Life 5:106 (c,4) Jl '82
--See also
    TOSCANINI, ARTURO

CONEY ISLAND, BROOKLYN,
  NEW YORK
--1885 colossal wooden elephant
  Am Heritage 36:64 (4) D '84
--Beach
  Nat Geog 163:606-7 (c,1) My
    '83
--Boardwalk
  Sports Illus 64:70 (c,3) Mr 24
    '86
--Ferris wheel
  Smithsonian 14:108 (c,1) Jl '83
--Nathan's Restaurant
  Trav/Holiday 159:4 (c,4) Ap
    '83
  Sports Illus 64:70-1 (c,1) Mr
    24 '86
Conferences. See
  MEETINGS
  PRESS CONFERENCES
CONIES
  Nat Geog 169:581 (c,4) My '86
--Rock hyrax
  Sports Illus 62:79 (c,4) My 27
    '85
CONNECTICUT
--Bow Bridge, Old Lyme
  Smithsonian 12:108 (paint-
    ing,c,2) Ja '82
--William Gillette castle
  Smithsonian 17:66 (c,4) D
    '86
--Goodspeed Opera House, East
    Haddam
  Smithsonian 14:96-7 (c,2) Je
    '83
  Trav/Holiday 166:8 (c,4) Ag
    '86
--Northwestern area
  Trav/Holiday 160:12-13 (c,1)
    D '83
--See also
  HARTFORD
  NEW HAVEN
Conservation. See
  ENVIRONMENT
  SOIL
CONSTABLE, JOHN
  Smithsonian 14:56 (paint-
    ing,c,4) My '83
--19th cent. English landscape
    paintings
  Smithsonian 14:52-9 (c,1) My
    '83
CONSTANTINE THE GREAT
--Depicted on Roman coin
  Nat Geog 164:722 (c,4) D '83

--Sculpture (Rome, Italy)
  Trav/Holiday 164:46-7 (c,1) O
    '85
Constantinople. See
  BYZANTINE EMPIRE--HISTORY
  ISTANBUL
Constellations. See issues of
  Natural History
  NEBULAE
  STARS
CONSTITUTION (SHIP)
  Trav/Holiday 158:30 (c,2) Jl '82
  Am Heritage 34:cov., 65-7 (paint-
    ing,c,1) Ap '83
CONSTRUCTION
--Construction site (Washington,
    D.C.)
  Smithsonian 15:20 (c,4) Je '84
--Playground (Iowa)
  Smithsonian 16:110-13 (c,4) Ag
    '85
--Scaffolding around Statue of Lib-
    erty
  Am Heritage 35:97 (c,1) Je '84
  Smithsonian 15:51-3 (c,1) Jl '84
  Nat Geog 170:9 (c,2) Jl '86
--Scaffolding on crumbling cliffs
    (Italy)
  Smithsonian 14:184 (c,1) N '83
--See also
  Specific architectural struc-
    tures--CONSTRUCTION
  BARNS
  BOATS
  BRIDGES
  BUILDINGS
  CANALS
  HOUSES
  ROADS
  SHIP BUILDING
CONSTRUCTION EQUIPMENT
  Nat Geog 166:350-1 (c,1) S '84
--Backhoe
  Sports Illus 63:155 (c,2) S 4 '85
--Cranes
  Nat Geog 162:780-1 (c,1) D '82
  Smithsonian 16:44-53 (c,1) S '85
--Cranes (Great Britain)
  Smithsonian 13:82-3 (c,2) Ag '82
--Cutting rock with jackhammer
  Smithsonian 14:57, 60 (c,4) Ap
    '83
--Earth mover (Sudan)
  Nat Geog 161:352-3 (c,1) Mr '82
--Jackhammer
  Sports Illus 59:2 (c,3) O 31 '83
--See also
  BULLDOZERS

CONSTRUCTION WORKERS
--China
    Nat Geog 164:64 (c,4) Jl '83
--India
    Nat Geog 167:528-9 (c,1) Ap
        '85
--Repairing cathedral spire
        (France)
    Nat Geog 161:504-5 (c,1) Ap
        '82
Containers. See
    BOTTLES
    BOXES
    CANS
    PACKAGING
CONTESTS
--1938 marathon dance contest
    Life 9:65 (2) Ag '86
--1949 Pillsbury Bake-off finalists
    Life 9:112 (2) Fall '86
--1950 Howdy Doody look-alike
        contest
    Life 9:205-6 (2) Fall '86
--Annual frisbee contest (Wash-
        ington, D.C.)
    Am Heritage 37:22-3 (c,1) Ap
        '86
--Judging mules (Missouri)
    Smithsonian 14:98 (c,1) N '83
--Marbles tournament (New Jersey)
    Sports Illus 63:52-3 (c,3) Jl 8
        '85
--"Miss Dumpy" (Maine)
    Nat Geog 163:448-9 (c,1) Ap
        '83
--Spear throwing (Tahiti)
    Sports Illus 64:138-9 (c,2) F
        10 '86
--Tug-of-war (Tibet)
    Nat Geog 165:311 (c,4) Mr '84
--World Frisbee Championships
        (California)
    Sports Illus 63:100 (c,4) O 21
        '85
--See also
    BEAUTY CONTESTS
    FISHING COMPETITIONS
    RACES
    SPORTS
CONVICTS
--17th cent. "Man in the Iron
        Mask" (France)
    Smithsonian 14:64 (drawing,4)
        Ag '83
--Cambodian political prisoners
    Nat Geog 161:600-1 (4) My
        '82

--In cells
    Ebony 38:44 (3) Ag '83
--In cells (Florida)
    Ebony 38:29 (4) S '83
--Juvenile detention center (China)
    Nat Geog 168:300 (c,4) S '85
--Man behind bars (Michigan)
    Life 5:42 (c,2) Ag '82
--Studying for ministry (New York)
    Ebony 38:154-8 (1) Ap '83
--Texas
    Life 5:36-44 (1) O '82
COOK, JAMES
    Smithsonian 13:79 (painting,c,4)
        Mr '83
--Death in Hawaii (1790)
    Nat Geog 164:568-9 (c,1) N '83
COOKING
    Sports Illus 59:36 (c,4) D 26 '83
    Ebony 39:86 (3) S '84
--19th cent. pioneers
    Am Heritage 33:24 (painting,c,4)
        Je '82
--Baking cookies
    Sports Illus 60:96 (c,4) F 13 '84
--Baking rolls in outdoor stone oven
        (Caribbean islands)
    Trav/Holiday 164:34 (c,4) N '85
--Barbecue
    Sports Illus 61:70 (c,3) S 17 '84
    Sports Illus 63:36 (c,2) Ag 5 '85
--Barbecue (Leeward Islands)
    Trav/Holiday 162:45 (c,4) O '84
--Chinese stir-frying
    Ebony 39:108 (c,4) Je '84
--Chopping vegetables
    Sports Illus 59:51 (c,4) Jl 18 '83
--Civil War army camp
    Am Heritage 33:72-3 (3) F '82
--Cookies
    Sports Illus 62:40 (c,4) Mr 11
        '85
--Cow (Sudan)
    Life 5:158-9 (c,1) D '82
--Eggs (Colorado)
    Life 6:78 (c,4) Ag '83
--Fast food chicken restaurant
    Ebony 38:84 (4) My '83
--Fish
    Ebony 38:102 (c,4) Ap '83
--Fish (Peru)
    Natur Hist 91:36-7 (c,4) Ja '82
--Fish barbecue (Alaska)
    Trav/Holiday 163:53 (c,4) F '85
--Frying eggs outdoors (Arizona)
    Trav/Holiday 166:18 (c,4) Jl '86
--Grain (Ethiopia)

COOKING (cont.)
  Natur Hist 94:30-1 (1) S '85
--Grinding cornmeal (Rhode Island)
  Natur Hist 92:96 (3) D '83
--Grinding sorghum into flour (Sudan)
  Nat Geog 161:346-7 (c,1) Mr '82
--In Arctic expedition tent
  Nat Geog 170:300, 323 (c,4) S '86
--Japanese food cooked at table
  Trav/Holiday 166:61 (c,4) S '86
--Lamb (Pennsylvania)
  Nat Geog 163:334-5 (c,1) Mr '83
--Maori tribal feast (New Zealand)
  Nat Geog 166:534 (c,3) O '84
--Matzoh brei (California)
  Life 9:150 (c,4) My '86
--Omelet
  Sports Illus 57:46 (c,2) D 13 '82
  Sports Illus 58:4 (4) Je 6 '83
--Over campfire (Yukon)
  Nat Wildlife 22:54-5 (c,2) D '83
--Pizza
  Sports Illus 57:57 (c,4) O 11 '82
--Planked salmon (Washington)
  Nat Geog 165:665 (c,4) My '84
--Porridge (Kenya)
  Nat Geog 161:130 (c,4) Ja '82
--Potatoes on outdoor fire (Wisconsin)
  Trav/Holiday 159:59 (c,4) My '83
--Pounding breadfruit (Micronesia)
  Natur Hist 94:38-9 (c,1) Mr '85
--Preparing barbecue (Kansas)
  Sports Illus 59:108 (c,4) S 1 '83
--Preparing meat for barbecue (Texas)
  Trav/Holiday 159:66 (c,4) Mr '83
--Restaurant (China)
  Nat Geog 168:310-11 (c,1) S '85
--Restaurant (Maryland)
  Trav/Holiday 163:6 (c,2) Je '85

--Restaurant (Pennsylvania)
  Trav/Holiday 159:39 (c,3) Ja '83
--Roasting corn outdoors (Maine)
  Trav/Holiday 157:63 (c,4) Ap '82
--Stuffing goat (Greece)
  Nat Geog 164:776 (c,4) D '83
--Tasting from pot on stove
  Ebony 40:98 (4) Mr '85
  Sports Illus 63:37 (c,4) Ag 5 '85
--Teriyaki (California)
  Nat Geog 169:513 (c,1) Ap '86
--Throwing pizza (Italy)
  Trav/Holiday 164:49 (c,4) O '85
--Throwing pizza at restaurant (Pennsylvania)
  Life 9:34-5 (c,1) Mr '86
--Tortillas (Mexico)
  Natur Hist 92:78 (c,4) Je '83
  Nat Geog 166:434 (c,4) O '84
  Nat Geog 167:726-7 (c,1) Je '85
--Working at stove
  Sports Illus 60:48 (c,4) Mr 19 '84
  Sports Illus 61:459 (c,3) Jl 18 '84
  Ebony 41:33 (c,4) Ap '86
--See also
    BREAD MAKING
    CHEFS
    DINNERS AND DINING
    FOOD PROCESSING
    RESTAURANTS
COOKING--EDUCATION
--Cooking class (Illinois)
  Ebony 38:102 (4) Mr '83
--Cooking school (Hyde Park, New York)
  Smithsonian 14:120-31 (c,1) D '83
COOKING UTENSILS
--Italian copper pans
  Natur Hist 92:63 (c,1) Ja '83
COOLIDGE, CALVIN
--Depicted on postage stamp
  Am Heritage 34:54 (c,4) D '82
COOPER, JAMES FENIMORE
  Smithsonian 14:102 (painting,c,3) Ag '83
COOPERSTOWN, NEW YORK
--Baseball Hall of Fame
  Trav/Holiday 166:28 (c,4) Ag '86
--Christmas street decorations
  Nat Geog 167:358 (c,4) Mr '85
--Museum displays
  Smithsonian 15:122-31 (c,2) Ap '84

COSMETICS (cont.)
--Cosmetologist
   Ebony 37:77 (3) Ap '82
--Facial
   Ebony 40:126 (c,4) Ja '85
--Geisha applying make-up
   (Japan)
   Natur Hist 92:46-8 (c,1) F '83
--Manicure
   Ebony 40:128 (c,4) Ja '85
--Pedicure
   Ebony 40:130 (c,4) Ja '85
--Polishing toenails
   Life 5:88 (c,2) My '82
--Pollen-mask facial (New York)
   Nat Geog 166:521 (c,1) O '84
--See also
     PERFUME
     THEATER--COSTUME
COSTA RICA
--Dry forest
   Smithsonian 17:112, 119 (c,1)
     D '86
--Montverde cloud forest
   Natur Hist 94:44-5 (c,3) F '85
--Rain forests
   Life 5:44-50 (map,c,1) S '82
   Nat Geog 163:48-65 (c,1) Ja
     '83
--Río Sixaola
   Nat Geog 169:475 (c,1) Ap '86
--Wildlife in national parks
   Nat Geog 163:48-65 (c,1) Ja
     '83
--See also
     SAN JOSE
Costume. See
     CHILDREN--COSTUME
     CLOTHING
     MASKS, CEREMONIAL
     MASQUERADE COSTUME
     MILITARY COSTUME
     U.S.--COSTUME
     individual countries--
       COSTUME
     specific religions--
       COSTUME
     list under OCCUPATIONS
     list under PEOPLE
COTTAGES
--Thatched (France)
   Natur Hist 91:44-5 (c,1) Ag
     '82
COTTON INDUSTRY--HARVESTING
--Arizona
   Smithsonian 13:49 (c,4) F '83
--Bales on field (Australia)

   Nat Geog 169:20-1 (c,2) Ja '86
--China
   Life 8:154 (c,3) D '85
COTTON INDUSTRY--TRANSPORTA-
   TION
--Trucking cotton (Paraguay)
   Nat Geog 162:264-9 (c,1) Ag '82
COTTONWOOD TREES
   Nat Geog 162:70 (c,1) Jl '82
   Nat Wildlife 21:42-3, 58-9 (c,1)
     O '83
   Nat Geog 165:68-9 (c,1) Ja '84
   Nat Wildlife 23:4-5 (c,1) D '84
   Natur Hist 94:36 (c,4) Ja '85
   Nat Wildlife 23:16 (c,1) Ap '85
   Natur Hist 94:66-7 (c,1) O '85
Cougars. See
     MOUNTAIN LIONS
Counseling. See
     THERAPY
COUPONS
--Coupon redemption center (Mexico)
   Nat Geog 167:733 (c,1) Je '85
COURTHOUSES
--Jefferson County, Washington
   Trav/Holiday 159:22 (drawing,4)
     Ja '83
--Monroe, Wisconsin
   Trav/Holiday 164:63 (c,4) O '85
--Vermont
   Life 5:36 (c,4) Jl '82
--See also
     SUPREME COURT BUILDING
COURTROOMS
--1873 (Rochester, New York)
   Am Heritage 37:29 (painting,2)
     D '85
--Conference with judge (1946 litho-
     graph)
   Am Heritage 33:85 (3) Je '82
--Florida
   Life 6:154 (c,3) N '83
--Local court (Ethiopia)
   Nat Geog 163:628-9 (c,1) My '83
--Newport, Rhode Island
   Life 6:124-5 (c,1) Ja '83
--San Francisco, California
   Life 5:100 (2) Ag '82
--See also
     JUSTICE, ADMINISTRATION OF
COVERED WAGONS
--Mid-19th cent.
   Nat Geog 170:cov., 146-61 (c,1)
     Ag '86
--1890 (New Mexico)
   Am Heritage 37:90-1 (1) D '85
--Wagon train (Teton National Forest,

CRANES (cont.)
--Sandhill
   Nat Wildlife 20:7 (c,2) Ap '82
   Natur Hist 93:68-75 (c,1) Ja
      '84
   Sports Illus 60:16 (drawing,c,4)
      My 28 '84
   Nat Wildlife 23:50-1 (c,1) O '85
   Nat Wildlife 24:48-50 (c,2) F
      '86
   Smithsonian 17:30 (c,4) Je '86
--Sandhill crane chick and eggs
   Life 9:17-18 (c,4) Jl '86
--Sandhill flock
   Nat Geog 162:86-7 (c,1) Jl '82
--Sandhill incubating eggs
   Smithsonian 14:28 (c,4) Jl '83
--See also
   WHOOPING CRANES
Cranes, construction. See
   CONSTRUCTION EQUIP-
      MENT
CRASHES
--1920s crashed air mail planes
   Smithsonian 13:88-9 (4) My
      '82
--1940s Navy blimp (California)
   Life 5:84 (3) Jl '82
--1955 tragic racing car accident
   (Le Mans, France)
   Sports Illus 64:80-96 (paint-
      ing,c,1) My 12 '86
--1956 auto collision
   Am Heritage 35:32 (paint-
      ing,c,4) F '84
--1982 rescue of Washington,
   D.C. plane crash survivors
   Life 6:109-12 (c,1) Ja '83
--Airplane on fire (Spain)
   Life 5:174-5 (c,1) N '82
--Airplane wreckage on mountain-
   side (Japan)
   Life 8:82-3 (1) O '85
--Artifacts from shot-down
   Korean airplane
   Life 7:99-108 (c,1) Ja '84
--Auto race crash
   Sports Illus 58:21 (c,4) F 28
      '83
   Sports Illus 60:68 (c,4) F 8
      '84
   Sports Illus 60:52-3 (c,4) F
      27 '84
   Life 8:86-7 (1) Ap '85
   Sports Illus 62:31 (c,3) My
      20 '85
   Sports Illus 63:14-15 (c,3)

      S 9 '85
   Sports Illus 64:90-2 (c,2) F 10
      '86
   Sports Illus 64:12-13 (c,1) F 24
      '86
--Automobile crash tests
   Nat Geog 164:26-7 (c,1) Jl '83
--B-52 bomber (California)
   Life 6:98-9 (c,1) F '83
--Bus accident (Texas)
   Life 8:58 (2) S '85
--Fiery crash at auto race
   Sports Illus 56:61 (c,4) My 24
      '82
--Hydroplane accident (Washington)
   Sports Illus 57:22-3 (c,3) Ag 9
      '82
--Mid-air plane collision (France)
   Life 6:173 (c,2) D '83
--Remains of allied World War II
   planes (Netherlands)
   Smithsonian 17:106-15 (c,1) Ap
      '86
--Rescue of plane crash victim
   (Japan)
   Life 9:142 (2) Ja '86
--Small plane crashed on highway
   (Rhode Island)
   Life 8:100-1 (1) N '85
--Stunt plane crash (New York)
   Life 8:68-9 (1) S '85
--Tractor-trailer hitting wall (New
   Mexico)
   Smithsonian 16:136-7 (c,4) My
      '85
--Train carrying toxic chemicals
   (Louisiana)
   Life 5:180-1 (c,1) D '82
--Wreckage of airplane (Bahamas)
   Nat Geog 162:372-3 (c,2) S '82
--Wreckage of airplane (Dallas,
   Texas)
   Smithsonian 17:79 (c,2) Je '86
--Wreckage of airplane (Florida)
   Nat Geog 162:190 (c,1) Ag '82
--Wreckage of airplane (Washington,
   D.C.)
   Life 5:108-9 (c,1) Mr '82
--See also
   ACCIDENTS
   DISASTERS
   SHIPWRECKS
CRATERS OF THE MOON NATIONAL
   MONUMENT, IDAHO
--Triple Twist Tree
   Trav/Holiday 158:4 (3) Jl '82

CRAYFISH
  Smithsonian 13:77 (c,4) N '82
  Natur Hist 94:32-7 (c,1) Ag
    '85
--Breaux Bridge Crawfish Festi-
    val, Louisiana
  Natur Hist 93:46-57 (c,1) Ap
    '84
--Spiny crayfish
  Nat Geog 165:142 (c,4) Ja '84
CRAZY HORSE (SIOUX INDIAN)
--Sculpture (South Dakota)
  Trav/Holiday 162:43 (c,3) Jl
    '84
CREDIT CARDS
  Smithsonian 17:43 (c,2) Jl '86
CREEKS
--Alaska
  Nat Wildlife 22:10 (c,4) Je '84
--Arizona
  Nat Wildlife 22:7 (c,4) F '84
--Washington
  Trav/Holiday 159:43 (c,1) My
    '83
CRETE
--Sites from the voyage of
    Ulysses
  Nat Geog 170:210-15 (c,1) Ag
    '86
Cribs. See
  BABY CRIBS
CRICK, FRANCIS
  Smithsonian 16:116 (4) Jl '85
CRICKET PLAYING
--Bermuda
  Ebony 38:122 (c,4) Ja '83
--Children (Australia)
  Nat Geog 169:754-5 (c,2) Je
    '86
--Great Britain
  Sports Illus 65:76-8, 84-7 (c,1)
    O 27 '86
CRICKETS
  Smithsonian 13:78 (c,4) N '82
  Nat Geog 164:376 (c,4) S '83
  Smithsonian 14:141 (paint-
    ing,c,4) Mr '84
CRIME AND CRIMINALS
--19th cent. Ned Kelly (Australia)
  Smithsonian 14:40-9 (c,1) Je
    '83
--1834 destruction of convent
    (Massachusetts)
  Am Heritage 33:100-5 (c,1) F
    '82
--Late 19th cent. counterfeit $50
    note

  Am Heritage 35:100-1 (2) Ag '84
--1876 plot to steal Lincoln's body
  Am Heritage 33:76-83 (1) Ap '82
--1914 Franz Ferdinand assassination
    site (Sarajevo)
  Sports Illus 56:50 (c,3) Mr 22
    '82
--1920s anti-lynching poster
  Ebony 39:51 (4) Jl '84
--1932 Lindbergh baby kidnaping
    case
  Life 5:40-4, 52 (c,1) Mr '82
--1935 assassination of Huey Long
    (Louisiana)
  Am Heritage 36:63 (painting,c,4)
    O '85
--1963 assassination of John F.
    Kennedy
  Life 6:cov., 48-71 (c,1) N '83
  Life 9:340-1 (c,1) Fall '86
--1965 assassination of Malcolm X
  Ebony 41:304 (4) N '85
--1968 assassination of Robert Ken-
    nedy
  Life 9:255 (3) Fall '86
--1968 assassination of Martin Luther
    King, Jr.
  Ebony 41:316 (3) N '86
  Life 9:342-3 (1) Fall '86
--1972 George Wallace assassination
    attempt
  Ebony 38:44 (4) S '83
--1981 assassination of Anwar Sadat
    (Egypt)
  Ebony 37:33 (4) Ja '82
  Life 5:14-16 (c,2) Ja '82
--1981 Pope assassination attempt
  Life 5:12-13 (c,4) Ja '82
--1981 Reagan assassination attempt
  Ebony 37:32 (4) Ja '82
  Life 5:8-11 (c,1) Ja '82
--1984 McDonald's massacre victims
    (San Ysidro, California)
  Life 8:76-86 (c,1) Ja '85
--Art forgeries
  Smithsonian 16:60-9 (c,1) O '85
--Butch Cassidy and Sundance Kid
  Am Heritage 37:56 (2) F '86
--Cattle rustling (Wyoming)
  Life 6:84-90 (c,1) D '83
--Child molesters
  Life 7:47-52 (1) D '84
--Counterfeit Cabbage Patch dolls
  Life 7:44-8 (c,1) S '84
  Life 9:49 (c,2) Ja '86
--Crime victims
  Life 7:32-42 (1) Ap '84

CRIME AND CRIMINALS (cont.)
--Disguise paraphernalia
    Life 6:94 (c,3) Jl '83
--Fighting counterfeit goods
    Smithsonian 17:34-43 (c,1) Jl
        '86
--Handcuffed prisoners
    Life 5:33 (c,4) Jl '82
    Sports Illus 61:82 (c,4) O 15
        '84
--Hauling 1935 gangland victim
        from river (New York)
    Sports Illus 64:40 (4) Je 30
        '86
--History of the Mafia (Italy)
    Life 8:cov., 28-38 (c,1) Mr
        '85
--Knife used on William H. Seward
        (1865)
    Am Heritage 34:6 (2) Ap '83
--Man robbing bank (Idaho)
    Life 6:94 (4) Jl '83
--McKinley's assassin Leon
        Czolgosz
    Am Heritage 38:26 (4) D '86
--Murder mystery game weekends
        (New Jersey)
    Life 7:109-14 (c,1) N '84
--Murder of a South African black
    Life 8:48-9 (1) S '85
--Murdered man (Utah)
    Life 8:115 (c,4) Je '85
--Bonnie Parker and Clyde Barrow
    Am Heritage 35:13 (4) Ap '84
--Police activities against drug
        smugglers (Florida)
    Life 8:58-64 (c,1) D '85
--Safecrackers depicted in movies
    Smithsonian 15:39 (4) Jl '84
--Serial murderers
    Life 7:58-74 (c,1) Ag '84
--Site of spy rendezvous (Mary-
        land)
    Life 9:10-11 (c,4) Ja '86
--Smuggling cigarettes from boat
        (Italy)
    Nat Geog 165:196-7 (c,1) F
        '84
--Smuggling parrots through
        U.S. Customs
    Smithsonian 16:58-67 (c,1) Ap
        '85
--Stealing from U.S. military
        bases (Philippines)
    Life 9:50-1 (c,1) Je '86
--Students acting out robbery
        scene (New Jersey)

    Smithsonian 12:70-1 (c,3) Ja '82
--Youth gang violence (Los Ange-
        les, California)
    Life 5:54-8 (c,1) My '82
--See also
        BOOTH, JOHN WILKES
        CAPITAL PUNISHMENT
        CAPONE, AL
        CONVICTS
        DEATH
        DETECTIVES
        DILLINGER, JOHN
        DRUG ABUSE
        JUSTICE, ADMINISTRATION
            OF
        LYNCHINGS
        POLICE WORK
        PROSTITUTION
        PRISONS
        PUNISHMENT
        SACCO AND VANZETTI
        SPIES
        TERRORISM
Crinoids. See
        SEA LILIES
CROCKETT, DAVEY
    Smithsonian 16:58-9, 67 (paint-
        ing,c,1) Mr '86
CROCODILES
    Smithsonian 13:137 (c,4) Jl '82
    Smithsonian 15:36 (c,4) My '84
    Nat Wildlife 23:15 (painting,c,4)
        Ap '85
    Nat Wildlife 23:13-15 (c,1) Je '85
--1586 drawing
    Am Heritage 36:86-7 (c,1) Ag '85
CROCUSES
    Nat Geog 163:397 (c,4) Mr '83
    Life 8:57 (c,4) Je '85
    Natur Hist 95:82 (c,4) S '86
CROP DUSTER PLANES
    Nat Geog 162:216 (c,1) Ag '82
    Nat Wildlife 24:28 (c,4) Ap '86
--Panama
    Nat Geog 169:475 (c,1) Ap '86
--Using ultralight plane for spray-
        ing
    Nat Geog 164:213 (c,3) Ag '83
CROQUET PLAYING
    Sports Illus 58:126 (drawing,c,4)
        Ap 4 '83
    Life 7:53-6 (c,1) Je '84
    Nat Geog 166:cov. (c,1) O '84
--Scotland
    Life 7:14 (3) Mr '84
CROSS COUNTRY
    Sports Illus 57:82, 86 (c,4) D

CROSS COUNTRY (cont.)
   6 '82
   Sports Illus 59:62-3 (c,3) D
     5 '83
   Sports Illus 62:26-7 (c,2) Mr
     11 '85
--Massachusetts
   Sports Illus 61:2-3, 53-4 (c,1)
     D 3 '84
--North Carolina
   Sports Illus 63:32-7 (c,2) D
     9 '85
--Texas
   Sports Illus 64:51 (c,3) Mr 17
     '86
--Training
   Sports Illus 64:34-5 (c,2) Je
     23 '86
--Training on sand dunes
   Sports Illus 59:58-9 (c,1) D
     26 '83
   Sports Illus 64:45 (c,2) Mr
     17 '86
--World Championships 1984 (New
    Jersey)
   Sports Illus 60:80, 83 (c,4) Ap
     2 '84
--World Cross Country Meet
    (Great Britain)
   Sports Illus 58:30-1 (c,2) Mr
     28 '83
Cross-country skiing. See
    SKIING--CROSS-COUNTRY
CROW INDIANS (MONTANA)--
    COSTUME
--1830s
   Sports Illus 58:68 (paint-
     ing,c,3) Ja 17 '83
CROWDS
--1780s mob of witch hunters
    (Philadelphia, Pa.)
   Am Heritage 34:6-11 (draw-
     ing,3) Ag '83
--1969 Woodstock concert, New
    York
   Life 9:344-5 (c,1) Fall '86
--Bicyclists commuting to work
    (China)
   Life 8:156 (c,2) D '85
--Buenos Aires street scene,
    Argentina
   Nat Geog 170:240-1 (c,1) Ag
     '86
--Commuters on bus (Madrid,
    Spain)
   Nat Geog 169:148-9 (c,1) F '86
--Commuters on Staten Island

    Ferry, New York City
   Nat Geog 170:32-3 (c,1) Jl '86
--Crowded street (New Delhi, India)
   Nat Geog 167:506-7 (c,1) Ap '85
--During papal visit (Guatemala)
   Life 7:14-15 (c,1) Ja '84
--Fasching Festival (West Germany)
   Trav/Holiday 161:77 (c,2) F '84
--Rimini beach, Italy
   Nat Geog 162:728-9 (c,1) D '82
--Viennese crowds watching Germans
    approaching (1938)
   Am Heritage 35:71 (2) Je '84
--See also
    AUDIENCES
    AUTOMOBILES--TRAFFIC
    SPECTATORS
    URBAN SCENES
CROWNS
--1806 queen (Bavaria)
   Nat Geog 168:210 (c,4) Ag '85
--Campus beauty queens
   Ebony 38:cov., 40-50 (c,2) My
     '83
   Ebony 39:118-24 (c,4) Ap '84
   Ebony 40:36-45 (c,3) Ap '85
   Ebony 41:132-43 (c,3) Ap '86
--European royalty
   Smithsonian 14:130-5 (c,1) O '83
--"Miss America"
   Life 7:136 (c,2) Ja '84
--Monaco
   Life 9:cov. (c,1) Ap '86
--St. Stephen (Hungary)
   Nat Geog 163:225 (c,4) F '83
CROWS
   Nat Geog 163:366-7 (c,2) Mr '83
   Nat Geog 169:50 (c,4) Ja '86
--Pet crow
   Smithsonian 13:118-32 (paint-
     ing,c,1) S '82
--See also
    NUTCRACKERS
CRUCIFIXES
--Apostolic Cross (Hungary)
   Smithsonian 14:140 (c,4) O '83
--Brandished by insane man (New
    York)
   Life 8:39 (2) F '85
--Cross carried by Christian pilgrim
    (Israel)
   Nat Geog 168:8 (c,3) Jl '85
--Coptic cross made of appliance
    parts (Egypt)
   Nat Geog 163:442 (c,4) Ap '83
--Cross shapes formed by everyday
    items

CRUCIFIXES (cont.)
Life 7:8-14 (c,2) Ap '84
--Mobile cross (Florida beach)
Nat Geog 162:203 (c,4) Ag '82
CRUISE SHIPS
Trav/Holiday 157:61 (c,3) Mr
'82
Trav/Holiday 160:59-72 (c,2)
O '83
Trav/Holiday 161:53 (3) Ja '84
Sports Illus 61:28-9 (c,2) D 10
'84
Life 8:149-56 (c,1) Ap '85
Trav/Holiday 165:56 (c,3) Ja
'86
Nat Geog 170:26-7 (c,1) Jl '86
--Late 19th cent.
Am Heritage 34:5 (painting,c,3)
Ag '83
--Construction
Trav/Holiday 162:48-51 (c,2) S
'84
--Egypt
Nat Geog 167:582-3 (c,1) My
'85
--Hong Kong
Trav/Holiday 160:14 (c,4) Jl
'83
--"Normandie"
Am Heritage 35:60-9, 114 (c,1)
D '83
Am Heritage 35:10 (2) Je '84
--Passengers on deck (Greece)
Trav/Holiday 160:58-9 (c,4) Ag
'83
--Shipboard activities
Trav/Holiday 162:56-77 (c,2)
O '84
Trav/Holiday 164:69-96 (c,1)
O '85
CRUSADERS
--Kolossi Castle, Limassol, Cyprus
Trav/Holiday 157:72 (c,4) Mr
'82
CRUSTACEANS
--Amphipods
Nat Geog 169:506-7 (c,1) Ap
'86
--Isopods
Smithsonian 15:125 (c,4) Mr
'85
--Krill
Nat Geog 165:626-43 (c,1) My
'84
Smithsonian 15:54-5 (c,3) N '84
--See also
BARNACLES

CRABS
CRAYFISH
LOBSTERS
SHRIMPS
CRYING
Smithsonian 15:102-14 (c,2) Je
'84
--Boxer after defeat
Sports Illus 62:70 (c,4) Ja 28
'85
CRYSTALS
--75 pound crystal
Natur Hist 95:92-3 (c,4) F '86
CUBA--COSTUME
--Anti-Castro guerrillas (Florida)
Nat Geog 162:196 (c,1) Ag '82
CUBA--HISTORY
--1962 Soviet missile site
Smithsonian 14:157 (4) Mr '84
--See also
CASTRO, FIDEL
CUBA--SOCIAL LIFE AND CUSTOMS
--Pinata (Florida)
Nat Geog 162:184 (c,4) Ag '82
CUCUMBERS
--Wild cucumber plants
Smithsonian 13:136 (c,4) O '82
CUERNAVACA, MEXICO
Trav/Holiday 157:57-8 (c,3) F
'82
CUMBERLAND MOUNTAINS, SOUTH-
EAST
Natur Hist 93:28 (c,3) S '84
CUMBERLAND RIVER, KENTUCKY
--Pineville
Sports Illus 61:96 (painting,c,3)
N 19 '84
CUMMINGS, EDWARD ESTLIN
--Manuscript by him
Smithsonian 14:145 (4) N '83
CURASSOWS (BIRDS)
Nat Geog 168:347 (drawing,4) S
'85
CURRENCY
--Late 19th cent. counterfeit $50
note
Am Heritage 35:100-1 (2) Ag '84
--Argentina
Nat Geog 170:232 (c,4) Ag '86
--U.S. dollar bills
Ebony 37:26-7 (1) Ja '82
Am Heritage 33:73 (4) Je '82
Sports Illus 58:61 (c,4) Ja 24 '83
--Watermarking paper for bank notes
(Great Britain)
Smithsonian 17:41 (c,4) Jl '86
--See also
COINS

CURRIER AND IVES
--Lithograph of George Washing-
    ton (1848)
    Am Heritage 35:14 (4) D '83
--Print of scene from "H.M.S.
    Pinafore"
    Smithsonian 14:112 (c,4) Mr
    '84
--"Sperm Whale in a Flurry"
    Natur Hist 95:2 (painting,4)
    Ag '86
CURTISS, GLENN
    Smithsonian 14:55 (4) Jl '83
    Am Heritage 36:107 (4) Je '85
CUSTER, GEORGE ARMSTRONG
    Smithsonian 15:184 (drawing,4)
    O '84
    Life 8:115, 122 (c,2) Mr '85
    Am Heritage 36:14 (drawing,4)
    Ap '85
    Nat Geog 170:787, 797 (4) D
    '86
--Battle of Little Big Horn (1876)
    Life 8:115-24 (c,1) Mr '85
    Natur Hist 95:cov., 46-55
    (map,c,1) Je '86
    Nat Geog 170:786-813 (c,1) D
    '86
--Reenactment of Custer at Fort
    Lincoln, North Dakota
    Trav/Holiday 164:56 (c,4) Jl '85
CUTLERY
--16th cent. (Great Britain)
    Smithsonian 15:77 (c,4) Ag '84
CUZCO, PERU
    Trav/Holiday 166:51-3 (c,3) N
    '86
CYCLONES
--Polynesia
    Nat Geog 165:144-5 (c,1) F '84
CYPRESS TREES
    Natur Hist 93:52 (c,4) N '84
CYPRUS
    Trav/Holiday 157:71-3 (c,1) Mr
    '82
CZECHOSLOVAKIA
--Karlstejn Castle
    Trav/Holiday 158:42 (2) Jl '82
--See also
    PRAGUE

-D-

DACHSHUNDS
    Smithsonian 15:115 (3) S '84
    Life 7:115 (c,2) D '84

DADDY LONGLEGS
    Smithsonian 13:83 (c,1) N '82
DA GAMA, VASCO
    Smithsonian 14:136 (drawing,c,4)
    F '84
DAGGERS
--Bedouin dagger (Saudi Arabia)
    Smithsonian 14:148 (c,4) Ap '83
--Ottoman empire (Turkey)
    Smithsonian 16:119 (c,4) F '86
DAIRYING
--Milking cow (1920s)
    Am Heritage 34:69 (3) Ag '83
--Milking cows (Minnesota)
    Sports Illus 63:85 (c,2) N 4 '85
--Milking goat (California)
    Natur Hist 92:86 (c,4) Ja '83
--See also
    CATTLE
    CHEESE INDUSTRY
    FARMING
    MILK INDUSTRY
DAISIES
    Nat Wildlife 24:56-7 (c,1) D '85
DAKAR, SENEGAL
    Nat Geog 168:228-9 (c,1) Ag '85
--Bathing fountain
    Ebony 37:50 (4) Jl '82
--Outdoor market
    Trav/Holiday 161:18 (c,4) Ap '84
DALI, SALVADOR
    Smithsonian 16:108 (painting,c,4)
    Je '85
    Smithsonian 17:62-70 (c,1) O '86
--"The Persistence of Memory"
    (1931)
    Smithsonian 17:68 (painting,c,3)
    O '86
--Self-portrait (1920s)
    Smithsonian 17:63 (painting,c,4)
    O '86
--Works by him
    Smithsonian 17:63-71 (c,3) O '86
DALLAS, TEXAS
    Ebony 38:52-8 (c,1) Ja '83
    Nat Geog 166:272-305 (map,c,1)
    S '84
    Trav/Holiday 166:40-3 (c,1) Jl
    '86
--Dallas Museum of Art
    Smithsonian 15:58-69 (c,1) My '84
--Galleria shopping center
    Nat Geog 166:294-5 (c,1) S '84
    Trav/Holiday 166:43 (c,4) Jl '86
    Ebony 42:54 (c,2) D '86
--Site of 1963 assassination of John
    F. Kennedy

DALLAS, TEXAS (cont.)
    Life 6:cov., 48-71 (c,1) N '83
DAMS
--Amazon River, Brazil
    Natur Hist 92:60-3 (map,c,1)
        Jl '83
--Angara River, Siberia, U.S.S.R.
    Trav/Holiday 165:54 (c,4) My
        '86
--Beaver dams
    Smithsonian 15:165, 170 (c,4)
        N '84
--Glen Canyon, Arizona
    Natur Hist 91:80-1 (c,1) Ja '82
    Nat Wildlife 23:44-5 (c,1) O
        '85
--Itaipú, Paraguay
    Nat Geog 162:246-7 (c,1) Ag
        '82
--Mississippi and Atchafalaya
        Rivers, Louisiana
    Natur Hist 94:64-5 (c,2) Je '85
--Quebec
    Nat Geog 161:407-13 (c,1) Mr
        '82
--Small dams
    Nat Wildlife 21:18-20 (c,1) O
        '83
--Storm-surge barrier across
        Oosterschelde, Netherlands
    Smithsonian 15:94-101 (c,1)
        Ag '84
--Summersville, West Virginia
    Life 5:78-9 (c,1) N '82
--Thames Barrier, England
    Nat Geog 163:788-91 (c,1) Je
        '83
--See also
    GRAND COULEE DAM
    HOOVER DAM
    LEVEES
Damselflies. See
    DRAGONFLIES
DANCERS
--19th cent. (Java, Indonesia)
    Smithsonian 13:138 (paint-
        ing,c,4) Ap '82
--Early 20th cent. "Florodora
        girls"
    Smithsonian 15:168 (4) D '84
--Cabaret (Hungary)
    Nat Geog 163:238 (c,2) F '83
--Chorus girls
    Sports Illus 56:142 (c,3) F 10
        '82
--Chorus girls (Nevada)
    Ebony 40:150, 154 (c,2) My '85

--Fan dancer Sally Rand
    Am Heritage 34:9 (3) Ap '83
--Hula dancer
    Trav/Holiday 157:26 (4) Ap '82
    Trav/Holiday 164:32 (c,4) O '85
--India
    Trav/Holiday 157:51 (c,4) Mr
        '82
--Nicholas Brothers
    Ebony 38:103-6 (3) My '83
--Night club (Trinidad & Tobago)
    Ebony 41:74 (c,4) My '86
--Rockettes (New York)
    Life 5:122-6 (c,1) D '82
    Smithsonian 14:102-3 (c,2) Je
        '83
--Yakan dancers (Philippines)
    Nat Geog 170:107 (c,1) Jl '86
--See also
    ASTAIRE, FRED
    NIJINSKY
DANCES
--1920 (Texas)
    Am Heritage 37:54-5 (1) F '86
--1954 teenage dance party (Colo-
        rado)
    Life 9:291 (1) Fall '86
--Ball (Vienna, Austria)
    Life 5:116 (c,3) D '82
    Nat Geog 167:422-3 (c,1) Ap '85
--Chendu, China
    Nat Geog 168:282-3 (c,1) S '85
--High school proms
    Life 8:85-90 (c,1) Jl '85
--Outdoor town dance (Texas)
    Nat Geog 165:212-13 (c,1) F '84
--White House party
    Life 5:148-9 (c,1) Ja '82
DANCING
--1938 marathon dance contest
    Life 9:65 (2) Ag '86
--1950s style jive
    Life 8:84 (c,3) Ag '85
--Angola
    Ebony 42:132 (c,4) D '86
--Basque (Nevada)
    Trav/Holiday 162:51 (c,3) Jl '84
--Belly dancing (Egypt)
    Trav/Holiday 163:77 (c,4) Mr '85
--Break dancing (Michigan)
    Sports Illus 63:72 (c,2) Jl 8 '85
--Break dancing (New York)
    Life 6:161-6 (c,1) Ja '83
--Break dancing (Samoa)
    Nat Geog 168:455 (c,3) O '85
--British royalty
    Life 9:148-9 (c,2) Ja '86

DANCING (cont.)

--Christmas Island, Pacific
Sports Illus 59:90-1 (c,4) D
26 '83

--Classical Thai dancing (Bangkok, Thailand)
Nat Geog 162:514-15 (c,1) O
'82

--Country-western (Louisiana)
Natur Hist 93:48 (c,1) Ap '84

--Disco club (Bermuda)
Trav/Holiday 157:49 (c,3) Je
'82

--Disco club (New York)
Life 6:117 (c,2) Jl '83

--Disco club (Papua New Guinea)
Nat Geog 162:143 (c,4) Ag
'82

--Ethiopia
Nat Geog 163:614-16 (c,1) My
'83

--Flamenco dancers (Spain)
Smithsonian 17:64 (drawing,4)
Je '86
Trav/Holiday 165:48-9 (c,3) Je
'86

--The Frug (1964)
Life 9:71 (4) Ag '86

--Geisha (Japan)
Natur Hist 92:53-5 (c,1) F '83

--Hopi Indians (Arizona)
Nat Geog 162:616-17 (c,2) N
'82

--Hula (Hawaii)
Trav/Holiday 158:19 (c,4) D
'82
Nat Geog 164:598-9 (c,1) N '83
Sports Illus 62:28 (c,2) Ja 7
'85

--In pub (British Columbia)
Nat Geog 170:67 (c,3) Jl '86

--Ivory Coast
Nat Geog 162:106-7, 113 (c,1)
Jl '82

--Kung people (Namibia)
Nat Geog 161:770 (c,1) Je '82

--Line of teenagers dancing
holding hands (East Ger-
many)
Nat Geog 164:460-1 (c,1) O
'83

--Middle Eastern (Israel)
Life 6:76-7 (c,1) N '83

--Morocco
Natur Hist 92:67-9 (c,1) O '83

--Panther dance (Ivory Coast)
Trav/Holiday 166:12 (c,4) Ag

'86

--Prince Charles break dancing
Life 8:72 (4) My '85

--Scottish Highland Fling (North
Carolina)
Smithsonian 13:114 (c,4) Jl '82

--Spanish (California)
Nat Geog 165:434 (c,4) Ap '84

--Spanish dancer (New Mexico)
Nat Geog 161:328 (c,4) Mr '82

--Square dancing (Alberta)
Nat Geog 165:385 (c,3) Mr '84

--Traditional bottle dance (Paraguay)
Nat Geog 162:251 (c,3) Ag '82

--Traditional male dance (Yap)
Nat Geog 170:488-9 (c,1) O '86

--Tu people (China)
Nat Geog 165:300 (c,3) Mr '84

--Wales
Nat Geog 164:40-1 (c,1) Jl '83

--Warm-up exercises
Ebony 39:33-8 (c,3) Jl '84

--See also
BALANCHINE, GEORGE
BALLET DANCING
FOLK DANCING

DANCING--EDUCATION

--Children learning two-step
(Florida)
Life 6:158 (2) N '83

--Dance class
Ebony 40:69-70 (3) F '85

--Following dancing manual (China)
Life 8:70-1 (1) Je '85

--Gourd dance class (Hawaii)
Nat Geog 164:596 (c,2) N '83

--Modern dance
Ebony 39:82-4 (3) Je '84
Ebony 40:48 (4) Ja '85

--See also
BALLET DANCING--
EDUCATION

DANCING, CONTEMPORARY
Ebony 37:78-9 (2) Ag '82

--The bump (Mexico)
Life 7:156 (c,2) N '84

--Japanese youth gang rockers
Natur Hist 94:48-57, 70 (c,1) Ag
'85

DANCING, MODERN
Ebony 37:150-1 (c,3) Ag '82
Ebony 37:84-6 (c,2) S '82
Ebony 38:74-5 (1) Mr '83
Ebony 39:164-8 (c,2) O '84
Ebony 41:204 (4) N '85
Smithsonian 16:86-97 (c,1) D '85

DANCING, MODERN (cont.)
--1923 (Germany)
   Sports Illus 65:54 (4) Ag 4
     '86
--Israel
   Nat Geog 168:39 (c,1) Jl '85
--Japan
   Nat Geog 170:630 (c,1) N '86
D'ANNUNZIO, GABRIELE
--Home (Gardone Riviera, Italy)
   Smithsonian 14:52-61 (c,1) Jl
     '83
--Scenes from his life
   Smithsonian 14:52-61 (c,1) Jl
     '83
DANTE ALIGHIERI
--Divine Comedy illustration
   Smithsonian 13:56-7 (paint-
     ing,c,2) S '82
DANUBE RIVER, AUSTRIA
--Dürnstein
   Nat Geog 167:435 (c,1) Ap '85
DANUBE RIVER, BUDAPEST,
     HUNGARY
   Nat Geog 163:228-9 (c,1) F '83
   Trav/Holiday 163:cov., 64-5
     (c,1) Mr '85
   Smithsonian 17:62-3 (c,1) N
     '86
DARIUS
--5th cent. bas-relief (Persepolis)
   Natur Hist 91:104 (4) Ja '82
DARROW, CLARENCE
   Smithsonian 14:202 (4) O '83
DARTERS (BIRDS)
   Nat Wildlife 21:cov. (c,1) Je
     '83
   Natur Hist 93:76-7 (c,1) Jl '84
DARTERS (FISH)
   Natur Hist 92:cov., 54-5 (c,2)
     Mr '83
   Natur Hist 95:32-3 (c,1) Ag '86
DARWIN, CHARLES
   Smithsonian 16:202 (4) Ap '85
--Cartoon of his head on an ape
   Life 5:48 (drawing,4) Ap '82
DATE INDUSTRY
--Egypt
   Nat Geog 161:207 (c,4) F '82
DAUMIER, HONORE
--1833 lithograph depicting ap-
     pendicitis attack
   Am Heritage 37:34 (3) Ap '86
DAVID, JACQUES LOUIS
--1788 portrait of Lavoisier
   Natur Hist 93:18 (painting,c,3)
     N '84

DAVIS, BETTE
   Life 9:190-1 (c,1) My '86
DAVIS, MILES
   Ebony 41:134 (2) N '85
DAY CARE CENTERS
   Life 9:67-72 (c,2) Ap '86
--Chicago, Illinois
   Ebony 37:48 (4) Ja '82
--Connecticut
   Ebony 38:36 (4) D '82
DEAD SEA, ISRAEL
   Nat Geog 168:24-5 (c,1) Jl '85
Deafness. See
     HEARING AIDS
DEATH
--18th cent. suicide (Great Britain)
   Smithsonian 14:74 (painting,c,3)
     N '83
--Body of sailor who died in 1846
     (Canada)
   Life 7:192-3 (c,1) N '84
   Smithsonian 16:117 (c,3) Je '85
--Dead Iranian soldier
   Life 5:100 (c,2) S '82
--Dead Iraqi soldiers
   Life 6:14-15 (c,1) Ja '83
--Dead Japanese soldier (1942)
   Life 8:6-7 (1) Spring '85
--Executed Guatemalan peasants
   Life 6:8 (c,4) Ja '83
--Mafia victim (Italy)
   Life 6:42-3 (1) F '83
   Life 8:28-9 (c,1) Mr '85
   Life 9:247 (c,4) Fall '86
--Man holding gun to his head
   Life 5:173 (c,2) N '82
--Matador killed by bull (Spain)
   Nat Geog 169:166 (4) F '86
--Murdered man (Utah)
   Life 8:115 (c,4) Je '85
--Nazi concentration camp victims
     (1945)
   Life 8:80-1 (1) Spring '85
--Putting dog to sleep
   Smithsonian 13:44 (4) S '82
--Victim of bomb (Lebanon)
   Life 7:12-13 (c,1) N '84
--Victims of mudslide (Ecuador)
   Nat Geog 165:166 (c,1) F '84
--Victims of shooting (El Salvador)
   Life 5:136-7 (1) My '82
   Life 6:8-9 (c,1) Ja '83
--Victims of soccer game riot (Bel-
     gium)
   Sports Illus 62:2-3 (c,1) Je 10
     '85
--See also

DEGAS, EDGAR (cont.)
    Smithsonian 14:99 (drawing,4)
        S '83
--Painting of Estelle Degas (1872)
    Am Heritage 38:54 (c,4) D '86
--Portrait of James Tissot (1868)
    Smithsonian 15:134 (painting,c,3)
        D '84
--Sculpture of dancer
    Smithsonian 14:104 (c,3) Ap '83
DE GAULLE, CHARLES
    Life 9:117 (4) Fall '86
--Sculpture by Marisol
    Smithsonian 14:58 (c,4) F '84
DEITIES
--19th cent. depictions of storm
        gods (Japan)
    Smithsonian 13:88, 91 (c,1) S
        '82
--Chola Dynasty goddess (India)
    Smithsonian 13:87 (sculp-
        ture,c,4) F '83
--Hindu deities (Tibet)
    Natur Hist 95:cov., 38-45
        (painting,c,1) Jl '86
--Indian sculpture
    Nat Geog 167:460 (c,2) Ap '85
--Kukailimoku (Hawaii)
    Nat Geog 164:573 (sculp-
        ture,c,4) N '83
--Statue of Hindu god Siva
    Natur Hist 93:16 (4) Ag '84
--See also
        BUDDHA
        JESUS CHRIST
        MYTHOLOGY
        specific religions
DELACROIX, FERDINAND
--"Liberty Leading the People"
    Smithsonian 15:48 (paint-
        ing,c,4) Jl '84
--Tableaux vivant of "Liberty
        Leading the People"
    Life 8:78-9 (1) D '85
DELAWARE
    Nat Geog 164:170-97 (map,c,1)
        Ag '83
--Du Pont's Winterthur estate
    Am Heritage 34:86-96 (c,1)
        Ap '83
    Smithsonian 14:98-109 (c,1) My
        '83
    Nat Geog 164:181 (c,4) Ag '83
--See also
        DELAWARE BAY
        WILMINGTON

DELAWARE BAY, DELAWARE/NEW
        JERSEY
    Natur Hist 95:68-71 (c,1) My '86
DELAWARE INDIANS--COSTUME
--Chief Lapowinsa (1735)
    Am Heritage 34:21 (painting,c,4)
        O '83
DELAWARE RIVER, NEW JERSEY
--Reenactment of Washington cross-
        ing the Delaware
    Trav/Holiday 166:32 (c,4) D '86
DELFT, NETHERLANDS
--Grote Markt
    Trav/Holiday 160:18 (4) Jl '83
--Making Delft porcelain
    Trav/Holiday 160:16, 20 (4) Jl
        '83
DELHI, INDIA
    Nat Geog 166:712-13 (c,1) D '84
    Nat Geog 167:506-33 (map,c,1)
        Ap '85
--Red Fort
    Nat Geog 167:464-5 (c,1) Ap '85
--Slum
    Smithsonian 16:44-5, 49 (c,1) Je
        '85
Demolition. See
        BUILDINGS--DEMOLITION
DEMONSTRATIONS
--1932 unemployed (San Francisco,
        California)
    Am Heritage 33:66 (3) Ag '82
--1968 demonstration at Democratic
        Convention (Chicago)
    Life 9:342 (2) Fall '86
--1970 Earth Day (New York City,
        New York)
    Nat Wildlife 24:31 (c,4) Ap '86
--1972 Republican National Conven-
        tion (Miami, Florida)
    Life 9:120 (2) Jl '86
--1974 football players picketing
        NFL
    Sports Illus 56:36 (c,4) F 1 '82
--Aerial view of anti-nuke rally
        (New York)
    Life 6:46-7 (c,1) Ja '83
--Against hydroelectric plant (Aus-
        tralia)
    Nat Geog 163:693 (c,3) My '83
--Anti acid rain (Massachusetts)
    Life 7:60-1 (c,1) N '84
--Anti apartheid (California)
    Life 8:63 (2) Je '85
--Anti apartheid (South Africa)
    Ebony 40:133-4, 140 (c,3) My '85
    Ebony 40:94 (3) Ag '85

DEMONSTRATIONS (cont.)
--Anti Berlin Wall (West Germany)
Nat Geog 161:10 (c,4) Ja '82
--Anti nuclear (Bonn, West Germany)
Life 5:38-9 (c,1) Ja '82
--Anti nuclear (California)
Nat Geog 165:455 (c,4) Ap '84
--Anti nuclear (Sicily, Italy)
Life 6:186 (c,2) N '83
--Anti nuclear human chain (West Germany)
Life 7:16-17 (1) Ja '84
--Anti statehood (Puerto Rico)
Nat Geog 163:520-1 (c,1) Ap '83
--Anti teacher competency tests (Texas)
Ebony 39:147-8, 153 (3) Mr '84
--Anti U.S. (Netherlands)
Nat Geog 170:514 (c,2) O '86
--Argentina
Nat Geog 170:226-7 (c,1) Ag '86
--Demonstrator being arrested (Georgia)
Ebony 38:42 (4) Jl '83
--Environmentalists (Australia)
Nat Geog 163:26-7 (c,3) Ja '83
--Farmers (Kansas)
Nat Geog 168:362 (c,4) S '85
--For Martin Luther King national holiday (Wash., D.C.)
Ebony 37:31 (2) Ja '82
Ebony 37:97 (3) Ap '82
--Hosing down 1963 civil rights demonstrators (Alabama)
Life 9:338-9 (1) Fall '86
--Iran
Nat Geog 168:114-15 (c,1) Jl '85
--Neo-Nazis (Sweden)
Life 8:68-9 (1) Je '85
--Political (Panama)
Nat Geog 169:472-3 (c,1) Ap '86
--Political (Philippines)
Nat Geog 170:76-80, 86 (c,1) Jl '86
--Pro Solidarity (Poland)
Life 6:38-9 (c,1) Ja '83
--Sinai Israelis
Nat Geog 161:446 (c,3) Ap '82
--U.S. flag upside-down in 1969 Vietnam War protest

Am Heritage 37:79 (4) Ap '86
--West Germany
Life 5:26-9 (c,1) Mr '82
--See also
CIVIL RIGHTS MARCHES
RIOTS
DEMPSEY, JACK
Life 7:171 (4) Ja '84
Sports Illus 63:131 (4) S 4 '85
DENALI NATIONAL PARK, ALASKA
Nat Wildlife 24:24 (c,1) Ap '86
Smithsonian 17:110-11 (c,1) Jl '86
Nat Wildlife 24:12-13 (c,1) Ag '86
DENMARK
Trav/Holiday 157:cov., 50-5 (c,1) Je '82
Trav/Holiday 161:63-7 (map,c,2) My '84
--Sites related to Hans Christian Andersen
Trav/Holiday 157:cov., 50-5 (c,1) Je '82
--See also
COPENHAGEN
FAEROE ISLANDS
VIKINGS
DENTISTRY
Ebony 40:53-6 (3) F '85
--19th-20th cent. dental equipment
Life 6:96 (c,2) D '83
--Braces on teeth
Sports Illus 63:26 (c,4) Ag 19 '85
Life 9:29 (c,2) Mr '86
--Cabbage Patch doll ripoff with braces
Life 9:49 (c,2) Ja '86
--Curbside dentist (China)
Nat Geog 165:303 (c,4) Mr '84
--Examining patient (South Africa)
Life 8:111 (c,4) N '85
DENTISTRY--EDUCATION
--Dental students (Washington, D.C.)
Ebony 39:85 (4) My '84
--Student working on patient (Washington, D.C.)
Ebony 40:142 (c,4) S '85
DENTISTS
Ebony 40:53-4 (3) F '85
--Dentist's office
Life 6:84 (c,4) O '83
DENVER, COLORADO
Nat Geog 166:200-1 (c,3) Ag '84
--Helen Bonfils Theatre Complex

DENVER, COLORADO (cont.)
  Smithsonian 16:84 (c,4) Jl '85
DEPRESSION
--1930s hoboes on boxcars
    (Utah)
  Am Heritage 36:62-3 (paint-
    ing,c,1) Ag '85
--1930s Okies traveling West
  Nat Geog 166:322-49 (map,c,1)
    S '84
--1932 demonstration (Scotland)
  Am Heritage 37:90-1 (1) Ag
    '86
--1932 unemployed marchers (San
    Francisco, California)
  Am Heritage 33:66 (3) Ag '82
--Scenes of the Depression in
    Europe
  Am Heritage 37:90-4 (1) Ag '86
--Urban scenes by Louis Lozowick
  Smithsonian 13:133 (drawing,4)
    Ja '83
--See also
    HOBOES
DES MOINES, IOWA
--Civic Center
  Trav/Holiday 164:6 (c,4) Jl '85
DESERTS
--Argentina
  Life 7:64-5 (c,1) Ap '84
  Smithsonian 16:72-3 (c,1) O '85
--Bonneville Salt Flats, Utah
  Nat Geog 167:712-13 (c,1) Je
    '85
--Central Desert, Australia
  Natur Hist 93:62-71 (map,c,1)
    Mr '84
--Chihuahuan Desert, New Mexico
  Nat Wildlife 24:27 (c,1) Ap '86
--Namib Desert
  Nat Geog 164:364-77 (c,1) S
    '83
--Peru
  Nat Geog 161:314-15 (c,1) Mr
    '82
--Pinnacles, Australia
  Sports Illus 62:124-5, 128-9
    (c,1) F 11 '85
--Sahel, Niger
  Nat Geog 164:484-5 (c,1) O '83
--Sonoran, Arizona
  Smithsonian 13:48 (c,4) F '83
  Natur Hist 93:47 (c,1) Ja '84
  Natur Hist 95:74-5 (c,1) Ap
    '86
--Tucson area, Arizona
  Trav/Holiday 159:cov. (c,1) F

    '83
--Western desert, Egypt
  Nat Geog 161:190-221 (c,1) F
    '82
--See also
    ARABIAN DESERT
    DEATH VALLEY
    GOBI DESERT
    KALAHARI DESERT
    OASES
    PAINTED DESERT
    SAHARA DESERT
DESIGN, DECORATIVE
--18th cent. Rococo style church
    interior (Austria)
  Nat Geog 167:415-17 (c,1) Ap
    '85
--Mid 19th cent. octagonal buildings
  Am Heritage 34:cov., 12-25 (c,1)
    Ag '83
--Early 20th cent. German design
  Smithsonian 17:122-31 (c,2) D
    '86
--1920s geometrical styles
  Smithsonian 12:110-19 (c,2) F '82
--1930s art deco cruise ship
  Am Heritage 35:60-9 (c,1) D '83
--1930s Moderne style (Miami Beach,
    Florida)
  Smithsonian 13:58-67 (c,2) D '82
--1930s use of newspaper wallpaper
  Natur Hist 91:4-14 (2) F '82
--1935 radio transmitting tower
    (New York)
  Am Heritage 36:68 (1) O '85
--Aerial view of new cars in lot
    (California)
  Life 8:84-5 (1) O '85
--Aerial views of U.S. countryside
  Nat Geog 166:390-9 (c,1) S '84
  Nat Wildlife 24:53-9 (c,1) O '86
--American Indian art
  Am Heritage 37:18-25 (c,1) Ag
    '86
--Animal skin seen through electron
    microscope
  Smithsonian 13:151-4 (3) Mr '83
--Art deco church interior (Tulsa,
    Oklahoma)
  Trav/Holiday 163:8 (c,4) Mr '85
--Art deco in Miami Beach, Florida
  Smithsonian 13:58-67 (c,2) D '82
  Trav/Holiday 160:49-53 (c,1) N
    '83
--Art deco window (Florida)
  Nat Geog 162:206 (c,4) Ag '82
--Danish housewares design

DESIGN, DECORATIVE (cont.)
   Trav/Holiday 166:29 (c,4) N
      '86
--Depictions of U.S. Victorian
      interiors
   Am Heritage 34:94-9 (draw-
      ing,c,1) D '82
--Fractal abstract patterns
   Smithsonian 14:cov., 110-17
      (c,1) D '83
--Pennsylvania Dutch hex signs
      (Pennsylvania)
   Trav/Holiday 165:79 (c,4) My
      '86
--Pond bottom seen through ice
   Smithsonian 17:cov., 168-72
      (c,1) N '86
--Yellin's wrought iron works
   Smithsonian 12:67-75 (c,1) Mr
      '82
DESKS
--17th cent. (France)
   Smithsonian 14:62 (c,4) Ag '83
--Late 18th cent. (Scotland)
   Sports Illus 58:48-9 (c,2) My
      9 '83
--1857 writing desk (Great Brit-
      ain)
   Am Heritage 34:108 (4) D '82
--Early 20th cent. writing desk
      (Austria)
   Smithsonian 17:76 (c,4) Ag '86
--Modern rolltop desk (Massachu-
      setts)
   Life 9:84 (c,4) Jl '86
--Office
   Sports Illus 56:54 (c,4) Ap 5
      '82
--Franklin Roosevelt's desktop
      items (1945)
   Life 9:212-13 (1) Fall '86
--School desk (Nicaragua)
   Nat Geog 168:781 (c,1) D '85
--White House Oval Office,
      Washington, D.C.
   Am Heritage 33:8 (1) F '82
   Am Heritage 34:108 (4) D '82
DETECTIVES
--Surveillance equipment
   Smithsonian 17:38-9 (c,4) Jl
      '86
--See also
      FEDERAL BUREAU OF IN-
         VESTIGATION
      HOLMES, SHERLOCK
      PINKERTON, ALLAN
      POLICE WORK

DETROIT, MICHIGAN
   Sports Illus 56:58 (c,4) Je 14
      '82
--1900
   Am Heritage 35:28-9 (2) Ap '84
--Renaissance Center
   Ebony 42:160 (2) D '86
--Satellite photo
   Nat Geog 164:322-3 (c,1) S '83
DEVILS
   Sports Illus 57:23 (drawing,c,4)
      S 13 '82
   Sports Illus 59:96 (drawing,c,4)
      N 7 '83
--17th cent. woodcut
   Am Heritage 35:81 (3) Ag '84
DEVILS TOWER NATIONAL MONU-
      MENT, WYOMING
   Trav/Holiday 157:121 (4) Ap '82
DEWEY, THOMAS
   Am Heritage 37:66, 70 (2) F '86
DIAMOND HEAD, OAHU, HAWAII
   Trav/Holiday 161:32, 44-5 (4)
      My '84
DIAMOND MINING
--Namibia
   Nat Geog 161:758-9, 790-1 (c,1)
      Je '82
DICKENS, CHARLES
   Smithsonian 16:123 (drawing,c,4)
      My '85
--19th cent. London sites related to
      Dickens novels
   Nat Geog 163:756-7 (c,1) Je '83
DIDRIKSON, BABE
   Sports Illus 61:143 (4) Jl 18 '84
   Sports Illus 63:84 (4) Ag 19 '85
--Depicted on postage stamp
   Sports Illus 61:76 (c,4) S 10 '84
DIETRICH, MARLENE
   Smithsonian 13:102 (4) F '83
   Sports Illus 65:54 (4) Ag 4 '86
DIK-DIKS
   Nat Geog 163:371 (c,4) Mr '83
   Natur Hist 94:44-5 (painting,c,1)
      Ag '85
DILLINGER, JOHN
--Scene of death at Biograph The-
      ater, Chicago, Illinois
   Trav/Holiday 158:52 (c,4) Ag
      '82
DIMAGGIO, JOE
   Sports Illus 57:56 (4) O 4 '82
   Life 9:65 (4) Fall '86
--1939 wedding
   Life 9:102 (4) Je '86
--1954 wedding to Marilyn Monroe

DIMAGGIO, JOE (cont.)
    Life 9:102 (4) Je '86
DINING ROOMS
--14th cent. Haddon Hall,
    England
    Nat Geog 168:660 (c,1) N '85
--17th cent. chateau (France)
    Smithsonian 14:65 (c,1) Ag
    '83
--17th cent. New England decor
    Am Heritage 34:92-3 (c,1) Ap
    '83
--18th cent. decor
    Am Heritage 34:91 (c,4) Ap
    '83
--Bahamas
    Ebony 39:49 (c,2) Ja '84
--Breakfast room (Los Angeles,
    California)
    Ebony 37:68 (c,4) Je '82
--California
    Ebony 38:40 (c,3) S '83
--Castle (Great Britain)
    Smithsonian 15:78 (c,4) Ag '84
--Decorator room
    Ebony 38:131 (c,2) My '83
--English country house
    Smithsonian 16:53 (c,2) O '85
--Formal (North Carolina)
    Ebony 40:34 (c,4) F '85
--French boarding school
    Nat Geog 161:160 (c,1) F '82
--Illinois mansion
    Ebony 41:96 (c,3) S '86
--Andrew Jackson's Hermitage,
    Tennessee
    Nat Geog 169:315 (c,4) Mr '86
--Medieval room (Great Britain)
    Smithsonian 16:46 (c,4) O '85
--Orient Express train
    Smithsonian 14:61, 68 (c,4)
    D '83
--Railroad dining car (India)
    Nat Geog 165:714-15 (c,1) Je
    '84
--Submarine mess hall
    Life 7:56 (c,4) N '84
DINNERS AND DINING
--1913 train dining car
    Am Heritage 36:114 (paint-
    ing,c,2) Je '85
--1932 banquet (Los Angeles,
    California)
    Am Heritage 33:67 (3) Ag '82
--1939 airplane dining
    Smithsonian 16:196 (4) N '85
--Aboard luxury barge (Belgium)

Trav/Holiday 159:76 (c,3) Mr
    '83
--Athlete eating pizza
    Sports Illus 60:58 (c,4) Mr 12
    '84
--Athlete having a snack in bed
    Sports Illus 60:2-3 (c,1) Mr 19
    '84
--Babies eating cake (Great Britain)
    Ebony 39:46 (3) Ap '84
--Banquet (Arkansas)
    Ebony 41:36-7 (c,2) S '86
--Banquet (South Africa)
    Sports Illus 59:72 (c,3) Jl 18 '83
--Bedouin communal meal (Saudi
    Arabia)
    Smithsonian 15:49-51 (c,3) D '84
    Smithsonian 15:16 (c,4) F '85
--Boxing arena refreshment stand
    (Los Angeles, California)
    Sports Illus 57:50-1 (c,3) Jl 12
    '82
--Breakfast
    Sports Illus 57:34 (c,4) D 27 '82
--Breakfast (California)
    Sports Illus 58:87 (c,4) Ap 25
    '83
--Breakfast in bed (French hotel)
    Life 6:79 (c,4) S '83
--British royalty
    Life 5:106-7 (c,1) Ap '82
    Life 6:64 (c,4) Ja '83
--Buffet
    Ebony 38:55 (2) D '82
--Buffet (Antigua)
    Ebony 37:106 (c,4) Ja '82
--Buffet aboard cruise ship
    Trav/Holiday 161:81 (c,3) My '84
    Trav/Holiday 162:80 (c,3) O '84
--Child eating ice cream cone
    Ebony 37:96 (c,2) Jl '82
--Children eating berries (Ohio)
    Nat Wildlife 20:3, 46-7 (c,4) Ag
    '82
--Chinese New Year's feast (Taiwan)
    Nat Geog 161:108-9 (c,1) Ja '82
--Communal feast (Tibet)
    Nat Geog 165:318-19 (c,1) Mr '84
--Dinner party (New Mexico)
    Nat Geog 161:325 (c,3) Mr '82
--Easter dinner (Greece)
    Nat Geog 164:777 (c,1) D '83
--Eating at diner (Connecticut)
    Smithsonian 17:98-9, 102 (c,3)
    N '86
--Eating at picnic table
    Sports Illus 61:513 (c,4) Jl 18 '84

DINNERS AND DINING (cont.)
--Elegant restaurant
    Trav/Holiday 162:cov. (c,1) D
        '84
    Trav/Holiday 166:cov. (c,1) D
        '86
--Elementary school cafeteria
        (North Carolina)
    Ebony 39:64 (c,4) Mr '84
--Family breakfast (1911)
    Am Heritage 38:58-9 (paint-
        ing,c,1) D '86
--Family breakfast (1943)
    Life 9:62 (2) Fall '86
--Family dinner
    Life 5:72-3 (1) Mr '82
    Ebony 37:61 (2) Ap '82
    Sports Illus 57:38, 232 (c,4)
        S 1 '82
    Sports Illus 58:49 (c,4) Ja
        17 '83
    Ebony 41:108-9 (c,1) Ag '86
--Family meal on terrace (Texas)
    Sports Illus 60:54 (c,4) My
        14 '84
--Fast food hamburger restaurant
    Sports Illus 59:43 (c,4) O 10
        '83
--Father feeding toddler
    Sports Illus 60:28-9 (c,4) Ap
        23 '84
--Feeding young child
    Sports Illus 59:92 (c,4) N 7
        '83
--Free meal service (Washington,
        D.C.)
    Nat Geog 163:119 (c,2) Ja '83
--French restaurant
    Sports Illus 59:37 (c,3) Ag
        22 '83
--Hasidic Jews at wedding ban-
        quet (New York)
    Life 8:64-5 (1) F '85
--Hot dog in stadium
    Sports Illus 60:76 (c,3) Ja 16
        '84
--Informal family dinner
    Sports Illus 60:75 (c,4) Ap 23
        '84
--Iowa farm dinner (1937)
    Life 9:280-1 (1) Fall '86
--Iowa politicians
    Life 7:32-3 (1) F '84
--Ireland
    Nat Geog 161:688-9 (c,1) My
        '82
--Japan

    Trav/Holiday 157:50 (c,4) Ja '82
    Natur Hist 92:52 (c,1) F '83
--Japanese food
    Sports Illus 61:422-3 (c,1) Jl
        18 '84
--Kentucky farm
    Nat Geog 161:526-7 (c,1) Ap '82
--Lobster bake (Maine)
    Trav/Holiday 157:59 (c,4) My '82
--Luau (Hawaii)
    Sports Illus 62:28-9 (c,1) Ja 7
        '85
--Lunch at French army base
        (Lebanon)
    Life 6:28-9 (c,2) Je '83
--Lunch in factory (China)
    Nat Geog 164:70-1 (c,1) Jl '83
--Maryland
    Ebony 37:28 (c,3) Jl '82
--Mock formal dinner (Massachusetts)
    Life 5:142 (c,2) N '82
--Munching popcorn in movie the-
        ater
    Sports Illus 64:32-3 (c,1) Mr
        24 '86
--Outdoor restaurant (California)
    Ebony 37:79 (4) Ag '82
--Outdoors (Jamaica)
    Trav/Holiday 158:38-9 (c,2) O
        '82
--Panda eating with silverware
        (China)
    Life 9:96 (c,2) Mr '86
--Potluck dinner buffet (Pitcairn
        Island)
    Nat Geog 164:523 (c,1) O '83
--Restaurant
    Sports Illus 56:32 (c,4) Ap 26
        '82
--Restaurant (China)
    Trav/Holiday 162:47 (c,3) S '84
    Trav/Holiday 164:48 (c,4) S '85
--Restaurant (Hong Kong)
    Trav/Holiday 165:58 (c,4) F '86
--Restaurant (Wisconsin)
    Trav/Holiday 164:62 (c,3) O '85
--St. Maarten hotel
    Trav/Holiday 157:57 (c,3) My '82
--School dining hall (France)
    Nat Geog 161:160 (c,1) F '82
--Scottish castle
    Trav/Holiday 159:43 (2) Ja '83
--Snacking
    Ebony 41:86 (3) S '86
--Snacking on boat
    Life 6:48 (c,2) Ag '83
--Snacking on clams

DISEASES (cont.)
  MALNUTRITION
  MEDICINE--PRACTICE
  MENTAL ILLNESS
  VACCINATIONS
  VIRUSES
DISEASES--HUMOR
--Effects of the common cold
  Smithsonian 14:48-9 (drawing,c,4) D '83
DISNEY, WALT
  Life 5:12 (c,4) Ag '82
  Nat Wildlife 24:50 (c,4) Ap '86
--See also
  AMUSEMENT PARKS
  DONALD DUCK
  MICKEY MOUSE
DISRAELI, BENJAMIN
--Caricature
  Smithsonian 13:212 (4) N '82
DIVING
  Sports Illus 58:49 (c,3) Mr 28 '83
  Sports Illus 58:61 (c,4) My 9 '83
  Sports Illus 59:12 (c,1) Ag 29 '83
  Sports Illus 60:126-9 (c,1) F 8 '84
  Life 7:62-3 (c,1) Summer '84
  Sports Illus 61:480-93 (c,1) Jl 18 '84
  Sports Illus 63:27 (c,4) Ag 5 '85
  Sports Illus 64:44 (c,3) Je 23 '86
--6th cent. B.C. Etruscan painting
  Smithsonian 15:52 (c,3) F '85
--1904 Olympics (St. Louis)
  Life 7:26-7 (2) Summer '84
--1984 Olympic trials
  Sports Illus 61:2-3, 42-3 (c,1) Jl 16 '84
--1984 Olympics (Los Angeles)
  Sports Illus 61:80-3 (c,2) Ag 20 '84
--Bride diving into pool (California)
  Life 5:112 (c,2) F '82
--Jumping into bay (Hawaii)
  Sports Illus 59:98 (c,4) O 17 '83
--Jumping into swimming pool (Indiana)
  Sports Illus 61:49 (c,2) Ag 6 '84

--Olympic athletes in slow motion
  Life 7:22-3 (c,3) Summer '84
--Pole-position dive
  Sports Illus 61:2-3 (c,1) Jl 16 '84
--Reverse dives
  Life 6:62-3 (c,1) Je '83
--Reverse 3½ tuck
  Sports Illus 58:60 (c,4) My 9 '83
--World Aquatic Championships 1982 (Ecuador)
  Sports Illus 57:12-13 (c,3) Ag 16 '82
--See also
  SKIN DIVING
DIXIE NATIONAL FOREST, UTAH
  Natur Hist 95:90-2 (map,c,1) My '86
DNA. See
  GENETICS
DNIEPER RIVER, U.S.S.R.
--Kiev
  Nat Geog 167:312-13 (c,1) Mr '85
--Smolensk
  Nat Geog 167:308 (c,1) Mr '85
DOBERMAN PINSCHERS
  Life 7:42 (3) Ap '84
  Smithsonian 15:28 (c,4) Je '84
  Sports Illus 65:86 (c,3) Jl 28 '86
DOCTORS
  Sports Illus 56:49 (c,4) My 24 '82
  Am Heritage 35:cov. (c,1) O '84
  Life 8:cov., 33-9 (c,1) My '85
--1880s
  Am Heritage 35:22 (painting,c,1) O '84
--Early 20th cent. house call
  Am Heritage 35:24-5 (drawing,c,1) Ap '84
--1904
  Am Heritage 35:112 (2) Ag '84
--Life of Colorado country doctor (1948)
  Life 9:140-2 (c,1) Fall '86
--Neurosurgeons
  Ebony 41:67 94) O '86
--Opthalmologists
  Ebony 39:94 (4) F '84
--Surgeons
  Life 5:24-8 (c,1) S '82
  Sports Illus 58:48 (c,4) Mr 7 '83
--U.S.S.R.
  Life 9:24-6 (c,3) Ag '86
--See also
  FREUD, SIGMUND

DOCTORS (cont.)
JUNG, CARL GUSTAV
MEDICINE--PRACTICE
PHARMACISTS
SHAMANS
SURGERY
THERAPY
VETERINARIANS
Dodgson, Charles. See
CARROLL, LEWIS
DODO BIRDS
Natur Hist 91:39 (paint-
ing,c,4) Mr '82
Smithsonian 13:98 (paint-
ing,c,4) Je '82
DOG SHOWS
Ebony 39:73 (c,3) Jl '84
--Phoenix, Arizona
Smithsonian 13:87 (3) Je '82
DOG SLEDS
Nat Geog 170:288-311 (c,1)
S '86
--Iditarod Trail Sled Dog Race
(Alaska)
Nat Geog 163:410-21 (c,1) Mr
'83
Sports Illus 62:28-9 (c,1) Ap
1 '85
Sports Illus 64:2-4, 90-107
(map,c,1) F 17 '86
Nat Wildlife 24:40-5 (c,1) F '86
DOGS
Sports Illus 56:106 (c,4) My
24 '82
Sports Illus 57:38 (c,4) Ag 9
'82
Ebony 37:58 (4) S '82
Smithsonian 15:113-17 (2) S '84
Life 7:115-22 (c,1) D '84
Life 8:66 (2) F '85
Sports Illus 64:25 (c,4) My 19
'86
--At animal shelters
Smithsonian 13:44-7 (4) S '82
--Attack training (Washington,
D.C.)
Nat Geog 163:118 (c,1) Ja '83
--Bathing dog
Life 9:50-1 (c,1) N '86
--Borzoi
Sports Illus 63:60 (c,2) O 21
'85
--Bouvier
Sports Illus 62:45 (c,4) Ap 1
'85
--Catching frisbee
Sports Illus 62:102 (c,4) Je

3 '85
--Dog sleeping in bed with child
(California)
Life 9:55 (c,3) N '86
--Graves of World War II K-9 corps
(Guam)
Life 8:101 (c,4) Spring '85
--Hunting dogs
Sports Illus 57:54 (painting,c,4)
N 22 '82
Sports Illus 58:95-100 (paint-
ing,c,1) Ja 24 '83
Smithsonian 16:78 (c,4) S '85
--Hunting dogs chasing stag (Great
Britain)
Nat Geog 170:548-9 (c,1) O '86
--Japanese chin
Sports Illus 61:122 (c,2) Jl 18
'84
--Livestock-guarding dogs
Smithsonian 13:cov., 64-73 (c,1)
Ap '82
Nat Wildlife 24:14-19 (c,1) Je '86
--Maremma puppy
Nat Wildlife 24:14-15 (c,1) Je '86
--Pekeapoos
Ebony 39:55 (c,3) N '83
--Pit bull
Sports Illus 62:42-3 (c,1) F 4
'85
--Posed for photographer
Life 6:8-14 (c,1) F '83
--Raccoon dogs
Natur Hist 95:cov., 38-45 (c,1)
Ag '86
--Shar peis
Life 7:122 (c,2) D '84
Life 9:322 (c,2) Fall '86
--Shih tzu
Life 7:38-9 (c,1) N '84
Life 8:110 (c,3) Mr '85
--Snoopy
Sports Illus 63:110 (c,2) D 23 '85
--Walking dogs
Sports Illus 57:58-9 (c,1) S 27
'82
Am Heritage 34:55 (painting,c,2)
F '83
--Wild dogs
Nat Geog 169:574-5 (c,1) My '86
--See also
AFFENPINSCHERS
ALASKAN MALAMUTES
BASSET HOUNDS
BEAGLES
BLOODHOUNDS
BOXERS

DOGS (cont.)
    BULLDOGS
    CHIHUAHUAS
    COLLIES
    COYOTES
    DACHSHUNDS
    DOBERMAN PINSCHERS
    GERMAN SHEPHERDS
    GOLDEN RETRIEVERS
    GREAT DANES
    GREAT PYRENEES DOGS
    KOMONDORS
    LABRADOR RETRIEVERS
    LHASA APSOS
    MASTIFFS
    PEKINGESES
    POINTERS
    POODLES
    RETRIEVERS
    ROTTWEILERS
    SAMOYEDS
    SHEEP DOGS
    SHETLAND SHEEP DOGS
    SIBERIAN HUSKIES
    SPANIELS
    TERRIERS
    WEIMARANERS
    WHIPPETS
    YORKSHIRE TERRIERS
DOGWOOD TREES
    Am Heritage 37:28 (c,2) Ap '86
--Berries
    Natur Hist 93:44-5 (c,1) Ag '84
Dollars. See
    CURRENCY
DOLLS
    Ebony 39:39 (c,3) N '83
    Ebony 39:30 (c,2) D '83
--1835 (Germany)
    Nat Geog 165:39 (c,4) Ja '84
--Late 19th cent. (France)
    Life 6:11-13 (c,1) D '83
--Late 19th cent. Eskimos
    (Alaska)
    Smithsonian 13:57 (c,4) My '82
    Nat Geog 163:203 (c,2) F '83
--Early 20th cent.
    Am Heritage 37:36-7 (c,1) Ag
    '86
--1916 (France)
    Life 6:20 (c,2) D '83
--1920s baby dolls
    Life 6:13 (c,4) D '83
--1940s Nazi doll (Germany)
    Life 6:86 (c,2) Jl '83
--Antique

    Am Heritage 33:22 (c,4) Ap '82
--Canada
    Nat Geog 163:186 (c,4) F '83
--Chinese dolls
    Sports Illus 62:30 (c,3) F 4 '85
--Counterfeit Cabbage Patch dolls
    Life 7:44-8 9c,1) S '84
    Life 9:49 (c,2) Ja '86
--Dream lover statuettes (Ivory
    Coast)
    Nat Geog 162:125 (c,1) Jl '82
--Dwight and Mamie Eisenhower
    dolls (1956)
    Life 6:16 (c,2) D '83
--Hopi kachina dolls
    Nat Geog 162:612 (c,4) N '82
    Smithsonian 13:120 (c,4) Ja '83
--Opium-smoking doll (Iran)
    Nat Geog 167:161 (c,4) F '85
--Maurice Sendak's "Wild Things"
    Smithsonian 12:88 (c,1) Ja '82
--Smurfs
    Life 6:120-1 (c,1) Ja '83
--See also
    PUPPETS
DOLOMITE MOUNTAINS, ITALY
    Nat Geog 165:200-1 (c,2) F '84
DOLPHINS
    Nat Wildlife 21:cov., 8-9 (c,1)
    Ag '83
    Nat Wildlife 22:34-5 (painting,c,2)
    Ag '84
    Natur Hist 95:70-3 (c,1) Ap '86
--Celebrating Flipper's birthday
    Life 9:38 (c,2) D '86
Domestic workers. See
    MAIDS
DOMINICAN REPUBLIC
--Casa de Campo resort
    Trav/Holiday 159:4 (c,4) My '83
--Puerto Plata
    Trav/Holiday 158:20 (4) Ag '82
DON QUIXOTE
--Sculpture (Spain)
    Trav/Holiday 161:73 (c,1) Ap '84
DONALD DUCK
    Life 7:130 (c,1) Je '84
DONKEYS
--Spotted asses
    Smithsonian 13:24 (c,4) O '82
DOORS
--1860 house (New York)
    Am Heritage 34:22 (c,1) Ag '83
--Church (Brooklyn, New York)
    Am Heritage 35:69 (c,3) D '83
--Dublin doorway, Ireland
    Trav/Holiday 163:66 (c,4) F '85

DOORS (cont.)
--Majorca, Spain
    Trav/Holiday 164:26 (c,4) Jl
        '85
--Palace door lock (Great Britain)
    Nat Geog 168:671 (c,3) N '85
--Yellin's wrought iron pieces
    Smithsonian 12:68-75 (c,1) Mr
        '82
DOUBLEDAY, ABNER
    Am Heritage 34:65 (4) Je '83
    Am Heritage 35:9 (4) Je '84
DOUGLAS FIR TREES
    Natur Hist 91:61 (c,1) O '82
    Life 5:114 (c,2) N '82
    Natur Hist 93:44-5 (c,2) Je '84
    Nat Geog 166:504-5 (c,2) O
        '84
    Nat Wildlife 23:15 (c,1) D '84
    Nat Wildlife 24:4-5 (c,1) F '86
--Cross section of rings
    Nat Geog 162:327 (c,2) S '82
    Smithsonian 16:46 (c,1) Jl '85
DOUGLASS, FREDERICK
    Ebony 39:76 (4) F '84
    Nat Geog 166:12 (painting,c,4)
        Jl '84
    Ebony 40:28 (4) F '85
DOURO (DUERO) RIVER, PORTU-
        GAL/SPAIN
    Nat Geog 166:460-88 (map,c,1)
        O '84
--Porto, Portugal
    Trav/Holiday 158:53 (c,2) O
        '82
DOVES
    Natur Hist 93:8 (c,3) F '84
    Nat Geog 170:326-7 (c,1) S
        '86
--See also
    MOURNING DOVES
DOYLE, SIR ARTHUR CONAN
    Life 7:154 (4) Ja '84
DRAGONFLIES
    Natur Hist 91:25 (c,1) Jl '82
    Smithsonian 13:66-7, 70-1
        (c,1) Jl '82
    Natur Hist 93:cov., 32-9 (c,1)
        Jl '84
    Nat Wildlife 22:2, 59 (c,2) O
        '84
    Smithsonian 17:131 (c,1) My
        '86
    Natur Hist 95:33 (c,4) Ag '86
DRAGONS
--15th cent. painting
    Smithsonian 12:32 (c,4) F '82

--Embroidered on silk (China)
    Nat Geog 165:2-3 (c,1) Ja '84
DRAGONS OF KOMODO
    Nat Wildlife 24:30 (4) O '86
DRAKE, SIR FRANCIS
--Late 16th cent. drawings from his
        voyages
    Am Heritage 36:81-95 (c,1) Ag
        '85
DREISER, THEODORE
    Am Heritage 35:72 (drawing,4)
        F '84
Dressing rooms. See
    THEATERS
DRIFTWOOD
--Hawaii beach
    Nat Wildlife 21:50-1 (c,1) Ag '83
DRINKING CUSTOMS
--1830s tavern (New Hampshire)
    Smithsonian 14:95 (painting,c,1)
        My '83
--Children at tea (Great Britain)
    Smithsonian 14:99 (c,3) Ja '84
--Coffeehouse (Madrid, Spain)
    Nat Geog 169:158-9 (c,1) F '86
--Drinking wine from bottle
    Sports Illus 60:35 (c,4) Mr 19
        '84
--Japanese tea ceremony (Hawaii)
    Trav/Holiday 164:62 (c,4) N '85
--Ojibwa Indian drinking beer (On-
        tario)
    Natur Hist 94:66 (4) Jl '85
--Opening champagne bottle
    Sports Illus 57:19 (c,4) Jl 26 '82
    Sports Illus 59:53 (c,4) Ag 1 '83
    Life 6:16 (c,2) S '83
--Pouring tea
    Ebony 41:146 (3) D '85
--"Quick tea" stand (China)
    Nat Geog 168:295 (c,3) S '85
--Schnaps (Austria)
    Trav/Holiday 157:80 (c,4) Ap '82
--Tea (China)
    Nat Geog 168:294-5 (c,3) S '85
--Tea (Japan)
    Life 6:103 (c,4) Ap '83
--Tea (Portugal)
    Nat Geog 166:466 (c,2) O '84
--Tea drinking through history
    Smithsonian 12:100-1 (c,4) F '82
--Tea served on cricket field (Great
        Britain)
    Nat Geog 168:672-3 (c,1) N '85
--Tea tray
    Nat Geog 163:404 (c,2) Mr '83
--Waitress carrying beer mugs

DRUG INDUSTRY
--Late 19th cent. pill-making
machine
Am Heritage 35:29 (c,4) O '84
--Opium (India)
Nat Geog 167:156-9 (c,1) F
'85
--Smelling armpits for deodorant
research
Nat Geog 170:330-1 (c,1) S
'86
--Tranquilizer production (Puerto
Rico)
Nat Geog 163:534 (c,4) Ap '83
DRUGS
--1880s belladonna jar
Am Heritage 35:30 (c,4) O '84
--1880s camphor jar
Am Heritage 35:25 (c,4) O '84
--19th cent. patent medicine label
Smithsonian 14:54 (c,4) D '83
--Late 19th cent. cocaine-based
drugs
Life 7:cov., 58-9 (c,4) My '84
--Early 20th cent. patent medi-
cines
Smithsonian 15:119 (c,3) Jl '84
--Calcium carbonate tablets
Nat Geog 168:207 (c,4) Ag '85
--Ecstasy
Life 8:88-94 (c,1) Ag '85
--Made from tree shavings (Zaire)
Nat Geog 163:39 (c,4) Ja '83
--Rhino horn drugs
Nat Geog 165:407, 410 (c,4)
Mr '84
--Steroids
Sports Illus 59:62-5 (c,1) Ag
1 '83
Sports Illus 62:40-1 (c,1) My
13 '85
--See also
PHARMACIES
DRUM PLAYING
Smithsonian 15:105 (c,1) D '84
--Bongo drums
Sports Illus 58:53 (c,4) My 2
'83
--Civil War
Am Heritage 33:2 (paint-
ing,c,1) F '82
--Conga drums
Ebony 38:85 (c,4) N '82
--Rock group
Ebony 38:126-8 (c,1) Jl '83
--Steel drums (Tobago)
Trav/Holiday 164:21 (c,4) D '85

DUBAI--COSTUME
Life 6:132 (c,2) Jl '83
--Sheik
Sports Illus 65:80-1, 90-2 (c,1)
D 1 '86
DUBLIN, IRELAND
Trav/Holiday 163:63-7, 83-4
(c,2) F '85
--See also
LIFFEY RIVER
DU BOIS, W. E. B.
Ebony 37:64 (4) F '82
Ebony 39:49-50 (3) Jl '84
Ebony 40:30 (4) F '85
Ebony 40:66 (4) Je '85
Ebony 41:64, 192, 296 (4) N '85
Ebony 41:126, 140 (3) Ag '86
Ebony 42:172 (4) N '86
--Reinterment (Ghana)
Ebony 42:172-8 (c,3) N '86
DUCKS
Smithsonian 13:66-72 (paint-
ing,c,1) Je '82
Natur Hist 91:cov. (c,1) Jl '82
Nat Geog 164:232-3 (c,3) Ag '83
Sports Illus 60:39 (c,3) Ja 16
'84
Nat Wildlife 22:57 (painting,c,4)
F '84
Nat Geog 166:564-99 (c,1) N '84
Life 8:94-5 (c,1) Mr '85
Nat Wildlife 24:51 (c,1) F '86
Trav/Holiday 166:54 (c,4) N '86
--Dead of diseases
Nat Geog 166:586-7 (c,2) N '84
--Decoys
Nat Geog 164:638-63 (c,1) N '83
--Duck stamps
Smithsonian 13:67-72 (painting,c,1)
Je '82
Nat Geog 166:582 (c,4) N '84
Nat Wildlife 24:9 (drawing,4) Ap
'86
--See also
CANVASBACKS
DONALD DUCK
GEESE
MALLARDS
MERGANSERS
SWANS
TEALS
WIDGEONS
WOOD DUCKS
DUELS
Life 5:66 (c,3) Ja '82
Duero River, Spain. See
DOURO RIVER

DUGONGS
--19th cent. illustration (Great
    Britain)
    Smithsonian 14:90 (4) Je '83
DULLES, JOHN FOSTER
    Am Heritage 37:59 (1) D '85
DULUTH, MINNESOTA
--Aerial Lift Bridge
    Trav/Holiday 162:14 (c,4) N
    '84
Dumps. See
    JUNKYARDS
DUNBAR, PAUL LAURENCE
    Ebony 37:49-51 (3) O '82
DURANTE, JIMMY
--Caricature
    Am Heritage 37:54 (4) Je '86
DURER, ALBRECHT
--"Adoration"
    Smithsonian 17:148 (paint-
    ing,c,4) D '86
--Drawing of hands
    Smithsonian 15:64 (4) N '84
--Engraving of Frederick the
    Wise
    Nat Geog 164:437 (4) O '83
DUSE, ELEONORA
    Smithsonian 14:54 (4) Jl '83
DUST STORMS
--1906 (New York)
    Am Heritage 37:24-5 (paint-
    ing,c,1) Je '86
--1930s
    Nat Wildlife 24:18-19 (1) Ap '86
--1937 (Oklahoma)
    Nat Geog 166:322-3 (1) S '84
--1977 (California)
    Nat Geog 166:354-5 (c,2) S
    '84
--Australia
    Life 7:186 (c,2) Ja '84
    Nat Geog 165:150-1 (c,1) F '84
--Iraq
    Nat Geog 167:94-5 (c,2) Ja '85
--Texas
    Nat Wildlife 23:21 (c,1) F '85
DYLAN, BOB
    Life 8:cov., 45 (c,1) Ap '85

-E-

EAGLES
    Life 6:62 (c,4) Ja '83
--Bald
    Smithsonian 13:104, 112-13
    (c,1) My '82

Nat Wildlife 21:3, 28-9 (c,2) D
    '82
Natur Hist 92:42-5 (c,1) Ag '83
Sports Illus 59:75 (c,4) S 26 '83
Nat Geog 165:68-9 (c,1) Ja '84
Nat Wildlife 22:cov. (c,1) Ap '84
Nat Wildlife 22:46 (c,1) O '84
Nat Wildlife 23:4-7 (c,1) D '84
Life 8:12-13 (c,1) F '85
Smithsonian 15:133 (c,2) Mr '85
Natur Hist 94:91 (painting,c,3)
    Ap '85
Nat Wildlife 24:28-9, 53, 66-7
    (c,1) Ap '86
Trav/Holiday 166:48 (c,4) S '86
--Bald eagle as U.S. symbol
    Smithsonian 13:104-13 (c,1) My
    '82
    Am Heritage 33:70 (c,4) Je '82
--Eagle mascot for 1984 Olympics
    Sports Illus 60:64-5 (c,1) Mr 5
    '84
--Eaglets
    Nat Wildlife 21:53 (c,1) Ap '83
    Nat Wildlife 24:16 (c,4) Ap '86
--Golden
    Nat Geog 162:626-7 (c,2) N '82
    Trav/Holiday 162:35 (c,2) S '84
    Natur Hist 94:96 (painting,c,3)
    Ap '85
--Sea eagles
    Nat Geog 164:256-7, 260-1 (c,1)
    Ag '83
--Used in Hopi ritual (Arizona)
    Nat Geog 162:626-7 (c,2) N '82
EAKINS, THOMAS
--1877 painting of William Rush
    sculpting
    Am Heritage 34:84 (c,3) F '83
--Portrait of Walt Whitman (1887)
    Am Heritage 34:21 (painting,c,4)
    O '83
--Self-portrait
    Smithsonian 14:134 (painting,4)
    Ap '83
EARHART, AMELIA
    Smithsonian 13:20 (4) Je '82
EARTH
--Animals of cretaceous and tertiary
    periods
    Nat Geog 170:408 (drawing,c,1)
    S '86
--Changes in the planet
    Nat Geog 168:142-81 (map,c,1)
    Ag '85
--Charts of growing world population
    centers

EARTH (cont.)
Nat Geog 166:180-5 (c,1) Ag
'84
--Continent formation theory
Smithsonian 15:67-75 (c,1) Ja
'85
--Cretaceous period cataclysm
Nat Geog 170:405-9 (draw-
ing,c,1) S '86
--Seen from the moon
Nat Geog 167:22-3 (c,1) Ja '85
Natur Hist 94:6 (c,4) O '85
--Seen from the moon (1969)
Life 9:12-13 (c,1) Fall '86
--See also
GEOLOGICAL PHENOMENA
WEATHER PHENOMENA
EARTH--MAPS
--1510 globe
Am Heritage 36:6 (c,2) Je '85
--Climate map
Smithsonian 13:88 (c,1) Ap '82
--Ice Age map
Natur Hist 95:8-10 (c,1) N '86
--Reproduction of 1492 globe
Nat Geog 170:563-5 (c,1) N
'86
--Satellite maps of earth
Nat Geog 164:282-3, 315-25,
334-5 (c,1) S '83
Life 7:10-16 (c,1) Jl '84
Trav/Holiday 165:6 (c,4) Je '86
--Tropical rain forests
Nat Geog 163:10-11 (c,2) Ja
'83
--See also
EARTHQUAKES--MAPS
GLOBES
MAPS
individual countries and
continents--MAPS
EARTHQUAKES
--1983 Borah Peak earthquake,
Idaho
Natur Hist 95:28-34 (map,c,1)
Je '86
--Ancient Chinese seismograph
Smithsonian 14:46 (c,4) Jl '83
--Anti-quake building design
Nat Geog 169:664-6 (c,1) My
'86
--Earthquake bolts protecting
house (South Carolina)
Nat Geog 164:820 (c,1) D '83
--Earthquake measurement equip-
ment
Nat Geog 169:672-3 (c,1) My

'86
--Examining seismograph
Trav/Holiday 159:6 (4) F '83
--Earthquake forecasting research
Smithsonian 14:41-7 (c,3) Jl '83
--Fukien, Japan (1948)
Life 8:168 (4) O '85
--School earthquake drill (California)
Nat Geog 169:668 (c,2) My '86
--Tokyo, Japan (1923)
Nat Geog 170:623 (painting,c,4)
N '86
--See also
SAN ANDREAS FAULT
EARTHQUAKES--DAMAGE
--1906 (San Francisco, California)
Am Heritage 34:36-45 (1) F '83
--1971 collapsed freeway (San Fer-
nando, California)
Smithsonian 14:40 (c,1) Jl '83
--Collapsed church (Colombia)
Smithsonian 15:138 (c,1) Mr '85
--Dead children (Turkey)
Life 7:20-1 (c,1) Ja '84
--Managua, Nicaragua (1972)
Nat Geog 168:788-9 (c,1) D '85
--Rescuing infant (Mexico City,
Mexico)
Life 9:140-1 (c,1) Ja '86
--Mexico City, Mexico (1985)
Life 8:67-9 (1) N '85
Nat Geog 169:654-63, 674 (c,1)
My '86
EARTHQUAKES--MAPS
--Earthquake sites (California)
Nat Geog 169:638-9, 669 (c,1)
My '86
--Pacific coast
Nat Geog 169:638-9 (c,1) My '86
--U.S. risk areas
Smithsonian 14:42-3, 48 (c,2) Jl
'83
Nat Geog 168:152-3 (c,1) Ag '85
EARTHWORMS
Nat Geog 166:373 (c,3) S '84
--Being eaten by snake
Nat Wildlife 22:50 (c,4) Je '84
EASTER
--Chocolate Easter eggs (Italy)
Life 7:122-6 (c,1) Ap '84
--Decorated eggs (Czechoslovakia)
Smithsonian 13:112 (c,4) S '82
--Easter Bunny costume
Sports Illus 58:54 (c,4) Ap 18
'83
--Easter procession (Jerusalem,
Israel)

EASTER (cont.)
Nat Geog 163:504-5 (c,1) Ap
'83
--Kárpathos, Greece
Nat Geog 164:768-77 (c,1) D
'83
--Rarámuri Indian festival (Mexico)
Natur Hist 92:58-67 (c,1) Mr
'83
--White House Easter egg roll,
Washington, D.C.
Nat Geog 163:111 (c,4) Ja '83
EASTER ISLAND, CHILE
--Stone sculptures
Nat Geog 170:784 (c,2) D '86
EASTERN U.S.
--Scenes along U.S. Route 1
Nat Geog 166:790-817
(map,c,1) D '84
--See also
APPALACHIAN TRAIL
CHESAPEAKE BAY
Eating. See
DINNERS AND DINING
EBRO RIVER, SPAIN
Nat Geog 165:122-3 (c,1) Ja
'84
ECHIDNAS
Smithsonian 14:75 (c,4) Ag '83
Natur Hist 94:2, 4 (draw-
ing,4) S '85
Echinoderms. See
SEA CUCUMBERS
SEA LILIES
SEA URCHINS
STARFISH
ECLIPSES
--Lunar eclipse diagram
Natur Hist 91:70 (4) Je '82
--Partial lunar eclipse
Natur Hist 92:68 (drawing,4)
Je '83
--Solar eclipse
Nat Geog 167:6-7 (c,1) Ja '85
Life 9:388-9 (c,1) Fall '86
ECUADOR
Trav/Holiday 160:57-61, 70
(map,c,1) Jl '83
--Peace Corps activities in
Cumbijín
Smithsonian 16:80-9 (c,1) F
'86
--See also
ANDES MOUNTAINS
GALAPAGOS ISLANDS
QUITO

ECUADOR--COSTUME
Trav/Holiday 160:57-60, 70 (c,1)
Jl '83
--Waorani tribe
Natur Hist 93:68-75 (c,1) S '84
ECUADOR--POLITICS AND GOVERN-
MENT
--Fist fight in Congress
Life 8:102-3 (1) O '85
EDDY, MARY BAKER
Am Heritage 33:110 (4) F '82
EDEN, SIR ANTHONY
Am Heritage 37:56 (3) D '85
EDINBURGH, SCOTLAND
Nat Geog 166:42-3 (c,1) Jl '84
EDISON, THOMAS ALVA
Am Heritage 36:112 (3) Ag '85
Am Heritage 36:71 (1) O '85
Smithsonian 17:124 (4) Je '86
EDMONTON, ALBERTA
Trav/Holiday 159:48, 53 (c,1)
Je '83
--Provincial legislature building
Trav/Holiday 159:48 (c,1) Je '83
--West Edmonton Mall
Trav/Holiday 159:53 (c,3) Je '83
Smithsonian 17:34-7, 42-3 (c,1)
D '86
EDUCATION
--McGuffey Readers
Smithsonian 15:182-208 (c,2) N
'84
--Nanny school (Colorado)
Life 8:104-5 (c,1) S '85
--Teaching imagination and visual
thinking
Smithsonian 16:44-55 (c,1) Ag
'85
--Teaching physics with dramatic
stunts
Smithsonian 17:112-21 (c,1) O
'86
--See also
ART EDUCATION
BLACKBOARDS
CLASSROOMS
COLLEGES AND UNIVERSITIES
COOKING--EDUCATION
DANCING--EDUCATION
DENTISTRY--EDUCATION
MEDICAL EDUCATION
MUSIC--EDUCATION
SCHOLARS
SCHOOLS
SCIENCE EDUCATION
WASHINGTON, BOOKER T.

EGYPT--COSTUME
  Nat Geog 161:204, 207 (c,2) F
    '82
  Trav/Holiday 157:cov., 36-41
    (c,1) F '82
  Nat Geog 167:578-9, 596-608
    (c,1) My '85
  Trav/Holiday 165:50-5 (c,1) Je
    '86
--Coptic Christian garbage col-
    lectors (Cairo)
  Nat Geog 163:442-6 (c,2) Ap
    '83
--Sinai Peninsula
  Nat Geog 161:422-43 (c,1) Ap
    '82
--Street vendors
  Trav/Holiday 166:4 (c,2) S '86
--See also
    BEDOUINS
Egypt--History. See
    EGYPT, ANCIENT
    SADAT, ANWAR
    SALADIN
EGYPT--MAPS
--Sinai Peninsula (1967-1982)
  Nat Geog 161:428-9 (c,1) Ap
    '82
Egypt, ancient. See
    CLEOPATRA
    RAMSES II
    ROSETTA STONE
    TUTANKHAMUN
EGYPT, ANCIENT--ARCHITECTURE
--3rd cent. B.C. Lighthouse of
    Pharos, Alexandria
  Smithsonian 14:59 (drawing,4)
    Mr '84
--Depiction of 13th cent. B.C.
    palace (Gaza)
  Nat Geog 162:754-5, 758-9
    (drawing,c,1) D '82
--See also
    PYRAMIDS
EGYPT, ANCIENT--ART
--Temple frieze of incense burn-
    ing (Karnak)
  Nat Geog 170:328 (c,4) S '86
EGYPT, ANCIENT--COSTUME
--13th cent. B.C.
  Nat Geog 162:754-5 (draw-
    ing,c,1) D '82
EGYPT, ANCIENT--HUMOR
--Letter writing in ancient Egypt
  Smithsonian 14:116-31 (draw-
    ing,c,3) Ap '83

EGYPT, ANCIENT--RELICS
--22nd cent. B.C. tombs (Balat)
  Nat Geog 161:219 (c,3) F '82
--1st cent. B.C. tomb
  Nat Geog 161:208-9 (c,1) F '82
--King Tut's death mask (Egypt)
  Life 6:131-2 (c,3) Je '83
--Late Bronze Age tomb contents
    (Gaza, Israel)
  Nat Geog 162:738-69 (c,1) D '82
--Pearl earrings
  Nat Geog 168:209 (c,4) Ag '85
EGYPT, ANCIENT--RITES AND
    CEREMONIES
--Funeral preparations
  Nat Geog 162:766-9 (drawing,c,1)
    D '82
Egypt, ancient--sculpture. See
    SCULPTURE--ANCIENT
    SPHINX
EIFFEL, ALEXANDRE GUSTAV
  Am Heritage 35:98 (4) Je '84
EIFFEL TOWER, PARIS, FRANCE
  Nat Geog 164:781 (c,1) D '83
  Trav/Holiday 161:88 (2) Mr '84
  Trav/Holiday 163:35 (c,1) Mr '85
EINSTEIN, ALBERT
  Life 9:372 (3) Fall '86
--Depicted on postage stamp
  Am Heritage 34:54 (c,4) D '82
--Manuscript by him
  Smithsonian 14:145 (4) N '83
EISENHOWER, DWIGHT DAVID
  Sports Illus 58:118 (4) Ap 4 '83
  Am Heritage 36:73 (3) Ap '85
  Am Heritage 36:112 (3) O '85
  Ebony 41:102, 266 (4) N '85
  Am Heritage 37:cov., 49-63 (c,1)
    D '85
  Am Heritage 37:8 (4) Je '86
  Life 9:211, 216-17 (c,1) Fall '86
--1940s
  Life 8:9 (1) Spring '85
--Depicted on postage stamp
  Am Heritage 34:56 (c,4) D '82
--Dolls of Dwight and Mamie (1956)
  Life 6:16 (c,2) D '83
--On golf course
  Sports Illus 58:72 (4) F 7 '83
  Sports Illus 64:118 (4) Ap 7 '86
--Political cartoons about him
  Am Heritage 37:50-61 (4) D '85
EISENSTAEDT, ALFRED
  Life 9:54-5 (c,2) Fall '86
EL PASO, TEXAS
  Nat Geog 167:740-1 (c,1) Je '85
  Life 9:3, 40-1 (c,1) Ag '86

EL PASO, TEXAS (cont.)
--Aerial view
   Life 8:58-9 (1) My '85
EL SALVADOR
--Red Cross relief operations
   Nat Geog 170:674-9 (c,1) N
      '86
EL SALVADOR--COSTUME
--President Duarte
   Life 8:94-5 (1) D '85
EL SALVADOR--POLITICS AND
      GOVERNMENT
--Executed rebels
   Life 6:8-9 (c,1) Ja '83
--Guerrilla struggle
   Nat Geog 170:674-9 (c,1) N '86
--Journalist victims of shooting
   Life 5:136-7 (1) My '82
--U.S. soldiers training military
   Life 6:32-8 (c,1) Mr '83
ELANDS
   Natur Hist 95:58 (c,4) Mr '86
   Sports Illus 65:60-1 (c,1) S 8
      '86
ELBA, ITALY
   Nat Geog 161:180 (c,4) F '82
ELDER TREES
--Elderberries
   Natur Hist 91:95 (4) My '82
ELECTIONS
--1856 Election Day riot (Balti-
      more, Maryland)
   Am Heritage 34:19 (drawing,3)
      F '83
--1860s blacks voting
   Ebony 39:114 (etching,4) Ag
      '84
   Ebony 40:120 (engraving,4) N
      '84
--1946 election problems (Athens,
      Tennessee)
   Am Heritage 36:72-8 (1) F '85
--Black voters at ballot box
      (Mississippi)
   Ebony 39:128 (2) Ag '84
--Blacks registering to vote
   Ebony 40:122 (4) N '84
--Outdoor municipal election (Swit-
      zerland)
   Nat Geog 169:104-5 (c,1) Ja
      '86
--Voting (Philippines)
   Nat Geog 170:89 (c,4) Jl '86
--See
      POLITICAL CAMPAIGNS
      WOMEN'S SUFFRAGE
         MOVEMENT

ELECTRICITY
--1900 Tesla coil electric discharge
   Smithsonian 17:122 (3) Je '86
--Early AC generators
   Smithsonian 17:128 (4) Je '86
--Early DC/AC transformer
   Smithsonian 17:130 (4) Je '86
--Generated from brine (Israel)
   Nat Geog 168:24-5 (c,1) Jl '85
--Lineman training (Papua New
      Guinea)
   Nat Geog 162:160-1 (c,1) Ag '82
--Work by Nikola Tesla
   Smithsonian 17:120-34 (c,1) Je
      '86
--See also
      EDISON, THOMAS ALVA
      LIGHTING
      TESLA, NIKOLA
ELECTRONICS
--Bar scanner technology
   Nat Geog 165:374-5 (c,1) Mr '84
--Diagram of circuitry (Israel)
   Nat Geog 168:3 (c,1) Jl '85
--Home entertainment centers
      (Illinois)
   Ebony 40:157-63 (3) N '84
--Lie detector
   Sports Illus 61:61 (c,4) O 22 '84
--Microchips
   Life 6:28-9 (c,1) Ap '83
   Ebony 39:59 (c,4) My '84
   Ebony 40:37 (c,4) N '84
--Microlaser chips
   Smithsonian 14:142-8 (c,2) O '83
--Microprocessor circuitry
   Nat Geog 162:430-1, 449 (c,1) O
      '82
--Russians stealing U.S. high tech
      secrets
   Life 6:28-36 (c,1) Ap '83
--Silicon chips
   Nat Geog 162:cov., 420-68 (c,1)
      O '82
--Telephone switching equipment
   Smithsonian 17:66-78 (c,2) N '86
--See also
      ANTENNAS
      CALCULATORS
      COMPUTER TERMINALS
      COMPUTERS
      ELECTRICITY
      MICROPHONES
      PHONOGRAPHS
      RADAR
      RADIOS
      RECORDING STUDIOS

ELECTRONICS (cont.)
>ROBOTS
>TAPE RECORDERS
>TELEPHONES
>TELEVISIONS
>VIDEO EQUIPMENT
ELECTRONICS INDUSTRY
--Silicon chip production
>Nat Geog 162:cov., 420-71
>(c,1) O '82
--Silicon Valley scenes, California
>Life 5:32-8 (c,1) Mr '82
--See also
>COMPUTER INDUSTRY
ELEPHANTS
>Nat Geog 161:778-9 (c,1) Je
>'82
>Nat Geog 162:122-3 (c,2) Jl '82
>Natur Hist 91:74-8 (c,2) S '82
>Life 5:9-13 (c,1) S '82
>Life 5:122 (drawing,c,3) N '82
>Nat Geog 163:283, 364-5, 372
>(c,1) Mr '83
>Nat Geog 164:254-5, 274-7
>(c,1) Ag '83
>Nat Wildlife 22:41 (c,3) D '83
>Nat Geog 165:cov., 180 (c,1)
>F '84
>Natur Hist 93:74-8 (c,3) Ap '84
>Life 7:18 (c,2) O '84
>Nat Geog 167:624-5 (c,1) My
>'85
>Sports Illus 62:70 (c,4) My
>27 '85
>Trav/Holiday 164:47 (c,2) Jl
>'85
>Natur Hist 94:38-9 (paint-
>ing,c,2) Ag '85
>Trav/Holiday 165:64 (c,4) Mr
>'86
>Nat Geog 169:597 (c,3) My '86
>Sports Illus 64:59-61, 71
>(painting,c,2) My 5 '86
>Life 9:96 (2) S '86
>Smithsonian 17:148 (4) N '86
>Life 9:112 (c,2) D '86
--"Babar"
>Smithsonian 15:90-6 (c,1) Jl
>'84
--Baby elephants
>Life 5:42-3 (c,1) Je '82
>Life 6:184 (c,2) N '83
--Baby elephant bathing in pool
>Smithsonian 15:25 (c,4) S '84
--Circus (New York)
>Ebony 39:74 (c,4) D '83
--Giving rides (India)

>Trav/Holiday 157:52 (c,3) Mr '82
--Jumbo (1880s)
>Am Heritage 33:6 (4) F '82
>Smithsonian 13:134-52 (c,1) My
>'82
--Riding elephants (Thailand)
>Trav/Holiday 166:62-3 (c,2) S
>'86
--Rolling logs (Thailand)
>Nat Geog 162:520-1 (c,2) O '82
--Shampooing elephant (New York)
>Life 6:134 (c,2) Jl '83
--Stuffed (Washington, D.C. mu-
>seum)
>Smithsonian 13:24 (c,4) S '82
--Swimming
>Natur Hist 95:50-1 (drawing,c,1)
>S '86
--Tusks
>Natur Hist 93:70-1, 76 (1) Ap
>'84
--War elephants at Round-up (Thai-
>land)
>Trav/Holiday 158:19 (4) N '82
--See also
>MASTODONS
ELIOT, T. S.
>Smithsonian 13:80 (4) S '82
>Life 9:117 (4) Fall '86
ELIZABETH I (GREAT BRITAIN)
>Nat Geog 168:681 (painting,c,4)
>N '85
--Actress depicting Elizabeth
>Life 8:64 (c,1) O '85
ELIZABETH II (GREAT BRITAIN)
>Life 5:140 (c,2) My '82
>Life 6:81-4 (c,1) Ja '83
>Smithsonian 14:144 (4) F '84
>Life 8:72 (3) Ag '85
>Life 9:356 (4) Fall '86
>Nat Geog 170:730-1 (c,1) D '86
>Life 9:10 (c,1) D '86
--1953 coronation
>Life 9:90 (c,4) Ap '86
--1953 coronation crown
>Smithsonian 14:134 (c,4) O '83
--Scenes from her life (1936-
>present)
>Life 9:87-90 (c,2) Ap '86
ELIZABETH, NEW JERSEY
--1889
>Am Heritage 37:90-1 (paint-
>ing,c,2) F '86
ELKS
>Nat Geog 162:360-1 (c,1) S '82
>Nat Wildlife 21:4 (c,1) Ap '83
>Nat Wildlife 22:33 (c,4) Ag '84

ELKS (cont.)
Nat Wildlife 23:12, 49 (c,3)
O '85
Nat Wildlife 24:cov., 68
(painting,c,1) D '85
Nat Wildlife 24:6-7 (c,1) F '86
--Antlers
Nat Wildlife 23:11-12, 17 (c,2)
O '85
--Roosevelt elks
Nat Wildlife 24:34-9 (c,1) O '86
--Tule elks
Nat Wildlife 21:28 (c,4) O '83
Nat Wildlife 22:6-7 (c,1) Je
'84
ELLINGTON, DUKE
Ebony 41:66 (4) N '85
Ebony 41:131 (4) F '86
ELM TREES
Am Heritage 37:97-101 (c,3)
O '86
--Killed by Dutch elm disease
Am Heritage 37:98 (c,3) O '86
EMBASSIES
--1983 bombed U.S. embassy
(Kuwait)
Life 8:131 (c,4) D '85
--British embassy interior (Wash-
ington, D.C.)
Life 8:52-5 (c,2) N '85
Embroidery. See
NEEDLEWORK
EMERALDS
--17th cent. ring
Nat Geog 161:237 (c,4) F '82
EMERSON, RALPH WALDO
Smithsonian 14:102 (paint-
ing,c,3) Ag '83
Smithsonian 16:125 (4) Ap '85
Am Heritage 37:78 (4) Je '86
--1840s caricature
Am Heritage 37:108 (drawing,4)
Ag '86
EMOTIONS
--Anguish of losing baseball
game
Sports Illus 65:38-43 (c,1) S
22 '86
--Child's delight at baby snake
Nat Wildlife 25:48 (c,4) D '86
--Losing basketball player pound-
ing floor in frustration
Sports Illus 58:31 (c,3) Ap 4
'83
--Mourning dead leader (Mozam-
bique)
Life 9:12-13 (c,1) D '86

--Shown in facial expressions
Smithsonian 16:112, 116 (c,1)
Mr '86
--Tweaking cheek affectionately
(Louisiana)
Nat Geog 164:230-1 (c,1) Ag '83
--Vietnam veterans embracing
(Washington, D.C.)
Life 8:56-7 (1) My '85
--Winner of soccer World Cup
Sports Illus 65:114-15 (c,1) D
22 '86
--See also
CRYING
GRIEF
KISSING
ROMANCE
SORROW
EMPIRE STATE BUILDING, NEW
YORK CITY, NEW YORK
Smithsonian 14:50 (c,3) O '83
ENERGY
--Ice ponds as source of energy
Smithsonian 14:105-13 (c,2) Ag
'83
--Wind-generated energy
Life 6:84-8 (c,1) N '83
--See also
ALASKA PIPELINE
ELECTRICITY
GASOLINE STATIONS
NUCLEAR ENERGY
OIL INDUSTRY
POWER PLANTS
SOLAR ENERGY
WINDMILLS
WOOD
ENERGY SHORTAGE
--1973 closed gas station
Nat Wildlife 24:32 (c,4) Ap '86
ENGINEERS
Ebony 40:33-6 (c,3) D '84
--Iraq
Nat Geog 167:90 (c,3) Ja '85
ENGINES
--19th cent. U.S. Navy cruiser
Am Heritage 37:88-9 (1) Je '86
--1880 portable agricultural steam
engine (France)
Smithsonian 16:200-1 (c,4) O '85
England. See
GREAT BRITAIN
ENGLISH CHANNEL
--Attempts to build tunnels under
English Channel
Smithsonian 17:66-7, 70-7 (c,1)
My '86

ESKIMOS (ALASKA)--COSTUME
--1899
  Smithsonian 13:57 (4) My '82
ESKIMOS (ALASKA)--RELICS
--Late 19th cent. artifacts
  Smithsonian 13:cov., 50-9
    (c,1) My '82
  Nat Geog 163:198-205 (c,1)
    F '83
--See also
  KAYAKS
  UMIAKS
ESKIMOS (CANADA)
  Nat Geog 169:694-7 (c,1) My
    '86
--Early 20th cent.
  Natur Hist 94:66-71 (1) Ja '85
--Hudson Bay area
  Nat Geog 161:380-403 (c,1) Mr
    '82
--Northwest Territories
  Nat Geog 163:144-5, 174-86
    (c,1) F '83
ESKIMOS (CANADA)--COSTUME
  Nat Geog 164:114-15 (c,1) Jl
    '83
--Inuit girl (Labrador)
  Trav/Holiday 166:52 (c,4) Jl
    '86
ESKIMOS (CANADA)--HISTORY
--11th cent. migration east from
    Alaska
  Nat Geog 164:100-26 (c,1)
    Jl '83
ESKIMOS (GREENLAND)
--Costume, lifestyle
  Nat Geog 163:190-3 (c,1) F '83
  Nat Geog 165:cov., 521-38
    (c,1) Ap '84
ESKIMOS (GREENLAND)--
    RELICS
--15th cent. mummies
  Nat Geog 167:cov., 190-207
    (c,1) F '85
ESSEN, WEST GERMANY
--Outdoor market
  Natur Hist 93:102 (c,3) Mr '84
ETHIOPIA
  Nat Geog 163:614-45 (map,c,1)
    My '83
--Eritrea
  Nat Geog 168:384-405 (map,c,1)
    S '85
--Fundraising concerts
  Life 9:80-5 (c,1) Ja '86
--Unloading imported grain
  Nat Geog 170:668 (c,2) N '86

--See also
  ADDIS ABABA
  NILE RIVER
ETHIOPIA--COSTUME
  Nat Geog 163:614-43 (c,1) My
    '83
  Life 8:124-34 (c,1) My '85
--Eritrea
  Nat Geog 168:384-405 (c,1) S '85
--Starving child
  Life 7:194 (c,2) D '84
  Life 8:8-9 (c,1) Ja '85
  Ebony 40:22 (4) F '85
--Starving people
  Life 8:124-34 (c,1) My '85
  Nat Geog 168:400-5 (c,1) S '85
  Natur Hist 94:30-1 (1) S '85
  Nat Geog 170:646, 668-75 (c,1)
    N '86
--Traditional dress (Indiana)
  Life 8:91, 94-5 (1) F '85
ETHIOPIA--HISTORY
--Depiction of battle vs. Italians
  Life 5:104-5 (c,1) N '82
--Haile Selassie
  Ebony 39:56 (4) O '84
ETHIOPIA--POLITICS AND GOV-
    ERNMENT
--Fighting Eritrean rebels
  Nat Geog 168:384-99 (c,1) S '85
EUROPE
--Scenes of Europe
  Trav/Holiday 165:45 (c,2) Mr '86
--See also
  ALPS
  DANUBE RIVER
  individual countries
EUROPE--MAPS
--1812
  Nat Geog 161:147-9 (c,1) F '82
--Ice Age Europe
  Smithsonian 17:80 (c,2) O '86
--Stone Age sites
  Natur Hist 95:74 (c,4) O '86
EVERGLADES NATIONAL PARK,
    FLORIDA
  Nat Wildlife 20:50-5 (c,1) O '82
  Natur Hist 93:46-57 (map,c,1)
    N '84
  Nat Wildlife 23:54-63 (map,c,1)
    Ap '85
  Trav/Holiday 165:44-7 9c,1) Ja
    '86
--Mangrove islands
  Smithsonian 15:123 (c,4) Mr '85
EVERGREEN TREES
  Nat Wildlife 23:12-17 (c,1) D '84

EVERS, MEDGAR
  Ebony 41:296 (4) N '85
EVOLUTION
--Animals of cretaceous and
    tertiary periods
  Nat Geog 170:408 (draw-
    ing,c,1) S '86
--See also
    DARWIN, CHARLES
    MAN, PREHISTORIC
EXERCISING
--Aerobic dancing
  Life 5:59-63 (c,1) Mr '82
  Sports Illus 61:75 (c,3) D 3
    '84
  Ebony 40:84 (3) Ag '85
--Aerobics done by football play-
    ers
  Sports Illus 57:28-9 (c,1) Jl
    26 '82
--Hanging upside-down
  Sports Illus 57:31 (c,3) Jl 26
    '82
--See also
    BODYBUILDING
    CALISTHENICS
    GYMNASTICS
    HEALTH CLUBS
    ROPE JUMPING
    YOGA
EXERCISING EQUIPMENT
  Smithsonian 13:67 (2) My '82
  Life 5:104 (c,4) Je '82
  Ebony 37:50-4 (c,2) Je '82
  Life 5:46-52 (c,1) O '82
  Life 6:59 (c,4) F '83
  Sports Illus 58:69 (c,4) F 7
    '83
  Ebony 38:112 (3) Mr '83
  Sports Illus 58:69 (c,4) F 7 '83
  Sports Illus 60:90 (c,4) F 6
    '84
  Sports Illus 60:42-3 (c,2) F
    13 '84
  Ebony 39:67, 78, 100 (c,4)
    My '84
  Ebony 39:58 (4) Jl '84
  Sports Illus 61:48, 130-1 (c,2)
    S 5 '84
  Ebony 39:98, 186 (3) O '84
  Sports Illus 61:81 (c,4) N 12
    '84
  Ebony 40:70 (4) Ap '85
  Ebony 40:56, 66 (c,4) O '85
  Sports Illus 64:54 (c,4) Mr 24
    '86
--Back-stretching "orthopod"

  machine
  Life 9:63 (c,2) My '86
--Ergometers
  Sports Illus 56:30 (c,4) F 22 '82
--Exercise bicycle
  Ebony 37:30 (c,4) My '82
  Ebony 38:82 (4) Je '83
  Sports Illus 59:80 (c,4) D 19 '83
  Sports Illus 60:98 (c,4) F 13 '84
--Health club
  Ebony 41:148 (3) Mr '86
--Home equipment
  Sports Illus 60:40 (c,4) Ap 16
    '84
--Jaw strengthener for boxers
  Sports Illus 64:41 (c,4) Je 9 '86
--Nautilus
  Sports Illus 61:82 (c,2) D 3 '84
--Sit up equipment
  Ebony 38:86 (4) My '83
--Strengthening knees
  Sports Illus 63:51 (c,3) Jl 29
    '85
--Swivel machine
  Sports Illus 64:49 (c,4) Ja 27
    '86
--Treadmill
  Ebony 39:186 (3) O '84
--Walking machine
  Ebony 39:52 (c,3) Ja '84
EXPLORERS
--1838 Wilkes' round the world trip
  Smithsonian 16:48-63 (map,c,1)
    N '85
--Matthew Henson
  Ebony 40:114 (4) S '85
--Sir Thomas Stamford Raffles
  Smithsonian 13:130 (painting,c,1)
    Ap '82
--See also
    AMERICA--DISCOVERY AND
      EXPLORATION
    ANTARCTIC EXPEDITIONS
    ARCTIC EXPEDITIONS
    CHAMPLAIN, SAMUEL DE
    COLUMBUS, CHRISTOPHER
    COOK, JAMES
    CORTES, HERNAN
    DA GAMA, VASCO
    DRAKE, SIR FRANCIS
    FREMONT, JOHN
    LA SALLE, SIEUR DE
    PEARY, ROBERT E.
    POLO, MARCO
    SAFARIS
EXPLOSIONS
--19th cent. dynamite used in

FACTORIES (cont.)
Nat Geog 169:692-3 (c,1) My
'86
--Linz, Austria
Nat Geog 167:429 (c,4) Ap '85
--Petrochemical plant (Puerto
Rico)
Nat Geog 163:529 (c,3) Ap '83
--Pulp and paper (New Hamp-
shire)
Nat Geog 162:776-7 (c,1) D '82
--Sugar refinery (Sudan)
Nat Geog 161:358 (c,4) Mr '82
--Uranium mill (South Dakota)
Life 7:108 (c,4) Jl '84
--See also
MANUFACTURING
MILLS
SAWMILLS
FACTORY WORKERS
--1940s women in defense plants
(U.S.)
Am Heritage 35:99-103 (4) F
'84
--American Samoa
Nat Geog 168:461 (c,1) O '85
--Cereal plant (Illinois)
Sports Illus 56:67-9 (c,4) Ap
5 '82
--Japan
Nat Geog 162:432-3 (c,1) O '82
--New York
Life 8:180 (c,2) O '85
--Nuclear power plants
Life 5:34-42 (c,1) My '82
--Steel workers (Pennsylvania)
Life 7:122, 124 (c,2) N '84
--Taiwan
Nat Geog 161:102-3 (c,2) Ja
'82
FADS
Life 6:117-22 (c,1) Ja '83
Life 7:158-66 (c,1) Ja '84
--1938-1985
Life 9:65-72 (c,2) Ag '86
--1938 marathon dance contest
Life 9:65 (2) Ag '86
--1950s
Life 8:cov., 77-84 (c,1) Ag
'85
--1975 streaker
Life 9:71 (4) Ag '86
--1985 fads
Life 9:105-10 (c,3) Ja '86
--1986 youth fads
Life 9:46-7 (drawing,c,2) Mr
'86

--Break dancing (New York)
Life 6:161-6 (c,1) Ja '83
--Deely Bobbers
Life 6:117 (c,2) Ja '83
--Hula hoops (1958)
Life 9:68 (3) Ag '86
--Pet Rock (1979)
Life 9:72 (c,4) Ag '86
--"Rocky Horror Picture Show" audi-
ence (Massachusetts)
Life 9:33 (c,4) D '86
--Rubik's cube (1981)
Life 9:72 (c,3) Ag '86
FAEROE ISLANDS
Life 9:8-9 (c,1) O '86
FAIRBANKS, DOUGLAS, JR.
Life 9:194 (c,2) My '86
FAIRS
--1876 Philadelphia Exposition Cen-
tennial fountain
Smithsonian 17:118 (drawing,4)
Jl '86
--1885 New Orleans Exposition
Am Heritage 36:61 (3) D '84
--1893 Chicago World's Fair
Am Heritage 35:74 (2) D '83
--1893 Chicago World's Fair ferris
wheel
Smithsonian 14:109 (3) Jl '83
--1893 Chicago World's Fair German
chocolate monument
Smithsonian 16:56 (c,4) F '86
--1893 Chicago World's Fair New
York State building
Am Heritage 35:78 (painting,c,4)
Ap '84
--1915 ticket booth (San Francisco,
California)
Am Heritage 34:112 (3) Ag '83
--1939 Perisphere and Trylon (New
York)
Am Heritage 35:78-9 (c,1) Ap
'84
Am Heritage 35:8 (4) Je '84
--1948 carnival
Am Heritage 37:77 (painting,c,2)
D '85
--1984 New Orleans Exposition
Smithsonian 15:54-5 (c,1) Je '84
Ebony 39:127-30 (c,2) Jl '84
--Expo 86, Vancouver, British
Columbia
Trav/Holiday 165:46-7 (c,1) F
'86
--Expo 86 Canada pavilion, Van-
couver, British Columbia
Nat Geog 170:74-5 (c,1) Jl '86

FAMILIES (cont.)
Sports Illus 59:31 (c,4) Ag
29 '83
--Parents and children
Sports Illus 61:52 (c,4) Ag 6
'84
Sports Illus 62:50 (c,4) Mr 4
'85
Sports Illus 63:77 (c,4) N 4
'85
--Parents and children (Japan)
Nat Geog 170:634-5, 638-9
(c,1) N '86
--Parents and children and dogs
Sports Illus 63:68 (c,2) Ag 5
'85
--Parents and children at pool
Sports Illus 63:33 (c,4) Ag
19 '85
--Several generations of large
family (New Jersey)
Life 6:48-9 (c,1) Jl '83
--Siblings hugging (New York)
Life 9:58-9 (1) D '86
FAMILY LIFE
--Family bicycle outing
Sports Illus 64:60 (c,3) Je 2
'86
--Family of 15 children (Australia)
Life 5:112 (c,2) Mr '82
--Family portrait (New York)
Life 5:88-9 (1) Je '82
--Family therapy session (New
York)
Life 5:74-80 (1) Mr '82
--Harlem, New York
Ebony 38:68-76 (2) Ag '83
--Mother awakened by son (1955)
Life 9:153 (2) Fall '86
--Parents and children at home
Ebony 40:88-94 (c,3) Jl '85
--Playing board game
Ebony 38:44 (c,4) Je '83
--Taiwanese immigrants (West
Virginia)
Life 8:145-50 (c,1) Je '85
--See also
BABIES
CHILDREN
LIFESTYLES
Family trees. See
GENEALOGY
FANS
--18th cent.
Smithsonian 14:199 (c,4) Mr '84
--1784 (China)
Natur Hist 93:64 (c,4) F '84

--1908 electric fan
Smithsonian 17:128 (c,4) D '86
--1920s promotional fan
Am Heritage 35:4 (c,1) Ag '84
--1960s Beatles fans
Life 7:58-67 (c,1) F '84
--Early Tesla electric fan
Smithsonian 17:128 (4) Je '86
--Rock group fans
Life 5:164, 170 (c,1) N '82
--See also
SPECTATORS
FARALLON ISLANDS, CALIFORNIA
Nat Wildlife 24:44-51 (c,1) Je
'86
FARM LIFE
--Alabama family
Ebony 38:112-16 (1) Ag '83
--Amish people (Pennsylvania)
Nat Geog 165:492-519 (c,1) Ap
'84
--Feeding hogs (Minnesota)
Sports Illus 63:81 (c,3) N 4 '85
--Forking hay (Massachusetts)
Am Heritage 33:42 (c,2) Ag '82
--Herding cows (Austria)
Trav/Holiday 164:52 (c,2) Ag '85
--Hosing down hog (Tennessee)
Nat Geog 169:613 (c,4) My '86
--Iowa farm dinner (1937)
Life 9:280-1 (1) Fall '86
--Livestock show (Great Britain)
Natur Hist 93:102-3 (c,3) N '84
--Milking goat (California)
Natur Hist 92:86 (c,4) Ja '83
--Nebraska
Life 8:145-50 (1) N '85
--Running for tornado storm cellar
(1929)
Am Heritage 37:28-9 (painting,c,1)
Je '86
--Tending farm animals (Florida)
Sports Illus 64:44-5, 55-6 (c,1)
Ap 7 '86
FARM MACHINERY
--1794 patent for Whitney's cotton
gin
Am Heritage 35:93 (c,2) Ag '84
--Barley mower (Greece)
Nat Geog 162:707 (c,4) D '82
--Windrower
Smithsonian 17:68-9 (c,1) S '86
--See also
COMBINES
CROP DUSTER PLANES
HARVESTERS
REAPING MACHINES
TRACTORS

FARM WORKERS
--1877 (Massachusetts)
    Nat Wildlife 21:18-20 (engrav-
        ing,2) D '82
--1950 migrant workers in cotton
    field (California)
    Ebony 41:212 (3) N '85
--Burma
    Nat Geog 166:104-5 (c,1) Jl '84
--California
    Nat Geog 166:325 (c,1) S '84
--Children of migrant workers
    (Florida)
    Life 6:147-58 (1) N '83
--China
    Nat Geog 165:34 (c,3) Ja '84
--Chinese (British Columbia)
    Nat Geog 170:71 (c,4) Jl '86
--Hawaii
    Nat Geog 169:516 (c,2) Ap '86
--Maintaining equipment (Missis-
    sippi)
    Ebony 41:48 (c,4) Je '86
--Migrant workers (California)
    Nat Geog 165:436-7 (c,2) Ap
        '84
    Nat Geog 167:743 (c,3) Je '85
--Portugal
    Trav/Holiday 158:cov. (c,1)
        O '82
--South Yemen
    Nat Geog 168:488 (c,4) O '85
--Spain
    Nat Geog 165:124-5 (c,2) Ja
        '84
    Sports Illus 63:76 (c,3) Jl 15
        '85
--Sri Lanka
    Trav/Holiday 165:54 (c,4) Ap '86
FARMERS
--Austria
    Trav/Holiday 164:52 (c,2) Ag
        '85
--Great Britain
    Trav/Holiday 164:40-1 (c,1) Jl
        '85
--Texas
    Sports Illus 59:38-9 (c,2) Jl 4
        '83
FARMHOUSES
--Late 18th cent. (Pennsylvania)
    Nat Geog 168:818 (3) D '85
--Bromfield's Malabar Farm, Ohio
    Trav/Holiday 159:25-9 (4) Ap
        '83
--New York
    Sports Illus 58:44 (drawing,c,4)

    Ja 31 '83
FARMING
--Agricultural research
    Smithsonian 12:54-63 (c,1) Mr
        '82
--Clearing land for crops (Bolivia)
    Nat Wildlife 22:17 (c,4) D '83
--Effects of groundwater depletion
    Nat Wildlife 24:50-5 (c,1) D '85
--Exotic fruits and vegetables
    (Florida)
    Smithsonian 16:36-41 (c,3) D '85
--Mexico
    Nat Geog 166:454-5 (c,2) O '84
--Pig farming (Florida)
    Sports Illus 64:44-5 (c,1) Ap 7
        '86
--Soil problems
    Nat Geog 166:350-89 (c,1) S '84
--Spain
    Natur Hist 94:68-75 (c,1) N '85
--See also
        DAIRYING
        IRRIGATION
        PEST CONTROL
        list of farmed products under
        INDUSTRIES
FARMING--PLANTING
--China
    Nat Geog 165:292 (c,1) Mr '84
--Corn (Hungary)
    Nat Geog 163:244-5 (c,1) F '83
--Corn (Kentucky)
    Nat Geog 161:542-3 (c,2) Ap '82
FARMING--PLOWING
--Horse-driven plow (Ohio)
    Nat Wildlife 20:48-9 (c,1) Ag '82
--Kenya
    Nat Geog 161:125 (c,3) Ja '82
--Mississippi
    Ebony 41:46-7, 50 (c,2) Je '86
--North Carolina
    Ebony 41:210 (4) N '85
--Ox-driven plow (France)
    Natur Hist 91:51 (c,1) Ag '82
--Rice paddy (Thailand)
    Smithsonian 13:99 (c,4) Ja '83
--Using mule and harrow (Pennsyl-
    vania)
    Nat Geog 165:504-5 (c,1) Ap '84
--Using water buffalo (India)
    Nat Geog 166:720-1 (c,1) D '84
--Yak pulling plow (Tibet)
    Natur Hist 95:60-1 (c,2) Ja '86
--Yoked cows (Spain)
    Natur Hist 94:68-9 (c,1) N '85

FARMS
  Nat Wildlife 20:12 (c,1) Ag '82
--1820s (Pennsylvania)
  Natur Hist 94:104 (paint-
    ing,c,4) Ap '85
--Aerial view (Iowa)
  Life 5:124 (c,1) O '82
--Aerial view of harvested field
    (California)
  Nat Wildlife 24:57 (c,2) O '86
--Aerial views of farm patterns
  Nat Geog 166:390-9 (c,1) S
    '84
  Nat Wildlife 24:53-9 (c,1) O
    '86
--Below sea level (Netherlands)
  Nat Geog 170:506-7 (c,1) O
    '86
--California
  Nat Wildlife 23:14 (c,1) F '85
--Decrepit scene (Nebraska)
  Trav/Holiday 159:12 (4) Ja '83
--Failing farm (Nebraska)
  Life 8:145-50 (1) N '85
--France
  Nat Geog 161:486-7 (c,1) Ap
    '82
--Great Britain
  Nat Geog 169:404-5 (c,1) Mr '86
--Herbs (California)
  Nat Geog 163:402-3 (c,2) Mr
    '83
--Hungary
  Nat Geog 163:242-3 (c,1) F '83
--Idaho
  Nat Geog 161:798-9 (c,1) Je '82
--Iowa
  Smithsonian 15:34-47 (1) Ag '84
--Israel
  Nat Geog 168:18-19 (c,1) Jl '85
--Ivory Coast
  Nat Geog 162:98-9 (c,1) Jl '82
--Jordan
  Nat Geog 165:250-1 (c,1) F '84
--Kashmir
  Trav/Holiday 166:61 (c,3) N
    '86
--Kentucky
  Nat Geog 161:522-46 (c,1) Ap
    '82
--Lancaster County, Pennsylvania
  Nat Geog 165:494-5, 508-9
    (c,1) Ap '84
--Midlands, England
  Natur Hist 94:42-51 (c,1) My
    '85
--Minnesota

Smithsonian 17:76-7 (c,1) S '86
--Nepal
  Nat Geog 161:710-11 (c,1) Je '82
--Paraguay
  Nat Geog 162:260-1 (c,1) Ag '82
--Pennsylvania
  Nat Geog 167:352-3 (c,1) Mr '85
  Smithsonian 15:158-9 (c,3) Mr
    '85
--Poor soil (Georgia)
  Nat Geog 166:352-3 (c,1) S '84
--Queensland, Australia
  Nat Geog 169:18-19 (c,1) Ja '86
--Reconstructed Viking farm (Ice-
    land)
  Smithsonian 16:118-19 (c,3) Ja
    '86
--Rice (Arkansas)
  Ebony 42:100-2 (c,1) D '86
--Rice (Australia)
  Nat Geog 168:262-3 (c,1) Ag '85
--Rice (Peru)
  Nat Geog 163:40-1 (c,3) Ja '83
--Rice terraces (Philippines)
  Trav/Holiday 159:33 (c,1) Ja '83
  Nat Geog 170:94-5 (c,1) Jl '86
--Sage (North Carolina)
  Nat Geog 163:408 (c,3) Mr '83
--Saskatchewan
  Nat Geog 166:572-3 (c,1) N '84
--Silos (Iowa)
  Smithsonian 15:38-41 (1) Ag '84
--Tasmania
  Nat Geog 167:174-5 (c,1) F '85
--Tennessee
  Nat Geog 169:610-11, 624-5 (c,1)
    My '86
--Texas
  Sports Illus 59:32-3 (c,1) Jl 4
    '83
  Nat Geog 165:214-15 (c,1) F '84
--Tobacco (North Carolina)
  Smithsonian 16:194 (4) Ap '85
--Vermont
  Trav/Holiday 162:55 (c,3) S '84
--Wales
  Nat Geog 164:58-9 (c,1) Jl '83
--Washington
  Nat Geog 161:804-7, 816-19 (c,1)
    Je '82
  Nat Geog 166:374-5 (c,3) S '84
--West Virginia
  Trav/Holiday 164:59 (c,2) O '85
--Wheat (Oregon)
  Nat Wildlife 24:38-9 (c,1) Ag '86
--Wisconsin
  Nat Wildlife 21:33 (c,3) Ap '83

FARMS (cont.)
--See also
    BARNS
    CORNFIELDS
    FARMHOUSES
    HORSE FARMS
    PLANTATIONS
    RANCHES
    STABLES
    VINEYARDS
    WHEAT FIELDS
FARRAGUT, DAVID GLASGOW
--Monument (New York)
    Am Heritage 36:47 (c,2) Je
      '85
FASHION SHOWS
    Ebony 37:106-10 (c,2) F '82
    Ebony 37:113-17 (c,2) Ap '82
    Ebony 37:115-18 (c,2) My '82
    Ebony 37:104-8 (c,1) Jl '82
    Ebony 37:104-8 (c,2) S '82
    Ebony 38:157-60 (c,3) N '82
    Ebony 38:100-2 (c,1) Jl '83
--East Germany
    Nat Geog 161:25 (c,3) Ja '82
--Netherlands
    Nat Geog 170:517 (c,1) O '86
--New York City, New York
    Smithsonian 16:cov., 30-1, 38,
      41 (c,1) Ag '85
--Peru
    Nat Geog 161:296-7 (c,1) Mr
      '82
Fat people. See
    OBESITY
FAULKNER, WILLIAM
    Sports Illus 64:39 (drawing,c,2)
      Ap 28 '86
--Home (Oxford, Mississippi)
    Trav/Holiday 166:56-7 (c,2) Jl
      '86
FEATHERS
    Nat Wildlife 21:21-4 (c,1) Je
      '83
--Bird feather fragments
    Smithsonian 12:98-101 (c,3) Mr
      '82
--Hopi prayer feathers (Arizona)
    Nat Geog 162:628-9 (c,1) N
      '82
--Pheasant
    Nat Geog 162:79 (c,4) Jl '82
FEDERAL BUREAU OF INVESTI-
    GATION
--Badge
    Ebony 37:48 (3) Ag '82
--FBI official seal

    Sports Illus 63:27 (c,4) N 18 '85
FEET
--Soles of feet that walked on fire
    (California)
    Life 8:42-3, 48 (c,1) Mr '85
FENCERS
--Spain
    Nat Geog 161:735 (c,2) Je '82
FENCES
--Farm wood and wire fence (Texas)
    Nat Geog 165:222-3 (c,1) F '84
--Horse farm (California)
    Nat Geog 165:459 (c,1) Ap '84
--Spruce garden fence (Newfound-
    land)
    Natur Hist 94:24 (c,3) Je '85
--Wooden log fence (Wyoming)
    Life 6:125 (c,4) N '83
--See also
    GATES
FENCING
    Sports Illus 62:86-8 (c,4) Mr 18
      '85
--1984 Olympics (Los Angeles)
    Life 8:122-3 (c,1) Ja '85
FER-DE-LANCE SNAKES
    Natur Hist 94:4 (c,3) Ap '85
FERNS
    Nat Wildlife 21:56 (c,1) Je '83
    Natur Hist 94:46-7 (c,1) F '85
    Smithsonian 16:51, 58 (c,4) My
      '85
--Curley-grass fern
    Smithsonian 14:87 (c,1) Jl '83
--Water ferns
    Smithsonian 16:154 (c,2) Ap '85
FERRETS
    Nat Geog 163:828-38 (c,1) Je '83
    Nat Wildlife 21:16-19 (1) Je '83
    Sports Illus 59:74 (c,4) S 26 '83
    Sports Illus 62:34 (c,3) F 18 '85
    Nat Wildlife 23:13 (c,4) Ap '85
    Natur Hist 95:cov., 62-71 (c,1)
      F '86
FERRIS WHEELS
    Smithsonian 14:108-18 (c,1) Jl
      '83
--1893 first ferris wheel (Chicago,
    Illinois)
    Smithsonian 14:109 (3) Jl '83
--Coney Island, Brooklyn, New
    York
    Smithsonian 14:108 (c,1) Jl '83
--History
    Smithsonian 14:108-18 (c,1) Jl
      '83
--Inventor George Ferris, Jr.

FERRIS WHEELS (cont.)
Smithsonian 14:110 (4) Jl '83
--Ohio
Life 8:38 (c,2) Ag '85
--West Virginia
Life 5:90 (2) N '82
FERRY BOATS
--Alaska
Nat Geog 165:59 (c,3) Ja '84
--Commuters on Staten Island
Ferry, New York City
Nat Geog 170:32-3 (c,1) Jl '86
--Long Island, New York
Trav/Holiday 165:87 (c,4) Ap
'86
--Maine
Trav/Holiday 157:63 (c,4) My
'82
--Pennsylvania
Nat Geog 167:364-5 (c,3) Mr
'85
--San Juan Islands, Washington
Trav/Holiday 16:58 (c,4) S '86
--Texas/Mexico ferry
Life 9:44-5 (c,1) Ag '86
FESTIVALS
Smithsonian 13:108-17 (c,1) S
'82
--1720 Ottoman festival (Turkey)
Smithsonian 16:120 (paint-
ing,c,3) F '86
--1830s Old West mountain men
rendezvous
Sports Illus 58:58-72 (paint-
ing,c,1) Ja 17 '83
--1880s Mardi Gras (New Orleans,
Louisiana)
Trav/Holiday 161:61, 70-1 (c,3)
F '84
--1886 Statue of Liberty opening
celebration, New York
Life 8:114 (2) S '85
Nat Geog 170:18 (2) Jl '86
--1897 dedication of Grant's
Tomb, New York City
Am Heritage 36:76-7 (painting,c,2) Ag '85
--1914 pageant (St. Louis, Missouri)
Am Heritage 33:54-5 (2) Ag
'82
--1924 carnival (New Mexico)
Am Heritage 33:104 (c,2) Ap
'82
--1936 christening of the U.S.S.
Enterprise
Life 8:39 (2) Spring '85

--Arkansas Folk Festival, Mountain
View
Trav/Holiday 161:52-4 (c,1) F
'84
--Basketball (Lowell, Michigan)
Sports Illus 63:62-76 (c,1) Jl 8
'85
--Basque games (Nevada)
Trav/Holiday 162:48-51 (c,1) Jl
'84
--Breaux Bridge Crawfish Festival,
Louisiana
Natur Hist 93:46-57 (c,1) Ap '84
--Calgary Stampede, Alberta
Nat Geog 165:385, 398-9 (c,1)
Mr '84
Trav/Holiday 163:66-9, 81 (c,1)
My '85
--Carnival (Panama)
Nat Geog 169:487 (c,2) Ap '86
--Carnival sideshow (Massachusetts)
Nat Geog 166:802 (c,1) D '84
--Cherry Blossom Festival, San
Francisco, California
Nat Geog 169:513-14 (c,1) Ap '86
--Cinco de Mayo (Denver, Colorado)
Nat Geog 166:200-1 (c,3) Ag '84
--Comic strips in "Hands Across
America" effort
Life 9:57-60 (1) Je '86
--Esala Perahera (Sri Lanka)
Nat Geog 164:254-5 (c,1) Ag '83
--Fasching (Munich, West Germany)
Trav/Holiday 161:77 (c,2) F '84
--Fasnacht Carnival (Basel, Switzer-
land)
Natur Hist 91:cov., 28-40 (c,1)
F '82
--Festival of Joan of Arc (Rouen,
France)
Nat Geog 161:506-7 (c,1) Ap '82
--Fête de Cuisinières (Guadeloupe)
Trav/Holiday 165:80 (c,1) Ap '86
--Fiesta (San Antonio, Texas)
Smithsonian 16:cov., 114-27 (c,1)
D '85
--Garlic festival (California)
Nat Geog 170:343 (c,2) S '86
--German Maifest (Missouri)
Trav/Holiday 160:54 (c,4) Jl '83
--"Hands Across America" event
(Pennsylvania)
Sports Illus 64:2-3 (c,1) Je 2
'86
--Harborfest, Norfolk, Virginia
Nat Geog 168:82-3 (c,1) Jl '85
--Mardi Gras

FIELDS (cont.)
    CORNFIELDS
    GRASSLANDS
    WHEAT FIELDS
FIG TREES
    Trav/Holiday 165:44 (c,1) F
        '86
FIGS
    Nat Geog 169:543-4 (c,1) Ap
        '86
FIGUREHEADS
    Smithsonian 15:122 (c,4) Ap
        '84
--Early 19th cent. U.S. ship
    Nat Geog 163:cov., 288-311
        (c,1) Mr '83
FIJI ISLANDS
    Trav/Holiday 163:10 (c,4) Mr
        '85
FIJI ISLANDS--HISTORY
--1840 lifestyle
    Smithsonian 16:58-9 (draw-
        ing,3) N '85
FIJI ISLANDS--RELICS
--1830s mask
    Smithsonian 16:54 (c,4) N '85
FINCHES
    Natur Hist 91:78 (c,4) Ja '82
    Natur Hist 91:44 (c,4) D '82
    Natur Hist 92:77-81 (c,2) S
        '83
    Nat Wildlife 22:31-2 (paint-
        ing,c,1) D '83
    Sports Illus 62:82 (c,3) My 27
        '85
    Natur Hist 94:66 (c,4) O '85
    Nat Wildlife 24:63 (c,4) D '85
    Natur Hist 95:84-5 (c,1) Ag
        '86
--See also
    BUNTINGS
    GOLDFINCHES
FINLAND
    Trav/Holiday 166:8-9 (map,c,3)
        D '86
--Lapp Folk Museum, Inari
    Trav/Holiday 158:8 (c,4) Jl '82
--See also
    HELSINKI
    TAMPERE
FINLAND--COSTUME
--Traditional
    Trav/Holiday 159:48 (4) Mr '83
FINLAND--MAPS
    Trav/Holiday 161:35 (4) My '84
FIR TREES
    Natur Hist 94:60-3 (c,1) Ja '85

--See also
    DOUGLAS FIR TREES
FIRE FIGHTERS
    Smithsonian 15:167-72 (c,2) Mr
        '85
--California
    Life 5:110-12 (c,1) N '82
--Chicago, Illinois
    Life 8:42-3 (1) F '85
--Forest smoke jumpers
    Nat Wildlife 20:37-9 (painting,2)
        Je '82
--Massachusetts
    Life 8:52 (c,4) Ap '85
--New Jersey
    Ebony 37:71 (2) Ag '82
--New York
    Life 5:18 (c,3) N '82
--"Smokey the Bear"
    Nat Geog 162:332 (drawing,c,4)
        S '82
--Trying to revive fire victim
        (Massachusetts)
    Life 8:92-3 (1) D '85
--Volunteer fire fighters
    Smithsonian 14:154-64 (c,2) N
        '83
FIRE FIGHTING
--Aboard cruise ship (1942)
    Am Heritage 35:65-7 (1) D '83
--Forest fire (California)
    Smithsonian 14:64 (c,4) Ap '83
--Forest fires
    Nat Geog 162:330-1 (c,1) S '82
--New York
    Smithsonian 14:154, 156 (c,2) N
        '83
--Plugging leak in gas pipe (Mary-
        land)
    Smithsonian 15:50 (c,4) Ap '84
FIRE FIGHTING EQUIPMENT
--Fire truck (Alabama)
    Ebony 37:56 (4) Jl '82
FIRE HYDRANTS
--1906 (San Francisco, California)
    Am Heritage 34:36-7 (1) F '83
--Brooklyn, New York
    Nat Geog 163:585 (c,2) My '83
--Connecticut
    Life 7:8 (c,4) Ap '84
FIREHOUSES
--Mount Carmel, Pennsylvania
    Nat Geog 167:369 (c,3) Mr '85
FIREPLACES
--Beverly Hills mansion, California
    Life 9:140 (c,2) My '86
--New Zealand

FIREPLACES (cont.)
    Trav/Holiday 166:50 (c,2) Ag
        '86
--Relaxing in front of fire at
        lodge
    Sports Illus 64:57 (c,4) Mr 3
        '86
--Washington hotel
    Trav/Holiday 159:44 (c,2) My
        '83
FIRES
    Nat Geog 164:435 (c,1) O '83
    Smithsonian 16:132-3 (c,1) My
        '85
--19th cent. Indians burning
        land (Midwest)
    Natur Hist 92:6, 8 (paint-
        ing,c,2) F '83
--1834 fire at Massachusetts con-
        vent
    Am Heritage 33:100 (c,1) F
        '82
--1854 fire at Westminster, Lon-
        don, England
    Nat Geog 170:738-9 (paint-
        ing,c,2) D '86
--1906 (San Francisco, California)
    Am Heritage 34:111 (3) D '82
    Am Heritage 34:38-9 (1) F '83
--1955 tragic racing car accident
        (Le Mans, France)
    Sports Illus 64:80-96 (paint-
        ing,c,1) My 12 '86
--Australian desert
    Sports Illus 62:128-9 (c,1) F
        11 '85
--Boston, Massachusetts
    Life 8:52-4 (c,4) Ap '85
--Cannes, France
    Life 9:10-11 (c,1) N '86
--Forest
    Nat Geog 162:326-32 (c,1) S
        '82
--Forest (Australia)
    Nat Geog 165:176-7 (c,2) F '84
--Forest (California)
    Life 5:110-12 (c,1) N '82
--Forest (Colorado)
    Natur Hist 95:60-1 (c,2) Ag
        '86
--Forest (Montana)
    Smithsonian 17:42-4 (c,2) Ag
        '86
--Gas tank carriers in flames
    Smithsonian 15:44-9 (c,1) Ap
        '84
--Houses (Philadelphia,

Pennsylvania)
    Life 8:41 (4) Jl '85
--Igniting forest fire by "heli-
        torch" (Oregon)
    Nat Geog 162:326 (c,1) S '82
--Marsh fire (Pacific coast)
    Nat Wildlife 21:25 (c,4) D '82
--New Jersey race track
    Sports Illus 62:44 (c,1) Ap 22
        '85
--Oxford University festival, Eng-
        land
    Nat Geog 163:766-7 (c,1) Je '83
--Soccer stadium, England
    Life 8:58-9 (1) Jl '85
--Tire junkyard on fire (Virginia)
    Life 7:86-7 (c,1) Mr '84
--Underground (Centralia, Pennsyl-
        vania)
    Nat Geog 167:368 (c,1) Mr '85
--University of Virginia rotunda
        (1895)
    Am Heritage 35:57 (2) Je '84
--See also
        CAMPFIRES
        FIRE FIGHTERS
        FIRE FIGHTING
        SMOKE
FIRES--DAMAGE
--1911 Triangle Shirtwaist Company
        fire, New York City
    Am Heritage 37:108 (3) F '86
--1967 Apollo I capsule damaged by
        fire
    Life 9:16 (4) Mr '86
--Cruise ship (1942)
    Am Heritage 35:65-7 (1) D '83
--Deodorizing smoke-damaged home
    Nat Geog 170:358-9 (c,1) S '86
--Destroyed town (Australia)
    Nat Geog 165:177 (c,3) F '84
--Destroyed neighborhood (Passaic,
        New Jersey)
    Life 8:96-7 (1) O '85
--Forest fire (Montana)
    Smithsonian 17:45-55 (c,1) Ag '86
--Remains of burned house (Texas)
    Life 6:32-3 (1) S '83
--Results of office arson fire (Ala-
        bama)
    Ebony 39:94 (3) Ap '84
--Southern California hillsides
    Smithsonian 13:132-43 (c,1) O
        '82
--Treating burn victim
    Life 9;243 (3) Fall '86

FIRETRUCKS
Smithsonian 14:160-2 (c,4) N
'83
--1889 (New Jersey)
Am Heritage 37:90-1 (paint-
ing,c,2) F '86
--Massachusetts
Life 8:54 (c,3) Ap '85
FIREWEED
Sports Illus 57:64 (c,4) Ag
16 '82
Nat Wildlife 24:35 (c,4) O '86
FIREWORKS
--1872 poster
Am Heritage 34:4 (c,1) Je '83
--1883 Brooklyn Bridge opening,
New York
Nat Geog 163:565 (drawing,c,4)
My '83
--1955 lawn fireworks (Texas)
Life 9:118 (c,2) Jl '86
--1984 Olympics (Los Angeles)
Sports Illus 61:98-9 (c,1) Ag
20 '84
Life 8:6-7 (c,1) Ja '85
--1986 Statue of Liberty celebra-
tion (New York City)
Life 9:396-7 (c,1) Fall '86
--Austin's sesquicentennial cele-
bration, Texas
Trav/Holiday 166:cov. (c,1) Jl
'86
--Celebration of Houston's 150th
birthday
Life 9:14-15 (c,1) Je '86
--Honoring General MacArthur
(1951; Chicago)
Am Heritage 35:95 (c,1) Ap '84
--Kentucky Derby festival, Ken-
tucky
Trav/Holiday 165:87 (c,2) Mr
'86
--New York City, New York
Life 5:134-5 (c,1) O '82
Life 7:10-11 (c,1) Ja '84
--North Korea
Life 5:42-3 (c,1) Jl '82
--Sports fans with sparklers
(New York)
Sports Illus 60:2-3 (c,1) My
14 '84
--Winter Carnival (St. Paul, Min-
nesota)
Life 9:6-7 (c,1) Ap '86
FISH
Life 5:48-9 (drawing,3) Ap '82
Smithsonian 16:185 (painting,c,4)

S '85
--18th cent. fanciful fishes (France)
Natur Hist 93:cov., 58-67 (paint-
ing,c,1) Ja '84
--Anglerfish
Natur Hist 91:14, 20 (drawing,4)
Jl '82
--Anthias school
Life 6:13 (c,2) Je '83
--Bigeye
Natur Hist 93:65 (c,1) D '84
--Blenny
Nat Geog 165:482 (c,2) Ap '84
Nat Wildlife 22:24 (c,4) Ag '84
--Butterfly fish
Sports Illus 64:124-5 (c,1) F 10
'86
Nat Wildlife 24:24 (sculpture,c,4)
Ag '86
--Cardinalfish
Nat Geog 161:278-9 (c,2) F '82
--Caribbean flashlight fish
Nat Wildlife 20:38-9 (2) Ap '82
--Caviar
Nat Wildlife 24:23 (c,1) D '85
--Clownfish
Smithsonian 13:132-3 (c,2) Mr
'83
Nat Wildlife 21:28 (c,3) Ap '83
Natur Hist 94:70-1 (c,3) Mr '85
Natur Hist 94:132-3 (c,1) Ap '85
Nat Wildlife 24:17 (c,3) F '86
--Croakers
Nat Geog 168:89 (c,4) Jl '85
--Damselfish
Nat Wildlife 22:22-3 (c,1) Je '84
Natur Hist 93:60 (c,4) D '84
--Flathead
Smithsonian 13:130 (c,4) Mr '83
--Freshwater fish (New York)
Natur Hist 92:cov., 48-57 (c,1)
Mr '83
--Glassy sweepers
Smithsonian 13:135 (c,2) Mr '83
Life 6:8-9 (c,1) Je '83
--Goby
Natur Hist 91:60-2, 66-7 (c,1)
D '82
Nat Geog 164:140-1 (c,1) Jl '83
Nat Geog 165:486 (c,4) Ap '84
--Goosefish
Natur Hist 93:28-33 (c,1) Ag '84
--Graysby
Nat Wildlife 21:47 (c,2) Ap '83
--Halfbeak fish
Nat Geog 161:279 (c,4) F '82
--Lookdowns

FISH (cont.)
  Nat Wildlife 21:54-5 (c,1) D
    '82
--Mahseer
  Sports Illus 63:90-1 (paint-
    ing,c,1) D 9 '85
--Mosquito fish
  Smithsonian 14:37 (c,2) Je '83
--Mudskippers
  Nat Geog 167:768 (c,4) Je '85
--Parrot fish
  Smithsonian 13:126-7 (c,1) Mr
    '83
  Nat Wildlife 21:26-7 (c,2) Ap
    '83
  Nat Geog 164:135 (c,4) Jl '83
  Nat Geog 167:804-5 (c,1) Je '85
--Razor fish
  Nat Geog 164:133, 138 (c,3)
    Jl '83
--Redside dace
  Natur Hist 92:55 (c,4) Mr '83
--School of fusiliers
  Life 6:10 (c,3) Je '83
--School of silversides
  Nat Geog 167:802-3 (c,1) Je
    '85
--Schools of fish
  Life 6:8-13 (c,1) Je '83
  Nat Wildlife 22:20 (c,1) Je '84
--Scorpion fish
  Nat Geog 165:483 (c,2) Ap '84
--Scrawled filefish
  Life 8:12 (c,4) Ap '85
--Sharks stuffed by taxidermist
    (Senegal)
  Nat Geog 168:235 (c,1) Ag '85
--Squawfish
  Nat Wildlife 23:48 (c,4) O '85
--Stargazers
  Nat Geog 164:130-1 (c,1) Jl
    '83
--Sushi (Japan)
  Nat Geog 162:238-9 (c,2) Ag
    '82
--Threadfin jack
  Life 8:12 (c,1) Ap '85
--Trumpetfish
  Nat Wildlife 22:60 (c,4) Ap '84
--Wrasses
  Nat Wildlife 21:25 (c,3) Ap '83
  Nat Geog 165:486 (c,3) Ap '84
  Nat Wildlife 22:24 (c,4) Je '84
--Yellow-finned goatfish school
  Life 6:10 (c,3) Je '83
--Yellowhead jawfish
  Nat Geog 167:805 (c,4) Je '85

--See also
  ANGELFISH
  ARCHERFISH
  BARRACUDAS
  BASS
  BLINDFISH
  CARP
  CATFISH
  CAVIAR INDUSTRY
  CHUBS
  DARTERS
  EELS
  FISHERMEN
  FISHING
  GROUPERS
  GRUNIONS
  GRUNTS
  HALIBUT
  HERRING
  MARINE LIFE
  MARLINS
  MINNOWS
  PERCH
  PICKERELS
  PIKE
  POND LIFE
  PORCUPINE FISH
  PUFFER FISH
  SAILFISH
  SCULPINS
  SEA HORSES
  SHARKS
  SOLE
  STURGEON
  SUCKERS
  TARPONS
  TOADFISH
  TROUT
  TUNA
  WOLF FISH
FISH, HAMILTON
  Smithsonian 16:89 (4) Mr '86
FISHERMEN
--19th cent. dorymen (Northeast)
  Am Heritage 33:58-62 (paint-
    ing,c,1) F '82
--1955
  Ebony 41:206 (4) N '85
--Egypt
  Nat Geog 167:596-9 (c,1) My '85
--France
  Trav/Holiday 161:84-5 (c,2) My
    '84
--Ghana
  Natur Hist 91:44-7 (c,1) Mr '82
--Gloucester Fisherman statue,
    Massachusetts

FISHING (cont.)
  Smithsonian 16:52 (c,4) D '85
--Mississippi
  Nat Wildlife 23:10 (c,4) Je '85
--New Hampshire
  Am Heritage 35:98 (c,1) D '83
--New York
  Trav/Holiday 162:50-1 (c,1)
    Ag '84
--Palau, Micronesia
  Smithsonian 17:50-1, 54 (c,2)
    S '86
--Pennsylvania
  Nat Geog 167:382-3 (c,1) Mr
    '85
--Poland
  Life 6:150 (c,2) O '83
--Sailfish mounted on wall
  Sports Illus 59:50 (c,4) D 26
    '83
--Salmon (Alaska)
  Nat Geog 169:202-3 (c,1) F '86
--Spearfishing (Wisconsin)
  Sports Illus 65:49 (c,2) Ag 11
    '86
--Sturgeon (Northwest)
  Smithsonian 17:84-5, 91 (c,3)
    Ag '86
--Tanzania
  Nat Geog 167:630-1 (c,1) My
    '85
--Tennessee
  Trav/Holiday 160:32 (4) Jl '83
--Texas
  Sports Illus 61:26 (3) O 8 '84
--350 lb. marlin mounted on wall
  Sports Illus 58:34 (c,3) Ja
    10 '83
--Trout
  Smithsonian 14:78 (c,3) My
    '83
--Trout (Connecticut)
  Sports Illus 64:46-51 (1) Ap 21
    '86
--Trout (Great Britain)
  Sports Illus 58:68-82 (c,1) My
    9 '83
--Trout (New York)
  Sports Illus 58:45-8 (draw-
    ing,c,4) Ja 31 '83
--Trout (Tennessee)
  Sports Illus 57:32-3 (c,2) Jl 5
    '82
--Trout (Washington)
  Life 6:80-1 (c,1) F '83
--Weighing catch (California)
  Trav/Holiday 158:27 (c,4) S '82

--Wyoming
  Nat Wildlife 24:36-7 (c,1) Ap '86
--See also
    CLAM DIGGING
    ICE FISHING
FISHING--HUMOR
  Sports Illus 62:200, 204-5 (paint-
    ing,c,3) F 11 '85
FISHING BOATS
--19th cent.
  Am Heritage 36:89 (painting,c,3)
    F '85
--Alaska
  Nat Wildlife 21:40-1 (c,1) Ag '83
  Smithsonian 17:96-109 (c,1) O
    '86
--Balsas (Peru)
  Nat Geog 161:318-19 (c,1) Mr '82
--Brazil
  Smithsonian 15:78 (c,2) D '84
--Burma
  Smithsonian 15:111 (c,1) My '84
--California
  Trav/Holiday 162:42 (c,4) N '84
--Cayman Islands
  Trav/Holiday 161:75 (c,2) My
    '84
--Delaware
  Nat Geog 164:183 (c,4) Ag '83
--Egypt
  Smithsonian 15:81 (c,1) D '84
--France
  Trav/Holiday 161:cov., 84-5 (c,1)
    My '84
--Greece
  Nat Geog 162:708-9 (c,1) D '82
--Japan
  Nat Geog 165:474-5 (c,1) Ap '84
--Lobster boat (Maine)
  Nat Geog 167:208-9 (c,1) F '85
--New England
  Smithsonian 16:104-17 (c,1) My
    '85
--New York City, New York
  Trav/Holiday 159:51 (c,2) Ap '83
--Zimbabwe
  Trav/Holiday 165:67 (c,2) Mr '86
FISHING COMPETITIONS
--New York
  Sports Illus 62:73-4 (c,3) Je 10
    '85
FISHING EQUIPMENT
--19th cent. Eskimos (Alaska)
  Nat Geog 163:204-5 (c,1) F '83
--Bamboo traps (Philippines)
  Nat Geog 170:98-9 (c,1) Jl '86
--Crab pots (Alaska)

FLAGS (cont.)
Vietnam War protest
Am Heritage 37:79 (4) Ap '86
--U.S. flag upside-down in 1972
demonstration (Florida)
Life 9:120 (2) Jl '86
--Vatican City
Nat Geog 168:728 (drawing,c,4)
D '85
--Wales
Nat Geog 164:40 (c,3) Jl '83
--West Berlin, West Germany
Nat Geog 161:8 (drawing,c,4)
Ja '82
--Western Samoa
Nat Geog 168:454 (drawing,c,4)
O '85
--Yap state
Nat Geog 170:460, 488 (c,4)
O '86
FLAMINGOS
Nat Wildlife 20:2 (c,1) F '82
Nat Wildlife 21:42-3 (paint-
ing,c,1) F '83
Nat Wildlife 22:53 (c,2) D '83
Sports Illus 60:118 (c,3) F 13
'84
Life 7:132 (c,2) O '84
Nat Wildlife 23:60 (c,1) F '85
Natur Hist 94:8-12 (paint-
ing,c,2) Mr '85
Nat Geog 169:567 (c,4) My '86
--16th cent. drawing
Am Heritage 36:95 (c,4) Ag '85
--Audubon painting
Sports Illus 63:128 (c,4) D 23
'85
--Flock
Nat Geog 163:382-3 (c,1) Mr
'83
--Stylized depiction on Florida
window
Smithsonian 13:59 (c,2) D '82
FLEA MARKETS
--Antique fair (Brazil)
Trav/Holiday 159:56 (c,4) Ja
'83
--Paris, France
Trav/Holiday 157:cov., 56 (c,1)
Mr '82
FLICKERS (BIRDS)
Nat Wildlife 21:49, 51, 60
(c,2) D '82
Nat Wildlife 23:2 (c,2) Ap '85
Nat Geog 167:679 (c,4) My '85
FLIES
Natur Hist 93:52-3 (c,1) D '84

--Dobsonflies
Natur Hist 95:34-5 (c,1) Ag '86
--Larva eating aphid
Nat Wildlife 21:48 (c,2) Je '83
--Mating crane flies
Smithsonian 13:67 (c,3) Jl '82
--Preserved in amber
Natur Hist 91:29, 31 (c,1) Je
'82
--See also
FRUIT FLIES
HORSEFLIES
TSETSE FLIES
FLOODS
--1850 (London, England)
Nat Geog 163:789 (engraving,4)
Je '83
--1870s (Louisiana)
Am Heritage 35:92-3 (draw-
ing,c,1) Je '84
--1910s Ford stuck in mud (Iowa)
Smithsonian 16:60-1 (3) Ag '85
--1919 molasses disaster (Boston,
Massachusetts)
Smithsonian 14:222-9 (4) N '83
--1983 Colorado River flood (South-
west)
Nat Wildlife 23:42-7 (map,c,1)
O '85
--Bangladesh
Nat Geog 165:738-41 (c,1) Je '84
--Cincinnati, Ohio (1937)
Am Heritage 37:46-7 (2) Je '86
--Cornfield (Pennsylvania)
Nat Wildlife 23:17 (c,3) F '85
--India
Nat Geog 166:722-3 (c,1) D '84
--Sandbagging levees (California)
Smithsonian 14:64 (c,4) Ap '83
--Storm-surge barrier across Ooster-
schelde, Netherlands
Smithsonian 15:94-101 (c,1) Ag
'84
--Thames Barrier, England
Smithsonian 13:79-87 (c,1) Ag
'82
Nat Geog 163:788-91 (c,1) Je
'83
--Utah
Nat Geog 165:160-1 (c,1) F '84
Nat Geog 167:694-717 (map,c,1)
Je '85
--Venice, Italy
Nat Geog 162:696-7 (c,1) D '82
--See also
LEVEES

FLOODS--DAMAGE
--Ecuador
    Nat Geog 165:146-7, 166 (c,1)
        F '84
--Indonesia
    Nat Geog 166:738-41, 744-5
        (c,1) D '84
--Victim of mudslide (Utah)
    Life 7:122 (2) Jl '84
FLORENCE, ITALY
    Trav/Holiday 159:36-41 (c,1)
        F '83
--Ponte Vecchio
    Smithsonian 13:60 (c,4) N '82
--See also
        MEDICI
        UFFIZI GALLERY
FLORIDA
    Nat Geog 162:173-219 (map,c,1)
        Ag '82
--Big Cypress Swamp
    Nat Geog 162:190 (c,1) Ag '82
--Biscayne Bay islands sur-
        rounded by pink plastic
    Life 6:37-41 (c,1) Je '83
--Captiva Island coast
    Trav/Holiday 163:14 (c,3) Ja
        '85
--Coconut Grove
    Nat Geog 162:187 (c,3) Ag '82
--Crystal River
    Nat Geog 166:402-3 (c,1) S
        '84
--Everglades City
    Life 7:68-86 (c,1) Je '84
--Highlands Hammocks State Park
    Trav/Holiday 157:54 (c,2) F '82
--Kissimmee River
    Nat Wildlife 20:52 (c,2) O '82
--Kissimmee River wetlands area
    Sports Illus 56:46-54 (map,c,2)
        Mr 15 '82
--Mangrove swamps
    Life 7:68-70, 77 (c,1) Je '84
--Marco Island
    Nat Geog 162:216 (c,1) Ag '82
--Ochopee post office
    Smithsonian 14:64-5 (c,1) Jl
        '83
--Palm Beach
    Life 6:93-8 (c,1) Mr '83
    Smithsonian 16:112-23 (c,1) S
        '85
--Pelican Island
    Nat Geog 162:353 (c,1) S '82
--Sawgrass golf course
    Sports Illus 56:38-45 (c,1)

        Mr 15 '82
    Sports Illus 56:26 (c,4) Mr 29 '82
--T. H. Stone Memorial Park
    Trav/Holiday 157:54 (c,3) F '82
--Warm Mineral Springs
    Smithsonian 17:72-83 (c,1) D '86
--See also
        EVERGLADES NATIONAL
            PARK
        FLORIDA KEYS
        KEY WEST
        LAKE OKEECHOBEE
        MIAMI
        MIAMI BEACH
        OCALA NATIONAL FOREST
        OKEFENOKEE SWAMP
        ORLANDO
        PENSACOLA
        ST. AUGUSTINE
        ST. PETERSBURG
        TAMPA
        WINTER PARK
FLORIDA--MAPS
--Leon Sinks area
    Natur Hist 94:78 (c,4) D '85
--West Florida (1781)
    Am Heritage 33:37 (3) Ap '82
FLORIDA KEYS
    Smithsonian 15:30 (c,4) Ag '84
--Seven Mile Bridge
    Nat Geog 166:816-17 (c,1) D '84
FLOWER INDUSTRY
--California
    Nat Geog 169:530-1 (c,2) Ap '86
--Fields of flowers (California)
    Nat Geog 165:426-7 (c,1) Ap '84
FLOWERING PLANTS
    Nat Wildlife 21:18-19 (drawing,c,1)
        Ag '83
--16th cent. sketches of New World
        plants
    Am Heritage 36:81-4 (c,4) Ag '85
--Brighamia plant
    Nat Wildlife 22:11 (c,2) Ag '84
--Brittlebush
    Natur Hist 95:31 (c,2) D '86
    Natur Hist 95:74-7 (c,1) Ap '86
--Cryogenic gene bank for endan-
        gered species
    Nat Wildlife 22:6-9 (c,1) Ag '84
--Cushion plant
    Nat Geog 163:682 (c,4) My '83
--Diapensia
    Natur Hist 94:24 (c,4) Jl '85
--Downingia
    Nat Wildlife 22:4-5 (c,1) Je '84
--Endangered species

FLOWERING PLANTS (cont.)
  Nat Wildlife 22:6-12 (c,1) Ag
    '84
--Fiddleneck
  Nat Wildlife 22:7 (c,4) Je '84
--Gayfeathers
  Life 9:112 (c,2) Jl '86
--Gila flowers
  Natur Hist 93:24 (c,4) Jl '84
--Goldfield flowers
  Nat Wildlife 22:6-7 (c,1) Je
    '84
--Hawkweed
  Nat Wildlife 22:55 (c,1) Je '84
--Jewelweed
  Nat Wildlife 21:21 (c,4) F '83
--New Jersey Pine Barrens
  Smithsonian 14:78-87 (c,1) Jl
    '83
--Pogonia
  Nat Wildlife 23:52 (c,1) Je '85
--Poker plants
  Nat Wildlife 22:2 (c,2) Je '84
--Protea plants
  Natur Hist 94:70-7 (c,1) My
    '85
--Ragwort
  Nat Wildlife 24:45 (c,1) Ap '86
--Silverswords
  Natur Hist 91:36-9 (c,1) D '82
--Spathe
  Natur Hist 92:cov. (c,1) Je
    '83
--Succulent frithia
  Natur Hist 95:64-7 (c,1) O '86
--Wildflowers
  Nat Geog 164:118-19 (c,1) Jl
    '83
  Nat Wildlife 22:4-7 (c,1) Je '84
  Natur Hist 93:26-31 (c,1) Jl
    '84
  Nat Wildlife 23:5 (c,3) Ap '85
--See also
        AFRICAN VIOLETS
        ASTERS
        AZALEAS
        BACHELOR'S-BUTTONS
        BAMBOO PLANTS
        BLADDERWORT PLANTS
        BLUEBONNETS
        BUNCHBERRIES
        BUTTERCUPS
        CACTUS
        CALLA LILIES
        CAMPANULAS
        CENTURY PLANTS
        CHRYSANTHEMUMS

COLUMBINES
COREOPSIS
CROCUSES
DAISIES
FIREWEED
FLOWER INDUSTRY
FLOWERS
FOXGLOVE
FUCHSIAS
GARDENS
GERANIUMS
GINSENG
GLADIOLI
GOLDENROD
HEATHER
HERBS
HOLLYHOCKS
HONEYSUCKLE
HUCKLEBERRY PLANTS
HYACINTHS
INDIAN PAINTBRUSH
INDIAN PIPES
IRISES
JACK-IN-THE-PULPIT
JIMSON WEED
LADY'S-SLIPPERS
LARKSPURS
LILACS
LILIES
LOBELIAS
LUPINES
MARSH MALLOWS
MAY APPLES
MONKEY FLOWERS
MOUNTAIN LAUREL
MUSTARD PLANTS
NASTURTIUMS
ORCHIDS
PASSIONFLOWERS
PEONIES
PHLOX
PITCHER PLANTS
POINTSETTIAS
POPPIES
PRIMROSES
RADISHES
RAFFLESIA
RHODODENDRONS
ROSES
SAGE
SAGEBRUSH
SPIREA PLANTS
SUCCULENTS
SUNDEW
SUNFLOWERS
THISTLES
TOUCH-ME-NOTS

FLOWERING PLANTS (cont.)
    TULIPS
    VENUS FLYTRAPS
    VIOLETS
    WATER HYACINTHS
    WATER LILIES
    ZINNIAS
Flowering plants, carnivorous.
    See
    BLADDERWORT PLANTS
    PITCHER PLANTS
    SUNDEW PLANTS
    VENUS FLYTRAPS
FLOWERS
    Sports Illus 61:20 (c,4) Ag 20
      '84
    Natur Hist 93:38-45 (c,1) Ap
      '84
    Smithsonian 15:100-7 (c,1) N
      '84
--18th cent. flower clock (Ger-
     many)
    Natur Hist 91:30 (c,4) O '82
--18th-19th cent. paintings of
    flowers
    Am Heritage 35:83-93 (c,1) F
      '84
--19th-20th cent. paintings of
    flowers
    Smithsonian 14:94-101 (c,1)
      Mr '84
--Late 19th cent. glass flowers
    (Germany)
    Smithsonian 13:100-7 (c,1) O
      '82
--Florist's shop (Washington)
    Natur Hist 94:89 (3) Ja '85
--Fossil flowers
    Natur Hist 93:56-61 (c,1) Mr
      '84
--Nosegay
    Nat Geog 163:393 (c,4) Mr '83
--X-ray pictures of flowers
    Smithsonian 17:cov., 88-92
      (1) O '86
    Smithsonian 17:16 (4) D '86
FLUTE PLAYING
--Israel
    Nat Geog 161:422 (c,2) Ap '82
--Platinum flute
    Nat Geog 164:706 (c,4) N '83
FLYCATCHERS
    Natur Hist 91:41-5 (c,1) S '82
    Nat Geog 164:266 (c,1) Ag '83
--See also
    KINGBIRDS
    WOOD PEWEES

FLYING FOXES
    Smithsonian 14:78 (c,4) Ja '84
    Nat Geog 169:540-57 (c,1) Ap '86
FLYING SQUIRRELS
    Smithsonian 16:56-67 (c,1) Je
      '85
    Nat Wildlife 24:30-2 (c,1) D '85
FLYNN, ERROL
    Am Heritage 35:47 (4) D '83
FOG
--Alaska
    Nat Geog 162:542-3 (c,2) O '82
    Nat Geog 164:338-9 (c,1) S '83
--British Columbian countryside
    Nat Geog 170:70-1 (c,1) Jl '86
--California coast
    Nat Geog 165:431 (c,1) Ap '84
--Cascade Mountain forest, Wash-
     ington
    Nat Wildlife 24:11 (c,1) F '86
--German village
    Nat Geog 164:450-1 (c,1) O '83
--Meteora, Greece
    Nat Geog 164:710-11 (c,1) D '83
--Minnesota forest
    Trav/Holiday 162:48 (c,1) O '84
--Mississippi Delta, Louisiana
    Nat Geog 164:248-9 (c,1) Ag '83
--Neblina mountain, Venezuela
    Natur Hist 93:16 (c,4) D '84
    Smithsonian 16:50 (c,1) My '85
--San Francisco, California
    Trav/Holiday 161:73 (c,2) Mr '84
FOLGER SHAKESPEARE LIBRARY,
    WASHINGTON, D.C.
    Smithsonian 13:118-27 (c,1) Ap
      '82
FOLK DANCING
--Filipino (Alaska)
    Nat Geog 164:355 (c,4) S '83
--German (Missouri)
    Trav/Holiday 160:54 (c,4) Jl '83
--Great Britain
    Trav/Holiday 164:6 (c,3) D '85
--Mexican (Texas)
    Life 6:58 (c,3) Mr '83
--Yugoslavia
    Trav/Holiday 159:58 (4) Mr '83
FONDA, HENRY
    Life 6:143 (4) Ja '83
FONTAINEBLEAU, FRANCE
    Nat Geog 161:178 (c,1) F '82
FOOD
--17th cent. methods of food preser-
     vation (New England)
    Natur Hist 91:38-49 (c,1) O '82
--1900 food package labels

FOOD (cont.)
    Nat Geog 162:238-9 (c,2) Ag
        '82
--Szechuan style
    Life 5:66-71 (c,1) Je '82
--Teenagers' diets
    Life 9:81 (c,3) Mr '86
--Tex-Mex dishes
    Life 6:52-7 (c,1) Mr '83
--Thanksgiving meal
    Ebony 38:108-12 (c,2) N '82
    Ebony 40:140-1 (c,1) N '84
--Tuscan specialties, Italy
    Trav/Holiday 165:56-7 (c,4)
        My '86
--Vegetable dishes
    Ebony 38:118-19 (c,1) My '83
--Wedding cake (Illinois)
    Ebony 40:122 (c,3) Ja '85
--Wedding cake (Kentucky)
    Nat Geog 161:532-3 (c,1) Ap
        '82
--Western Samoa feast food
    Nat Geog 168:471 (c,4) O '85
--See also
        BREAD
        CHEESE
        COOKING
        DINNERS AND DINING
        DRINKING CUSTOMS
        FOOD MARKETS
        FRUIT
        HERBS
        RESTAURANTS
FOOD--HUMOR
--History of French cuisine
    Smithsonian 16:134-46 (draw-
        ing,c,1) S '85
FOOD MARKETS
--1891 produce market (New Or-
        leans, Louisiana)
    Am Heritage 38:68 (2) D '86
--1918 supermarket (Memphis,
        Tennessee)
    Am Heritage 36:22-3 (1) O
        '85
--1922 fruit stand (Florida)
    Nat Geog 166:793 (4) D '84
--1930 supermarket (Queens,
        New York)
    Am Heritage 36:24 (3) O '85
--Bagging food at supermarket
    Sports Illus 62:22 (c,3) My 13 '85
--Bananas sold from boat (Hon-
        duras)
    Nat Geog 164:629 (c,3) N '83
--Cheese (Alkmaar, Netherlands)

Trav/Holiday 163:58-9 (c,1) Je
    '85
--China
    Trav/Holiday 158:49 (c,4) Jl '82
--Cooked ducks in Chinatown store
        window
    Trav/Holiday 159:51 (c,4) Ja '83
--Crab (Maryland)
    Natur Hist 91:90-2 (3) F '82
--Farmer's market (Lancaster, Penn-
        sylvania)
    Natur Hist 92:78 (4) Ag '83
--Fish (India)
    Natur Hist 95:70 (4) Ag '86
--Fish (Italy)
    Natur Hist 94:80 (3) D '85
--Fish (Portugal)
    Nat Geog 166:464 (c,3) O '84
--Fish (Tunisia)
    Nat Geog 162:735 (c,4) D '82
--Floating (Thailand)
    Trav/Holiday 163:58 (c,1) Ap
        '85
--Fruit market (Siberia, U.S.S.R.)
    Trav/Holiday 165:54 (c,4) My '86
--Fruit stand (India)
    Trav/Holiday 165:50 (c,3) Ap '86
--Fruit stand (Lima, Peru)
    Trav/Holiday 157:44 (c,4) Ja '82
--Fruit stand (New Zealand)
    Trav/Holiday 164:57 (c,2) S '85
    Trav/Holiday 166:51 (c,2) Ag '86
--Fruit stand (Portugal)
    Natur Hist 95:78-9 (c,3) D '86
--Fruit stand (Puerto Rico)
    Nat Geog 163:538-9 (c,1) Ap '83
--Fruit stand (Vancouver, British
        Columbia)
    Natur Hist 92:75 (3) Je '83
--Fulton Fish Market, New York
    Trav/Holiday 157:73 (c,4) Ap
        '82
    Natur Hist 95:72-7 (c,1) Ag '86
--Garlic (Spain)
    Natur Hist 92:86 (4) My '83
--Grand Central Market, Los Ange-
        les, California
    Natur Hist 91:100-3 (c,2) O '82
    Natur Hist 91:100, 104 (c,2) N
        '82
--History of supermarkets
    Am Heritage 36:22-32, 114 (c,1)
        O '85
--Hong Kong
    Trav/Holiday 161:46 (c,4) Ja '84
--Hunts Point Market, Bronx, New
        York

FOOTBALL--COLLEGE (cont.)
    Sports Illus 57:29 (c,3) N 15
      '82
    Sports Illus 63:20-1 (c,3) O
      7 '85
--Mascots
    Sports Illus 59:22 (c,4) N 21
      '83
    Sports Illus 60:12 (c,4) Mr
      26 '84
    Sports Illus 61:94 (c,4) N 12
      '84
--Orange Bowl 1982 (Clemson
    vs. Nebraska)
    Sports Illus 56:cov., 14-17
      (c,1) Ja 11 '82
--Orange Bowl 1983 (Nebraska
    vs. LSU)
    Sports Illus 58:26 (c,3) Ja 10
      '83
--Orange Bowl 1984 (Miami vs.
    Nebraska)
    Sports Illus 60:cov., 14-19
      (c,1) Ja 9 '84
    Sports Illus 60:32 (c,3) F 8
      '84
--Orange Bowl 1986 (Oklahoma
    vs. Penn State)
    Sports Illus 64:82-5 (c,2) Ja
      13 '86
--Passing
    Sports Illus 57:36 (c,4) O 18
      '82
    Sports Illus 57:cov., 28-31
      (c,1) N 8 '82
    Sports Illus 58:18 (c,4) Ja 10
      '83
    Sports Illus 58:40-1 (c,2) Ap
      18 '83
    Sports Illus 59:28, 55 (c,3) N
      7 '83
    Sports Illus 59:61 (c,4) N 14
      '83
    Sports Illus 60:32-3 (c,4) F
      8 '84
    Sports Illus 60:38 (c,4) F 27
      '84
    Sports Illus 60:28 (c,2) Mr 12
      '84
    Sports Illus 61:42 (c,4) N 12
      '84
    Sports Illus 61:cov., 22-4 (c,1)
      D 3 '84
--Pep talk by coach
    Sports Illus 59:67 (c,4) O 24
      '83
--Place-kicking

    Sports Illus 57:41 (c,4) O 18 '82
    Sports Illus 61:23 (c,4) O 1 '84
--Receiving
    Sports Illus 57:24 (c,4) O 4 '82
    Sports Illus 57:34 (c,4) O 11 '82
    Sports Illus 57:35 (c,4) O 18 '82
    Sports Illus 57:44-5 (c,2) N 22
      '82
    Sports Illus 59:20-1 (c,1) S 26
      '83
    Sports Illus 59:52-4 (c,3) O 17
      '83
    Sports Illus 59:61 (c,4) N 14 '83
    Sports Illus 61:cov. (c,1) S 10
      '84
    Sports Illus 63:18-19 (c,1) O 7
      '85
--Receiving touchdown pass
    Sports Illus 59:45 (c,4) N 21 '83
    Sports Illus 61:40-1 (c,2) N 12
      '84
--Referee
    Sports Illus 59:3 (c,2) O 17 '85
--Rose Bowl 1982 (Washington vs.
    Iowa)
    Sports Illus 56:24-5 (c,4) Ja 11
      '82
--Rose Bowl 1983 (UCLA vs. Michi-
    gan)
    Sports Illus 58:23-5 (c,2) Ja 10
      '83
--Rose Bowl 1986 (UCLA vs. Iowa)
    Sports Illus 64:86-7 (c,2) Ja 13
      '86
--Running
    Sports Illus 56:22 (c,3) Mr 1 '82
    Sports Illus 57:74-9 (c,1) S 1
      '82
    Sports Illus 57:cov., 16-17 (c,1)
      S 13 '82
    Sports Illus 57:25-6 (c,2) O 4 '82
    Sports Illus 57:18-23 (c,1) N 1
      '82
    Sports Illus 59:20-1 (c,3) S 12
      '83
    Sports Illus 59:30-1 (c,2) O 31
      '83
    Sports Illus 60:cov. (c,1) Ja 9
      '84
    Sports Illus 60:30-1 (c,2) F 8 '84
    Sports Illus 61:cov., 18-21 (c,1)
      O 1 '84
--Sideshow acts
    Sports Illus 59:202-11 (c,1) S 1
      '83
--Single wing play
    Sports Illus 57:44-54 (c,4) S 20

FOOTBALL TEAMS (cont.)
  Sports Illus 65:34-5 (c,2) Jl
    7 '86
--High school
  Sports Illus 57:70 (c,4) N 1
    '82
FOOTBALLS
  Sports Illus 63:86 (c,4) N 18
    '85
--Deflated
  Sports Illus 57:cov. (c,1) S
    27 '82
FOOTWEAR
--16th cent. leather shoe (Great
    Britain)
  Nat Geog 163:660-1 (c,2) My
    '83
--17th cent. shoe (Massachusetts)
  Smithsonian 13:106-7 (c,1) Je
    '82
--18th cent. shoe (Great Britain)
  Nat Geog 165:10 (c,2) Ja '84
--1889 cowboy boots (Texas)
  Am Heritage 37:58-9 (1) F '86
--1910 shoeshine boy (New York)
  Natur Hist 94:88 (4) O '85
--1925 women's evening shoes
  Smithsonian 17:159 (c,4) N '86
--1930s cowboy boots
  Sports Illus 63:102-3 (c,1) D
    23 '85
--1947 high school coeds
  Life 9:65 (4) Ag '86
--Ancient hobnailed boot (Great
    Britain)
  Smithsonian 16:77 (c,4) Ap
    '85
--Fred Astaire's shoes
  Life 9:360 (2) Fall '86
--Ballet toe shoes
  Smithsonian 15:88-99 (c,1) Je
    '84
  Trav/Holiday 163:58 (c,1) My
    '85
--Basketball shoes
  Sports Illus 65:2-3, 21 (c,1)
    N 17 '86
--Pat Boone's white bucks (1958)
  Life 9:68 (4) Ag '86
--Clogs (1972)
  Life 9:72 (c,4) Ag '86
--Cowboy boots
  Sports Illus 57:7 (4) S 6 '82
  Nat Geog 167:742 (c,1) Je '85
--Hiking shoes
  Sports Illus 57:46-7 (c,2) S 6
    '82

Nat Geog 163:684 (c,3) My '83
--Hunting boots
  Sports Illus 63:96, 91 (c,2) D 2
    '85
--Motorcycle boot
  Sports Illus 63:100 (c,4) D 2 '85
--Red shoes
  Life 7:8-18 (c,1) O '84
--Reptile skin footwear and fakes
  Life 9:96-8 (c,1) D '86
--Ruby slippers from "Wizard of
    Oz"
  Life 7:9 (c,4) O '84
--Shoes (Korea)
  Life 7:104-5 (c,1) Ja '84
--Sioux Indian beaded sneakers
  Natur Hist 95:76 (c,4) Jl '86
--See also
    SNOWSHOES
FORD, GERALD
  Life 5:139 (c,4) My '82
  Ebony 39:144 (4) D '83
  Life 9:211, 224-5, 327 (c,1) Fall
    '86
--Betty Ford
  Life 9:110 (c,2) Jl '86
--On golf course
  Sports Illus 56:35 (c,4) Ap 5
    '82
FORD, HENRY
  Smithsonian 15:202 (4) N '84
  Am Heritage 37:112 (2) Ag '86
  Am Heritage 37:4, 49-64 (c,2)
    O '86
--Depicted on postage stamp
  Am Heritage 34:53 (c,4) D '82
--Edsel Ford
  Smithsonian 16:38 (painting,c,4)
    F '86
FORESTS
  Nat Wildlife 20:48-9 (c,4) Je '82
  Nat Geog 162:306-38 (map,c,1)
    S '82
  Sports Illus 62:68-9 (painting,c,1)
    Mr 18 '85
--Ailing trees (West Germany)
  Smithsonian 16:211-30 (c,2) N '85
--Autumn scenes (Eastern U.S.)
  Life 9:38-48 (c,1) O '86
--Bob Marshall Wilderness, Montana
  Nat Geog 167:664-92 (map,c,1)
    My '85
  Smithsonian 17:42-55 (map,c,1)
    Ag '86
--California
  Natur Hist 94:78-81 (c,1) S '85
--Caribou, Northwest

FORESTS (cont.)
  Nat Geog 162:308-9 (c,1) S '82
--Colorado
  Natur Hist 94:58-65 (c,1) Ja
    '85
--Cumberland Mountains, South-
    east
  Natur Hist 93:28 (c,3) S '84
--Damaged by acid rain (North
    Carolina)
  Life 7:70 (c,2) N '84
--Deforested hillside (Mexico)
  Natur Hist 94:54 (4) Mr '85
--Flooded (Brazil)
  Natur Hist 92:64-5 (c,1) Jl '83
--Fire (Colorado)
  Natur Hist 95:60-1 (c,2) Ag
    '86
--Fire (Montana)
  Smithsonian 17:42-4 (c,2) Ag
    '86
--Georgia
  Trav/Holiday 163:90 (c,2) Mr
    '85
--Hawaii
  Natur Hist 91:16-17 (c,1) D
    '82
  Trav/Holiday 162:37 (c,1) O
    '84
--Maine
  Life 9:38-9 (c,1) O '86
--Map of U.S. National Forests
  Nat Wildlife 21:6-7 (c,1) Ap
    '83
--New York
  Natur Hist 91:64 (c,4) My '82
--Northwest
  Natur Hist 91:54-63 (c,1) O
    '82
  Nat Wildlife 24:4-11 (c,1) F '86
--Paraguay
  Natur Hist 93:56-7 (c,3) Jl '84
--Pennsylvania
  Nat Geog 167:366-7 (c,1) Mr
    '85
--Tanzania
  Smithsonian 13:50-1 (c,1) Ag
    '82
--Trees stripped by moths (Mary-
    land)
  Smithsonian 15:47, 50 (c,4) My
    '84
--U.S.S.R.
  Nat Geog 167:310-11 (c,1) Mr
    '85
--Venezuela
  Nat Geog 168:333 (c,1) S '85

--Washington
  Trav/Holiday 159:47 (c,1) My
    '83
  Nat Geog 165:646-7 (c,1) My '84
--See also
    AUTUMN
    BLACK FOREST
    NATIONAL PARKS
    RAIN FORESTS
    TREES, and these national
      forests:
    ALLEGHENY
    ANGELES
    BIG THICKET
    CORONADO
    DIXIE
    GEORGE WASHINGTON
    GUNNISON
    MONONGAHELA
    OCALA
    PRESCOTT
    SHAWNEE
    SIERRA
    TETON
    TONGASS
    TONTO
    WHITE MOUNTAIN
    WHITE RIVER
FORREST, EDWIN
  Smithsonian 16:169-82 (c,4) O
    '85
--1849 fight between actors Forrest
    and MacReady (N.Y.)
  Smithsonian 16:168-90 (draw-
    ing,c,2) O '85
FORT SUMTER, CHARLESTON,
    SOUTH CAROLINA
--1861 shelling
  Am Heritage 37:98 (4) Ap '86
--1863
  Am Heritage 38:60-1 (paint-
    ing,c,3) D '86
FORTRESSES
--12th cent. Muslim (Sinai, Egypt)
  Nat Geog 161:424-5 (c,1) Ap '82
--King Herod's palace (Israel)
  Nat Geog 165:260 (c,2) F '84
--Naarden, Netherlands
  Nat Geog 170:518-19 (c,1) O '86
--Urbino, Italy
  Nat Geog 165:204 (c,1) F '84
--See also
    CITADELS
    MONT SAINT MICHEL
FORTS
--Baltit, Pakistan
  Smithsonian 13:51 (c,4) Ap '82

FORTS (cont.)
--Boonesborough, Kentucky (1778)
   Nat Geog 168:828-9 (draw-
      ing,c,1) D '85
--DeRussy, Hawaii
   Nat Wildlife 21:8 (c,3) Ap '83
--El Castillo, Tulum, Mexico
   Trav/Holiday 163:62-3 (c,1) Ja
      '85
--El Morro, Puerto Rico
   Nat Geog 163:518-19 (c,1) Ap
      '83
--Fort Hawkins blockhouse,
      Macon, Georgia
   Trav/Holiday 163:72 (c,4) My
      '85
--Fort Lincoln, North Dakota
   Trav/Holiday 164:56 (c,4) Jl
      '85
--Fort McHenry, Baltimore,
      Maryland (1874 painting)
   Am Heritage 33:22-3 (c,2) Je
      '82
--Fort William, Ontario
   Trav/Holiday 163:14, 121-2
      (c,3) Ap '85
--Housesteads, England
   Smithsonian 16:78 (c,3) Ap '85
--Jefferson, Florida
   Nat Geog 162:201 (c,2) Ag '82
--Lowell storehouse, Tucson,
      Arizona
   Am Heritage 33:84-5 (c,2) Ap
      '82
--Point, San Francisco, California
   Trav/Holiday 159:65 (4) Je '83
--St. Angelo, Malta
   Smithsonian 12:124 (c,4) Ja '82
--Torna, India
   Nat Geog 167:488 (c,1) Ap '85
--See also
         CITADELS
         FORT SUMTER
         FORTRESSES
FOSSILS
   Smithsonian 13:153 (c,3) F '83
   Nat Geog 168:171, 182-91 (c,1)
      Ag '85
--Ammonite shell fossil
   Natur Hist 93:34-40 (c,1) Ag
      '84
--Ancient man
   Nat Geog 168:cov., 563-629
      (c,1) N '85
--Animal fragments
   Smithsonian 15:99-103 (c,3)
      Jl '84

--Antarctica
   Natur Hist 95:60-7 (c,1) My '86
--Butterfly
   Natur Hist 93:106 (4) Ap '84
--Cambrian period
   Natur Hist 94:30, 34-9 (c,1) D
      '85
--Conodont animals
   Natur Hist 92:14, 16 (c,3) Jl '83
--Fossil flowers
   Natur Hist 93:56-61 (c,1) Mr '84
   Natur Hist 93:38-45 (c,1) Ap '84
   Smithsonian 15:100-7 (c,1) N '84
--Rhinoceros jaw (Greece)
   Nat Geog 162:704 (c,4) D '82
--Sequoia twig (Yukon)
   Nat Geog 168:638 (c,4) N '85
--Snail shells
   Natur Hist 92:16 (4) Ap '83
--Trilobites
   Smithsonian 15:70, 72 (c,3) Ja
      '85
   Natur Hist 94:37 (c,4) D '85
--Tsetse fly fossil
   Nat Geog 170:825 (c,4) D '86
FOUNTAINS
--Albquerque, New Mexico
   Trav/Holiday 161:62 (c,2) Ja '84
--Berlin, East Germany
   Trav/Holiday 165:6 (c,4) Ap '86
--Children playing in fountain
      (Philadelphia, Pa.)
   Nat Geog 163:342-3 (c,1) Mr '83
--Cincinnati, Ohio
   Ebony 37:38 (c,2) O '82
--Drinking fountain
   Nat Wildlife 22:14 (c,1) F '84
--French chateau
   Smithsonian 14:60-1 (c,3) Ag '83
--Las Vegas hotel, Nevada
   Sports Illus 56:83 (c,3) Je 7 '82
--Loring Park, Minneapolis, Minne-
      sota
   Trav/Holiday 158:50 (c,1) Jl '82
--Louisiana plantation
   Trav/Holiday 158:38 (c,4) S '82
--Red-dyed water (Iran)
   Nat Geog 168:111 (c,4) Jl '85
--Trevi Fountain, Rome, Italy
   Trav/Holiday 164:50 (c,4) O '85
--Unpredictable trick fountain
      (U.S.S.R.)
   Nat Geog 167:299 (c,3) Mr '85
--Wolf fountain (Rome, Italy)
   Trav/Holiday 164:49 (c,4) O '85
FOURTH OF JULY
--1941 (Arizona)

FRANCE (cont.)
  Nat Geog 161:478-511 (map,c,1)
    Ap '82
--Rochecorbon
  Smithsonian 14:52 (c,4) Je '83
--Roquefort
  Smithsonian 13:57 (c,4) F '83
--Roussillon
  Life 5:69 (c,3) Ap '82
--St. Tropez
  Nat Geog 162:730-1 (c,1) D '82
--Tignes
  Trav/Holiday 163:57-9 (c,3)
    Ja '85
--Vaux-le-Vicomte chateau
  Smithsonian 14:56-65 (c,1) Ag
    '83
--See also
    ALPS
    BORDEAUX
    CARCASSONNE
    CORSICA
    ENGLISH CHANNEL
    FONTAINEBLEAU
    LE HAVRE
    MONT ST. MICHEL
    NICE
    NIMES
    PARIS
    RHONE RIVER
    RIVIERA
    ROUEN
    SEINE RIVER
    VERSAILLE PALACE
FRANCE--ARCHITECTURE
--Drawings of architectural styles
  Smithsonian 17:64 (4) Je '86
FRANCE--ART
--20th cent. works
  Trav/Holiday 158:33-7 (c,1) Jl
    '82
FRANCE--COSTUME
--17th cent. aristocrat
  Smithsonian 14:57 (painting,4)
    Ag '83
--17th cent. warrior
  Smithsonian 15:54 (painting,c,2)
    Ja '85
--18th cent. coat and waistcoat
  Nat Geog 165:11 (c,1) Ja '84
--1804
  Nat Geog 161:144-5 (paint-
    ing,c,1) F '82
--Late 19th cent.
  Smithsonian 15:134-43 (paint-
    ing,c,2) D '84
  Smithsonian 16:58 (4) S '85

--1882 women
  Smithsonian 14:77 (painting,c,1)
    Jl '83
--1890s men's wear shown on dolls
  Life 6:13 (c,4) D '83
--1912 (Normandy)
  Smithsonian 14:112-13 (1) Ja '84
--Basque costume (Western U.S.)
  Trav/Holiday 162:48-51 (c,1) Jl
    '84
--Jurade wine officials (St. Emilion)
  Trav/Holiday 160:62 (c,3) S '83
--Mardi Gras (Nice)
  Trav/Holiday 161:cov., 67-8 (c,1)
    F '84
--Norman costume (Rouen)
  Nat Geog 161:506-7 (c,1) Ap '82
FRANCE--HISTORY
--16th cent. French witch trials
  Natur Hist 95:11, 15 (2) O '86
--1520 summit between Henry VIII
    and François I
  Smithsonian 17:60-1 (painting,c,2)
    S '86
--1545 attack on Portsmouth, Eng-
    land
  Nat Geog 163:648-51 (painting,c,1)
    My '83
--19th cent. Empress Eugénie
  Am Heritage 34:4 (painting,4)
    Ap '83
--1803 engraving of possible French
    attack on England
  Smithsonian 17:66-7 (1) My '86
--1807-1808 summits between Napo-
    leon and Alexander I
  Smithsonian 17:62, 67 (paint-
    ing,c,2) S '86
--1940 British sinking of French
    ships (Algeria)
  Smithsonian 16:122-38 (c,3) Jl
    '85
--1940 German strategy for invading
    France
  Smithsonian 16:130 (diagram,c,4)
    F '86
--1940 invasion of France by Ger-
    man tanks
  Smithsonian 16:125 (3) F '86
--1940 rescue of intellectuals from
    Vichy France
  Am Heritage 34:82-92 (1) Je '83
--1944 D-Day landing sites (Nor-
    mandy)
  Life 7:38-45 (c,1) Je '84
--Humorous history of French cuisine
  Smithsonian 16:134-46 (drawing,c,1)

FRISBEE PLAYING
--Annual frisbee contest (Wash-
   ington, D.C.)
   Am Heritage 37:22-3 (c,1) Ap
      '86
--China
   Life 8:168 (c,2) N '85
--Frisbee Championships (Califor-
   nia)
   Sports Illus 63:100 (c,4) O 21
      '85
FROGS
   Nat Geog 161:88-9 (c,1) Ja '82
   Smithsonian 13:79 (c,4) N '82
   Nat Wildlife 21:19 (4) Ap '83
   Natur Hist 93:34 (c,4) S '84
   Natur Hist 95:93 (c,3) Ap '86
--Caribbean frogs mating
   Natur Hist 95:106-7 (c,1) O
      '86
--Frog eggs
   Natur Hist 95:93 (c,3) Ap '86
--Frog embryos in eggs
   Natur Hist 93:cov., 60-1 (c,1)
      Ap '84
--Glass frog
   Smithsonian 17:124 (c,4) My '86
--Leaf frogs
   Nat Geog 163:62 (c,4) Ja '83
   Smithsonian 17:88 (c,4) S '86
--Poison dart frogs
   Life 5:47 (c,4) S '82
   Nat Geog 163:cov., 48, 62-4
      (c,1) Ja '83
--Tadpole attacked by water bug
   Smithsonian 13:62 (c,1) Jl '82
--Tadpoles
   Natur Hist 93:cov., 60-9 (c,1)
      Ap '84
   Smithsonian 17:124 (c,4) My '86
--Túngara frogs
   Natur Hist 95:36-43 (c,1) Je
      '86
--See also
   BULLFROGS
   TREE FROGS
FROST, ROBERT
--Caricature
   Am Heritage 37:53 (4) Je '86
FRUIT FLIES
   Natur Hist 91:54-9 (c,1) D '82
--Mediterranean fruit flies
   Natur Hist 91:70, 74-5 (2) My
      '82
FRUITS
   Life 5:46-7 (c,1) My '82
   Trav/Holiday 161:16 (c,4) F '84

--Carambola
   Natur Hist 95:88 (c,3) D '86
--Exotic fruits
   Smithsonian 16:34-43 (c,1) D '85
--See also
   APPLES
   APRICOTS
   BANANAS
   BERRIES
   BLUEBERRIES
   BREADFRUIT
   BUNCHBERRIES
   CHERRIES
   COCONUTS
   CRAB APPLES
   CRANBERRIES
   DATES
   FIGS
   GRAPES
   MULBERRIES
   OLIVES
   ORANGES
   QUINCE
   STRAWBERRIES
   TOMATOES
   WATERMELONS
FUCHSIA PLANTS
--X-ray photo
   Smithsonian 17:88 (1) O '86
Fugu. See
   PUFFER FISH
FULLER, ALFRED
   Am Heritage 37:28 (4) Ag '86
FULTON, ROBERT
--1806 self-portrait
   Am Heritage 34:9 (c,4) D '82
FUNERAL RITES AND CEREMONIES
--Mid-19th cent. pioneers heading
   west
   Nat Geog 170:170-1 (c,1) Ag '86
--1860 slave burial (Louisiana)
   Am Heritage 34:36-7 (painting,c,1)
      Je '83
--1913 victims of staircase stampede
   (Calumet, Michigan)
   Am Heritage 37:47 (4) Ap '86
--1926 horse-drawn hearse (Montana)
   Nat Geog 169:93 (3) Ja '86
--1938 Suzanne Lenglen funeral
   (Paris, France)
   Sports Illus 57:79 (4) S 13 '82
--Africa funerary sculpture
   Smithsonian 12:144 (c,4) Ja '82
--Ancient Egyptian funeral prepara-
   tions
   Nat Geog 162:766-9 (drawing,c,1)
      D '82

FUNERAL RITES AND CERE-
    MONIES (cont.)
--Ancient funerary urns (Mali)
    Nat Geog 162:396-7 (c,1) S
    '82
--Ancient Maya rites (Guatemala)
    Nat Geog 169:422-4, 434-5
    (painting,c,1) Ap '86
--Black Americans (North Carolina)
    Nat Geog 166:810-11 (c,2) D
    '84
--Cardinal lying in state (Illinois)
    Life 5:126 (2) Je '82
--Carrying coffin (Alabama)
    Sports Illus 65:20 (c,2) S 8
    '86
--Winston Churchill (1965)
    Life 8:167 (c,4) O '85
--Ethiopia
    Nat Geog 168:400-1 (c,3) S '85
--French sailors (1940)
    Smithsonian 16:138 (3) Jl '85
--French soldiers killed in Lebanon
    (Paris, France)
    Life 7:52-3 (c,1) Ja '84
--Funeral of former Nazi colonel
    (1984)
    Life 7:120-1 (c,1) Jl '84
--Indira Ghandi (1984)
    Life 8:18 (c,1) Ja '85
    Nat Geog 167:510-11 (c,3) Ap
    '85
--Hand-holding memorial ceremony
    (California)
    Life 5:46 (c,3) D '82
--Hindu customs (Benares, India)
    Nat Geog 169:220-1, 249 (c,1)
    F '86
--Hong Kong funeral (China)
    Nat Geog 164:79 (c,1) Jl '83
--IRA hunger strike victim
    (Northern Ireland)
    Life 5:48 (2) Ja '82
--Jewish burial (Poland)
    Nat Geog 170:370-1 (c,1) S '86
--Kansas City, Missouri
    Ebony 37:75 (3) S '82
--John F. Kennedy (1963)
    Life 6:60-7 (c,1) N '83
--Martin Luther King, Jr. (1968)
    Ebony 41:206, 316 (3) N '85
    Ebony 41:98-103 (1) Ja '86
--Joe Louis (Virginia)
    Ebony 37:30 (4) Ja '82
--Maoris (New Zealand)
    Nat Geog 166:530-1 (c,1) O '84
--Newfoundland

Life 5:85-7 (1) Ap '82
--Pallbearers carrying coffin (New
    York)
    Sports Illus 63:20 (c,4) N 18
    '85
--Pearl Harbor victims (1941)
    Life 8:4-5 (1) Spring '85
--Pohnpei, Micronesia
    Nat Geog 170:482-3 (c,1) O '86
--Putting human remains in orbit
    Life 8:76-7 (1) Ap '85
--Reinterment of W. E. B. Du Bois
    (Ghana)
    Ebony 42:172-8 (c,3) N '86
--Sacrificing lamb (South Africa)
    Sports Illus 59:73 (c,4) Jl 18 '83
--Setting Indira Ghandi's pyre
    ablaze (India)
    Life 7:198 (2) D '84
--South African blacks
    Life 8:108-10 (2) Je '85
--Taiwan
    Nat Geog 161:108 (c,3) Ja '82
--U.S. soldiers in Vietnam (1970s)
    Ebony 38:42 (3) Ag '83
--See also
    CEMETERIES
    COFFINS
    DEATH MASKS
    GRIEF
    TOMBS
    TOMBSTONES
FUNGI
    Smithsonian 13:82 (c,4) N '82
--Parasitic carnivorous fungus
    Natur Hist 95:94-5 (c,3) Ap '86
--See also
    MUSHROOMS
    SLIME MOLD
    TRUFFLES
FUR INDUSTRY
--Arctic fox garment factory (Can-
    ada)
    Nat Geog 161:390 (c,4) Mr '82
--Slaughtering seals (Alaska)
    Life 7:179-84 (1) N '84
FURNITURE
--1st cent. A.D. (Herculaneum,
    Italy)
    Nat Geog 165:592-3 (c,4) My '84
--18th cent. (U.S.)
    Am Heritage 36:36-47 (c,1) F '85
--1725 highboy (Massachusetts)
    Am Heritage 36:40 (c,2) F '85
--1760s Philadelphia Chippendale
    parlor
    Smithsonian 14:98-9 (c,1) My '83

FURNITURE (cont.)
--1783 Chippendale bureau (Massachusetts)
Am Heritage 36:36-7 (c,1) F '85
--1790s sideboard (New York)
Am Heritage 36:42-3 (c,1) F '85
--1800 fire screen (Massachusetts)
Am Heritage 36:38-9 (c,2) F '85
--Early 19th cent. Chinese sewing table
Am Heritage 33:47 (c,3) F '82
--19th cent. Shaker room (New Hampshire)
Am Heritage 34:94-5 (c,1) Ap '83
Smithsonian 14:103 (c,4) My '83
--Late 19th cent. (Illinois)
Smithsonian 15:236 (c,4) N '84
--Early American decor
Am Heritage 34:87-95 (c,1) Ap '83
Smithsonian 14:98-109 (c,1) My '83
--Modern
Smithsonian 16:176 (c,4) My '85
--See also
BABY CRIBS
BATHTUBS
BEDS
BENCHES
CHAIRS
CHESTS
DESKS
HOME FURNISHINGS
LAMPS
SOFAS
TABLES
FUTURE
--Future city
Smithsonian 13:46-7 (drawing,c,4) O '82

-G-

GABLE, CLARK
Smithsonian 13:103 (4) F '83
Am Heritage 37:112 (2) D '85
Smithsonian 16:128 (4) Mr '86
Life 9:187 (1) Fall '86
GABON--ART
--19th cent. statuette
Nat Geog 168:773 (c,4) D '85
GAINSBOROUGH, THOMAS
--"Blue Boy" painting
Smithsonian 12:73 (c,1) F '82
GALAPAGOS ISLANDS, ECUADOR
Nat Geog 165:168-9 (c,3) F '84
Trav/Holiday 161:77-9 (c,1) Mr '84
GALAXIES
Natur Hist 91:60 (4) Jl '82
--NGC 1265
Nat Geog 163:739 (c,4) Je '83
--NGC 2997
Nat Geog 163:708-9 (c,1) Je '83
--See also
CONSTELLATIONS
MILKY WAY
NEBULAE
STARS
GALLINULES (BIRDS)
Natur Hist 93:48-9 (c,1) N '84
Nat Wildlife 23:61 (c,1) Ap '85
GALVESTON, TEXAS
--Beach
Ebony 41:78 (c,3) My '86
GAMBIA
Nat Geog 168:225-51 (map,c,1) Ag '85
--See also
BANJUL
GAMBIA--COSTUME
Nat Geog 168:225-51 (c,1) Ag '85
GAMBLING
--1941 crapshooters
Am Heritage 34:39 (painting,c,3) Je '83
--Bingo (Iowa)
Smithsonian 14:160-1 (c,2) N '83
--Bookie (Australia)
Trav/Holiday 158:51 (c,4) Ag '82
--Roulette wheel (Bahamas)
Ebony 38:118 (c,4) Ap '83
--Roulette wheel (New Jersey)
Trav/Holiday 158:39 (c,2) Ag '82
--Slot machines (Las Vegas, Nevada)
Sports Illus 59:70 (c,3) D 5 '83
--Slot machines (New Jersey)
Ebony 40:154 (c,4) My '85
--See also
CARD PLAYING
GAMBLING CASINOS
--Atlantic City, New Jersey
Trav/Holiday 158:39-43 (c,2) Ag '82
--Baden-Baden, West Germany
Trav/Holiday 157:45 (c,4) Je '82

GAMBLING CASINOS (cont.)
--Las Vegas, Nevada
    Ebony 37:45 (c,4) Ja '82
    Sports Illus 56:80-94 (c,1) Je
        7 '82
--Monte Carlo, Monaco
    Trav/Holiday 161:47 (c,4) Je
        '84
--North Dakota
    Sports Illus 65:64-6 (c,4) O
        27 '86
--San Pellegrino, Italy
    Smithsonian 15:115 (c,1) O '84
GAME PLAYING
--19th cent. walrus tusk crib-
        bage board (Alaska)
    Nat Geog 163:200-1 (c,2) F
        '83
--1941 crapshooters
    Am Heritage 34:39 (painting,c,3)
        Je '83
--1950s simulated war game
    Am Heritage 34:58 (2) Je '83
--Annual frisbee contest (Wash-
        ington, D.C.)
    Am Heritage 37:22-3 (c,1) Ap
        '86
--Cat's cradle (Greenland)
    Nat Geog 165:531 (c,4) Ap '84
--Catching frisbee (Cayman Is-
        lands)
    Nat Geog 167:824 (c,3) Je '85
--Children's hand slapping game
        (South)
    Life 6:58 (c,4) Ag '83
--Dice game
    Sports Illus 62:34-5 (c,2) My
        27 '85
--Dominoes
    Nat Geog 167:122-3 (c,2) Ja '85
--Dungeons & Dragons
    Life 5:17, 20 (2) Mr '82
--Jigsaw puzzles
    Sports Illus 59:120 (c,4) O 31
        '83
    Sports Illus 65:120-30 (c,1) N
        19 '86
--Korean Jang-Ki (New York)
    Life 7:40 (c,4) O '84
--"Monopoly"
    Sports Illus 61:67 N 19 '84
--Murder mystery weekends (New
        Jersey)
    Life 7:109-14 (c,1) N '84
--National Survival Game (New
        Hampshire)
    Life 6:68-72 (c,1) My '83

--Ouija boards
    Am Heritage 34:24-7 (3) F '83
--Photon
    Sports Illus 64:19 (c,4) F 3 '86
--Rubik's cube inventor (Hungary)
    Nat Geog 163:235 (c,3) F '83
--Rubik's Cube played by Indians
        (French Guiana)
    Nat Geog 163:67 (c,1) Ja '83
--"Scrabble"
    Ebony 38:124 (4) S '83
--"Scrabble" (Israel)
    Life 5:39 (4) S '82
--"Scrabble" tournament (Boston,
        Massachusetts)
    Sports Illus 63:94, 98-102 (c,4)
        N 18 '85
--Table hockey
    Sports Illus 64:40 (c,4) Mr 3 '86
--Video game operating controls
    Sports Illus 56:31 (c,4) Mr 1 '82
--Video games
    Smithsonian 13:93 (c,3) Jl '82
    Sports Illus 57:223 (c,4) S 1 '82
    Natur Hist 91:70-80 (c,1) N '82
    Life 6:72-3 (c,1) Ja '83
    Nat Geog 164:385 (c,3) S '83
    Nat Geog 169:704-5 (c,1) Je '86
--See also
        BILLIARDS
        CARD PLAYING
        CHESS PLAYING
        CROQUET PLAYING
        FRISBEE PLAYING
        GAMBLING
        PINBALL MACHINES
        REBUSES
        SPORTS
        TABLE TENNIS
        TOYS
GAMES
--1899 "Ports & Commerce"
    Am Heritage 34:110-11 (c,4) O
        '83
--Rubik's cube (1981)
    Life 9:72 (c,3) Ag '86
GANGES RIVER, INDIA
--Benares
    Smithsonian 16:82-93 (c,1) S '85
    Nat Geog 169:222-31, 250-1
        (map,c,1) F '86
GARBAGE
    Nat Geog 163:cov., 424-57 (c,1)
        Ap '83
--Coral reefs created on sunken
        garbage
    Nat Wildlife 24:12-17 (c,1) F '86

GARBAGE (cont.)
--Sculpture made from trash
  Nat Geog 163:cov., 428-9,
    452-3 (c,1) Ap '83
  Smithsonian 14:82-91 (c,1) Ag
    '83
--See also
    JUNKYARDS
    REFUSE DISPOSAL
GARBAGE CANS
--Mouth of sculpture used as
    trash can (Washington,
    D.C.)
  Life 8:88-9 (1) O '85
--On beach (California)
  Sports Illus 63:4 (c,4) Jl 22
    '85
GARBO, GRETA
  Smithsonian 13:100 (2) F '83
  Lie 8:120 (c,2) S '85
GARDEN OF THE GODS, COLO-
    RADO
  Life 6:48 (c,4) Ap '83
GARDENERS
--1903 (Great Britain)
  Smithsonian 16:178 (4) Ap '85
GARDENING
--1910 lawn sprinkler
  Am Heritage 35:21 (4) F '84
--Clipping hedges
  Ebony 40:85 (c,4) N '84
--Groundkeeping at stadium
    (Kansas City, Missouri)
  Sports Illus 56:42-9 (c,2) My
    17 '82
--Mowing golf course (Florida)
  Sports Illus 56:38 (c,4) Mr 15
    '82
--Mowing lawn (1880s)
  Am Heritage 35:114 (c,4) F '84
--Mowing lawn (Indiana)
  Nat Wildlife 23:18-19 (c,2) O
    '85
--Mowing lawn (Midway)
  Nat Wildlife 23:10 (c,3) F '85
--Mowing lawn on garden tractor
    (Ohio)
  Sports Illus 63:51 (c,4) Jl 15
    '85
--New York City slums
  Nat Geog 166:384-5 (c,1) S '84
--Straw coats on plants for win-
    ter protection (Japan)
  Smithsonian 15:94-101 (c,1) F
    '85
--Watering baseball field (North
    Carolina)

Sports Illus 56:55 (c,4) Ap 26
    '82
--Watering plants (1951)
  Am Heritage 35:26 (painting,c,1)
    F '84
--See also
    GARDENERS
    GREENHOUSES
    LAWN MOWERS
GARDENS
--6th cent. B.C. Hanging Gardens
    of Babylon
  Smithsonian 14:59 (drawing,4)
    Mr '84
--15th cent. cloister garden
  Smithsonian 15:36 (painting,c,2)
    Je '84
--Early 20th cent. gardens by
    Beatrix Ferrand
  Am Heritage 37:66-77 (c,1) Je
    '86
--Arnold Arboretum, Jamaica Plains,
    Massachusetts
  Life 8:58 (c,2) Je '85
--Backyard habitats
  Nat Wildlife 21:36 (c,4) O '83
--Botanical (San Diego, California)
  Trav/Holiday 158:28 (c,2) S '82
--Butchart Gardens, Victoria, Brit-
    ish Columbia
  Trav/Holiday 160:47 (c,2) Ag '83
--Cactus at Exotic Garden, Monaco
  Trav/Holiday 161:49 (c,3) Je '84
--Castel Gandolfo, Italy
  Nat Geog 168:762-3 (c,1) D '85
--Delaware mansion
  Am Heritage 34:96 (c,4) Ap '83
  Smithsonian 14:106 (c,4) My '83
--Dumbarton Oaks, Washington, D.C.
  Life 8:56-7 (c,1) Je '85
  Am Heritage 37:68-74 (c,3) Je
    '86
--Filoli gardens, Woodside, California
  Life 8:52-3 (c,1) Je '85
--Isabella Stewart Gardner Museum,
    Boston, Massachusetts
  Trav/Holiday 163:70 (c,1) Mr '85
--Hampshire estate, England
  Smithsonian 17:56 (c,2) My '86
--Het Loo Palace, Netherlands
  Nat Geog 170:510-11 (c,1) O '86
--Huntington Library, San Marino,
    California
  Smithsonian 12:71 (c,3) F '82
--Japan
  Nat Geog 165:762-3 (c,1) Je '84
  Smithsonian 15:94-101 (c,1) F '85

GARDENS (cont.)
--Japanese (California)
  Trav/Holiday 158:40 (c,1) O
    '82
--Maine estate
  Am Heritage 37:66-76 (c,1) Je
    '86
--Monticello, Charlottesville,
    Virginia
  Smithsonian 15:68-77 (c,1) Jl
    '84
--National Herb Garden, Wash-
    ington, D.C.
  Nat Geog 163:394-5 (c,1) Mr
    '83
--New York
  Nat Wildlife 20:30-1 (c,1) Ap '82
--New York Botanical Garden rose
    garden sketches (1916)
  Am Heritage 37:76 (4) Je '86
--Plantation grounds (Louisiana)
  Trav/Holiday 158:37-8 (c,1)
    S '82
--Potato garden (Newfoundland)
  Natur Hist 94:24 (c,3) Je '85
--Roof gardens (London, Eng-
    land)
  Smithsonian 15:42 (c,4) Mr '85
--Seal Harbor public garden,
    Maine
  Life 8:60 (c,2) Je '85
--Southern France
  Smithsonian 14:144-5 (c,2) Mr
    '84
--Stratford-Upon-Avon, England
  Nat Geog 163:392-3 (c,2) Mr
    '83
--Thailand
  Life 7:78-9 (c,1) My '84
--U.S. public gardens
  Life 8:52-60 (c,1) Je '85
--Vegetable garden
  Nat Wildlife 23:20 (c,4) F '85
--See also
    FLOWERS
    GARDENING
    GREENHOUSES
    PLANTS
GARIBALDI, GIUSEPPE
  Sports Illus 64:39 (paint-
    ing,c,3) Je 30 '86
GARLAND, JUDY
  Am Heritage 35:46, 49 (1) D
    '83
  Smithsonian 15:113 (4) D '84
  Smithsonian 17:114-15 (2) Jl
    '86

--Ruby slippers from "Wizard of
    Oz"
  Life 7:9 (c,4) O '84
GARLIC
--Garlic festival (California)
  Nat Geog 170:343 (c,2) S '86
GARMENT INDUSTRY
--Arctic fox factory (Canada)
  Nat Geog 161:390 (c,4) Mr '82
--Jeans (Italy)
  Nat Geog 165:186 (c,4) F '84
--New York City, New York
  Smithsonian 16:cov., 30-41 (c,1)
    Ag '85
--Sportswear (Italy)
  Life 7:159-66 (c,1) N '84
--Underwear plant (Kentucky)
  Nat Geog 161:536 (c,3) Ap '82
--See also
    CLOTHING
    FOOTWEAR
    TEXTILE INDUSTRY
GARRISON, WILLIAM LLOYD
  Nat Geog 166:12 (painting,c,4)
    Jl '84
GARTER SNAKES
  Natur Hist 92:64-9 (c,1) Ap '83
  Smithsonian 16:57 (drawing,c,4)
    N '85
GARY, INDIANA
--Civic Center
  Ebony 38:62-3 (c,1) Jl '83
GASOLINE STATIONS
--1936 (Utah)
  Am Heritage 36:66-7 (painting,c,1)
    Ag '85
--Abandoned (Georgia)
  Nat Geog 166:794 (c,3) D '84
--China
  Nat Geog 164:66-7 (c,3) Jl '83
--Closed station during 1973 energy
    shortage
  Nat Wildlife 24:32 (c,4) Ap '86
--Filling tank
  Life 5:74 (c,4) D '82
--Papua New Guinea
  Nat Geog 162:151 (c,1) Ag '82
GASPE PENINSULA, QUEBEC
  Trav/Holiday 165:82-3 (map,c,2)
    Mr '86
GATES
--Palm Beach mansion, Florida
  Trav/Holiday 165:116 (4) Mr '86
--Yellin's wrought iron designs
  Smithsonian 12:69 (c,4) Mr '82

GATEWAY ARCH, ST. LOUIS,
    MISSOURI
    Smithsonian 14:60 (c,4) Mr '84
    Trav/Holiday 165:63 (c,3) My
        '86
GAUGUIN, PAUL
--1893 painting of woman with
        breadfruit
    Natur Hist 94:34 (c,1) Mr '85
--"D'ou Venons Nous?" (1897)
    Natur Hist 93:14 (painting,c,4)
        N '84
--"Les Drames de la Mer"
    Smithsonian 17:164 (draw-
        ing,c,4) D '86
GAURS (CATTLE)
--Calf
    Life 5:47 (c,4) Je '82
GAZELLES
    Life 5:47 (c,4) Je '82
    Nat Geog 167:226-33 (c,4) F '85
    Nat Geog 170:346 (c,3) S '86
--Gerenuks
    Natur Hist 92:68 (4) Jl '83
GECKOS (LIZARDS)
    Nat Geog 164:368 (c,4) S '83
    Natur Hist 93:92 (c,4) S '84
GEESE
    Natur Hist 92:102 (drawing,4)
        Ap '83
    Natur Hist 166:374-5 (c,3) S
        '84
    Nat Geog 167:391 (c,3) Mr '85
    Nat Wildlife 24:54 (c,4) Ap '86
    Nat Wildlife 24:4-11 (c,1) Je
        '86
--Diagram of flying goose
    Natur Hist 92:33, 36 (c,4) S
        '83
--Flock in flight
    Nat Wildlife 23:33 (painting,c,2)
        O '85
--Snow
    Nat Wildlife 21:30-1 (c,1) D '82
    Natur Hist 92:36-43 (c,1) Ja
        '83
    Sports Illus 65:126 (c,1) S 3
        '86
--Snow geese in flight
    Smithsonian 14:35 (c,4) Ja '84
    Nat Wildlife 24:46-7 (c,1) F '86
--See also
    CANADA GEESE
Gems. See
    JEWELRY
    JEWELS
    list under MINERALS

GEMSBOKS
    Nat Geog 161:777, 796-7 (c,1)
        Je '82
    Nat Geog 163:370 (c,3) Mr '83
    Natur Hist 92:42-4 (c,1) Mr '83
GENEALOGY
--Family trees
    Am Heritage 33:10-18, 114 (c,2)
        Ag '82
--Study of heraldry (Great Britain)
    Smithsonian 15:cov., 86-95 (c,1)
        My '84
GENETICS
--Biotechnology
    Nat Geog 166:819-47 (c,1) D '84
--Computer image of DNA
    Smithsonian 16:115-19 (c,1) Jl
        '85
--DNA model
    Nat Geog 164:179 (c,4) Ag '83
    Nat Geog 166:822-5 (drawing,c,1)
        D '84
    Life 9:98 (c,2) Fall '86
--Research on the origins of life
    Smithsonian 15:42-5 (c,1) Je '84
--RNA model
    Smithsonian 15:46 (c,4) Je '84
--See also
    CRICK, FRANCIS
    PAULING, LINUS
    WATSON, JAMES
GENEVA, SWITZERLAND
--Outdoor cafe
    Trav/Holiday 164:30 (c,4) Ag '85
--See also
    LAKE GENEVA
GENGHIS KHAN
--1258 siege of Baghdad by Genghis
        Khan's grandson Hulegu
    Smithsonian 17:162 (painting,c,3)
        O '86
GEOLOGICAL PHENOMENA
--Coriolis effect
    Smithsonian 13:66-73 (c,1) F '83
--Earth mima mounds (Western U.S.)
    Natur Hist 93:36-45 (map,c,1)
        Je '84
--Soil problems and research
    Nat Geog 166:350-89 (c,1) S '84
--Wetlands areas
    Nat Geog 166:568-85 (c,1) N '84
--Winter Park sinkhole, Florida
    Nat Geog 162:214-15 (c,1) Ag '82
    Smithsonian 13:56 (c,4) Mr '83
--See also
    ANTARCTICA
    ARCTIC

GEOLOGICAL PHENOMENA (cont.)
    BEACHES
    CAVES
    CLIFFS
    DESERTS
    EARTH
    EARTHQUAKES
    FARMS
    FIELDS
    FLOODS
    FORESTS
    GEYSERS
    GLACIERS
    GRASSLANDS
    GROUND WATER
    HOT SPRINGS
    ICEBERGS
    ISLANDS
    MARSHES
    MOUNTAINS
    MUD
    NORTH POLE
    RAIN FORESTS
    ROCKS
    SAND DUNES
    SOIL
    VOLCANOES
    WATER FORMATIONS
    WEATHER PHENOMENA
GEORGE III (GREAT BRITAIN)
    Smithsonian 14:57 (paint-
      ing,c,4) S '83
GEORGE VI (GREAT BRITAIN)
--1937 coronation
    Life 9:88 (4) Ap '86
--Playing tennis
    Sports Illus 56:76 (4) Je 21 '82
GEORGE, HENRY
    Am Heritage 37:14 (draw-
      ing,4) O '86
GEORGE WASHINGTON BRIDGE,
    NEW YORK/NEW JERSEY
--1933
    Smithsonian 13:136 (4) N '82
GEORGE WASHINGTON NATIONAL
    FOREST, VIRGINIA
--Ramsey's Draft
    Natur Hist 94:76-8 (map,c,2)
      N '85
GEORGIA
--Chattooga River area, Rabun
    County
    Nat Geog 163:458-77 (map,c,1)
      Ap '83
--The Cloister, Sea Island
    Trav/Holiday 162:44-5 (c,1) Jl
      '84

--Harris Neck
    Ebony 38:36-41 (c,3) Jl '83
--Jekyll Island
    Trav/Holiday 158:48-9 (4) N '82
--Panther Creek Cove
    Natur Hist 95:98-100 (map,c,1)
      F '86
--Sapelo Island marshes
    Nat Wildlife 22:18-19 (c,1) F '84
--Sky Valley resort
    Nat Geog 163:466-7 (c,1) Ap '83
--See also
    ATLANTA
    AUGUSTA
    BLUE RIDGE MOUNTAINS
    MACON
    OKEFENOKEE SWAMP
    SAVANNAH
    SAVANNAH RIVER
    STONE MOUNTAIN
GERANIUMS
    Nat Geog 163:408 (c,4) Mr '83
GERMAN SHEPHERDS
    Ebony 37:36 (3) Mr '82
    Nat Wildlife 21:44 (painting,c,1)
      D '82
    Sports Illus 57:28-9 (c,1) D 20
      '82
    Sports Illus 58:56 (c,4) My 16
      '83
    Ebony 39:38 (c,2) Je '84
    Life 7:120 (c,2) D '84
    Sports Illus 64:2-3, 74-5, 88
      (c,1) Ap 28 '86
GERMANY--ART
--Early 20th cent. works
    Smithsonian 17:122-31 (c,2) D
      '86
GERMANY--COSTUME
--16th cent.
    Nat Geog 164:418-59 (paint-
      ing,c,1) O '83
--Children (1912)
    Sports Illus 65:52 (4) Ag 4 '86
--Nazi officers (France)
    Life 8:69 (2) F '85
GERMANY--HISTORY
--1806 Bavarian crown
    Nat Geog 168:210 (c,4) Ag '85
--1932 Hitler campaign poster
    Am Heritage 37:92 (4) Ag '86
--1940 German strategy for invad-
    ing France
    Smithsonian 16:130 (diagram,c,4)
      F '86
--1940 invasion of France by German
    tanks

GERMANY--HISTORY (cont.)
Smithsonian 16:125 (3) F '86
--1945 ashamed German graffiti
(Munich)
Am Heritage 34:6 (4) D '82
--1945 license and press for post-
war newspaper
Am Heritage 33:90, 92 (3) Je
'82
--Carrying Olympic torch through
Berlin (1936)
Life 7:102-3 (1) Summer '84
--See also
CONCENTRATION CAMPS
GOEBBELS, PAUL JOSEPH
HITLER, ADOLPH
LUTHER, MARTIN
NAZISM
ROMMEL, ERWIN
WORLD WAR I
WORLD WAR II
GERMANY, EAST
--Eisleben's Market Square
Trav/Holiday 160:14 (4) O '83
--Wittenberg
Nat Geog 164:446-7, 452-3,
456 (c,1) O '83
--Wittenberg (16th cent.)
Nat Geog 164:419 (c,1) O '83
--See also
BERLIN
BERLIN WALL
ERFURT
GERMANY, EAST--COSTUME
--East Berlin
Nat Geog 161:cov., 3-33 (c,1)
Ja '82
--Guard at war memorial (East
Berlin)
Nat Geog 161:cov., 3-4 (c,1)
Ja '82
GERMANY, WEST
--Assmannshausen
Trav/Holiday 162:56-7 (c,1) S
'84
--Castles
Trav/Holiday 163:73-5 (c,2) Ap
'85
--Hannoversch-Muenden
Trav/Holiday 166:26 (c,4) Ag
'86
--Lindau
Trav/Holiday 160:38 (c,1) Jl '83
--Marburg
Nat Geog 164:450-1 (c,1) O '83
--Oberwesel
Trav/Holiday 161:106 (4) Mr '84

--Rhineland
Trav/Holiday 162:56-61, 70 (c,1)
S '84
--Scenes of Bavaria
Trav/Holiday 158:12 (c,2) D '82
--See also
BADEN-BADEN
BERCHTESGADEN
BERLIN
BERLIN WALL
BLACK FOREST
COLOGNE
ESSEN
FRANKFURT
HAMBURG
KASSEL
LAKE CONSTANCE
MUNICH
NUREMBERG
RHINE RIVER
GERMANY, WEST--COSTUME
--Motorcycle gang
Life 5:24-5 (c,1) Mr '82
--Traditional Bavarian costume
Trav/Holiday 159:50 (4) Mr '83
--Traditional guardsman's outfit
Trav/Holiday 163:74 (c,4) Ap '85
--West Berlin
Nat Geog 161:6-13, 34-51 (c,1)
Ja '82
GERMANY, WEST--HOUSING
--Half-timbered houses (Hannoversch-
Muenden)
Trav/Holiday 166:26 (c,4) Ag '86
GERMANY, WEST--POLITICS AND
GOVERNMENT
--Youth demonstrations
Life 5:26-9 (c,1) Mr '82
GERMANY, WEST--RITES AND
FESTIVALS
--Oktoberfest (Munich)
Trav/Holiday 165:38 (c,1) Ja '86
GERMANY, WEST--SOCIAL LIFE
AND CUSTOMS
--Reenactment of Pied Piper story
(Hamelin)
Trav/Holiday 163:102 (4) My '85
GERRY, ELBRIDGE
--Tombstone (Washington, D.C.)
Am Heritage 33:67 (c,4) Je '82
GERSHWIN, IRA
Life 7:173 (4) Ja '84
GETTY, J. PAUL
Life 8:112-13, 126 (1) D '85
--J. Paul Getty Museum, Malibu,
California
Trav/Holiday 164:64-6 (c,1) Ag '85

GEYSERS
--Old Faithful, Yellowstone,
    Wyoming
    Nat Wildlife 21:6 (c,4) Ap '83
    Trav/Holiday 165:18 (c,4) Ja
    '86
--Yellowstone in winter
    Nat Wildlife 20:37-9 (c,1) F '82
GHANA
--See also
    ASANTE CIVILIZATION
GHANA--COSTUME
    Ebony 42:172-8 (c,3) N '86
--Children
    Natur Hist 91:44-7 (c,1) Mr
    '82
    Natur Hist 91:38 (c,3) Jl '82
GHANA--HISTORY
--19th cent. Asante civilization
    relics
    Natur Hist 93:62-73, 106 (c,1)
    O '84
GHANDI, MOHANDAS
    Life 8:10 (4) My '85
--1910 letter from Ghandi to
    Tolstoy
    Nat Geog 169:787 (c,4) Je '86
GHIRLANDAIO, DOMENICO
--1480 fresco of the Last Supper
    (Florence, Italy)
    Nat Geog 164:682-3 (c,1) N
    '83
GHOST TOWNS
--Butte, Montana
    Trav/Holiday 164:16 (c,4) Ag
    '85
--Coloma, California
    Trav/Holiday 163:20 (c,4) Ja
    '85
--Cumberland, Wyoming
    Sports Illus 56:88 (4) My 17
    '82
--Nevada City, Montana
    Trav/Holiday 164:61 (c,4) S '85
--See also
    VIRGINIA CITY
GIACOMETTI, ALBERTO
    Smithsonian 13:191 (4) O '82
GIBBONS
    Smithsonian 14:119-22 (c,2)
    Mr '84
    Smithsonian 16:104 (c,4) D '85
GIBRALTAR
--Seen in fog
    Nat Geog 162:700-1 (c,1) D '82
GILA MONSTERS
    Natur Hist 91:59 (c,4) S '82

GILBERT, SIR WILLIAM
    Smithsonian 14:110, 114 (4) Mr
    '84
--Scenes from Gilbert and Sullivan
    operettas
    Smithsonian 14:cov., 104-15 (c,1)
    Mr '84
Gilbert Islands. See
    TARAWA ATOLL
GILLESPIE, JOHN BIRKS (DIZZY)
    Ebony 39:78 (3) F '84
    Trav/Holiday 161:69 (c,4) Ap '84
    Smithsonian 15:162 (3) My '84
    Ebony 41:126 (4) N '85
    Ebony 41:50-6 (c,2) S '86
GINGER
    Smithsonian 14:111 (c,3) D '83
GINSENG
    Nat Wildlife 21:16 (drawing,4) F
    '83
--1817 engraving
    Natur Hist 93:74 (c,4) F '84
GIOTTO
--"Adoration of the Magi" (1303)
    Life 8:32 (painting,c,4) O '85
    Smithsonian 16:162 (painting,c,4)
    N '85
GIPP, GEORGE
    Smithsonian 16:131-48 (2) D '85
--Portrayed by Ronald Reagan
    (1940)
    Smithsonian 16:130, 146-8 (2) D
    '85
    Life 9:95 (3) My '86
GIRAFFES
    Smithsonian 12:94-103 (c,1) Ja
    '82
    Smithsonian 13:128-9 (c,4) Ap
    '82
    Nat Geog 163:348-9, 358 (c,1)
    Mr '83
    Nat Wildlife 22:36 (4) D '83
    Life 7:200 (c,2) N '84
    Nat Wildlife 24:12 (c,4) D '85
    Trav/Holiday 165:cov. (c,1) Mr
    '86
    Nat Geog 169:596 (c,4) My '86
    Ebony 42:62 (c,4) N '86
--See also
    OKAPIS
GIRL SCOUTS
--1920
    Am Heritage 33:113 (2) Ap '82
--1930s Brownie
    Am Heritage 33:114 (drawing,c,3)
    Je '82
--History

GLOBES (cont.)
--Prague, Czechoslovakia
    Trav/Holiday 158:40 (c,4) Jl
        '82
--Reproduction of 1492 globe
    Nat Geog 170:563-5 (c,1) N '86
GLOUCESTER, ENGLAND
--Gloucester Cathedral
    Trav/Holiday 164:43 (c,2) Jl '85
GLOUCESTER, MASSACHUSETTS
    Trav/Holiday 157:22 (4) Ap '82
GLOVES
--16th cent. (Great Britain)
    Smithsonian 15:77 (c,4) Ag '84
--Golf gloves
    Sports Illus 59:38-9 (c,1) Jl
        25 '83
--Newspaper reading gloves
    Life 9:149 (c,4) Fall '86
--Riding gloves
    Life 5:78 (c,4) Ag '82
GOATS
    Smithsonian 13:110-19 (c,1) D
        '82
    Life 7:162 (c,2) Ja '84
    Sports Illus 60:67 (c,4) Je 4
        '84
    Life 8:96 (c,2) Mr '85
    Natur Hist 95:cov., 40-7 (c,1)
        N '86
--Depictions in art works
    Smithsonian 13:110-13 (c,3) D
        '82
--Himalayan tahrs
    Nat Geog 161:717 (c,1) Je '82
--Milking goat (California)
    Natur Hist 92:86 (c,4) Ja '83
--Takins
    Nat Geog 169:294-5 (c,1) Mr
        '86
--See also
        IBEXES
GOBI DESERT, MONGOLIA
    Nat Geog 167:262-3 (c,1) F '85
GODDARD, ROBERT
--Depicted on postage stamp
    Am Heritage 34:54 (c,4) D '82
Gods and goddesses. See
        DEITIES
        MYTHOLOGY
        specific religions
GOEBBELS, PAUL JOSEPH
    Sports Illus 65:56 (4) Ag 4 '86
GOGGLES
--Late 19th cent. wooden Eskimo
        goggles (Alaska)
    Smithsonian 13:54 (c,4) My '82

--1920s pilots
    Smithsonian 13:90-1 (1) My '82
--Border patrol night vision goggles
        (California)
    Nat Geog 167:728-9 (c,1) Je '85
--Metal workers
    Nat Geog 163:592 (c,4) My '83
--Swimming goggles
    Life 5:134 (2) D '82
GOLD
    Smithsonian 15:89 (c,4) Ap '84
--Gold bars
    Nat Geog 163:441 (c,1) Ap '83
--Spanish gold ingots
    Smithsonian 14:78 (c,1) O '83
--Treasures from 17th cent. Spanish
        shipwreck
    Nat Geog 161:228-37 (c,1) F '82
GOLD MINING
--Brazil
    Nat Geog 163:6-7 (c,1) Ja '83
    Smithsonian 15:88-97 (c,1) Ap
        '84
--South Africa
    Nat Geog 168:175 (c,3) Ag '85
--South Dakota
    Life 9:32 (c,2) Jl '86
--See also
        PROSPECTING
GOLD RUSH
--1898 prospectors (Alaska)
    Am Heritage 36:98-9 (2) O '85
--1898 prospectors climbing mountain
        (Alaska)
    Nat Geog 165:85 (4) Ja '84
--Abandoned gold dredger (Califor-
        nia)
    Trav/Holiday 166:75 (c,4) O '86
--Recreation of Sutter's 1848 mill
        (California)
    Smithsonian 13:97 (c,1) D '82
GOLDEN GATE BRIDGE, SAN
        FRANCISCO, CALIFORNIA
    Smithsonian 13:98-107 (c,1) Jl
        '82
    Trav/Holiday 159:65 (4) Je '83
    Trav/Holiday 161:73 (c,2) Mr '84
GOLDEN GATE NATIONAL RECREA-
        TION AREA, CALIFORNIA
--Coastline
    Trav/Holiday 159:16 (c,4) Je '83
GOLDEN RETRIEVERS
    Life 6:66 (c,2) Mr '83
    Nat Geog 165:446-7 (c,1) Ap '84
    Life 7:104 (c,4) Ap '84
GOLDENROD
    Nat Wildlife 20:21-4 (c,2) Ag '82

GOLDENROD (cont.)
  Natur Hist 95:70 (c,4) S '86
--Made of glass
  Smithsonian 13:105 (c,4) O '82
GOLDFINCHES
  Nat Wildlife 20:52 (c,1) Ag '82
  Nat Wildlife 22:33-4 (paint-
    ing,c,1) D '83
GOLDMAN, EMMA
  Trav/Holiday 164:37 (4) Jl '85
GOLF
--Child putting
  Sports Illus 56:46 (c,4) Ap 19
    '82
--Miniature golf (Florida)
  Trav/Holiday 160:19 (4) D '83
--Putting
  Sports Illus 61:38 (c,2) D 10
    '84
--Sand trap
  Sports Illus 61:116 (c,4) S 5
    '84
--Six-year-old champion
  Ebony 38:93-8 (c,3) N '82
--Swing
  Ebony 37:71 (2) Ja '82
  Sports Illus 56:45 (c,4) Ap 19
    '82
  Sports Illus 57:56 (c,4) Ag 30
    '82
  Sports Illus 62:cov. (c,1) Mr
    11 '85
GOLF--COLLEGE
--NCAA Championships 1986 (North
    Carolina)
  Sports Illus 64:48-51 (c,4) Je
    9 '86
GOLF--EDUCATION
  Trav/Holiday 157:14 (4) Ap '82
GOLF--HUMOR
  Sports Illus 65:36-40 (draw-
    ing,c,1) S 8 '86
GOLF--PROFESSIONAL
  Sports Illus 58:138-41 (c,1) F
    16 '83
  Sports Illus 59:28-35 (c,1) D 5
    '83
  Ebony 41:67-8 (c,2) D '85
--Lining up putt
  Sports Illus 57:21 (c,3) S 6
    '82
  Sports Illus 59:18 (c,3) Jl 25
    '83
  Sports Illus 60:26 (c,4) Ap 23
    '84
--Putting
  Sports Illus 56:58 (c,4) My 3

    '82
  Sports Illus 57:35 (c,4) Jl 5 '82
  Ebony 37:104 (4) O '82
  Sports Illus 58:43 (painting,c,4)
    Ap 25 '83
--Searching for balls (Great Britain)
  Sports Illus 63:24-5 (c,1) Jl 29
    '85
--Seniors
  Sports Illus 61:66-8 (c,3) S 17
    '84
--Swinging
  Sports Illus 58:50 (c,4) F 28 '83
GOLF--PROFESSIONAL--WOMEN
  Sports Illus 58:34-5 (c,2) Ap 11
    '83
  Sports Illus 60:36-7 (c,1) Mr 19
    '84
  Sports Illus 60:2-3, 68, 73 (c,2)
    Ap 16 '84
--Swinging
  Sports Illus 59:30-1 (c,1) Ag 8
    '83
GOLF BAGS
  Sports Illus 57:57 (c,4) Ag 30
    '82
GOLF BALLS
  Sports Illus 65:18 (c,4) D 8 '86
GOLF CARTS
  Sports Illus 56:44 (c,4) Mr 15
    '82
  Ebony 38:94 (4) N '82
  Nat Geog 164:394 (c,4) S '83
  Sports Illus 60:38 (c,4) Ap 9 '84
  Sports Illus 63:61 (c,4) Jl 8 '85
--Man pulling cart (Ireland)
  Sports Illus 60:65 (c,4) Je 4 '84
GOLF CLUBS
--Repairing clubs
  Sports Illus 56:30-1 (c,2) Ap 5
    '82
GOLF COURSES
  Trav/Holiday 164:44-9 (c,1) Ag
    '85
--Augusta National, Georgia
  Sports Illus 64:98-113 (c,1) Ap
    7 '86
--Augusta National's Sarazen Bridge,
    Georgia
  Sports Illus 62:61 (3) Ap 8 '85
--Australia
  Nat Geog 169:36-7 (c,1) Ja '86
--Edinburgh, Scotland
  Nat Geog 166:42-3 (c,1) Jl '84
--Fairway Oaks, Abilene, Texas
  Sports Illus 57:77 (c,4) O 18 '82
--Ireland

GOLF TOURNAMENTS (cont.)
--Masters 1982 (Augusta, Georgia)
Sports Illus 56:cov., 16-19
(c,1) Ap 19 '82
--Masters 1983 (Augusta, Georgia)
Sports Illus 58:30-5 (c,1) Ap
18 '83
--Masters 1984 (Augusta, Georgia)
Sports Illus 60:20-7 (c,1) Ap
23 '84
--Masters 1985 (Augusta, Georgia)
Sports Illus 62:2-3, 26-35 (c,1)
Ap 22 '85
--Masters 1986 (Augusta, Georgia)
Sports Illus 64:cov., 2-3, 18-
25 (c,1) Ap 21 '86
Sports Illus 64:46-50, 54 (c,4)
Ap 28 '86
--Oregon
Sports Illus 57:52-3 (c,4) Jl 19
'82
--PGA 1982 (Tulsa, Oklahoma)
Sports Illus 57:26-7 (c,4) Ag
16 '82
--PGA 1983 (Pacific Palisades,
California)
Sports Illus 59:16-17 (c,2) Ag
15 '83
--PGA 1984 (Shoal Creek, Alabama)
Sports Illus 61:28-30 (c,2) Ag
27 '84
--PGA 1985 (Cherry Hills, Denver,
Colorado)
Sports Illus 63:20-3 (c,1) Ag
19 '85
--PGA 1986 (Inverness Club, Tole-
do, Ohio)
Sports Illus 65:20-1 (c,2) Ag
18 '86
Sports Illus 65:75, 82 (c,3) Ag
18 '86
--Senior Open 1985 (Tahoe)
Sports Illus 63:56, 61 (c,3) Jl
8 '85
--Texas
Sports Illus 62:62-4 (c,4) My
6 '85
--Tournament Players Champion-
ship 1982 (Florida)
Sports Illus 56:24-31 (c,2) Mr
29 '82
--Tournament Players Champion-
ship 1985 (Florida)
Sports Illus 62:40-7 (c,2) Ap
8 '85
--Tournament Players Champion-
ship 1986 (Florida)

Sports Illus 64:36-43 (c,3) Ap
7 '86
--U.S. Open 1913 (Brookline, Mas-
sachusetts)
Sports Illus 58:62 (3) Je 6 '83
--U.S. Open 1930 (Minneapolis,
Minnesota)
Sports Illus 58:63 (4) Je 6 '83
--U.S. Open 1950 (Merion, Penn-
sylvania)
Sports Illus 58:65 (4) Je 6 '83
--U.S. Open 1982 (Pebble Beach,
California)
Sports Illus 56:14-19 (c,2) Je
28 '82
--U.S. Open 1983 (Oakmont, Penn-
sylvania)
Sports Illus 58:28-31 (c,2) Je
27 '83
--U.S. Open 1984 (Mamaroneck,
New York)
Sports Illus 60:30-5 (c,1) Je
25 '84
Sports Illus 61:50 (c,3) Ag 6 '84
--U.S. Open 1985 (Birmingham,
Michigan)
Sports Illus 62:cov., 20-5 (c,1)
Je 24 '85
--U.S. Open 1986 (Southhampton,
New York)
Sports Illus 64:cov., 18-23 (c,1)
Je 23 '86
--Women's U.S. Open 1982 (Sacra-
mento, California)
Sports Illus 57:14-15 (c,2) Ag
2 '82
--Women's U.S. Open 1984 (Pea-
body, Massachusetts)
Sports Illus 61:2, 20-1 (c,2) Jl
23 '84
--Women's U.S. Open 1985 (Baltus-
rol, New Jersey)
Sports Illus 63:28-9 (c,2) Jl 22
'85
--Women's U.S. Open 1986 (Ketter-
ing, Ohio)
Sports Illus 65:18-19 (c,2) Jl 21
'86
--Worst avid golfer tournament
(Florida)
Sports Illus 63:18-19 (c,4) Jl 1
'85
GOLFERS
Sports Illus 58:36-7 (painting,c,2)
Ap 25 '83
--Wearing plus fours
Sports Illus 60:6 (c,3) Ap 23 '84

GOLFERS (cont.)
--Wearing plus fours (1923)
    Sports Illus 60:117 (4) My 28
        '84
--See also
    DIDRIKSON, BABE
    HOGAN, BEN
    JONES, BOBBY
    PALMER, ARNOLD
GONDOLAS
--Late 19th cent. (Venice, Italy)
    Am Heritage 35:40-1 (paint-
        ing,c,1) Je '84
--Naples Island, Long Beach,
        California
    Trav/Holiday 165:78 (c,3) Ap
        '86
--Venice, Italy
    Smithsonian 17:59-60 (c,3) Jl
        '86
GONGS
--Burma
    Sports Illus 56:60 (c,4) F 15
        '82
GOPHERS
    Natur Hist 93:41 (c,4) Je '84
    Life 8:26 (c,4) S '85
GORILLAS
    Natur Hist 91:cov., 48-59, 84
        (c,1) Mr '82
    Life 5:48 (c,4) Je '82
    Life 5:116-17, 130 (draw-
        ing,c,1) N '82
    Natur Hist 92:68 (4) Ag '83
    Smithsonian 14:32 (c,4) Mr '84
    Nat Wildlife 23:8-11 (c,1) D
        '84
    Nat Geog 167:cov., 110-13
        (c,1) Ja '85
    Smithsonian 15:74-5 (c,1) Mr
        '85
    Nat Geog 167:826 (c,3) Je '85
    Life 8:22-8 (c,1) Jl '85
    Smithsonian 16:105 (c,4) D '85
    Life 9:65 (c,4) N '86
GOSHAWKS
    Natur Hist 91:cov. (c,1) Ap
        '82
    Smithsonian 15:80 (c,4) N '84
    Nat Wildlife 24:24 (paint-
        ing,c,3) O '86
Government. See
    ELECTIONS
    GOVERNMENT--LEGISLA-
        TURES
    POLITICAL CAMPAIGNS
    TAXATION

U.S. PRESIDENTS
    specific countries--POLITICS
        AND GOVERNMENT
    list under STATESMEN
GOVERNMENT--LEGISLATURES
--California
    Ebony 39:56-8, 148 (c,2) Ag '84
--Cayman Islands assembly
    Nat Geog 167:816 (c,3) Je '85
--Fist fight in Congress (Ecuador)
    Life 8:102-3 (1) O '85
--House Budget Committee meeting
    Ebony 40:35 (c,3) My '85
--House of Commons (Great Britain)
    Nat Geog 170:734-5 (c,1) D '86
--Iran
    Nat Geog 168:134-5 (c,1) Jl '85
--New Hampshire
    Nat Geog 162:772-3 (c,1) D '82
--Provincial legislature building
        (Edmonton, Alberta)
    Trav/Holiday 159:48 (c,1) Je '83
--Sark Island Parliament, Channel
        Islands
    Smithsonian 17:95 (c,3) My '86
GOVERNMENT BUILDINGS
--18th cent. Treasury Dept. Build-
        ing, Washington, D.C.
    Am Heritage 37:74 (drawing,c,3)
        Ag '86
--Clock in U.S. House of Repre-
        sentatives (1915)
    Am Heritage 33:2 (2) Je '82
--Early U.S. government buildings
        by George Hadfield
    Am Heritage 37:74-80 (c,3) Ag
        '86
--Old Executive Office Building,
        Washington, D.C.
    Smithsonian 16:84-95 (c,1) Mr
        '86
--Palace of Westminster, London,
        England
    Nat Geog 170:729-57 (c,1) D '86
--Peace Tower, Ottawa, Ontario
    Trav/Holiday 166:4 (c,3) Ag '86
--Senate office building rotunda,
        Washington, D.C.
    Life 5:68 (4) My '82
--U.S. Department of Interior Build-
        ing, Washington, D.C.
    Smithsonian 14:36-7 (c,4) F '84
--See also
    CAPITOL BUILDINGS
    CITY HALLS
    COURTHOUSES
    POST OFFICES

GOVERNMENT BUILDINGS (cont.)
    SUPREME COURT BUILDING
    WHITE HOUSE
GOYA, FRANCISCO
--"He-Goat" (1794)
    Smithsonian 13:113 (paint-
        ing,c,4) D '82
GRABLE, BETTY
    Am Heritage 35:42-3, 47 (1)
        D '83
    Life 8:88 (2) Spring '85
--World War II leggy pinup
    Life 8:88 (4) Spring '85
GRAFFITI
--1945 German graffiti (Munich)
    Am Heritage 34:6 (4) D '82
--New York City, New York
    Nat Geog 163:604-5 (c,1) My
        '83
--New York City subway
    Am Heritage 34:cov., 22
        (painting,c,1) F '83
    Nat Geog 163:604-5 (c,1) My
        '83
    Smithsonian 16:89 (1) My '85
--On statue of Lincoln (Newark,
    New Jersey)
    Am Heritage 35:12-13 (1) F
        '84
--Scotland
    Nat Geog 166:56-7 (c,1) Jl '84
--World War II "Kilroy was Here"
    Life 8:20 (4) Spring '85
GRAHAME, KENNETH
    Smithsonian 14:170 (4) D '83
GRAIN INDUSTRY
--Grain elevator (Kansas)
    Nat Geog 168:382-3 (c,1) S
        '85
--Grain elevator (Minnesota)
    Life 9:117 (c,3) Ja '86
--Grain elevators (Arkansas)
    Ebony 42:100-2 (c,4) D '86
--Grain elevators (Colorado)
    Nat Geog 166:206-7 (c,1) Ag
        '84
--Threshing barley (Nepal)
    Smithsonian 16:cov., 136-7,
        254 (c,1) N '85
--See also
    CORN INDUSTRY
    OAT INDUSTRY
    RICE INDUSTRY
    RYE INDUSTRY
    WHEAT INDUSTRY
GRAND CANYON, ARIZONA
    Natur Hist 91:74-82 (map,c,1)

        Ja '82
    Nat Geog 162:608-9 (c,1) N '82
    Smithsonian 13:55 (c,1) F '83
    Sports Illus 62:96-110 (c,1) Ap
        8 '85
--Early 20th cent. concessions in
    park
    Natur Hist 91:14, 20 (3) Je '82
--Caves
    Natur Hist 95:10-14 (c,3) Ap '86
--See also
    COLORADO RIVER
GRAND COULEE DAM, COLUMBIA
    RIVER, WASHINGTON
    Smithsonian 14:64 (c,3) Mr '84
GRAND TETON NATIONAL PARK,
    WYOMING
    Nat Wildlife 21:10-11 (c,2) Ap
        '83
GRANGE, "RED" HAROLD
    Sports Illus 63:114-35 (1) S 4
        '85
GRANT, ULYSSES S.
--Home (Galena, Illinois)
    Trav/Holiday 160:16 (4) S '83
--Shortly before death
    Am Heritage 35:13 (4) Ap '84
    Am Heritage 36:64 (4) D '84
--Statue (Washington, D.C.)
    Am Heritage 37:26 (c,4) Ap '86
--See also
    GRANT'S TOMB
GRANT'S TOMB, NEW YORK CITY,
    NEW YORK
--History of the monument
    Am Heritage 36:70-9 (c,1) Ag
        '85
GRAPE INDUSTRY. See also
    VINEYARDS
    WINE INDUSTRY
GRAPE INDUSTRY--HARVESTING
--Bordeaux, France
    Trav/Holiday 160:66 (c,3) S '83
--Champagne region, France
    Nat Geog 161:487 (c,3) Ap '82
--Spain
    Nat Geog 165:124-5 (c,2) Ja '84
GRAPES
    Trav/Holiday 160:50 (4) Ag '83
    Trav/Holiday 164:35 (c,4) S '85
GRASS
--Artificial turf in stadiums
    Sports Illus 63:34-62 (c,1) Ag
        12 '85
--Cheatgrass
    Natur Hist 93:42-4 (c,2) F '84
--Nepal park

GREAT BRITAIN--COSTUME
Smithsonian 14:46 (c,1) Ag
'83
--17th cent.
Am Heritage 37:25 (paint-
ing,c,1) F '86
--17th-18th cent. nobles
Smithsonian 15:74-5 (painting,c,4) Ag '84
--18th cent.
Smithsonian 13:78-9, 84
(painting,c,4) Mr '83
--Late 18th cent.
Smithsonian 16:120-1 (draw-
ing,c,1) My '85
--Late 18th cent. (Bath)
Smithsonian 15:122-3, 128-32
(drawing,c,1) N '84
--1792 children
Smithsonian 14:172 (paint-
ing,c,2) O '83
--1860 gentlemen fishermen
Sports Illus 58:80 (4) My 9
'83
--1903 gardener
Smithsonian 16:178 (4) Ap '85
--1940
Am Heritage 37:27 (2) O '86
--1940s children
Am Heritage 33:87, 89 (2) Je
'82
--Armor
Smithsonian 13:64-73 (c,1) O
'82
--Beefeaters (London)
Trav/Holiday 161:6 (c,3) Ja '84
Life 8:102 (c,2) Mr '85
Sports Illus 65:cov. (c,1) Ag
11 '86
--College of Heralds
Smithsonian 15:86 (c,4) My '84
--Court of Common Council,
London
Smithsonian 13:90 (c,3) N '82
--Duke and Duchess of Windsor
Life 9:95-9 (2) Je '86
Am Heritage 38:106 (4) D '86
--Judges
Nat Geog 170:735, 749 (c,3)
D '86
--Palace guards
Life 7:96 (c,2) Ag '84
--Prince Harry
Life 7:cov., 154-62 (c,1) D '84
Lie 8:104 (c,2) F '85
--Prince of Wales (1930s)
Am Heritage 37:46 (4) Ag '86

--Prince William
Life 5:98-9 (c,1) S '82
Life 6:97 (c,2) F '83
Life 7:155-62 (c,1) D '84
--Princess
Ebony 37:104 (c,4) Ja '82
Life 5:105-12 (c,2) My '82
Life 7:cov., 154-64 (c,1) D '84
Life 8:cov., 29, 43-50 (c,1) N
'85
Life 9:375 (c,2) Fall '86
--Queen's Guard, Buckingham Palace
Trav/Holiday 157:23, 26 (4) Je
'82
--Rear admiral
Life 6:84 (c,2) Ja '83
--Royal children
Life 9:50, 54 (c,2) S '86
--Royal children (1956)
Life 9:61 (2) Fall '86
--Royalty
Life 5:104-9 (c,1) Ap '82
Life 5:98-9 (c,1) S '82
Life 5:cov., 51-6 (c,1) D '82
Life 6:34-9 (c,1) Ag '83
Smithsonian 14:113 (c,4) N '83
Life 7:138 (painting,c,2) Ap '84
Life 7:cov., 154-64 (c,1) D '84
Life 8:cov., 29, 43-50 (c,1) N
'85
Life 9:148-9 (c,2) Ja '86
--Sark, Channel Islands
Smithsonian 17:94-104 (c,2) My
'86
--Sentry at Windsor Castle, England
Life 7:16 (2) Mr '84
--Society wedding reception (Oxford)
Nat Geog 163:768-9 (c,1) Je '83
--Traditional ceremonial costume
(London)
Smithsonian 13:89-91 (c,3) N '82
--Traditional outfits for Royal
Regatta (Henley)
Sports Illus 57:36-49 (c,1) Jl 5
'82
Nat Geog 163:750-1, 770-1 (c,1)
Je '83
GREAT BRITAIN--HISTORY
--11th cent. Domesday Book
Smithsonian 17:82-94 (c,1) Jl '86
--13th cent. Parliament
Nat Geog 170:738 (painting,c,3)
D '86
--1520 summit between Henry VIII
and François I
Smithsonian 17:60-1 (painting,c,2)
S '86

GREAT BRITAIN--HISTORY
(cont.)
--1530 petition to Pope to annul
Henry VIII marriage
Nat Geog 168:774-5 (c,1) D
'85
--1530 wax seals of British nobles
Nat Geog 168:774-5 (c,1) D
'85
--1545 French attack on Portsmouth
Nat Geog 163:648-51 (painting,c,1) My '83
--1653 Parliament
Nat Geog 170:739 (drawing,4)
D '86
--1791 artifacts from shipwreck
Nat Geog 168:431-51 (c,1) O
'85
--1791 shipwreck of boat carrying
"Bounty" mutineers
Nat Geog 168:422-51 (c,1) O
'85
--19th cent. landscapes by Constable
Smithsonian 14:52-9 (c,1) My
'83
--19th cent. London sites related
to Dickens novels
Nat Geog 163:756-7 (c,1) Je
'83
--1803 engraving of possible
French attack on England
Smithsonian 17:66-7 (1) My '86
--1840 Chinese Opium War (Dinghai)
Nat Geog 167:152-3 (painting,c,1) F '85
--1937 coronation of George VI
Life 9:88 (4) Ap '86
--1953 coronation of Elizabeth II
Life 9:90 (c,4) Ap '86
--1940 British evacuation of Dun-
kirk
Smithsonian 13:172-208 (c,1)
N '82
--1940 British sinking of French
ships (Algeria)
Smithsonian 16:122-38 (c,3) Jl
'85
--Churchill's Cabinet War Rooms
(London)
Trav/Holiday 165:86 (4) Ja '86
--Descendants of Bounty mutineers
(Pitcairn/Norfolk Isles)
Nat Geog 164:510-41 (c,1) O
'83

--History of Bath, England
Smithsonian 15:122-35 (c,1) N '84
--See also
BLIGH, WILLIAM
CHARLES II
CHURCHILL, WINSTON
DISRAELI, BENJAMIN
EDEN, SIR ANTHONY
EDWARD IV
EDWARD VI
EDWARD VII
ELIZABETH I
ELIZABETH II
GEORGE III
GEORGE VI
HENRY VII
HENRY VIII
KIPLING, RUDYARD
MARY OF TECK
MARY QUEEN OF SCOTS
MONTGOMERY, BERNARD
NELSON, HORATIO
REVOLUTIONARY WAR
RICHARD I
RICHARD III
WAR OF 1812
WATERLOO, BATTLE OF
WORLD WAR I
WORLD WAR II
GREAT BRITAIN--HOUSING
--English country houses
Smithsonian 16:44-59 (c,1) O '85
Nat Geog 168:658-94 (map,c,1)
N '85
Life 8:30-8 (c,1) N '85
GREAT BRITAIN--MAPS
--Channel Islands
Smithsonian 17:102 (c,4) My '86
--Map of English country houses
Nat Geog 168:662-3 (c,1) N '85
--Thames River sights
Nat Geog 163:760-1 (c,1) Je '83
GREAT BRITAIN--POLITICS AND
GOVERNMENT
--13th cent. Parliament
Nat Geog 170:738 (painting,c,3)
D '86
--1653 Parliament
Nat Geog 170:739 (drawing,4) D
'86
--Court of Common Council, London,
England
Smithsonian 13:90 (c,3) N '82
--House of Lords in session
Life 6:174-5 (c,1) D '83
--Palace of Westminster, London
Nat Geog 170:729-57 (c,1) D '86

GREENLAND (cont.)
  ESKIMOS
  NUUK
GREENLAND--COSTUME
--15th cent. Inuit mummies
  Nat Geog 167:cov., 190-207
    (c,1) F '85
--Eskimos
  Nat Geog 165:cov., 521-38
    (c,1) Ap '84
--Inuits
  Nat Geog 163:190-3 (c,1) F '83
GREETING CARDS
--19th cent. valentines
  Am Heritage 33:25-9 (c,2) F
    '82
--1881 advertisement for cards
  Smithsonian 13:158 (c,4) D
    '82
--History of Hallmark
  Am Heritage 34:71-9 (c,3) D
    '82
GRENADA
  Nat Geog 166:688-709 (c,1) N
    '84
  Trav/Holiday 164:54-7 (c,1) Ag
    '85
--St. George's
  Trav/Holiday 164:54-5 (c,1) Ag
    '85
GRENADA--COSTUME
  Nat Geog 166:689-709 (c,1) N
    '84
  Trav/Holiday 164:55-7 (c,3) Ag
    '85
GRENADA--POLITICS AND GOV-
    ERNMENT
--U.S. invasion (1983)
  Life 6:34-7 (c,1) D '83
GRIEF
--1971 earthquake survivor (Peru)
  Smithsonian 14:51 (c,1) Jl '83
--Mother of earthquake victims
    (Turkey)
  Life 7:20-1 (c,1) Ja '84
--Mourning dead soldiers (Israel)
  Nat Geog 163:515 (c,1) Ap '83
--Mourning princess (Monaco)
  Life 6:52 (c,2) Ja '83
--Relatives of dead soldiers (Iran)
  Nat Geog 168:120 (c,4) Jl '85
--See also
    CRYING
    SORROW
GRIFFINS
--Sculpture (Great Britain)
  Smithsonian 13:86 (c,4) N '82

GRIFFITH, DAVID WARK
  Smithsonian 16:116 (4) N '85
--Depicted on postage stamp
  Am Heritage 34:53 (c,4) D '82
GRIMM BROTHERS
  Smithsonian 17:108-11 (paint-
    ing,c,2) My '86
--Illustrations from their fairy tales
  Smithsonian 17:109-18 (c,4) My
    '86
GRIZZLY BEARS
  Nat Wildlife 20:9 (c,2) Ap '82
  Life 5:105-6 (c,2) D '82
  Nat Wildlife 21:14-15 (2) F '83
  Nat Wildlife 22:37, 52 (c,1) D '83
  Natur Hist 93:20 (c,3) Ja '84
  Sports Illus 61:62-76 (paint-
    ing,c,1) Jl 23 '84
  Life 7:cov., 38-46 (c,1) Ag '84
  Nat Wildlife 22:2 (c,2) Ag '84
  Nat Geog 168:642 (c,4) N '85
  Nat Geog 169:182-213 (c,1) F '86
  Nat Wildlife 24:38-9 (c,1) Ap '86
  Sports Illus 65:92 (c,3) O 20 '86
  Life 9:400 (2) Fall '86
--Cub
  Nat Wildlife 24:2 (c,2) Je '86
GROS MORNE NATIONAL PARK,
    NEWFOUNDLAND
  Trav/Holiday 162:43 (c,3) S '84
GROSBEAKS
  Nat Wildlife 22:cov., 23 (c,1) D
    '83
  Nat Wildlife 23:34 (painting,c,1)
    D '84
  Nat Wildlife 24:17 (painting,c,4)
    D '85
GROSZ, GEORGE
  Smithsonian 14:169 (4) D '83
GROUND WATER
--Effects of ground water depletion
  Nat Wildlife 24:50-5 (c,1) D '85
--Study of ground water
  Smithsonian 13:50-9 (c,1) Mr '83
Groundhogs. See
    WOODCHUCKS
GROUPERS (FISH)
  Nat Wildlife 21:66-7 (c,1) D '82
  Smithsonian 13:133 (c,4) Mr '83
  Nat Wildlife 22:24 (c,4) Je '84
GROUSE
  Nat Wildlife 21:26-7 (c,1) D '82
  Nat Geog 168:643 (c,4) N '85
  Nat Wildlife 24:40 (c,4) Ag '86
--Ruffed grouse
  Nat Wildlife 23:38-41 (c,1) Ap
    '85

GROUSE (cont.)
--See also
    PRAIRIE CHICKENS
    PTARMIGANS
GRUNIONS (FISH)
    Nat Wildlife 21:33-6 (c,1) Je
    '83
GRUNTS (FISH)
    Nat Wildlife 24:14 (c,4) F '86
    Natur Hist 95:88-9 (c,1) Jl '86
GUADALCANAL, SOLOMON IS-
    LANDS
--1942 battle for Guadalcanal
    Am Heritage 36:49-55 (map,c,1)
    O '85
GUADELOUPE
    Trav/Holiday 165:80-3 (c,1) Ap
    '86
GUADELOUPE--COSTUME
    Trav/Holiday 165:80-3 (c,1) Ap
    '86
GUADELOUPE--RITES AND
    FESTIVALS
--Fête de Cuisinières
    Trav/Holiday 165:80 (c,1) Ap
    '86
GUAM, MARIANA ISLANDS
--World War II battle sites
    Life 8:100-1 (c,1) Spring '85
GUANACOS
    Smithsonian 16:77 (c,4) O '85
GUANAJUATO, MEXICO
    Trav/Holiday 159:10-11 (4) Ap
    '83
GUARDS
--Beefeaters (London, England)
    Trav/Holiday 161:6 (c,3) Ja
    '84
    Life 8:102 (c,2) Mr '85
    Life 8:71 (2) D '85
    Sports Illus 65:cov. (c,1) Ag
    11 '86
--Changing of the Guard (Lima,
    Peru)
    Trav/Holiday 157:44-5 (c,1)
    Ja '82
--Guardian Angels (Virginia)
    Sports Illus 63:76 (c,3) S 4
    '85
--Palace guards (Great Britain)
    Life 7:96 (c,2) Ag '84
--Park guards watching for
    poachers (Kenya)
    Nat Geog 165:414-15 (c,1) Mr
    '84
--President's Palace, Lisbon,
    Portugal

Trav/Holiday 160:cov. (c,1) Ag
    '83
--Queen's Guard, Buckingham
    Palace, England
    Trav/Holiday 157:23, 26 (4) Je
    '82
--Sentry at Windsor Castle, England
    Life 7:16 (2) Mr '84
--Swiss guard (Vatican)
    Trav/Holiday 164:49 (c,4) O '85
    Nat Geog 168:738-41 (c,1) D '85
--Texas prisons
    Life 5:36-44 (1) O '82
--U.S. Customs officials
    Life 7:48 (c,2) S '84
--U.S. Marine guarding sentry post
    (Lebanon)
    Life 6:38 (2) D '83
GUATEMALA
--Ancient Mayan tombs (Rio Azul
    region)
    Nat Geog 166:137-137B (c,3) Ag
    '84
    Nat Geog 169:420-61 (map,c,1)
    Ap '86
--Lake Atitlán
    Natur Hist 92:68, 70 (c,3) F '83
--Mayan ruins (Tikal)
    Natur Hist 94:44-5 (c,3) Ap '85
    Smithsonian 17:39 (c,3) My '86
--Mexican border area
    Nat Geog 168:514-42 (map,c,1)
    O '85
--Usumacinta River
    Nat Geog 168:514-42 (map,c,1)
    O '85
GUATEMALA--COSTUME
    Natur Hist 91:cov., 62-9 (1) N
    '82
    Nat Geog 168:515-39 (c,1) O '85
--Indian worker
    Natur Hist 92:68 (c,3) F '83
Guatemala--History. See
    MAYAN CIVILIZATION
GUATEMALA--POLITICS AND GOV-
    ERNMENT
--Fighting guerrillas
    Nat Geog 168:522-3, 533-5 (c,1)
    O '85
GUITAR PLAYING
    Life 5:90 (2) Je '82
    Nat Geog 162:549 (c,3) O '82
    Ebony 38:85 (c,4) N '82
    Ebony 38:78 (c,4) Ap '83
    Ebony 38:80 (4) Je '83
    Ebony 38:128-30 (c,4) Jl '83
    Ebony 38:157-8 (2) O '83

GUNS (cont.)
   Nat Geog 165:818 (2) Je '84
--Copy of Soviet automatic rifle
   (China)
   Nat Geog 161:262 (c,1) F '82
--Gatling gun
   Sports Illus 65:66 (c,4) S 8 '86
--Gun store (Pakistan)
   Nat Geog 167:794 (c,1) Je '85
--Handguns
   Life 5:cov., 30-6 (c,1) Ap '82
--Machine guns
   Life 9:30-1 (c,1) Mr '86
--Machine guns (Northern Ire-
   land)
   Life 8:46 (c,3) O '85
--Making sawed-off shotgun
   (California)
   Life 5:57 (c,3) My '82
--Punt gun for hunting
   Nat Geog 164:646 (c,4) N '83
--Revolver
   Nat Geog 162:197 (c,3) Ag '82
--Sacco's automatic pistol (1921)
   Am Heritage 37:108 (4) Je '86
--Shooting paint-filled pellets
   Life 6:68-72 (c,1) My '83
--World War II Japanese gun
   emplacement (Palau)
   Smithsonian 17:55 (c,1) S '86
--World War II mortars
   Nat Geog 170:126 (4) Jl '86
--See also
      ARMS
      BLOWGUNS
      RIFLES
      SHOOTING
GYMNASIUMS
--Dedication (Paraguay)
   Nat Geog 162:256-7 (c,1) Ag
   '82
--Panama
   Sports Illus 59:84 (c,4) N 7
   '83
GYMNASTICS
   Ebony 38:42-4 (1) Ja '83
   Ebony 38:52-6 (c,1) S '83
   Sports Illus 59:62, 65 (c,4)
   N 7 '83
   Sports Illus 59:68-9 (c,1) D
   26 '83
   Sports Illus 60:138-9 (c,1) F
   8 '84
   Sports Illus 61:462-71 (c,1) Jl
   18 '84
   Sports Illus 63:90-2 (c,4) N
   18 '85

   Sports Illus 65:67 (c,4) Jl 28
   '86
   Sports Illus 65:cov., 52-4 (c,1)
   S 1 '86
--1980 Olympics (Moscow)
   Life 7:110-11 (c,1) Summer '84
--1984 Olympics (Los Angeles)
   Sports Illus 61:cov., 42-59
   (c,1) Ag 13 '84
   Sports Illus 61:33, 38 (c,2) D
   24 '84
   Life 8:118-19 (c,1) Ja '85
--Back walkover
   Sports Illus 58:4 (4) F 14 '83
--Balance beam
   Sports Illus 58:70 (c,4) Je 13
   '83
   Ebony 38:52-6 (c,1) S '83
   Trav/Holiday 160:65 (c,4) N '83
--Children doing chin-ups
   Sports Illus 58:60-1 (c,1) F 7
   '83
--China
   Life 6:56-7 (c,1) D '83
--Hanging upside down
   Sports Illus 63:63 (c,2) Jl 1 '85
--Headstand
   Life 5:106 (c,4) Jl '82
--High bar (East Germany)
   Nat Geog 161:22 (c,1) Ja '82
--Olympic athletes in slow motion
   Life 7:18-21 (c,1) Summer '84
--On basketball court
   Sports Illus 63:2-3 (c,2) D 9 '85
--Paraguay
   Nat Geog 162:256-7 (c,1) Ag '82
--Rhythmic gymnastics
   Life 7:34-5 (c,1) Summer '84
   Sports Illus 61:220-39 (c,1) Jl
   18 '84
GYPSIES
--Carnival bear act (Turkey)
   Nat Geog 164:734-5 (c,1) D '83
GYPSUM
   Nat Geog 162:713 (c,4) D '82
GYPSY MOTHS
   Smithsonian 15:46-54 (c,1) My
   '84

-H-

HAARLEM, NETHERLANDS
--1670 painting
   Smithsonian 13:50 (c,2) Je '82
HADRIAN
--Bronze sculpture of him

HADRIAN (cont.)
  Nat Geog 168:22 (c,4) Jl '85
--Depicted on Roman coin
  Smithsonian 16:72 (c,4) Ap '85
--Hadrian's Wall, Northumbria,
    England
  Smithsonian 16:70-81 (c,1) Ap
    '85
  Nat Geog 169:414-15 (c,2) Mr
    '86
THE HAGUE, NETHERLANDS
--Mauritshuis
  Smithsonian 13:46 (c,4) Je '82
--Scheveningen
  Smithsonian 16:84-5 (paint-
    ing,c,1) Ag '85
HAIDA INDIANS (NORTHWEST)--
    ART
--Basket weaving
  Natur Hist 91:40-7 (c,1) My
    '82
HAIR
--Hair transplants
  Ebony 37:44-8 (3) Je '82
HAIR DRYERS
--East Germany
  Nat Geog 161:28-9 (c,1) Ja '82
HAIRDRESSING--MEN
--19th cent. barbershop (Japan)
  Smithsonian 14:170 (c,4) N
    '83
--Barber cutting hair (Arkansas)
  Life 8:90-1 (1) D '85
--Barbershop (Colorado)
  Lie 8:112 (c,2) Mr '85
--Barbershop (Kentucky)
  Nat Geog 163:814 (c,2) Je '83
--Braiding man's long hair (Texas)
  Life 6:80-1 (c,1) Ag '83
--Cutting boxer's hair
  Sports Illus 59:78-9 (c,1) N 7
    '83
--Cutting man's hair
  Sports Illus 60:81 (c,4) Ja 16
    '84
--Cutting man's hair aboard ship
  Sports Illus 61:100 (c,4) O 1
    '84
--Father cutting son's hair
  Ebony 38:68 (4) D '82
--Trimming hair in street (Greece)
  Nat Geog 164:772-3 (c,1) D '83
--See also
      BARBERSHOPS
      HAIRSTYLES--MEN
HAIRDRESSING--WOMEN
--1907 painting

  Am Heritage 34:9 (c,2) F '83
--Hair in curlers
  Life 9:67 (c,2) Je '86
--See also
      BEAUTY PARLORS
HAIRSTYLES--CHILDREN
--Redheaded children
  Life 5:8-12 (c,1) Jl '82
HAIRSTYLES--MEN
--1984 trendy styles
  Life 8:110 (c,4) Ja '85
--1985 teenage styles
  Life 9:292 (c,4) Fall '86
--Long hair and head band
  Life 6:cov. (c,1) Ag '83
--Mohawk cut
  Sports Illus 65:22 (c,4) S 3 '86
  Sports Illus 65:29 (c,4) S 15 '86
--Punk styles (Great Britain)
  Sports Illus 65:184-5 (c,2) S 3
    '86
--See also
      BALDNESS
HAIRSTYLES--WOMEN
  Ebony 39:110-12 (c,2) Ja '84
--1610s Flemish hair roll
  Nat Geog 161:74 (engraving,4)
    Ja '82
--1947 high school girls
  Life 9:292 (1) Fall '86
--1984 trendy styles
  Life 8:110 (c,4) Ja '85
--Afros
  Ebony 37:79-84 (4) Je '82
--Braids (Golok woman; Tibet)
  Natur Hist 91:53 (c,3) S '82
--Himbas (Namibia)
  Nat Geog 161:774 (c,1) Je '82
--Punk styles (Great Britain)
  Sports Illus 65:184-5 (c,2) S 3
    '86
--Unmarried Hopi Indian (Arizona)
  Nat Geog 162:629 (c,4) N '82
HAITI
  Trav/Holiday 165:cov., 49-53
    (map,c,1) F '86
--The Citadelle
  Trav/Holiday 157:44 (4) Ap '82
  Trav/Holiday 165:51 (c,4) F '86
--Waterfalls
  Nat Geog 167:396-9 (c,1) Mr '85
--See also
      PORT-AU-PRINCE
HAITI--COSTUME
  Nat Geog 167:394-407 (c,1) Mr
    '85
  Trav/Holiday 165:cov., 49, 51

HAITI--COSTUME (cont.)
  (c,1) F '86
--Woman with basket on head
  Trav/Holiday 165:cov., 49
  (c,1) F '86
HAITI--RITES AND FESTIVALS
--Voodoo
  Nat Geog 167:394-408 (c,1)
  Mr '85
HALEAKALA NATIONAL PARK,
  MAUI, HAWAII
  Natur Hist 91:cov., 38-9
  (c,1) D '82
  Trav/Holiday 162:38 (c,1) O
  '84
HALIBUT
  Trav/Holiday 165:68 (c,4) Mr '86
--Caught by fisherman
  Life 7:182 (4) N '84
HALLEY, EDMUND
  Natur Hist 94:6 (painting,4)
  Ag '85
  Life 8:32 (painting,c,4) O '85
HALLEY'S COMET
  Trav/Holiday 165:cov., 6 (c,1)
  Ja '86
  Nat Geog 170:758-84 (c,1) D
  '86
--164 B.C. Babylonian cuneiform
  tablet mention
  Life 8:33 (c,1) O '85
  Natur Hist 94:16 (3) D '85
--1909
  Natur Hist 94:118-19 (4) Ap
  '85
--1910 souvenirs
  Am Heritage 36:6 (c,2) O '85
  Life 8:34-5 (c,2) O '85
--Path of Halley's Comet
  Natur Hist 94:32 (c,3) F '85
  Natur Hist 94:88 (c,3) Mr '85
  Natur Hist 94:126 (c,3) Ap '85
  Natur Hist 94:84 (c,3) My '85
  Natur Hist 94:80 (c,3) Je '85
  Natur Hist 94:76 (c,3) Jl '85
  Natur Hist 94:22 (c,3) Ag '85
  Natur Hist 94:96 (c,3) S '85
  Natur Hist 94:104-6 (c,3) O
  '85
  Natur Hist 94:100 (c,4) N '85
  Natur Hist 94:74-5 (4) D '85
  Natur Hist 95:85 (4) Ja '86
  Natur Hist 95:88, 80 (4) Mr
  '86
--References to it throughout
  history
  Life 8:30-6 (c,1) O '85

Smithsonian 16:162-3 (c,3) N '85
--Vega image of comet (U.S.S.R.)
  Smithsonian 17:128, 140 (c,1) Jl
  '86
HALLOWEEN
--Children in Halloween costumes
  (1960)
  Life 9:238-9 (c,1) Fall '86
--Costumes
  Natur Hist 92:cov., 42-51 (c,1)
  O '83
--Frankenstein and bride costumes
  Sports Illus 60:46-7 (c,1) My 28
  '84
HALS, FRANS
--"Head of a Young Boy" (1620s)
  Smithsonian 13:51 (painting,c,4)
  Je '82
HAMBURG, WEST GERMANY
--Buildings at docks
  Trav/Holiday 163:40 (c,3) Mr
  '85
HAMILTON, ALEXANDER
  Am Heritage 34:109 (4) F '83
HAMILTON, BERMUDA
  Trav/Holiday 157:46 (c,4) Je '82
HAMMOCKS
  Nat Wildlife 22:19 (c,4) Ag '84
--For baby (Quebec)
  Nat Geog 161:416-17 (c,1) Mr
  '82
--Panama
  Nat Geog 169:489-91 (c,1) Ap
  '86
--Nancy Reagan in hammock
  Life 6:22 (4) D '83
--Thailand
  Nat Geog 162:502-3 (c,1) O '82
--Venezuela
  Nat Geog 168:334-5 (c,1) S '85
HAMPTON, LIONEL
  Ebony 41:134 (4) N '85
HAMPTON ROADS, VIRGINIA
  Trav/Holiday 157:39-40, 66
  (c,1) Je '82
  Nat Geog 168:72-107 (map,c,1)
  Jl '85
HAND SHAKING
--15th cent. drawing
  Smithsonian 14:50 (4) Mr '84
--Football players before game
  Sports Illus 57:128-9 (c,2) S 1
  '82
--"High five"
  Sports Illus 57:27 (c,4) Jl 5 '82
  Sports Illus 57:58 (c,4) D 6 '82
  Sports Illus 62:27 (c,4) My 27

HAND SHAKING (cont.)
    '85
    Sports Illus 63:15 (c,4) Ag 5
    '85
    Ebony 40:50 (painting,c,3) Ag
    '85
    Sports Illus 64:56 (c,4) Ap 14
    '86
    Sports Illus 65:22-3 (c,4) Ag
    18 '86
    Sports Illus 65:cov. (c,1) O
    20 '86
HANDBALL PLAYING
    Sports Illus 57:52 (c,4) Jl 26
    '82
HANDICAPPED PEOPLE
--Aided by labrador retriever
    Life 9:50-5 (c,1) N '86
--Ancient Anasazi Indian crutches
    (New Mexico)
    Nat Geog 162:559 (c,2) N '82
--Armless boy (Namibia)
    Nat Geog 161:780 (c,4) Je '82
--Artificial arms
    Life 6:30 (c,2) F '83
--Boxer with amputated foot
    Sports Illus 64:50-2 (c,2) F 3
    '86
--Boy with no legs (Pennsylvania)
    Life 7:70-3 (1) F '84
--Child on crutches
    Ebony 39:115 (2) My '84
--Children with cancer at camp
    (California)
    Life 7:32-40 (c,1) S '84
--Deafness
    Life 5:74-86 (1) S '82
--Disabled children using com-
    puters
    Smithsonian 14:42-7 (3) F '84
--Elderly woman walking with
    cane
    Ebony 38:39 (2) Mr '83
--Electronic arms
    Nat Geog 162:422-3 (c,1) O '82
--One-armed man
    Ebony 38:96-8 (2) Je '83
--One-legged man
    Sports Illus 60:94 (c,4) My 14
    '84
--One-legged marathon runner
    Life 5:23 (4) Mr '82
--People in wheelchairs
    Ebony 37:100 (4) Ag '82
    Life 6:122 (c,4) Jl '83
    Life 7:47-51 (c,2) Je '84
--People with missing limbs

    (Afghanistan)
    Nat Geog 167:784-5, 790-1 (c,1)
    Je '85
--Quadriplegiac
    Sports Illus 59:28-9 (painting,c,1)
    S 5 '83
    Ebony 38:68-74 (4) O '83
    Ebony 39:75-80 (c,1) S '84
--Quadriplegiacs aided by trained
    capuchin monkeys
    Smithsonian 17:125-33 (c,1) O '86
--Retarded athletes
    Life 6:121-4 (c,1) Jl '83
--Teaching deaf to blow bubbles
    (New Mexico)
    Nat Geog 161:337 (c,2) Mr '82
--See also
    BLINDNESS
    HEARING AIDS
    INJURED PEOPLE
    KELLER, HELEN
    MEDICAL INSTRUMENTS
    THERAPY
    WHEELCHAIRS
HANDS
    Ebony 37:26-7 (1) Ja '82
--Farmer (U.S.S.R.)
    Nat Geog 169:781 (c,1) Je '86
--Nails notched for combing silk
    (Japan)
    Nat Geog 165:45 (c,4) Ja '84
--Six week old embryo
    Life 6:cov. (c,2) Ap '83
--Woman with dyed hands (North
    Yemen)
    Nat Geog 168:cov. (c,2) O '85
--Wrinkled hands of old person
    Ebony 39:30 (4) F '84
HANDY, W.C.
    Ebony 41:280 (2) N '85
HANG GLIDING
--California
    Nat Geog 167:64-5 (c,1) Ja '85
    Life 9:21 (c,3) D '86
--Colorado
    Nat Geog 166:191 (c,1) Ag '84
--Florida
    Smithsonian 13:63 (c,4) Je '82
--Hawaii
    Sports Illus 64:22 (c,4) My 19
    '86
--North Carolina
    Sports Illus 65:2-3 (c,1) O 6 '86
--Squirrel hang gliding
    Life 6:100 (c,2) Mr '83
Hanging. See
    CAPITAL PUNISHMENT
    LYNCHINGS

HANOI, VIETNAM
--Community pond
    Life 9:44 (c,2) Jl '86
HARARE, ZIMBABWE
--Cecil Square
    Trav/Holiday 165:64-5 (c,1)
        Mr '86
HARBORS
--Avalon, California
    Trav/Holiday 157:68 (c,1) Mr
        '82
--Bahamas
    Nat Geog 162:380-1 (c,1) S
        '82
--Baltimore, Maryland
    Trav/Holiday 163:67 (c,1) Je
        '85
--Camden, New Jersey (1941)
    Am Heritage 36:114-15 (1) D
        '84
--Dry dock (Great Britain)
    Am Heritage 35:36-7 (c,1) Ap
        '84
--Dutch Harbor, Unalaska Island,
        Alaska
    Nat Geog 164:350-1 (c,1) S
        '83
--Eritrea, Ethiopia
    Nat Geog 168:391 (c,3) S '85
--Hobart, Tasmania
    Trav/Holiday 163:4 (c,3) Ja
        '85
--Ischia, Italy
    Trav/Holiday 161:49 (c,4) Ja
        '84
--Juneau, Alaska
    Trav/Holiday 157:48 (c,4) My
        '82
--Le Havre, France
    Nat Geog 161:508-9, 511 (c,1)
        Ap '82
--Monaco
    Trav/Holiday 161:46-7 (c,2) Je
        '84
--Montrose, Chicago, Illinois
    Trav/Holiday 158:55 (c,3) Ag
        '82
--New York Harbor scenes
    Sports Illus 64:28-51 (map,c,1)
        Je 30 '86
    Nat Geog 170:19-43 (map,c,1)
        Jl '86
    Smithsonian 17:68-79 (c,1) Jl
        '86
--Norfolk, Virginia
    Nat Geog 168:82-3 (c,1) Jl '85
--Pago Pago, American Samoa

    Nat Geog 168:458-9 (c,1) O '85
--Portland, Maine
    Nat Geog 167:224-5 (c,1) F '85
--Roche, San Juan Island, Washing-
        ton
    Trav/Holiday 166:59 (c,2) S '86
--St. George's, Grenada, Windward
        Islands
    Trav/Holiday 164:54-5 (c,1) Ag
        '85
--St. Tropez, France
    Trav/Holiday 158:36 (c,4) Jl '82
--See also
    MARINAS
    PIERS
HARDING, WARREN GAMALIEL
--Depicted on postage stamp
    Am Heritage 34:54 (c,4) D '82
Hardware. See
    LADDERS
    LOCKS
    NAILS
    TOOLS
Hares. See
    RABBITS
Hari, Mata. See
    MATA HARI
Harlem, New York. See
    NEW YORK CITY
HARLOW, JEAN
    Smithsonian 13:105 (4) F '83
HARP PLAYING
--1903 painting
    Smithsonian 12:105 (c,4) Ja '82
--Austria
    Trav/Holiday 157:80 (c,4) Ap
        '82
HARPERS FERRY, WEST VIRGINIA
    Trav/Holiday 160:54-5 (c,1) O
        '83
    Nat Geog 166:32-3 (c,1) Jl '84
HARPOONS
--16th cent. (Newfoundland)
    Nat Geog 168:54 (c,4) Jl '85
--19th cent. Eskimos (Alaska)
    Nat Geog 163:202, 204 (c,3) F
        '83
HARPS
    Life 9:194 (c,2) My '86
HARPSICHORDS
    Smithsonian 14:53 (c,2) Je '83
HARRIMAN, EDWARD HENRY
    Am Heritage 33:75, 82 (2) Je
        '82
HARRIMAN, W. AVERELL
--As a youth
    Am Heritage 33:75, 82 (2) Je '82

HARTFORD, CONNECTICUT
    Ebony 38:31-4 (c,3) D '82
--Knights of Columbus building
    Smithsonian 13:97 (c,1) Ag
        '82
HARVARD UNIVERSITY, CAM-
        BRIDGE, MASSACHUSETTS
    Am Heritage 37:98-9 (c,1) Ag
        '86
    Life 9:24-35 (c,1) S '86
--19th-20th cent. scenes
    Smithsonian 17:140-60 (3) S
        '86
--Harvard Lampoon castle
    Life 5:133 (c,2) N '82
--See also
        LOWELL, ABBOTT LAW-
            RENCE
HARVESTERS
    Ebony 40:151 (4) Je '85
    Nat Wildlife 24:54-5 (c,1) D '85
Harvesting. See
        specific crops--HARVESTING
HATS
--17th cent. (New England)
    Smithsonian 13:106-7 (c,3) Je
        '82
--19th cent. leather Asante hats
        (Ghana)
    Natur Hist 93:68 (c,3) O '84
--1820 ad for men's beaver hats
    Smithsonian 15:168 (4) N '84
--1899 woman's hat
    Am Heritage 34:94 (1) Ag '83
--1925 woman's hat
    Am Heritage 34:65 (2) Ag '83
--Basketry hats by Haida Indians
        (Northwest)
    Natur Hist 91:40-7 (c,1) My
        '82
--Cowboy hats (Texas)
    Nat Geog 165:218 (c,4) F '84
--Sherlock Holmes deerstalker
        hats
    Smithsonian 17:61, 66 (c,4) D
        '86
--Men's hats
    Nat Geog 166:288 (c,4) S '84
--Mexican sombrero
    Sports Illus 60:29 (c,4) Ja
        16 '84
    Smithsonian 16:cov., 115, 120
        (c,1) D '85
--Outback hat (Australia)
    Nat Geog 169:30 (c,3) Ja '86
--Pressman's paper hats
    Am Heritage 34:111 (drawing,4)

    Ag '83
--Sailing cap
    Sports Illus 59:40 (c,4) Ag 29
        '83
--Straw
    Sports Illus 60:72 (c,4) Mr 12
        '84
--Straw (China)
    Nat Geog 164:81 (c,2) Jl '83
--Thailand
    Trav/Holiday 163:cov., 58 (c,1)
        Ap '85
--Top hats
    Am Heritage 33:7 (4) F '82
    Nat Geog 163:331 (c,4) Mr '83
--Harry S Truman's hat
    Am Heritage 35:84 (c,4) Ap '84
--U.S. general's hat
    Trav/Holiday 157:66 (4) Je '82
    Am Heritage 35:85 (c,4) Ap '84
--Various hats and helmets
    Sports Illus 59:92-3 (c,4) O 17
        '83
--Women's hats
    Ebony 37:92-6 (c,2) Je '82
    Ebony 39:108-14 (c,2) Ap '84
--See also
        HEADGEAR
        HELMETS
HAWAII
    Natur Hist 91:entire issue
        (map,c,1) D '82
    Nat Geog 164:562-95 (map,c,1)
        N '83
    Life 7:10-16 (c,1) Ag '84
--18th cent. history
    Nat Geog 164:558-85 (paint-
        ing,c,1) N '83
--19th cent. royalty
    Nat Geog 164:587 (4) N '83
--Ala Wai Canal, Oahu
    Trav/Holiday 160:8 (c,4) S '83
--Countryside
    Trav/Holiday 157:59-60 (c,2) Ja
        '82
    Trav/Holiday 163:27, 80-3 (c,1)
        Mr '85
--Hana Coast, Maui
    Trav/Holiday 160:40-5 (c,1) N
        '83
--Historical relics
    Smithsonian 12:164 (c,4) Mr '82
--Hula dancing
    Sports Illus 62:28 (c,2) Ja 7 '85
--Iolani Palace interior
    Nat Geog 164:586-7 (c,1) N '83
--Japanese influences

HAWAII (cont.)
    Trav/Holiday 164:60-3 (c,1)
        N '85
--King Kamehameha
    Smithsonian 12:164 (paint-
        ing,c,4) Mr '82
    Nat Geog 164:558, 572, 581
        (painting,c,1) N '83
--Lahaina, Maui
    Trav/Holiday 166:6 (c,4) N '86
--Maui
    Nat Wildlife 22:56-7 (c,1) Ap
        '84
--Molokai
    Trav/Holiday 163:44 (c,3) Ap
        '85
--National parks
    Trav/Holiday 162:34-8 (map,c,1)
        O '84
--Northwestern islands wildlife
    Nat Wildlife 21:4-12 (map,c,1)
        F '83
--Postage stamp commemorating
        statehood
    Am Heritage 34:56 (c,4) D '82
    Nat Geog 164:554 (c,4) N '83
--Pu'uhonua O Honaunau
    Trav/Holiday 165:14 (c,4) Mr
        '86
--Sunset off Kona coast
    Trav/Holiday 159:58 (c,1) F
        '83
--Waikiki
    Nat Geog 164:564-5 (c,1) N '83
--Waikiki Beach
    Nat Wildlife 21:8 (c,3) Ap '83
    Trav/Holiday 166:58-61 (c,1)
        Ag '86
--Waimea, Kauai (1778)
    Natur Hist 91:34-5 (engrav-
        ing,3) D '82
--See also
    DIAMOND HEAD
    HALEAKALA NATIONAL
        PARK
    HAWAII VOLCANOES NA-
        TIONAL PARK
    HILO
    KALAUPAPA NATIONAL PARK
    KILAUEA VOLCANO
    PEARL HARBOR
HAWAII VOLCANOES NATIONAL
    PARK, HAWAII
    Trav/Holiday 157:60 (c,2) Ja
        '82
    Trav/Holiday 162:37 (c,1) O '84
    Trav/Holiday 166:62 (c,4) Jl '86

--Pu'u O'o eruption
    Natur Hist 95:81 (c,4) D '86
HAWKS
    Nat Geog 164:108-9 (c,1) Jl '83
    Trav/Holiday 166:54 (c,4) N '86
--In flight
    Smithsonian 13:188 (c,2) O '82
    Nat Wildlife 21:24 (c,4) Je '83
--Red-tailed
    Smithsonian 15:80 (c,4) N '84
--See also
    CARACARAS
    FALCONS
    GOSHAWKS
    OSPREYS
    VULTURES
HAWTHORNE, NATHANIEL
    Smithsonian 13:132 (4) Jl '82
    Smithsonian 14:102 (painting,c,3)
        Ag '83
HAY INDUSTRY--HARVESTING
--Minnesota
    Smithsonian 17:68-79 (c,1) S '86
HAYES, HELEN
    Life 9:52-3 (c,1) Fall '86
HEADGEAR
--1955 Davy Crockett coonskin cap
    Life 9:66 (2) Ag '86
--Arabian
    Life 5:10-21 (c,1) D '82
--Bathing caps
    Sports Illus 56:34 (c,4) Mr 29
        '82
    Sports Illus 61:95 (c,1) Jl 18 '84
--Buckingham Palace guards, Eng-
        land
    Trav/Holiday 157:23, 26 (4) Je
        '82
--Clay and ostrich feather head-
        dress (Ethiopia)
    Nat Geog 163:623 (c,4) My '83
--Decorative head adornments (Afri-
        ca)
    Nat Geog 166:600-33 (c,1) N '84
--Dunce caps (Texas)
    Sports Illus 63:17 (c,4) N 4 '85
--Fez (Morocco)
    Nat Geog 169:330-1 (c,1) Mr '86
--Makah Indian headdress (Washing-
        ton)
    Nat Geog 165:663 (c,4) My '84
--Miners' hats (West Virginia)
    Smithsonian 17:165 (c,4) O '86
--Nigerian president
    Ebony 37:67 (4) F '82
--Niska headdress (British Columbia)
    Smithsonian 14:152 (c,4) F '84

HEADGEAR (cont.)
--Papal tiara
   Smithsonian 13:130 (c,4) Je
      '82
--Rarámuri Indian headdress
      (Mexico)
   Natur Hist 92:67 (c,1) Mr '83
--Turbans (India)
   Trav/Holiday 165:61 (c,4) Je
      '86
--Yarmulkes (Israel)
   Nat Geog 168:9 (c,3) Jl '85
--Yorba tribe headdress (Nigeria)
   Trav/Holiday 157:44 (4) F '82
--See also
      CROWNS
      HATS
      HELMETS
      MASKS, CEREMONIAL
      WIGS
HEADPHONES
   Life 5:77 (4) S '82
   Smithsonian 14:45 (4) F '84
--Listening to music
   Sports Illus 62:82-3 My 13 '85
--Sports announcer
   Sports Illus 58:73 (c,4) Je 13
      '83
HEALTH CLUBS
   Sports Illus 61:72-86 (c,1) D
      3 '84
--Illinois
   Ebony 41:148 (3) Mr '86
HEARING AIDS
--Ear implant
   Nat Geog 162:423 (c,4) O '82
HEARST, WILLIAM RANDOLPH
   Smithsonian 16:65 (4) D '85
--Hearst castle, San Simeon,
      California
   Nat Geog 165:450-3 (c,1) Ap
      '84
   Smithsonian 16:60-71 (c,1) D
      '85
HEARTS
--1829 drawing (France)
   Am Heritage 34:101 (c,4) Ag
      '83
--Artificial hearts
   Life 6:28-9 (c,1) F '83
   Am Heritage 34:104 (c,4) Ag
      '83
--Electronic depictions
   Am Heritage 34:102-3 (c,4) Ag
      '83
--Marfan syndrome
   Sports Illus 64:31 (drawing,c,4)

   F 17 '86
HEATERS
--Portable heaters
   Sports Illus 59:204 (c,4) S 1 '83
HEATHER
   Smithsonian 13:48 (c,4) Ag '82
HEATING
--Solar reflector boiling water
      (China)
   Nat Geog 165:302 (c,1) Mr '84
HEBRIDES, SCOTLAND
--Blanket bogs
   Natur Hist 91:54-5 (c,1) N '82
HEDGEHOGS
--Museum specimens
   Life 6:92 (c,4) D '83
HELD, JOHN, JR.
   Smithsonian 17:94, 100 (4) S '86
--Illustration from dog story
   Smithsonian 17:18 (c,4) N '86
--Works by him
   Smithsonian 17:cov., 95-105
      (painting,c,1) S '86
HELENA, MONTANA
   Trav/Holiday 164:16 (c,4) Ag '85
HELICOPTERS
   Smithsonian 13:44 (c,4) Jl '82
   Life 7:147 (c,2) My '84
   Trav/Holiday 163:46-7 (c,1) Ja
      '85
   Sports Illus 62:72 (painting,c,2)
      Mr 18 '85
   Sports Illus 62:40-1 (c,1) My 27
      '85
   Ebony 40:138 (c,4) Je '85
--1965 U.S. military helicopter
   Am Heritage 35:50-1 (1) F '84
--Airlifting goats out of park
      (Washington)
   Smithsonian 15:105 (c,3) Ag '84
--Airlifting Vietnam War wounded
   Am Heritage 35:76-7 (c,1) O '84
--Australia
   Smithsonian 16:126 (c,4) Ag '85
--Dusting crops (Hungary)
   Nat Geog 163:250-1 (c,1) F '83
--Mexico
   Nat Geog 167:178-9 (c,1) F '85
--New Zealand
   Nat Geog 170:552-3 (c,1) O '86
--Rescuing man from water (Oregon)
   Life 8:92-3 (1) Ap '85
--Rescuing plane crash survivors
      (Japan)
   Life 8:82-3 (1) O '85
--U.S. Army
   Life 5:68-9 (c,1) Mr '82

HELICOPTERS (cont.)
--U.S. Presidential helicopter
  Am Heritage 35:35 (c,3) Je '84
--Venezuela
  Smithsonian 16:62 (c,3) My '85
HELLMAN, LILLIAN
  Life 8:143 (4) Ja '85
HELMETS
--20th cent. U.S. Army helmets
  Am Heritage 35:86-8 (4) Ag
    '84
--1930s flying helmets
  Smithsonian 17:144 (1) N '86
--1952 football helmet
  Life 9:297 (c,1) Fall '86
--Argentine military helmet
  Life 5:33 (c,4) S '82
--Auto racing helmet
  Sports Illus 61:35 (c,4) N 5
    '84
--Early football headgear
  Sports Illus 63:97 (c,2) D 23
    '85
--Football
  Sports Illus 58:40-1 (c,1) Mr
    7 '83
  Sports Illus 59:2, 52 (c,4) N
    14 '83
  Sports Illus 60:36 (c,2) F 27
    '84
  Sports Illus 61:cov. (c,1) Jl
    30 '84
  Sports Illus 65:cov. (c,1) Ag
    18 '86
--Football helmet on lion sculpture
    (Chicago, Illinois)
  Sports Illus 63:2-3 (c,1) D 16
    '85
--Hard hats
  Nat Geog 163:592 (c,4) My '83
  Trav/Holiday 162:51 (c,4) S
    '84
  Life 9:39 (c,2) Je '86
  Smithsonian 17:100-1 (c,4) D
    '86
HELSINKI, FINLAND
  Trav/Holiday 166:8-9 (c,3) D
    '86
HEMINGWAY, ERNEST
  Am Heritage 33:13 (4) Ap '82
  Am Heritage 35:113 (3) F '84
  Am Heritage 35:cov., 50-6
    (c,1) Ap '84
  Smithsonian 15:118 (4) D '84
  Sports Illus 64:cov., 58 (paint-
    ing,c,2) My 5 '86
  Life 9:cov., 91-3 (c,1) Je '86

  Natur Hist 95:4 (4) O '86
  Life 9:333, 356 (3) Fall '86
--On crutches (1918)
  Smithsonian 17:162 (4) My '86
HENIE, SONJA
  Smithsonian 15:113 (4) D '84
  Sports Illus 64:122 (4) My 19
    '86
  Sports Illus 64:53 (4) Je 30 '86
HENRI, ROBERT
  Smithsonian 15:145 (4) My '84
--Paintings by him
  Smithsonian 15:144-53 (c,2) My
    '84
HENRY VII (GREAT BRITAIN)
  Smithsonian 15:92 (painting,c,4)
    Mr '85
HENRY VIII (GREAT BRITAIN)
  Nat Geog 163:658-9 (painting,c,1)
    My '83
  Smithsonian 17:60-1 (painting,c,2)
    S '86
--1530 petition to Pope to annul
    Henry VIII marriage
  Nat Geog 168:774-5 (c,1) D '85
--Armor
  Smithsonian 13:68-9 (c,2) O '82
HEPBURN, KATHARINE
  Life 9:20, 180 (c,2) Fall '86
HERBS
  Nat Geog 163:386-409 (c,1) Mr
    '83
  Ebony 40:112 (c,4) Ag '85
--Pink willow herbs
  Nat Geog 164:119 (c,4) Jl '83
--See also
    BASIL
    GINSENG
    LAVENDER
    THYME
HERCULANEUM, ITALY
--Reconstruction of ancient city
  Nat Geog 165:578-85, 596 (c,1)
    My '84
--Relics of ancient city
  Nat Geog 162:686-93 (c,1) D '82
  Nat Geog 165:cov., 556-605 (c,1)
    My '84
HERCULES
--16th cent. Bandinelli sculpture
    (Florence, Italy)
  Trav/Holiday 159:41 (c,2) F '83
HERMIT CRABS
  Smithsonian 12:124 (c,3) Mr '82
  Nat Geog 164:144 (c,2) Jl '83
  Smithsonian 15:124-5 (c,3) Mr
    '85

HINDUISM--SHRINES AND
        SYMBOLS (cont.)
    '82
--Vishnu's Iron Pillar, Delhi,
        India
    Nat Geog 167:533 (c,2) Ap '85
HIPPOPOTAMI
    Sports Illus 56:96 (c,4) F 8
        '82
    Nat Geog 165:178-9 (c,2) F '84
    Nat Geog 167:627 (c,4) My '85
    Nat Geog 169:582-3 (c,1) My
        '86
--Extinct dwarf hippos
    Natur Hist 95:54-5 (drawing,4)
        S '86
--Pygmy
    Natur Hist 91:36-7 (paint-
        ing,c,3) Ag '82
HIRSCHFELD, AL
--Cartoon about the Automat
    Smithsonian 16:59 (4) Ja '86
--Drawing of Robert Benchley
    Am Heritage 37:87 (4) Ap '86
History. See
        specific countries--
            HISTORY
        list under People and
            Civilizations
HITLER, ADOLF
    Life 6:19, 22 (2) Je '83
    Life 8:20 (c,4) Spring '85
    Sports Illus 65:48, 56 (4) Ag
        4 '86
    Am Heritage 37:26 (4) O '86
--1932 Hitler campaign poster
        (Germany)
    Am Heritage 37:92 (4) Ag '86
--Eva Braun's roadster (1940s)
    Life 6:84-5 (c,1) Jl '83
--See also
    NAZISM
HOARFROST
    Nat Geog 162:355 (c,1) S '82
    Nat Wildlife 21:49-50 (c,4) F
        '83
Hoaxes. See
        CARDIFF GIANT
        PILTDOWN MAN
Hobbies. See
        list under AMUSEMENTS
HOBOES
--1930s hoboes on boxcars (Utah)
    Am Heritage 36:62-3 (paint-
        ing,c,1) Ag '85
--Buffalo nickels recarved by
        hoboes

    Am Heritage 34:81-3, 114 (c,2)
        Ag '83
HOCKEY
    Sports Illus 58:38-9, 46 (c,1)
        Mr 28 '83
--1924 Olympics (Chamonix)
    Sports Illus 59:114 (4) D 26 '83
--1984 Olympics (Sarajevo)
    Sports Illus 60:22-5 (c,2) F 20
        '84
--Backyard hockey
    Sports Illus 60:102 (drawing,c,4)
        My 28 '84
--Field hockey
    Sports Illus 61:402-18 (draw-
        ing,c,2) Jl 18 '84
    Sports Illus 63:21 (c,2) Ag 5 '85
--Frogmen's underwater hockey
    Sports Illus 63:20 (c,4) D 16 '85
--Giant hockey puck (Canada)
    Sports Illus 65:14 (c,4) N 3 '86
--Net
    Sports Illus 59:74-5 (c,1) D 26
        '83
HOCKEY--AMATEUR
    Sports Illus 59:2, 86-7, 92-4
        (c,1) D 12 '83
    Sports Illus 59:2-3, 64 (c,2) D
        19 '83
--Checking
    Sports Illus 60:24 (c,2) F 20 '84
--Goal-tending
    Sports Illus 59:38-9, 44 (c,1) N
        14 '83
HOCKEY--COLLEGE
    Sports Illus 60:56 (c,4) Ja 30
        '84
--Champions celebrating
    Sports Illus 58:102-3 (c,2) Ap 4
        '83
--Goal-tending
    Sports Illus 56:48 (c,4) F 8 '82
    Sports Illus 64:6-7 (c,1) Ap 7
        '86
--Mascot (Wisconsin)
    Sports Illus 56:46 (drawing,c,4)
        F 8 '82
--NCAA Championships 1982 (North
        Dakota vs. Wisconsin)
    Sports Illus 56:20-1 (c,3) Ap 5
        '82
--NCAA Championships 1984
    Sports Illus 60:2-3 (c,2) Ap 2
        '84
--NCAA Championships 1985 (RPI
        vs. Providence)
    Sports Illus 62:86-8 (c,3) Ap 8

HONDURAS
    Nat Geog 164:608-37 (map,c,1)
        N '83
--See also
    TEGUCIGALPA
HONDURAS--COSTUME
    Nat Geog 164:610-37 (c,1) N
        '83
HONEY BEARS
    Nat Geog 164:262 (c,4) Ag '83
    Smithsonian 14:81 (c,1) Ag '83
HONEYSUCKLE
    Smithsonian 13:76 (draw-
        ing,c,2) Mr '83
HONG KONG
    Trav/Holiday 159:61 (c,4) F
        '83
    Trav/Holiday 161:44-6 (c,2) Ja
        '84
    Trav/Holiday 165:58-63 (map,c,3)
        F '86
HOOVER, HERBERT
    Am Heritage 36:13 (4) D '84
    Smithsonian 16:146-60 (1) My
        '85
--1900 China trip
    Smithsonian 16:146-60 (1) My
        '85
--1932 Hoover campaign button
    Am Heritage 38:25 (4) D '86
--Caricature
    Smithsonian 15:179 (draw-
        ing,c,2) N '84
--Depicted on postage stamp
    Am Heritage 34:55 (c,4) D '82
--Mrs. Lou Hoover
    Smithsonian 16:148-60 (4) My
        '85
HOOVER DAM, SOUTHWEST
    Smithsonian 13:52-3 (c,2) F '83
--Commemorated on postage stamp
    Am Heritage 34:55 (c,4) D '82
HOPE, BOB
    Sports Illus 62:2-3 (c,2) Ja
        21 '85
HOPI INDIANS (ARIZONA)
--Costume, lifestyle
    Nat Geog 162:606-29 (map,c,1)
        N '82
    Natur Hist 93:40-5 (c,1) My
        '84
HOPI INDIANS (ARIZONA)--
        RELICS
--Kachina dolls
    Nat Geog 162:612 (c,4) N '82
    Smithsonian 13:120 (c,4) Ja
        '83

HOPPER, EDWARD
--"Automat" (1927)
    Smithsonian 16:61 (painting,c,2)
        Ja '86
--"Corn Belt City" (1947)
    Smithsonian 13:117 (painting,4)
        Mr '83
--"People in the Sun" (1960)
    Am Heritage 37:34-5 (painting,c,1)
        Je '86
--"Room in New York" (1932)
    Am Heritage 33:25 (painting,c,3)
        O '82
HORN PLAYING
--Baritone horn (Austria)
    Nat Geog 167:438 (c,4) Ap '85
--Swiss carnival
    Natur Hist 91:39 (c,3) F '82
HORNBILLS
    Nat Geog 164:267 (c,3) Ag '83
    Natur Hist 94:40-1 (c,1) S '85
HORNE, LENA
    Ebony 39:48, 104 (4) Je '84
    Ebony 41:90, 124 (c,2) N '85
HORSE FARMS
--Fences (California)
    Nat Geog 165:459 (c,1) Ap '84
--Pennsylvania
    Nat Geog 167:380-1 (c,1) Mr '85
--See also
    STABLES
HORSE JUMPING EVENTS
    Sports Illus 57:41-2 (c,2) O 4
        '82
--Norfolk Island, Australia
    Nat Geog 164:536-7 (c,1) O '83
HORSE RACING
    Sports Illus 56:134-5 (c,2) F 10
        '82
    Sports Illus 56:44 (c,4) F 15 '82
    Sports Illus 56:78 (c,4) Mr 8 '82
    Sports Illus 56:69 (c,3) Mr 15
        '82
    Sports Illus 56:60 (c,4) Ap 5 '82
    Sports Illus 56:26-8 (c,1) Ap 12
        '82
    Sports Illus 57:54 (c,4) Jl 5 '82
    Sports Illus 57:60 (c,3) Ag 9
        '82
    Sports Illus 57:32 (c,3) S 27 '82
    Sports Illus 58:93 (c,4) F 14 '83
    Sports Illus 58:24 (c,4) F 21 '83
    Sports Illus 58:52 (c,3) F 28 '83
    Ebony 38:60-1 (c,2) My '83
    Sports Illus 58:42-6 (c,1) My 9
        '83
    Sports Illus 59:22-3 (c,2) S 26 '83

HORSE RACING (cont.)
Sports Illus 59:63-4 (c,3) O
24 '83
Sports Illus 60:14-19 (c,1) Mr
12 '84
Sports Illus 60:2-3 (c,1) Mr
26 '84
Sports Illus 60:36-7 (c,2) My
7 '84
Sports Illus 61:48, 51 (c,3)
Jl 30 '84
Sports Illus 61:38-9, 58-61
(c,2) Ag 27 '84
Sports Illus 61:12-15 (c,1) S 3
'84
Sports Illus 61:24-5 (c,3) O 1
'84
Sports Illus 61:24-5 (c,2) O 8
'84
Sports Illus 62:24-5 (c,2) Mr
11 '85
--1867 "Races at Longchamps" by
Manet
Smithsonian 14:98-9 (paint-
ing,c,1) S '83
--Accident on track
Sports Illus 63:2-3 (c,1) O 14
'85
--Ancient Greece
Natur Hist 93:60-1 (paint-
ing,c,1) Je '84
--Belmont Stakes 1982
Sports Illus 56:54 (c,4) Je 14
'82
--Belmont Stakes 1983
Sports Illus 58:18-21 (c,1) Je
20 '83
Sports Illus 60:71 (c,3) Ap 23
'84
--Belmont Stakes 1984
Sports Illus 60:2-3 (c,1) Je 18
'84
--Belmont Stakes 1986
Sports Illus 64:48, 51 (c,4) Je
16 '86
--Breeders' Cup 1984 (Hollywood
Park)
Sports Illus 61:36-43, 87 (c,1)
N 19 '84
Sports Illus 63:5-11 (c,1) O 21
'85
--Breeder's Cup 1985 (Aqueduct,
New York)
Sports Illus 63:46-8 (c,2) N 11
'85
--Breeder's Cup 1986 (Santa Anita,
California)

Sports Illus 65:22-5 (c,2) N 10
'86
--Chuck wagon race (Calgary, Al-
berta)
Nat Geog 165:398-9 (c,1) Mr '84
--Delaware
Nat Geog 164:180-1 (c,1) Ag '83
--English Derby 1981
Sports Illus 58:28 (c,3) F 21 '83
--English Derby 1985
Sports Illus 62:38-40 (c,2) Je 17
'85
--Florida Derby 1986
Sports Illus 64:12-15 (c,1) Mr
10 '86
--Kentucky Derby 1968
Sports Illus 63:57 (c,3) Jl 15
'85
--Kentucky Derby 1974
Sports Illus 60:76-7 (c,4) Ap 23
'84
--Kentucky Derby 1976
Sports Illus 60:76 (c,4) Ap 23
'84
--Kentucky Derby 1981
Sports Illus 56:132-3 (c,1) F 10
'82
--Kentucky Derby 1982
Sports Illus 56:32-7 (c,1) My 10
'82
--Kentucky Derby 1983
Sports Illus 58:40-9 (painting,c,1)
My 2 '83
Sports Illus 58:cov., 30-3 (c,1)
My 16 '83
--Kentucky Derby 1984
Sports Illus 60:26-31 (c,1) My
14 '84
--Kentucky Derby 1985
Sports Illus 62:24-9 (c,1) My 13
'85
--Kentucky Derby 1986
Sports Illus 64:5-14 (c,2) Ap 28
'86
Sports Illus 64:18-24 (c,1) My
12 '86
--Mule race (New Mexico)
Smithsonian 14:102 (3) N '83
--Preakness Stakes 1980
Sports Illus 60:70 (c,4) Ap 23
'84
--Preakness Stakes 1982
Sports Illus 56:98, 101 (c,3) My
24 '82
--Preakness Stakes 1983
Sports Illus 58:74-5 (c,2) My 30
'83

HOTELS (cont.)
  Trav/Holiday 163:55 (c,1) Ja
    '85
--Barbados
  Trav/Holiday 162:46 (c,4) Ag
    '84
--Birdsville Hotel, Queensland,
    Australia
  Nat Geog 169:13 (c,3) Ja '86
--Chateau Frontenac, Quebec
  Trav/Holiday 157:38 (c,4) My
    '82
  Trav/Holiday 161:38 (4) My
    '84
  Trav/Holiday 165:80-1 (c,1)
    Mr '86
--Cataract Hotel, Egypt
  Nat Geog 167:607 (c,4) My '85
--Chelsea Hotel, New York City,
    New York
  Smithsonian 14:94-107 (c,1)
    D '83
--Cocktail lounge (India)
  Trav/Holiday 157:52 (c,2) Mr
    '82
--Country inn bedroom (Con-
    necticut)
  Trav/Holiday 160:13 (c,4) D
    '83
--Egypt
  Trav/Holiday 163:76-9 (c,1) Mr
    '85
--Guesthouse (Nepal)
  Nat Geog 161:714 (c,1) Je '82
--Hawaii
  Trav/Holiday 159:10 (4) Ja '83
--Hawaiian hotel atrium
  Trav/Holiday 161:78 (4) My
    '84
--The Homestead, Hot Springs,
    Virginia
  Trav/Holiday 159:104 (4) Mr
    '83
--Hotel corridor
  Ebony 39:102 (4) Mr '84
--Hotel del Coronado, San Diego,
    California
  Trav/Holiday 158:26 (c,4) S
    '82
--Hotel room (Virginia)
  Life 5:50 (c,3) N '82
--Hotel room trashed by rock
    group
  Life 5:166-7 (c,1) N '82
--Hotel rooms (Mexico)
  Sports Illus 57:32 (c,4) Ag 30
    '82

--Inns (Puerto Rico)
  Trav/Holiday 166:62-4 (c,2) N
    '86
--Japanese guest house interiors
  Trav/Holiday 157:50 (c,4) Ja
    '82
--Lake District, England
  Trav/Holiday 163:69 (c,3) Ap
    '85
--Lodge fireplace (Washington)
  Trav/Holiday 159:44 (c,2) My
    '83
--Luxury (Baghdad, Iraq)
  Nat Geog 167:91 (c,4) Ja '85
--Luxury (Las Vegas, Nevada)
  Sports Illus 56:80-94 (c,1) Je
    7 '82
--Luxury (San Juan, Puerto Rico)
  Nat Geog 163:540 (c,3) Ap '83
--Luxury (Tunisia)
  Life 6:100-1 (c,1) F '83
--Modern (Togo)
  Trav/Holiday 158:36 (c,2) Ag
    '82
--Modern lobby (Spain)
  Trav/Holiday 163:71 (c,2) Ap
    '85
--Motel sign (California)
  Smithsonian 17:69 (c,1) D '86
--New Orleans, Louisiana
  Trav/Holiday 159:40 (c,4) Ja '83
--Resort hotel (Elat, Israel)
  Nat Geog 168:16-17 (c,2) Jl '85
--Resort hotel (Haiti)
  Trav/Holiday 165:52-3 (c,2) F '86
--Resort hotel (Jamaica)
  Nat Geog 167:138-9 (c,1) Ja '85
--Resort hotel (San Juan Islands,
    Washington)
  Trav/Holiday 166:54-5 (c,1) S
    '86
--Resort hotel (Singapore)
  Trav/Holiday 165:71, 73 (c,2) Ap
    '86
--St. Moritz, Switzerland
  Trav/Holiday 164:14 (c,3) N '85
--St. Nicholas Hotel, New York
    City (1850s)
  Am Heritage 33:18-19 (paint-
    ing,c,1) Je '82
--St. Petersburg, Florida
  Nat Geog 162:204-5 (c,1) Ag '82
--Small inns (Mexico)
  Trav/Holiday 164:49-53 (c,1) Jl
    '85
--Small San Francisco hotels,
    California

HOTELS (cont.)
    Trav/Holiday 157:40, 43 (c,1)
        Ja '82
--Taiwan
    Nat Geog 161:104-5 (c,2) Ja
        '82
    Trav/Holiday 160:41 (c,3) Ag
        '83
--Wayside inn (Bumi, Pakistan)
    Smithsonian 13:53 (c,4) Ap '82
--See also
    RESORTS
Hounds. See
    BASSET HOUNDS
    BLOODHOUNDS
HOUSEBOATS
--Great Britain
    Nat Geog 163:782-3 (c,1) Je
        '83
--Iowa
    Trav/Holiday 162:51 (c,4) O
        '84
--Kashmir
    Trav/Holiday 166:56-9 (c,1) N
        '86
--Kentucky
    Trav/Holiday 159:95 (4) Mr '83
--Mississippi
    Nat Geog 169:381 (c,4) Mr '86
--Seattle, Washington
    Sports Illus 57:64 (c,4) Jl 19
        '82
--Seine River, France
    Nat Geog 161:492-7 (c,1) Ap
        '82
HOUSEHOLD ACTIVITIES
--Carrying water buckets on head
        (Kenya)
    Sports Illus 56:95 (c,4) F 8
        '82
--Carrying water buckets on head
        (South Africa)
    Nat Geog 165:183 (c,4) F '84
--Child pumping water (China)
    Natur Hist 93:80-1 (c,1) N
        '84
--Children carrying water (Cam-
        bodia)
    Nat Geog 161:623 (c,1) My '82
--Polishing floor
    Sports Illus 61:62 (c,3) O 22
        '84
--Preparing yak dung for fuel
        (Tibet)
    Natur Hist 95:61 (c,4) Ja '86
--Raking leaves (Kansas)
    Nat Geog 168:354-5 (c,1) S '85

--Swatting flies
    Life 6:124-5 (c,1) N '83
--Washing car (California)
    Sports Illus 57:59 (c,4) N 15
        '82
--Washing dishes
    Sports Illus 58:86 (4) Je 13 '83
    Sports Illus 60:91 (c,3) F 6 '84
--Washing dishes at Boy Scout
        camp
    Smithsonian 16:37 (c,4) Jl '85
--Women hauling water (Niger)
    Nat Geog 164:486-7 (c,1) O '83
--See also
    BATHING
    BREAD MAKING
    CANDLE MAKING
    COOKING
    GARDENING
    IRONING
    LAUNDRY
    LOG SPLITTING
    SEWING
    SHAVING
    SWEEPING
    TYPING
    VACUUMING
HOUSES
--19th cent. (Key West, Florida)
    Nat Geog 162:199 (c,4) Ag '82
--19th cent. (Massachusetts)
    Am Heritage 33:43 (c,1) Ag '82
--19th-20th cent. suburban homes
    Am Heritage 35:20-36 (c,1) F
        '84
--Mid-19th cent. (Oregon)
    Nat Geog 170:176 (3) Ag '86
--Mid-19th cent. octagonal buildings
    Am Heritage 34:cov., 12-25 (c,1)
        Ag '83
    Am Heritage 35:109-10 (c,4) D
        '83
--1860s 16-sided house (Massachu-
        setts)
    Am Heritage 34:26-7 (c,1) Ag
        '83
--Late 19th cent. (Ohio)
    Am Heritage 37:100-5 (2) F '86
--Early 20th cent. mail-order houses
    Smithsonian 16:90-101 (c,1) N
        '85
--Abandoned buildings (Brooklyn,
        New York)
    Nat Geog 163:602-3 (c,1) My '83
--Ancient mud-brick house (Mali)
    Nat Geog 162:412-13 (c,1) S '82
--Barbados

HOUSES (cont.)
Natur Hist 94:38-44 (c,4) O
'85
--Brownstones (Brooklyn, New
York)
Trav/Holiday 159:48 (c,2) Ap
'83
Nat Geog 163:588-9 (c,1) My
'83
--California
Ebony 37:34 (c,4) My '82
Nat Geog 162:474 (c,4) O '82
--Chalets (Austria)
Trav/Holiday 157:78-9, 83
(c,1) Ap '82
--Depictions of U.S. Victorian
interiors
Am Heritage 34:96-9 (draw-
ing,c,1) D '82
--Designed by Frank Lloyd
Wright (1901)
Am Heritage 36:106-7 (draw-
ing,2) D '84
--East Berlin, East Germany
Nat Geog 161:26-7 (c,1) Ja '82
--Expensive homes (Kentucky)
Nat Geog 163:806-7 (c,1) Je
'83
--Flounder house (Alexandria,
Virginia)
Trav/Holiday 166:12 (c,4) N
'86
--Illustrated house facades (Swit-
zerland)
Trav/Holiday 166:38 (c,4) N
'86
--Made of trash (New Mexico)
Nat Geog 163:454-5 (c,1) Ap
'83
--Middle class cave dwellings
(France)
Smithsonian 14:50-9 (c,1) Je
'83
--New Mexico
Ebony 39:38-44 (c,1) O '84
--Ohio
Sports Illus 57:42 (c,2) Ag 30
'82
--On stilts (Burma)
Smithsonian 15:102 (c,3) My '84
--Palm-thatched house (Pacific
Islands)
Trav/Holiday 165:16 (c,4) Ja
'86
--Pre-fabricated (Northwest
Territories)
Nat Geog 163:180 (c,2) F '83

--Pre-fabricated cardboard units
(Antarctica)
Nat Geog 164:475 (c,3) O '83
--Pyramid-shaped home (Illinois)
Life 9:6-7 (c,1) O '86
--Restoring brownstones (Washing-
ton, D.C.)
Ebony 40:155, 162 (3) Ap '85
--Row houses (Baltimore, Maryland)
Life 9:119 (c,4) Ja '86
--Row houses (Harlem, New York)
Ebony 41:58 (4) My '86
--Solar-heated (New Mexico)
Nat Geog 161:324-5 (c,1) Mr '82
--Stone house (Pakistan)
Trav/Holiday 164:43 (c,2) Ag '85
--Texas
Ebony 38:34 (c,4) N '82
--Townhouses (Georgetown, Wash-
ington, D.C.)
Am Heritage 37:31 (c,1) Ap '86
--Tudor mansion (Illinois)
Ebony 37:27, 34 (c,3) F '82
--U.S.
Life 9:58-61 (c,2) N '86
--Victorian style (Los Angeles,
California)
Trav/Holiday 158:43 (c,4) O '82
--Victorian style (Portsmouth,
Virginia)
Nat Geog 168:84-5 (c,1) Jl '85
--Victorian style (San Diego, Cali-
fornia)
Trav/Holiday 158:26 (c,4) S '82
--West Germany
Trav/Holiday 162:58 (c,4) S '84
--Working class shacks (Honduras)
Nat Geog 164:264-5 (c,1) N '83
--See also
ARCHITECTURAL FEATURES
ARCHITECTURAL STRUC-
TURES
ARCHITECTURE
HOUSING
HOUSES--CONSTRUCTION
Sports Illus 61:34 (c,3) S 5 '84
--1855
Am Heritage 35:22 (engraving,4)
F '84
--Brazil
Nat Geog 165:680 (c,3) My '84
--Hungary
Nat Geog 163:240-1 (c,1) F '83
--Log cabin (Northwest Territories)
Nat Geog 163:181 (c,4) F '83
--Mixing concrete (Louisiana)
Sports Illus 59:40-1 (c,2) O 24 '83

HOUSES--CONSTRUCTION (cont.)
--Thatching hut roof (Mexico)
  Nat Geog 168:518-19 (c,1) O
    '85
--Thatching hut roof (Nepal)
  Smithsonian 14:166 (c,4) Mr
    '84
--Replacing roof after volcano
    damage (Mexico)
  Nat Geog 162:670-1 (c,1) N
    '82
--Thatching roof (Stanton, Eng-
    land)
  Trav/Holiday 159:64 (c,2) Ap
    '83
--Wood skeleton of house
  Ebony 39:143 (c,4) S '84
--Yap, Micronesia
  Nat Geog 170:491 (c,4) O '86
HOUSEWARES
--12th cent. candlesticks (Af-
    ghanistan)
  Smithsonian 16:225 (c,4) O '85
--13th cent. canteen (Syria)
  Smithsonian 16:225 (c,4) O '85
--18th cent. snuff bottles (China)
  Natur Hist 93:68 (c,1) F '84
--1871 products made in Philadel-
    phia
  Am Heritage 36:34-9 (2) Ag
    '85
--1880s vaporizer
  Am Heritage 35:26 (c,4) O '84
--1890s apple parer
  Am Heritage 37:41 (c,4) Ag
    '86
--Early 20th cent. (U.S.)
  Am Heritage 37:34-43 (c,1) Ag
    '86
--1933 pencil sharpener
  Smithsonian 17:164 (4) N '86
--Ancient mortar and pestle
    (Chile)
  Natur Hist 94:80 (c,4) O '85
--Concealed in 19th cent. cane
  Smithsonian 14:156 (c,4) My
    '83
--Danish housewares design
  Trav/Holiday 166:29 (c,4) N
    '86
--Pepper mills
  Smithsonian 14:148 (c,4) F '84
--Unpacking pots and pans
  Sports Illus 60:47 (c,4) F 13
    '84
--See also
  BOTTLES

BROOMS
BRUSHES
CALENDARS
CANDLES
CHINAWARE
CLOCKS
COOKING UTENSILS
CUTLERY
FANS
GARBAGE CANS
GLASSWARE
INKWELLS
MATCHBOXES
QUILTS
SPONGES
TEAKETTLES
TEAPOTS
TOASTERS
WALKING STICKS
HOUSING
--Cliff dwellings (Cappadocia, Tur-
    key)
  Trav/Holiday 166:cov., 40-2 (c,1)
    S '86
--Prehistoric cave dwellings (Reig-
    nac, France)
  Smithsonian 17:76-7 (c,2) O '86
--See also
  ADOBE HOUSES
  APARTMENT BUILDINGS
  CABINS
  CAGES
  CASTLES
  CAVES
  CHATEAUS
  COTTAGES
  FARMHOUSES
  HOUSEBOATS
  HOUSES
  HOUSING DEVELOPMENTS
  HUTS
  IGLOOS
  KIBBUTZIM
  LOG CABINS
  MANSIONS
  MOBILE HOMES
  PALACES
  PLANTATIONS
  SLUMS
  SOD HOUSES
  STILT HOUSES
  TENTS
  TEPEES
  YURTS
  geographical entries--HOUSING
    (e.g. CHINA--HOUSING)

HOUSING DEVELOPMENTS
--1953 moving-in scene (Los
        Angeles, California)
    Am Heritage 35:36 (4) F '84
--Abidjan, Ivory Coat
    Nat Geog 162:102-3 (c,2) Jl
        '82
--Aerial view
    Natur Hist 92:82 (c,3) S '83
--Australia
    Nat Geog 161:650 (c,3) My '82
--Calgary, Alberta
    Nat Geog 165:393 (c,3) Mr '84
--Chicago, Illinois
    Ebony 40:38 (3) Ag '85
--Dallas, Texas
    Nat Geog 166:280-1 (c,1) S '84
--Florida
    Nat Wildlife 20:42-3 (c,1) Je
        '82
--Greenland
    Nat Geog 163:192-3 (c,2) F '83
--Israel's West Bank
    Nat Geog 168:32-3 (c,1) Jl '85
--Jerusalem, Israel
    Nat Geog 163:492-3 (c,1) Ap
        '83
--Mobile home park (Arizona)
    Natur Hist 93:46 (c,3) Mr '84
--Scottsdale, Arizona
    Nat Wildlife 24:22-3 (c,1) Ap
        '86
--Sinai Peninsula, Israel
    Nat Geog 161:420-1 (c,1) Ap
        '82
--Tucson, Arizona
    Nat Geog 166:516 (c,1) O '84
--Washington, D.C.
    Nat Geog 163:116 (c,1) Ja '83
HOUSTON, SAM
    Nat Geog 169:310-29 (c,1) Mr
        '86
HOUSTON, TEXAS
    Trav/Holiday 158:40-2 (c,1) N
        '82
    Smithsonian 16:94 (c,4) O '85
--Celebration of Houston's 150th
        birthday
    Life 9:14-15 (c,1) Je '86
--Houston Ship Canal
    Smithsonian 16:88-99 (map,c,1)
        O '85
--View from Ship Channel Bridge
    Sports Illus 63:87 (c,2) Ag 26
        '85
HOWITZERS
    Sports Illus 56:82 (c,4) Ap 19

        '82
HOWLERS (MONKEYS)
    Nat Geog 168:332 (c,4) S '85
--Red howler monkeys
    Natur Hist 93:54-61 (c,1) Ag '84
HUCKLEBERRY PLANTS
    Nat Wildlife 22:4-7 (c,1) O '84
HUDSON, W. H.
    Smithsonian 14:123 (4) Je '83
HUDSON BAY, CANADA
    Nat Geog 161:380-401 (c,1) Mr
        '82
HUDSON RIVER, NEW YORK/NEW
        JERSEY
--19th cent. construction of Hudson
        River tunnels
    Smithsonian 17:74-6 (2) My '86
HUGHES, CHARLES EVANS
    Am Heritage 38:37 (drawing,4)
        D '86
HUGHES, LANGSTON
    Ebony 37:53-5 (3) My '82
    Ebony 41:148 (3) N '85
HUMBOLDT, ALEXANDER VON
    Nat Geog 168:319-30 (c,2) S '85
--Life and works
    Nat Geog 168:319-48 (c,1) S '85
HUMMINGBIRDS
    Nat Geog 161:222-7 (c,1) F '82
    Nat Wildlife 22:2, 40 (c,2) Je
        '84
    Natur Hist 93:28-9 (c,2) Jl '84
    Nat Wildlife 23:42-4 (paint-
        ing,c,4) Ap '85
    Natur Hist 94:cov., 56-63 (c,1)
        Jl '85
    Nat Wildlife 24:2 (c,2) Ag '86
    Nat Wildlife 25:2 (c,2) D '86
HUMPHREY, HUBERT H.
    Ebony 39:50 (4) Ag '84
HUNGARY
    Nat Geog 163:224-60 (map,c,1)
        F '86
--See also
        BUDAPEST
        DANUBE RIVER
HUNGARY--COSTUME
    Nat Geog 163:224-60 (c,1) F '83
--1956 street fighters
    Smithsonian 17:52-7 (1) N '86
--Budapest
    Trav/Holiday 163:66-9 (c,1) Mr
        '85
    Smithsonian 17:52-61 (c,1) N '86
HUNGARY--HISTORY
--1956 revolution
    Smithsonian 17:52-61 (1) N '86

HUNTING (cont.)
--Trapping arctic foxes (Canada)
    Nat Geog 161:402-3 (c,2) Mr
    '82
--Turkey calling
    Sports Illus 59:18 (c,4) N 28
    '83
--Turkeys
    Sports Illus 56:41 (paint-
    ing,c,4) Mr 22 '82
--Turtles (Brazil)
    Nat Geog 165:678-9, 692-3
    (c,1) My '84
--Whales (Alaska)
    Nat Geog 163:158-9, 164-5
    (c,1) F '83
--Whales (Canada)
    Nat Geog 164:113-15 (c,1) Jl
    '83
--Whales (Faeroe Islands)
    Life 9:8-9 (c,1) O '86
--Wild pig (Papua New Guinea)
    Nat Geog 162:167 (c,1) Ag '82
--See also
        FOX HUNTING
        SAFARIS
HUNTING--HUMOR
--1916 cartoon of duck hunting
    Smithsonian 13:70 (2) Je '82
HUNTING EQUIPMENT
--19th cent. decoys
    Am Heritage 33:28 (c,4) Ap '82
--1900 field kit
    Nat Geog 164:647 (c,4) N '83
--Ancient Clovis spearpoints
    (New Mexico)
    Natur Hist 95:22 (drawing,4)
    D '86
--Bamboo hunting spears (Nepal)
    Nat Geog 169:806 (c,4) Je '86
--Daniel Boone's hunting bag and
    powder horn
    Nat Geog 168:821, 836-7 (c,1)
    D '85
--Duck decoys
    Nat Geog 164:638-63 (c,1) N
    '83
--Hunting boots
    Sports Illus 63:86, 91 (c,2)
    D 2 '85
--Wild turkey calls
    Nat Wildlife 22:48-9 (c,1) O
    '84
    Life 7:84-5 (c,1) D '84
--See also
        GUNS
        HARPOONS

HUNTSVILLE, ALABAMA
--Antebellum depot
    Trav/Holiday 163:36 (c,4) Ap
    '85
--Rocket Park
    Trav/Holiday 163:6 (c,4) Ap '85
HURDLING
    Sports Illus 56:17 (c,3) Ja 25
    '82
    Sports Illus 56:91 (c,4) F 8 '82
    Sports Illus 56:18 (c,2) F 22
    '82
    Sports Illus 56:cov., 35 (c,1)
    Ap 26 '82
    Sports Illus 56:32-3 (c,4) My
    31 '82
    Sports Illus 57:72 (c,3) S 20 '82
    Sports Illus 58:60-1 (c,1) F 16
    '83
    Sports Illus 58:27 (c,4) F 28 '83
    Sports Illus 58:80 (c,4) My 23
    '83
    Sports Illus 58:84 (c,4) Je 6
    '83
    Sports Illus 59:22 (c,2) Ag 22
    '83
    Sports Illus 59:cov., 16 (c,1)
    S 12 '83
    Sports Illus 60:58-9 (c,2) F 8
    '84
    Ebony 39:95-6 (c,1) My '84
    Life 7:64-5, 88 (c,1) Summer '84
    Sports Illus 61:2-3, 18-19, 31
    (c,1) Jl 2 '84
    Sports Illus 61:43, 69, 196 (c,2)
    Jl 18 '84
    Sports Illus 61:54-5 (c,3) Jl 30
    '84
    Sports Illus 64:20 (c,3) Ja 27
    '86
    Sports Illus 65:85 (c,2) N 24
    '86
--1932 Olympics (Los Angeles)
    Sports Illus 57:96 (4) N 22 '82
--1984 Olympics (Los Angeles)
    Sports Illus 61:38, 42, 50 (c,4)
    Ag 20 '84
    Sports Illus 61:32-3 (c,2) D 24
    '84
--Into water
    Sports Illus 59:20 (c,2) Ag 29 '83
HURRICANES
--1938 (Fire Island, New York)
    Am Heritage 37:30-1 (paint-
    ing,c,1) Je '86
--1985 Elena (Gulf of Mexico)
    Life 9:14-15 (c,1) Ja '86

HURRICANES (cont.)
--1985 Gloria (Northeast)
  Life 8:76-7 (1) N '85
--Arctic hurricanes
  Natur Hist 95:66-72 (c,1) D '86
HURRICANES--DAMAGE
--1900 (Galveston, Texas)
  Smithsonian 13:90-1 (3) S '82
Huskies. See
  SIBERIAN HUSKIES
HUSTON, JOHN
  Am Heritage 33:8-15 (c,1) Ap
    '82
HUTS
--Botswana
  Nat Geog 165:148-9 (c,1) F '84
--Costa Rican rain forest
  Trav/Holiday 163:10 (c,4) My
    '85
--Mexican Indians (Chiapas)
  Trav/Holiday 162:42 (c,4) O
    '84
--Mexico
  Nat Geog 168:518-19 (c,1) O
    '85
--Ovambo tribe (Namibia)
  Nat Geog 161:760-1 (c,1) Je
    '82
--Papua New Guinea
  Nat Geog 164:150-1 (c,1) Ag
    '83
--Thatched (Sudan)
  Nat Geog 161:350-1 (c,1) Mr
    '82
--Thatched (Togo)
  Trav/Holiday 158:35 (c,4) Ag
    '82
--Waorani wood-and-palm-leaf
    houses (Ecuador)
  Natur Hist 93:68-9 (c,1) S '84
--Yap, Micronesia
  Trav/Holiday 162:59 (c,4) N
    '84
HYACINTHS
  Nat Wildlife 20:48-9 (c,1) Je
    '82
HYDRAS
  Smithsonian 13:68 (c,4) Jl '82
HYDROPLANES
  Sports Illus 57:62 (c,4) Jl 19
    '82
HYENAS
  Nat Geog 163:359 (c,3) Mr '83
  Natur Hist 92:44-5, 46-7 (c,1)
    Mr '83
  Life 7:137 (c,4) N '84
  Natur Hist 94:90-1 (c,1) Mr '85

--See also
  AARDWOLVES

-I-

IBEXES
  Nat Geog 163:638 (c,4) My '83
--Ancient Bactrian sculpture
  Natur Hist 94:68 (c,4) D '85
IBISES
  Nat Wildlife 20:54 (c,3) O '82
  Natur Hist 94:38-45 (c,1) Ja '85
  Nat Wildlife 23:cov. (c,1) Ap
    '85
ICE
  Nat Wildlife 22:4-13 (c,1) D '83
--Antarctic ice pack
  Trav/Holiday 158:55 (c,1) N '82
--Cutter ships breaking ice (Massa-
    chusetts)
  Smithsonian 13:45 (c,1) Jl '82
--Frost on trees (China)
  Life 8:152 (c,3) D '85
--Frostbitten feet
  Nat Geog 170:306 (c,1) S '86
--Hanging from berries
  Nat Wildlife 21:62 (c,4) D '82
--Ice castle (Minnesota)
  Life 9:6-7 (c,1) Ap '86
--Ice cave (Yukon)
  Nat Geog 168:649 (c,1) N '85
--Ice chunks under water (Antarc-
    tica)
  Nat Geog 169:502-3, 508-9 (c,1)
    Ap '86
--Ice mining (Ecuador)
  Natur Hist 95:40-2 (c,1) F '86
--Ice ponds as source of energy
  Smithsonian 14:105-13 (c,2) Ag
    '83
--Ice sculpture (Japan)
  Trav/Holiday 163:48 (c,4) Ja '85
--Polar bear ice sculpture (U.S.S.R.)
  Sports Illus 62:86 (c,4) Ap 29
    '85
--Pond bottom seen through ice
  Smithsonian 17:cov., 168-72
    (c,1) N '86
--Rescuing truck from partly frozen
    lake (New Hampshire)
  Nat Geog 162:793 (c,3) D '82
--Surrounding branches
  Nat Wildlife 22:8 (c,4) D '83
--Testing aircraft in icy conditions
  Life 9:14-15 (c,1) N '86
--See also

ICE (cont.)
GLACIERS
HOARFROST
IGLOOS
Ice Age. See
MAN, PREHISTORIC
ICE FISHING
--Drilling through ice (Lake
Champlain, Northeast)
Sports Illus 62:82 (c,4) Je 10
'85
--New Hampshire
Life 7:94 (4) Ap '84
--Rescuing ice fishermen from
cracked ice (U.S.S.R.)
Life 9:10-11 (1) Ap '86
--U.S.S.R.
Sports Illus 62:82-4 (c,1) Ap
29 '85
Ice skating. See
SKATING
ICEBERGS
Nat Wildlife 22:6-7 (c,1) D '83
Nat Geog 165:638-9 (c,1) My
'84
Smithsonian 15:66-7 (paint-
ing,c,1) My '84
--Alaska
Nat Wildlife 24:40-1 (c,1) D
'85
--Antarctica
Nat Geog 163:558-61 (c,1) Ap
'83
Nat Geog 166:658-9 (c,1) N '84
--Greenland
Sports Illus 57:67 (c,4) Ag 16
'82
ICELAND
Smithsonian 16:114-25 (c,1) Ja
'86
Trav/Holiday 166:44-7 (map,c,1)
N '86
--Eyjafjordur
Trav/Holiday 166:46-7 (c,1) N
'86
--Krafla volcano
Smithsonian 12:52-61 (c,1) Ja
'82
--Jökulsá á Fjöllum River
Nat Geog 166:308-21 (map,c,1)
S '84
--Reconstructed Viking farm
Smithsonian 16:118-19 (c,3) Ja
'86
--Stapi
Trav/Holiday 163:42 (3) Mr '85
--Vatnajökull Glacier

Nat Geog 166:308-16 (map,c,1)
S '84
--See also
REYKJAVIK
IDAHO
Sports Illus 61:78-92 (paint-
ing,c,1) N 5 '84
--Borah Peak earthquake (1983)
Natur Hist 95:28-34 (map,c,1)
Je '86
--Coeur d'Alene area
Life 9:22 (c,4) N '86
--Hells Canyon
Smithsonian 15:69 (c,4) Ja '85
--Palouse country
Nat Geog 161:798-819 (map,c,1)
Je '82
--Sawtooth mountains
Trav/Holiday 165:42-5 (map,c,1)
My '86
--See also
BOISE
CRATERS OF THE MOON
NATIONAL MONUMENT
SNAKE RIVER
IGLOOS
--Antarctica
Smithsonian 15:56 (c,4) O '84
IGUAÇU FALLS, SOUTH AMERICA
Trav/Holiday 159:57 (c,1) F '83
Nat Geog 170:236-7 (c,1) Ag '86
IGUANAS
Smithsonian 13:137 (c,4) Jl '82
Trav/Holiday 161:78 (c,4) Mr
'84
--Pet iguana
Sports Illus 64:79 (c,4) My 12
'86
ILLINOIS
--Alton riverfront
Nat Wildlife 23:9 (c,1) Je '85
--St. Charles post office
Nat Wildlife 21:8 (c,4) Ap '83
--Waverly street
Life 5:56 (c,2) O '82
--See also
CHICAGO
ILLINOIS RIVER
SHAWNEE NATIONAL FOREST
ILLINOIS RIVER, ILLINOIS
Smithsonian 17:68-9 (c,1) Ap '86
Illnesses. See
DISEASES
IMMIGRANTS
--Early 20th cent. immigrants arriv-
ing (New York City)
Sports Illus 64:32 (4) Je 30 '86

IMMIGRANTS (cont.)
  Nat Geog 170:17 (2) Jl '86
--Early 20th cent. immigrants to
    U.S.
  Trav/Holiday 164:36-9 (4) Jl
    '85
--Early 20th cent. prejudice
    against Japanese (California)
  Nat Geog 169:518-19 (2) Ap
    '86
--1940 refugees on ship (New
    York)
  Am Heritage 37:24 (2) O '86
--Amerasians
  Life 8:98-103 (c,1) Ag '85
--Ellis Island, New York City,
    New York
  Life 6:44-9 (c,1) Jl '83
  Trav/Holiday 164:34-9 (c,1) Jl
    '85
INCA CIVILIZATION. See also
    MACHU PICCHU
INCA CIVILIZATION--RELICS
--Drinking cup
  Natur Hist 91:86 (4) D '82
INCENSE BURNERS
--8th cent. (Egypt)
  Smithsonian 16:225 (c,4) O '85
--Middle East
  Nat Geog 168:482 (c,4) O '85
--Peru
  Nat Geog 161:288 (c,1) Mr '82
--Ancient Egypt
  Nat Geog 170:328 (painting,c,4)
    S '86
--Thailand
  Nat Geog 162:508 (c,4) O '82
Inch worms. See
    MEASURING WORMS
INDEPENDENCE, MISSOURI
--Truman home and library
  Trav/Holiday 159:6 (4) Mr '83
INDIA
  Nat Geog 165:cov., 696-748
    (map,c,1) Je '84
  Nat Geog 167:460-93, 506-33
    (map,c,1) Ap '85
  Trav/Holiday 165:56-61
    (map,c,1) Je '86
--Benares
  Smithsonian 16:82-93 (c,1) S
    '85
  Nat Geog 169:214-51 (map,c,1)
    F '86
--Deccan Mountains
  Nat Geog 167:488 (c,4) Ap '85
--Golden Temple, Amritsar

  Life 8:163-8 (c,1) Ja '85
--Keoladeo Ghana game preserve
  Trav/Holiday 158:44 (c,2) O '82
--Monsoon season
  Nat Geog 166:712-27 (c,1) D '84
--Mysore City
  Sports Illus 6384 (painting,c,2)
    D 9 '85
--Ranthambhor National Park
  Nat Geog 166:750-1, 764-7 (c,1)
    D '84
--See also
    BOMBAY
    DELHI
    GANGES RIVER
    HINDUISM
    JAIPUR
    KASHMIR
    MONGOL EMPIRE
    NEW DELHI
    TAJ MAHAL
INDIA--ART
  Smithsonian 16:180 (c,4) Je '85
INDIA--COSTUME
  Nat Geog 165:cov., 697-743
    (c,1) Je '84
  Nat Geog 166:712-27 (c,1) D '84
  Natur Hist 94:70 (c,2) F '85
  Nat Geog 167:464-93, 506-33
    (c,1) Ap '85
  Smithsonian 16:82-93 (c,1) S '85
  Trav/Holiday 165:56-61 (c,1) Je
    '86
--1948 servants
  Life 8:8-9 (1) My '85
--Benares
  Nat Geog 169:214-51 (c,1) F '86
--Child workers
  Nat Geog 165:32-3 (c,1) Ja '84
--Indira Ghandi
  Life 7:198-200 (2) D '84
--Hindu pilgrims (Kashmir)
  Natur Hist 92:44-51 (c,1) Jl '83
--Jaipur
  Trav/Holiday 157:50-2 (c,1) Mr
    '82
--Jawaharial Nehru doing headstand
    (1948)
  Life 8:10 (2) My '85
--New Delhi
  Nat Geog 167:506-33 (c,1) Ap
    '85
--Performers
  Smithsonian 16:cov., 44-53 (c,1)
    Je '85
--Saris
  Nat Geog 169:239 (c,1) F '86

INDIANS OF NORTH AMERICA
(cont.)
    INDIAN RESERVATIONS
    INDIAN WARS
    KIOWA
    MANDAN
    NAVAJO
    PUEBLO
    SCALPING
    SEMINOLE
    SIOUX
    SITTING BULL
    TEPEES
    TLINGIT
    TOTEM POLES
    UTE
    ZUNI
INDIANS OF NORTH AMERICA--
    ARCHITECTURE
--Anasazi pueblos (New Mexico)
    Nat Geog 162:555-91 (c,1) N
    '82
INDIANS OF NORTH AMERICA--
    ART
--Pueblo pottery
    Nat Geog 162:cov., 593-605
    (c,1) N '82
INDIANS OF NORTH AMERICA--
    COSTUME
--1830s
    Smithsonian 15:149 (paint-
    ing,c,4) Ja '85
    Am Heritage 36:2 (painting,c,2)
    Ap '85
--Early 20th cent.
    Smithsonian 12:160 (4) F '82
    Smithsonian 15:154-74 (3) Ap
    '84
--Cheslatta Indians (British
    Columbia)
    Nat Geog 170:57 (c,4) Jl '86
--Tigua leader (Texas)
    Trav/Holiday 66:45 (c,2) Jl '86
INDIANS OF NORTH AMERICA--
    HOUSING
--Acoma mud houses, New Mexico
    Life 9:34 (c,4) Jl '86
--See also
    IGLOOS
    TEPEES
INDIANS OF NORTH AMERICA--
    RELICS
--11th cent. rock painting (New
    Mexico)
    Smithsonian 15:143 (c,4) S '84
--Early 20th cent. Kiowa cradle-
    board

Smithsonian 15:136 (c,4) Ag '84
--Anasazi Indians (New Mexico)
    Nat Geog 162:572-3 (c,1) N '82
--Ancient sculpture (Woodland re-
    gion)
    Natur Hist 94:72-5 (c,1) S '85
--Ceremonial mask (Northwest)
    Natur Hist 95:74 (c,4) Jl '86
--Indian shields
    Am Heritage 37:18-25 (c,1) Ag
    '86
--Makah Indian kerfed box
    Natur Hist 95:76 (c,4) Jl '86
INDIANS OF NORTH AMERICA--
    RITES AND FESTIVALS
--Oglala Indians Kettle Dance (1919)
    Natur Hist 95:10, 14-15 (3) F
    '86
INDONESIA
    Natur Hist 93:22-32 (c,2) Mr '84
--Bali
    Trav/Holiday 165:49 (c,2) Ap '86
--Borobudur Temple, Java
    Natur Hist 163:126-42 (c,1) Ja
    '83
--Flood damage
    Nat Geog 166:738-41, 744-5 (c,1)
    D '84
--Java
    Nat Geog 167:752-9 (map,c,1) Je
    '85
--Java (1750)
    Smithsonian 13:134 (painting,c,4)
    Ap '82
--See also
    KRAKATOA VOLCANO
INDONESIA--COSTUME
    Nat Geog 163:132-3 (c,1) Ja '83
    Natur Hist 93:22-32 (c,2) Mr
    '84
    Nat Geog 166:738-47 (c,1) D '84
--19th cent.
    Smithsonian 13:138 (painting,c,4)
    Ap '82
--Malnourished child (East Timor)
    Nat Geog 170:658-61 (c,1) N '86
--Nias
    Trav/Holiday 163:132 (4) Ap '85
INDONESIA--HOUSING
--1883 thatched houses
    Nat Geog 167:754 (drawing,4) Je
    '85
--Transmigration program houses
    Natur Hist 93:24 (c,2) Mr '84
Industries. See
    ALFALFA
    APRICOTS

INGERSOLL, ROBERT
INJURED PEOPLE
--1942 wounded British soldier
(Africa)
--Administering first aid to boxer
in ring
--Atomic bomb victims (Micronesia)
--Bandaged nose (Israel)
--Bandaging foot
--Baseball players
--Basketball players
--Boxer on stretcher

INJURED PEOPLE (cont.)
--Boxer's injured eye
   Ebony 39:27 (4) Mr '84
--Boxers
   Sports Illus 57:59 (c,4) Ag 9
      '82
   Life 8:78 (2) Mr '85
--Bus accident victims (Texas)
   Life 8:58 (2) S '85
--Cambodian guerrillas (Thailand)
   Nat Geog 170:664-5 (c,1) N
      '86
--Dying soldier (Nicaragua)
   Nat Geog 168:806-7 (c,1) D
      '85
--Football players
   Ebony 38:68-70 (4) O '83
   Ebony 39:51 (c,2) Mr '84
   Sports Illus 60:31 (c,4) Mr 12
      '84
   Sports Illus 60:32 (c,4) Ap
      30 '84
   Sports Illus 63:2-3 (c,1) N
      25 '85
   Sports Illus 65:16-20 (c,1) N
      10 '86
--Frostbitten feet
   Nat Geog 170:306 (c,1) S '86
--Hockey players
   Sports Illus 59:61 (c,3) O 10
      '83
   Sports Illus 63:62 (3) Ag 5
      '85
--Ice packs on basketball player's
      knees
   Nat Geog 163:332 (c,4) Mr
      '83
--Korean War soldier on stretcher
      (1950)
   Ebony 41:258 (2) N '85
--Man mauled by polar bear
      (Manitoba)
   Life 7:54 (c,3) F '84
--Man on crutches
   Sports Illus 61:53 (c,4) O 29
      '84
   Sports Illus 63:74 (c,4) D 2
      '85
   Sports Illus 64:93 (c,4) Ap 7
      '86
--Man wounded by grizzly bear
      (Yukon)
   Nat Geog 168:644-5 (c,1) N '85
--Napalm victim (Ethiopia)
   Nat Geog 168:394-5 (c,1) S '85
--Napalm victim (Vietnam)
   Smithsonian 12:122 (4) Ja '82

--Plane crash victims (Japan)
   Life 5:111 (2) Ap '82
--PLO prisoner (Lebanon)
   Life 6:12 (c,4) Ja '83
--Rescuing mountain climber (Kenya)
   Sports Illus 62:77 (c,4) My 27
      '85
--Runner
   Sports Illus 60:54 (c,3) F 8 '84
--Signing leg cast
   Ebony 37:70 (c,4) O '82
--Skiing leg injury
   Sports Illus 58:32-3 (c,3) F 21
      '83
--Sports injuries caused by artificial
      turf
   Sports Illus 63:48-50, 56-7, 62
      (c,2) Ag 12 '85
--Track star
   Sports Illus 61:22-5 (c,3) Ag
      20 '84
--Treating burn victim
   Life 9:243 (3) Fall '86
--Treating hurt knee
   Sports Illus 64:78 (c,4) F 3 '86
--U.S. soldiers in Vietnam (1966)
   Life 9:18-19 (c,1) Fall '86
--Victim of land mine accident
      (Israel)
   Nat Geog 168:7 (c,4) Jl '85
--Victims of bombing (Great Britain)
   Life 7:192-3 (1) D '84
--Victims of Chernobyl nuclear dis-
      aster, U.S.S.R.
   Life 9:cov., 20-6 (c,1) Ag '86
--Victims of exploding mines (Falk-
      lands)
   Life 5:34-5 (c,3) S '82
--Victims of shooting (Illinois)
   Life 5:34 (c,2) Ap '82
--Victims of war (Beirut, Lebanon)
   Life 5:24-6 (c,1) Ag '82
--Volcano victims (Colombia)
   Life 9:12-13, 139 (c,1) Ja '86
--World War I American soldiers
      (France)
   Am Heritage 35:6, 70-1 (1) O
      '84
--World War II American soldier
      (Italy)
   Am Heritage 35:72-3 (1) O '84
--World War II G.I. in cast
   Life 9:146 (2) Fall '86
--See also
      HANDICAPPED PEOPLE
      MEDICINE--PRACTICE
      THERAPY

INKWELLS
--12th-13th cents. (Middle East)
   Smithsonian 14:63 (c,4) Je '83
INNESS, GEORGE
--19th cent. landscapes by him
   Am Heritage 36:32-41 (c,1) Ap
   '85
INNSBRUCK, AUSTRIA
   Trav/Holiday 162:36 (c,4) Ag
   '84
--Cafes
   Trav/Holiday 157:80 (c,2) Ap
   '82
--Street scene
   Nat Geog 167:442 (c,4) Ap '85
INSECTS
--Assassin bugs
   Natur Hist 92:40-7 (c,1) My
   '83
   Smithsonian 15:51 (c,4) My '84
   Nat Wildlife 23:24-5 (c,1) F '85
--Collared peripatus
   Natur Hist 94:cov., 54-61 (c,1)
   S '85
--Hobomok skippers
   Nat Wildlife 22:57 (c,3) O '84
--Inhabiting river
   Smithsonian 14:77 (c,2) My '83
--Leaf-footed bugs
   Natur Hist 93:100-1 (c,1) Ja '84
--Parasitoids
   Natur Hist 93:52-7 (c,1) D '84
--Pephricus paradoxus
   Natur Hist 92:30 (3) My '83
--Pond life
   Smithsonian 13:62-71 (c,1) Jl
   '82
--Pseudoscorpion
   Natur Hist 95:100-1 (c,1) Mr
   '86
--Shield bugs
   Natur Hist 93:100-1 (c,1) Mr
   '84
--Trapped in amber
   Natur Hist 91:26-31 (c,1) Je
   '82
--Treehoppers
   Natur Hist 94:62-9 (c,1) S '85
--Waterstriders
   Natur Hist 95:35 (c,4) Ag '86
--See also
      ANTS
      APHIDS
      BEES
      BEETLES
      BOLL WEEVILS
      BUTTERFLIES

      CATERPILLARS
      COCKROACHES
      COCOONS
      CRICKETS
      DRAGONFLIES
      EGGS
      FLIES
      FRUIT FLIES
      GRASSHOPPERS
      GYPSY MOTHS
      KATYDIDS
      LACEWINGS
      LADYBUGS
      LEAFHOPPERS
      MANTIDS
      MAY FLIES
      MEASURING WORMS
      MITES
      MOSQUITOS
      MOTHS
      NESTS
      PEST CONTROL
      POND LIFE
      SILKWORMS
      TERMITES
      TICKS
      TSETSE FLIES
      WASPS
      WATER BUGS
      YELLOW JACKETS
INSTRUMENTS
--1622 gunsight (Germany)
   Natur Hist 93:51 (2) Ja '84
--Metal detector used to seek
   meteorites
   Nat Geog 170:414 (c,1) S '86
--Surveillance equipment
   Smithsonian 17:38-9 (c,4) Jl '86
--Surveying equipment
   Ebony 39:61 (c,3) Ja '84
--See also
      BINOCULARS
      CLOCKS
      COMPASSES
      MEDICAL INSTRUMENTS
      MUSICAL INSTRUMENTS
      NAVIGATION INSTRUMENTS
      RADAR
      SCALES
      SCIENTIFIC INSTRUMENTS
      TELESCOPES
INTERIOR, DEPARTMENT OF
--Headquarters building, Washing-
   ton, D.C.
   Sports Illus 59:102-3 (c,2) O 3
   '83

Inuits. See
    ESKIMOS
INVENTIONS
--14th cent. fanciful hand-
    washing contraption (Egypt)
    Smithsonian 14:69 (drawing,c,2)
    Je '83
--17th-18th cents.
    Natur Hist 93:48-57 (c,1) Ja
    '84
--1785 automatic grist mill
    Am Heritage 36:108 (engrav-
    ing,4) Ag '85
--19th cent. patent models
    Smithsonian 14:120-6 (c,2) F
    '84
--Energy machine (Mississippi)
    Life 9:19 (c,4) S '86
--Unusual items
    Sports Illus 56:52-8 (c,2) My
    10 '82
--See also
    INVENTORS
    PATENTS
Inventors. See
    BELL, ALEXANDER GRAHAM
    CURTISS, GLENN
    EDISON, THOMAS ALVA
    FIELD, CYRUS WEST
    FORD, HENRY
    FRANKLIN, BENJAMIN
    FULTON, ROBERT
    GODDARD, ROBERT
    MARCONI, GUGLIELMO
    MORSE, SAMUEL F. B.
    STEINMETZ, CHARLES
    TESLA, NIKOLA
    VON BRAUN, WERNHER
    WESTINGHOUSE, GEORGE
    WHITNEY, ELI
    WRIGHT, WILBUR & ORVILLE
INVERNESS, SCOTLAND
--1877 castle
    Trav/Holiday 159:42-3 (2) Ja
    '83
IOWA
--Farms
    Smithsonian 15:34-47 (1) Ag '84
--Reinbeck
    Smithsonian 15:45 (4) Ag '84
--See also
    DES MOINES
IRAN
    Nat Geog 168:108-35 (map,c,1)
    Jl '85
--Qum
    Life 8:94-100 (c,1) S '85

--State jewels
    Nat Geog 168:210-11 (c,1) Ag
    '85
--See also
    MESHED
    TEHRAN
IRAN--COSTUME
    Nat Geog 168:108-35 (c,1) Jl '85
--Ayatollah Khomeini
    Nat Geog 168:112, 118 (paint-
    ing,c,1) Jl '85
    Life 8:98 (c,4) S '85
--Military recruits
    Life 8:78-9 (1) My '85
--Shi'ite Moslems
    Life 8:94-100 (c,1) S '85
--Soldiers
    Life 6:130-1 (c,1) Jl '83
--Wounded soldiers
    Nat Geog 170:656 (c,1) N '86
IRAN--HISTORY
--History of Middle Eastern As-
    sassin sect
    Smithsonian 17:145-62 (c,3) O
    '86
IRAN--POLITICS AND GOVERN-
    MENT
--1985 view of U.S. Embassy (Teh-
    ran)
    Nat Geog 168:124-5 (c,1) Jl '85
--Anti USA poster
    Nat Geog 167:160 (c,1) F '85
--Soldiers marching on painted
    U.S. flag
    Life 6:130-1 (c,1) Jl '83
IRAN, ANCIENT--SCULPTURE
--Bronze goat
    Smithsonian 13:86 (c,4) F '83
IRAQ. See also
    BAGHDAD
    MESOPOTAMIA
    TIGRIS RIVER
IRAQ--COSTUME
    Nat Geog 167:80-109 (c,1) Ja
    '85
--Dead soldiers
    Life 6:14-15 (c,1) Ja '83
IRAQ--HISTORY
--1258 siege of Baghdad by Genghis
    Khan's grandson
    Smithsonian 17:162 (painting,c,3)
    O '86
IRELAND
--Blarney Castle, Cork
    Trav/Holiday 164:64 (c,3) S '85
--Donegal
    Trav/Holiday 157:64 (c,4) My '82

IRELAND (cont.)
--Golf courses
    Sports Illus 60:54-69 (c,1) Je
        '84
--See also
        CORK
        DUBLIN
        LIFFEY RIVER
        NORTHERN IRELAND
IRELAND--COSTUME
--Dublin
    Trav/Holiday 163:64-7, 83 (c,2)
        F '85
IRELAND--HISTORY
--19th cent. U.S. cartoon about
        potato famine
    Nat Geog 161:689 (drawing,4)
        My '82
IRELAND--HOUSING
--Thatching roof (Ardara)
    Trav/Holiday 157:64 (c,4) My
        '82
IRISES
    Nat Wildlife 21:22 (c,4) F '83
    Nat Wildlife 22:57 (c,3) O '84
    Life 8:54-5 (c,1) Je '85
--X-ray photo
    Smithsonian 17:91 (4) O '86
IRON MINES
--Australia
    Nat Geog 168:174-5 (c,1) Ag
        '85
--Ore Mountain, Austria
    Nat Geog 167:428-9 (c,1) Ap
        '85
IRONING
--Amish people (Pennsylvania)
    Nat Geog 165:495 (c,3) Ap '84
--In hotel room
    Sports Illus 59:60 (c,4) N 28 '83
--Indiana
    Life 8:96 (4) F '85
--Steaming wrinkles
    Sports Illus 60:88 (c,4) Ap
        16 '84
IRRAWADDY RIVER, BURMA
    Smithsonian 15:98-111 (c,1)
        My '84
IRRIGATION
--1910 lawn sprinkler
    Am Heritage 35:21 (4) F '84
--Apple orchard (Washington)
    Smithsonian 17:122 (c,1) S '86
--Center-pivot sprinklers (Texas)
    Nat Geog 165:214-15 (c,1) F
        '84
--Drip irrigation (Israel)

    Nat Geog 168:19 (c,4) Jl '85
--Dry irrigation ditch (Arizona)
    Smithsonian 13:57 (c,3) Mr '83
--Sprinklers at stadium (Kansas
        City, Missouri)
    Sports Illus 56:49 (c,4) My 17
        '82
--Sprinklers on farm (Australia)
    Nat Geog 168:270-1 (c,1) Ag '85
--Sudan
    Nat Geog 167:580-1 (c,1) My '85
IRVING, WASHINGTON
    Smithsonian 14:93-4, 102 (paint-
        ing,c,3) Ag '83
--Home (Irvington, New York)
    Smithsonian 14:92-5 (c,1) Ag '83
--Illustrations from his tales
    Smithsonian 14:96-8 (painting,c,2)
        Ag '83
Islam. See
        MOSLEMS
ISLANDS
--Bahamas
    Nat Geog 162:368-9 (c,1) S '82
    Nat Geog 170:570-1, 590-1, 595
        (c,1) N '86
--Bikini
    Nat Geog 169:830-1 (c,1) Je '86
--Gorée, Senegal
    Nat Geog 168:237 (c,4) Ag '85
--Grand Cayman Island
    Nat Geog 167:813 (c,3) Je '85
--Kili, Micronesia
    Nat Geog 169:828 (c,4) Je '86
--Norfolk Island, Australia
    Nat Geog 164:530 (c,3) O '83
--Palau
    Nat Geog 161:267-9 (c,1) F '82
--Ponape, Micronesia
    Natur Hist 92:52-3 (c,1) D '83
--Robinson Crusoe Island, Chile
    Trav/Holiday 165:6 (c,4) F '86
--Rock Islands, Palau
    Smithsonian 17:46-7 (c,3) S '86
    Nat Geog 170:462-3 (c,1) O '86
--Whale-Skate, Hawaii
    Nat Wildlife 21:4-5 (c,1) F '83
ISLE ROYAL NATIONAL PARK,
        MICHIGAN
    Nat Geog 167:534-49 (c,1) Ap
        '85
ISRAEL
    Nat Geog 168:2-39 (map,c,1)
        Jl '85
--Elat
    Nat Geog 168:16-17 (c,2) Jl '85
--Masada

ISRAEL (cont.)
 Nat Geog 168:22-3 (c,1) Jl '85
--Shrine of Abraham (Hebron)
 Nat Geog 165:266-7 (c,1) F
 '84
--Silwan
 Smithsonian 13:79 (c,3) Jl '82
--Sinai Peninsula
 Nat Geog 161:420-61 (map,c,1)
 Ap '82
--West Bank town of Maaleh
 Adumim
 Nat Geog 165:264-5 (c,1) F
 '84
--See also
 DEAD SEA
 JERUSALEM
 KIBBUTZIM
 TEL AVIV
ISRAEL--COSTUME
 Nat Geog 163:478-515 (c,1) Ap
 '83
 Life 6:74-82 (c,1) N '83
 Life 7:66-72 (c,1) D '84
 Nat Geog 168:2-39 (c,1) Jl '85
--Hasidim
 Nat Geog 168:28-31 (c,1) Jl
 '85
--Military
 Life 5:26, 31 (1) Je '82
 Life 5:38-9 (1) S '82
--Palestinians
 Life 5:26-34 (1) Je '82
 Life 6:74-82 (c,2) N '83
--Sinai Peninsula
 Nat Geog 161:445-60 (c,1) Ap
 '82
--Women's dress requirements in
 religious district
 Nat Geog 168:30 (c,4) Jl '85
ISRAEL--HISTORY
--Historical maps of Jerusalem
 Nat Geog 163:486-7 (c,1) Ap
 '83
--See also
 MEIR, GOLDA
ISRAEL--MAPS
--Gaza excavation sites
 Nat Geog 162:738-69 (c,1) D
 '82
--Jerusalem
 Nat Geog 163:487, 499 (c,1)
 Ap '83
--Landsat satellite map
 Nat Geog 165:244 (c,1) F '84
--Sinai Peninsula (1967-1982)
 Nat Geog 161:428-9 (c,1) Ap '82

ISRAEL--POLITICS AND GOVERN-
 MENT
--Palestinian resistance activities
 Life 5:26-34 (1) Je '82
--Returning terrorists to Lebanon
 Life 8:44-5 (1) Jl '85
--Victims of PLO terrorists
 Life 7:80-8 (c,1) Jl '84
ISRAEL, ANCIENT
--Rendering of 10th cent. B.C.
 Jerusalem
 Smithsonian 13:80-2 (c,1) Jl '82
ISTANBUL, TURKEY
 Nat Geog 164:719-26 (c,1) D '83
--Bosporus bridge
 Nat Geog 167:170-1 (c,1) F '85
 Smithsonian 17:130-1 (c,3) N
 '86
--Byzantine Constantinople
 Nat Geog 164:719-21 (map,c,1)
 D '83
--Suleymaniye mosque
 Trav/Holiday 162:12 (c,3) S '84
--Topkapi Palace Museum
 Smithsonian 16:112-23 (c,1) F
 '86
--View from water at twilight
 Nat Geog 162:736-7 (c,1) D '82
--See also
 ST. SOPHIA CATHEDRAL
ITALIAN AMERICANS
--Brooklyn, New York
 Nat Geog 163:608-11 (c,1) My
 '83
ITALY
 Nat Geog 165:184-209 (map,c,1)
 F '84
--Apulia olive trees
 Smithsonian 15:98-9 (c,1) Mr '85
--Bormio
 Sports Illus 62:16-17 (c,1) F 18
 '85
--Carrara
 Nat Geog 162:42-59 (c,1) Jl '82
--Cremona street scene
 Smithsonian 14:90 (c,2) O '83
 Sports Illus 61:54 (c,2) N 12 '84
--Ercolano
 Nat Geog 162:689 (c,1) D '82
 Nat Geog 165:582-5 (c,1) My '84
--Etruscan necropolis (Cerveteri)
 Smithsonian 15:56 (c,4) F '85
--Formia
 Sports Illus 58:71 (c,3) My 23
 '83
--Gardone Riviera mansion
 Smithsonian 14:52-61 (c,1) Jl '83

ITALY (cont.)
--Mafia victims (Sicily)
  Life 6:92-5 (1) F '83
--Orvieto
  Smithsonian 14:184-91 (c,1) N
  '83
--Pozzuoli
  Nat Geog 165:614-25 (c,1) My '84
--Prato
  Sports Illus 57:43 (c,4) Ag 16
  '82
--Rimini beach
  Nat Geog 7:28-9 (c,1) D '82
--Stromboli volcano
  Nat Geog 162:694-5 (c,1) D
  '82
--Urbino (aerial view)
  Nat Geog 165:204 (c,1) F '84
--World War II German bunker
  (Gela, Sicily)
  Life 8:36 (c,3) Mr '85
--See also
    ALPS
    BOLOGNA
    DOLOMITE MOUNTAINS
    ELBA
    FLORENCE
    MATTERHORN
    MILAN
    MOUNT ETNA
    NAPLES
    PISA
    POMPEII
    ROMAN EMPIRE
    ROME
    SARDINIA
    SICILY
    STROMBOLI
    TURIN
    VENICE
    VESUVIUS
ITALY--ART
--Renaissance art works
  Smithsonian 13:cov., 59-71
  (c,1) N '82
ITALY--COSTUME
  Nat Geog 165:184-209 (c,1) F
  '84
--17th cent.
  Smithsonian 13:94 (paint-
  ing,c,4) S '82
--Bride and groom
  Nat Geog 165:612-13 (c,1) My
  '84
--Pozzuoli
  Nat Geog 165:614-25 (c,1) My
  '84

--Sardinia
  Natur Hist 92:cov., 54-63 (c,1)
  Ja '83
--Sicily
  Life 6:92-5 (1) F '83
ITALY--HISTORY
--Cosimo I (Florence)
  Smithsonian 13:61 (painting,c,4)
  N '82
--Napoleon stealing bronze Venetian
  horses (1797)
  Smithsonian 13:103 (3) S '82
--Punishing Nazi collaborator (1945)
  Life 8:81 (4) Spring '85
--See also
    D'ANNUNZIO, GABRIELE
    GARIBALDI, GIUSEPPE
    HERCULANEUM
    MEDICI
    MUSSOLINI, BENITO
    NERO
    ROMAN EMPIRE
ITALY--MAPS
--Bay of Naples
  Nat Geog 162:721 (c,4) D '82
ITALY--SOCIAL LIFE AND CUSTOMS
--Chocolate Easter eggs (Italy)
  Life 7:122-6 (c,1) Ap '84
ITALY, ANCIENT--RELICS
--Etruscan works
  Smithsonian 15:cov., 48-57 (c,1)
  F '85
IVAN IV, THE TERRIBLE (U.S.S.R.)
--Crown
  Smithsonian 14:135 (c,4) O '83
IVES, CHARLES
  Life 9:267 (4) Fall '86
IVORY
--19th cent. Eskimo carvings
  (Alaska)
  Nat Geog 163:198-205 (c,2) F '83
--Carved puzzle balls (China)
  Natur Hist 93:72 (c,2) Ap '84
--Walrus tusks
  Nat Geog 165:827 (2) Je '84
IVORY COAST
  Nat Geog 162:94-125 (map,c,1)
  Jl '82
--Cacao bean farming
  Nat Geog 166:664-7 (c,1) N '84
--See also
    ABIDJAN
IVORY COAST--COSTUME
  Nat Geog 162:94-125 (c,1) Jl
  '82

JESUS CHRIST (cont.)
    Nat Geog 164:708 (c,1) D '83
--Byzantine mosaics (Italy)
    Life 7:181-8 (c,1) D '84
--Depicted in Leonardo's "Last
    Supper"
    Nat Geog 164:cov., 664-85
        (painting,c,1) N '83
--Depicted in Renaissance paint-
    ings (Italy)
    Smithsonian 13:68-70 (c,4) N
        '82
--Depictions based on Shroud of
    Turin image
    Life 7:36-9 (c,1) F '84
--Handing key to heaven to St.
    Peter (1482 fresco)
    Smithsonian 15:42 (c,3) F '85
--Jeweled altarpiece (St. Mark's,
    Venice, Italy)
    Nat Geog 164:752-3 (c,1) D
        '83
--Michelangelo's "Pietà"
    Nat Geog 168:768-9 (c,1) D
        '85
--Painting by Titian
    Life 7:20 (painting,c,4) Ap '84
--Shroud of Turin
    Smithsonian 14:157 (c,4) S '83
    Life 7:37 (c,3) F '84
--Soldiers casting lots for his
    clothes (15th cent. paint-
    ing)
    Smithsonian 16:54 (c,3) Ap '85
--Statue of Christ blindfolded
    (Nicaragua)
    Nat Geog 168:783 (c,1) D '85
--Virgin and Child icon (Yugo-
    slavia)
    Nat Geog 164:cov. (c,1) D
        '83
--Walking on water
    Smithsonian 14:145 (paint-
    ing,c,4) S '83
JEWELRY
--13th cent. B.C. (Egypt)
    Nat Geog 162:750-1 (c,1) D
        '82
--4th cent. B.C. gold bracelets
    (Colchis)
    Nat Geog 168:419 (c,4) S '85
--1st cent. A.D. (Italy)
    Nat Geog 165:560-3 (c,1) My
        '84
--1830 brooch of Medusa
    Smithsonian 12:122 (c,4) Mr
        '82

--African people
    Nat Geog 166:600-33 (c,1) N '84
--Ancient Bactrian gold jewelry
    Natur Hist 94:70 (c,3) D '85
--Beaded Indian earrings (Florida)
    Trav/Holiday 165:46 (c,4) Ja '86
--Bedouin (Saudi Arabia)
    Smithsonian 14:148 (c,4) Ap '83
--Bracelets (Thailand)
    Natur Hist 94:78 (c,4) F '85
--British royal family
    Life 8:44-8 (c,2) N '85
--Carving jade (Hong Kong)
    Smithsonian 17:33 (c,4) Ag '86
--Church treasures (Colombia)
    Smithsonian 15:138-47 (c,1) Mr
        '85
--Earrings (Mali)
    Nat Geog 162:406-7 (c,3) S '82
--European royal jewels
    Smithsonian 14:130-41 (c,1) O
        '83
--Fabergé eggs
    Smithsonian 14:cov., 46-53 (c,1)
        Ap '83
--Jade pieces
    Smithsonian 17:36-7 (c,4) Ag
        '86
--Jeweler wearing magnifier
    Ebony 38:80 (4) Je '83
--NBA championshp ring
    Sports Illus 60:62-3 (c,1) F 8
        '84
--Ndebele neck rings (South Africa)
    Nat Geog 169:cov., 261, 274-5
        (c,1) F '86
--Necklaces
    Life 7:56-8 (c,1) Ja '84
--Nose pendant (Egypt)
    Nat Geog 161:204 (c,2) F '82
--Nose rings (Mali)
    Nat Geog 162:406-7 (c,3) S '82
--Ostrich egg beads (Egypt)
    Nat Geog 161:219 (c,4) F '82
--Pearl jewelry
    Smithsonian 15:48-9 (c,3) Ja '85
    Nat Geog 168:209-11, 216-22
        (c,1) Ag '85
--Platinum earrings
    Nat Geog 164:697 (c,3) N '83
--Ring belonging to Sam Houston
    Nat Geog 169:311 (c,4) Mr '86
--School ring
    Sports Illus 63:20 (c,4) Jl 1 '85
--Silver jewelry (Miao people;
    China)
    Nat Geog 165:282-3, 324-5 (c,1)

JORDAN (cont.)
--See also
    AMMAN
    PETRA
JORDAN--COSTUME
    Nat Geog 165:237-67 (c,1) F
    '84
--Royalty
    Nat Geog 165:252-3 (c,1) F '84
JOSEPHINE
    Nat Geog 161:144-6, 169 (paint-
    ing,c,1) F '82
JOURNALISTS
--1863 Civil War reporters
    Am Heritage 36:28-9 (2) Je
    '85
--1910 fantasy of press at sign-
    ing of Declaration of Inde-
    pendence
    Am Heritage 33:2 (drawing,1)
    O '82
--1983 Grenada invasion
    Am Heritage 36:33 (3) Je '85
--See also
    BROUN, HEYWOOD
    GREELEY, HORACE
    HEARST, WILLIAM RAN-
        DOLPH
    LIPPMANN, WALTER
    NEWSPAPER INDUSTRY
    PULITZER, JOSEPH
    PYLE, ERNIE
    SPORTS ANNOUNCERS
    SWOPE, HERBERT BAYARD
    TELEVISION NEWSCASTERS
    THOMPSON, DOROTHY
JOYCE, JAMES
    Smithsonian 14:117 (4) Ag '83
JUAN FERNANDEZ ARCHIPELAGO,
    CHILE
--Robinson Crusoe Island
    Trav/Holiday 165:6 (c,4) F '86
JUDAISM
--Studying at yeshiva (Jeru-
    salem, Israel)
    Nat Geog 163:488 (c,4) Ap '83
JUDAISM--COSTUME
--Hasidim (Brooklyn, New York)
    Nat Geog 163:584-5 (c,1) My
    '83
    Life 7:117-23 (c,1) Je '84
--Hasidim (Israel)
    Nat Geog 168:28-31 (c,1) Jl '85
--Hasidim (New York)
    Life 8:64-5 (1) F '85
--Israel
    Nat Geog 163:482-513 (c,1)

Ap '83
--Modern Poland
    Nat Geog 170:362-89 (c,1) S '86
--Ultra-Orthodox sect (Israel)
    Nat Geog 163:484-5, 488 (c,1)
    Ap '83
--Yemeni bride (Israel)
    Nat Geog 168:2 (c,4) Jl '85
JUDAISM--HISTORY
--1938 Jewish child (Warsaw,
    Poland)
    Smithsonian 14:130 (4) Ja '84
--1940 rescue of intellectuals from
    Vichy France
    Am Heritage 34:82-92 (1) Je '83
--1940s deportations from Prague,
    Czechoslovakia
    Life 7:84, 89 (3) N '84
--1940s Zyklon gas cannister
    Am Heritage 35:94 (c,2) Ag '84
--1945 death list from Mauthausen
    concentration camp
    Am Heritage 35:94 (c,2) Ag '84
--Chagall works of early 20th cent.
    Jewish life (U.S.S.R.)
    Smithsonian 16:68-71 (paint-
    ing,c,1) My '85
--Jewish Museum, Prague, Czecho-
    slovakia
    Life 7:84-90 (c,1) N '84
--See also
    CONCENTRATION CAMPS
    FRANK, ANNE
    NAZISM
JUDAISM--RELICS
--Shofars
    Life 7:86 (c,4) N '84
JUDAISM--RITES AND FESTIVALS
--Hasidic marriage rites (New York)
    Life 7:117-23 (c,1) Je '84
--Boy studying Hebrew (Poland)
    Nat Geog 170:364-5 (c,1) S '86
--Passover (Poland)
    Nat Geog 170:366-9 (c,1) S '86
--Simchas Torah festival (Israel)
    Nat Geog 168:9 (c,3) Jl '85
--Yemeni wedding celebration
    (Israel)
    Nat Geog 163:512-13 (c,1) Ap '83
JUDAISM--SHRINES AND SYMBOLS
--Jewish cemeteries (Poland)
    Nat Geog 170:370-1, 388-9 (c,1)
    S '86
--Jewish cemetery (Morocco)
    Nat Geog 169:352 (c,4) Mr '86
--Matzoh (Poland)
    Nat Geog 170:366-7 (c,1) S '86

JUDAISM--SHRINES AND SYM-
BOLS (cont.)
--Tomb of Abraham, Hebron,
Israel
Nat Geog 165:266-7 (c,1) F
'84
--See also
JERUSALEM
WAILING WALL
JUDGES
Ebony 38:48 (4) N '82
Sports Illus 59:34 (draw-
ing,c,4) Ag 15 '83
Ebony 39:90 (4) F '84
Ebony 39:136 (3) Ag '84
Ebony 41:101-2 (c,2) D '85
Ebony 41:37-8 (c,2) F '86
--Bermuda
Ebony 37:42 (c,4) S '82
--Gambia
Nat Geog 168:225 (c,4) Ag '85
--Great Britain
Nat Geog 170:735, 749 (c,3)
D '86
--Texas
Life 5:38-9 (1) O '82
--See also
BEAN, JUDGE ROY
SUPREME COURT JUSTICES
JUDO
Sports Illus 61:424-5 (c,3) Jl
18 '84
Sports Illus 61:72 (c,4) D 24
'84
Sports Illus 63:55-6 (c,4) N 11
'85
Sports Illus 64:224 (c,4) F 10
'86
Sports Illus 64:58-69 (c,1) Mr
24 '86
--Training Swiss guards (Vatican
City)
Nat Geog 168:740 (c,3) D '85
JUGGLERS
Smithsonian 15:110-18 (c,1) N
'84
Sports Illus 65:47-8 (c,2) Ag
18 '86
--15th cent. painting
Smithsonian 12:32 (c,4) F '82
JUKEBOXES
Trav/Holiday 163:76 (c,4) Ap
'85
Sports Illus 63:4, 48 (c,2) N
20 '85
Sports Illus 64:62 (c,3) My 12
'86

JUMPING
Sports Illus 56:20 (c,2) Mr 1
'82
Sports Illus 56:27 (c,4) Mr 8
'82
Life 5:70-1 (c,1) S '82
Sports Illus 58:32-3 (c,1) Je 27
'83
Sports Illus 59:20-1 (c,1) Ag
22 '83
Ebony 38:139, 142 (c,1) S '83
Sports Illus 60:18-21 (c,1) F 6
'84
Sports Illus 60:58, 60 (c,4) Mr
19 '84
Sports Illus 60:27 (c,4) Je 25
'84
Sports Illus 61:25 (c,2) Jl 2 '84
Sports Illus 62:61 (c,4) Mr 18
'85
Sports Illus 62:18-21 (c,1) My
27 '85
Sports Illus 65:13 (c,2) Jl 21 '86
Sports Illus 65:20 (c,2) Ag 11
'86
Ebony 41:77-8 (c,2) O '86
--1904 Olympics (St. Louis)
Life 7:24-5 (1) Summer '84
--1960 Olympics (Rome)
Ebony 39:144 (4) Je '84
--1984 Olympics (Los Angeles)
Sports Illus 61:26-7 (c,2) Ag 20
'84
--China
Life 6:60 (c,2) D '83
--NCAA Championships
Sports Illus 60:2-3 (c,1) Je 11
'84
--Triple jump
Sports Illus 56:62 (c,4) My 17
'82
--See also
HIGH JUMPING
ROPE JUMPING
Jumping rope. See
ROPE JUMPING
JUNEAU, ALASKA
Nat Geog 162:292-3 (c,1) S '82
Nat Geog 165:62-3 (c,1) Ja '84
Trav/Holiday 163:50-3 (c,1) F
'85
--Gold Creek Avalanche (1972)
Nat Geog 162:292-3 (c,1) S '82
--Harbor
Trav/Holiday 157:48 (c,4) My '82
JUNG, CARL GUSTAV
Smithsonian 13:186 (4) Mr '83

JUNG, CARL GUSTAV (cont.)
  Am Heritage 35:15 (4) Ag '84
Jungles. See
    RAIN FORESTS
JUNKS
--China
    Nat Geog 162:36-7 (c,1) Jl '82
    Smithsonian 15:80 (c,2) D '84
--Singapore
    Trav/Holiday 157:37 (4) Ap
      '82
JUNKYARDS
    Nat Geog 163:424-54 (c,1) Ap
      '83
--Alaska
    Natur Hist 92:44-5 (c,1) Ag
      '83
--Automobiles (California)
    Smithsonian 15:cov., 52-63 (c,1)
      Mr '85
--Automobiles (Michigan)
    Life 5:38-9 (c,1) Ag '82
--Automobiles (Montana)
    Life 6:106-7 (c,1) Jl '83
--Hazardous waste sites
    Nat Geog 167:cov., 318-51
      (c,1) Mr '85
--Junkyard scavengers (Philip-
    pines)
    Life 9:50 (c,4) Je '86
--Landfill (Nebraska)
    Nat Geog 166:383 (c,1) S '84
--Marshall Islands
    Nat Geog 170:474-5 (c,1) O '86
--Tire junkyard on fire (Virginia)
    Life 7:86-7 (c,1) Mr '84
JUPITER (PLANET)
    Natur Hist 93:88-9 (paint-
      ing,c,4) Mr '84
    Nat Geog 167:34-9 (c,1) Ja '85
--Moon Io
    Nat Geog 167:38-9 (c,1) Ja '85
--Rings
    Natur Hist 91:64 (3) Ag '82
JUSTICE, ADMINISTRATION OF
--1900 trial (Texas)
    Am Heritage 37:57 (4) F '86
--Courtroom trial scenes (Florida)
    Life 6:40-3 (1) O '83
--Examination of witness at trial
    Am Heritage 36:36-7 (draw-
      ing,c,1) Je '85
--Martin Luther's defense at Diet
    of Worms (1521)
    Nat Geog 164:420-1 (paint-
      ing,c,1) O '83
--Trial

Sports Illus 65:22-7 (drawing,c,2)
      Jl 7 '86
--Trial (China)
    Nat Geog 168:300-1 (c,1) S '85
--Trial (Iran)
    Nat Geog 168:130 (c,4) Jl '85
--See also
      CAPITAL PUNISHMENT
      COURTHOUSES
      COURTROOMS
      CRIME AND CRIMINALS
      JUDGES
      POLICE WORK
      PRISONS
      PUNISHMENT
      SUPREME COURT JUSTICES
JUSTINIAN THE GREAT
    Nat Geog 164:715-18 (mosaic,c,1)
      D '83

-K-

KABUL, AFGHANISTAN
    Nat Geog 167:494-505 (map,c,1)
      Ap '85
KALAHARI DESERT, BOTSWANA
    Life 7:128-46 (c,1) N '84
    Smithsonian 17:54-65 (c,1) Ap
      '86
KALAUPAPA NATIONAL PARK,
    HAWAII
    Trav/Holiday 163:80-1 (c,1) Mr
      '85
KALEIDOSCOPES
    Smithsonian 13:98-108 (c,1) N
      '82
Kampuchea. See
    CAMBODIA
KANDINSKY, VASILY
    Smithsonian 14:85 (4) Ja '84
--"Landscape with Red Spots No. 2"
    (1913)
    Smithsonian 17:64 (painting,c,4)
      Jl '86
--Paintings by him
    Smithsonian 14:84-93 (c,1) Ja '84
--"Yellow, Red, Blue"
    Smithsonian 14:17 (painting,c,4)
      Mr '84
KANGAROOS
    Trav/Holiday 160:47 (drawing,4)
      O '83
    Life 6:180 (2) D '83
    Nat Geog 165:173 (c,4) F '84
    Natur Hist 93:cov. (c,1) Mr '84
    Life 7:134 (2) O '84

KANGAROOS (cont.)
    Nat Geog 168:254 (c,4) Ag '85
    Nat Geog 169:36-7 (c,1) Ja
        '86
    Sports Illus 64:83 (c,4) Je 2
        '86
KANSAS
    Nat Geog 168:352-83 (map,c,1)
        S '85
--Coffeyville
    Sports Illus 61:196-7 (c,2) S
        5 '84
--Lawrence (1860s)
    Nat Geog 170:153 (3) Ag '86
--St. Marys ranch
    Sports Illus 65:76-7 (c,3) O
        6 '86
--U.S. geographic center (Leb-
        anon)
    Trav/Holiday 159:40 (4) My
        '83
--See also
    WICHITA
KANSAS CITY, MISSOURI
    Trav/Holiday 161:58-9 (c,1)
        Je '84
--Office buildings
    Am Heritage 34:71 (c,3) D '82
--Westport Landing (mid-19th
        cent.)
    Nat Geog 170:152-3 (draw-
        ing,c,1) Ag '86
Karakoram Range. See
    HIMALAYAN MOUNTAINS,
        PAKISTAN
KARATE
    Ebony 37:55 (4) Ja '82
    Sports Illus 57:102 (c,4) O 4
        '82
    Sports Illus 57:31 (c,4) D 20
        '82
    Ebony 38:149, 152 (2) Mr '83
    Ebony 38:38 (4) My '83
    Ebony 39:76 (c,4) Je '84
    Sports Illus 63:60 (c,4) S 30
        '85
    Ebony 41:92 (c,4) My '86
--Children
    Sports Illus 63:2-3 (c,1) N 11
        '85
--Japan
    Ebony 37:52 (4) S '82
--National Championships 1985
        (Florida)
    Sports Illus 63:2-3, 72-3 (c,1)
        N 11 '85

KARATE--PROFESSIONAL
    Sports Illus 58:36-9, 78-9 (c,2)
        Ja 24 '83
KASHMIR, INDIA/PAKISTAN
    Trav/Holiday 166:56-61, 72 (c,1)
        N '86
--Amarnath Hindu shrine
    Natur Hist 92:44-51 (c,1) Jl '83
--Dal Lake
    Nat Geog 167:478-9 (c,1) Ap '85
    Trav/Holiday 166:56-7 (c,1) N
        '86
KASSEL, WEST GERMANY
--1842
    Smithsonian 17:119 (drawing,c,2)
        My '86
KATMAI NATIONAL PARK, ALASKA
    Trav/Holiday 159:57-8 (c,2) Ap
        '83
KATYDIDS
    Life 5:46 (c,4) S '82
    Nat Geog 163:58 (c,4) Ja '83
    Natur Hist 92:71-5 (c,1) O '83
--Attacked by tarantula
    Nat Geog 163:56-7 (c,1) Ja '83
KAYAKING
    Sports Illus 60:92 (drawing,c,4)
        Mr 19 '84
--Aerial view
    Smithsonian 17:180 (4) S '86
--Greenland
    Sports Illus 57:56-67 (c,1) Ag
        16 '82
    Nat Geog 165:524-5, 532-4 (c,1)
        Ap '84
--Iceland
    Nat Geog 166:308-21 (c,1) S '84
--Idaho
    Nat Wildlife 22:46 (c,3) Je '84
--Massachusetts
    Nat Wildlife 24:66 (c,4) D '85
--Rapids (Bhutan)
    Life 5:80-2 (c,1) N '82
--Snake River, Northwest
    Trav/Holiday 164:61 (c,4) S '85
KAYAKS
--19th cent. carved ivory model
        kayak (Alaska)
    Nat Geog 163:202 (c,4) F '83
--Construction (Greenland)
    Nat Geog 165:528-9 (c,1) Ap '84
KEATON, BUSTER
    Smithsonian 15:120 (4) Jl '84
    Life 9:117 (4) Fall '86
KELLER, HELEN
--Depicted on postage stamp

KELLER, HELEN (cont.)
Am Heritage 34:59 (c,4) D '82
KELVIN, LORD
Natur Hist 93:28 (4) F '84
KENNAN, GEORGE F.
Am Heritage 37:65 (4) Ap '86
KENNEDY, JOHN FITZGERALD
Nat Geog 162:274 (c,3) Ag '82
Am Heritage 34:51 (4) F '83
Am Heritage 34:cov., 12-26
(c,1) Je '83
Life 6;cov., 3, 23-71 (c,1)
N '83
Am Heritage 35:50, 58-9
(painting,c,2) D '83
Ebony 39:98 (4) S '84
Smithsonian 15:68 (4) O '84
Ebony 41:286, 294 (4) N '85
Am Heritage 37:63 (1) D '85
Nat Wildlife 24:50 (4) Ap '86
Sports Illus 64:122 (4) My 19
'86
Life 9:42 (4) S '86
Life 9:211, 218-19 (c,2) Fall
'86
--1953 marriage to Jackie (Rhode
Island)
Life 6:34 (2) N '83
Life 9:104 (2) Je '86
--1963 assassination
Life 6:cov., 48-71 (c,1) N '83
Life 9:340-1 (c,1) Fall '86
--1963 funeral
Ebony 41:299 (4) N '85
--Caroline Kennedy's wedding
(Massachusetts)
Life 9:cov., 38-44 (c,1) S '86
Life 9:26-7 (c,1) Fall '86
--Family
Am Heritage 35:52-5 (paint-
ing,c,2) D '83
--Grave (Arlington, Virginia)
Am Heritage 34:24-5 (3) Je '83
--Jacqueline Kennedy Onassis
Life 9:110 (c,4) Jl '86
Life 9:69, 218-19 (c,2) Fall '86
--Postage stamp depicting him
Am Heritage 34:59 (c,4) D '82
--Scenes from Caroline Kennedy's
life
Life 9:cov., 13, 38-44 (c,1)
S '86
KENNEDY, JOSEPH P.
--Home (Hyannis Port, Massachu-
setts)
Am Heritage 34:17 (4) Je '83
--Home (Palm Beach, Florida)

Am Heritage 34:19 (4) Je '83
KENNEDY, ROBERT
Am Heritage 34:23-5 (3) Je '83
Am Heritage 35:57 (painting,c,4)
D '83
Ebony 39:102 (4) Ag '84
--1968 assassination
Life 9:255 (3) Fall '86
KENTUCKY
Trav/Holiday 162:58-61 (c,2)
Ag '84
--Daniel Boone's wilderness road
Nat Geog 168:826-7 (c,2) D '85
--Boonesborough State Park
Trav/Holiday 162:60 (c,4) Ag '84
--Bourbon County
Trav/Holiday 165:58-61 (c,1) Ja
'86
--Coal mining area
Nat Geog 163:800-19 (map,c,1)
Je '83
--Hatfield clan (1880s)
Am Heritage 33:107 (4) Ag '82
--Heartland region
Nat Geog 161:522-46 (map,c,1)
Ap '82
--Pikeville
Nat Geog 163:794-5 (c,1) Je '83
--Pineville
Sports Illus 61:88-102 (paint-
ing,c,1) N 19 '84
--Rebels Rock
Nat Geog 168:820 (c,2) D '85
--Red River Gorge
Natur Hist 95:68-70 (map,c,1)
S '86
--See also
APPALACHIAN MOUNTAINS
CUMBERLAND MOUNTAINS
CUMBERLAND RIVER
MAMMOTH CAVE NATIONAL
PARK
OHIO RIVER
KENYA
Nat Geog 161:122-39 (c,1) Ja
'82
Sports Illus 56:92-108 (map,c,1)
F 8 '82
Trav/Holiday 160:44-9 (c,1) S
'83
--Amboseli National Park
Natur Hist 93:58-9 (c,3) F '84
--Lake Bororia
Nat Geog 168:560-1 (c,1) N '85
--Lake Turkana
Nat Geog 168:624-7 (c,1) N '85
--Meru National Park

KENYA (cont.)
  Nat Geog 165:414-15 (c,1) Mr
    '84
--Samburu Hills
  Nat Geog 168:580-1 (c,1) N
    '85
--Tsavo National Park
  Natur Hist 93:74, 78 (c,3) Ap
    '84
--See also
    LAKE VICTORIA
    MOUNT KENYA
KENYA--COSTUME
  Sports Illus 56:92-5 (c,1) F 8
    '82
  Trav/Holiday 160:44-5 (c,1) S
    '83
  Sports Illus 62:67-9 (c,4) My
    27 '85
--Masai people
  Nat Geog 170:816-19 (c,1) D
    '86
--Masai warriors
  Nat Geog 166:608-9 (c,2) N '84
--Pokot people
  Nat Geog 161:121-39 (c,1) Ja
    '82
--Rendille people
  Nat Geog 166:610-11 (c,2) N
    '84
--Traditional
  Ebony 40:156 (c,3) O '85
KENYA--POLITICS AND GOV-
    ERNMENT
--1963 independence celebration
  Ebony 41:299 (4) N '85
KENYA--SOCIAL LIFE AND
    CUSTOMS
--Carrying water buckets on
    head
  Sports Illus 56:95 (c,4) F 8
    '82
KESTRELS
  Natur Hist 91:38 (c,1) Mr '82
  Smithsonian 13:96 (c,4) Je '82
  Sports Illus 64:138 (c,4) My
    19 '86
KETCHIKAN, ALASKA
  Nat Geog 165:79 (c,3) Ja '84
  Trav/Holiday 161:58 (c,4) F
    '84
  Trav/Holiday 165:69-71 (c,1)
    Mr '86
KEY WEST, FLORIDA
  Nat Geog 162:198-9, 201 (c,1)
    Ag '82

KHARTOUM, SUDAN
  Nat Geog 161:360-2 (c,1) Mr '82
KHRUSHCHEV, NIKITA
  Life 9:269 (c,4) Fall '86
KIBBUTZIM
--Ashdot Yaaqov, Israel
  Nat Geog 168:18-19 (c,1) Jl '85
KIEV, U.S.S.R.
  Nat Geog 167:312-13 (c,1) Mr
    '85
KILAUEA VOLCANO, HAWAII
--1983 eruption
  Nat Geog 164:583 (c,1) N '83
--Erupting
  Natur Hist 91:68-9 (c,2) D '82
  Trav/Holiday 162:34-5 (c,1) O
    '84
  Nat Geog 168:144-5 (c,1) Ag '85
KILIMANJARO, TANZANIA
  Smithsonian 13:38-51 (c,1) Ag
    '82
KILLER WHALES
  Trav/Holiday 160:22 (drawing,4)
    Ag '83
  Nat Wildlife 22:47-51 (c,1) F '84
  Nat Geog 166:220-37 (c,1) Ag
    '84
  Life 8:136-7 (c,1) Ap '85
KING, MARTIN LUTHER, JR.
  Am Heritage 33:51 (3) Je '82
  Ebony 38:31 (4) Ap '83
  Ebony 39:71 (c,1) Ja '84
  Ebony 39:114 (2) F '84
  Ebony 39:33-40 (2) Ap '84
  Ebony 40:32 (4) F '85
  Ebony 40:74 (3) Mr '85
  Ebony 41:70, 160, 164-8, 296,
    302 (2) N '85
  Ebony 41:entire issue (c,1) Ja
    '86
  Life 9:118 (4) Jl '86
--1956 arrest in Montgomery bus
    boycott
  Ebony 41:44 (4) Ja '86
--1965 poster of King as Communist
    (Alabama)
  Am Heritage 33:60-1 (2) Je '82
--1968 assassination (Tennessee)
  Ebony 41:316 (3) N '85
  Life 9:342-3 (1) Fall '86
--1968 funeral (Georgia)
  Ebony 41:206, 316 (3) N '85
  Ebony 41:98-103 (1) Ja '86
--Center for Nonviolent Social
    Change, Atlanta, Georgia
  Ebony 38:120-7 (c,2) F '83
--Crypt (Atlanta, Georgia)

LAKES (cont.)
    Nat Geog 170:416-17 (c,1) S
        '86
--Kennebago, Maine
    Life 6:9 (c,2) F '83
--Kluane, Yukon, Canada
    Trav/Holiday 157:84 (c,2) Ap
        '82
--Little Rock Lake, Wisconsin
    Life 7:64 (c,2) N '84
--Mono, California
    Sports Illus 58:76-86 (c,1)
        My 30 '83
--Lake Nasser, Egypt
    Nat Geog 167:592-7 (c,1) My
        '85
--Man-made lake (Oklahoma)
    Trav/Holiday 165:54 (c,1) F
        '86
--Navajo Lake, Utah
    Natur Hist 95:90 (c,4) My '86
--North Dakota
    Trav/Holiday 164:57 (c,2) Jl
        '85
--Patzcuaro, Mexico
    Trav/Holiday 165:14 (c,3) Ap
        '86
--Powell, Arizona
    Natur Hist 91:80-1 (c,1) Ja
        '82
--Shandur, Pakistan
    Smithsonian 13:48-9 (c,2) Ap
        '82
--Shek Ngam, China
    Nat Geog 164:76-7 (c,3) Jl '83
--Sun Moon Lake, Taiwan
    Nat Geog 161:110-11 (c,2) Ja
        '82
--Tonle Sap, Cambodia
    Nat Geog 161:612-13 (c,1) My
        '82
--Underwater scenes (Palau Is-
        lands)
    Nat Geog 161:264-81 (c,1) F
        '82
--Victoria, Africa
    Nat Geog 167:628-9 (c,1) My
        '85
--Washington, Seattle, Washington
    Sports Illus 57:58 (c,3) Jl 19
        '82
--See also
        GREAT SALT LAKE
        LAKE CHAMPLAIN
        LAKE CONSTANCE
        LAKE GENEVA
        LAKE GEORGE

    LAKE LOUISE
    LAKE OKEECHOBEE
    LAKE SUPERIOR
    LAKE TITICACA
    LAKE VICTORIA
    LAKE WINNIPESAUKEE
LAMAISM--COSTUME
--Dalai Lama and followers (India)
    Smithsonian 14:82-91 (c,1) Mr
        '84
--Lamas (Mongolia)
    Nat Geog 167:256 (c,3) F '85
LAMPS
--Outdoor lamps
    Nat Geog 164:578-9 (c,1) N '83
--Outside house (New Mexico)
    Nat Geog 161:324 (c,4) Mr '82
LANDON, ALFRED M.
    Nat Geog 168:360 (c,4) S '85
LANGDON, HARRY
    Am Heritage 35:46 (4) D '83
LAPP PEOPLE (FINLAND)--
        HOUSING
--Log cabins (Inari, Finland)
    Trav/Holiday 158:8 (c,4) Jl '82
LAPP PEOPLE (NORWAY)
    Nat Geog 163:194-7 (c,1) F '83
LARCH TREES
--Alpine larch
    Nat Wildlife 22:7 (c,4) O '84
LARKSPURS
    Natur Hist 93:28-31 (c,1) Jl '84
LAS VEGAS, NEVADA
    Ebony 37:45 (c,4) Ja '82
    Sports Illus 56:80-94 (c,1) Je 7
        '82
LA SALLE, SIEUR DE
--Claiming Mississippi River for
        France (1682)
    Am Heritage 33:6 (4) Ap '82
LASERS
    Nat Geog 165:334-77 (c,1) Mr
        '84
--Measuring earthquake movement
        (California)
    Nat Geog 169:672-3 (c,1) My '86
--Use in medicine
    Life 5:cov., 129-34 (c,1) My '82
--Used to treat herpes
    Life 6:88 (4) Ja '83
--See also
        HOLOGRAPHY
LATIN AMERICA--HISTORY
--1940s anti-Nazi propaganda
    Am Heritage 35:105-9 (c,4) Ap
        '84

LATIN AMERICA--ART
--Primitive sculpture
    Smithsonian 12:42-9 (c,1) F
        '82
LATVIA--SOCIAL LIFE AND
        CUSTOMS
--Jumping over campfire in
        "White Night" celebration
    Nat Geog 167:294-5 (c,1) Mr
        '85
LAUNDRY
--19th cent. clothespins
    Smithsonian 14:123 (c,4) F '84
--1912 electric washing machine
    Am Heritage 37:40 (c,4) Ag
        '86
--1916 laundry (Wyoming)
    Am Heritage 36:38 (4) O '85
--Aboard houseboat (France)
    Nat Geog 161:496-7 (c,2) Ap
        '82
--Frozen on clothesline (New-
        foundland)
    Nat Geog 169:696-7 (c,1) My
        '86
--Hanging clothes on clothesline
        (1887)
    Am Heritage 37:85 (paint-
        ing,c,4) F '86
--Hanging clothes on clothesline
        (1943; Ohio)
    Life 9:288 (1) Fall '86
--Hanging clothes on clothesline
        (Michigan)
    Life 5:40 (c,4) Ag '82
--Hanging clothes on clothesline
        (Minnesota)
    Life 6:84 (c,3) Mr '83
--Hanging clothes on clothesline
        (Mississippi)
    Sports Illus 60:70 (c,4) F 20
        '84
--Hanging on line (Naples, Italy)
    Nat Geog 162:724-5 (c,1) D
        '82
--Shirtpressing industry (New
        York)
    Smithsonian 13:70-1, 76 (1)
        Ja '83
--Washing in public trough
        (Mexico)
    Trav/Holiday 166:37 (c,4) S
        '86
--Washing in river (India)
    Nat Geog 165:720-1 (c,1) Je
        '84
    Nat Geog 169:226-7 (c,1) F '86

--Washing in river (Ivory Coast)
    Nat Geog 162:116-17 (c,1) Jl '82
--Washing in river (Mexico)
    Trav/Holiday 164:55 (c,4) N '85
LAUREL AND HARDY
    Am Heritage 37:45 (4) Ag '86
--Depicted by actors
    Life 9:75 (c,2) My '86
--Posters from their films
    Life 9:75 (c,2) My '86
LAUREL TREES
    Natur Hist 94:26-7 (c,3) Jl '85
--See also
        MOUNTAIN LAUREL
LAVA
--Underwater pillows (Hawaii)
    Natur Hist 91:69 (4) D '82
--Made into sculpture (Italy)
    Nat Geog 162:714 (c,4) D '82
LAVA BEDS NATIONAL MONUMENT,
        CALIFORNIA
    Smithsonian 15:154 (c,4) F '85
LAVENDER
    Nat Geog 163:408 (c,4) Mr '83
LAVOISIER, ANTOINE LAURENT
--Portrait by David
    Natur Hist 93:18 (painting,c,3)
        N '84
Law. See
        JUSTICE, ADMINISTRATION
            OF
LAWN MOWERS
    Nat Geog 166:490-1 (c,1) O '84
LAWRENCE, JAMES
    Am Heritage 38:30 (drawing,4)
        D '86
Lawyers. See
        DARROW, CLARENCE
        JUDGES
        JUSTICE, ADMINISTRATION
            OF
        SUPREME COURT JUSTICES
LAZARUS, EMMA
    Nat Geog 170:16 (4) Jl '86
--Manuscript of Statue of Liberty
        sonnet
    Nat Geog 170:16 (c,4) Jl '86
LEAFHOPPERS
    Nat Wildlife 24:63 (c,1) Ap '86
LEAKEY, LOUIS S. B.
    Nat Geog 162:274-5 (2) Ag '82
LEAR, EDWARD
--Painting of wildlife
    Natur Hist 94:cov., 58-67 (c,1)
        D '85
LEATHER INDUSTRY
--Dyed animal skins drying

LEATHER INDUSTRY (cont.)
(Morocco)
Nat Geog 169:332-3 (c,1) Mr
'86
LEAVES
Smithsonian 16:150-5 (c,1) Ap
'85
--Aspen
Nat Wildlife 21:58, 60 (c,1)
O '83
--Autumn leaves
Natur Hist 95:82 (c,4) O '86
--Closeups of decaying leaves
Natur Hist 95:54-7 (c,1) Ag
'86
--Full of insect holes
Natur Hist 92:20-1, 24-5 (c,3)
My '83
--Maple
Natur Hist 163:477 (c,1) Ap
'83
Natur Hist 92:45 (c,4) Je '83
Sports Illus 65:90 (c,4) O 20
'86
Nat Wildlife 24:4-5 (c,1) O '86
--Oak leaves
Nat Wildlife 23:60 (c,1) O '85
--On forest floor
Nat Wildlife 21:13 (c,1) Ap '83
--Raking leaves (Kansas)
Nat Geog 168:354-5 (c,1) S
'85
LEBANON. See also
BEIRUT
LEBANON--COSTUME
--Beirut
Nat Geog 163:262-85 (c,1) F
'83
--Woman
Life 8:60-1 (1) F '85
LEBANON--POLITICS AND GOV-
ERNMENT
--Aftermath of 1982 Israeli in-
vasion (Beirut)
Nat Geog 163:262-85 (c,1) F
'83
--Aftermath of U.S. Marine head-
quarters bombing (Beirut)
Life 7:46-51 (c,1) Ja '84
--Bombing victim
Life 7:12-13 (c,1) N '84
--Political kidnaping
Life 8:70-1 (1) Ap '85
--Rescuing U.S. Marine from
bombed headquarters (Beirut)
Life 6:32-3 (c,1) D '83
--Victims of war (Beirut)

Life 5:4, 22-30 (c,1) Ag '82
LEE, ROBERT E.
Smithsonian 13:168 (4) My '82
Smithsonian 16:164 (painting,c,4)
O '85
LEECHES
Nat Wildlife 20:30 (3) Ap '82
LEEWARD ISLANDS
--Anguilla
Trav/Holiday 159:45-7 (map,c,2)
Ja '83
--Antigua
Ebony 37:104-9 (c,3) Ja '82
Trav/Holiday 166:50-3 (map,c,1)
S '86
--Dominica
Trav/Holiday 166:26 (c,4) Jl '86
--Montserrat
Trav/Holiday 162:44-7 (c,1) O
'84
--Nevis
Trav/Holiday 163:72-4 (c,4) F
'85
--St. Kitts
Trav/Holiday 163:72-5 (c,1) F
'85
--St. Maarten
Trav/Holiday 157:54-7, 80 (c,3)
My '82
--See also
VIRGIN ISLANDS
LEEWARD ISLANDS--COSTUME
--Antigua
Ebony 37:104-9 (c,3) Ja '82
LEEWARD ISLANDS--SOCIAL LIFE
AND CUSTOMS
--Antigua independence celebration
Ebony 37:104-9 (c,3) Ja '82
LEGER, FERNAND
Trav/Holiday 158:37 (4) Jl '82
--Paintings by him
Trav/Holiday 158:34-7 (c,2) Jl
'82
Legislatures. See
GOVERNMENT--LEGISLATURES
LE HAVRE, FRANCE
Nat Geog 161:508-9 (c,1) Ap '82
LEMURS
Nat Wildlife 21:31 (4) Je '83
Smithsonian 16:102, 105 (c,4) D
'85
Life 9:108 (c,4) Je '86
LENIN, NIKOLAI
--Depicted in Rivera mural (New
York)
Smithsonian 17:18 (4) Ap '86

LENINGRAD, U.S.S.R.
--Cemetery of World War II victims
Life 8:54-5 (c,1) Spring '85
--Chesme Church
Smithsonian 13:66 (c,4) Mr '83
--St. Nicholas Cathedral
Smithsonian 13:73 (c,1) Mr '83
--See also
NEVA RIVER
LENNON, JOHN
Smithsonian 13:107 (4) Mr '83
Life 9:62 (4) Fall '86
--His 1956 Bentley car
Nat Geog 164:32-3 (c,2) Jl '83
--Strawberry Fields memorial, Central Park, New York
Life 8:61-4 (c,1) N '85
LEONARDO DA VINCI
--"Last Supper"
Nat Geog 164:cov., 664-85 (painting,c,1) N '83
LEOPARDS
Smithsonian 13:72-81 (c,1) My '82
Nat Geog 163:357 (c,2) Mr '83
Nat Geog 164:268-9 (c,1) Ag '83
Smithsonian 14:169 (c,3) Mr '84
Nat Geog 167:750-1, 765 (c,1) Je '85
Natur Hist 94:40-1 (painting,c,1) Ag '85
Life 9:255 (c,4) Fall '86
--Cub
Smithsonian 14:102 (c,4) Jl '83
--Snow leopards
Nat Geog 169:cov., 798-809 (map,c,1) Je '86
LEOPOLD III (BELGIUM)
Smithsonian 14:65 (4) D '83
LEVEES
--Mississippi River, Louisiana
Nat Geog 164:234 (c,3) Ag '83
LEWIS, JOHN L.
Am Heritage 33:59 (4) Ap '82
LEWIS, SINCLAIR
Am Heritage 36:42-3, 47 (c,1) O '85
Smithsonian 16:48 (4) D '85
--Home (Sauk Center, Minnesota)
Smithsonian 16:50 (c,4) D '85
--Home town of Sauk City, Minnesota
Am Heritage 36:44 (4) O '85
Smithsonian 16:46-57 (c,1) D '85

LHASA APSO DOGS
Life 5:82-5 (c,1) Mr '82
Life 7:116-17 (c,1) D '84
Smithsonian 17:67 (1) Jl '86
LIBERTY, STATUE OF, NEW YORK CITY, NEW YORK
Life 6:10-14 (c,1) Mr '83
Ebony 38:133 (4) O '83
Am Heritage 35:cov., 97-109 (c,1) Je '84
Smithsonian 15:cov., 46-55 (c,1) Jl '84
Trav/Holiday 164:cov., 39 (c,1) Jl '85
Life 8:110-14 (c,1) S '85
Sports Illus 64:2-3, 28-9 (c,1) Je 30 '86
Am Heritage 37:6 (c,2) Je '86
Nat Geog 170:cov., 3-20 (c,1) Jl '86
Life 9:cov., 3, 47-80, 124 (c,1) Jl '86
--1880s construction (France)
Trav/Holiday 164:84 (4) Jl '85
Life 8:112 (2) S '85
Am Heritage 37:10 (4) Je '86
Nat Geog 170:10-12, 18 (1) Jl '86
Life 9:50-5 (c,1) Jl '86
--1886 grand opening day
Life 8:114 (2) S '85
Nat Geog 170:18 (2) Jl '86
--1986 centennial celebration
Life 9:396-7 (c,1) Fall '86
--Chocolate sculpture
Nat Geog 166:cov., 687 (c,1) N '84
--Covered with scaffolding
Life 8:49 (c,1) Ja '85
Nat Geog 170:9 (c,2) Jl '86
--Depicted in political cartoons
Smithsonian 15:54-5 (c,4) Jl '84
--Depicted on 1954 postage stamp
Am Heritage 34:51 (c,4) D '82
--Fiberglass copy (Mexico)
Life 8:86-7 (1) Je '85
--Manuscript of Emma Lazarus sonnet
Nat Geog 170:16 (c,4) Jl '86
--Rear view
Life 9:39 (c,2) Je '86
--Restoration of statue
Smithsonian 17:68-75 (c,1) Je '86
Nat Geog 170:3-9, 12-13 (c,1) Jl '86
Life 9:67-73 (c,1) Jl '86
--Souvenirs

LIBERTY, STATUE OF, NEW
YORK CITY, NEW YORK
(cont.)
Nat Geog 170:14-15 (c,1) Jl
'86
Life 9:76-9 (c,3) Jl '86
--See also
BARTHOLDI, FREDERIC
AUGUSTE
LIBERTY BELL, PHILADELPHIA,
PENNSYLVANIA
Am Heritage 36:104 (4) Je '85
--1939 replica made of pearls
Nat Geog 168:213 (c,4) Ag
'85
--View from beneath the bell
Nat Geog 163:324 (c,1) Mr '83
LIBRARIES
--1690s country house (Great
Britain)
Smithsonian 16:55 (c,4) O '85
--17th cent. mansion (Great
Britain)
Nat Geog 168:683 (c,3) N '85
Life 8:30-1 (c,1) N '85
--Bookmobile (Nebraska)
Smithsonian 16:129 (c,1) O '85
--Chicago public library stacks,
Illinois
Ebony 37:101 (2) My '82
--College (Tennessee)
Ebony 39:58 (3) Ja '84
--College library card catalog
(Ohio)
Ebony 40:40 (3) D '84
--English country house (Chats-
worth)
Smithsonian 16:56-7 (c,1) O
'85
--Harvard Law Library stacks
Sports Illus 61:71 (c,3) O 29
'84
--High school library (Illinois)
Ebony 41:68 (c,4) Ag '86
--Home (Colorado)
Sports Illus 57:34 (c,4) Ag 9
'82
--Home (Florida)
Life 7:112-13 (c,1) Jl '84
--Home (North Carolina)
Ebony 37:133 (4) F '82
--Home (Switzerland)
Life 8:144 (c,4) Ja '85
--Home bookshelves
Life 8:19 (c,2) F '85
--Huntington, San Marino, Cali-
fornia

Smithsonian 12:66-7 (c,3) F '82
--Lyndon Baines Johnson Library,
U. of Texas, Austin
Smithsonian 14:150 (c,4) N '83
Trav/Holiday 166:46 (c,1) Jl '86
--John F. Kennedy Library exterior,
Boston, Massachusetts
Trav/Holiday 158:cov. (c,1) Jl
'82
--Oxford University, England
Smithsonian 15:63 (c,4) D '84
--Palace of Westminster, London,
England
Nat Geog 170:755 (c,1) D '86
--Photo archive (New York)
Life 9:54-5 (c,1) Fall '86
--St. Vincent
Trav/Holiday 159:48 (c,2) F '83
--Schomburg Center, New York
City
Ebony 37:62-6 (3) S '82
--Sketch of 1893 home library (New-
port, Rhode Island)
Am Heritage 35:77 (c,2) Ap '84
--Tibetan monastic library (India)
Smithsonian 14:84 (c,4) Mr '84
--Harry S Truman's home library
(Missouri)
Life 7:108-9 (c,1) My '84
--Vatican City
Nat Geog 168:766-7 (c,1) D '85
--White House Library, Washington,
D.C.
Smithsonian 16:85, 92 (c,1) Mr
'86
--See also
FOLGER SHAKESPEARE
LIBRARY
LIBRARY OF CONGRESS
LIBRARY OF CONGRESS, WASH-
INGTON, D.C.
--1941 photograph
Am Heritage 33:27 (3) Ag '82
LIBYA
--Sahabi desert area
Natur Hist 91:34-40 (map,c,1)
Ag '82
LIBYA--POLITICS AND GOVERN-
MENT
--Libyan diplomat killed by terrorist
(Rome, Italy)
Life 8:51 (2) Mr '85
LICENSE PLATES
Life 5:4 (4) My '82
--Souvenir California 1984 Olympics
plates
Sports Illus 60:66 (c,4) Mr 5 '84

LICHENS
  Natur Hist 91:30-1 (c,1) Mr
    '82
  Nat Wildlife 20:42 (c,4) Ag '82
  Smithsonian 15:134-43 (c,1) Ap
    '84
LICHTENSTEIN, ROY
  Life 9:78 (c,2) Je '86
--"Mural with Blue Brushstroke"
  Life 9:74-7 (c,1) Je '86
LIFEGUARDS
--Australia
  Nat Geog 161:643 (c,3) My '82
  Sports Illus 62:132-56 (c,1)
    F 11 '85
--Children training to be life
    savers (Australia)
  Sports Illus 62:148-56 (c,2) F
    11 '85
LIFESTYLES
--1840s Fruitlands Utopian com-
    munity (Massachusetts)
  Am Heritage 37:72-5 (3) F '86
--1934 black lifestyle (New Or-
    leans, Louisiana)
  Am Heritage 38:60 (paint-
    ing,c,2) D '86
--1940 small town Saturday night
    (Indiana)
  Life 9:286-7, 302 (1) Fall '86
--1949 chart of hi-, middle-, and
    low-brow lifestyles
  Am Heritage 34:44-5 (1) Je
    '83
--1969 commune family (Oregon)
  Life 9:157 (c,2) Fall '86
--Affluent woman stepping from
    limousine (Texas)
  Nat Geog 166:274-5 (c,1) S '84
--Androgynous rock stars
  Life 8:94-100 (c,1) Ja '85
--British royalty
  Life 5:104-9 (c,1) Ap '82
  Life 9:32-9 (c,1) N '86
--Debutante at play
  Life 6:76-80 (c,1) S '83
--Hermits (U.S.)
  Life 6:140-50 (c,1) D '83
--Home life of rock singer
  Life 8:23-8 (c,1) Ag '85
--Ice Age lifestyle
  Smithsonian 17:74-85 (c,1) O
    '86
--Lifestyle of affluent teenage
    girl (Texas)
  Life 9:38-42 (c,1) Mr '86
--Lifestyle of inner-city teenage

  boy (Detroit, Michigan)
  Life 9:51-6 (1) Mr '86
--Lifestyle of a middle-class drug
    addict (California)
  Life 9:cov., 28-35 (c,1) O '86
--Reenacting 1950s fads
  Life 8:cov., 77-84 (c,1) Ag '85
--Rural Alabama
  Nat Geog 169:384-7 (c,1) Mr '86
--Small town recreation and sports
    (Appleton, Wisconsin)
  Sports Illus 65:32-65 (c,1) Ag
    11 '86
--Teenagers' Saturday night activ-
    ities
  Life 9:3, 28-35 (c,1) Mr '86
--Tennessee
  Nat Geog 169:602-37 (c,1) My
    '86
--Wealthy (Palm Beach, Florida)
  Life 6:93-8 (c,1) Mr '83
--Wealthy tycoon (California)
  Life 5:77-84 (c,1) O '82
--World War II homefront fads and
    artifacts
  Life 8:20-4, 85-94 (c,2) Spring
    '85
--See also
    COLLEGE LIFE
    FAMILY LIFE
    FARM LIFE
    POVERTY
    U.S.--SOCIAL LIFE AND
      CUSTOMS
LIFESTYLES--HUMOR
--Athlete roommate conflicts
  Sports Illus 58:70-84 (draw-
    ing,c,1) My 2 '83
LIFFEY RIVER, DUBLIN, IRELAND
  Trav/Holiday 163:63 (c,3) F '85
LIGHTHOUSES
--3rd cent. B.C. lighthouse of
    Pharos, Egypt
  Smithsonian 14:59 (drawing,4)
    Mr '84
--13th cent. (Lindau, West Ger-
    many)
  Trav/Holiday 160:38 (c,1) Jl '83
--1920s poster of Evanston light-
    house, Illinois
  Am Heritage 37:36 (c,2) D '85
--Anacapa, California
  Trav/Holiday 157:98 (4) Mr '82
--Australia
  Sports Illus 58:59 (c,4) My 30
    '83
--Bagdad, Mexico

LIGHTHOUSES (cont.)
    Life 9:46-7 (c,1) Ag '86
--Biloxi, Mississippi
    Trav/Holiday 157:77 (c,4) Mr
        '82
--Cape Arago, Oregon
    Trav/Holiday 162:14 (c,4) Ag
        '84
--Gibraltar
    Nat Geog 162:700-1 (c,1) D '82
--Lighthouse keeper (New York
        City, New York)
    Nat Geog 170:24-5 (c,1) Jl
        '86
--Marina del Rey, California
    Trav/Holiday 166:22 (c,4) N
        '86
--Portland, Maine
    Trav/Holiday 166:26 (c,3) S
        '86
--Saugerties, New York
    Trav/Holiday 164:4 (c,2) O '85
--Town light hung on tree
        (Bahamas)
    Nat Geog 170:594-5 (c,1) N
        '86
--Vermont
    Am Heritage 33:21 (c,4) Ap
        '82
--West Quoddy, Maine
    Nat Geog 167:241 (c,4) F '85
LIGHTING
--Bridge beacon (Delaware)
    Nat Geog 164:170-1 (c,1) Ag
        '83
--Chandelier (Virginia)
    Nat Geog 168:78-9 (c,1) Jl '85
--Chandelier in mansion (Beverly
        Hills, California)
    Life 9:132-3 (c,1) My '86
--Chandeliers (Manila hotel,
        Philippines)
    Trav/Holiday 165:123 (c,2) Ap
        '86
--Cigarette lighter flames in
        darkness (France)
    Life 9:14-15 (c,1) D '86
--Coleman lantern
    Nat Geog 168:372 (c,4) S '85
--Mobile stadium lights
    Sports Illus 57:101 (c,4) S 1
        '82
--See also
        LAMPS
        STREET LIGHTS
        TRAFFIC LIGHTS

LIGHTNING
    Natur Hist 91:35 (c,4) Jl '82
    Natur Hist 92:22 (c,4) Jl '83
    Nat Wildlife 22:54-5 (c,4) D '83
    Life 7:182-3 (1) Ja '84
    Nat Geog 166:206-7 (c,1) Ag '84
    Smithsonian 16:133 (c,3) My '85
    Nat Geog 168:352-3 (c,1) S '85
    Am Heritage 37:112 (2) Ap '86
    Am Heritage 37:43 (3) Je '86
--Artificially created in lab (Utah)
    Life 5:170-1 (c,1) D '82
--Lightning detector
    Smithsonian 17:46 (c,4) Ag '86
LILACS
    Life 8:58 (c,2) Je '85
LILIES
    Nat Wildlife 21:22 (c,4) F '83
    Nat Wildlife 24:62 (c,2) D '85
--Made of glass
    Smithsonian 13:100 (c,2) O '82
--See also
        CALLA LILIES
        HYACINTHS
        TULIPS
Lilies, water. See
        WATER LILIES
LIMA, PERU
    Trav/Holiday 157:44-9 (c,1) Ja
        '82
    Nat Geog 161:294-7 (c,1) Mr '82
LIMESTONE
--Caverns (Great Britain)
    Nat Geog 169:406-7 (c,1) Mr '86
LIMPETS
    Natur Hist 92:24 (drawing,4)
        Ag '83
LINCOLN, ABRAHAM
    Am Heritage 34:56-63 (c,1) F
        '83
    Life 6:96 (1) O '83
    Am Heritage 35:cov., 112-13
        (statue, c,2) F '84
    Smithsonian 14:189 (4) Mr '84
    Sports Illus 64:33 (4) F 17 '86
    Am Heritage 38:30 (drawing,4)
        D '86
--1860 Presidential campaign flag
    Am Heritage 36:108 (4) O '85
--1864 cartoon
    Am Heritage 33:106 (4) F '82
--1876 plot to steal his body
    Am Heritage 33:76-83 (1) Ap '82
--1908 sketch of unbuilt memorial
        to Lincoln
    Am Heritage 37:6 (c,2) D '85

LINCOLN, ABRAHAM (cont.)
--Eyeglasses belonging to him
    Sports Illus 64:93 (c,4) Mr 10
      '86
--Log cabin birthplace (Kentucky)
    Trav/Holiday 157:75 (c,4) Mr
      '82
    Am Heritage 37:6 (c,2) F '86
--Log cabin boyhood home
      (Lincoln City, Indiana)
    Trav/Holiday 159:28 (4) F '83
--Mary Todd Lincoln
    Am Heritage 34:63 (paint-
      ing,c,4) F '83
    Life 6:98 (4) O '83
--Statue (Hodgenville, Kentucky)
    Nat Geog 161:534-5 (c,2) Ap
      '82
--See also
      BOOTH, JOHN WILKES
LINCOLN, NEBRASKA
--1872
    Nat Geog 162:84-5 (1) Jl '82
LINCOLN CENTER, NEW YORK
      CITY, NEW YORK
--Metropolitan Opera House
    Ebony 39:164 (c,4) O '84
LINCOLN MEMORIAL, WASHING-
      TON, D.C.
    Nat Geog 166:38-9 (c,2) Jl '84
LINDBERGH, CHARLES A.
    Smithsonian 16:184 (4) N '85
--1932 Lindbergh baby kidnaping
      case
    Life 5:40-4, 52 (c,1) Mr '82
--Fake photo of Paris parade
      (1927)
    Am Heritage 33:53 (3) O '82
LINDEN TREES
    Nat Geog 169:770 (c,1) Je '86
LIONS
    Life 5:144 (c,2) O '82
    Nat Geog 162:cov., 800-19
      (c,1) D '82
    Smithsonian 13:97 (drawing,c,1)
      Ja '83
    Nat Geog 163:346, 376-7 (c,1)
      Mr '83
    Smithsonian 14:99-101 (c,3)
      Jl '83
    Natur Hist 92:cov., 54-63
      (c,1) Ag '83
    Trav/Holiday 160:45 (c,4) S '83
    Natur Hist 93:46-7 (c,2) Ja
      '84
    Life 7:12 (c,3) S '84
    Life 7:130-46 (c,3) N '84

Nat Geog 167:626 (c,1) My '85
    Trav/Holiday 164:22 (c,3) Jl '85
    Nat Geog 169:cov., 566-9, 578-
      9, 590 (c,1) My '86
--Brass Asante sculpture (Ghana)
    Natur Hist 93:62-3 (c,1) O '84
--Cub
    Nat Geog 169:cov. (c,1) My '86
    Natur Hist 95:92-3 (c,1) D '86
--Depicted in coats of arms (Great
      Britain)
    Smithsonian 15:92-4 (drawing,c,4)
      My '84
--Teeth
    Life 7:144 (c,4) N '84
--See also
      MOUNTAIN LIONS
LIPPMANN, WALTER
    Am Heritage 33:66 (4) O '82
LIPSCHITZ, JACQUES
    Am Heritage 34:92 (4) Je '83
LIPTON, SIR THOMAS J.
    Sports Illus 64:18 (4) Je 2 '86
LIQUOR INDUSTRY
--17th cent. still head
    Nat Geog 161:57 (4) Ja '82
--1870s whiskey still (North Caro-
      lina)
    Am Heritage 34:39 (painting,c,3)
      Je '83
--Fermentation vat (Kentucky)
    Trav/Holiday 165:60 (c,4) Ja '86
--Testing proof of moonshine whis-
      key (Georgia)
    Nat Geog 163:468 (c,4) Ap '83
LISZT, FRANZ
    Smithsonian 17:144 (drawing,c,4)
      Je '86
    Smithsonian 17:112, 118, 124
      (1) Ag '86
--Liszt's choral music manuscript
    Smithsonian 17:114 (c,4) Ag '86
LITTLE ROCK, ARKANSAS
    Ebony 37:130-1 (2) Ap '82
LIVESTOCK INDUSTRY
--Pigs
    Life 6:48-9 (c,1) F '83
--Veal calves in stalls (Wisconsin)
    Life 6:44-5 (c,1) F '83
LIVING ROOMS
--California
    Ebony 37:31 (c,2) Ap '82
--Florida mansion
    Sports Illus 57:34 (c,1) D 13 '82
--Illinois mansion
    Ebony 37:28-9 (c,2) F '82
--Palm Beach mansion, Florida

LIVING ROOMS (cont.)
　Nat Geog 162:207 (c,1) Ag '82
LIVINGSTON, ROBERT
　Am Heritage 37:104 (painting,4)
　　O '86
Lizards. See
　　REPTILES
LLAMAS
　Ebony 38:128 (c,4) D '82
　Life 6:90 (c,4) Ag '83
　Ebony 39:54 (c,4) N '83
　Ebony 39:163 (c,4) My '84
　Trav/Holiday 166:72-3 (c,1) O
　　'86
LOBELIAS
　Smithsonian 13:48 (c,4) Ag '82
LOBSTER INDUSTRY
--Lobster traps (Maine)
　Nat Geog 167:216-17 (c,1) F
　　'85
　Trav/Holiday 165:111 (c,4) Ap
　　'86
LOBSTERS
--Blue lobster
　Nat Wildlife 24:20 (c,4) O '86
LOCH NESS MONSTER (SCOT-
　　LAND)
　Life 5:36 (4) Ag '82
LOCKER ROOMS
--Baseball
　Sports Illus 56:46-7 (c,1) Mr
　　8 '82
　Ebony 39:66 (c,4) Je '84
　Life 8:116-17 (c,1) My '85
　Sports Illus 64:28-30 (c,2) Je
　　16 '86
--College crew team (Massachu-
　　setts)
　Life 5:78-9 (c,1) My '82
--Empty
　Sports Illus 59:55 (c,3) D 12
　　'83
--Football
　Sports Illus 57:49 (c,4) O 18
　　'82
　Sports Illus 64:98 (paint-
　　ing,c,3) My 19 '86
　Sports Illus 65:36 (c,4) Jl 7
　　'86
　Sports Illus 65:95 (c,4) O 13
　　'86
--Hockey
　Sports Illus 63:43 (c,3) O 14
　　'85
--New York City school lockers
　Smithsonian 13:60-1 (1) My '82
--Racquetball

　Sports Illus 64:27 (c,3) Ja 13
　　'86
--Wimbledon, England
　Sports Illus 56:74 (c,4) Je 21
　　'82
LOCKS
--18th cent. padlock (China)
　Smithsonian 15:37 (c,4) Jl '84
--Ancient locks
　Smithsonian 15:36-7 (c,4) Jl '84
--Locks on safes
　Smithsonian 15:34-42 (c,1) Jl '84
LOCOMOTIVES
--Early 19th cent. history of the
　　locomotive (New York)
　Am Heritage 35:65-9 (paint-
　　ing,c,1) Ag '84
--1925 steam locomotive (Mississippi)
　Trav/Holiday 166:63 (c,3) O '86
--Antique (California)
　Trav/Holiday 158:45 (c,1) Jl '82
--Antique steam engines (Great
　　Britain)
　Smithsonian 14:120-6 (c,2) O '83
--Steam engine (Essex, Connecticut)
　Trav/Holiday 166:8 (c,4) Ag '86
--See also
　　RAILROADS
　　TRAINS
LOG CABINS
--Late 18th cent. (Pennsylvania)
　Smithsonian 15:188 (c,4) N '84
--Late 19th cent. (Montana)
　Nat Geog 169:72-3 (c,1) Ja '86
--Late 19th cent. frontier
　Smithsonian 13:108-9 (paint-
　　ing,c,1) S '82
--1956 (Mississippi)
　Ebony 41:144 (4) Ag '86
--Cabin built by Daniel Boone
　　(Missouri)
　Nat Geog 168:812 (4) D '85
--Construction of log home (North-
　　west Territories)
　Nat Geog 163:181 (c,4) F '83
--Idaho
　Trav/Holiday 165:42 (c,4) My '86
--Lapp cottages (Inari, Finland)
　Trav/Holiday 158:8 (c,4) Jl '82
--Lincoln's birthplace (Kentucky)
　Trav/Holiday 157:75 (c,4) Mr
　　'82
　Am Heritage 37:6 (c,2) F '86
--Lincoln's boyhood home (Indiana)
　Trav/Holiday 159:28 (4) F '83
--Minnesota
　Life 9:17 (c,4) Ag '86

LOG SPLITTING
  Sports Illus 57:31 (c,3) Jl 26
    '82
Logging. See
  LUMBERING
LOMBARD, CAROLE
  Smithsonian 13:105 (3) F '83
LONDON, JACK
  Am Heritage 35:78 (drawing,4)
    F '84
LONDON, ENGLAND
  Smithsonian 13:86-95 (c,1) N
    '82
--1759 painting
  Smithsonian 16:163 (c,3) N
    '85
--19th cent. India House sales-
    room
  Smithsonian 13:132 (paint-
    ing,c,4) Ap '82
--1827 near-disaster in Thames
    tunnel
  Smithsonian 17:68 (cartoon,c,3)
    My '86
--1850 flood
  Nat Geog 163:789 (engraving,4)
    Je '83
--Churchill's Cabinet War Rooms
  Trav/Holiday 165:86 (4) Ja '86
--Double-decker bus
  Trav/Holiday 157:22 (4) Je '82
--Kensington Gardens statue
  Smithsonian 14:96 (c,1) Ja '84
--Palace of Westminster
  Nat Geog 170:729-57 (c,1) D
    '86
--Palace of Westminster fire
    (1834)
  Nat Geog 170:738-9 (paint-
    ing,c,2) D '86
--Reform Club exterior
  Trav/Holiday 165:16 (drawing,4)
    Je '86
--Roof gardens
  Smithsonian 15:42 (c,4) Mr '85
--St. Paul's Cathedral
  Life 5:86-7 (c,1) Ja '82
  Smithsonian 13:88-9 (c,1) N
    '82
--Sherlock Holmes Pub exterior
  Trav/Holiday 161:114 (4) Ap
    '84
--Thames River scenes
  Nat Geog 163:756-7, 778-83
    (c,1) Je '83
--Tower Bridge
  Nat Geog 163:780-1 (c,1) Je '83

--See also
  BANK OF ENGLAND
  BIG BEN CLOCK TOWER
  BUCKINGHAM PALACE
  THAMES RIVER
  TOWER OF LONDON
  WESTMINSTER ABBEY
LONG, HUEY
  Am Heritage 36:22 (4) D '84
  Am Heritage 36:56-63 (c,1) O
    '85
  Am Heritage 37:8 (4) F '86
LONG BEACH, CALIFORNIA
  Trav/Holiday 165:cov., 74-9
    (map,c,1) Ap '86
LONG ISLAND, NEW YORK
--North Fork
  Trav/Holiday 165:84-7 (c,2) Ap
    '86
LONGFELLOW, HENRY WADSWORTH
  Smithsonian 14:102 (painting,c,3)
    Ag '83
LOONS
  Natur Hist 92:94 (painting,c,4)
    S '83
  Nat Geog 166:574-5 (c,2) N '84
  Nat Wildlife 24:46-51 (c,1) Ag
    '86
  Natur Hist 95:cov., 58-65 (c,1)
    S '86
  Nat Wildlife 24:28 (painting,c,3)
    O '86
LOS ANGELES, CALIFORNIA
  Trav/Holiday 160:cov., 60-5
    (c,1) N '83
  Trav/Holiday 162:8 (c,4) S '84
--1931 urban housing scene
  Am Heritage 36:96 (painting,c,2)
    D '84
--1932 Olympics
  Am Heritage 33:64-71 (c,1) Ag
    '82
--Aerial view of freeway
  Nat Geog 164:30-1 (c,1) Jl '83
--Boxing's Olympic Auditorium
  Sports Illus 57:40-1 (c,1) Jl 12
    '82
--Grand Central Market
  Natur Hist 91:100-3 (c,2) O '82
  Natur Hist 91:100, 104 (c,2) N
    '82
--Museums
  Smithsonian 17:88-99 (c,1) Je
    '86
LOUIS, JOE
  Ebony 37:30 (4) Ja '82
  Life 5:99 (2) Ja '82

LOUIS, JOE (cont.)
  Smithsonian 14:136 (paint-
    ing,c,4) Je '83
  Ebony 39:104 (4) Je '84
  Ebony 40:66 (4) Je '85
  Sports Illus 63:cov., 80-101
    (c,1) S 16 '85
  Sports Illus 63:74-90 (c,1) S
    23 '85
  Ebony 41:70, 340 (4) N '85
--1981 funeral (Virginia)
  Ebony 37:30 (4) Ja '82
  Sports Illus 63:90 (2) S 23 '85
--Birthplace (Alabama)
  Sports Illus 63:84 (4) S 16 '85
--Caricature
  Am Heritage 37:53 (4) Je '86
LOUIS XIV (FRANCE)
--Bedroom tapestry (Versailles,
    France)
  Smithsonian 17:112-13 (c,1) N
    '86
LOUISIANA
--1870s
  Am Heritage 35:92-5 (draw-
    ing,c,1) Je '84
--1870s black governor P.B.S.
    Pinchback
  Ebony 37:94 (3) O '82
  Ebony 42:116 (2) N '86
--Atchafalaya River delta
  Natur Hist 94:60-71 (map,c,1)
    Je '85
--Avery Island
  Smithsonian 15:73-83 (c,1) My
    '84
--Breaux Bridge Crawfish Festival
  Natur Hist 93:46-57 (c,1) Ap
    '84
--Mississippi River Delta area
  Nat Geog 164:226-53 (map,c,1)
    Ag '83
--Oak Alley Plantation
  Trav/Holiday 159:96 (4) Mr '83
--Plantation gardens
  Trav/Holiday 158:37-8 (c,1) S
    '82
--See also
    LONG, HUEY
    NEW ORLEANS
LOUISIANA--MAPS
--New Orleans (1755)
  Am Heritage 33:32 (c,2) Ap '82
LOUVRE, PARIS, FRANCE
--1833 Morse painting "Gallery of
    the Louvre"
  Smithsonian 13:144-5 (c,1) O '82

LOW, JULIETTE
  Am Heritage 33:39 (painting,c,1)
    Je '82
LOWELL, ABBOTT LAWRENCE
  Smithsonian 17:157 (4) S '86
LOWELL, PERCIVAL
  Am Heritage 35:38 (2) F '84
LOWELL, MASSACHUSETTS
--19th cent. factory
  Am Heritage 34:48-9 (c,1) Je '83
--Replica of 1901 trolley
  Trav/Holiday 164:12 (c,4) O '85
LUCE, HENRY
  Life 9:8 (4) Fall '86
LUCERNE, SWITZERLAND
  Trav/Holiday 161:87, 108 (c,4)
    Mr '84
  Trav/Holiday 162:35 (c,4) Ag
    '84
Luge. See
    BOBSLEDDING
LUGGAGE
--1875 travel dressing case (Great
    Britain)
  Smithsonian 17:175 (4) My '86
LUMBER CAMPS
--Late 19th cent. (Michigan)
  Natur Hist 95:10-11 (1) Ja '86
--Sudan
  Nat Geog 161:376-7 (c,1) Mr '82
LUMBERING
--Late 19th cent. (Michigan)
  Natur Hist 95:10-16 (1) Ja '86
--1920s (Oregon)
  Am Heritage 34:106-7 (c,2) F '83
--Australia
  Nat Geog 168:262 (c,2) Ag '85
--Clear-cut lands (Montana)
  Nat Geog 167:692 (c,4) My '85
--Clear-cut lands (Oregon)
  Nat Geog 162:320-1 (c,1) S '82
  Nat Wildlife 22:34 (4) Ap '84
--Cutting mahogany log (Zaire)
  Nat Geog 163:25 (c,1) Ja '83
--Deforested areas (British Colum-
    bia)
  Nat Geog 170:58 (c,4) Jl '86
--Felling tree (Florida)
  Sports Illus 64:62 (c,4) Ap 7 '86
--Felling tree (Pennsylvania)
  Nat Geog 167:364 (c,2) Mr '85
--Lathe in mill
  Nat Geog 162:316 (c,3) S '82
--Logging contest (Washington)
  Nat Geog 165:658-9 (c,1) My '84
--Northwest
  Nat Wildlife 24:4 (c,4) F '86

LUMBERING (cont.)
--Oregon
  Nat Geog 162:320-2 (c,1) S '82
--Papua New Guinea
  Nat Geog 163:2-3, 28-33 (c,1)
    Ja '83
--Reforestation (China)
  Smithsonian 15:35 (c,4) Ap '84
--Stripped area (Canada)
  Life 6:110-11 (c,1) Jl '83
--Teak (Burma)
  Nat Geog 166:102-3 (c,1) Jl '84
--Washington
  Nat Geog 165:670 (c,3) My '84
--See also
  SAWMILLS
LUMBERING--TRANSPORTATION
--19th cent. timber rafting
    (Pennsylvania)
  Nat Geog 167:364-5 (3) Mr '85
--Elephants rolling logs (Thai-
    land)
  Nat Geog 162:520-1 (c,2) O
    '82
--Truck (Alaska)
  Nat Geog 162:318 (c,1) S '82
LUMBERJACKS
--1880 Cajun lumberjacks (Louisi-
    ana)
  Natur Hist 94:63 (3) Je '85
--1891
  Natur Hist 91:88-9 (2) My '82
LUPINES
  Life 8:20-1 (c,1) S '85
LUTE PLAYING
--East Germany
  Nat Geog 164:454 (c,3) O '83
--Spain
  Nat Geog 169:152-3 (c,1) F
    '86
LUTHER, MARTIN
  Nat Geog 164:418-63 (paint-
    ing,c,1) O '83
  Smithsonian 14:52 (painting,c,4)
    N '83
--Life and works
  Nat Geog 164:418-63 (c,1) O
    '83
--Monument (Eisleben, East Ger-
    many)
  Trav/Holiday 160:14 (4) O '83
Luxembourg. See
  LUXEMBOURG CITY
LUXEMBOURG CITY, LUXEM-
    BOURG
  Trav/Holiday 163:44 (c,4) Mr '85

LYNCHINGS
--1951
  Ebony 41:264 (3) N '85
LYNXES
  Nat Geog 161:776 (c,4) Je '82
  Nat Wildlife 24:64-5 (c,1) Ap
    '86
--Audubon painting
  Sports Illus 63:129 (c,4) D 23
    '85

-M-

MacARTHUR, DOUGLAS
  Am Heritage 35:86-95 (c,1) Ap
    '84
  Life 8:112 (4) Spring '85
  Life 8:168 (3) O '85
  Life 9:118 (4) Jl '86
--MacArthur returning to the
    Philippines (1945)
  Life 9:240 (3) Fall '86
--Memorial (Norfolk, Virginia)
  Trav/Holiday 157:66 (4) Je '82
MACAWS
  Nat Wildlife 20:cov., 3-11 (c,1)
    Je '82
  Smithsonian 13:38-9 (c,2) Ja '83
  Nat Geog 166:814 (c,4) D '84
  Life 8:28 (c,4) F '85
  Smithsonian 16:58-61 (c,1) Ap
    '85
MACHINERY
--Restoring 19th cent. machinery
  Smithsonian 16:193-209 (c,2) O
    '85
--Transformer rotor
  Am Heritage 36:74-5 (1) O '85
--See also
  CONSTRUCTION EQUIPMENT
  ENGINES
  FARM MACHINERY
MACHU PICCHU, PERU
  Nat Geog 161:300-1 (c,1) Mr '82
  Trav/Holiday 166:49 (c,1) N '86
MACKENZIE RIVER, NORTHWEST
    TERRITORIES
  Nat Geog 163:182 (c,1) F '83
MACLEISH, ARCHIBALD
  Am Heritage 33:22-32 (1) Ag '82
  Life 6:143 (4) Ja '83
  Smithsonian 14:55-65 (2) O '83
--Home (Conway, Massachusetts)
  Smithsonian 14:56-9, 65 (c,2) O
    '83

MACON, GEORGIA
Trav/Holiday 163:70-3, 82
(c,1) My '85
--Hay House
Trav/Holiday 163:70, 82 (c,1)
My '85
MADRID, SPAIN
Nat Geog 169:142-81 (map,c,1)
F '86
--El Escorial
Nat Geog 169:178 (c,2) F '86
--Plaza Mayor
Nat Geog 169:146-7 (c,1) F
'86
MAGAZINES
--1733 Poor Richard's Almanack
Am Heritage 34:10 (4) D '82
--1896 Celebrities Monthly
Am Heritage 33:64-7 (2) F '82
--1911 Ladies' Home Journal cover
Am Heritage 36:101 (c,4) D
'84
--1921 St. Nicholas cover
Am Heritage 37:46 (c,2) D '85
--1923 St. Nicholas cover
Am Heritage 37:41 (c,4) D '85
--Comic books
Sports Illus 56:42 (c,2) My 3
'82
--Cover of first American Heritage
(1949)
Am Heritage 37:9 (4) O '86
--Covers of Jet
Ebony 37:34 (4) Ja '82
Ebony 41:262 (2) N '85
--First Life magazine (1936)
Life 9:50-6 (4) Fall '86
--Inland Printer covers
Am Heritage 34:106-9 (c,2) Ap
'83
--On newsstand
Ebony 39:65 (c,3) Ja '84
--On newsstand (Greece)
Natur Hist 92:85 (3) D '83
--St. Nicholas children's magazine
(early 20th cent.)
Am Heritage 37:41-7 (c,2) D
'85
--The Sporting News archival mate-
rial
Sports Illus 64:68-82 (c,1) Mr
17 '86
--See also
BOK, EDWARD
LUCE, HENRY
McCLURE, SAMUEL S.

MAGIC ACTS
--1949 act (U.S.S.R.)
Sports Illus 60:78 (4) Ap 30 '84
--Escape artist in straitjacket
Life 8:18 (c,4) Ag '85
MAGNESIUM INDUSTRY
--Salt evaporation ponds (Utah)
Nat Geog 167:705 (c,4) Je '85
MAGNETS
--Superconductivity of cold metals
Smithsonian 15:78-89 (c,1) Jl
'84
MAGNOLIA TREES
--Fruit
Natur Hist 93:50 (c,2) Ag '84
--Leaf
Natur Hist 95:98-9 (c,1) F '86
--X-ray photo of magnolias
Smithsonian 17:90 (4) O '86
MAGPIES
Nat Wildlife 21:45 (painting,c,4)
O '83
Natur Hist 93:34-5 (c,1) Je '84
MAGRITTE, RENE
--"Voice of Space" (1931)
Smithsonian 17:64 (painting,c,4)
Jl '86
MAIDS
--Early 20th cent.
Am Heritage 35:23 (drawing,c,2)
Ap '84
Am Heritage 38:34 (drawing,2)
D '86
--Cleaning ladies (Great Britain)
Nat Geog 168:666-7 (c,1) N '85
MAILBOXES
--Mobile home park (Indiana)
Natur Hist 93:56-61 (c,4) Mr '84
--On side of trailer home
Smithsonian 16:77 (c,4) D '85
--Patriotic (Kentucky)
Nat Geog 161:522-3 (c,1) Ap '82
--Rural box
Sports Illus 61:292 (c,4) Jl 18
'84
--Rural box (Kansas)
Nat Geog 168:366 (c,4) S '85
--Rural box (Mississippi)
Sports Illus 59:51 (c,3) O 24 '83
--U.S. mail box
Sports Illus 62:88 (c,4) Ja 14
'85
MAILER, NORM
Life 6:4, 64-74 (c,1) F '83
MAINE
--Atlantic coastal areas
Nat Geog 167:208-41 (map,c,1)

MAINE (cont.)
F '85
--Countryside
Nat Geog 166:790-1, 798-9
(c,1) D '84
--Field
Nat Wildlife 22:48-9 (c,1) Je
'84
--Gouldsboro Bay
Smithsonian 14:104-11 (c,1) S
'83
--Lake Kennebago
Life 6:9 (c,2) F '83
--Maine islands
Trav/Holiday 157:cov., 58-63
(c,1) My '82
--Seal Harbor public garden
Life 8:60 (c,2) Je '85
--View from Mount Katahdin
Trav/Holiday 165:38 (c,4) Mr
'86
--Vinalhaven
Nat Geog 167:228-9 (c,1) F
'85
--See also
ACADIA NATIONAL PARK
PORTLAND
MAJORCA, SPAIN
--Reenactment of battle of Mata-
moros
Trav/Holiday 164:26 (c,4) Jl
'85
MALAYSIA
Trav/Holiday 165:66-9 (map,c,2)
Ap '86
--Jengka Triangle plantation
Nat Geog 163:4-5 (c,1) Ja '83
--See also
KUALA LUMPUR
MALCOLM X
Ebony 40:32 (4) F '85
Ebony 40:146A (4) Ap '85
Ebony 41:70, 212 (4) N '85
--1965 assassination (New York)
Ebony 41:304 (4) N '85
MALI
Trav/Holiday 159:8-9 (c,3) Mr
'83
--Jenne-jeno
Nat Geog 162:396-418 (map,c,1)
S '82
--See also
NIGER RIVER
TIMBUKTU
MALI--COSTUME
Nat Geog 162:396-418 (c,1) S
'82

MALI--SCULPTURE
--Bamana tribe antelope
Ebony 40:31 (c,2) Jl '85
MALI, ANCIENT--RELICS
--Jenne-jeno
Nat Geog 162:396-418 (c,1) S
'82
MALLARDS
Nat Wildlife 20:31-2 (drawing,c,1)
O '82
Nat Wildlife 22:9 (c,1) D '83
Nat Geog 166:572-3 (c,3) N '84
Natur Hist 94:110 (painting,c,4)
Ap '85
Nat Wildlife 24:21 (c,4) Ap '86
MALNUTRITION
--Africa
Ebony 40:44-8 (2) Mr '85
--Ethiopia
Life 7:194 (c,2) D '84
Life 8:8-9 (c,1) Ja '85
Ebony 40:22 (4) F '85
Life 8:124-34 (c,1) My '85
Nat Geog 168:400-5 (c,1) S '85
Nat Geog 170:646, 668-75 (c,1)
N '86
--Fundraising concerts
Life 9:80-5 (c,1) Ja '86
--Indonesia
Nat Geog 170:658-61 (c,1) N '86
--Peru
Nat Geog 161:678 (c,3) My '82
--Starving child (Philippines)
Nat Geog 170:100 (c,1) Jl '86
--Sudan
Life 8:52-3 (1) S '85
MALTA
Trav/Holiday 162:24-5 (map,4)
Jl '84
--Fort St. Angelo
Smithsonian 12:124 (c,4) Ja '82
MAMMOTH CAVE NATIONAL PARK,
KENTUCKY
Smithsonian 13:52-3 (c,2) Mr '83
MAN, PREHISTORIC
--Australopithecus head
Natur Hist 93:36-8 (c,4) S '84
--Australopithecus skeleton Lucy
Natur Hist 93:28 (c,3) O '84
--Evolutionary stages of early man
Nat Geog 168:564-77, 584-5 (c,1)
N '85
--Ice Age life
Smithsonian 17:74-85 (c,1) O '86
--Neanderthal man bones
Natur Hist 93:6 (c,4) D '84
--Origins of mankind

MANNEQUINS
--Constructed for museum use
  (Maryland)
    Smithsonian 16:167-71 (c,1)
    Ap '85
--Football player stand-in
    Sports Illus 63:2-3 (c,1) Ag
    19 '85
--Heads
    Sports Illus 59:62 (c,4) Ag 15
    '83
--Street art at Vienna Festival,
    Austria
    Nat Geog 167:411 (c,1) Ap '85
MANSIONS
--1858 parlor (Mississippi)
    Trav/Holiday 166:55 (c,4) Jl
    '86
--1920 (Pennsylvania)
    Am Heritage 36:112-13 (1) D
    '84
--1920s villa (Atlanta, Georgia)
    Trav/Holiday 164:12 (c,1) D
    '85
--Biltmore's banquet hall, Ashe-
    ville, North Carolina
    Trav/Holiday 166:48 (c,4) S
    '86
--California
    Ebony 37:50-1 (c,1) Mr '82
    Ebony 40:44-5 (c,1) My '85
    Ebony 40:100-4 (c,2) S '85
    Trav/Holiday 164:10 (c,4) D
    '85
    Ebony 41:164-5 (c,2) My '86
--Calke Abbey, Ticknall, England
    Smithsonian 16:102, 110-11
    (c,1) Jl '85
--Caramoor bedroom, Katonah,
    New York
    Trav/Holiday 166:32 (c,4) Jl
    '86
--Gabriele D'Annunzio's home
    (Italy)
    Smithsonian 14:52-61 (c,1) Jl
    '83
--Great Britain
    Sports Illus 57:42-3 (c,1) Jl 5
    '82
--Du Pont's Winterthur, Delaware
    Am Heritage 34:86-96 (c,1)
    Ap '83
    Smithsonian 14:98-109 (c,1) My
    '83
    Nat Geog 164:181 (c,4) Ag '83
--Du Pont's Granogue estate,
    Delaware

    Nat Geog 164:174-5 (c,1) Ag '83
--English country houses
    Smithsonian 16:44-59 (c,1) O '85
--Estate (France)
    Life 6:71-3 (c,1) D '83
--Homes of movie stars (California)
    Life 9:132-42 (c,1) My '86
--Houston, Texas
    Trav/Holiday 158:42 (c,3) N '82
--Japan
    Trav/Holiday 158:52 (c,4) N '82
--Landscaped gardens
    Life 8:52-60 (c,1) Je '85
--Long Island, New York
    Sports Illus 61:2-3 (c,1) S 17
    '84
--Longuevue, New Orleans, Louisi-
    ana
    Trav/Holiday 161:64 (c,2) Ap
    '84
--Longwood, Natchez, Mississippi
    Trav/Holiday 159:44 (2) F '83
    Am Heritage 36:100-2 (c,3) O
    '85
    Am Heritage 37:13 (4) F '86
--Maryland
    Ebony 40:88 (c,3) Jl '85
--Mexico
    Sports Illus 63:34 (c,3) Jl 8 '85
--New Jersey
    Ebony 40:58-66 (c,1) O '85
--Newport, Rhode Island
    Trav/Holiday 160:43, 47 (c,1) Jl
    '83
    Am Heritage 35:42-3, 48 (c,1)
    Ag '84
--North Carolina
    Ebony 40:34-6 (c,3) F '85
--Palm Beach, Florida
    Smithsonian 16:112-23 (c,1) S
    '85
--Provence, France
    Smithsonian 15:108 (c,3) O '84
--Rochester, New York
    Trav/Holiday 165:33 (c,4) Mr '86
--Sark, Channel Islands
    Smithsonian 17:96-7 (c,2) My '86
--Tennessee
    Nat Geog 169:620-1 (c,1) My '86
--Waverly, Mississippi
    Nat Geog 169:378-9 (c,1) Mr '86
--Wrigley, Pasadena, California
    Trav/Holiday 158:43 (c,2) O '82
--See also
    PLANTATIONS
MANTIDS
    Nat Geog 165:268-80 (c,1) F '84

MANTIDS (cont.)
  Nat Wildlife 22:8 (c,1) O '84
  Smithsonian 15:125 (c,4) Mr
    '85
  Nat Wildlife 24:59 (c,3) D '85
  Nat Wildlife 24:6 (c,4) O '86
MANTLE, MICKEY
  Sports Illus 62:cov., 70-84
    (c,1) Mr 25 '58
MANUFACTURING
--1918 blueprint of Ford plant
    production line (Michigan)
  Am Heritage 37:54 (2) O '86
--1920s automobile plant (Michigan)
  Am Heritage 37:36 (2) O '86
--Aircraft (Israel)
  Nat Geog 168:34 (c,1) Jl '85
--Auto manufacturing mural by
    Diego Rivera (Michigan)
  Smithsonian 16:43-5 (c,1) F
    '86
--Automobiles
  Nat Geog 164:6-11 (c,1) Jl '83
--Automobiles (India)
  Nat Geog 167:518 (c,4) Ap '85
--Buses (Hungary)
  Nat Geog 163:230-1 (c,2) F '83
--Communications equipment
    (Illinois)
  Ebony 37:44-6 (1) S '82
--Computers
  Nat Geog 162:442 (c,1) O '82
--Computers (Minnesota)
  Ebony 37:31-2 (3) Je '82
--Computers (New Hampshire)
  Nat Geog 162:785 (c,4) D '82
--Electrical generators (West Ger-
    many)
  Nat Geog 161:42 (c,4) Ja '82
--Motorcycles (West Germany)
  Nat Geog 161:43 (c,4) Ja '82
--Paper (Michigan)
  Ebony 37:88-90 (2) O '82
--Pianos (Queens, New York)
  Life 7:36 (c,3) O '84
--Semiconductor circuits (Philip-
    pines)
  Nat Geog 170:102 (c,2) Jl '86
--Sheepskin (Mongolia)
  Nat Geog 167:248-9 (c,1) F '85
--Shoes (New York)
  Nat Geog 167:361 (c,3) Mr '85
--Silk (China)
  Nat Geog 165:28-31 (c,1) Ja
    '84
--Steel
  Life 7:120-4 (c,1) N '84

--Sunfish sailboats (Connecticut)
  Sports Illus 57:76-7 (c,3) S 20
    '82
--Televisions (India)
  Nat Geog 167:518 (c,4) Ap '85
--Toy cars (China)
  Nat Geog 164:72-3 (c,2) Jl '83
--Using robots (Delaware)
  Nat Geog 162:454-5 (c,1) O '82
--Using robots (Japan)
  Nat Geog 164:11 (c,4) Jl '83
  Smithsonian 16:165 (c,1) Ap '85
--Warehouse (Maine)
  Nat Geog 167:221 (c,4) F '85
--Wooden boxes (Japan)
  Nat Geog 163:29 (c,3) Ja '83
--See also
    FACTORIES
    FOOD PROCESSING
    specific products (e.g.,
      PAPER, PLASTIC, POT-
      TERY)
    list under INDUSTRIES
MAO ZEDONG
  Life 9:192 (4) Fall '86
--Statue (Chengdu, China)
  Nat Geog 168:284-5 (c,1) S '85
MAORI PEOPLE (NEW ZEALAND)
  Nat Geog 166:523-41 (c,1) O '84
--19th cent.
  Natur Hist 94:36-43 (1) Jl '85
MAORI PEOPLE (NEW ZEALAND)--
  ART
--Carvings
  Natur Hist 93:cov., 54-9 (c,1)
    S '84
  Nat Geog 166:542-53 (c,1) O '84
  Smithsonian 16:48, 55 (c,1) N
    '85
MAPLE TREES
--Autumn
  Nat Geog 161:808-9 (c,1) Je '82
  Life 9:40-1, 44-8 (c,1) O '86
--Covered with frost
  Nat Wildlife 21:49 (c,4) F '83
--Glass maple leaves
  Smithsonian 13:104 (c,4) O '82
--Leaves
  Nat Geog 163:477 (c,1) Ap '83
  Natur Hist 92:45 (c,4) Je '83
  Sports Illus 65:90 (c,4) O 20 '86
  Nat Wildlife 24:4-5 (c,1) O '86
--Red maple flowers
  Nat Wildlife 23:4 (c,1) Ap '85
--Sugar maple
  Natur Hist 95:80 (c,1) O '86

MAPS
--1519 New World
  Nat Geog 170:598 (c,1) N '86
--1546 world map (Canadian area)
  Nat Geog 168:71 (c,3) Jl '85
--17th cent. world map (Japan)
  Natur Hist 93:66-7 (c,4) My
    '84
--19th cent. rebus map (Japan)
  Natur Hist 93:70 (c,4) My '84
--Behavioral geography
  Smithsonian 15:123-9 (c,3) My
    '84
--Maps of possible Columbus
    routes
  Nat Geog 170:584-5, 588-9,
    596 (c,1) N '86
--Revised world map with Aus-
    tralia on top
  Smithsonian 15:123 (c,4) My
    '84
--Sites of early man
  Nat Geog 168:586-7 (c,1) N
    '85
  Natur Hist 95:8-10 (c,1) N '86
--See also
    EARTH--MAPS
    GLOBES
    individual countries--MAPS
      (e.g., JAPAN--MAPS)
MARATHONS
--1896 Olympics (Athens)
  Life 7:14 (2) My '84
--1908 Olympics (London)
  Life 7:10-11 (1) Summer '84
--1984 Olympic trials
  Sports Illus 60:56, 60 (c,4) My
    21 '84
  Sports Illus 60:72-4, 114 (c,3)
    Je 4 '84
--1984 Olympics (Los Angeles)
  Sports Illus 62:64-5 (c,1) Mr
    4 '85
--Australia
  Sports Illus 57:60, 64 (c,4)
    O 18 '82
--Japan
  Sports Illus 59:75-6 (c,4) D
    12 '83
--New York (1981)
  Sports Illus 56:144 (c,4) F 10
    '82
  Sports Illus 56:71 (c,4) Mr 22
    '82
--New York (1982)
  Sports Illus 57:24-5 (c,2) N 1
    '82

Sports Illus 58:144 (c,2) F 16
  '83
--New York (1983)
  Sports Illus 59:2-3, 94-6 (c,1)
    O 31 '83
  Sports Illus 60:144 (c,2) F 8 '84
--Rotterdam, Netherlands
  Sports Illus 58:70-5 (c,4) Ap 18
    '83
--Winner receiving laurels (Finland)
  Sports Illus 61:356-7 (c,1) Jl 18
    '84
--See also
    BOSTON MARATHON
MARBLE INDUSTRY
--Carrara, Italy
  Nat Geog 162:42-58 (c,1) Jl '82
--Quarrying (India)
  Nat Geog 167:490 (c,3) Ap '85
MARBLES
--Marbles tournament (New Jersey)
  Sports Illus 63:52-3 (c,3) Jl 8
    '85
--Playing marbles (Tennessee)
  Nat Geog 169:626-7 (c,1) My '86
Marching bands. See
    BANDS, MARCHING
MARCONI, GUGLIELMO
  Smithsonian 12:126-42 (c,3) Mr
    '82
  Smithsonian 17:125 (4) Je '86
MARCOS, FERDINAND (PHILIP-
    PINES)
  Life 9:50-4 (c,1) F '86
  Nat Geog 170:84 (c,4) Jl '86
MARCOS, FERDINAND
--Sculpture of head (Philippines)
  Life 7:150 (c,2) My '84
MARIANA ISLANDS
  Nat Geog 170:464-5, 468-70
    (map,c,1) O '86
--World War II battle sites
  Life 8:96-102 (c,1) Spring '85
--See also
    GUAM
    SAIPAN
    TINIAN
MARIE ANTOINETTE
--Jewelry
  Smithsonian 14:136 (c,4) O '83
MARIJUANA
--Harvesting crop (Jamaica)
  Nat Geog 167:135 (c,1) Ja '85
--Listed on coffeehouse menu (Am-
    sterdam, Netherlands)
  Nat Geog 170:516 (c,4) O '86
--Marijuana farming (Northern

MARIJUANA (cont.)
    California)
      Life 5:40-6 (c,1) D '82
--Marijuana plants
    Nat Geog 169:633 (c,4) My '86
--Smoke shops (New York)
    Life 5:127-30 (c,1) O '82
--Smoking marijuana
    Life 5:128-9 (c,1) O '82
MARINAS
--California
    Trav/Holiday 160:65 (c,4) N
      '83
--Charlestown, Massachusetts
    Trav/Holiday 158:29 (c,1) Jl
      '82
--Ketchikan, Alaska
    Nat Geog 165:79 (c,3) Ja '84
--Long Beach, California
    Trav/Holiday 165:cov. (c,1)
      Ap '86
--St. Tropez, France
    Nat Geog 162:730-1 (c,1) D '82
--San Diego, California
    Trav/Holiday 161:6 (c,4) Ja
      '84
--Vancouver, British Columbia
    Trav/Holiday 160:44 (c,3) Ag
      '83
--See also
      BOATHOUSES
      HARBORS
MARINE LIFE
--Antarctica
    Nat Geog 169:494-511 (c,1) Ap
      '86
--Brittle stars
    Nat Wildlife 21:46-7 (c,1) Ap '83
--Fora minifera
    Natur Hist 94:60-7 (c,1) Mr '85
--Hawaii
    Nat Wildlife 22:56-63 (c,1) Ap
      '84
--Izu Oceanic Park, Japan
    Nat Geog 165:462-91 (c,1) Ap
      '84
--Life on coral reef
    Nat Wildlife 24:46-7 (draw-
      ing,c,1) D '85
--Red Sea
    Nat Geog 164:128-44 (c,1) Jl
      '83
--Sea moths
    Nat Geog 164:138-9 (c,1) Jl '83
--Tide pools
    Nat Geog 169:252-9 (c,1) F '86
--See also

      ECHINODERMS
      FISH
      POND LIFE
      SEA LILIES
      SEA SQUIRTS
Marionettes. See
      PUPPETS
MARKETS
--19th cent. porcelain shop (China)
    Smithsonian 15:188 (painting,c,4)
      My '84
--1872 (San Francisco, California)
    Am Heritage 36:92-3 (paint-
      ing,c,1) D '84
--Baskets (Dominican Republic)
    Trav/Holiday 165:10 (c,4) Ja '86
--Birds (Peru)
    Nat Wildlife 20:8 (4) Je '82
--Cairo, Egypt
    Trav/Holiday 157:41 (c,3) F '82
    Natur Hist 93:111 (4) N '84
--Cambodia
    Nat Geog 161:618-19 (c,1) My
      '82
--Carpets (Turkey)
    Trav/Holiday 166:45 (c,1) S '86
--Cartagena, Colombia
    Trav/Holiday 160:4 (c,4) Jl '83
--Dakar, Senegal
    Trav/Holiday 161:18 (c,4) Ap '84
--Delft, Netherlands
    Trav/Holiday 160:18 (4) Jl '83
--Fabric (Pakistan)
    Smithsonian 13:54 (c,4) Ap '82
--Flowers (Washington)
    Natur Hist 94:89 (3) Ja '85
--Indian (Santa Fe, New Mexico)
    Nat Geog 161:329 (c,1) Mr '82
--Jerusalem, Israel
    Nat Geog 163:500-1 (c,1) Ap '83
--Kyoto, Japan
    Trav/Holiday 160:24 (c,4) Jl '83
--Mexico
    Trav/Holiday 157:58 (c,3) F '82
--Mexico City, Mexico
    Trav/Holiday 162:52-5 (c,2) Jl
      '84
    Nat Geog 166:152-3 (c,2) Ag '84
--Outdoor (Bahamas)
    Ebony 38:118 (c,4) Ap '83
--Outdoor (Ecuador)
    Trav/Holiday 160:58-9 (c,1) Jl
      '83
--Outdoor (Managua, Nicaragua)
    Nat Geog 168:790-1 (c,1) D '85
--Outdoor (Philippines)
    Trav/Holiday 159:34 (c,4) Ja '83

MARKETS (cont.)
--Outdoor (Thera, Greece)
    Trav/Holiday 165:79 (c,1) Mr
    '86
--Pots (Kashmir)
    Trav/Holiday 166:58 (c,4) N
    '86
--Rug merchant (Tunisia)
    Trav/Holiday 158:50 (c,2) O
    '82
--Togo
    Trav/Holiday 158:33 (c,2) Ag
    '82
--Used hardware (Greece)
    Natur Hist 95:85 (2) Jl '86
--Wood (India)
    Natur Hist 95:87 (2) N '86
--See also
        FLEA MARKETS
        FOOD MARKETS
        SHOPPING CENTERS
        STORES
        STREET VENDORS
MARLINS
--Mounted on wall
    Sports Illus 58:34 (c,3) Ja 10
    '83
MARMOTS
    Nat Wildlife 22:33-6 (c,1) F
    '84
    Natur Hist 165:648 (c,4) My
    '84
    Sports Illus 93:102-3 (c,1) S
    '84
    Nat Wildlife 23:48 (c,1) Ag '85
MARRIAGE RITES AND CUSTOMS
    Sports Illus 63:36 (c,3) S 4
    '85
    Life 8:80-1 (1) O '85
--16th cent. Indians (West Indies)
    Am Heritage 36:92 (draw-
        ing,c,2) Ag '85
--1805
    Am Heritage 36:87 (paint-
        ing,c,4) Je '85
--1831 ring ceremony
    Am Heritage 33:15 (drawing,4)
        Je '82
--1925
    Am Heritage 34:39 (4) O '83
--1930 (Great Britain)
    Life 5:148 (4) D '82
--1945 Agta people (Philippines)
    Natur Hist 95:4 (3) N '86
--1953 marriage of John and
        Jackie Kennedy (Rhode
        Island)

Life 6:34 (2) N '83
--1959
    Ebony 37:121 (4) O '82
--Bride feeding cake to groom
        (1948)
    Ebony 40:74 (4) Mr '85
--Celebrities' weddings (1945-1981)
    Life 9:101-6 (c,2) Je '86
--China
    Nat Geog 168:306-7 (c,1) S '85
--Grover Cleveland's wedding (1886)
    Am Heritage 37:109 (drawing,4)
        Je '86
--Courtship rituals (Niger)
    Nat Geog 164:496-503 (c,1) O
    '83
--Eastern Orthodox (Romania)
    Nat Geog 164:728-9 (c,1) D '83
--Examining presents (1880)
    Am Heritage 36:83 (painting,c,2)
        Je '85
--Fitting the bridal gown (1910)
    Am Heritage 36:84 (painting,c,4)
        Je '85
--Flower girl (Newfoundland)
    Nat Geog 169:686 (c,4) My '86
--Hasidic Jews (Brooklyn, New
        York)
    Life 7:117-23 (c,1) Je '84
--Hindu wedding (Netherlands)
    Nat Geog 170:504-5 (c,1) O '86
--Hopi Indians (Arizona)
    Nat Geog 162:616-21 (c,1) N '82
--Illinois
    Ebony 40:116-23 (c,3) Ja '85
--Japan
    Nat Geog 165:766-7 (c,1) Je '84
--Kazak people (China)
    Nat Geog 165:298-9 (c,1) Mr '84
--Caroline Kennedy's wedding
        (Massachusetts)
    Life 9:cov., 38-44 (c,1) S '86
--Kentucky
    Nat Geog 161:532-3 (c,1) Ap '82
--Las Vegas, Nevada
    Life 8:84-5 (4) Je '85
--Louisiana
    Ebony 41:84 (c,2) Ag '86
--Maoris (New Zealand)
    Nat Geog 166:534-5 (c,1) O '84
--Mass wedding ceremony for
        Moonies (New York)
    Life 5:94-5 (1) Ag '82
    Life 6:48-9 (c,1) Ja '83
--Morocco
    Nat Geog 169:336-7, 342-4, 348-9
        (c,1) Mr '86

MARSH MALLOWS (PLANTS)
Nat Wildlife 22:19 (c,4) F '84
MARSHALL, JOHN
Am Heritage 36:104 (drawing,4)
Je '85
MARSHALL, THURGOOD
Ebony 41:70, 306, 312 (4) N
'85
Ebony 42:76 (2) D '86
MARSHALL ISLANDS
Nat Geog 170:464-5, 472-5
(map,c,1) O '86
MARSHES
--Alaska
Nat Geog 168:552-3 (c,1) O '85
--Atchafalaya River, Louisiana
Natur Hist 94:60-71 (c,1) Je
'85
--Big Cypress Swamp, Florida
Nat Geog 162:190 (c,1) Ag
'82
--Blanket bogs (Great Britain)
Natur Hist 91:48-55 (c,1) N
'82
--Bogs
Nat Wildlife 20:45 (c,1) Je '82
--Florida
Smithsonian 14:30 (c,4) Je '83
Life 7:68-70, 77 (c,1) Je '84
Nat Wildlife 23:25-7 (c,1) D
'84
--Georgia
Nat Geog 164:812-13 (c,1) D
'83
--Louisiana
Nat Geog 164:234-5 (c,1) Ag
'83
--Maryland
Nat Wildlife 22:10-11 (c,1) Ap
'84
--Monongahela forest bog, West
Virginia
Natur Hist 94:28-30 (map,c,1)
Ag '85
--Northwest
Nat Geog 161:628-9 (c,3) My
'82
--Potomac River, Virginia
Smithsonian 14:30 (c,4) Ap '83
--Sapelo Island, Georgia
Nat Wildlife 22:18-19 (c,1) F
'84
--See also
OKEFENOKEE SWAMP,
FLORIDA/GEORGIA
MARSUPIALS
--Ancient animals (Australia)

Nat Geog 169:38-9 (drawing,c,1)
Ja '86
--Quokkas
Nat Geog 161:655 (c,3) My '82
--See also
KANGAROOS
KOALAS
OPOSSUMS
TASMANIAN DEVILS
TASMANIAN TIGERS
MARTENS
Nat Wildlife 23:2 (c,2) F '85
Natur Hist 94:108-9 (c,1) N '85
MARTIAL ARTS
Sports Illus 65:21 (c,2) S 3 '86
--Defense training (Palau)
Nat Geog 170:495 (c,4) O '86
--Tae kwon do kick (California)
Sports Illus 65:38 (c,4) S 1 '86
--Wu shu (China)
Life 6:60 (c,4) D '83
--See also
KARATE
MARTIAL ARTS--EDUCATION
--Self-defense class for U.S. em-
bassy employees (Kuwait)
Life 8:132-3 (c,1) D '85
MARTINIQUE--COSTUME
--Flower seller
Trav/Holiday 165:23 (c,4) Mr '86
--Traditional
Trav/Holiday 157:55 (4) Ap '82
MARTINS (BIRDS)
--Purple martins
Smithsonian 16:36, 40-1 (c,4)
O '85
MARX BROTHERS
Sports Illus 59:124 (4) O 31 '83
--Caricature of Groucho Marx
Am Heritage 37:55 (c,1) Je '86
--Groucho Marx mask
Life 9:152 (c,4) My '86
--Harpo Marx
Life 7:53 (4) Je '84
MARY OF TECK (GREAT BRITAIN)
Sports Illus 57:73 (4) S 13 '82
MARY, QUEEN OF SCOTS (GREAT
BRITAIN)
--Hairnet belonging to her
Smithsonian 15:77 (c,4) Ag '84
--Pearl necklace belonging to her
Nat Geog 168:210 (c,4) Ag '85
MARYLAND
--Blackwater National Wildlife
Refuge
Nat Wildlife 22:10-11 (c,1) Ap
'84

MARYLAND (cont.)
--Chesapeake Bay area
Nat Wildlife 22:6-15 (c,1) Ap
'84
--See also
ANNAPOLIS
BALTIMORE
CHESAPEAKE BAY
MASEFIELD, JOHN
Smithsonian 16:141 (4) Jl '85
MASKS
--1940s proposed Mickey Mouse
gas mask for children
Am Heritage 36:6 (draw-
ing,c,2) Ag '85
--1941 gas mask
Am Heritage 36:45 (3) Ag '85
--Baseball players' Halloween
masks
Sports Illus 63:2-3 (c,1) Ag
5 '85
--Gas masks
Life 8:118-19 (c,1) N '85
--Gas masks (Switzerland)
Nat Geog 169:111 (c,4) Ja '86
--Groucho Marx mask
Life 9:152 (c,4) My '86
--Hog costume masks
Sports Illus 63:2-3 (c,1) N
18 '85
--Protective winter face masks
(China)
Nat Geog 166:737 (c,4) D '84
--Self-portraits (Vermont)
Smithsonian 14:131-7 (c,2) N
'83
--See also
DEATH MASKS
MASQUERADE COSTUME
MASKS, CEREMONIAL
--18th cent. (Hawaii)
Natur Hist 91:34 (engraving,4)
D '82
--19th cent. Maori mask (New
Zealand)
Natur Hist 93:57 (c,4) S '84
--1830s mask (Fiji)
Smithsonian 16:54 (c,4) N '85
--Late 19th cent. Eskimos (Alaska)
Smithsonian 13:56, 58-9 (c,1)
My '82
Nat Geog 163:199 (c,2) F '83
--Abelam people (Papua New
Guinea)
Smithsonian 13:117 (c,1) S '82
--Africa
Smithsonian 14:18 (c,4) Jl '83

--Aztec masks (Mexico)
Natur Hist 91:49, 54 (c,1) Jl
'82
--Carnival masks (Italy)
Nat Geog 164:750 (c,3) D '83
--Fasnacht Carnival, Basel, Switzer-
land
Natur Hist 91:cov., 28-40 (c,1)
F '82
--Ivory Coast
Nat Geog 162:112 (c,4) Jl '82
--Mask factory (China)
Trav/Holiday 165:37 (c,4) My '86
--Nigeria
Ebony 40:34 (c,4) Jl '85
--Northwestern Indians
Natur Hist 95:74 (c,4) Jl '86
--Papua New Guinea
Nat Geog 162:148-9 (c,1) Ag '82
Nat Geog 164:141, 146-69 (c,1)
Ag '83
Trav/Holiday 166:76 (4) Ag '86
--U.S. Indians
Trav/Holiday 161:54 (c,4) Ap
'84
--Zaire
Ebony 40:34 (c,4) Jl '85
--See also
DEATH MASKS
MASQUERADE COSTUME
MASONRY
--Masonic temple (Wyoming)
Am Heritage 36:35 (1) O '85
MASQUERADE COSTUME
--1883 Venetian princess costume
(New York)
Am Heritage 34:7 (4) F '83
--Castro costume
Life 9:61 (4) F '86
--Children in Halloween costumes
(1960)
Life 9:238-9 (c,1) Fall '86
--Christmas mummers in costume
(Newfoundland)
Nat Geog 169:678-9 (c,1) My '86
--Easter Bunny
Sports Illus 58:54 (c,4) Ap 18
'83
--Fasnacht Carnival (Basel, Swit-
zerland)
Natur Hist 91:cov., 28-40 (c,1)
F '82
--Frankenstein and bride costumes
Sports Illus 60:46-7 (c,1) My 28
'84
--Halloween costumes
Natur Hist 92:cov., 42-51 (c,1)

MASQUERADE COSTUME (cont.)
O '83
--Mardi Gras costumes
Trav/Holiday 161:cov., 61-77
(c,1) F '84
Life 7:46-52 (c,1) My '84
--Men in ape costumes
Life 6:160-1 (c,1) N '83
--Men in Santa Claus costumes
(New York)
Life 8:11, 16 (c,4) D '85
--Mexican Indian dancer
Trav/Holiday 162:41 (c,2) O
'84
--Panda costume
Life 8:153-8 (1) O '85
--Rabbit costume
Life 7:34-5 (c,1) N '84
--Schemenlauf festival (Austria)
Nat Geog 167:449 (c,1) Ap
'85
--Venice carnival, Italy
Nat Geog 165:209 (c,1) F '84
MASS TRANSIT
--1920s posters along Chicago
transit lines
Am Heritage 37:33-9, 114
(c,2) D '85
--Commuters on Staten Island
Ferry, New York City
Nat Geog 170:32-3 (c,1) Jl
'86
--See also
BUSES
COMMUTERS
SUBWAYS
TAXICABS
TRANSIT WORKERS
TROLLEY CARS
MASSACHUSETTS
--1834 burning of Charlestown
convent
Am Heritage 33:100-5 (c,1) F
'82
--Arnold Arboretum, Jamaica
Plains
Life 8:58 (c,2) Je '85
--Cape Ann
Trav/Holiday 157:22, 105 (4)
Ap '82
--Concord River scenes
Am Heritage 34:94-101
(map,c,1) Je '83
--Conway Bank (1855)
Am Heritage 35:27 (1) Ap '84
--Countryside
Life 9:120 (c,3) Ja '86

--Jamaica Plain (early 20th cent.)
Am Heritage 35:30 (3) F '84
--Newburyport
Nat Geog 166:803 (c,3) D '84
--Old Sturbridge Village
Am Heritage 33:33-43 (c,1) Ag
'82
--Plimouth Plantation
Natur Hist 91:38-49 (c,1) O '82
--See also
BOSTON
BUNKER HILL, BATTLE OF
CAMBRIDGE
GLOUCESTER
LOWELL
MERRIMACK RIVER
NEW BEDFORD
MASSAGES
Life 7:135 (c,4) D '84
Life 9:66 (c,4) My '86
--Massaging feet
Sports Illus 64:32 (c,4) Je 9 '86
MASTIFFS
--Medieval dog in armor
Smithsonian 14:141 (drawing,4)
My '83
--See also
BULLDOGS
GREAT DANES
MASTODONS
Natur Hist 91:58-9 (paint-
ing,c,2) F '82
Natur Hist 91:38 (drawing,3)
Ag '82
MATA HARI
Smithsonian 14:64 (4) D '83
Smithsonian 17:132-58 (2) My
'86
MATADORS
--Matador killed by bull (Spain)
Nat Geog 169:166 (4) F '86
--Peru
Nat Geog 161:298-9 (c,1) Mr '82
--Spain
Nat Geog 166:489 (c,1) O '84
MATCHBOXES
--Antique match safes
Am Heritage 33:2, 97-9 (c,2)
Ag '82
Smithsonian 14:204 (c,4) O '83
MATHER, COTTON
Smithsonian 16:125 (painting,4)
Ap '85
MATISSE, HENRI
Smithsonian 13:190 (4) O '82
Smithsonian 17:81, 91 (c,1) N '86
Life 9:259 (c,3) Fall '86

MATISSE, HENRI (cont.)
--"Ivy in Flower" (1953)
   Smithsonian 15:65 (collage,c,4)
   My '84
--"Jazz VIII"
   Smithsonian 14:166 (c,3) D '83
--Self-portrait (1918)
   Smithsonian 17:81 (paint-
   ing,c,4) N '86
--Works by him
   Smithsonian 17:80-90 (c,2) N
   '86
MATTERHORN, ALPS, EUROPE
   Trav/Holiday 160:33 (4) S '83
   Trav/Holiday 164:24 (c,4) S
   '85
   Sports Illus 64:176 (c,4) F
   10 '86
MAURITIUS
   Natur Hist 91:40 (map,c,4) Mr
   '82
   Smithsonian 13:94-103 (c,1) Je
   '82
   Trav/Holiday 162:46-8 (c,1) N
   '84
MAURY, MATTHEW FONTAINE
   Smithsonian 14:171-82 (4) Mr
   '84
--Monument to him (Richmond,
   Virginia)
   Smithsonian 14:186 (c,2) Mr
   '84
MAY APPLE PLANTS
   Nat Wildlife 23:6 (c,1) Ap '85
MAY DAY
--1628 Merry Mount Maypole
   (Massachusetts)
   Am Heritage 37:82, 86 (paint-
   ing,c,1) O '86
--East Berlin, East Germany
   Nat Geog 161:14-15 (c,1) Ja
   '82
--Maypole dance (New York)
   Smithsonian 13:88 (3) Je '82
--Parade (Italy)
   Nat Geog 165:189 (c,4) F '84
MAY FLIES
   Nat Wildlife 24:30-3 (c,4) Ag
   '86
MAYAN CIVILIZATION (MEXICO)
--Chiapas, Mexico
   Trav/Holiday 162:40-3 (c,2)
   O '84
MAYAN CIVILIZATION--
      ARCHITECTURE
--Ancient ruins (Mexico)
   Natur Hist 94:52 (4) Mr '85

--El Castillo, Tulum, Mexico
   Trav/Holiday 163:62-3 (c,1) Ja
   '85
--Mexico
   Trav/Holiday 158:cov. 31-2 (c,1)
   S '82
--Palenque, Mexico
   Nat Geog 162:682-3 (c,1) N '82
   Trav/Holiday 163:68 (c,4) Ja
   '85
   Natur Hist 94:55 (c,1) Jl '85
MAYAN CIVILIZATION--ART
--6th cent. wooden figure
   Smithsonian 12:42 (c,4) F '82
--Sculpture
   Smithsonian 17:38-49 (c,1) My
   '86
MAYAN CIVILIZATION--COSTUME
--1940s Lacandon Maya
   Natur Hist 94:50-9 (1) Mr '85
MAYAN CIVILIZATION--RELICS
   Smithsonian 17:38-49 (c,1) My
   '86
--Belize
   Nat Geog 162:130-40 (c,1) Jl '82
--Carved pottery bowl
   Natur Hist 92:72 (3) Ag '83
--Chichen Itza, Mexico
   Trav/Holiday 163:64 (c,4) Ja
   '85
--Glyphs (Guatemala)
   Nat Geog 169:cov., 420, 452-6,
   462-3 (c,1) Ap '86
--Guatemala
   Nat Geog 166:137A-B (c,3) Ag
   '84
   Nat Geog 169:cov., 420-65 (c,1)
   Ap '86
--Hieroglyphics (Mexico)
   Nat Geog 168:541 (c,2) O '85
--"Madrid Codex" manuscript
   Nat Geog 169:462-3 (c,2) Ap '86
--Mexico
   Trav/Holiday 163:68-9 (c,3) Ja
   '85
   Natur Hist 94:43-9 (c,1) Ap '85
--Yaxchilán, Mexico
   Nat Geog 168:520-1, 538-9 (c,1)
   O '85
MAYAN CIVILIZATION--RITES AND
      FESTIVALS
--Funeral rites (Guatemala)
   Nat Geog 169:422-4, 434-5
   (painting,c,1) Ap '86
MAYAN CIVILIZATION--RUINS
--Ancient tombs (Río Azul region,
   Guatemala)

MAYAN CIVILIZATION--RUINS
(cont.)
Nat Geog 166:137-137B (c,3)
Ag '84
Nat Geog 169:434-5, 458-61
(c,1) Ap '86
--Tikal, Guatemala
Natur Hist 94:44-5 (c,3) Ap
'85
Smithsonian 17:39 (c,3) My '86
MAYER, LOUIS B.
Life 9:20-1 (c,1) Fall '86
MAYS, WILLIE
Sports Illus 62:cov., 70-84
(c,1) Mr 25 '85
--"The Catch" in 1954 World
Series
Sports Illus 65:16 (4) O 6 '86
McCARTHY, JOSEPH
Am Heritage 37:50-1 (2) D '85
--Bust (Wisconsin)
Sports Illus 65:36 (c,4) Ag 11
'86
McCLURE, SAMUEL S.
Am Heritage 34:26, 31 (1) Ag
'83
McCORMACK, JOHN
Am Heritage 33:18 (4) F '82
McCORMICK, CYRUS HALL
--1850 reaper
Am Heritage 35:14 (drawing,4)
Je '84
McKINLEY, WILLIAM
--Depicted on postage stamp
Am Heritage 34:52 (c,4) D
'82
--McKinley's assassin Leon Czol-
gosz
Am Heritage 38:26 (4) D '86
McPHERSON, AIMEE SEMPLE
Sports Illus 61:17 (4) Jl 18
'84
MEAD, MARGARET
Smithsonian 14:66-75 (c,1) Ap
'83
Smithsonian 15:118-40 (1) S '84
MEADOWLARKS
Nat Geog 162:78-9 (c,1) Jl '82
Nat Wildlife 24:57 (c,2) Ap '86
MEASURING WORMS
Nat Geog 164:218-25 (c,1) Ag
'83
MECCA, SAUDI ARABIA
--Haram Mosque
Nat Geog 168:508-9 (c,1) O
'85

MEDALS
--19th cent. Cross of Hanover
(Great Britain)
Smithsonian 16:128 (c,4) Je '85
--1925 Boy Scout merit badges
Am Heritage 36:68 (4) F '85
--1927 Boy Scout badge
Am Heritage 36:114 (c,2) F '85
--Legion of Honor (France)
Nat Geog 161:161 (c,4) F '82
--Olympics
Life 7:15 (c,1) Summer '84
--Olympics (1912)
Sports Illus 57:48 (c,4) O 25
'82
--Olympics (1932)
Sports Illus 61:109 (c,4) Jl 18
'84
--Purple Heart
Life 6:40 (2) D '83
--Purple Heart (1951)
Am Heritage 33:111 (4) F '82
--Running
Sports Illus 57:60-1 (c,1) D 27
'82
--Skating
Sports Illus 59:47 (c,4) N 21
'83
--Special Olympics
Life 6:124 (c,4) Jl '83
--Swimming
Sports Illus 56:39 (c,4) My 31
'82
--U.S. Army medals
Life 9:31, 39 (c,4) Jl '86
--World War II (Sudan)
Nat Geog 161:379 (c,1) Mr '82
--World War II (U.S.S.R.)
Nat Geog 167:314-15 (c,1) Mr
'85
--World War II honorable discharge
pin (U.S.)
Life 8:24 (c,4) Spring '85
--See also
NOBEL PRIZE
MEDICAL EDUCATION
--Grenada medical school
Nat Geog 166:700 (c,2) N '84
--Lecture room (Massachusetts)
Am Heritage 35:47 (c,1) O '84
--Medical school classroom (Georgia)
Ebony 38:75-8 (3) N '82
--Meharry Medical College, Nash-
ville, Tennessee
Ebony 41:42-50 (3) Mr '86
--Switzerland
Nat Geog 169:111 (c,2) Ja '86

MEDICINE--PRACTICE (cont.)
    MEDICAL INSTRUMENTS
    NURSES
    PLASTIC SURGERY
    SURGERY
    THERAPY
    VACCINATIONS
    VETERINARIANS
    X-RAYS
Medicines. See
    DRUGS
Meditating. See
    PRAYING
MEDITERRANEAN SEA
--Extinct animals of Mediter-
    ranean islands
    Natur Hist 95:52-7 (map,c,1)
    S '86
--Lands along the coast
    Nat Geog 162:694-737 (c,1) D
    '82
MEDITERRANEAN SEA--MAPS
--Byzantine empire
    Nat Geog 164:712-14 (c,1) D
    '83
--Topographical map
    Nat Geog 162:710-11 (c,1) D
    '82
MEDUSA
--1830 brooch depicting her
    Smithsonian 12:122 (c,4) Mr
    '82
MEETINGS
    Ebony 37:46 (c,3) Ja '82
    Ebony 38:40 (c,4) Je '83
--Conference room (Alaska)
    Nat Geog 165:72 (c,4) Ja '84
--Conference room (Washington,
    D.C.)
    Ebony 39:124 (3) Je '84
--Informal conference
    Sports Illus 57:14-15 (c,1) S
    27 '82
--Presentation using overheads
    Life 6:63 (4) D '83
--See also
    PRESS CONFERENCES
MEGAPHONES
--Papua New Guinea
    Nat Geog 162:168 (c,1) Ag '82
MEIR, GOLDA
--Dressed as Statue of Liberty
    (1919)
    Smithsonian 15:14 (4) S '84
MELBOURNE, AUSTRALIA
    Trav/Holiday 164:64-7, 118
    (map,c,2) O '85

MELLON, ANDREW W.
    Smithsonian 14:98 (painting,c,2)
    Ap '83
MELVILLE, HERMAN
    Sports Illus 64:39 (4) Je 30 '86
MEMORIAL DAY
--Puerto Rico
    Nat Geog 163:543 (c,1) Ap '83
Memorials. See
    MONUMENTS
MEMPHIS, TENNESSEE
    Nat Geog 169:634-5 (c,1) My '86
--Elvis Presley's Graceland
    Life 5:124 (c,2) Je '82
MENCKEN, HENRY LOUIS
--Caricature
    Am Heritage 37:54 (4) Je '86
MENDELSSOHN, FELIX
    Smithsonian 14:73 (4) Mr '84
MENNINGER, KARL A.
    Nat Geog 168:376 (c,4) S '85
MENNONITES
--Paraguay
    Nat Geog 162:260 (c,4) Ag '82
--Tennessee
    Nat Geog 169:614-15 (c,1) My
    '86
--See also
    AMISH PEOPLE
    PENNSYLVANIA DUTCH
        PEOPLE
MENTAL ILLNESS
--Insane man brandishing a crucifix
    (New York)
    Life 8:39 (2) F '85
--Insane World War II survivor
    (Poland)
    Life 9:96 (1) Fall '86
--See also
    THERAPY
    list under PSYCHOLOGISTS
MENUHIN, YEHUDI
    Smithsonian 14:76 (c,4) Mr '84
MERCURY (PLANET)
    Nat Geog 167:17 (3) Ja '85
MERGANSERS (DUCKS)
    Smithsonian 12:153 (painting,c,4)
    Mr '82
    Nat Wildlife 21:46 (painting,c,3)
    F '83
    Natur Hist 92:69 (painting,c,3)
    S '83
    Nat Geog 166:580-1 (c,2) N '84
MERMAIDS
--18th cent. painting (France)
    Natur Hist 93:66-7 (c,2) Ja '84
--Character from movie "Splash"

MEXICO (cont.)
  Trav/Holiday 158:cov., 31-5
    (map,c,1) S '82
--Baja
  Trav/Holiday 165:54-7 (c,1)
    Ja '86
--Beaches
  Am Heritage 33:8 (c,1) Ap '82
--Cancun
  Trav/Holiday 163:62-7 (c,1)
    Ja '85
--Chiapas
  Trav/Holiday 162:40-3, 93
    (map,c,2) O '84
--Chichen Itza
  Trav/Holiday 158:cov., 32
    (c,1) S '82
  Trav/Holiday 163:64 (c,4) Ja
    '85
--Cholula pyramid
  Nat Geog 168:326-7 (c,1) S '85
--Cozumel
  Trav/Holiday 161:50 (c,2) Ja
    '84
--Guanajuato
  Trav/Holiday 159:62 (c,2) Mr
    '83
--Guatemala border area
  Nat Geog 168:514-42 (map,c,1)
    O '85
--Janitzio
  Trav/Holiday 165:14 (c,3) Ap
    '86
--Las Hadas
  Trav/Holiday 163:8 (c,3) Ap
    '85
--Netzahualcóyotl
  Nat Geog 166:176-8 (c,1) Ag
    '84
--Mayan Palenque palace, Chiapas
  Trav/Holiday 163:68 (c,4) Ja
    '85
--Poppy fields
  Nat Geog 167:178-9 (c,1) F '85
--Puerto Vallarta
  Trav/Holiday 164:52-5 (c,2) N
    '85
--Reynosa
  Nat Geog 167:735 (c,3) Je '85
--San Miguel de Allende
  Trav/Holiday 160:20-1 (c,2) D
    '83
--Selva Lacandona forest (1940s)
  Natur Hist 94:50-9 (1) Mr '85
--Small inns
  Trav/Holiday 164:49-53 (c,1)
    Jl '85

--Socorro Island
  Natur Hist 93:12 (c,4) F '84
--Texas border areas
  Life 9:40-1, 44-5 (c,1) Ag '86
--Tijuana
  Nat Geog 167:735-7, 763-7 (c,1)
    Je '85
--Towns along U.S. border
  Nat Geog 167:720-49 (map,c,1)
    Je '85
--Usumacinta River
  Nat Geog 168:514-42 (map,c,1)
    O '85
--See also
    CUERNAVACA
    GUANAJUATO
    MEXICO CITY
    OAXACA
    ORIZABA MOUNTAIN
    POPOCATEPETL
MEXICO--COSTUME
  Nat Geog 166:425-55 (c,1) O '84
  Nat Geog 168:518-42 (c,1) O '85
--Chiapas
  Natur Hist 93:91 (c,4) D '84
--Mayan descendants (Chiapas)
  Trav/Holiday 162:41-3 (c,2) O
    '84
--Rarámuri Indians
  Natur Hist 92:58-67 (c,1) Mr
    '83
--Mexico City
  Nat Geog 166:cov., 138-74 (c,1)
    Ag '84
--U.S. border towns
  Nat Geog 167:723-49 (c,1) Je
    '85
MEXICO--HISTORY
--1519 conquest by Cortés
  Nat Geog 166:420-59 (map,c,1)
    O '84
--Depicted on Rivera mural
  Trav/Holiday 162:56 (c,2) Jl '84
  Smithsonian 16:40-2 (c,1) F '86
--Scenes of 1835-36 Texas fight
    against Mexico
  Nat Geog 169:316-23 (map,c,1)
    Mr '86
--See also
    ALAMO
    AZTEC CIVILIZATION
    MAYAN CIVILIZATION
    SANTA ANNA
MEXICO--RITES AND FESTIVALS
--Paper spirit images used in heal-
    ing Otomi Indians
  Natur Hist 95:66-73 (c,1) Ja '86

MICHIGAN (cont.)
    Natur Hist 95:88-90 (map,c,1)
        Ja '86
--Staircase scene of 74 deaths
        during 1913 fire stampede
        (Calumet)
    Am Heritage 37:38-9, 47 (c,1)
        Ap '86
    Am Heritage 37:9 (c,4) Ag '86
--See also
        ANN ARBOR
        DETROIT
        ISLE ROYAL NATIONAL
            PARK
        LAKE SUPERIOR
MICKEY MOUSE
    Am Heritage 35:cov. (draw-
        ing,c,1) D '83
    Life 7:68 (c,4) Ja '84
    Sports Illus 61:41 (c,4) Ag 13
        '84
    Ebony 41:72 (c,4) My '86
--1940s proposed Mickey Mouse
        gas mask for children
    Am Heritage 36:6 (draw-
        ing,c,2) Ag '85
--Mickey Mouse balloon
    Life 9:35 (c,4) D '86
--Mickey Mouse doll
    Sports Illus 65:178 (c,4) S 3
        '86
Micronesia. See
        PACIFIC ISLANDS
MICROPHONES
    Life 5:61 (2) My '82
    Sports Illus 57:69 (c,4) O 4
        '82
    Sports Illus 59:69, 78 (c,3)
        Ag 8 '83
--Headsets
    Sports Illus 57:33 (c,4) O 11
        '82
    Sports Illus 57:47 (c,4) O 25
        '82
MICROSCOPES
    Smithsonian 14:127 (c,3) S '83
    Life 6:154 (3) N '83
    Nat Geog 165:601 (c,4) My '84
    Ebony 39:61 (4) S '84
    Nat Geog 166:508 (c,4) O '84
    Sports Illus 62:18 (c,4) Ja
        21 '85
    Smithsonian 16:144 (c,4) Je '85
--Animals seen through electron
        microscope
    Smithsonian 15:168 (4) Je '84

MIDDLE AGES
--9th cent. "Book of Kells" (Ire-
        land)
    Trav/Holiday 163:66 (c,4) F '85
--16th cent. Germany
    Nat Geog 164:418-59 (paint-
        ing,c,1) O '83
--Dining room (Great Britain)
    Smithsonian 16:46 (c,4) O '85
--Dog wearing armor
    Smithsonian 14:141 (drawing,4)
        My '83
--See also
        CASTLES
        CRUSADERS
        DRAGONS
        FORTRESSES
        KNIGHTS
        POLO, MARCO
MIDDLE AGES--COSTUME
--Worn at Renaissance fairs
    Trav/Holiday 161:cov., 38-45
        (c,1) Je '84
MIDDLE EAST
--Arabian frankincense areas
    Nat Geog 168:474-513 (map,c,1)
        O '85
MIDDLE EAST--HISTORY
--History of Middle Eastern Assas-
        sin sect
    Smithsonian 17:145-62 (c,3) O
        '86
Migrant workers. See
        FARM WORKERS
MILAN, ITALY
--Monastery damaged by bombs
        (1943)
    Nat Geog 164:676-7 (2) N '83
MILITARY COSTUME
--1805 (France)
    Nat Geog 161:166-7 (c,1) F '82
--1860s Confederate soldiers
    Am Heritage 36:70-84 (paint-
        ing,1) D '84
--1860s Union soldiers
    Smithsonian 13:12 (4) Jl '82
--1870s U.S. Army lieutenant
    Life 8:118 (4) Mr '85
--1898 (U.S.)
    Am Heritage 34:95 (1) Ag '83
--20th cent. U.S. Army helmets
    Am Heritage 35:86-8 (4) Ag '84
--1908 U.S. Navy uniform
    Am Heritage 34:38 (4) Ap '83
--1910s France
    Smithsonian 17:150 (4) My '86
--1910s U.S. soldier

MILITARY COSTUME (cont.)
  Life 5:46 (c,4) Jl '82
--Panamanian general
  Nat Geog 169:472 (c,4) Ap '86
--Paraguay
  Nat Geog 162:241 (c,1) Ag '82
--ROTC cadets
  Life 5:67-70 (c,1) Mr '82
--South Africa
  Nat Geog 161:762-3 (c,1) Je
    '82
--Spain
  Nat Geog 169:172-3 (c,1) F '86
--Spanish security forces
  Sports Illus 56:33 (c,4) Je 21
    '82
--Switzerland
  Nat Geog 169:109 (c,2) Ja '86
--Taiwanese air force cadets
  Nat Geog 161:116-17 (c,2) Ja
    '82
--U.S. Air Force
  Ebony 40:94-6 (3) Mr '85
  Life 9:10-11 (c,1) Jl '86
--U.S. Army general
  Ebony 41:64-8 (c,3) My '86
--U.S. battleship crew
  Life 7:36 (c,2) Mr '84
--U.S. dog tag
  Nat Geog 170:692 (c,4) N '86
--U.S. general's hat
  Trav/Holiday 157:66 (4) Je '82
--U.S. major general
  Ebony 40:50-2 (3) Jl '85
--U.S. Marines
  Life 8:17-18 (c,2) S '85
--U.S. military women
  Ebony 37:90-4 (2) Ag '82
  Ebony 41:140-2 (2) D '85
--U.S. National Guard
  Nat Geog 165:831 (2) Je '84
--U.S. Navy
  Ebony 38:74-8 (c,3) F '83
  Ebony 41:45-50 (c,2) D '85
--U.S. Navy cadets (Maryland)
  Trav/Holiday 161:40 (c,2) Ja
    '84
--U.S. soldiers
  Nat Geog 161:cov., 3-4 (c,1)
    Ja '82
  Life 7:8-9 (1) Ja '84
  Life 9:30-1 (c,1) Mr '86
--U.S. women Marines
  Ebony 38:92-4 (2) D '82
--U.S. soldiers (Korea)
  Life 5:72-6 (c,1) N '82
--World War I paraphernalia (U.S.)

Smithsonian 15:106 (c,4) Ja '85
Military leaders. See
  CHURCHILL, WINSTON
  CUSTER, GEORGE ARM-
    STRONG
  DE GAULLE, CHARLES
  EISENHOWER, DWIGHT DAVID
  FARRAGUT, DAVID GLASGOW
  GARIBALDI, GIUSEPPE
  HITLER, ADOLF
  HOUSTON, SAM
  JONES, JOHN PAUL
  LAWRENCE, JAMES
  LEE, ROBERT E.
  MacARTHUR, DOUGLAS
  MONTGOMERY, BERNARD
  MUSSOLINI, BENITO
  NAPOLEON
  NELSON, HORATIO
  NIMITZ, CHESTER
  ROMMEL, ERWIN
  SANTA ANNA
  SCHLEY, WINFIELD SCOTT
  SHERMAN, WILLIAM TECUM-
    SEH
  WILKES, CHARLES
  ZAPATA, EMILIANO
MILITARY TRAINING
--1940 citizens drill (Lexington,
    Massachusetts)
  Am Heritage 37:30-1 (1) O '86
--Afghanistan
  Nat Geog 167:795 (c,3) Je '85
--The Citadel, South Carolina
  Nat Geog 164:824 (c,1) D '83
--Girls' school (Egypt)
  Nat Geog 161:442 (c,4) Ap '82
--Honduras
  Nat Geog 164:622-3 (c,3) N '83
--IRA guerrillas (Northern Ireland)
  Life 8:40-6 (c,1) O '85
--Iran
  Life 8:78-9 (1) My '85
--ROTC programs
  Life 5:67-70 (c,1) Mr '82
--Survival training (Florida)
  Nat Geog 162:197 (c,4) Ag '82
--U.S. military women
  Ebony 37:90-4 (2) Ag '82
  Ebony 38:92-4 (2) D '82
--U.S. trainers in El Salvador
  Life 6:32-8 (c,1) Mr '83
--U.S. Young Marine program
  Life 8:17-18 (c,2) S '85
--Virginia
  Nat Geog 168:94-5 (c,1) Jl '85

MILK INDUSTRY
--Early 20th cent. milkman
  Am Heritage 35:21 (draw-
  ing,c,4) Ap '84
MILK INDUSTRY--TRANSPORTA-
  TION
--Carrying milk cans to market
  by train (India)
  Nat Geog 165:724 (c,2) Je '84
MILKWEED
  Natur Hist 93:42-3 (c,1) Ja
  '84
  Trav/Holiday 163:14 (c,4) F
  '85
--Milkweed pods
  Nat Wildlife 24:7 (c,4) O '86
MILKY WAY
  Nat Geog 163:707A-B (c,1) Je
  '83
  Nat Geog 170:760-1 (c,1) D
  '86
MILL, JOHN STUART
  Smithsonian 14:72 (painting,4)
  Mr '84
MILLAIS, SIR JOHN EVERETT
--Paintings by him
  Smithsonian 14:72-80 (paint-
  ing,c,1) N '83
MILLER, ARTHUR
  Smithsonian 14:97 (c,4) D '83
--1956 marriage to Marilyn Monroe
  Life 9:102 (2) Je '86
MILLER, HENRY
  Am Heritage 35:67 (drawing,4)
  F '84
MILLIPEDES
  Sports Illus 56:96 (c,4) F 8
  '82
  Smithsonian 13:78 (c,4) N '82
MILLS
--1785 automatic grist mill
  Am Heritage 36:108 (engrav-
  ing,4) Ag '85
--19th cent. style water wheel
  (Georgia)
  Smithsonian 16:208-9 (c,4) O
  '85
--1917 lumber mill (Wyoming)
  Am Heritage 36:40-1 (1) O '85
--Grinding cacao beans (Nether-
  lands)
  Nat Geog 166:678-9 (c,2) N
  '84
--Grist mill (Rhode Island)
  Natur Hist 92:96 (3) D '83
--Grist mill (West Virginia)
  Trav/Holiday 160:53 (c,1) O '83

--Paper (Florida)
  Nat Geog 162:213 (c,3) Ag '82
--Recreation of Sutter's 1848 mill
  (California)
  Smithsonian 13:97 (c,1) D '82
--Steel mill (Pennsylvania)
  Nat Geog 167:373 (c,4) Mr '85
--Sugar mill (Nevis, Leeward Is-
  lands)
  Trav/Holiday 163:74 (c,4) F '85
--Water mill (Georgia)
  Nat Geog 163:468-9 (c,1) Ap '83
--See also
    FACTORIES
    MANUFACTURING
    SAWMILLS
MILTON, JOHN
--"Paradise Lost" illustration
  Smithsonian 12:69 (c,4) F '82
  Smithsonian 13:59 (painting,c,2)
  S '82
Minerals. See
    AMBER
    COAL
    CRYSTALS
    DIAMONDS
    EMERALDS
    GOLD
    GYPSUM
    IRON
    JADE
    JEWELRY
    LIMESTONE
    MAGNESIUM
    MARBLE
    PEARLS
    PLATINUM
    QUARTZ
    QUARTZITE
    RUBIES
    SILVER
    SULFUR
    TOPAZ
MINERS
--Coal (Pennsylvania)
  Ebony 37:72 (3) Ag '82
--Coal (Wales)
  Nat Geog 164:46 (c,4) Jl '83
--Coal (West Virginia)
  Nat Geog 163:792, 798-9 (c,1)
  Je '83
--Gold miners (Philippines)
  Nat Geog 170:115 (c,3) Jl '86
--Gold miners (South Dakota)
  Life 9:32 (c,2) Jl '86
--Miners' hats (West Virginia)
  Smithsonian 17:165 (c,4) O '86

MINERS (cont.)
--Zinc (Tennessee)
   Nat Geog 169:604-5 (c,1) My
   '86
MINES
--Denuded strip mine (Ohio)
   Natur Hist 95:30-1 (c,1) Ag
   '86
MINES, EXPLODING
--Land mines (Iran)
   Nat Geog 168:116-17 (c,1) Jl
   '85
--World War I minelaying in North
   Sea
   Am Heritage 34:36-47 (c,1) Ap
   '83
MINING
--1907 Monongah, West Virginia
   mine disaster
   Am Heritage 34:11 (4) D '82
--1913 Calumet copper miners
   strike (Michigan)
   Am Heritage 37:38-47 (c,1) Ap
   '86
--Ice mining (Ecuador)
   Natur Hist 95:40-2 (c,1) F '86
--Staircase scene of 74 deaths
   during 1913 fire stampede
   (Calumet, Michigan)
   Am Heritage 37:38-9, 47 (c,1)
   Ap '86
   Am Heritage 37:9 (c,4) Ag '86
--Tourists panning for rubies
   (North Carolina)
   Trav/Holiday 165:41 (c,4) Ap
   '86
--Training miners (Colorado)
   Nat Geog 166:212-13 (c,1) Ag
   '84
--See also
      COAL
      DIAMONDS
      GOLD
      IRON
      MARBLE
      OPALS
      PLATINUM
      PROSPECTING
      SALT
      SILVER
      SULFUR
MINKS
   Nat Wildlife 24:21-3 (c,1) F
   '86
   Nat Wildlife 24:24 (painting,c,3)
   O '86

MINNEAPOLIS, MINNESOTA
   Trav/Holiday 158:50-2, 58 (c,1)
   Jl '82
--Loring Park
   Trav/Holiday 158:50 (c,1) Jl '82
--Southdale Mall
   Smithsonian 17:39 (c,4) D '86
MINNESOTA
--Glenville
   Sports Illus 63:78-92 (c,1) N 4
   '85
--Sauk Center
   Smithsonian 16:46-57 (c,1) D '85
--Sauk Center (1920s)
   Am Heritage 36:44 (4) O '85
--See also
      DULUTH
      MINNEAPOLIS
      ST. PAUL
MINNOWS
   Natur Hist 92:48-9, 54-5 (c,1)
   Mr '83
   Nat Geog 169:46-7 (c,1) Ja '86
MIRO, JOAN
   Life 7:75 (c,2) F '84
--"Birdcatchers"
   Life 7:18 (lithograph,4) Ap '84
--Outdoor sculpture (France)
   Trav/Holiday 158:33-4 (c,1) Jl
   '82
--Paintings by him
   Life 7:75 (c,2) F '84
--"The Tilled Field" (1924)
   Natur Hist 93:12 (painting,c,3)
   N '84
MIRRORS
--Used with lasers
   Life 6:32-3 (c,1) Ap '83
MISSILES
   Life 6:52-6 (1) Jl '83
--Antiaircraft missile
   Life 6:65 (4) D '83
--Atlas abandoned missile site
   (Wyoming)
   Life 9:48 (c,2) D '86
--Cruise missiles
   Life 5:32-3 (c,1) F '82
--MX
   Life 5:34-5 (c,1) F '82
   Life 9:43-6 (c,1) D '86
--Nuclear warheads
   Life 5:30 (c,2) Mr '82
--Submarine missile controls
   Life 7:52-5 (c,1) N '84
MISSIONS
--Queen of the Missions, Santa
   Barbara, California

MISSIONS (cont.)
Nat Geog 165:434-5 (c,2) Ap
'84
MISSISSIPPI
Nat Geog 169:364-83 (map,c,1)
Mr '86
--William Faulkner's home (Oxford)
Trav/Holiday 166:56-7 (c,2)
Jl '86
--Money
Ebony 41:53 (c,2) Mr '86
--Oxford
Trav/Holiday 166:54-7 (c,1)
Jl '86
--Tennessee-Tombigbee Waterway
Nat Geog 169:364-83 (map,c,1)
Mr '86
--See also
NATCHEZ
TOMBIGBEE RIVER
MISSISSIPPI RIVER, U.S.
Nat Wildlife 23:4-11 (map,c,1)
Je '85
--1860s sketches of river scenes
Am Heritage 35:86-95 (c,1)
Je '84
MISSISSIPPI RIVER, LOUISIANA
Natur Hist 94:60-71 (map,c,1)
Je '85
--1870s sketches
Am Heritage 35:92-5 (c,1) Je
'84
--Delta area
Nat Geog 164:226-53 (map,c,1)
Ag '83
Natur Hist 94:60-71 (map,c,1)
Je '85
MISSISSIPPI RIVER, MISSOURI
--St. Louis (aerial view)
Nat Wildlife 21:4-5 (c,1) Je '83
MISSISSIPPI RIVER, TENNESSEE
--Memphis
Nat Geog 169:634-5 (c,1) My
'86
MISSOURI
--German festival (Hermann)
Trav/Holiday 160:54 (c,4) Jl
'83
--Hercules Glade
Natur Hist 94:82-5 (map,c,3)
Mr '85
--Sunset along river
Life 7:92-3 (c,1) Je '84
--See also
GATEWAY ARCH
INDEPENDENCE
KANSAS CITY

MISSOURI RIVER
OZARK NATIONAL SCENIC
RIVERWAYS
ST. LOUIS
MISSOURI RIVER, MISSOURI
Nat Wildlife 23:45 (c,1) F '85
MITES
Nat Geog 166:370 (c,4) S '84
Natur Hist 94:58 (drawing,4)
Jl '85
--Preserved in amber
Natur Hist 91:29-30 (c,4) Je '82
MOBILE, ALABAMA
Nat Geog 169:383 (c,4) Mr '86
--Africatown
Life 9:13-14 (c,4) S '86
MOBILE HOMES
Natur Hist 93:42-51 (c,1) Mr
'84
--Early 20th cent. motor homes
Am Heritage 37:98-105 (c,2) D
'85
--Improvised truck home
Sports Illus 58:54 (c,2) My 16
'83
MOCKINGBIRDS
Natur Hist 93:10 (c,3) F '84
Nat Wildlife 23:31 (painting,c,1)
D '84
--Audubon painting
Sports Illus 63:142 (c,4) D 23
'85
MODELS
--Fashion models posing
Life 5:145-50 (c,1) N '82
--See also
FASHION SHOWS
MANNEQUINS
MODIGLIANI, AMADEO
--"Boy in Short Pants"
Smithsonian 15:60 (painting,c,4)
My '84
Mold. See
SLIME MOLD
MOLLUSKS
--Ammonite shell fossils
Natur Hist 93:34-40 (c,1) Ag
'84
Nat Geog 168:183 (c,1) Ag '85
--Ancient gastropod shell
Natur Hist 95:60-1 (c,1) My '86
--Tritons
Smithsonian 14:29 (c,4) Ag '83
--See also
CLAMS
CONCHES
LIMPETS

MOLLUSKS (cont.)
    MUSSELS
    NAUTILUSES
    OCTOPI
    OYSTERS
    SLUGS
    SNAILS
    SQUID
MONACO
    Trav/Holiday 161:46-9 (map,c,2)
      Je '84
--Royal palace
    Life 5:73 (c,2) Ag '82
MONACO--COSTUME
--1956 bride Princess Grace
    Life 9:106 (4) Je '86
--Princess Grace
    Life 9:177 (c,2) Fall '86
--Royalty
    Life 6:cov., 4, 22-9 (c,1) Mr
      '83
    Life 7:56-60 (c,1) Ja '84
    Life 9:cov., 76-82 (c,1) Ap
      '86
Monarchs. See
    RULERS AND MONARCHS
MONASTERIES
--Buddhist (China)
    Nat Geog 165:20-1 (c,1) Ja '84
--Catherine's, Sinai, Egypt
    Nat Geog 161:436 (c,3) Ap '82
--Cistercian abbey, Wilhering,
      Austria
    Nat Geog 167:415-17 (c,1) Ap
      '85
--Eastern Orthodox (New York)
    Life 6:162-70 (c,1) D '83
--Germany
    Nat Geog 164:447 (c,4) O '83
--Mandalay, Burma
    Nat Geog 166:118-19 (c,1) Jl
      '84
--Meteora, Greece
    Nat Geog 164:710-11 (c,1) D
      '83
    Trav/Holiday 162:52-4 (c,1)
      O '84
--Milan, Italy
    Nat Geog 164:676 (c,3) N '83
--Monastery of the Caves, Kiev,
      U.S.S.R.
    Nat Geog 167:312-13 (c,1) Mr
      '85
--Mount Athos, Greece
    Nat Geog 164:738-45 (c,1) D
      '83
--Nebraska

Life 9:24-5 (c,4) Mr '86
--Pechory, Pskov, U.S.S.R.
    Nat Geog 167:296-7 (c,1) Mr
      '85
--Rila Monastery, Sofia, Bulgaria
    Trav/Holiday 163:cov., 54-5
      (c,1) F '85
--Shey, Tibet
    Smithsonian 14:88-9 (c,1) Mr
      '84
--See also
    MONT ST. MICHEL
    MONTSERRAT
MONDRIAN, PIET
--1925 painting
    Smithsonian 12:110-11 (c,3) F
      '82
--"Blue Tree" (1909)
    Smithsonian 15:65 (c,4) My '84
--Studio (1930)
    Smithsonian 12:116 (4) F '82
MONET, CLAUDE
    Smithsonian 14:75 (painting,c,3)
      Jl '83
--Home (Giverny, France)
    Nat Geog 161:502-3 (c,2) Ap '82
Money. See
    COINS
    CURRENCY
    WALLETS
MONGOL EMPIRE
--13th cent. naval invasions of
      Japan
    Nat Geog 162:634-49 (paint-
      ing,c,1) N '82
--1258 siege of Baghdad by Genghis
      Khan's grandson Hulegu
    Smithsonian 17:162 (painting,c,3)
      O '86
--16th-19th cent. occupation of In-
      dia
    Nat Geog 167:462-93 (map,c,1)
      Ap '85
--Mongol occupation of Afghanistan
    Nat Geog 167:498 (c,4) Ap '85
--See also
    GENGHIS KHAN
    KUBLAI KHAN
MONGOL EMPIRE--RELICS
--13th cent.
    Nat Geog 162:640, 646-7 (c,2)
      N '82
MONGOLIA
    Nat Geog 167:242-69 (map,c,1)
      F '85
--See also
    GOBI DESERT
    ULAN BATOR

MONTANA (cont.)
   Nat Geog 167:664-92 (map,c,1)
      My '85
   Smithsonian 17:42-55 (map,c,1)
      Ag '86
--Nevada City
   Trav/Holiday 164:61 (c,4) S
      '85
--Paintings by Charles Marion
      Russell
   Nat Geog 169:cov., 66-94
      (c,1) Ja '86
--Square Butte
   Nat Geog 169:76-7 (c,1) Ja
      '86
--See also
      BUTTE
      GLACIER NATIONAL PARK
      HELENA
      ROCKY MOUNTAINS
MONTEREY, CALIFORNIA
--Monterey Bay Aquarium
   Smithsonian 16:94-100 (c,1)
      Je '85
MONTESQUIEU
--Chateau de la Brède home,
      Graves, France
   Trav/Holiday 160:59 (c,2) S
      '83
MONTEVIDEO, URUGUAY
   Trav/Holiday 159:33-4 (4) Ap
      '83
MONTGOMERY, ALABAMA
--Capitol Building
   Ebony 37:146 (4) My '82
   Am Heritage 33:63 (4) Je '82
MONTGOMERY, BERNARD
   Life 8:8 (1) Spring '85
MONTICELLO, CHARLOTTES-
      VILLE, VIRGINIA
   Smithsonian 15:68-77 (c,1) Jl
      '84
--Skyroom under dome
   Am Heritage 36:6 (c,2) Ap '85
MONTPELIER, VERMONT
--Capitol Building
   Life 5:34-5 (c,1) Jl '82
MONTREAL, QUEBEC
   Trav/Holiday 157:38, 41 (c,2)
      My '82
--City Hall
   Trav/Holiday 162:63 (4) Jl '84
--Lord Nelson monument
   Sports Illus 59:18 (c,2) Jl 18
      '83
--Notre Dame Church interior
   Trav/Holiday 162:4 (c,3) Jl '84

--Place Jacques Cartier
   Trav/Holiday 166:33 (c,4) S '86
MONTSERRAT MONASTERY, SPAIN
   Nat Geog 165:110-11 (c,1) Ja
      '84
MONUMENT VALLEY NAVAJO
      TRIBAL PARK, ARIZONA/
      UTAH
   Trav/Holiday 162:4 (c,3) Ag '84
MONUMENTS
--1908 sketch of unbuilt memorial
      to Lincoln
   Am Heritage 37:6 (c,2) D '85
--1945 Soviet victory over Germany
      (Budapest, Hungary)
   Nat Geog 163:228-9 (c,1) F '83
--El Angel, Mexico City, Mexico
   Nat Geog 166:160-1 (c,1) Ag
      '84
--Commemorating war dead (Iraq)
   Nat Geog 167:88-9 (c,1) Ja '85
--Confederacy memorial (Tuskegee,
      Alabama)
   Ebony 37:52 (3) Jl '82
--Field's "Historical Monument of
      American Republic"
   Smithsonian 15:64-7 (c,1) Ag
      '84
--Japanese World War II shrine
      (Papua New Guinea)
   Nat Geog 162:165 (c,3) Ag '82
--Martin Luther King, Jr. memorials
   Ebony 41:64-72 (2) Ja '86
--Matthew Maury monument (Rich-
      mond, Virginia)
   Smithsonian 14:186 (c,2) Mr '84
--Memorial to Australian soldiers
      (Brisbane)
   Trav/Holiday 162:28 (4) O '84
--Memorial to U.S. Vietnam dead
      (Washington, D.C.)
   Life 6:55-8 (c,1) Ja '83
   Nat Geog 167:cov., 551-72 (c,1)
      My '85
   Life 8:56-7 (1) My '85
   Ebony 41:122-3 (c,1) Ap '86
--Mountainside sculpture of Marcos
      (Philippines)
   Nat Geog 170:90-1 (c,1) Jl '86
--Lord Horatio Nelson (Montreal,
      Quebec)
   Sports Illus 59:18 (c,2) Jl 18
      '83
--Philippine World War II memorial
      (Corregidor)
   Nat Geog 170:129 (c,3) Jl '86
--Elvis Presley statue (Memphis,

MONUMENTS (cont.)
    Tennessee)
      Trav/Holiday 160:53 (4) S '83
--Sherman Monument, New York
    City, New York
      Am Heritage 36:44-5 (1) Je
      '85
--Tomb of the Unknown Soldier
    (Warsaw, Poland)
      Trav/Holiday 165:18 (c,4) F
      '86
--U.S.S. Arizona Memorial, Pearl
    Harbor, Hawaii
      Trav/Holiday 164:34 (4) O '85
--Vietnam veterans memorial
    (New York City, New York)
      Life 9:44-5 (c,1) Ja '86
--See also
      ARC DE TRIOMPHE
      EIFFEL TOWER
      GATEWAY ARCH
      GRANT'S TOMB
      JEFFERSON MEMORIAL
      LIBERTY, STATUE OF
      LINCOLN MEMORIAL
      MOUNT RUSHMORE
      STONE MOUNTAIN
      WASHINGTON MONUMENT
      WORLD TRADE CENTER
MOON
    Nat Wildlife 21:cov. (c,1) F
    '83
    Natur Hist 93:98-9 (4) N '84
    Nat Geog 167:22-3 (c,1) Ja
    '85
--Footsteps on moon
    Life 7:19 (c,2) Jl '84
--Man walking on moon (1969)
    Life 9:344 (c,2) Fall '86
--U.S. flag on moon (1969)
    Life 9:118 (c,4) Jl '86
--See also
    ECLIPSES
MOORE, HENRY
    Life 6:118-24 (1) My '83
    Life 6:19 (4) Jl '83
--"Large Spindle Piece"
    Smithsonian 15:158 (sculp-
    ture,c,2) N '84
--Sculpture by him
    Life 6:3, 118-24 (1) My '83
    Smithsonian 15:60-1 (c,3) My
    '84
--"Two Piece Reclining Figure:
    Points"
    Smithsonian 15:156 (sculp-
    ture,c,4) N '84

MOOSE
    Nat Wildlife 21:58-9 (c,1) D '82
    Nat Wildlife 21:10-11 (c,2) Ap
    '83
    Ebony 38:158 (c,4) My '83
    Nat Wildlife 22:16-21 (c,1) O
    '84
    Nat Wildlife 23:58-9 (c,1) D '84
    Nat Geog 167:536-7, 541, 546 (c,1)
    Ap '85
    Nat Wildlife 23:14-15 (c,1) O
    '85
    Nat Wildlife 24:16B-C (paint-
    ing,c,1) D '85
    Nat Geog 169:206-7 (c,1) F '86
    Natur Hist 95:62 (c,1) Mr '86
    Nat Wildlife 24:34-5 (c,1) Ap
    '86
    Smithsonian 17:98-111 (c,1) Jl
    '86
--Antlers
    Nat Wildlife 23:14-15 (c,1) O '85
    Natur Hist 95:62 (c,1) Mr '86
    Smithsonian 17:98-108 (c,1) Jl
    '86
--Calf
    Nat Wildlife 22:21 (c,1) O '84
MORE, SIR THOMAS
    Smithsonian 15:220 (drawing,4)
    N '84
MORGUES
--El Salvador
    Life 5:136-7 (1) My '82
MORMONS
--Recruiting converts (South Amer-
    ica)
    Sports Illus 63:84-101 (c,1) S
    4 '85
--See also
    YOUNG, BRIGHAM
MOROCCO
    Trav/Holiday 160:4-5, 10 (c,2)
    D '83
--Jahjouka
    Natur Hist 92:60-9 (c,1) O '83
--See also
    CASABLANCA
    FEZ
    RABAT
MOROCCO--COSTUME
    Natur Hist 92:60-9 (c,1) O '83
--Ayt Brahim women
    Natur Hist 92:72 (c,2) Je '83
--Fez
    Nat Geog 169:330-53 (c,1) Mr
    '86
--Snake charmer

MOROCCO--COSTUME (cont.)
    Trav/Holiday 160:5 (c,2) D
        '83
--See also
    BERBER PEOPLE
MOROCCO--POLITICS AND
    GOVERNMENT
--Moroccan prisoners of Western
    Saharan Polisarios
    Nat Geog 170:648-9, 654-5
        (c,1) N '86
MOROCCO--RITES AND FESTI-
    VALS
--Rolling out carpets for visit-
    ing ruler
    Nat Geog 169:345 (c,1) Mr
        '86
MORSE, SAMUEL F. B.
    Smithsonian 13:144-7 (paint-
        ing,c,1) O '82
--"Gallery of the Louvre" (1833)
    Smithsonian 13:144-5 (paint-
        ing,c,1) O '82
MOSAICS
--13th cent. (St. Mark's Cathe-
    dral, Venice, Italy)
    Smithsonian 15:42-53 (c,1) S
        '84
--Ancient fishermen (Tunisia)
    Nat Geog 162:734 (c,1) D '82
--Byzantine
    Nat Geog 164:708-49 (c,1) D
        '83
--Byzantine (Cyprus)
    Trav/Holiday 157:73 (3) Mr '82
--Byzantine (Italy)
    Life 7:181-8 (c,1) D '84
MOSCOW, U.S.S.R.
--Bolshoi Theater interior
    Nat Geog 169:774-5 (c,1) Je
        '86
--Churches
    Smithsonian 13:65-7 (c,2) Mr
        '83
--Museum space exploration exhi-
    bit
    Nat Geog 170:446 (c,2) O '86
--Novodevichy
    Smithsonian 13:66-7 (c,2) Mr
        '83
--Red Square
    Nat Geog 161:175 (c,1) F '82
--St. Basil's Cathedral
    Smithsonian 13:65 (c,2) Mr '83
    Trav/Holiday 163:61 (c,2) My
        '85
    Sports Illus 65:13 (c,4) Jl 21

    '86
--Space exploration monument
    (1964)
    Smithsonian 17:142 (c,2) Jl '86
MOSLEMS--ART
--Medieval Islamic metalwork
    Smithsonian 16:225 (c,4) O '85
MOSLEMS--COSTUME
--12th-19th cents.
    Smithsonian 14:60-9 (c,2) Je '83
--Shi'ite terrorist
    Life 8:45 (2) Ag '85
--White-robed woman (Thailand)
    Nat Geog 162:529 (c,2) O '82
--Yugoslavia
    Trav/Holiday 159:47 (c,4) Je
        '83
MOSLEMS--HISTORY
--History of Middle Eastern Assas-
    sin sect
    Smithsonian 17:145-62 (c,3) O
        '86
--See also
    SALADIN
MOSLEMS--RELICS
--12th-19th cents.
    Smithsonian 14:60-9 (c,2) Je
        '83
MOSLEMS--RITES AND FESTIVALS
--Circumcision (Morocco)
    Nat Geog 169:343 (c,4) Mr '86
--Great Magal pilgrimage (Senegal)
    Nat Geog 168:248-9 (c,1) Ag
        '85
--Observance of Ashura (Qum,
    Iran)
    Life 8:94-100 (c,1) S '85
--Ramadan observance (Senegal)
    Nat Geog 168:244-5 (c,1) Ag '85
MOSLEMS--SHRINES AND SYMBOLS
--The Koran
    Nat Geog 168:112-13 (c,1) Jl
        '85
--Qum, Iran
    Life 8:94-100 (c,1) S '85
--Shrine of Imam Reza, Meshed,
    Iran
    Nat Geog 168:129 (c,1) Jl '85
MOSQUES
--Al-Kazimayn, Baghdad, Iraq
    Nat Geog 167:104-5 (c,1) Ja '85
--Baghdad, Iraq
    Nat Geog 167:82-3, 104-5 (c,1)
    Ja '85
--Chitral, Pakistan
    Smithsonian 13:46 (c,1) Ap '82
--Dome of the Rock, Jerusalem,

MOTION PICTURES (cont.)
   Am Heritage 35:47 (4) D '83
--Movie stars in bathtubs
   Life 9:159-67 (c,2) My '86
--Munching popcorn in movie
      theater
   Sports Illus 64:32-3 (c,1) Mr
      24 '86
--"Murder on the Orient Ex-
      press" (1974)
   Smithsonian 14:66 (4) D '83
--"The Natural" (1984)
   Sports Illus 60:92-106 (c,1)
      My 7 '84
   Sports Illus 60:71 (c,4) My
      21 '84
   Smithsonian 15:153 (c,4) O
      '84
--"Niagara" poster (1952)
   Smithsonian 14:111 (c,3) Ja '84
--"Norman ... is that You?"
      (1976)
   Ebony 37:52 (4) Ap '82
--"An Officer and a Gentleman"
      (1982)
   Ebony 37:112-14 (2) S '82
   Ebony 38:26 (4) N '82
   Ebony 38:146 (4) D '82
   Life 6:104 (c,2) Ja '83
   Ebony 38:168 (4) Ag '83
--Olympic athletes in film roles
   Life 7:82-3 (c,1) Summer '84
--"On the Waterfront" (1954)
   Sports Illus 64:42 (4) Je 30
      '86
--"One Down, Two to Go"
   Ebony 38:172 (4) Ag '83
--"Outward Bound" (1930)
   Am Heritage 35:10 (4) Ap '84
--"Paris Blues" (1961)
   Ebony 41:127-8 (4) Je '86
--"Personal Best" (1982)
   Sports Illus 56:80 (c,4) F 8
      '82
--"The Petrified Forest" (1936)
   Am Heritage 35:34 (4) D '83
--"Places in the Heart" (1986)
   Ebony 41:86 (3) Mr '86
--"Porgy and Bess" (1959)
   Ebony 41:126-7 (4) Je '86
--"The Professionals" (1966)
   Ebony 37:142 (4) Je '82
--"The Public Enemy" (1931)
   Am Heritage 35:36 (4) D '83
--"Purple Rain" (1984)
   Ebony 40:66-8 (c,1) N '84
--"Quest for Fire" (1981)

Ebony 37:126 (4) Je '82
--"Race to the Pole"
   Ebony 39:80-1 (c,1) N '83
--"Radio Days"
   Life 9:16 (c,4) My '86
--"Ragtime" (1981)
   Ebony 37:115 (2) F '82
--"A Raisin in the Sun" (1961)
   Ebony 39:84 (3) S '84
--"Red Headed Stranger" (1986)
   Life 9:56-62 (c,1) Ag '86
--"Reds"
   Am Heritage 33:43 (4) Ap '82
--"Return of the Jedi" (1983)
   Ebony 38:126, 132 (c,4) Je '83
   Life 6:cov., 84, 100 (c,1) Je '83
--"The Roaring Twenties" (1939)
   Am Heritage 35:34 (4) D '83
--"Rocky III" (1982)
   Sports Illus 56:70 (c,4) Je 7 '82
--"Rocky Horror Picture Show"
      audience (Massachusetts)
   Life 9:33 (c,4) D '86
--Safecrackers depicted in movies
   Smithsonian 15:39 (4) Jl '84
--Scenes from John Huston films
   Am Heritage 33:10-11 (4) Ap '82
--Scenes from Robert Benchley films
   Smithsonian 12:134-42 (4) F '82
--"Shanghai Surprise" (1986)
   Life 9:16 (c,4) My '86
--Shown in 1911 song slide
   Am Heritage 36:98 (c,2) Ag '85
--"Silverado" (1986)
   Ebony 41:86 (2) Mr '86
--"A Soldier's Story" (1984)
   Ebony 40:112-16 (3) N '84
   Ebony 40:60-2 (4) D '84
--"Song of the Islands" (1942)
   Am Heritage 35:42-3 (1) D '83
--"Spartacus" (1960)
   Ebony 37:140 (4) Je '82
--"Splash" mermaid
   Life 7:38 (c,4) Mr '84
--"Star Trek" (1979)
   Ebony 40:150, 154 (3) Ag '85
--"A Streetcar Named Desire"
   Life 7:73-6 (c,1) Mr '84
--"Superman" (1978)
   Am Heritage 33:45 (2) O '82
--"Superman III" (1983)
   Ebony 38:168 (4) Ag '83
--"Teacher's Pet" (1958)
   Am Heritage 33:43 (4) O '82
--"That Championship Season"
   Sports Illus 57:71 (c,4) D 13 '82
--"They Wanted to Marry" (1937)

MOUNT FUJI, JAPAN (cont.)
Nat Geog 170:612-13, 616
(c,1) N '86
--Seen from ships (1940s)
Am Heritage 36:27 (4) Ag '85
MOUNT HOOD, OREGON
Sports Illus 64:16 (c,4) My 26
'86
MOUNT KENYA, KENYA
Sports Illus 62:66-9 (c,1) My
27 '85
MOUNT McKINLEY, ALASKA
Nat Geog 168:166-7 (c,1) Ag
'85
MOUNT MITCHELL, NORTH
CAROLINA
Life 7:70 (c,2) N '84
MOUNT RAINIER, WASHINGTON
Sports Illus 57:58 (c,3) Jl 19
'82
Nat Wildlife 22:4-5 (c,1) O '84
MOUNT RAINIER NATIONAL
PARK, WASHINGTON
Nat Wildlife 20:64 (c,1) O '82
MOUNT RUSHMORE, SOUTH
DAKOTA
Trav/Holiday 157:22 (4) F '82
Nat Geog 162:341 (c,1) S '82
Trav/Holiday 162:cov. (c,1)
Jl '84
MOUNT ST. HELENS, WASH-
INGTON
Trav/Holiday 161:6 (c,4) My
'84
Nat Geog 168:180-1 (c,1) Ag
'85
--1980 eruption
Sports Illus 62:63 (c,4) F 25
'85
Life 8:21 (c,4) S '85
--Animal life after 1980 eruption
Natur Hist 91:19-24 (map,3)
My '82
Nat Wildlife 24:34-8 (c,1) O
'86
--Land recovering from 1980
eruption
Life 8:20-6 (c,1) S '85
Nat Wildlife 24:34-8 (c,1) O '86
MOUNT SHASTA, CALIFORNIA
Trav/Holiday 166:77 (c,2) O
'86
Mount Vernon. See
WASHINGTON, GEORGE
MOUNT WASHINGTON, NEW
HAMPSHIRE
Nat Geog 162:790-1 (c,1) D

'82
Sports Illus 58:120-2 (map,c,4)
Ap 4 '83
MOUNTAIN ASH TREES
Nat Wildlife 22:7 (c,4) O '84
--Berries
Natur Hist 93:42-3 (c,1) Ag '84
MOUNTAIN CLIMBING
--China
Nat Geog 161:246-7 (c,1) F '82
--France
Sports Illus 64:180 (c,3) F 10
'86
--Himalayan Mountains, Asia
Smithsonian 14:106-17 (c,2) O '83
Sports Illus 65:96 (c,4) D 8 '86
--Italy
Sports Illus 64:190 (c,4) F 10
'86
--Japan
Nat Geog 166:238-9 (c,1) Ag '84
--Kenya
Sports Illus 62:72 (2) My 27 '85
--Mount Everest, Nepal
Sports Illus 59:90-102 (c,1) N 14
'83
Nat Geog 166:70-1, 78-89 (c,1)
Jl '84
Life 9:230 (c,4) Fall '86
--Pakistan
Life 8:74-5 (1) D '85
--Pik Pobedy, U.S.S.R.
Nat Geog 170:256-71 (map,c,1)
Ag '86
--St. Elias Range, Yukon
Nat Geog 168:656-7 (c,1) N '85
--Taiwan
Nat Geog 161:118 (c,2) Ja '82
--See also
ROCK CLIMBING
MOUNTAIN CLIMBING EQUIPMENT
--Ice screws
Sports Illus 59:90 (c,4) N 14 '83
Mountain goats. See
ROCKY MOUNTAIN GOATS
MOUNTAIN LAUREL
--Made of glass
Smithsonian 13:107 (c,1) O '82
MOUNTAIN LIONS
Nat Wildlife 20:46-56 (c,1) Ap '82
Natur Hist 91:35 (c,2) Jl '82
Life 5:107 (c,2) D '82
Nat Wildlife 21:45 (painting,c,4)
O '83
Nat Wildlife 23:38-42 (c,1) Ag '85
Smithsonian 16:cov., 68-79 (c,1)
S '85

MOUNTAINS
--Adam's Peak, Sri Lanka
  Nat Geog 162:20 (c,3) Jl '82
--Aftermath of 1975 San Gabriel
    Mountains fire, Calif.
  Smithsonian 13:134-5 (c,3) O
    '82
--Bradshaw Mountains, Arizona
  Natur Hist 95:30-2 (map,c,1)
    Jl '86
--Brooks Range, Alaska
  Nat Geog 163:170-1 (c,1) F
    '83
--Chilkat Mountains, Alaska
  Life 8:16 (c,2) F '85
--Dachstein Mountains, Austria
  Nat Geog 167:446-7 (c,1) Ap
    '85
--Deccan Mountains, India
  Nat Geog 167:488 (c,1) Ap '85
--Japan
  Nat Geog 166:238-59 (c,1) Ag
    '84
--Kailas, Tibet
  Smithsonian 13:94-8 (c,1) My
    '82
--Min Shan range, China
  Nat Geog 165:284-5 (c,1) Mr
    '84
--Mount Anne, Tasmania, Aus-
    tralia
  Nat Geog 163:682-3 (c,1) My
    '83
--Mount Huang, China
  Life 7:48-54 (c,1) Mr '84
--Mount Magazine, Arkansas
  Natur Hist 94:82-5 (map,c,1)
    O '85
--Mount Stephen, British Colum-
    bia
  Nat Geog 162:296 (c,2) S '82
--Neblina Mountain, Brazil/Vene-
    zuela
  Natur Hist 93:89 (c,3) S '84
  Natur Hist 93:16 (c,4) D '84
  Smithsonian 16:50-63 (c,1) My
    '85
--Nepal
  Smithsonian 16:128-43 (c,1) N
    '85
--Roan Mountain, North Carolina
  Natur Hist 94:38-41 (c,1) Ap
    '85
--Ruwenzori Range, Uganda/
    Zaire
  Nat Geog 167:633 (c,4) My '85
--San Juan range, Colorado

  Nat Geog 166:190-1 (c,1) Ag '84
--Sandia Peak tramway, New Mexico
  Smithsonian 14:69 (c,3) F '84
--Satsuma Fuji, Kyushu, Japan
  Trav/Holiday 158:51 (c,2) N '82
--Sawtooth mountains, Idaho
  Trav/Holiday 165:42-5 (map,c,1)
    My '86
--Simien, Ethiopia
  Nat Geog 163:638-9 (c,1) My '83
--Superstition Mountains, Arizona
  Trav/Holiday 160:40-3 (c,2) O '83
  Natur Hist 95:28-9, 31 (c,1) D
    '86
--Torngat Mountains, Labrador,
    Newfoundland
  Trav/Holiday 166:50-1 (c,1) Jl
    '86
--Wallowa, Oregon
  Trav/Holiday 157:16 (4) Je '82
--White Mountains, California
  Natur Hist 94:38-41 (c,1) My '85
--See also
    ALASKA RANGE
    ADIRONDACK MOUNTAINS
    ALPS
    ANDES
    APPALACHIAN MOUNTAINS
    AVALANCHES
    BLUE RIDGE MOUNTAINS
    CASCADE RANGE
    CUMBERLAND MOUNTAINS
    DOLOMITES
    GREEN MOUNTAINS
    HIMALAYAN MOUNTAINS
    HINDU KUSH MOUNTAINS
    KILIMANJARO
    MATTERHORN
    MOUNT EVEREST
    MOUNT FUJI
    MOUNT HOOD
    MOUNT KENYA
    MOUNT McKINLEY
    MOUNT MITCHELL
    MOUNT RAINIER
    MOUNT RUSHMORE
    MOUNT ST. HELENS
    MOUNT SHASTA
    MOUNT WASHINGTON
    OLYMPIC MOUNTAINS
    ORIZABA
    POPOCATEPETL
    ROCKY MOUNTAINS
    ST. ELIAS RANGE
    SIERRA NEVADA
    TETON RANGE
    VESUVIUS

MOUNTAINS (cont.)
    WASATCH RANGE
    WHITE MOUNTAINS
MOURNING DOVES
    Nat Wildlife 24:16A (paint-
      ing,c,2) D '85
Movies. See
    MOTION PICTURES
MOVING INDUSTRY
--1953 suburban moving-in scene
    (Los Angeles, California)
    Am Heritage 35:36 (4) F '84
--Family moving (Italy)
    Nat Geog 165:624-5 (c,1) My
      '84
MOZAMBIQUE--COSTUME
--Military costume
    Life 9:12-13 (c,1) D '86
MOZART, WOLFGANG AMADEUS
    Smithsonian 14:71 (paint-
      ing,c,4) Mr '84
--Depicted in movie "Amadeus"
    Life 7:66-70 (c,1) S '84
MUD
--1910s Ford stuck in mud (Iowa)
    Smithsonian 16:60-1 (3) Ag '85
--Covering football players
    Sports Illus 63:34, 36, 41
      (c,2) N 25 '85
MUIR, JOHN
    Am Heritage 33:81 (4) Je '82
MULBERRIES
    Natur Hist 95:102 (c,4) O '86
MULBERRY TREES
    Nat Geog 165:22-3 (c,1) Ja '84
    Am Heritage 37:72 (3) F '86
MULE DEER
    Natur Hist 91:cov., 50-7 (c,1)
      Je '82
    Nat Wildlife 21:5 (c,1) D '82
    Nat Geog 167:675 (c,3) My '85
    Nat Wildlife 24:49 (c,4) F '86
MULES
    Smithsonian 14:cov., 98-109
      (c,1) N '83
    Nat Geog 165:504-5 (c,1) Ap
      '84
--Races (New Mexico)
    Smithsonian 14:102 (3) N '83
MUNICH, WEST GERMANY
    Trav/Holiday 165:38-43 (c,1)
      Ja '86
--Marienplatz
    Trav/Holiday 161:77 (c,2) F
      '84
MURALS
--Anasazi Indians (New Mexico)

    Nat Geog 162:554 (c,2) N '82
--Ancient (Saudi Arabia)
    Smithsonian 14:49 (c,3) S '83
--Child mourning dead soldier
    (Iran)
    Nat Geog 168:110 (c,1) Jl '85
--Cincinnati, Ohio
    Ebony 37:39 (c,4) O '82
--Copies of Picassos (Spain)
    Life 5:100-2 (c,1) Ap '82
--Mexico City, Mexico
    Trav/Holiday 162:56, 59 (c,2)
      Jl '84
    Smithsonian 16:40-2 (c,1) F '86
--Nassau street, Bahamas
    Nat Geog 162:366-7 (c,1) S '82
--San Antonio barrio, Texas
    Smithsonian 16:122 (c,3) D '85
--Works by Diego Rivera
    Trav/Holiday 162:56 (c,2) Jl '84
    Smithsonian 16:39-45 (c,1) F '86
Murder. See
    CRIME AND CRIMINALS
    DEATH
MURRAY RIVER, AUSTRALIA
    Nat Geog 168:254-77 (map,c,1)
      Ag '85
MURRES
--In flight
    Nat Geog 162:546 (c,1) O '82
MUSEUMS
--African sculpture exhibit (North
    Carolina)
    Ebony 40:38 (c,4) Jl '85
--Albertina palace treasures, Vienna,
    Austria
    Smithsonian 15:cov., 62-9 (c,1)
      N '84
--Art works of the Vatican Palace
    Smithsonian 13:120-31 (c,1) D '82
    Life 5:58-70 (c,1) D '82
    Nat Geog 168:764-77 (c,1) D '85
--Ashmolean, Oxford, England
    Smithsonian 14:122 (c,4) S '83
--Baseball Hall of Fame, Coopers-
    town, New York
    Smithsonian 15:129 (c,4) Ap '84
    Trav/Holiday 166:28 (c,4) Ag '86
--Boston Museum of Fine Arts,
    Massachusetts
    Trav/Holiday 163:72 (c,4) Mr '85
--Boston Museum of Science exhibits,
    Massachusetts
    Trav/Holiday 163:73 (c,2) Mr '85
--California State Railroad Museum,
    Sacramento
    Trav/Holiday 158:45 (c,1) Jl '82

MUSEUMS (cont.)
Smithsonian 16:112-23 (c,1)
F '86
--Vatican City
Nat Geog 168:766-7 (c,1) D '85
--See also
FOLGER SHAKESPEARE
LIBRARY
LOUVRE
METROPOLITAN MUSEUM
OF ART
NATIONAL ARCHIVES
SMITHSONIAN INSTITUTION
UFFIZI GALLERY
MUSHROOMS
Life 7:102 (c,4) Ja '84
Natur Hist 95:92 (c,3) Ja '86
--Morels
Nat Wildlife 21:44 (painting,c,4)
O '83
Sports Illus 60:98 (c,4) My 14
'84
--Scarlet hygrophorus mushrooms
Nat Wildlife 24:8 (c,4) O '86
--Toadstools
Nat Geog 163:cov., 48 (c,1)
Ja '83
--Unusual varieties
Nat Wildlife 23:4-9 (c,1) O '85
--Wild mushrooms
Nat Geog 167:539 (c,4) Ap '85
MUSIC
--Collages depicting jazz by
Romare Bearden
Am Heritage 33:86-95 (c,1) F
'82
MUSIC--EDUCATION
Ebony 39:80 (4) F '84
--Indiana University School of
Music
Smithsonian 16:130-48 (1) Ja
'86
--Violin lesson
Nat Geog 165:388 (c,4) Mr '84
MUSIC--HISTORY
--1910s Tin Pan Alley, New York
City
Am Heritage 34:88 (c,2) O '83
MUSICAL INSTRUMENTS
--Balaphone
Ebony 38:80 (c,3) Ap '83
--Blowing jug (South)
Life 6:56-7 (c,1) Ag '83
--Bowed piano
Life 6:139 (c,2) N '83
--Didgeridoo (Australia)
Nat Geog 161:664-5 (c,1) My '82

--Latin American instruments
Trav/Holiday 166:24-5 (c,2) D
'86
--Lotar (Morocco)
Natur Hist 92:62 (c,3) O '83
--Morin Khour (Mongolia)
Nat Geog 167:251 (c,4) F '85
--Pickin' bow (Arkansas)
Trav/Holiday 157:82 (4) My '82
--Sarod (India)
Nat Geog 167:522 (c,3) Ap '85
--Shofars
Life 7:86 (c,4) N '84
--Sitar (Pakistan)
Nat Geog 167:cov., 482-3 (c,1)
Ap '85
--Unusual modern instruments
Life 6:139-44 (c,1) N '83
--See also
ACCORDIONS
BAGPIPES
BANDS
BANDS, MARCHING
BANJO PLAYING
BASS PLAYING
BELLS
BUGLES
CELLOS
CONCERTS
CONDUCTORS, MUSIC
DRUMS
FLUTES
FRENCH HORNS
GUITARS
HARPS
HARPSICHORDS
HORNS
LUTES
MANDOLINS
MUSICAL SCORES
MUSICIANS
ORGANS
PIANOS
SAXOPHONES
TRUMPETS
UKULELES
VIOLINS
XYLOPHONES
MUSICAL SCORES
--16th-17th cents. (Great Britain)
Smithsonian 14:116 (c,4) S '83
--Early 20th cent. baseball song
illustrations
Am Heritage 34:76-9, 114 (c,4)
Je '83
--Early 20th cent. dream-related song
covers

MUSICAL SCORES (cont.)
   Am Heritage 34:90-1 (c,4) O
      '83
--Early 20th cent. silent films
   Am Heritage 36:99-107 (2) Ag
      '85
--Early 20th cent. song covers
   Am Heritage 34:90-1, 94 (c,4)
      O '83
--1908 "Take Me Out to the Ball
   Game" score and slides
   Am Heritage 34:76-7 (c,4) Je
      '83
--1918 Appalachian ballad
   Smithsonian 16:188-9 (4) Ap
      '85
--Liszt's choral music manuscript
   Smithsonian 17:114 (c,4) Ag
      '86
--World War II song covers
   Life 8:94 (c,4) Spring '85
--Writing song at piano
   Ebony 38:78 (c,4) Ap '83
--"Yes! We Have no Bananas"
   cover (1923)
   Am Heritage 34:94 (c,4) O '83
MUSICIANS
--Blues musicians (Tennessee)
   Trav/Holiday 160:50 (c,3) S
      '83
--Calypso (Jamaica)
   Ebony 38:122 (c,4) Ja '83
--Folk musicians
   Life 6:96 (c,3) N '83
--Jazz
   Trav/Holiday 161:69-70 (c,4)
      Ap '84
   Smithsonian 15:154-62 (2) My
      '84
--Morocco
   Natur Hist 92:60-9 (c,1) O '83
--Rock musicians
   Ebony 39:36, 40 (c,3) Je '84
   Life 7:102-5 (c,1) D '84
   Ebony 40:32 (c,3) S '85
--Russian jazz combo
   Smithsonian 14:121 (draw-
      ing,c,1) Jl '83
--Street guitarist (Jerusalem,
   Israel)
   Nat Geog 163:482-3 (c,1) Ap
      '83
--Street musicians (Colorado)
   Trav/Holiday 159:33 (c,4) Je
      '83
--Symphony orchestra (Oregon)
   Ebony 40:36-7 (2) S '85

--See also
   ARMSTRONG, LOUIS
   BANDS
   BASIE, COUNT
   BLAKE, EUBIE
   CONCERTS
   CONDUCTORS, MUSIC
   DAVIS, MILES
   ELLINGTON, DUKE
   GILLESPIE, JOHN BIRKS
      (DIZZY)
   HAMPTON, LIONEL
   HANDY, W. C.
   MENUHIN, YEHUDI
   PARKER, CHARLIE
   RACHMANINOFF, SERGEI
   SEGOVIA, ANDRES
   SOUSA, JOHN PHILIP
   TOSCANINI, ARTURO
MUSK OXEN
   Nat Wildlife 22:37-41 (c,1) Ap '84
   Life 8:95-110 (c,2) My '85
   Nat Geog 169:137 (c,2) Ja '86
   Smithsonian 16:cov., 68-77 (c,1)
      F '86
MUSKRATS
   Nat Wildlife 23:12 (painting,c,4)
      F '85
   Natur Hist 95:26-7 (c,4) Mr '86
MUSSELS
   Smithsonian 14:104, 108 (c,1) S
      '83
MUSSOLINI, BENITO
   Life 8:20 (c,4) Spring '85
MUSTACHES
--1886 gentleman
   Am Heritage 37:86 (painting,c,2)
      F '86
--Handlebar mustache
   Sports Illus 60:20-1 (c,2) Je 18
      '84
--Unusual shape
   Sports Illus 59:74-5 (c,1) Ag 22
      '83
MUSTANGS
   Smithsonian 14:88-96 (c,1) F '84
MUSTARD PLANTS
   Natur Hist 93:70 (c,3) Jl '84
MYCENAE, GREECE
--Ancient ruins
   Nat Geog 170:203 (c,1) Ag '86
MYTHOLOGY
--Ancient Maya mythology
   Nat Geog 169:464-5 (c,4) Ap '86
--Depictions of jungle spirits (Brazil)
   Natur Hist 92:14-20 (drawing,4)
      Ag '83

MYTHOLOGY (cont.)
--Irish myths
    Smithsonian 15:106-13 (draw-
      ing,c,1) F '85
--Kingdom of Shambhala (Tibet)
    Natur Hist 92:54-63 (c,1) Ap
      '83
--Ramayana (India)
    Smithsonian 14:168-9 (paint-
      ing,c,2) F '84
--Reenactment of Pied Piper story
    (Hamelin, W. Germany)
    Trav/Holiday 163:102 (4) My
      '85
--Sites associated with Iceland
    myths
    Smithsonian 16:120-5 (c,4) Ja
      '86
--Thor sculpture (Iceland)
    Smithsonian 16:120 (c,4) Ja '86
--See also
    DEITIES
    DRAGONS
    MERMAIDS
    UNICORNS
MYTHOLOGY--GREEK AND
    ROMAN
--5th cent. B.C. Greek vase
    depicting Jason and Athena
    Nat Geog 168:409 (c,4) S '85
--1st cent. Roman Laocoön sculp-
    ture
    Nat Geog 168:772-3 (c,1) D
      '85
--Late 19th cent. bronze Diana
    weathervane (New York)
    Am Heritage 35:44 (c,3) Ag
      '84
--Apollo Belvedere
    Smithsonian 13:122-3 (sculp-
      ture,c,3) D '82
--Diana sculpture by Saint-
    Gaudens
    Am Heritage 36:51 (4) Je '85
--Greek weather god Aeolus
    Smithsonian 13:90 (c,4) S '82
--Icarus
    Nat Geog 164:200 (drawing,4)
      Ag '83
--"Laocoön" (El Greco painting)
    Smithsonian 13:48-9 (c,1) Jl
      '82
--Niobe
    Smithsonian 15:105 (sculp-
      ture,4) Je '84
--Pan
    Smithsonian 13:110 (sculpture,4)

    D '82
--Reenacting Jason and Argonauts'
    voyage
    Nat Geog 168:406-20 (map,c,1)
      S '85
--Statue of Clio, muse of history
    Am Heritage 33:2 (2) Je '82
--Sun-god Mithras
    Smithsonian 16:73 (sculpture,c,4)
      Ap '85
--See also
    ATHENA
    GRIFFINS
    HERCULES
    MEDUSA
    MERMAIDS
    ULYSSES
    VENUS

-N-

NAACP
--History
    Ebony 39:49-52 (3) Jl '84
NAGASAKI, JAPAN
--1945 ruins of city
    Life 8:14-15, 83 (1) Spring '85
NAILS
--16th cent. (Great Britain)
    Nat Geog 163:673 (c,4) My '83
NAMIBIA
    Nat Geog 161:754-97 (map,c,1)
      Je '82
--Etosha National Park
    Nat Geog 163:344-85 (c,1) Mr '83
--Kuiseb River area
    Natur Hist 92:44-5 (c,2) Mr '83
--Namib Desert
    Nat Geog 164:364-77 (c,1) S '83
--See also
    WINDHOEK
NAMIBIA--COSTUME
    Nat Geog 161:754-95 (c,1) Je '82
NAPLES, ITALY
--Spanish quarter
    Nat Geog 162:724-5 (c,1) D '82
NAPOLEON
    Nat Geog 161:143-89 (c,1) F '82
    Smithsonian 13:76-85 (painting,c,1)
      Ap '82
    Smithsonian 17:62, 67 (paint-
      ing,c,2) S '86
--1832 cast iron stove decoration
    (New York)
    Natur Hist 91:70-1 (c,1) Ja '82
--Birthplace (Corsica)

NAPOLEON (cont.)
    Nat Geog 161:153 (c,4) F '82
--Clothing order placed by
    Napoleon
    Nat Geog 165:10 (c,4) Ja '84
--Home (St. Helena)
    Smithsonian 13:80 (paint-
      ing,c,4) Ap '82
--Items belonging to him
    Nat Geog 170: 332-3 (c,1) S '86
--Scenes from his life and cam-
    paigns
    Nat Geog 161:143- 89 (c,1) F
      '82
--Theory of death by poisoning
    Smithsonian 13:76-85 (paint-
      ing,c,1) Ap '82
--Tomb (Paris, France)
    Nat Geog 161:188 (c,4) F '82
--See also
    JOSEPHINE
NAPOLEON III (FRANCE)
--Displaying royal infant
    Smithsonian 15:38 (engrav-
      ing,4) S '84
NARWHALS
    Nat Geog 169:354-63 (c,1) Mr
      '86
--Killed in hunt (Greenland)
    Nat Geog 165:536-7 (c,1) Ap
      '84
NASHVILLE, TENNESSEE
    Nat Geog 169:606-7 (c,1) My
      '86
NASSAU, BAHAMAS
    Nat Geog 162:366-7, 394-5
      (c,1) S '82
--Street market
    Ebony 38:118 (c,4) Ap '83
NAST, THOMAS
--Cartoons about Boss Tweed
    and Tammany Hall
    Am Heritage 38:81- 96 (draw-
      ing,2) D '86
NASTURTIUMS
    Nat Geog 165:58 (c,1) Ja '84
NATCHEZ, MISSISSIPPI
--Longwood mansion
    Trav/Holiday 159:44 (2) F '83
    Am Heritage 36:100-2 (c,3) O
      '85
    Am Heritage 37:13 (4) F '86
NATIONAL ARCHIVES, WASH-
    INGTON, D.C.
    Smithsonian 17:134-43 (c,1)
      O '86

NATIONAL GEOGRAPHIC SOCIETY
--Washington, D.C. headquarters
    Nat Geog 166:554-60 (c,1) O '84
NATIONAL PARKS
    Nat Wildlife 21:4-11 (map,c,1)
      Ap '83
--Early 20th cent. concessions at
    parks
    Natur Hist 91:14-24 (3) Je '82
--Amboseli, Kenya
    Natur Hist 93:58-9 (c,3) F '84
--Bob Marshall Wilderness, Montana
    Nat Geog 167:664-92 (map,c,1)
      My '85
--Boma, Sudan
    Sports Illus 59:50-64 (map,c,1)
      S 5 '83
--Chitawan, Nepal
    Smithsonian 14:164-9 (c,1) Mr '84
--Etosha, Namibia
    Nat Geog 163:344-85 (c,1) Mr '83
--Manú, Peru
    Smithsonian 13:34-43 (c,1) Ja '83
--Meru National Park, Kenya
    Nat Geog 165:414-15 (c,1) Mr '84
--Plitvice, Yugoslavia
    Sports Illus 59:96 (c,3) O 24 '83
--Ranthambhor National Park
    Nat Geog 166:750-1, 764-7 (c,1)
      D '84
--Serengeti National Park, Tanzania
    Nat Geog 169:560-601 (c,1) My
      '86
--Tsavo National Park, Kenya
    Natur Hist 93:74, 78 (c,3) Ap '84
--See also
    ACADIA
    APPALACHIAN TRAIL
    BANDELIER NATIONAL MONU-
      MENT
    BANFF
    BIG BEND
    BIG THICKET NATIONAL
      MONUMENT
    BRYCE CANYON
    CRATERS OF THE MOON
    DENALI
    DEVILS TOWER
    EVERGLADES
    GLACIER
    GOLDEN GATE NATIONAL
      RECREATION AREA
    GRAND CANYON
    GRAND TETON
    GREAT SAND DUNES NATIONAL
      MONUMENT
    GREAT SMOKY MOUNTAINS

NATIONAL PARKS (cont.)
>   GROS MORNE
>   HALEAKALA
>   HAWAII VOLCANOES
>   ISLE ROYAL
>   KALAUPAPA
>   KATMAI
>   KLUANE
>   LAVA BEDS NATIONAL
>   MONUMENT
>   MAMMOTH CAVE
>   MOUNT RAINIER
>   MOUNT RUSHMORE
>   OLYMPIC
>   OZARK NATIONAL SCENIC
>   RIVERWAYS
>   ROCKY MOUNTAIN
>   SEQUOIA
>   SUNSET CRATER NATIONAL
>   MONUMENT
>   THEODORE ROOSEVELT
>   WILDLIFE REFUGES
>   YELLOWSTONE
>   YOHO
>   YOSEMITE
>   and list under FORESTS
NATIONAL WILDLIFE FEDERA-
    TION
--History
    Nat Wildlife 24:46-53 (c,1) Ap
    '86
NATURALISTS
--Edward W. Nelson
    Smithsonian 13:53 (4) My '82
--Constantine Samuel Rafinesque
    Am Heritage 36:58 (paint-
    ing,c,1) Je '85
--See also
>   AGASSIZ, LOUIS
>   AUDUBON, JOHN JAMES
>   BURROUGHS, JOHN
>   MUIR, JOHN
NAUTILUSES (MOLLUSKS)
    Natur Hist 91:64-8 (c,1) O '82
    Natur Hist 93:cov., 36-41
    (c,1) Ag '84
NAVAJO INDIANS (ARIZONA)--
    ART
--Rock paintings
    Nat Geog 162:72 (c,4) Jl '82
NAVAJO INDIANS (ARIZONA)--
    COSTUME
    Nat Geog 162:616-17 (c,2) N
    '82
--Papoose
    Natur Hist 95:80 (4) S '86

NAVIGATION INSTRUMENTS
--1911 gyrocompass
    Am Heritage 36:76 (1) O '85
--1921 ship's gyroscope
    Am Heritage 36:77 (4) O '85
--Channel markers (Maryland)
    Nat Wildlife 22:12 (c,4) Ap '84
--Found on wrecks of allied World
    War II planes
    Smithsonian 17:106-15 (c,1) Ap
    '86
--Navigation tower (Alaska)
    Nat Geog 162:543 (c,4) O '82
--See also
>   ASTROLABES
>   COMPASSES
>   LIGHTHOUSES
>   MAURY, MATTHEW FONTAINE
>   RADAR
>   SEXTANTS
Navy. See
>   MILITARY COSTUME
>   SAILORS
>   U.S. NAVY
NAZISM
--1934 Nazi rally (Germany)
    Sports Illus 65:50 (2) Ag 4 '86
--1940s Zyklon gas cannister
    Am Heritage 35:94 (c,2) Ag '84
--1945 death list from Mauthausen
    concentration camp
    Am Heritage 35:94 (c,2) Ag '84
--Funeral of former S.S. colonel
    (1984)
    Life 7:120-1 (c,1) Jl '84
--Nazi artifacts
    Life 6:83-8 (c,1) Jl '83
--Nazi flag
    Am Heritage 35:75 (2) Je '84
--Nazi officers (France)
    Life 8:69 (2) F '85
--Neo-Nazi march (Sweden)
    Life 8:68-9 (1) Je '85
--Nuremberg arena
    Am Heritage 36:62-3 (1) Ap '85
--War criminal Josef Mengele
    Life 8:70-1 (1) Ag '85
--War criminals
    Life 8:70-1 (1) Ag '85
--See also
>   CONCENTRATION CAMPS
>   FRANK, ANNE
>   GOEBBELS, PAUL JOSEPH
>   HITLER, ADOLF
>   WORLD WAR II
NEBRASKA
    Nat Geog 162:70-85 (c,1) Jl '82

NEBRASKA (cont.)
--Late 1880s scenes
  Natur Hist 94:44-51 (1) S '85
--Badlands countryside
  Smithsonian 15:101 (c,3) Jl
    '84
--Chimney Rock
  Nat Geog 170:162 (c,4) Ag '86
--Countryside
  Smithsonian 16:118-29 (c,1) O
    '85
--One-room schoolhouses
  Smithsonian 16:118-28 (c,1) O
    '85
--Verdigre
  Life 8:145-50 (1) N '85
--See also
    LINCOLN
    PLATTE RIVER
NEBULAE
--Crab Nebula
  Natur Hist 91:84 (3) O '82
--Horsehead Nebula
  Nat Geog 163:cov. (c,1) Je '83
--See also
    GALAXIES
    MILKY WAY
    STARS
Necklaces. See
    JEWELRY
NEEDLEWORK
--17th-18th cent. embroidered
    samplers
  Smithsoniand 14:201 (c,4) Mr
    '84
--19th cent. embroideries of
    ships (Great Britain)
  Smithsonian 17:13 (c,4) Ag '86
--Crocheting
  Sports Illus 57:64 (c,4) O 25
    '82
--Football player doing needle-
    point
  Sports Illus 63:69 (c,4) S 4
    '85
--See also
    SEWING
    TAPESTRIES
NEHRU, JAWAHARIAL
--Doing headstand (1948)
  Life 8:10 (2) My '85
NELSON, HORATIO
  Sports Illus 65:74 (paint-
    ing,c,4) Jl 21 '86
--Depicted with two arms as ship
    figurehead
  Nat Geog 163:288-9, 294-5

  (c,1) Mr '83
--Monument (Montreal, Quebec)
  Sports Illus 59:18 (c,2) Jl 18 '83
--Nelson doll
  Sports Illus 64:78 (c,4) Je 23 '86
NEMATODES
  Smithsonian 12:58 (c,4) Mr '82
  Nat Geog 166:368 9c,4) S '84
Neon signs. See
    SIGNS AND SIGNBOARDS
NEPAL
  Smithsonian 13:cov., 50-61 (c,1)
    O '82
--Chitawan National Park
  Smithsonian 14:164-9 (c,1) Mr
    '84
--Dolpo
  Smithsonian 16:cov., 128-43 (c,1)
    N '85
--Langu Gorge
  Nat Geog 169:794-801 (map,c,1)
    Je '86
--Sagarmatha Park, Mount Everest
  Nat Geog 161:699, 706-25
    (map,c,1) Je '82
--See also
    HIMALAYAN MOUNTAINS
    MOUNT EVEREST
NEPAL--COSTUME
  Nat Geog 161:705-23 (c,1) Je '82
  Smithsonian 13:52-7 (c,2) O '82
  Trav/Holiday 159:37 (4) My '83
  Nat Geog 166:729-33 (c,1) D '84
  Smithsonian 16:128-43 (c,1) N '85
  Trav/Holiday 165:57 (c,4) Je '86
--Holy man
  Trav/Holiday 166:6 (c,4) S '86
NEPTUNE (PLANET)
  Nat Geog 167:50 (c,2) Ja '85
NERO
--Head on 68 A.D. coin
  Nat Geog 162:690 (c,4) D '82
NESTS
--Bees
  Life 7:26 (c,4) Ag '84
--Dinosaur nest
  Natur Hist 94:26 (4) Mr '85
--Termites
  Natur Hist 92:42 (c,3) My '83
--Wasps
  Nat Geog 163:58 (c,4) Ja '83
--See also
    BIRD NESTS
NETHERLANDS
  Nat Geog 170:500-37 (map,c,1)
    O '86
--Alkmaar cheese market

NETHERLANDS (cont.)
 Trav/Holiday 163:58-9 (c,1)
  Je '85
--Enkhuizen
 Trav/Holiday 163:60-1 (c,1) Je
  '85
--Het Loo Palace
 Nat Geog 170:510-11 (c,1) O
  '86
--Naarden Fortress
 Nat Geog 170:518-19 (c,1) O
  '86
--Oosterschelde Barrier
 Nat Geog 170:526-37 (map,c,1)
  O '86
--Storm-surge barrier across
  Oosterschelde
 Smithsonian 15:94-101 (c,1) Ag
  '84
--Zaandam
 Nat Geog 166:678-9 (c,2) N '84
--See also
  AMSTERDAM
  DELFT
  HAARLEM
  THE HAGUE
  ROTTERDAM
  UTRECHT
NETHERLANDS--ART
--17th cent. paintings
 Smithsonian 13:47-53 (c,1) Je
  '82
--Making Delft porcelain
 Trav/Holiday 160:16, 20 (4) Jl
  '83
NETHERLANDS--COSTUME
 Nat Geog 170:503-25 (c,1) O
  '86
--1940s Dutch officers
 Life 6:12 (4) Ap '83
--Queen Beatrix
 Nat Geog 170:509-11 (c,2) O
  '86
--Royalty
 Smithsonian 13:44 (4) My '82
NETHERLANDS--HOUSING
--Amsterdam houses
 Trav/Holiday 163:48 (c,3) Mr
  '85
NETHERLANDS--RITES AND
  FESTIVALS
--Katwijk mayor eating season's
  first heering
 Nat Geog 170:521 (c,3) O '86
NETHERLANDS ANTILLES
--Bonaire
 Sports Illus 60:112-20

 (map,c,3) F 13 '84
--Curaçao
 Trav/Holiday 159:54-8 (c,1) Je
  '83
--See also
  ARUBA
NEVA RIVER, LENINGRAD, U.S.S.R.
 Smithsonian 13:73 (c,1) Mr '83
NEVADA
--Goldfield (1905)
 Am Heritage 36:41 (4) O '85
--Granite Range
 Natur Hist 95:37-9 (c,1) Ap '86
--Rural highway
 Life 9:28-9 (c,1) Jl '86
--See also
  HOOVER DAM
  LAS VEGAS
  VIRGINIA CITY
NEW BEDFORD, MASSACHUSETTS
--Late 19th cent.
 Am Heritage 34:110 (4) Ap '83
NEW BRUNSWICK
 Trav/Holiday 163:84-7 (c,1) Mr
  '85
--See also
  ST. JOHN
NEW DELHI, INDIA
 Nat Geog 167:506-33 (map,c,1)
  Ap '85
NEW HAMPSHIRE
 Nat Geog 162:770-99 (map,c,1)
  D '82
--19th cent. scene near North Con-
  way
 Smithsonian 16:58-9 (painting,c,1)
  Jl '85
--1830s Indian Stream Republic
 Smithsonian 14:87-95 (painting,c,1)
  My '83
--Early 20th cent. paintings of Mt.
  Monadnock
 Am Heritage 34:30 (c,4) D '82
--Alpine Garden
 Natur Hist 94:22-7 (map,c,1) Jl
  '85
--Franconia Notch
 Trav/Holiday 160:26 (4) Ag '83
--Silver Cascade
 Trav/Holiday 162:52-3 (c,1) S '84
--Washington
 Nat Geog 162:770-1 (c,1) D '82
--See also
  LAKE WINNIPESAUKEE
  MERRIMACK RIVER
  MOUNT WASHINGTON
  PORTSMOUTH

NEW HAMPSHIRE (cont.)
WHITE MOUNTAIN NA-
TIONAL FOREST
WHITE MOUNTAINS
NEW HAVEN, CONNECTICUT
--1906 sketch for railroad station
Am Heritage 35:69 (c,4) Ap
'84
--See also
YALE UNIVERSITY
NEW JERSEY
--Pine Barrens
Smithsonian 14:cov., 78-87
(c,1) Jl '83
--Woodbridge Center Mall
Smithsonian 17:40-1 (c,2) D
'86
--See also
ATLANTIC CITY
CAMDEN
DELAWARE BAY
DELAWARE RIVER
ELIZABETH
GEORGE WASHINGTON
BRIDGE
HUDSON RIVER
NEWARK
PRINCETON UNIVERSITY
NEW MEXICO
--Early 20th cent. paintings by
John Sloan
Am Heritage 33:98-107 (c,1)
Ap '82
--Acoma
Life 9;34 (c,4) Jl '86
--Bosque del Apache wildlife
refuge
Nat Wildlife 24:46-51 (c,1) F
'86
--Chapel
Nat Geog 162:92-3 (c,1) Jl '82
--Chihuahuan Desert
Nat Wildlife 24:27 (c,1) Ap '86
--Cimarron Canyon
Trav/Holiday 164:cov. (c,1) O
'85
--Countryside
Am Heritage 38:62-3 (paint-
ing,c,1) D '86
--Drought landscape (1938)
Am Heritage 37:30-1 (paint-
ing,c,1) Je '86
--Northern New Mexico
Trav/Holiday 164:cov., 52-5
(c,1) O '85
--Postage stamp commemorating
statehood (1962)

Am Heritage 34:53 (c,4) D '82
--Red Rock Cliff
Sports Illus 60:58-9 (c,1) Mr 26
'84
--Rio Grande Rift
Nat Geog 168:178-9 (c,1) Ag '85
--Ruins of Anasazi civilization
Nat Geog 162:554-91 (c,1) N '82
--Sandia Peak tramway
Smithsonian 14:69 (c,3) F '84
--Tajique Canyon
Natur Hist 95:81-2 (map,c,4) O
'86
--See also
ALBUQUERQUE
BANDELIER NATIONAL
MONUMENT
SANTA FE
TAOS
NEW ORLEANS, LOUISIANA
Ebony 39:107-8 (c,4) Ja '84
Trav/Holiday 161:63-4 (c,2) Ap
'84
Ebony 41:120-1 (c,2) Jl '86
--1755 map
Am Heritage 33:32 (c,2) Ap '82
--1878 street
Am Heritage 35:57 (engraving,3)
O '84
--1880s Mardi Gras
Trav/Holiday 161:61, 70-1 (c,3)
F '84
--1885 New Orleans Exposition
Am Heritage 36:61 (3) D '84
--1934 black lifestyle
Am Heritage 38:60 (painting,c,2)
D '86
--1984 Exposition
Smithsonian 15:54-5 (c,1) Je '84
Ebony 39:127-30 (2) Jl '84
--Cemetery
Life 6:160 (2) D '83
--Mardi Gras
Ebony 37:44 (3) Ja '82
--Piazza d'Italia
Smithsonian 15:61 (c,1) Je '84
--Small hotels
Trav/Holiday 159:40 (c,4) Ja '83
NEW YEAR'S DAY
--1887 New Year ad for almanac
Am Heritage 34:15 (c,4) D '82
--Chinese New Year celebration
(China)
Natur Hist 94:52-61 (c,1) F '85
--Chinese New Year's feast (Taiwan)
Nat Geog 161:108-9 (c,1) Ja '82
--Mummers Parade (Philadelphia,

NEW YEAR'S DAY (cont.)
    Pennsylvania)
    Nat Geog 163:338-9 (c,1) Mr
      '83
--New Year's stilt celebration
    (China)
    Life 8:152 (c,3) D '85
--Splashing water to celebrate
    (Burma)
    Nat Geog 166:90-1 (c,1) Jl '84
NEW YEAR'S EVE
--Kansas City, Missouri
    Smithsonian 14:100-1 (c,2) Je
      '83
NEW YORK
--Adirondack region
    Trav/Holiday 162:49-53, 62
      (c,1) Ag '84
--Auburn prison (1831 and 1970)
    Am Heritage 33:12 (4) Je '82
--Catskill Mountain lake
    Trav/Holiday 165:6 (c,4) Mr
      '86
--Great Gull Island
    Natur Hist 93:9-14 (c,2) My
      '84
--Love Canal area
    Natur Hist 92:10 (map,c,3) O
      '83
--Saugerties
    Trav/Holiday 164:4 (c,2) O '85
--Watkins Glen
    Trav/Holiday 159:20 (4) Mr '83
--See also
      ADIRONDACK MOUNTAINS
      COOPERSTOWN
      ERIE CANAL
      HARRIMAN, W. AVERELL
      HUDSON RIVER
      LAKE CHAMPLAIN
      LAKE GEORGE
      LONG ISLAND
      NEW YORK CITY
      NIAGARA FALLS
      ROCHESTER
      SUSQUEHANNA RIVER
      THOUSAND ISLANDS
NEW YORK--MAPS
--New York City
    Sports Illus 64:33, 50-1 (c,1)
      Je 30 '86
--New York Harbor
    Nat Geog 170:19 (c,2) Jl '86
--Physical map
    Natur Hist 92:50-1 (c,1) Mr
      '83

NEW YORK CITY, NEW YORK
    Trav/Holiday 157:73-7 (c,4) Ap
      '82
--19th cent. asylum (Blackwell's
    Island)
    Am Heritage 34:20 (c,4) Ag '83
--19th cent. rule of Boss Tweed
    Am Heritage 38:81-96 (draw-
      ing,2) D '86
--1850s St. Nicholas Hotel
    Am Heritage 33:18-19 (paint-
      ing,c,1) Je '82
--Late 19th cent. book on the hor-
    rors of the big city
    Am Heritage 35:111 (4) Ag '84
--1910s Tin Pan Alley (West 28th
    Street)
    Am Heritage 34:88 (c,2) O '83
--1911 Triangle Shirtwaist Company
    fire damage
    Am Heritage 37:108 (3) F '86
--1930s apartment building
    Am Heritage 35:23 (1) Ag '84
--1934 construction of Hayden
    Planetarium
    Natur Hist 94:4 (3) O '85
--1986 Statue of Liberty centennial
    celebration
    Life 9:396-7 (c,1) Fall '86
--Aerial view from satellite
    Sports Illus 64:50-1 (c,2) Je 30
      '86
--Aerial view of Central Park anti-
    nuke rally
    Life 6:46-7 (c,1) Ja '83
--Aerial view of Water Street
    Am Heritage 34:40 (c,1) Ag '83
--Astoria film studio, Queens (1929)
    Smithsonian 16:110-11 (1) N '85
--Battery Park area
    Smithsonian 16:92 (c,3) D '85
--Carnegie Hall
    Life 5:94 (2) F '82
    Ebony 37:49-50 (c,3) My '82
--Central Park
    Natur Hist 92:28-39 (c,1) Ag '83
    Nat Wildlife 22:33-4 (c,2) O '84
--Central Park (19th cent.)
    Natur Hist 92:30-8 (c,1) Ag '83
--Central Park's Sheep Meadow
    Smithsonian 15:158 (c,2) N '84
--Central Park's Strawberry Fields
    Life 8:61-4 (c,1) N '85
--Chelsea Hotel
    Smithsonian 14:94-107 (c,1) D '83
--Chrysler Building
    Smithsonian 17:160, 162 (c,4) N '86

NEW YORK CITY, NEW YORK
(cont.)
--Commuters on Staten Island
Ferry, New York City
Nat Geog 170:32-3 (c,1) Jl '86
--The Dakota apartment building
Life 7:91-8 (c,1) D '84
--Ellis Island
Life 6:44-9 (c,1) Jl '83
Trav/Holiday 164:34-9 (c,1) Jl
'85
--Federal Hall
Life 5:62-3 (c,1) Mr '82
--Five Points (1829 painting)
Am Heritage 34:17 (c,3) F '83
--Flatiron Building-shaped penny
bank
Smithsonian 14:168 (c,4) S '83
--Ford Foundation building
Smithsonian 13:90 (c,1) Ag '82
--Fulton Fish Market
Nat Geog 170:40-1 (c,1) Jl '86
Natur Hist 95:72-7 (c,1) Ag
'86
--Garment center area
Smithsonian 16:cov., 30-41
(c,1) Ag '85
--Harlem
Ebony 38:80-4 (1) Ja '83
Life 8:124, 140 (c,2) O '85
--Harlem (1920s)
Ebony 38:81 (4) Ja '83
--Harlem row houses
Ebony 41:58 (4) My '86
--Harlem's Cotton Club (1930s)
Ebony 41:92 (3) D '85
--Hester Street (1890s)
Natur Hist 94:90-1 (4) O '85
--Hudson River piers (1942)
Am Heritage 35:66-7 (1) D '83
--Lower Broadway (1830s)
Am Heritage 34:18-19 (paint-
ing,c,4) O '83
--Lower East Side rubble
Life 5:26 (c,3) N '82
--McSorley's bar (1912)
Am Heritage 34:22-3 (paint-
ing,c,1) O '83
--Mulberry Street (1888)
Am Heritage 34:21 (2) F '83
--New York Harbor scenes
Sports Illus 64:28-51 (map,c,1)
Je 30 '86
Nat Geog 170:19-43 (map,c,1)
Jl '86
Smithsonian 17:68-79 (c,1) Jl
'86

--New York Harbor (1885)
Life 9:50-1 (1) Jl '86
--Night scene
Life 9:296-7 (c,1) Fall '86
--Pulitzer Building (1890)
Am Heritage 33:68 (4) O '82
--Queens
Life 7:36-44 (c,3) O '84
--Radio City Music Hall
Trav/Holiday 157:74 (c,4) Ap '82
Life 5:122-3 (c,1) D '82
Smithsonian 14:102-3 (c,2) Je '83
--Schomburg Center
Ebony 37:62-6 (3) S '82
Ebony 38:82 (4) Ja '83
--Skyline
Life 7:126-7 (c,1) D '84
Sports Illus 64:30-1 (c,1) Je 30
'86
Sports Illus 65:2-3 (c,1) Jl 14
'86
--Skyline (1920s)
Smithsonian 17:105 (painting,c,2)
S '86
--Skyline at night
Life 5:98-9 (c,1) Mr '82
Nat Geog 166:804-5 (c,2) D '84
--Skyline of lower Manhattan
Nat Geog 163:567-70 (1) My '83
--Skyline of lower Manhattan (1876)
Nat Geog 163:567-70 (1) My '83
--Skyscrapers
Smithsonian 14:43-51 (c,1) O '83
--Slum area gardens
Nat Geog 166:384-5 (c,1) S '84
--Streets during 1981 garbage strike
Nat Geog 163:434 (c,1) Ap '83
--Temple Emanu-El interior
Smithsonian 13:161 (c,4) N '82
--U.N. Building lit up for 40th
anniversary
Life 8:80-1 (1) D '85
--Union Square (1882)
Am Heritage 33:110 (2) Ag '82
--Vietnam veterans memorial
Life 9:44-5 (c,1) Ja '86
--View from Central Park
Life 5:9 (c,4) Mr '82
--Wall Street
Sports Illus 59:40 (c,1) Ag 1 '83
--Yankee Stadium, Bronx
Sports Illus 60:102-3 (c,1) Je 4
'84
--See also
BRONX
BROOKLYN
BROOKLYN BRIDGE

NEWSPAPER OFFICES (cont.)
--Paraguay
Nat Geog 162:254 (c,3) Ag '82
NEWSPAPERS
--1861 New York Herald war head-
lines
Am Heritage 36:26 (4) Je '85
--1912 headlines of Titanic sink-
ing
Smithsonian 17:56-7 (c,1) Ag
'86
--1945 license and press for post-
war newspaper (Germany)
Am Heritage 33:90, 92 (3) Je
'82
--History of The New York World
Am Heritage 33:62-73 (c,2) O
'82
--Stacked in piles
Life 5:132 (2) D '82
--See also
READING
NIAGARA FALLS, NEW YORK/
ONTARIO
--19th cent. souvenirs
Smithsonian 14:106-11 (c,2) Ja
'84
--Late 19th cent.
Am Heritage 36:106 (4) Je '85
--Paintings of the Falls
Smithsonian 16:126-31 (c,1) S
'85
NICARAGUA
Nat Geog 168:776-811 (map,c,1)
D '85
--See also
MANAGUA
NICARAGUA--COSTUME
Nat Geog 168:777-811 (c,1) D
'85
--1920s rebels
Am Heritage 36:53-61 (2) Ag
'85
Nat Geog 168:786-7 (4) D '85
--Refugees (Honduras)
Nat Geog 164:610-11, 637 (c,1)
N '83
--Augusto Sandino
Am Heritage 36:51, 56-7, 61
(2) Ag '85
Nat Geog 168:786 (4) D '85
--Upper class lifestyles
Life 6:24-30 (c,1) S '83
NICARAGUA--HISTORY
--1933 ejection of U.S. troops
by Sandino
Am Heritage 36:51-61 (c,2)

Ag '85
NICARAGUA--HOUSING
Nat Geog 168:798-9, 805 (c,2) D
'85
NICARAGUA--POLITICS AND GOV-
ERNMENT
--Contra activities (Costa Rica)
Life 8:25-8 (c,1) F '85
--Contras executing government
agent
Life 8:80-1 (2) Je '85
--Revolution
Nat Geog 168:806-11 (c,1) D '85
NICE, FRANCE
--Beach
Trav/Holiday 158:34 (c,4) Jl '82
--Mardi Gras parade
Trav/Holiday 161:cov., 67-8
(c,1) F '84
NICKELODEONS
--Illustrated song slides
Smithsonian 12:cov., 76-83 (c,1)
Mr '82
--Slides illustrating baseball songs
Am Heritage 34:76-9, 114 (c,4)
Je '83
NIGER
Nat Geog 164:482-508 (c,1) O '83
NIGER--COSTUME
Life 8:80-90 (c,1) Mr '85
--Wodaabe tribe
Nat Geog 164:cov., 482-508 (c,1)
O '83
Nat Geog 166:633 (c,1) N '84
NIGER--HOUSING
Life 8:84 (c,4) Mr '85
NIGER RIVER, MALI
Nat Geog 162:400-1 (map,c,1) S
'82
--See also
LAGOS
NIGERIA--ART
--16th cent. ivory spoon
Smithsonian 13:88 (c,4) F '83
--Bronze sculpture done in lost wax
process
Nat Geog 166:618-19 (c,2) N '84
--Yoruba area
Ebony 40:34 (c,4) Jl '85
NIGERIA--COSTUME
Ebony 37:67, 74-5 (4) F '82
Sports Illus 59:106-7, 114-28 (c,1)
N 28 '83
--President
Ebony 37:67 (4) F '82
--Yorba headdress
Trav/Holiday 157:44 (4) F '82

NIGERIA--POLITICS AND
GOVERNMENT
--1960 independence celebration
Ebony 41:204-5 (2) N '85
NIGHT CLUBS
--1930s Cotton Club, Harlem,
New York
Ebony 41:92 (3) D '85
--1930s Cotton Club acts, Har-
lem, New York
Ebony 41:90-2 (2) D '85
--1940s (Paris, France)
Ebony 39:59 (3) D '83
--Bermuda
Trav/Holiday 157:49 (c,3) Je
'82
--Dallas, Texas
Nat Geog 166:302-3 (c,1) S '84
--Madrid, Spain
Nat Geog 169:144-5 (c,1) F
'86
--Ticket booth (Oklahoma)
Nat Geog 164:400 (c,3) S '83
--See also
DANCING
SINGERS
NIJINSKY
Life 9:356 (4) Fall '86
NILE RIVER, AFRICA
Nat Geog 167:576-633 (map,c,1)
My '85
NILE RIVER, EGYPT
Trav/Holiday 165:50-1, 54-5
(c,1) Je '86
--Cairo
Trav/Holiday 157:38 (c,3) F
'82
NILE RIVER, ETHIOPIA
--Blue Nile Falls
Nat Geog 163:645 (c,1) My '83
NIMES, FRANCE
--Maison Carree
Am Heritage 35:54 (4) Je '84
NIMITZ, CHESTER
Am Heritage 33:36 (paint-
ing,c,2) F '82
Ebony 40:114 (4) S '85
NIXON, RICHARD M.
Life 5:139 (c,4) My '82
Am Heritage 33:17 (4) Je '82
Am Heritage 34:49 (4) F '83
Life 8:30 (c,2) Ja '85
Am Heritage 37:34 (3) O '86
Life 9:211, 222-3 (c,1) Fall '86
--Gifts he received in office
Am Heritage 35:96 (c,2) Ag '84
--Leaving the Presidency (1974)

Am Heritage 35:22 (c,1) Je '84
--Pat Nixon
Life 9:109 (c,4) Jl '86
--Tricia Nixon's 1971 wedding
Life 9:222-3 (c,1) Fall '86
NOAH'S ARK
--13th cent. mosaic (Venice, Italy)
Smithsonian 15:48-9 (c,1) S '84
--1483 Nuremburg Bible depiction
Smithsonian 14:89 (woodcut,c,4)
Je '83
NOBEL PRIZE
--Nobel medal
Am Heritage 35:53 (c,4) O '84
NOMADS
--Golog tribe (China)
Nat Geog 161:244-63 (c,1) F '82
--Golok tribe (Tibet)
Natur Hist 91:48-57 (c,1) S '82
--Kazak people (China)
Nat Geog 165:296-7 (c,1) Mr '84
--Kirghiz people (U.S.S.R.)
Nat Geog 170:258-9 (c,3) Ag '86
--Qalandar people (Pakistan)
Natur Hist 92:50-8 (c,1) My '83
--Rashaidas (Sudan)
Nat Geog 161:375 (c,3) Mr '82
--Tibet
Natur Hist 95:56-65 (c,1) Ja '86
--See also
BEDOUINS
BERBER PEOPLE
GYPSIES
NORFOLK, VIRGINIA
Nat Geog 168:72-3, 88-9 (c,1) Jl
'85
--Fishing pier
Trav/Holiday 157:40 (c,3) Je '82
NORFOLK ISLAND
Nat Geog 164:530-41 (map,c,1) O
'83
NORFOLK ISLAND--COSTUME
Nat Geog 164:531-41 (c,1) O '83
NORTH CAROLINA
--Albemarle Country
Trav/Holiday 157:53 (c,3) My '82
--Catawba County history
Am Heritage 33:100-5 (paint-
ing,c,1) Ag '82
--MacRae Meadows Scottish festival
Smithsonian 13:109-16 (c,3) Jl '82
--Roan Mountain
Natur Hist 94:38-41 (c,1) Ap '85
--Sodom Laurel (1916)
Smithsonian 16:184 (3) Ap '85
--Outer Banks
Trav/Holiday 159:38-41 (c,2) Je '83

NORTH CAROLINA (cont.)
--See also
    ASHEVILLE
    BLUE RIDGE MOUNTAINS
    CHARLOTTE
    GREAT SMOKY MOUNTAINS
        NATIONAL PARK
    MOUNT MITCHELL
NORTH CAROLINA--MAPS
--1585 Roanoke Island
    Am Heritage 34:34 (c,4) Ag
        '83
--Croatan National Forest
    Natur Hist 94:34 (c,4) Je '85
NORTH DAKOTA
--Countryside
    Nat Geog 166:568-9 (c,1) N
        '84
--Minnewaukan
    Life 5:158 (3) N '82
--Tornado in village (1895)
    Am Heritage 37:38-9 (1) Je '86
--See also
    BADLANDS
    THEODORE ROOSEVELT
        NATIONAL PARK
NORTH POLE
    Smithsonian 13:52-4 (c,4) D
        '82
    Nat Geog 170:314-15, 322-3
        (c,1) S '86
NORTH YEMEN
    Nat Geog 168:485, 498-504
        (map,c,1) O '85
NORTH YEMEN--COSTUME
    Trav/Holiday 163:28 (c,4) Je
        '85
    Nat Geog 168:cov., 498-504
        (c,1) O '85
--Woman with dyed hands
    Nat Geog 168:cov. (c,2) O '85
NORTHERN IRELAND--COSTUME
--IRA guerrillas
    Life 8:40-6 (c,1) O '85
NORTHERN IRELAND--POLITICS
        AND GOVERNMENT
--Funeral of IRA hunger striker
    Life 5:48 (2) Ja '82
--Police shooting at crowd
    Life 7:128-9 (1) O '84
Northern Lights. See
    AURORA BOREALIS
NORTHWEST TERRITORIES,
        CANADA
--Arctic region
    Nat Geog 163:148-9, 174-89
        (map,c,1) F '83

--Hood River area of 1821 Franklin
        expedition
    Nat Geog 169:128-40 (map,c,1)
        Ja '86
NORWAY
--1940 German attack on Norwegian
        village
    Am Heritage 37:22-3 (1) O '86
--Arctic region
    Nat Geog 163:148-9, 194-7
        (map,c,1) F '83
--See also
    LAPP PEOPLE
    OSLO
    VIKINGS
NORWAY--ARCHITECTURE
--Model of 12th cent. Norwegian
        church (Wisconsin)
    Trav/Holiday 164:60-1 (c,1) O
        '85
NORWAY--COSTUME
--Lapp people
    Nat Geog 163:194-7 (c,1) F '83
NOTRE DAME CATHEDRAL, PARIS,
        FRANCE
    Trav/Holiday 158:61 (c,4) N '82
NOVA SCOTIA
--Christmas tree industry
    Sports Illus 61:110-21 (c,1) D
        24 '84
NUCLEAR ENERGY
--Anti nuke demonstration (Bonn,
        West Germany)
    Life 5:38-9 (c,1) Ja '82
--Anti nuke demonstration (Califor-
        nia)
    Nat Geog 165:455 (c,4) Ap '84
--Anti nuke demonstration (Sicily,
        Italy)
    Life 6:186 (c,2) N '83
--Drums of radioactive waste
    Nat Wildlife 21:20-3 (1) Ap '83
--Fusion laser equipment (California)
    Nat Geog 165:354-5 (c,1) Mr '84
--Nuclear testing (Mururoa, Pacific)
    Sports Illus 63:32 (c,4) S 2 '85
--Victims of Chernobyl nuclear
        disaster, U.S.S.R.
    Life 9:cov., 20-6 (c,1) Ag '86
--See also
    BOHR, NIELS
    NUCLEAR POWER PLANTS
NUCLEAR POWER PLANTS
    Life 5:34-42 (c,1) My '82
--Diablo Canyon, California
    Nat Geog 165:455 (c,3) Ap '84
--Pennsylvania

NUCLEAR POWER PLANTS
(cont.)
Natur Hist 91:26-7 (c,2) Jl '82
--TVA cooling tower (Tennessee)
Nat Geog 169:609 (c,4) My '86
--Three Mile Island, Pennsylvania
Life 5:34 (c,1) My '82
Nat Geog 167:378-9 (c,1) Mr
'85
--Victims of Chernobyl nuclear
disaster, U.S.S.R.
Life 9:cov., 20-6 (c,1) Ag '86
Nudibranches. See
SLUGS
NURFMBERG, WEST GERMANY
--1940s Nazi arena
Am Heritage 36:62-3 (1) Ap
'85
--Christmas Market
Trav/Holiday 158:12 (c,4) D
'82
NURSES
Ebony 37:62 (4) Jl '82
Ebony 37:68 (c,4) Ag '82
--See also
BARTON, CLARA
NUT INDUSTRY--HARVESTING
--Picking macadamia nuts (Hawaii)
Trav/Holiday 166:63 (c,3) Jl
'86
NUTCRACKERS
--Clark's nutcrackers
Natur Hist 92:60-3 (c,1) S '83
Nutrias. See
COYPUS
Nuts. See
ALMOND TREES
CHESTNUTS
NUT INDUSTRY
NUUK, GREENLAND
Nat Geog 163:192-3 (c,2) F '83

-O-

OAK TREES
Natur Hist 92:14 (c,3) My '83
Nat Wildlife 22:4 (c,1) F '84
Smithsonian 15:83 (c,1) My '84
Nat Geog 169:396-7 (c,1) Mr '86
--Oak leaves
Nat Wildlife 23:60 (c,1) O '85
OAKLAND, CALIFORNIA
--Tribune building
Ebony 40:105 (c,2) Je '85
OAKLEY, ANNIE
Smithsonian 13:63 (4) Ja '83

Am Heritage 36:63 (4) D '84
OASES
--California
Smithsonian 15:40 (c,4) My '84
--Namibia
Nat Geog 163:348-9, 352-3 (c,1)
Mr '83
OAT FIELDS
Natur Hist 93:108 (c,4) Ap '84
OAT INDUSTRY--HARVESTING
--Ohio
Nat Wildlife 20:48 (c,4) Ag '82
OAXACA, MEXICO
Trav/Holiday 166:10 (c,4) O '86
Natur Hist 95:61 (c,4) D '86
OBESITY
Ebony 38:86 (3) N '82
Ebony 39:118 (4) F '84
Life 7:25, 28 (c,2) Mr '84
Ebony 39:67 (c,4) My '84
Ebony 42:142 (c,4) N '86
--Fat mouse
Smithsonian 14:121 (c,1) My '83
--Fat people
Ebony 41:39-40, 52 (3) Ap '86
--Heavy man
Sports Illus 59:34 (c,4) Ag 22 '83
--Obese rat
Smithsonian 16:92 (c,2) Ja '86
--Obesity research
Smithsonian 16:90-7 (c,1) Ja '86
--Trousers for 500 lb. man
Ebony 38:66-8 (2) Ja '83
OBSERVATORIES
--France
Nat Geog 163:792-3 (c,1) Je '83
--Jantar Mantar, Delhi, India
Nat Geog 167:532 (c,1) Ap '85
--Mauna Kea, Hawaii
Nat Geog 163:724-5 (c,1) Je '83
--See also
TELESCOPES
OCALA NATIONAL FOREST, FLORIDA
--Juniper Springs
Natur Hist 93:32-4 (map,c,1) D
'84
O'CASEY, SEAN
Smithsonian 15:126 (4) Ag '84
Occupations. See
ABOLITIONISTS
ACROBATS
ACTORS
AIRPLANE PILOTS
ANIMAL TRAINERS
ARCHAEOLOGY
ARCHITECTS
ARTISTS

OCCUPATIONS (cont.)
  ASTRONAUTS
  ATHLETES
  AUTOMOBILE MECHANICS
  BAKERS
  BARBERSHOPS
  BARTENDERS
  BEE KEEPING
  BEGGARS
  BLACKSMITHS
  BUSINESSMEN
  BUTCHERS
  CARPENTRY
  CARTOONISTS
  CHEFS
  CONDUCTORS, MUSIC
  CONSTRUCTION WORKERS
  DENTISTS
  DISC JOCKEYS
  DOCTORS
  ENGINEERS
  FACTORY WORKERS
  FARM WORKERS
  FARMERS
  FIRE FIGHTERS
  FISHERMEN
  GARDENERS
  GUARDS
  HOBOES
  HUNTERS
  INVENTORS
  JOCKEYS
  JUDGES
  JUGGLERS
  LABORERS
  LIFEGUARDS
  LUMBERJACKS
  MAIDS
  MATADORS
  METALWORKING
  MILITARY COSTUME
  MINERS
  MODELS
  NURSES
  PAINTERS
  PHOTOGRAPHERS
  PIRATES
  PLUMBERS
  PORTERS
  RAILROAD WORKERS
  SAILORS
  SALESMEN
  SANITATION WORKERS
  SCHOLARS
  SHEPHERDS
  SNAKE CHARMERS
  SOCIAL WORKERS

  SPIES
  SPORTS ANNOUNCERS
  STATESMEN
  STREET VENDORS
  TELEVISION NEWSCASTERS
  TRANSIT WORKERS
  TRUCK DRIVERS
  VETERINARIANS
  WAITERS
  WAITRESSES
OCEAN CRAFT
--1920s research vessel (Germany)
  Natur Hist 95:53-4 (4) O '86
--1940s research vessel
  Natur Hist 95:51, 53-4 (3) O '86
--Remotely piloted vehicles
  Nat Geog 163:312-13 (c,2) Mr '83
--Submersibles
  Nat Geog 162:822-3 (c,1) D '82
  Nat Geog 164:cov., 104A-C (c,1)
    Jl '83
  Smithsonian 17:64 (c,4) Ag '86
  Nat Geog 170:706-7 (drawing,c,1)
    D '86
Oceania. See
  PACIFIC ISLANDS
OCEANOGRAPHY
--Discovery of Mid-Atlantic Ridge
  Natur Hist 95:48-62 (c,1) O '86
OCEANS
--Atlantic Ocean currents
  Natur Hist 94:48-9 (c,1) Je '85
--See also
  ATLANTIC OCEAN
  PACIFIC OCEAN
  WAVES
OCEANS--MAPS
--Map of ocean terrain
  Nat Geog 162:822-3 (c,3) D '82
OCELOTS
  Smithsonian 13:41 (c,4) Ja '83
  Nat Wildlife 21:14-17 (c,2) O '83
  Nat Geog 167:744 (c,4) Je '85
OCTOPI
  Smithsonian 13:128 (c,4) Mr '83
  Life 8:10-11 (c,1) Ap '85
Odors. See
  SMELL
OFFICE BUILDINGS
--1890 (New York City, New York)
  Am Heritage 33:68 (4) O '82
--1921 van der Rohe skyscraper
    model (Germany)
  Smithsonian 17:124 (4) D '86
--Architect's model of planned build-
    ings (China)
  Nat Geog 164:66-7 (c,2) Jl '83

OFFICE BUILDINGS (cont.)
--Calgary, Alberta
  Nat Geog 165:380-1 (c,1) Mr
    '84
--Chrysler Building, New York
    City, New York
  Smithsonian 17:160, 162 (c,4)
    N '86
--Cutting ribbon of new building
    (Washington, D.C.)
  Ebony 38:85 (4) Jl '83
--Dallas, Texas
  Nat Geog 166:272-3 (c,1) S '84
  Trav/Holiday 166:40 (c,1) Jl
    '86
--Flatiron Building-shaped penny
    bank
  Smithsonian 14:168 (c,4) S '83
--Houston, Texas
  Trav/Holiday 158:40-1 (c,1) N
    '82
--Kansas City, Missouri
  Am Heritage 34:71 (c,3) D '82
--Los Angeles, California
  Trav/Holiday 160:cov. (c,1) N
    '83
--Modern Kevin Roche buildings
  Smithsonian 13:90-7 (c,1) Ag
    '82
--Modern lobby (Wichita, Kansas)
  Nat Geog 168:372-3 (c,1) S
    '85
--New York City skyscrapers,
    New York
  Smithsonian 14:43-51 (c,1) O
    '83
--Park Avenue Atrium, New York
    City, New York
  Smithsonian 13:108 (c,1) F '83
--Prefabricated (Silicon Valley,
    California)
  Nat Geog 162:460-1 (c,1) O '82
--Renaissance Center, Detroit,
    Michigan
  Ebony 42:160 (2) D '86
--Seoul, South Korea
  Sports Illus 65:40 (c,4) S 29
    '86
--Sao Paulo, Brazil
  Trav/Holiday 159:56 (c,3) Ja
    '83
--Tokyo, Japan
  Nat Geog 170:618 (c,1) N '86
--Unusual skyscrapers
  Smithsonian 14:42-51 (c,1) O
    '83
--See also

  EMPIRE STATE BUILDING
  WORLD TRADE CENTER
  list under ARCHITECTURAL
    STRUCTURES
OFFICE BUILDINGS--CONSTRUCTION
  Smithsonian 16:44-53 (c,1) S '85
OFFICE WORK
--Vehicle registration files (Mexico)
  Nat Geog 166:168-9 (c,1) Ag '84
OFFICES
  Ebony 38:108 (2) Ap '83
--Alabama
  Sports Illus 59:82 (c,2) S 19 '83
--Board room
  Ebony 38:86 (3) Jl '83
--Dentist's office
  Life 6:84 (c,4) O '83
--Filing cabinets
  Life 8:144-6 (2) D '85
--Filing cabinets at U.S. National
    Archives
  Am Heritage 35:89 (c,4) Ag '84
--Graphics studio (New York)
  Smithsonian 15:118-19 (c,3) F '85
--Open plan (California)
  Nat Geog 162:462 (c,1) O '82
--See also
    DESKS
    MEETINGS
    NEWSPAPER OFFICES
OHIO
--Late 19th cent. houses (Licking
    County)
  Am Heritage 37:100-5 (2) F '86
--Malabar Farm
  Trav/Holiday 159:25-9 (4) Ap '83
--Steubenville
  Life 5:84-90 (1) N '82
--See also
    CINCINNATI
    CLEVELAND
    OHIO RIVER
    SANDUSKY
OHIO RIVER, CINCINNATI, OHIO
  Am Heritage 34:96-101 (c,1) O
    '83
OHIO RIVER, OHIO/KENTUCKY
  Nat Geog 166:18 (c,1) Jl '84
OIL INDUSTRY
--1930s backyard derricks (Texas)
  Am Heritage 37:64 (2) F '86
--Alaska
  Natur Hist 91:8-18 (map,c,2) O
    '82
--Exploration activities (Wyoming)
  Ebony 39:60-3 (c,1) Ja '84
--Offshore oil lines (California)

OIL INDUSTRY (cont.)
Nat Geog 165:424-5 (c,1) Ap
'84
--Oil wells (Texas)
Smithsonian 14:141 (3) N '83
--Refinery (Bahamas)
Ebony 38:118 (c,4) Ap '83
--Refinery (Delaware)
Nat Geog 164:176 (c,4) Ag '83
--Refinery (Houston, Texas)
Smithsonian 16:96 (c,3) O '85
--Refinery (Tulsa, Oklahoma)
Nat Geog 164:382-3 (c,1) S
'83
--Scotland
Nat Geog 166:46-7 (c,2) Jl '84
--Shale oil operation (Colorado)
Nat Geog 166:212 (c,4) Ag '84
--Sinai, Egypt
Nat Geog 161:434-5 (c,1) Ap
'82
--Uncoupling drill pipe (Louisiana)
Nat Geog 164:236-7 (c,1) Ag
'83
--Welding a pipeline (Peru)
Nat Geog 161:313 (c,3) Mr '82
OIL INDUSTRY--DRILLING
--Capsized offshore oil rig (New-
foundland)
Life 5:85-90 (c,1) Ap '82
--Offshore (Ivory Coast)
Nat Geog 162:120 (c,4) Jl '82
--Offshore oil rig (Alaska)
Natur Hist 91:8, 18 (c,2) O
'82
Nat Geog 163:154 (c,1) F '83
--Offshore oil rig (Louisiana)
Ebony 38:139-42 (c,2) Mr '83
--Offshore oil rigs (Arctic)
Natur Hist 95:66-7 (c,1) D '86
--Thailand
Nat Geog 162:520 (c,4) O '82
Oil industry--transportation. See
ALASKA PIPELINE
TANKERS
OKAPIS
Life 5:46-7 (c,1) Je '82
O'KEEFFE, GEORGIA
Smithsonian 13:10 (c,4) Ja '83
--1926 painting of black iris
Smithsonian 14:99 (c,4) Mr '84
--"Red Hills, Grey Sky" (1935)
Natur Hist 94:63 (painting,c,4)
N '85
--"Shelton Hotel, New York, No.
1" (1926)
Smithsonian 13:132 (painting,c,3)

N '82
--Wooden sculpture of her by Mari-
sol
Smithsonian 14:55 (c,4) F '84
OKEFENOKEE SWAMP, FLORIDA/
GEORGIA
Nat Geog 166:815 (c,1) D '84
OKLAHOMA
--Eastern Oklahoma
Trav/Holiday 165:54-7 (map,c,1)
F '86
--Kenton
Nat Geog 166:330-1 (c,1) S '84
--Postage stamp commemorating
statehood (1957)
Am Heritage 34:53 (c,4) D '82
--See also
TULSA
OLIVE INDUSTRY
--Olive oil production (Italy)
Smithsonian 15:98-107 (c,1) Mr
'85
--Pressing by hand (Egypt)
Nat Geog 161:206 (c,4) F '82
OLIVE TREES
Smithsonian 15:98-9 (c,1) Mr '85
Life 9:167 (c,4) Fall '86
OLIVIER, SIR LAURENCE
--Life and works
Life 5:139-54 (c,1) D '82
OLMSTEAD, FREDERICK LAW
Nat Wildlife 20:41 (painting,c,1)
Je '82
Natur Hist 92:29 (4) Ag '83
OLYMPIA, GREECE
Smithsonian 15:64-73 (c,1) Je '84
Natur Hist 93:62-72 (c,2) Je '84
Life 7:8-9 (c,1) Summer '84
OLYMPIC MOUNTAINS, WASHINGTON
Trav/Holiday 159:42 (c,3) My '83
--Mount Olympus
Nat Geog 165:650-1 (c,1) My '84
OLYMPIC NATIONAL PARK, WASH-
INGTON
Trav/Holiday 159:42-3, 147 (c,1)
My '83
Nat Geog 165:644-54, 673 (c,1)
My '84
--Olympic National Forest
Natur Hist 95:30-2 (map,c,1) Mr
'86
--See also
OLYMPIC MOUNTAINS
OLYMPICS
--20th cent. female Olympic athletes
Life 7:38-45 (c,1) Summer '84
--20th cent. souvenirs

OLYMPICS (cont.)
   Life 7:92-7 (c,1) Summer '84
--History of summer Olympics
   Life 7:entire issue (c,1)
      Summer '84
--Olympics ring symbol
   Sports Illus 61:56 (c,3) Jl 16
      '84
--Olympics symbol with broken
      ring
   Sports Illus 60:cov. (c,1) My
      21 '84
--Olympic torch
   Sports Illus 59:15 (paint-
      ing,c,4) O 3 '83
   Sports Illus 61:5-6 (c,1) Jl 18
      '84
--Special Olympics
   Life 6:121-4 (c,1) Jl '83
--Stamp commemorating Olympics
      (Philippines)
   Sports Illus 61:66 (c,4) Jl 16
      '84
OLYMPICS--1896 SUMMER
      (ATHENS)
   Life 7:10-14 (1) My '84
OLYMPICS--1904 SUMMER (ST.
      LOUIS)
   Life 7:24-30 (1) Summer '84
OLYMPICS--1908 SUMMER (LON-
      DON)
--Marathon
   Life 7:10-11 (1) Summer '84
OLYMPICS--1912 SUMMER
      (STOCKHOLM)
--Awards ceremony
   Life 7:106-7 (1) Summer '84
OLYMPICS--1912 SUMMER
      (STOCKHOLM)
--Jim Thorpe's medal
   Sports Illus 57:48 (c,4) O 25
      '82
OLYMPICS--1924 WINTER
      (CHAMONIX)
   Sports Illus 59:102-16 (1) D
      26 '83
OLYMPICS--1932 SUMMER (LOS
      ANGELES)
   Am Heritage 33:64-71 (c,1)
      Ag '82
   Sports Illus 57:96, 98 (4) N
      22 '82
   Life 7:70-3 (4) Summer '84
   Sports Illusd 61:109-35, 146
      (c,4) Jl 18 '84
OLYMPICS--1936 SUMMER (BERLIN)
   Sports Illus 65:48, 51, 58-9

   (2) Ag 4 '86
--Carrying Olympic torch through
      Nazi Berlin
   Life 7:102-3 (1) Summer '84
--Track events
   Ebony 39:140-2 (3) D '83
   Ebony 39:140 (2) Je '84
OLYMPICS--1948 SUMMER (LONDON)
--Track events
   Sports Illus 58:108 (4) F 14 '83
   Ebony 39:142 (4) Je '84
OLYMPICS--1952 WINTER (OSLO)
--Speed skating
   Sports Illus 65:64 (4) Jl 7 '86
OLYMPICS--1960 SUMMER (ROME)
   Ebony 39:144 (4) Je '84
--Track
   Sports Illus 58:94 (4) My 16 '83
   Ebony 39:84 (4) F '84
   Life 7:118-19 (1) Summer '84
OLYMPICS--1968 SUMMER (MEXICO
      CITY)
--Black power fist symbol at award
      ceremony
   Ebony 39:148 (4) Je '84
   Life 7:106 (c,4) Summer '84
   Ebony 41:102 (4) N '85
OLYMPICS--1972 SUMMER (MUNICH)
--Disputed basketball game
   Life 7:104-5 (c,4) Summer '84
--Opening ceremonies
   Life 7:12-13 (c,1) Summer '84
OLYMPICS--1976 SUMMER (MON-
      TREAL)
--Track
   Sports Illus 61:61 (c,4) Jl 30 '84
OLYMPICS--1980 SUMMER (MOSCOW)
   Life 7:6-7, 110-11 (c,1) Summer
      '84
--Acrobats tumbling
   Life 9:390-1 (c,1) Fall '86
OLYMPICS--1980 WINTER (LAKE
      PLACID)
--Slalom
   Sports Illus 56:89 (c,4) Ja 18 '82
OLYMPICS--1984 SUMMER (LOS
      ANGELES)
   Sports Illus 61:cov., 2-3, 24-46
      (c,1) Ag 6 '84
   Sports Illus 61:cov., 2-3, 18-85
      (c,1) Ag 13 '84
   Sports Illus 61:cov., 2-3, 22-106
      (c,1) Ag 20 '84
   Ebony 39:172-80 (c,3) O '84
   Life 8:6-7, 116-26 (c,1) Ja '85
   Ebony 40:70 (4) Ja '85
--Bicycling

OMAN--COSTUME (cont.)
--Camel herder
    Nat Geog 168:486 (c,4) O '85
O'NEILL, EUGENE
--Depicted on postage stamp
    Am Heritage 34:54 (c,4) D '82
ONTARIO
--Old Fort William
    Trav/Holiday 163:14, 121-2
        (c,3) Ap '85
--See also
        HUDSON BAY
        NIAGARA FALLS
        OTTAWA
        THOUSAND ISLANDS
        TORONTO
OPAL MINING
--Australia
    Trav/Holiday 163:140 (4) Mr '85
Opera. See
        THEATER
Opera houses. See
        THEATERS
OPIUM
    Nat Geog 167:144-67 (c,1) F
        '85
OPIUM INDUSTRY
--1840s (China)
    Am Heritage 37:4, 50-63 (c,2)
        Ag '86
--Harvesting poppies (Thailand)
    Nat Geog 162:532 (c,4) O '82
--India
    Nat Geog 167:156-9 (c,1) F '85
--Thailand
    Nat Geog 167:164-7 (c,1) F '85
OPOSSUMS
    Nat Wildlife 21:65 (c,2) D '82
    Nat Wildlife 21:2 (c,1) O '83
    Nat Wildlife 23:20-3 (c,1) D
        '84
OPPENHEIMER, J. ROBERT
    Am Heritage 34:55 (4) Je '83
OPTICAL ILLUSIONS
    Smithsonian 16:98-104 (c,4) Ap
        '85
OPTICAL PRODUCTS
--Mid 19th cent. optician's tools
    Sports Illus 64:93 (c,4) Mr
        10 '86
--Eye chart
    Sports Illus 64:55 (c,4) Mr 31
        '86
--See also
        EYEGLASSES
ORANGE INDUSTRY--HARVESTING
--Florida

    Nat Geog 162:211 (c,4) Ag '82
ORANGUTANS
    Nat Wildlife 21:8 (c,4) Ag '83
    Smithsonian 16:103 (c,3) D '85
    Nat Wildlife 25:53 (c,3) D '86
ORCHIDS
    Trav/Holiday 157:60 (c,4) Ja '82
    Smithsonian 13:97 (c,4) Je '82
    Nat Wildlife 21:68 (c,1) D '82
    Smithsonian 14:83 (c,4) Jl '83
    Nat Geog 165:268-9 (c,1) F '84
    Nat Wildlife 22:9 (c,2) Ag '84
    Natur Hist 93:74-7 (c,1) O '84
    Nat Geog 167:548 (c,4) Ap '85
    Smithsonian 16:55 (c,4) My '85
    Smithsonian 16:168-81 (c,1) N
        '85
    Nat Wildlife 24:10 (c,4) F '86
OREGON
--Cape Arago lighthouse
    Trav/Holiday 162:14 (c,4) Ag '84
--Coastline
    Nat Geog 168:158-9 (c,2) Ag '85
--Proxy Falls
    Nat Wildlife 21:52 (c,1) Ag '83
--Wallowa Mountains
    Trav/Holiday 157:16 (4) Je '82
--See also
        CASCADE RANGE
        MOUNT HOOD
        PORTLAND
        SNAKE RIVER
ORGAN PLAYING
    Ebony 39:50 (c,4) Ja '84
    Ebony 41:48 (c,4) S '86
ORGAN PLAYING--HUMOR
--History of organ
    Sports Illus 57:58-70 (draw-
        ing,c,1) Ag 30 '82
ORGANS (MUSICAL INSTRUMENT)
    Smithsonian 13:109 (c,4) F '83
ORINOCO RIVER, VENEZUELA
    Trav/Holiday 157:62 (c,3) Mr '82
    Nat Geog 168:331 (c,1) S '85
ORIOLES
    Natur Hist 91:50-1 (c,1) O '82
    Nat Wildlife 22:19, 24, 28 (c,4)
        D '83
ORIZABA MOUNTAIN, MEXICO
    Nat Geog 166:430-1 (c,1) O '84
ORKNEY ISLANDS, SCOTLAND
    Nat Geog 166:51, 60-1 (c,1) Jl
        '84
ORLANDO, FLORIDA
--Disney World
    Life 9:111 (c,3) Fall '86
--Epcot Center

ORLANDO, FLORIDA (cont.)
Life 5:138-9 (c,1) O '82
Life 5:I-XXIII (c,1) D '82
Ebony 38:122 (c,4) Ja '83
Am Heritage 35:70, 75, 79 (c,1)
D '83
--Epcot geosphere
Nat Geog 162:176-7 (c,1) Ag
'82
ORWELL, GEORGE
Am Heritage 35:65, 71 (draw-
ing,2) F '84
OSLO, NORWAY
--Aerial view
Sports Illus 65:56-7 (c,2) Jl
7 '86
--Bislett Stadium
Sports Illus 65:54-68 (c,1) Jl
7 '86
OSPREYS
Trav/Holiday 157:60 (c,4) My
'82
Trav/Holiday 162:36 (c,4) S
'84
OSTRICHES
Nat Geog 161:cov. (c,1) Je '82
Nat Geog 163:362-3 (c,2) Mr
'83
Sports Illus 60:24-5 (c,1) Ap
9 '84
Life 8:74-5 (1) Ap '85
Sports Illusd 65:63 (c,4) S 8
'86
Sports Illus 95:cov., 34-41
(c,1) D '86
OTTAWA, ONTARIO
Trav/Holiday 157:38 (c,4) My
'82
--Chateau Laurier
Trav/Holiday 162:26 (c,3) D '84
--Peace Tower
Trav/Holiday 166:4 (c,3) Ag
'86
OTTERS
Sports Illus 57:72-86 (c,1) D
13 '82
Nat Wildlife 22:21 (c,4) F '84
Smithsonian 14:125 (c,1) Mr '84
--Sea otters
Nat Wildlife 20:10-11 (c,1) Ap
'82
Nat Wildlife 21:6-7 (c,1) Ag '83
Nat Wildlife 24:58-9 (c,1) Ap
'86
Nat Wildlife 25:17-20 (c,1) D
'86
--Swimming in river (Peru)

Smithsonian 13:37 (c,4) Ja '83
OTTOMAN EMPIRE. See also
SULEYMAN
OTTOMAN EMPIRE--RELICS
--Treasures of Topkapi Museum,
Istanbul, Turkey
Smithsonian 16:114-23 (c,1) F
'86
OTTOMAN EMPIRE--RITES AND
FESTIVALS
--1720 Ottoman festival (Turkey)
Smithsonian 16:120 (painting,c,3)
F '86
OUTHOUSES
--Outhouse race (Yukon)
Trav/Holiday 164:63 (c,2) Ag '85
OVENBIRDS
Smithsonian 13:180 (c,4) O '82
OWENS, JESSE
Ebony 39:140-6 (3) D '83
Ebony 39:140 (2) Je '84
Ebony 39:55, 68 (3) Jl '84
Life 7:100-1, 112 (1) Summer '84
Ebony 41:339 (4) N '85
Sports Illus 65:58 (4) Ag 4 '86
Am Heritage 37:109 (4) Ag '86
OWLS
Nat Geog 164:262-3 (c,1) Ag '83
Nat Wildlife 22:51 (c,1) Je '84
Nat Wildlife 22:60 (c,1) O '84
Smithsonian 16:150 (c,4) O '85
Nat Wildlife 23:34-9 (c,1) O '85
--Barn
Natur Hist 92:cov., 56-9 (c,1)
S '83
Nat Wildlife 23:2 (c,2) Je '85
--Barred
Nat Wildlife 22:28 (painting,4) D
'83
--Boreal
Nat Wildlife 23:36 (c,4) O '85
--Burrowing
Nat Wildlife 20:29-32 (c,1) Ag '82
Trav/Holiday 166:54 (c,4) N '86
--Elf
Smithsonian 15:cov., 122-31 (c,1)
D '84
--Great gray
Nat Wildlife 20:8 (c,4) O '82
Nat Geog 166:122-36 (c,1) Jl '84
Nat Wildlife 23:38-9 (c,1) O '85
--Great-horned
Nat Wildlife 21:45 (painting,c,4)
F '83
Sports Illus 58:82 (c,4) My 30
'83
Nat Wildlife 22:62-3 (c,1) D '83

OWLS (cont.)
  Nat Wildlife 22:58 (paint-
    ing,c,2) F '84
  Nat Wildlife 22:50-5 (c,1) Ap
    '84
--Hawk owls
  Nat Wildlife 23:37 (c,1) O '85
--Horned
  Natur Hist 91:32-3 (c,1) Jl '82
  Smithsonian 15:180 (drawing,4)
    Ap '84
--Long-eared owlets
  Nat Wildlife 22:2 (c,2) F '84
--Northern spotted
  Nat Wildlife 24:10 (c,3) F '86
--Saw-whet
  Sports Illus 64:100 (c,4) Je 2
    '86
--Screech
  Nat Wildlife 21:43 (drawing,4)
    Je '83
  Nat Wildlife 21:45 (sculpture,c,4)
    O '83
  Nat Wildlife 23:12-13 (c,1) Ag
    '85
  Natur Hist 95:56-64 (c,1) Je
    '86
--Short-eared
  Nat Wildlife 23:18-19 (c,1) D
    '84
--Snowy
  Nat Wildlife 21:cov. (c,1) F '83
  Trav/Holiday 160:39 (c,4) O
    '83
  Natur Hist 94:114 (paint-
    ing,c,2) Ap '85
  Nat Wildlife 23:34-5 (c,1) O
    '85
  Nat Wildlife 24:23 (paint-
    ing,c,2) O '86
  Nat Wildlife 25:25 (c,1) D '86
--Stuffed great-horned
  Nat Wildlife 23:22 (c,1) Ag '85
OXFORD, ENGLAND
  Nat Geog 163:766 (c,4) Je '83
OXFORD UNIVERSITY, ENGLAND
  Nat Geog 163:766-7 (c,1) Je
    '83
--Pembroke College library
  Smithsonian 15:63 (c,4) D '84
OYSTER INDUSTRY
--Louisiana
  Nat Geog 164:250-1 (c,1) Ag
    '83
--Maryland
  Nat Wildlife 22:6 (c,4) Ap '84

OYSTERS
  Nat Geog 168:196-7 (c,1) Ag '85
OZARK NATIONAL SCENIC RIVER-
    WAYS, MISSOURI
  Sports Illus 56:64-76 (map,c,1)
    Je 28 '82

-P-

PACIFIC ISLANDS
  Trav/Holiday 157:61-4 (c,1) F
    '82
--Kili, Micronesia
  Nat Geog 169:828 (c,4) Je '86
--Micronesia
  Trav/Holiday 162:56-61 (map,c,1)
    N '84
--Runit depository of radioactive
    wastes
  Nat Geog 169:826-7 (2) Je '86
--See also
    AMERICAN SAMOA
    ASIAN TRIBES
    BIKINI ATOLL
    CHRISTMAS ISLAND
    GUADALCANAL
    GUAM
    KIRIBATI
    KOSRAE
    MARIANA ISLANDS
    MARSHALL ISLANDS
    NORFOLK ISLAND
    PALAU ISLANDS
    PAPUA NEW GUINEA
    PITCAIRN ISLAND
    POHNPEI STATE
    PONAPE
    SAIPAN
    SANTA CRUZ ISLANDS
    SOCIETY ISLANDS
    TAHITI
    TARAWA ATOLL
    TINIAN
    TONGA ISLANDS
    TRUK ISLANDS
    TUAMOTU ISLANDS
    WESTERN SAMOA
    YAP STATE
PACIFIC ISLANDS--ART
--Primitive sculpture
  Smithsonian 12:38-47 (c,2) F '82
PACIFIC ISLANDS--COSTUME
--1839 mother and child
  Smithsonian 16:22 (painting,c,4)
    D '85
--Agta people (Philippines)

PAINTINGS (cont.)
--1920s geometrical styles
    Smithsonian 12:110-19 (c,2) F
    '82
--American Impressionists
    Smithsonian 13:8-9 (c,4) Je
    '82
--American Impressionists (New
    England)
    Smithsonian 12:105-11 (c,2)
    Ja '82
--Depicting comets
    Smithsonian 16:160-5 (c,2) N
    '85
--Depicting people reading news-
    papers (19th-20th cents.)
    Am Heritage 33:cov., 16-27
    (c,1) O '82
--Fake J. M. W. Turner painting
    (1830)
    Am Heritage 37:89 (c,4) D '85
--Italian Renaissance works
    Smithsonian 13:cov., 59-71
    (c,1) N '82
--Modern works by Red Grooms
    Smithsonian 16:104-15 (c,1) Je
    '85
--Paintings of birds
    Natur Hist 92:66-75, 94 (c,1)
    S '83
    Nat Wildlife 24:23-8 (c,1) O
    '86
--Paintings of the Western U.S.
    Natur Hist 94:cov., 58-67
    (c,1) N '85
--Paintings of wildlife
    Nat Wildlife 4:14-19 (c,1) D '85
--Pre-Raphaelites (Great Britain)
    Smithsonian 14:72-83 (c,1) N
    '83
--LeConte Stewart's paintings of
    Utah
    Am Heritage 36:62-9 (c,1) Ag
    '85
--U.S. ships (19th-20th cents.)
    Am Heritage 34:78-85 (c,1) Ap
    '83
--Wildlife stamps
    Nat Wildlife 24:16 (c,4) D '85
--Works by Henry Alexander
    Smithsonian 12:108-17 (c,1) Mr
    '82
--Works by John White Alexander
    Am Heritage 36:82-9 (c,1) O
    '85
--Works by Milton Avery
    Smithsonian 13:110-17 (c,2) O
    '82
--Works by Henri Fantin-Latour
    Smithsonian 14:72-7 (c,1) Jl '83
--Works by Friedensreich Hundert-
    wasser
    Smithsonian 16:74-85 (c,1) Ja '86
--Works by Erastus Salisbury Field
    Smithsonian 15:60-9 (c,1) Ag '84
--Works by Everett Shinn
    Am Heritage 37:66-77 (c,1) D '85
--Works by Abbott Thayer
    Am Heritage 34:4, 24-31 (c,1)
    D '82
--Works by James Tissot
    Smithsonian 15:134-43 (c,2) D '84
--See list under ART WORKS
PAKISTAN
    Smithsonian 13:46-55 (map,c,1)
    Ap '82
    Nat Geog 165:698-709 (map,c,1)
    Je '84
    Trav/Holiday 164:38-43 (map,c,1)
    Ag '85
--Poppy fields
    Nat Geog 167:146-7 (c,1) F '85
--See also
    HIMALAYAN MOUNTAINS
    KASHMIR
    SHALIMAR GARDENS
PAKISTAN--COSTUME
    Smithsonian 13:47-55 (c,1) Ap '82
    Nat Geog 165:707-9 (c,10 Je '84
    Nat Geog 167:148-9 (c,1) F '85
    Nat Geog 167:cov., 470, 476,
    482-5 (c,1) Ap '85
    Trav/Holiday 164:39-43 (c,1) Ag
    '85
--President
    Life 6:74 (c,4) D '83
--Qalandar people
    Natur Hist 92:50-8 (c,1) My '83
PAKISTAN--HOUSING
--Afghan refugee camps
    Nat Geog 167:778-9 (c,1) Je '85
--Stone house (Karakoram Mountains)
    Trav/Holiday 164:43 (c,2) Ag '85
PAKISTAN--POLITICS AND GOVERN-
    MENT
--Benazir Bhutto's political campaign
    Life 9:50-8 (c,1) O '86
PALACES
--Amman, Jordan
    Nat Geog 165:252-3 (c,1) F '84
--Bangkok, Thailand
    Nat Geog 162:490 (c,3) O '82
--Bedroom at Schonbrunn, Vienna,
    Austria

PALACES (cont.)
    Nat Geog 161:171 (c,3) F '82
--Belvedere Palace, Austria
    Smithsonian 15:61-2 (c,2) Ja
      '85
--Blenheim, England
    Nat Geog 168:668-9 (c,1) N
      '85
--Blenheim dining room, England
    Smithsonian 16:53 (c,2) O '85
--Blenheim interior, England
    Trav/Holiday 159:62-3 (c,1)
      Ap '83
--Catherine Palace, Pushkin,
    U.S.S.R.
    Smithsonian 13:70-1 (c,2) Mr
      '83
--Fez, Morocco
    Nat Geog 169:345 (c,1) Mr '86
--Forbidden City, Beijing, China
    Natur Hist 95:42-3 (c,1) S '86
--Gwalior, India
    Nat Geog 167:474-5 (c,1) Ap
      '85
--Hampton Court, England
    Nat Geog 163:774-5 (c,1) Je
      '83
--Hawa Mahal, Jaipur, India
    Trav/Holiday 157:50 (c,1) Mr
      '82
--Het Loo, Netherlands
    Nat Geog 170:510-11 (c,1) O
      '86
--Imperial, Beijing, China
    Trav/Holiday 164:48-9 (c,2) S
      '85
--Iolani bandstand, Hawaii
    Trav/Holiday 164:39 (4) O '85
--Iolani interior, Hawaii
    Nat Geog 164:586-7 (c,1) N '83
--King Herod's Palace (Israel)
    Nat Geog 165:260 (c,2) F '84
--Luxembourg, Paris, France
    Trav/Holiday 157:56 (c,3) Mr
      '82
--Monaco
    Life 5:73 (c,2) Ag '82
--Palenque, Chiapas, Mexico
    Trav/Holiday 163:68 (c,4) Ja
      '85
--Summer Palace, Beijing, China
    Natur Hist 95:40-1 (c,1) S '86
--Topkapi Palace Museum, Istan-
    bul, Turkey
    Smithsonian 16:112-23 (c,1) F
      '86
--Torre Tagle courtyard, Lima,

    Peru
    Trav/Holiday 157:45 (c,4) Ja '82
--Westminster, London, England
    Nat Geog 170:729-57 (c,1) D '86
--See also
      BUCKINGHAM PALACE
      LOUVRE
      VERSAILLES
PALAU ISLANDS, MICRONESIA
    Nat Geog 161:267-9 (c,1) F '82
    Smithsonian 17:44-55 (map,c,1)
      S '86
    Nat Geog 170:462-5, 592-7
      (map,c,1) O '86
--Peleliu World War II sites
    Nat Geog 170:496-7 (c,1) O '86
PALAU--COSTUME
    Smithsonian 17:44-54 (c,1) S '86
    Nat Geog 170:494-5 (c,1) O '86
PALESTINIANS
--Anti-Israeli resistance (Israel)
    Life 5:26-34 (1) Je '82
--Israel
    Life 6:74-82 (c,2) N '83
    Nat Geog 168:36-7 (c,1) Jl '85
--Jordan
    Nat Geog 165:262-3 (c,2) F '84
--Lebanon
    Life 5:24-30 (c,1) Ag '82
PALM TREES
    Trav/Holiday 157:59 (c,2) Ja '82
    Smithsonian 13:102 (c,4) Je '82
--Babassu palms
    Natur Hist 94:40-7 (c,1) D '85
--Fan palms
    Natur Hist 94:cov., 64-73 (c,1)
      O '85
PALMER, ARNOLD
    Sports Illus 58:65 (4) Je 6 '83
--1962 biorhythm chart
    Natur Hist 91:93 (4) O '82
--With 1962 British Open trophy
    Natur Hist 91:92 (4) O '82
Palo Alto, California. See
    STANFORD UNIVERSITY
PANAMA
    Nat Geog 169:466-93 (map,c,1)
      Ap '86
--See also
      PANAMA CANAL
      PANAMA CITY
      PORTOBELO
PANAMA--COSTUME
    Nat Geog 169:466-93 (c,1) Ap '86
--Cuna Indian woman
    Trav/Holiday 159:36 (4) My '83
--Cuna Indians

PANAMA--COSTUME (cont.)
  Nat Geog 169:488-93 (c,1) Ap
    '86
--Guaymi Indians
  Nat Geog 169:474 (c,4) Ap '86
--Panamanian general
  Nat Geog 169:472 (c,4) Ap '86
--President Eric Delvalle
  Nat Geog 169:471 (c,3) Ap '86
PANAMA--RITES AND FESTIVALS
--Feast of the Black Christ
  Nat Geog 169:476-7 (c,1) Ap
    '86
PANAMA CANAL, PANAMA
  Nat Geog 169:468, 480-1 (c,1)
    Ap '86
--Commemorated on 1913 postage
    stamp
  Am Heritage 34:52 (c,4) D '82
--People descending into lock
  Smithsonian 14:68 (c,4) F '84
PANAMA CITY, PANAMA
  Nat Geog 169:482-3 (c,1) Ap
    '86
--Slum
  Sports Illus 59:82 (c,4) N 7
    '83
PANDAS
  Life 5:50 (c,2) Ja '82
  Life 5:48 (c,2) Je '82
  Smithsonian 14:145-64 (3) D
    '83
  Nat Wildlife 22:36 (4) D '83
  Smithsonian 14:26 (c,4) Mr '84
  Trav/Holiday 161:63 (c,4) Mr
    '84
  Nat Wildlife 22:10-11 (c,1) O
    '84
  Trav/Holiday 164:46 (c,4) Jl
    '85
  Nat Geog 169:cov., 285-309
    (map,c,1) Mr '86
--Eating with silverware (China)
  Life 9:96 (c,2) Mr '86
--Panda costume
  Life 8:153-8 (1) O '85
PANGOLINS
  Nat Geog 163:381 (c,3) Mr '83
  Smithsonian 14:77 (c,4) Ag '83
PANTHEON, ROME, ITALY
  Am Heritage 35:54 (drawing,4)
    Je '84
PANTHERS
  Nat Wildlife 22:35 (4) Ap '84
  Nat Wildlife 23:15, 62-3 (c,1)
    Ap '85
  Nat Wildlife 24:14-15 (c,1)

Ap '86
--Black panthers
  Smithsonian 13:77 (c,4) My '82
PAPER INDUSTRY
--Making parchment (Great Britain)
  Smithsonian 17:86 (c,4) Jl '86
--See also
  MILLS
PAPUA NEW GUINEA
  Nat Geog 162:cov., 142-71
    (map,c,1) Ag '82
  Trav/Holiday 166:54-7, 76 (c,1)
    Ag '86
--Lumbering industry
  Nat Geog 163:2-3, 28-33 (c,1)
    Ja '83
PAPUA NEW GUINEA--ART
--Masks
  Nat Geog 162:148-9 (c,1) Ag '82
  Nat Geog 164:141, 146-69 (c,1)
    Ag '83
  Trav/Holiday 166:76 (4) Ag '86
PAPUA NEW GUINEA--COSTUME
  Nat Geog 162:cov., 142-71 (c,1)
    Ag '82
  Trav/Holiday 166:54-7 (c,1) Ag
    '86
--Abelam people mask
  Smithsonian 13:117 (c,1) S '82
--Gahuku-Gama man
  Natur Hist 95:24 (3) Je '86
--Gimi people
  Nat Geog 164:141, 146-69 (c,1)
    Ag '83
--Sepik River warrior
  Trav/Holiday 166:54-5 (c,1) Ag
    '86
PAPUA NEW GUINEA--SOCIAL LIFE
    AND CUSTOMS
--Gimi people performances
  Nat Geog 164:141, 146-69 (c,1)
    Ag '83
PAPYRUS
--Ancient Rome
  Nat Geog 165:600-1 (c,1) My '84
PARACHUTES
  Nat Geog 164:210, 214-15 (c,1)
    Ag '83
--U.S. Marines parachuting into
    Grenada
  Life 6:34-5 (c,1) D '83
PARACHUTING
--BASE jumpers
  Sports Illus 63:82-92 (c,1) Ag 26
    '85
--Forest fire smoke jumpers
  Nat Wildlife 20:37 (painting,2)

PARIS, FRANCE (cont.)
   Ebony 37:84 (c,3) My '82
--Napoleon's tomb
   Nat Geog 161:188 (c,4) F '82
--Pont Neuf wrapped in nylon
   by Christo
   Life 8:74-5 (1) N '85
--Printemps store
   Ebony 39:150 (c,3) Je '84
--Sewers
   Life 8:56-7 (1) Jl '85
--See also
      ARC DE TRIOMPHE
      EIFFEL TOWER
      LOUVRE
      NOTRE DAME
PARKER, CHARLIE
   Ebony 41:272 (4) N '85
   Ebony 41:131 (4) F '86
PARKER, DOROTHY
   Smithsonian 12:128 (4) F '82
PARKING LOTS
--Trailers (New York)
   Smithsonian 16:74-5 (c,1) D
   '85
PARKMAN, FRANCIS
   Am Heritage 38:31 (4) D '86
PARKS
--Early 20th cent. (St. Louis,
   Missouri)
   Am Heritage 33:48 (2) Ag '82
--Auckland, New Zealand
   Trav/Holiday 166:52 (c,2) Ag
   '86
--Central Park, New York City,
   New York
   Natur Hist 92:28-39 (c,1) Ag
   '83
--Central Park, New York City,
   New York (19th cent.)
   Natur Hist 92:30-8 (c,1) Ag
   '83
--Central Park's Sheep Meadow,
   New York City, New York
   Smithsonian 15:158 (c,2) N '84
--Central Park's Strawberry
   Fields, New York City
   Life 8:61-4 (c,1) N '85
--Florida state parks
   Trav/Holiday 157:53-4 (c,2)
   F '82
--French regional parks
   Natur Hist 91:cov., 42-51, 76
   (c,1) Ag '82
--Gas Works Park, Seattle, Wash-
   ington
   Sports Illus 57:60 (c,3) Jl

   19 '82
--Gazebo (California)
   Life 6:60-1 (c,1) F '83
--Japan
   Trav/Holiday 158:52 (c,4) N '82
--Khabarousk, Siberia, U.S.S.R.
   Trav/Holiday 165:55 (c,2) My '86
--Lubéron regional park, France
   Natur Hist 91:34 (4) N '82
--Melbourne, Australia
   Trav/Holiday 164:64 (c,3) O '85
--Spokane, Washington
   Trav/Holiday 161:56 (c,2) Ap '84
--Willow Grove Park, Philadelphia,
   Pennsylvania (1929)
   Am Heritage 36:116-17 (1) D '84
--See also
      AMUSEMENT PARKS
      GARDEN OF THE GODS
      GARDENS
      OLMSTEAD, FREDERICK LAW
      PLAYGROUNDS
      WILFLIFE REFUGES
      list under NATIONAL PARKS
PARLORS
--185h cent. (Pennsylvania)
   Am Heritage 34:87 (c,4) Ap '83
   Smithsonian 14:98-9, 101 (c,1)
   My '83
--18th plantation home (Mississippi)
   Trav/Holiday 166:55 (c,4) Jl '86
--Late 19th cent. "cozy corners"
   (Pennsylvania)
   Am Heritage 33:109 (3) F '82
--Blenheim Palace drawing room,
   England
   Nat Geog 168:670 (c,1) N '85
PARROTS
   Sports Illus 58:34-5 (c,2) Ja 17
   '83
   Sports Illus 59:30-1 (c,1) D 19
   '83
   Sports Illus 60:54-5 (c,1) Ja 9
   '84
   Sports Illus 61:32, 34, 38 (c,2)
   S 3 '84
   Smithsonian 16:58-67 (c,1) Ap '85
   Sports Illus 63:70 (c,4) O 21 '85
   Nat Wildlife 24:4-7 (c,1) Ag '86
--Lorikeets
   Natur Hist 94:38-9 (c,3) F '85
--See also
      COCKATOOS
      MACAWS
      PARAKEETS
PARTHENON, ATHENS, GREECE
   Smithsonian 12:44-53 (c,1) Mr '82

PARTHENON, ATHENS, GREECE
(cont.)
Trav/Holiday 161:116 (3) Mr
'84
PARTIES
--1954 teenage dance party
(Colorado)
Life 9:291 (1) Fall '86
--Black-tie charity affair (Wash-
ington, D.C.)
Nat Geog 163:102 (c,1) Ja
'83
--Block party (Brooklyn, New
York)
Nat Geog 163:596-7 (c,1) My
'83
--Street fair (Washington, D.C.)
Nat Geog 163:117 (c,3) Ja '83
--See also
BIRTHDAY PARTIES
DANCES
MASQUERADE COSTUME
PASADENA, CALIFORNIA
--City Hall
Ebony 37:113 (c,2) Ag '82
PASSENGER PIGEONS
Nat Wildlife 24:16A (paint-
ing,c,2) D '85
PASSIONFLOWERS
Natur Hist 94:62-3 (c,1) Jl '85
PATENTS
--1785 automatic grist mill
Am Heritage 36:108 (engrav-
ing,4) Ag '85
--1794 patent for Whitney's cotton
gin
Am Heritage 35:93 (c,2) Ag
'84
--19th cent. patent models
Smithsonian 14:120-6 (c,2) F
'84
--1835 Colt revolver patent draw-
ing
Am Heritage 37:106 (4) F '86
PAULING, LINUS
Smithsonian 14:55 (c,2) D '83
Smithsonian 16:116 (4) Jl '85
PEACE CORPS
--Peace Corps activities (Ecuador)
Smithsonian 16:80-9 (c,1) F
'86
PEACOCKS
Smithsonian 12:117 (paint-
ing,c,2) Mr '82
Nat Geog 166:726 (c,4) D '84
Trav/Holiday 164:44 (c,1) Jl
'85

--Feathers
Nat Wildlife 21:22 (c,4) Je '83
--Perched on motorcycle (Kenya)
Sports Illus 56:75 (c,4) F 8 '82
PEALE, CHARLES WILLSON
--Painting of Benjamin Franklin
Am Heritage 34:10 (c,4) D '82
--Portrait of woman crying
Smithsonian 15:103 (painting,c,2)
Je '84
PEANUT INDUSTRY
--Africa
Nat Geog 168:230-1 (c,2) Ag '85
PEANUTS
Natur Hist 93:98-9 (c,4) S '84
Nat Geog 168:91 (c,4) Jl '85
PEAR TREES
Nat Geog 166:502-3 (c,1) O '84
PEARL HARBOR, HAWAII
--U.S.S. Arizona Memorial
Trav/Holiday 164:34 (4) O '85
PEARL INDUSTRY
Smithsonian 15:cov., 40-51 (c,1)
Ja '85
Nat Geog 168:192-222 (c,1) Ag
'85
--China
Nat Geog 168:214-15 (c,1) Ag
'85
--French Polynesia
Nat Geog 168:194-7 (c,1) Ag '85
--Japan
Nat Geog 168:198-205 (c,1) Ag
'85
--Tennessee
Nat Geog 168:218-19 (c,2) Ag '85
PEARLS
Smithsonian 15:cov., 40-51 (c,1)
Ja '85
Nat Geog 168:192-222 (c,1) Ag
'85
PEARY, ROBERT E.
--1909 Arctic expedition
Nat Geog 170:295 (4) S '86
PEAT MOSS
--Sphagnum
Natur Hist 91:52 (c,3) N '82
PEKINGESE DOGS
Life 7:118 (c,2) D '84
PELICANS
Natur Hist 91:cov., 38-42 (c,1)
Ja '82
Nat Wildlife 20:46-7 (c,1) Je '82
Nat Geog 164:261 (c,3) Ag '83
Nat Wildlife 22:56 (c,1) Je '84
Trav/Holiday 163:19 (c,4) Ja '85
Nat Geog 168:348-9 (c,1) S '85

PELICANS (cont.)
  Trav/Holiday 165:56 (c,3) F
    '86
--Brown pelicans
  Nat Geog 164:232-3 (c,1) Ag
    '83
--Chicks
  Natur Hist 91:42 (c,4) Ja '82
  Nat Wildlife 21:29 (c,4) D '82
--In flight
  Smithsonian 15:32 (c,4) Ja '85
PENCILS
--1791 mechanical pencil (Great
    Britain)
  Nat Geog 168:451 (c,1) O '85
PENGUINS
  Nat Geog 161:789 (c,1) Je '82
  Trav/Holiday 158:56 (c,4) N
    '82
  Nat Geog 163:550-1 (c,1) Ap
    '83
  Nat Wildlife 22:4-5 (c,1) D '83
  Nat Wildlife 22:52-3 (c,4) F '84
  Life 7:cov., 60-8 (c,1) Ap '84
  Sports Illus 61:54-5 (c,1) O 15
    '84
  Smithsonian 15:53 (c,4) O '84
  Nat Geog 166:635-63 (c,1) N
    '84
  Smithsonian 15:50, 52 (c,4) N
    '84
  Nat Wildlife 23:cov. (c,1) D '84
  Trav/Holiday 163:27 (4) Mr '85
  Smithsonian 16:42 (c,4) My '85
  Nat Geog 168:349 (c,4) S '85
  Natur Hist 95:58-9 (c,4) F '86
  Nat Geog 169:497-9 (c,1) Ap
    '86
PENN, WILLIAM
  Am Heritage 33:106 (paint-
    ing,c,4) Ag '82
--Statue on Philadelphia City Hall,
    Pennsylvania
  Trav/Holiday 165:100 (4) Mr '86
Pennants. See
    BANNERS
PENNSYLVANIA
--1895 Wellsboro
  Am Heritage 34:87 (4) Ag '83
--Brandywine Valley
  Smithsonian 15:150-63 (c,1) Mr
    '85
--Centralia
  Nat Geog 167:368-9 (c,1) Mr
    '85
--Easton
  Ebony 37:118-20 (c,3) S '82

--Enola railroad switchyard
  Nat Geog 167:372-3 (c,1) Mr '85
--Lancaster County
  Nat Geog 165:492-519 (map,c,1)
    Ap '84
--Meadowcroft archaeological site
  Natur Hist 95:20-2 (map,c,3) D
    '86
--Susquehanna River area
  Nat Geog 167:352-83 (c,1) Mr '85
--Three Mile Island
  Life 5:34 (c,1) My '82
  Nat Geog 167:378-9 (c,1) Mr '85
--Warren (1862)
  Am Heritage 36:88-9 (paint-
    ing,c,1) Je '85
--See also
    ALLEGHENY NATIONAL FOR-
      EST
    ALLEGHENY RIVER
    AMISH PEOPLE
    MONONGAHELA RIVER
    PENN, WILLIAM
    PHILADELPHIA
    PITTSBURGH
    SCRANTON
    SUSQUEHANNA RIVER
PENNSYLVANIA DUTCH PEOPLE--
    ART
--Folk art (Pennsylvania)
  Trav/Holiday 165:79 (c,4) My '86
PENS
--1920s fountain pen
  Am Heritage 35:10 (c,4) F '84
--Cartoonist's pen
  Life 9:57 (c,4) Je '86
PENSACOLA, FLORIDA
  Trav/Holiday 162:20-2 (map,c,3)
    D '84
PEONIES
  Natur Hist 93:78-80 (painting,c,4)
    My '84
PEOPLE
--Early 20th cent. giant man
  Trav/Holiday 164:38 (4) Jl '85
--Carnival attractions
  Life 6:115-18 (c,3) Je '83
--Dwarf
  Sports Illus 58:53 (c,3) Mr 28 '83
--7'6" tall man
  Ebony 42:59-60 (c,2) D '86
--7'8" tall man
  Ebony 38:110-14 (3) D '82
--Tall basketball players
  Sports Illus 65:54-9 (c,1) N 3
    '86

PEOPLE AND CIVILIZATIONS.
  See also
  ABORIGINES
  AFRICAN TRIBES
  AGED
  AMISH PEOPLE
  ASANTE CIVILIZATION
  ASIAN TRIBES
  AZTEC CIVILIZATION
  BABIES
  BEDOUINS
  BLACK AMERICANS
  BOY SCOUTS
  BUDDHISM
  BYZANTINE EMPIRE
  CHILDREN
  CHINESE AMERICANS
  COLLEGE LIFE
  COMMUTERS
  CROWDS
  CRUSADERS
  ESKIMOS
  FAMILIES
  FAMILY LIFE
  FARM LIFE
  GIRL SCOUTS
  GYPSIES
  HANDICAPPED PEOPLE
  HOBOES
  IMMIGRANTS
  INCA CIVILIZATION
  INDIANS OF LATIN AMERICA
  INDIANS OF NORTH AMERICA
  INJURED PEOPLE
  ITALIAN AMERICANS
  JAPANESE AMERICANS
  JUDAISM
  KU KLUX KLAN
  LAPP PEOPLE
  LIFESTYLES
  MAN, PREHISTORIC
  MAORIES
  MASONRY
  MAYAN CIVILIZATION
  MENNONITES
  MIDDLE AGES
  MONGOL EMPIRE
  MORMONS
  MOSLEMS
  NOMADS
  OBESITY
  OTTOMAN EMPIRE
  PALESTINIANS
  PENNSYLVANIA DUTCH
  PERSIAN EMPIRE
  REFUGEES
  RENAISSANCE

  SHAKERS
  TOURISTS
  TWINS
  VIKINGS
  YOUTH
People's Republic of China. See
  CHINA
PEPPER INDUSTRY
--Drying chili peppers (China)
  Life 5:72 (c,3) Je '82
--Drying peppercorns (India)
  Nat Geog 162:15 (c,4) Jl '82
--History
  Smithsonian 14:128-48 (c,1) F '84
--Tabasco processing (Louisiana)
  Smithsonian 15:72-83 (c,1) My
  '84
PEPPER INDUSTRY--HARVESTING
--14th cent. (India)
  Smithsonian 14:128-9 (paint-
  ing,c,1) F '84
--Kashmir
  Trav/Holiday 166:60 (c,3) N '86
PEPPERCORNS
  Smithsonian 14:128, 130 (c,4) F
  '84
PEPPERS
--Chili peppers
  Nat Geog 161:324 (4) Mr '82
--Jalapeño
  Smithsonian 16:157 (drawing,c,4)
  D '85
--Red rocotillo capsicum
  Natur Hist 94:76 (drawing,c,3)
  Ag '85
PERCH
--Pike perch
  Life 6:188 (c,2) N '83
Performers. See
  ACTORS
  ENTERTAINERS
  SINGERS
PERFUME
--16th cent. pomander (Great Brit-
  ain)
  Nat Geog 163:660 (c,4) My '83
--Research on smells
  Nat Geog 170:324-61 (c,1) S '86
PERFUME INDUSTRY
--Perfume research
  Nat Geog 170:324-5, 335 (c,1) S
  '86
PERON, JUAN
--Sculpture of Juan and Evita Peron
  Nat Geog 162:58 (c,4) Jl '82
PERSIAN EMPIRE. See also
  DARIUS

PERSIAN EMPIRE--ART
--5th cent. bas-relief of Darius
    (Persepolis)
    Natur Hist 91:104 (4) Ja '82
PERTH, AUSTRALIA
    Nat Geog 161:638-67
        (map,c,1) My '82
    Trav/Holiday 160:44 (c,4) O
        '83
    Trav/Holiday 166:44-7, 69
        (map,c,1) Ag '86
PERU
    Nat Geog 161:284-321
        (map,c,1) Mr '82
    Trav/Holiday 166:49-53
        (map,c,1) N '86
--Amazon area
    Natur Hist 95:40 (c,3) Mr '86
--Manú National Park
    Smithsonian 13:34-43 (c,1) Ja
        '83
--Manú River
    Smithsonian 13:34 (c,1) Ja '83
--Nazca Indian lines drawn on
        the pampa
    Life 7:169-76 (c,1) N '84
    Trav/Holiday 166:50 (c,3) N
        '86
--Prison
    Life 5:50-2, 62 (1) Je '82
--Ucayali River basin
    Nat Wildlife 22:17 (c,3) D '83
--See also
        ANDES MOUNTAINS
        CUZCO
        LAKE TITICACA
        LIMA
        MACHU PICCHU
PERU--COSTUME
    Nat Geog 161:284-321 (c,1)
        Mr '82
    Nat Geog 162:60-9 (c,1) Jl '82
    Trav/Holiday 166:cov., 51
        (c,1) N '86
--Farmers
    Nat Geog 161:672-5 (c,1) My
        '82
--Jívaro Indians
    Nat Geog 168:356-7 (c,1) S '85
--Lima
    Trav/Holiday 157:44-9 (c,1)
        Ja '82
--Old woman (1970)
    Smithsonian 14:51 (c,1) Jl '83
--Uru Indians
    Natur Hist 91:34-7 (c,1) Ja
        '82

PERU--RITES AND CEREMONIES
--Changing of the Guard (Lima)
    Trav/Holiday 157:44-5 (c,1) Ja
        '82
--Snow Star Pilgrimage
    Nat Geog 162:60-9 (c,1) Jl '82
PEST CONTROL
--Plane spraying insecticides
        (Florida)
    Smithsonian 14:34-5 (c,2) Je '83
--Plane spraying insecticides (Zim-
        babwe)
    Nat Geog 170:832-3 (c,2) D '86
PETAIN, MARSHAL
    Smithsonian 16:127 (4) Jl '85
PETRA, JORDAN
    Nat Geog 165:236, 246-7 (c,2) F
        '84
    Trav/Holiday 163:29 (c,4) Je '85
    Nat Geog 168:512-13 (c,1) O '85
PETRELS
    Smithsonian 16:57 (drawing,c,4)
        N '85
Petroglyphs. See
        CAVE PAINTINGS
        ROCK CARVINGS
        ROCK PAINTINGS
PETS
--Pet gazelle's hutch (France)
    Life 6:71 (c,2) D '83
--Pet pigs
    Smithsonian 16:146-57 (c,1) N
        '85
--Unusual pets of celebrities
    Ebony 39:52-6 (c,2) N '83
--See also
        AQUARIUMS
        CATS
        DOGS
PHALAROPES
    Sports Illus 58:82 (c,4) My 30
        '83
    Natur Hist 94:59-65 (c,1) Ag '85
PHARMACIES
--17th cent. mortars and pestles
        (Spain)
    Nat Geog 161:238 (c,4) F '82
--Early 19th cent. engraving of
        pharmacist
    Am Heritage 35:28 (4) O '84
--Reproduction of 19th cent. Ver-
        mont drug store
    Am Heritage 33:24 (c,1) Ap '82
PHEASANTS
    Nat Geog 161:716 (c,4) Je '82
--Ring-necked
    Nat Wildlife 21:8 (c,4) D '82

PHEASANTS (cont.)
    Nat Wildlife 22:20-1 (c,1) Ap
      '84
    Nat Wildlife 23:19 (c,4) F '85
    Nat Wildlife 23:cov. (c,1) O '85
    Nat Wildlife 25:26-7 (c,1) D '86
PHIDIAS
--5th cent. B.C. statue of
    Olympian Zeus
    Smithsonian 14:59 (drawing,4)
      Mr '84
PHILADELPHIA, PENNSYLVANIA
    Ebony 37:86 (4) F '82
    Nat Geog 163:314-43 (c,1) Mr
      '83
--City Hall
    Ebony 39:44-5 (c,1) My '84
--City Hall statue of William Penn
    Trav/Holiday 165:100 (4) Mr
      '86
--Humorous sculpture of its his-
    tory
    Life 5:45-8 (c,1) Ag '82
--Society Hill
    Trav/Holiday 157:106 (4) Ap
      '82
--Willow Grove Park (1929)
    Am Heritage 36:116-17 (1) D
      '84
--See also
      LIBERTY BELL
PHILIPPINES
    Nat Geog 170:76-117 (map,c,1)
      Jl '86
--Cordillera area
    Trav/Holiday 159:33-6
      (map,c,1) Ja '83
--Farms
    Nat Geog 161:684-5 (c,1) My
      '82
--Marcos palace interior
    Nat Geog 170:81-3 (c,1) Jl '86
--See also
      CORREGIDOR
      MANILA
      MARCOS, FERDINAND
PHILIPPINES--COSTUME
    Trav/Holiday 159:34-6 (c,1)
      Ja '83
    Life 9:47-52 (c,1) Je '86
    Nat Geog 170:76-117 (c,1) Jl
      '86
--Agta people
    Natur Hist 95:36-43 (c,1) My
      '86
--Agta people (1945)
    Natur Hist 95:4, 6 (3) N '86

--Corazon Aquino
    Life 9:51-4 (c,2) F '86
    Nat Geog 170:80, 85 (c,3) Jl '86
--Folk dancer (Alaska)
    Nat Geog 164:355 (c,4) S '83
--Guerrillas
    Nat Geog 170:93 (c,1) Jl '86
--Traditional (Ontario)
    Trav/Holiday 161:63 (c,1) Je '84
Philippines--History. See
    MARCOS, FERDINAND
PHILIPPINES--RITES AND FESTI-
    VALS
--Agta wedding dance (1945,
    Natur Hist 95:4 (3) N '86 *
PHILIPPINES--SCULPTURE
--Mountainside sculpture of Marcos
    Nat Geog 170:90-1 (c,1) Jl '86
Philosophers. See
    WRITERS
PHLOX
--Sky pilots
    Natur Hist 94:28-35 (c,1) Jl '85
PHNOM PENH, CAMBODIA
    Nat Geog 161:606-11 (c,1) My
      '82
PHOENIX, ARIZONA
    Trav/Holiday 161:68, 71 (c,2)
      Mr '84
PHONOGRAPHS
--Early 20th cent.
    Am Heritage 33:63 (4) Ag '82
--Early gramophone
    Am Heritage 37:38 (c,4) Ag '86
--Thomas Edison's phonograph
    Smithsonian 17:124 (4) Je '86
PHOTOGRAPHERS
--1948 newspaper photographers
    Am Heritage 37:69 (3) F '86
--Famous photographers
    Life 5:115-26 (1) My '82
--Guatemala
    Natur Hist 91:62-4 (1) N '82
--News photographers (New York)
    Life 5:53 (2) Ja '82
--See also
      ABBOTT, BERENICE
      BOURKE-WHITE, MARGARET
      BRADY, MATHEW
      EISENSTAEDT, ALFRED
      STIEGLITZ, ALFRED
PHOTOGRAPHY
--Early 20th cent. aerial views
    (New Jersey/Pennsylvania)
    Am Heritage 36:111-17 (1) D '84
--Early 20th cent. shots of U.S.
    urban architecture

PHOTOGRAPHY (cont.)
  Smithsonian 13:131-40 (3) N
    '82
--Advances in amateur equipment
  Life 5:8-16 (c,1) My '82
--Aerial shots of U.S. landscapes
  Natur Hist 91:cov., 74-7 (c,1)
    O '82
--History of aerial photography
  Smithsonian 14:150-61 (c,2)
    Mr '84
--Panoramics technique
  Life 6:8-12 (c,1) Ag '83
--Parafoil used for aerial photos
  Smithsonian 15:122 (c,3) O
    '84
--Photo archive (New York)
  Life 9:54-5 (c,1) Fall '86
--Photos of earth from space
  Life 7:10-16 (c,1) Jl '84
--Photos retouched for political
    reasons (U.S.S.R.)
  Life 9:67-8 (4) D '86
--Photographs used in photo-
    therapy
  Life 5:15-22 (c,2) O '82
--Tableau photography
  Life 6:10-16 (c,1) My '83
--Unusual wedding photography
    techniques
  Life 5:8-14 (c,1) Je '82
--Using light meter (New Mexico)
  Nat Geog 161:338 (c,4) Mr '82
--Works of F. W. Guerin
  Am Heritage 33:65-75 (1) Ap
    '82
--See also
    CAMERAS
    MOTION PICTURE
      PHOTOGRAPHY
    PHOTOGRAPHERS
PHOTOGRAPHY--PICTURE-
    TAKING
  Life 5:44 (c,3) Ap '82
  Sports Illus 58:74-5 (c,1) Je
    13 '83
--Shooting animals from blinds
  Nat Wildlife 22:25-8 (c,1) O
    '84
--Shooting wildflowers
  Nat Wildlife 24:45 (c,1) Ap '86
--Snapping athletes
  Sports Illus 56:66-7 (c,1) My
    31 '82
  Sports Illus 60:52-3 (c,1) F
    8 '84
--Thailand

  Nat Geog 162:494 (c,4) O '82
PIAF, EDITH
--Tombstone (Paris, France)
  Trav/Holiday 157:56 (c,4) Mr '82
PIANO PLAYING
  Ebony 37:92 (4) Jl '82
  Life 6:85 (c,1) Mr '83
  Life 6:72-3, 86 (c,1) Ap '83
  Ebony 39:134 (c,2) N '83
  Sports Illus 62:40 (c,3) Je 3 '85
  Sports Illus 65:35 (c,4) S 1 '86
  Ebony 42:140 (c,4) N '86
--1962 child's recital (Iowa)
  Life 9:256 (3) Fall '86
--Child practicing
  Ebony 37:44 (4) My '82
  Ebony 37:50 (4) Ag '82
  Ebony 38:70 (3) D '82
  Ebony 39:32 (4) Mr '84
--Family
  Sports Illus 59:56 (c,4) Ag 8 '83
  Life 9:19 (c,4) Ag '86
--Father and son duet
  Ebony 37:31 (c,3) Jl '82
--Jazz
  Ebony 38:28 (4) My '83
  Ebony 39:87 (3) D '83
--Rock musician on keyboard
  Ebony 38:130 (c,4) Jl '83
PIANOS
  Ebony 40:124 (3) Mr '85
--Construction (Queens, New York)
  Life 7:36 (c,3) O '84
--White piano
  Life 9:35 (c,4) D '86
PICASSO, PABLO
  Life 9:351 (c,2) Fall '86
--"La Baignade" (1937)
  Smithsonian 17:64 (c,4) Jl '86
--Copies of his paintings on town
    walls (Caltojar, Spain)
  Life 5:100-2 (c,1) Ap '82
--"Guernica"
  Nat Geog 169:162-3 (painting,c,2)
    F '86
--Outdoor sculpture (Chicago, Illi-
    nois)
  Life 5:24 (4) Ja '82
--Self-portrait (1973)
  Smithsonian 15:179 (c,4) My '84
PICKERELS (FISH)
--Grass pickerel
  Natur Hist 92:52-3 (c,2) Mr '83
PICKFORD, MARY
  Smithsonian 16:188 (4) N '85
--Bloomers belonging to her
  Life 9:125 (c,4) My '86

PICNICS
Trav/Holiday 165:84-5 (c,2)
Mr '86
--Australia
Trav/Holiday 159:54 (c,4) My
'83
--Barbeque (Massachusetts)
Sports Illus 59:44 (c,4) S 26
'83
--California
Trav/Holiday 158:28 (c,2) S
'82
--Colorado
Trav/Holiday 159:37 (c,2) Je
'83
--Farm workers (Hungary)
Nat Geog 163:252 (c,3) F '83
--France
Nat Geog 161:482-3 (c,2) Ap
'82
--Freeze-dried foods
Smithsonian 14:90 (c,2) Jl '83
--Jamaica beach
Trav/Holiday 163:84 (c,2) Ap
'85
--Norfolk Island, Australia
Nat Geog 164:538-9 (c,1) O '83
--Picnic foods
Life 6:59-80 (c,1) Jl '83
--Romantic scene (Michigan)
Sports Illus 57:55 (c,4) D 6
'82
--Spain
Nat Geog 166:486-7 (c,1) O '84
PIED PIPER OF HAMELIN
--Reenactment of 13th cent. story
(Hamelin, W. Germany)
Trav/Holiday 163:102 (4) My
'85
PIERCE, FRANKLIN
Am Heritage 36:47 (1) Ag '85
PIERS
--Amusement piers
Smithsonian 13:60-9 (c,1) S
'82
--Providence wharf, Rhode Island
(1878)
Am Heritage 38:69 (paint-
ing,c,4) D '86
PIGEONS
Sports Illus 64:22-3 (c,1) Ja
6 '86
--Pink pigeons
Natur Hist 91:42 (c,4) Mr '82
Smithsonian 13:98, 103 (c,1)
Je '82
--Used as laboratory subjects

Nat Wildlife 21:12-13 (c,2) Ag
'83
--See also
PASSENGER PIGEONS
PIGS
Trav/Holiday 162:41 (c,4) Ag '84
Smithsonian 15:162-3 (c,1) Mr
'85
Nat Geog 168:cov. (c,1) S '85
Sports Illus 64:44-5 (c,1) Ap 7
'86
Nat Geog 170:823 (c,4) D '86
--Pet pigs
Smithsonian 16:146-57 (c,1) N
'85
--Piglet
Smithsonian 14:46 (c,1) Ag '83
--Raised for food
Life 6:48-50 (c,1) F '83
--Sow
Smithsonian 14:53 (c,4) Ag '83
PIKAS
Natur Hist 92:50-7 (c,1) Je '83
PIKE (FISH)
Nat Wildlife 23:12 (painting,c,4)
F '85
--Caught by fisherman
Sports Illus 58:74 (c,4) My 9 '83
Pilots. See
AIRPLANE PILOTS
PILTDOWN MAN (1911)
--Skull
Life 5:18 (4) F '82
PINBALL MACHINES
Life 6:59 (c,4) F '83
--Canada
Nat Geog 161:389 (c,3) Mr '82
PINE TREES
Nat Geog 164:529 (c,1) O '83
--Longleaf pine sprout
Natur Hist 94:77 (c,4) D '85
--Piñon pine cones
Natur Hist 95:44-5 (c,3) D '86
--Piñon pine trees
Natur Hist 95:44-7 (c,1) D '86
--Remains of pine forest (Michigan)
Natur Hist 95:cov. (c,1) Ja '86
--White pine
Natur Hist 92:12 (c,3) My '83
--See also
BRISTLECONE PINE TREES
DOUGLAS FIR TREES
LARCH TREES
SPRUCE TREES
Ping pong. See
TABLE TENNIS

PINKERTON, ALLAN
    Nat Geog 166:12 (paint-
        ing,c,4) Jl '84
Pioneers. See
    WESTERN FRONTIER LIFE
PIPE SMOKING
    Smithsonian 13:79 (c,4) Ap '82
    Smithsonian 13:111 (c,2) Ag
        '82
--19th cent. woman (Japan)
    Nat Geog 170:643 (paint-
        ing,c,4) N '86
--Switzerland
    Nat Geog 169:127 (c,1) Ja '86
--Wisconsin
    Sports Illus 65:52 (c,2) Ag 11
        '86
Pipelines. See
    ALASKA PIPELINE
PIPES, TOBACCO
--12th cent. B.C. opium pipe
        (Cyprus)
    Nat Geog 167:152 (c,4) F '85
--1610s (Great Britain)
    Nat Geog 161:70 (c,4) Ja '82
--Ethiopia
    Nat Geog 163:632-3 (c,1) My
        '83
PIRATES
--Parody of baseball owner as
        pirate
    Sports Illus 56:40-1 (draw-
        ing,c,1) My 10 '82
PISA, ITALY
    Trav/Holiday 163:36 (c,4) Mr
        '85
PITCAIRN ISLAND
    Nat Geog 164:512-29 (c,1) O
        '83
PITCAIRN ISLAND--COSTUME
    Nat Geog 164:512-29 (c,1) O
        '83
PITCHER, MOLLY
--Depicted on postage stamp
    Am Heritage 34:59 (c,4) D '82
PITCHER PLANTS
    Nat Wildlife 20:41-5 (c,1) Ap
        '82
    Smithsonian 14:82 (c,4) Jl '83
    Natur Hist 93:90 (c,2) S '84
    Nat Wildlife 23:52 (c,4) D '84
    Smithsonian 16:63 (c,1) My '85
    Natur Hist 94:32 (c,1) Je '85
PITTSBURGH, PENNSYLVANIA
    Trav/Holiday 163:52-5 (c,1)
        My '85
--1940s

    Sports Illus 62:72 (3) Je 17 '85
--Mexican War streets area
    Sports Illus 57:78-9 (c,3) Ag
        23 '82
--PPG Place
    Smithsonian 14:14 (c,4) D '83
PLANETARIUMS
--1934 construction of Hayden
        Planetarium, New York
    Natur Hist 94:4 (3) O '85
--1935 Zeiss Star Projector
    Natur Hist 94:96-7 (c,2) O '85
PLANETS
    Nat Geog 167:4-50 (c,1) Ja '85
--See also
    ASTEROIDS
    EARTH
    JUPITER
    MARS
    MERCURY
    NEPTUNE
    PLUTO
    SATURN
    URANUS
    VENUS
PLANTATIONS
--Longwood, Natchez, Mississippi
    Am Heritage 36:100-2 (c,3) O '85
    Am Heritage 37:13 (4) F '86
--Louisiana
    Trav/Holiday 158:37-8 (c,1) S
        '82
    Nat Geog 166:26 (c,1) Jl '84
--Oak Alley, Louisiana
    Trav/Holiday 159:96 (4) Mr '83
--Waverly, Mississippi
    Nat Geog 169:378-9 (c,1) Mr '86
Planting. See
    FARMING--PLANTING
    GARDENING
PLANTS
--Bromeliads
    Smithsonian 16:cov. (c,1) Ap '85
    Smithsonian 16:60-1 (c,1) My '85
--Cobra plants
    Natur Hist 92:46-51 (c,1) Ap '83
--Genetic research
    Nat Geog 166:834-5 (c,1) D '84
--Groundnuts
    Nat Wildlife 23:43 (c,4) Ag '85
--House plants
    Nat Wildlife 23:10 (drawing,2) Ag
        '85
    Ebony 41:60-2 (c,3) S '86
--Illusions of human faces on plants
    Smithsonian 13:152-3 (c,4) S '82
--Pollen

POISON OAK
  Smithsonian 16:88, 95 (c,4) Ag
    '85
Poisonous plants. See
    PITCHER PLANTS
    POISON IVY
    POISON OAK
    SUMAC
POLAND
--Detention camp
  Life 5:110-11 (1) F '82
--See also
    WARSAW
POLAND--ART
--Posters
  Smithsonian 13:cov., 89-96
    (c,1) Ja '83
POLAND--COSTUME
  Life 5:108-16 (c,1) Ja '82
--1938 Jewish child (Warsaw)
  Smithsonian 14:130 (4) Ja '84
--Jews
  Nat Geog 170:362-89 (c,1) S
    '86
POLAND--HOUSING
--Apartment interior
  Nat Geog 170:364-5 (c,1) S '86
POLAND--MAPS
  Nat Geog 170:378 (c,4) S '86
POLAND--POLITICS AND GOV-
    ERNMENT
--Scenes of martial law
  Life 5:106-11 (1) F '82
--Solidarity movement
  Life 5:110-16 (c,3) Ja '82
  Life 6:38-9 (c,1) Ja '83
--Solidarity symbol
  Smithsonian 13:88-91 (c,4) Ja
    '83
--Youths doing victory handsign
  Life 5:142 (2) O '82
POLAR BEARS
  Nat Geog 161:393-5 (c,1) Mr
    '82
  Life 5:cov. (c,1) Je '82
  Nat Wildlife 21:37-43 (c,1) D
    '82
  Smithsonian 14:137 (c,4) Ap
    '83
  Life 6:94 (c,2) S '83
  Nat Geog 164:469 (c,4) O '83
  Trav/Holiday 160:cov., 38-9
    (c,1) O '83
  Natur Hist 92:42-3 (c,1) D '83
  Nat Wildlife 22:38-9, 60 (c,2)
    D '83
  Life 7:3, 42-54 (c,1) F '84

  Natur Hist 93:84-5 (c,1) Je '84
  Natur Hist 93:cov., 38-47 (c,1)
    D '84
  Smithsonian 16:40-51 (c,1) Mr
    '86
  Nat Wildlife 25:53 (c,4) D '86
POLE VAULTING
  Sports Illus 56:90 (c,4) F 8 '82
  Sports Illus 56:21 (c,4) F 22 '82
  Sports Illus 56:21 (c,4) Mr 1 '82
  Sports Illus 56:31 (c,4) My 31
    '82
  Sports Illus 56:21 (c,4) Je 28
    '82
  Sports Illus 58:30-3 (c,2) F 7
    '83
  Sports Illus 58:87 (c,3) F 14 '83
  Sports Illus 59:21 (c,4) Jl 4 '83
  Sports Illus 59:22-3 (c,3) S 1 '83
  Sports Illus 60:55 (c,4) F 20 '84
  Life 7:68-9, 90-1, 117 (c,1)
    Summer '84
  Sports Illus 61:38 (c,2) Jl 2 '84
  Sports Illus 63:2-3 (c,1) Jl 22
    '85
  Sports Illus 64:18-19 (c,1) Ja 27
    '86
  Sports Illus 64:18-19 (c,3) F 17
    '86
  Sports Illus 64:60-1 (c,2) F 24
    '86
  Sports Illus 64:2-3 (c,1) Mr 10
    '86
--1904 Olympics (St. Louis)
  Life 7:28-9 (1) Summer '84
--1984 Olympics (Los Angeles)
  Sports Illus 61:50-1 (c,4) Ag 20
    '84
POLICE WORK
--Abscam sting
  Life 5:62 (4) My '82
--Analyzing fingerprints
  Nat Geog 165:353 (c,4) Mr '84
--Apprehending criminals (New York
    City, New York)
  Life 7:30-6 (c,1) Jl '84
--Bloodhound hunting escaped con-
    vict (Georgia)
  Nat Geog 170:353 (c,1) S '86
--Bomb squad (Israel)
  Life 7:66-72 (c,1) D '84
--Catching illegal Mexican immigrants
    (California)
  Nat Geog 167:728-9 (c,1) Je '85
--Citizens patrol (Queens, New York)
  Life 7:44 (c,3) O '84
--Detectives on motorcycle chasing

POLICEMEN (cont.)
Life 7:194 (c,2) N '84
--Royal Canadian Mounted Police
(Alberta)
Trav/Holiday 163:67 (c,2) My
'85
--San Diego, California
Life 8:86 (c,2) Ja '85
--Seoul, South Korea
Sports Illus 65:45 (c,4) S 29
'86
--Sheriff (Alabama)
Ebony 37:56 (4) Jl '82
--Sheriff (Georgia)
Ebony 41:92, 96 (3) Mr '86
--Sheriffs (Northern California)
Life 5:40-1 (c,1) D '82
--Sheriff's badge
Sports Illus 56:80 (c,4) Ja 11
'82
--South Carolina
Nat Geog 166:797 (c,4) D '84
--South Korea
Sports Illus 61:81 (c,4) D 24
'84
--Strapping on ankle holster (New
York)
Life 7:36 (c,2) Jl '84
--Sudan
Life 8:52-3 (1) S '85
--Texas
Life 5:34 (4) D '82
--Tulsa, Oklahoma
Nat Geog 164:388-9 (c,1) S '83
--See also
DETECTIVES
FEDERAL BUREAU OF
INVESTIGATION (FBI)
POLICE WORK
POLITICAL CAMPAIGNS
--1848 Zachary Taylor campaign
scarf
Am Heritaged 38:28 (c,4) D
'86
--1860 Lincoln campaign flag
Am Heritage 36:108 (4) O '85
--1904 Teddy Roosevelt campaign
banner
Am Heritage 38:28 (c,4) D '86
--1908 William Jennings Bryan
speech
Am Heritage 35:108 (2) O '84
--1920s Jimmy Walker mayoral
campaign artifact (N.Y.)
Am Heritage 33:107 (4) Ag '82
--1932 Hitler campaign poster
(Germany)

Am Heritage 37:92 (4) Ag '86
--1932 Hoover campaign button
Am Heritage 38:25 (4) D '86
--1932-1984 cartoons about presidential races
Am Heritage 35:81-9, 114 (c,1)
O '84
--1940 FDR presidential campaign
speech
Am Heritage 37:28 (2) O '86
--1948 Presidential campaign debate
Am Heritage 37:66-70 (2) F '86
--1952 Republican National Convention (Chicago, Illinois)
Am Heritage 37:49 (3) D '85
--1960 presidential campaign
Life 6:24-5 (2) N '83
--1960 Adlai Stevenson presidential
campaign
Am Heritage 35:49-53, 64 (1) Ag
'84
Am Heritage 36:12 (3) D '84
--1980 Democratic National Conven-
tion delegates
Life 6:65 (4) My '83
--1984 Jesse Jackson presidential
campaign
Ebony 39:92-8 (c,1) Ag '84
Ebony 40:144 (3) Ag '85
--1984 presidential campaign
Life 7:82-98 (c,1) Ap '84
Life 8:10-11, 61-8 (c,1) Ja '85
--1984 Reagan presidential campaign
Life 7:75-80 (c,1) N '84
--1986 Congressional campaign of
Joe Kennedy, Jr. (Mass.)
Life 9:42-4 (c,1) Ap '86
--Artifacts from U.S. presidential
campaigns
Am Heritage 38:24-32 (c,4) D '86
--Cartoons about 20th cent. presi-
dential races
Am Heritage 35:81-9, 114 (c,1)
O '84
--JFK campaign button and poster
Am Heritage 34:23 (c,4) Je '83
--Politician in car (California)
Life 5:32 (4) O '82
--Talking to voters
Life 5:56-60 (c,2) O '82
--Willkie waving from a car (1940)
Am Heritage 33:22 (4) F '82
--See also
ELECTIONS
PUBLIC SPEAKING
U.S.--POLITICS AND GOVERN-
MENT

POLITICAN CAMPAIGNS--HUMOR
--Politics in ancient Rome
  Smithsonian 15:130-8 (drawing,c,1) O '84
POLITICAL CARTOONS
--1783 reconciliation between U.S.
    and England
  Smithsonian 14:58 (3) S '83
--1864 Abraham Lincoln cartoon
  Am Heritage 33:106 (4) F '82
--1932-1984 cartoons about presidential races
  Am Heritage 35:81-9, 114 (c,1)
    O '84
--1950s cartoons about Eisenhower
  Am Heritage 37:50-61 (4) D '85
--1954 cartoon about Joseph
    McCarthy
  Am Heritage 37:50 94) D '85
--1964 U.S. involvement in Vietnam
  Am Heritage 35:16 (4) Ag '84
--American treatment of Tories
    during Revolutionary War
  Smithsonian 14:58 (drawing,4)
    S '83
--Thomas Nast cartoons about
    Boss Tweed
  Am Heritage 38:81-96 (2) D '86
--Satellite competition with
    U.S.S.R. (1957-58)
  Smithsonian 13:149, 160 (drawing,4) O '82
--See also
    NAST, THOMAS
Politicians. See
    POLITICAL CAMPAIGNS
    STATESMEN
    U.S.--POLITICS AND GOVERNMENT
Politics and government. See
    DEMONSTRATIONS
    ELECTIONS
    GOVERNMENT--LEGISLATURES
    POLITICAL CAMPAIGNS
    U.S.--POLITICS AND GOVERNMENT
    specific countries--POLITICS
      AND GOVERNMENT
POLLOCK, JACKSON
--"Direction" (1945)
  Smithsonian 17:64 (painting,c,4) Jl '86
POLLAIUOLO, ANTONIO DEL
--"Portrait of a Woman" (1491)
  Smithsonian 13:59 (paint-

ing,c,2) N '82
POLLUTION
--Cartoons about determining safe
    pollutant levels
  Nat Wildlife 22:29-32 (4) Ag '84
--Drums of radioactive waste
  Nat Wildlife 21:20-3 (1) Ap '83
--Hazardous waste sites
  Nat Geog 167:cov., 318-51 (c,1)
    Mr '85
--Testing for toxic wastes
  Nat Wildlife 23:38-41 (c,1) Je '85
Pollution. See
    AIR POLLUTION
    ENVIRONMENTAL PROTECTION
      AGENCY
    WATER POLLUTION
POLO
  Sports Illus 62:43, 46 (c,3) Mr
    18 '85
--1935 (New York)
  Sports Illus 65:118 (4) N 3 '86
--Pakistan
  Smithsonian 13:53 (c,4) Ap '82
--Polocrosse (Papua New Guinea)
  Nat Geog 162:157 (c,1) Ag '82
--Texas
  Life 7:103-7 (c,1) O '84
--See also
    WATER POLO
POLO, MARCO
--Modern scenes along 13th cent.
    "Silk Road" (Pakistan)
  Smithsonian 13:46-55 (map,c,1)
    Ap '82
Polynesia. See
    PACIFIC ISLANDS
POLYPS
  Nat Geog 165:478-9 (c,1) Ap '84
POMPADOUR, MARQUISE DE
--Painting by Boucher
  Smithsonian 16:108 (c,4) Mr '86
POMPEII, ITALY
  Nat Geog 165:608-9 (c,1) My '84
PONAPE
  Trav/Holiday 162:58, 60 (c,2) N
    '84
--Nan Madol
  Natur Hist 92:50-61 (map,c,1) D
    '83
PONAPE--COSTUME
  Natur Hist 92:56-9 (c,1) D '83
POND LIFE
  Smithsonian 13:62-71 (c,1) Jl '82
--Freshwater springs (Florida)
  Natur Hist 92:90-3 (c,1) D '83
--Stream wildlife

POND LIFE (cont.)
  Nat Wildlife 24:30-5 (c,1) Ag
      '86
PONDS
--Aerial view (Florida)
  Life 5:122 (c,4) O '82
--China
  Nat Geog 168:214-15 (c,1) Ag
      '85
--Manitoba
  Natur Hist 94:64 (c,4) Ag '85
--Maryland
  Smithsonian 13:63 (c,3) Jl '82
--Pond bottom seen through ice
  Smithsonian 17:cov., 168-72
      (c,1) N '86
--Toxic waste in New York pond
  Nat Wildlife 24:30-1 (c,1) Ap
      '86
PONY EXPRESS
  Am Heritage 36:22 (drawing,4)
      Ap '85
POODLES
  Life 5:37 (1) S '82
  Ebony 38:90 (2) Mr '83
  Sports Illus 60:84 (c,4) Ap 9
      '84
  Smithsonian 17:96 (4) My '86
--Toy poodle
  Ebony 37:28 (c,4) Jl '82
  Nat Geog 166:325 (c,1) S '84
Pool playing. See
      BILLIARD PLAYING
Pools. See
      SWIMMING POOLS
POPCORN
--Poured on man's head
  Smithsonian 16:55 (c,1) Ag '85
POPES
--Clement VIII's 16th cent.
      chasuble
  Smithsonian 13:130 (c,4) D '82
--Clement IX
  Life 5:58-9 (painting,c,1) D
      '82
--John XXIII
  Ebony 41:284 (3) N '85
--John Paul II
  Sports Illus 56:41 (c,4) F 15
      '82
  Ebony 37:63, 66 (c,3) Ap '82
  Life 6:64 (c,3) Ja '83
  Nat Geog 164:414 (c,4) O '83
  Life 8:52-3 (1) Mr '85
  Life 8:63 (4) Jl '85
  Nat Geog 168:723-5, 753, 763
      (c,1) D '85

Life 9:15 (c,4) D '86
--John Paul II (1959)
  Life 9:368 (4) Fall '86
--John Paul II's 1981 assassination
      attempt
  Life 5:12-13 (c,4) Ja '82
--Leo X
  Nat Geog 164:434 (sculpture,c,4)
      O '83
--Papal tiara
  Smithsonian 13:130 (c,4) Je '82
--Pius IX image on ring
  Nat Geog 168:764 (c,4) D '85
POPLAR TREES
  Nat Wildlife 21:54-60 (c,1) O '83
--See also
      ASPEN TREES
      COTTONWOOD TREES
POPOCATEPETL, MEXICO
  Nat Geog 166:452-3 (c,1) O '84
POPPIES
  Smithsonian 13:142-3 (c,1) O '82
  Nat Wildlife 22:7 (c,4) Je '84
  Nat Geog 167:142-79 (c,1) F '85
  Nat Wildlife 24:27 (c,1) Ap '86
  Nat Wildlife 25:60 (c,1) D '86
--Poppy seeds
  Nat Geog 167:172-3 (c,2) F '85
POPPY INDUSTRY
  Nat Geog 167:142-89 (c,1) F '85
POPULATION
--Charts of growing world population
      centers
  Nat Geog 166:180-5 (c,1) Ag '84
Porcelain. See
      GLASSWARE
      POTTERY
PORCUPINE FISH
  Nat Geog 165:480-1 (c,1) Ap '84
  Nat Geog 166:262 (c,1) Ag '84
PORCUPINES
  Nat Wildlife 20:5 (c,1) O '82
  Nat Wildlife 21:56 (c,1) Ap '83
  Nat Wildlife 22:54 (c,2) O '84
  Natur Hist 94:62-9, 99 (c,1) My
      '85
  Nat Wildlife 24:14-19 (c,1) O '86
--Baby porcupine
  Nat Wildlife 21:56 (c,1) Ap '83
Porpoises. See
      DOLPHINS
      KILLER WHALES
PORT-AU-PRINCE, HAITI
  Trav/Holiday 165:51 (c,4) F '86
PORTER, COLE
  Smithsonian 14:154 (4) F '84

PORTERS
--Carrying luggage on head (India)
   Nat Geog 165:717 (c,2) Je '84
--Railroad porter
   Ebony 39:87-90 (c,3) Ja '84
PORTLAND, MAINE
   Nat Geog 167:222-5 (c,1) F '85
--Lighthouse
   Trav/Holiday 166:26 (c,3) S '86
PORTLAND, OREGON
--1880s cable cars
   Am Heritage 36:96 (2) Ap '85
PORTO, PORTUGAL
   Trav/Holiday 158:53-4 (c,2) O '82
   Nat Geog 166:460-9 (c,1) O '84
--See also
   DOURO RIVER
PORTOBELO, PANAMA
   Nat Geog 169:476 (c,1) Ap '86
PORT-OF-SPAIN, TRINIDAD AND TOBAGO
   Ebony 40:104, 108 (c,4) N '84
Ports. See
   HARBORS
PORTSMOUTH, NEW HAMPSHIRE
   Nat Geog 162:782-3 (c,1) D '82
PORTSMOUTH, VIRGINIA
   Nat Geog 168:72-3, 84-5 (c,1) Jl '85
PORTUGAL
   Trav/Holiday 160:cov., 53-4 (c,1) Ag '83
--Cascais
   Trav/Holiday 160:66 (3) Ag '83
--Northern provinces
   Trav/Holiday 158:cov., 53-5 (c,1) O '82
--Sesimbra
   Trav/Holiday 160:54 (c,2) Ag '83
--See also
   DOURO RIVER
   PORTO
PORTUGAL--COSTUME
   Nat Geog 166:462-81 (c,1) O '84
--Farm worker
   Trav/Holiday 158:cov. (c,1) O '82
--Guard at palace (Lisbon)
   Trav/Holiday 160:cov. (c,1)

   Ag '83
PORTUGUESE MAN-OF-WAR
   Natur Hist 93:20 (drawing,4) D '84
POST, EMILY
   Am Heritage 35:93 (painting,c,4) O '84
POST OFFICES
--1899 letter box (Washington, D.C.)
   Nat Geog 164:413 (c,4) S '83
--General Post Office, Washington, D.C. (1850)
   Smithsonian 15:26 (engraving,4) F '85
--Interior (Lost Springs, Wyoming)
   Life 6:126 (c,4) N '83
--Old Post Office, Washington, D.C.
   Nat Geog 164:404-15 (c,1) S '83
--St. Charles, Illinois
   Nat Wildlife 21:8 (c,4) Ap '83
--Small town post offices
   Smithsonian 14:62-9 (c,1) Jl '83
POSTAGE STAMPS
--20th cent. U.S. stamps
   Am Heritage 34:50-9 (c,4) D '82
--1926 U.S. air mail stamp
   Am Heritage 33:113 (3) O '82
--Commemorating Alaska's statehood
   Nat Geog 164:554 (c,4) N '83
--Commemorating Hawaii's statehood
   Nat Geog 164:554 (c,4) N '83
--Commemorating Olympics (Philippines)
   Sports Illus 61:66 (c,4) Jl 16 '84
--Domesday Book commemorative (Great Britain)
   Smithsonian 17:85 (c,4) Jl '86
--Honoring Roberto Clemente
   Sports Illus 61:64 (c,4) Ag 27 '84
--Honoring Babe Didrikson
   Sports Illus 61:76 (c,4) S 10 '84
--Honoring Bobby Jones
   Sports Illus 61:76 (c,4) S 10 '84
--Honoring Martin Luther King, Jr.
   Am Heritage 34:59 (c,4) D '82
   Ebony 41:82-4 (c,4) Ja '86
--Honoring Jackie Robinson
   Sports Illus 57:99 (c,4) N 1 '82
--Illustrated with sunfish sailboats (Bahamas)
   Sports Illus 57:82 (c,4) S 20 '82
--Knights of Malta
   Smithsonian 12:126 (c,4) Ja '82
--Norfolk Island, Australia
   Nat Geog 164:535 (c,4) O '83
--U.S. duck stamps

POSTERS (cont.)
Nat Geog 169:156-7 (c,1) F
'86
--Classic movie posters
Life 9:75-82 (c,2) My '86
--European ads for mineral water
Smithsonian 15:112-13 (c,4) O
'84
--European posters of U.S.
movies
Smithsonian 17:176 (c,4) My
'86
--Movie posters (Japan)
Life 6:106 (c,2) Ap '83
--Poland
Smithsonian 13:cov., 89-96
(c,1) Ja '83
--Toronto festival poster
Trav/Holiday 161:62 (c,4) Je
'84
--World War I U.S. Navy recruit-
ment poster
Am Heritage 34:2 (drawing,c,1)
Ap '83
--World War II "loose lips" post-
ers (U.S.)
Life 8:92 (c,4) Spring '85
--See also
ADVERTISING
POTATO INDUSTRY
Nat Geog 161:668-92 (c,1) My
'82
--Sorting potatoes (Delaware)
Nat Geog 164:186-7 (c,1) Ag
'83
POTATO INDUSTRY--HARVESTING
--Peru
Nat Geog 161:672-3 (c,1) My
'82
POTATOES
Nat Geog 161:668-91 (c,1) My
'82
POTOMAC RIVER, SOUTHEAST
Nat Geog 163:90-1 (c,1) Ja '83
Nat Geog 166:806-7 (c,1) D
'84
--1838 view
Smithsonian 16:163 (paint-
ing,c,3) O '85
--Marshy area (Virginia)
Smithsonian 14:30 (c,4) Ap '83
POTTERY
--12th-13th cent. bowl (Iran)
Smithsonian 14:66 (c,4) Je '83
--16th cent. Chinese porcelain
Nat Geog 162:481 (c,4) O '82
--17th-19th cents. (Japan)

Smithsonian 17:162 (c,4) Ap '86
--17th cent. German jug
Smithsonian 13:111 (c,4) Je '82
--1620 (Virginia)
Am Heritage 34:38 (c,4) Ag '83
--19th cent. Wedgwood anti-slavery
medallion (Great Britain)
Natur Hist 95:18 (4) Ap '86
--Ancient Thailand
Smithsonian 13:98-107 (c,1) Ja
'83
--Carved Maya bowl (Central Amer-
ica)
Natur Hist 92:72 (3) Ag '83
--Early Pennsylvania German family
platters
Am Heritage 34:80-1, 114 (c,4) D
'82
--Mayan civilization
Smithsonian 17:40 (c,4) My '86
--Mayan civilization (Belize)
Nat Geog 162:136-7 (c,4) Jl '82
--Pueblo Indians (New Mexico)
Nat Geog 162:cov., 593-605 (c,1)
N '82
--Spain
Trav/Holiday 166:19 (4) S '86
--Staffordshire
Am Heritage 34:88 (c,2) Ap '83
--Zuni Indians (Southwest)
Smithsonian 16:141 (c,4) Ag '85
POTTERY MAKING
--Hand-painting Delft porcelain
(Netherlands)
Trav/Holiday 160:16, 20 (4) Jl
'83
--Kentucky
Trav/Holiday 162:60 (c,3) Ag '84
--Mali
Nat Geog 162:409 (c,1) S '82
--Mexico
Nat Geog 166:440-1 (c,1) O '84
--Pueblo Indians (Southwest)
Nat Geog 162:603-5 (c,3) N '82
--Spain
Nat Geog 161:748 (c,4) Je '82
--Thailand
Smithsonian 13:103 (c,4) Ja '83
POVERTY
--1888 homeless orphans (New York
City)
Smithsonian 17:94 (2) Ag '86
--1936 soup line (Vienna, Austria)
Am Heritage 37:94 (3) Ag '86
--1956 sharecropping family (Missis-
sippi)
Ebony 41:144 (4) Ag '86

POVERTY
--Breadline (Poland)
  Life 5:108-9 (c,1) Ja '82
--Children of migrant workers
    (Florida)
  Life 6:147-58 (1) N '83
--Family living in campground
    (New Mexico)
  Life 6:42-3 (c,1) Ja '83
--Food stamp distribution (Puerto
    Rico)
  Nat Geog 163:528-9 (c,1) Ap
    '83
--Free meal service (Washington,
    D.C.)
  Nat Geog 163:119 (c,2) Ja '83
--Poor family saying grace (1894
    painting)
  Ebony 38:38 (c,2) D '82
--Relief center (Ethiopia)
  Nat Geog 168:390-1 (c,1) S '85
--Sick Brazilian boy (1961)
  Life 9:154 (2) Fall '86
--Street life of runaway teens
    (Washington)
  Life 6:34-42 (1) Jl '83
--Unemployment line
  Ebony 38:46 (3) Ag '83
  Ebony 40:60 (3) F '85
  Ebony 41:62 (2) Ag '86
--See also
    BEGGARS
    DEPRESSION
    MALNUTRITION
    SLUMS
POWER PLANTS
--France
  Nat Geog 161:491 (c,3) Ap '82
--Geothermal plants (Iceland)
  Trav/Holiday 166:44 (c,4) N
    '86
--Hydropower project (Quebec)
  Nat Geog 161:406-18 (c,1) Mr
    '82
--Hydropower station controls
    (Papua New Guinea)
  Nat Geog 162:160 (c,3) Ag '82
--Maryland
  Nat Geog 165:552-3 (c,1) Ap
    '84
--Small hydroelectric power sta-
    tions (California)
  Smithsonian 13:87-96 (c,2) D
    '82
--See also
    NUCLEAR POWER PLANTS

PRAGUE, CZECHOSLOVAKIA
  Trav/Holiday 158:39-42 (c,1) Jl
    '82
  Life 7:66-7 (c,1) S '84
  Life 7:88-90 (c,1) N '84
--Charles Bridge
  Life 6:120 (c,2) D '83
--Jewish Museum
  Life 7:84-90 (c,1) N '84
PRAIRIE CHICKENS
  Nat Wildlife 25:28 (c,4) D '86
PRAIRIE DOGS
  Nat Wildlife 20:2 (c,1) Ap '82
  Nat Geog 162:361 (c,3) S '82
  Nat Wildlife 20:cov. (c,1) O '82
  Sports Illus 59:75 (c,4) S 26 '83
  Trav/Holiday 162:42 (c,4) Jl '84
  Nat Geog 166:386-7 (c,1) S '84
  Nat Wildlife 23:48-53 (c,1) Ap
    '85
  Nat Wildlife 23:2 (c,2) O '85
  Natur Hist 95:74 (c,2) F '86
  Nat Wildlife 24:17 (c,1) Ap '86
PRAYING
--1777 Congressional prayer session
  Am Heritage 35:77 (painting,4)
    Ag '84
--Afghans (Pakistan)
  Nat Geog 167:790-1 (c,1) Je '85
--Buddhist prayer wheel (China)
  Nat Geog 161:257 (c,2) F '82
--Cheerleaders before football game
  Sports Illus 57:168 (c,4) S 1 '82
--Children (Western Samoa)
  Nat Geog 168:468 (c,3) O '85
--Football players
  Sports Illus 57:39 (c,4) D 27 '82
  Sports Illus 60:16 (c,2) Ja 9 '84
--Iranian soldiers
  Nat Geog 168:116 (c,3) Jl '85
--Mass prayer service (Iran)
  Nat Geog 168:122-3 (c,1) Jl '85
--Meditating (California)
  Life 5:43 (c,1) D '82
--Meditating (Colorado)
  Nat Geog 166:211 (c,4) Ag '84
--Moslems (Senegal)
  Nat Geog 168:244-5 (c,1) Ag '85
--Muslim (California)
  Sports Illus 61:68-9 (1) O 8 '84
  Ebony 40:142 (3) Mr '85
--Muslim (Egypt)
  Nat Geog 161:426-7 (c,1) Ap '82
--Muslims at Jama Masjid Mosque,
    Delhi, India
  Nat Geog 167:524-5 (c,1) Ap '85
--Nicaraguan contras

PRAYING (cont.)
Nat Geog 168:808 (c,3) D '85
--Oman
Nat Geog 162:32 (c,3) Jl '82
--Philippine guerrillas
Nat Geog 170:93 (c,1) Jl '86
--Policeman (Oklahoma)
Nat Geog 164:388-9 (c,1) S '83
--Poor family saying grace (1894
painting)
Ebony 38:38 (c,2) D '82
--Prayer flags (Tibet)
Natur Hist 91:50-1 (c,3) S '82
--Saying grace at dinner (Penn-
sylvania)
Nat Geog 165:507 (c,3) Ap '84
--Tibet
Smithsonian 13:101 (c,1) My '82
--Transcendental Meditation
Ebony 40:84 (4) Ag '85
PREGNANCY
Life 5:66 (2) S '82
--Line of pregnant women (Kansas)
Life 9:26-7 (c,1) Jl '86
--Medical exam
Ebony 38:106 (2) D '82
--Midwife examining pregnant
woman (Mexico)
Nat Geog 166:150 (c,3) Ag '84
--Pregnant woman
Ebony 40:cov., 80 (c,1) Mr '85
Ebony 41:38 (c,3) Ag '86
--Princess of Wales
Life 5:105-12 (c,2) My '82
--Queen Elizabeth II (1948)
Life 9:89 (4) Ap '86
--Sonogram of 19-week fetus
Smithsonian 14:68 (c,4) Ja '84
--Teenage pregnancies
Life 6:102-11 (1) D '83
--28-week-old human fetus
Life 9:100-1 (c,1) Fall '86
--See also
CHILDBIRTH
REPRODUCTION
Prehistoric man. See
MAN, PREHISTORIC
PRESCOTT, WILLIAM HICKLING
Smithsonian 14:102 (paint-
ing,c,3) Ag '83
PRESCOTT NATIONAL FOREST,
ARIZONA
Natur Hist 95:30-2 (map,c,1)
Jl '86
Presidents. See
U.S. PRESIDENTS

PRESLEY, ELVIS
Life 8:60-1 (1) Mr '85
Life 9:371 (2) Fall '86
--Artifacts and impersonators
Life 7:76-82 (c,1) Ag '84
--Graceland, Memphis, Tennessee
Life 7:78-9 (c,1) Ag '84
--Graceland's "Jungle Room" (Mem-
phis, Tennessee)
Life 5:124 (c,2) Je '82
--Grave (Memphis, Tennessee)
Nat Geog 169:619 (c,3) My '86
--Japanese Elvis imitators
Natur Hist 94:56-7 (c,1) Ag '85
--Monument (Memphis, Tennessee)
Trav/Holiday 160:53 (4) S '83
--Wax likeness
Smithsonian 16:171 (c,1) Ap '85
PRESS CONFERENCES
--Franklin D. Roosevelt (1933)
Am Heritage 33:15 (4) F '82
PRIBILOF ISLANDS, ALASKA
Nat Geog 162:536-51 (map,c,1)
O '82
--Killing seals
Life 7:179-84 (1) N '84
PRIMATES
Smithsonian 16:100-5 (c,3) D '85
--Amphipithecus
Natur Hist 94:30 (drawing,4) O
'85
--Family tree diagram
Natur Hist 94:32 (c,4) O '85
--Vervets
Smithsonian 15:73 (c,4) Mr '85
--See also
APES
LEMURS
MONKEYS
PRIMROSES
Smithsonian 12:38 (c,4) Mr '82
Natur Hist 94:84 (c,4) Mr '85
PRINCE EDWARD ISLAND, CANADA
Trav/Holiday 161:58-60 (c,1) Ap
'84
--Aerial view
Trav/Holiday 159:40 (4) Ap '83
PRINCETON UNIVERSITY, NEW
JERSEY
Trav/Holiday 165:47-9 (c,1) My
'86
Am Heritage 37:73 (c,3) Je '86
PRINTING INDUSTRY
--1870 printing shop
Am Heritage 34:99 (drawing,c,1)
D '82
--1945 newspaper printing press

Psychology. See
>FREUD, SIGMUND
>JUNG, CARL GUSTAV
>MENNINGER, KARL A.
>THERAPY

PTARMIGANS
>Nat Wildlife 20:48 (c,1) F '82

PUBLIC SPEAKING
--1908 William Jennings Bryan
>presidential campaign
>Am Heritage 35:108 (2) O '84
--1940 FDR presidential campaign
>speech
>Am Heritage 37:28 (2) O '86
--At rally for Martin Luther King
>national holiday (D.C.)
>Ebony 37:97 (3) Ap '82
--Politician (Illinois)
>Ebony 38:28-9 (c,1) Jl '83
--Politician atop car (Illinois)
>Life 5:58 (c,2) O '82
--Politician's victory speech
>Ebony 38:36 (3) F '83
--Presentation using overheads
>Life 6:63 (4) D '83
--Standing in front of microphones
>Life 5:61 (2) My '82

PUBLISHING
--Harvard Lampoon staff
>Life 5:133-42 (c,1) N '82
--Preservation techniques for
>U.S. documents
>Smithsonian 17:134-43 (c,1) O
>'86
--See also
>BARTLETT, JOHN
>BOOKS
>MAGAZINES
>NEWSPAPER INDUSTRY
>PRINTING INDUSTRY

PUEBLO INDIANS. See also
>HOPI INDIANS
>ZUNI INDIANS

PUEBLO INDIANS--RELICS
--19th cent. buffalo-hide shield
>Am Heritage 37:21 (c,4) Ag '86

PUERTO RICO
>Nat Geog 163:517-43 (map,c,1)
>Ap '83
--El Yunque rain forest
>Trav/Holiday 159:52, 61 (c,2)
>Ja '83
--Inns
>Trav/Holiday 166:62-4 (c,3) N
>'86
--See also
>SAN JUAN

PUFFER FISH
>Nat Wildlife 22:58-9 (c,1) Ap '84
>Nat Geog 166:260-9 (c,1) Ag '84
--See also
>PORCUPINE FISH

PUFFINS
>Trav/Holiday 157:51 (c,4) F '82
>Nat Geog 164:362-3 (c,2) S '83
>Nat Wildlife 23:4-9 (c,1) Ag '85
>Nat Wildlife 24:17 (painting,c,4)
>D '85
>Nat Wildlife 24:50-1 (c,1) Je '86

PULITZER, JOSEPH
>Nat Wildlife 33:62-3 (c,1) O '82
--1896 cartoon
>Am Heritage 33:62 (c,2) O '82

PUMPKINS
>Am Heritage 33:43 (c,1) Ag '82
>Trav/Holiday 162:54 (c,4) S '84

Pumps. See
>WATER

PUNISHMENT
--Saboteurs in chains (Sudan)
>Nat Geog 161:361 (c,4) Mr '82
--Wooden horse (Civil War camp)
>Am Heritage 33:77 (3) F '82
--See also
>CAPITAL PUNISHMENT
>LYNCHINGS
>PRISONS
>SCALPING

PUPPETS
--Howdy Doody
>Life 9:205-6 (2) Fall '86
--Latex celebrities
>Life 9:84 (c,2) O '86
--Marionette
>Life 6:19 (2) Ap '83
--Medieval-costumed marionettes
>Smithsonian 14:cov., 68-73 (c,1)
>Ag '83
--Muppets
>Trav/Holiday 159:37 (c,4) Je '83
--Peregrine falcon dummy
>Life 6:54-5 (c,1) Je '83

PURSES
--1945 women's handbags and con-
>tents
>Life 9:171-2 (4) Fall '86
--Reptile skin accessories and fakes
>Life 9:96-8 (c,1) D '86

Puzzles. See
>GAME PLAYING
>REBUSES

PYGMIES--COSTUME
--1930s (Congo)
>Smithsonian 17:154 (4) N '86

PYLE, ERNIE
   Am Heritage 36:33 (3) Je '85
PYRAMIDS
--Belize
   Nat Geog 162:130-3 (c,1) Jl
      '82
--Cholula, Mexico
   Nat Geog 168:326-7 (c,1) S '85
--Egypt
   Nat Geog 161:cov., 158-9 (c,1)
      F '82
   Trav/Holiday 157:36-7 (c,1) F
      '82
   Nat Geog 163:457 (c,1) Ap '83
   Nat Geog 167:576-7 (c,1) My
      '85
   Smithsonian 17:78-93 (c,1) Ap
      '86
--Mayan (Uxmal, Mexico)
   Natur Hist 94:48-9 (c,1) Ap
      '85
--Mexico
   Trav/Holiday 158:32 (c,3) S
      '82
--Sudan
   Nat Geog 161:348-9 (c,1) Mr '82
   Nat Geog 167:610-11 (c,1) My
      '85
PYTHONS
   Life 5:60-1 (c,1) Ja '82
   Sports Illus 56:98 (c,4) F 8 '82
   Smithsonian 13:137 (c,4) Jl '82
   Life 7:12 (c,3) S '84

                  -Q-

QUAIL
   Nat Wildlife 22:54-5 (paint-
      ing,c,1) F '84
   Sports Illus 61:58-9 (c,3) S
      10 '84
   Natur Hist 94:90 (drawing,4)
      F '85
--Bobwhites
   Nat Wildlife 22:24 (c,3) O '84
   Nat Wildlife 23:31 (drawing,4)
      O '85
   Nat Wildlife 24:26-7 (paint-
      ing,c,1) O '86
QUARTZ
   Nat Geog 162:426 (c,4) O '82
QUARTZITE
   Nat Geog 163:682 (c,4) My '83
QUEBEC
--Hydropower project
   Nat Geog 161:406-18 (map,c,1)

   Mr '82
QUEBEC. See also
   GASPE PENINSULA
   MONTREAL
   QUEBEC CITY
   ST. LAWRENCE RIVER
QUEBEC CITY, QUEBEC
   Trav/Holiday 157:38, 42-3 (c,4)
      My '82
   Ebony 38:158 (c,4) My '83
   Trav/Holiday 161:38 (4) My '84
   Trav/Holiday 165:80-1 (c,1) Mr
      '86
--Winter Carnival
   Trav/Holiday 159:42 (c,2) F '83
QUETZALS (BIRDS)
   Nat Geog 163:65 (c,1) Ja '83
QUILTING
--Amish people (Pennsylvania)
   Nat Geog 165:502-3 (c,2) Ap '84
--Arkansas
   Trav/Holiday 161:54 (c,2) F '84
QUILTS
--Hand-made (South)
   Life 6:52-3 (c,1) Ag '83
QUINCE FRUITS
   Natur Hist 91:79 (1) Ag '82
QUITO, ECUADOR
   Trav/Holiday 160:57-8 (c,1) Jl
      '83

                  -R-

RABAT, MOROCCO
   Trav/Holiday 160:4 (c,4) D '83
RABBITS
   Life 6:66-9 (c,1) Ap '83
   Nat Wildlife 21:14-15 (c,1) Ag '83
   Nat Wildlife 21:36 (c,4) O '83
   Ebony 39:52 (c,3) N '83
   Smithsonian 15:28 (c,4) Je '84
   Trav/Holiday 166:67 (c,4) N '86
--Arctic hare
   Nat Geog 164:468 (c,4) O '83
   Natur Hist 95:100-1 (c,1) Ja '86
--Arctic hare on hind feet
   Natur Hist 93:93 (c,2) D '84
--Black-naped hare
   Nat Geog 164:259 (c,4) Ag '83
--Cottontail
   Nat Wildlife 21:cov. (painting,c,1)
      D '82
   Nat Wildlife 22:64 (c,1) Ap '84
--Rabbit costume
   Life 7:34-5 (c,1) N '84
--Snowshoe hares

RABBITS (cont.)
    Nat Wildlife 22:54 (c,2) Je '84
    Nat Wildlife 24:64-5 (c,1) Ap
        '86
    Nat Wildlife 25:24 (c,4) D '86
--See also
    CONIES
    JACK RABBITS
    PIKAS
RACCOONS
    Natur Hist 93:6-10 (c,1) Jl '84
    Nat Wildlife 22:59 (c,3) O '84
    Nat Wildlife 23:20-4 (c,1) Je
        '85
    Smithsonian 16:29 (c,4) Ja '86
    Nat Wildlife 24:22 (c,4) Ap '86
--Rabid raccoons
    Life 6:3, 44-7 (c,1) My '83
--Residing in tree
    Nat Wildlife 20:2 (c,2) O '82
RACE TRACKS
--Aqueduct, Queens, New York
    Sports Illus 63:8 (c,4) O 21
        '85
--Charlotte, North Carolina
    Trav/Holiday 165:87 (c,4) Mr
        '86
--Churchill Downs, Kentucky
    Sports Illus 60:26-7 (c,1) My
        14 '84
    Sports Illus 62:28 (c,3) My 13
        '85
    Sports Illus 64:9-14 (c,4) Ap
        28 '86
--Garden State Park, Cherry Hill,
    New Jersey
    Sports Illus 62:44-50 (c,1) Ap
        22 '85
--Grand Prix track (Detroit,
    Michigan)
    Sports Illus 56:58-65 (c,3) Je
        14 '82
--Grand Prix track (Las Vegas,
    Nevada)
    Sports Illus 56:88 (c,4) Je 7
        '82
--Hialeah, Florida
    Sports Illus 56:83 (c,4) Mr 8
        '82
    Sports Illus 56:70 (c,4) Mr 15
        '82
--Hippodrome, Beirut, Lebanon
    Nat Geog 163:274-5 (c,4) F '83
--Indianapolis 500 track, Indiana
    Sports Illus 58:66 (c,2) My 23
        '83
--Keeneland, Kentucky

Smithsonian 17:128-9 (c,1) Ap
    '86
--Latonia, Florence, Kentucky
    Sports Illus 58:96 (c,4) Ap 4 '83
--Ontario harness track
    Sports Illus 61:63 (c,3) D 10 '84
--Pimlico, Baltimore, Maryland
    Sports Illus 62:10 (4) Ap 1 '85
--Red Mile harness track, Lexington,
    Kentucky
    Am Heritage 35:110 (c,4) D '83
--Santa Anita barn area, California
    Sports Illus 62:72-3, 83 (c,4)
        My 6 '85
--See also
    STABLES
RACES
--1928 cross-country foot race
    Life 6:80 (c,4) Je '83
--All-terrain vehicles (Oklahoma)
    Nat Geog 164:398 (c,4) S '83
--Armadillo races (Texas)
    Trav/Holiday 166:66 (c,3) Jl '86
--Bedouin camel race (Saudi Arabia)
    Smithsonian 15:56-7 (c,1) D '84
--Bedouril Race Meeting (Queensland,
    Australia)
    Nat Geog 169:2-3 (c,1) Ja '86
--Beginning of running race
    Sports Illus 57:86-7 (drawing,c,1)
        D 27 '82
--Blimp race (New York)
    Sports Illus 65:2-3 (c,1) Jl 14
        '86
--Camel race (Florida)
    Sports Illus 62:6-7 (c,1) Mr 11
        '85
--Chuck-wagon race (Calgary, Al-
    berta)
    Nat Geog 165:398-9 (c,1) Mr '84
--Computer analysis of race walking
    Nat Geog 162:424 (c,1) O '82
--Cross-country sled dog race
    Smithsonian 13:88-97 (c,1) Mr '83
--Crossing finish line
    Sports Illus 58:72 (c,4) Ap 18 '83
--Fifth Avenue Mile, New York City,
    New York
    Sports Illus 59:70-1 (c,3) Jl 18
        '83
--Gasparilla (Florida)
    Sports Illus 56:20-1 (c,4) F 15
        '82
--Iditarod Trail Sled Dog Race
    (Alaska)
    Nat Geog 163:410-21 (c,1) Mr '83
    Sports Illus 62:28-9 (c,1) Ap 1 '85

RAIN (cont.)
    Nat Geog 166:716-17 (c,1) D
        '84
--Hawaii
    Nat Geog 164:594-5 (c,1) N '83
--Pedestrian avoiding splashing
        car (Sweden)
    Life 9:404 (2) Fall '86
--Rain falling on golf course
        (Ohio)
    Sports Illus 65:18-19 (c,2) Jl
        21 '86
--Rain falling on patio furniture
    Life 8:110 (c,2) Ag '85
--Rainmakers
    Natur Hist 94:20-8 (4) S '85
--See also
        MONSOONS
        STORMS
RAIN FORESTS
    Nat Geog 163:2-65 (map,c,1)
        Ja '83
--Brazil
    Smithsonian 16:101-11 (c,1) D
        '85
--Chile
    Smithsonian 16:85 (c,1) O '85
--Costa Rica
    Life 5:44-50 (c,1) S '82
    Nat Geog 163:48-65 (c,1) Ja '83
    Natur Hist 94:42-7 (c,1) F '85
    Trav/Holiday 163:10 (c,4) My
        '85
--El Yunque, Puerto Rico
    Trav/Holiday 159:52, 61 (c,2)
        Ja '83
--Peru
    Smithsonian 17:80-90 (c,3) S '86
--Rwanda
    Natur Hist 91:50-5 (c,1) Mr '82
--Venezuela
    Natur Hist 92:70-8 (c,1) Ap '83
--Washington
    Natur Hist 94:48-9 (c,1) F '85
    Natur Hist 95:30-2 (map,c,1)
        Mr '86
RAINBOWS
    Nat Wildlife 20:12-15 (c,1) Ap
        '82
    Smithsonian 13:127 (c,1) My '82
    Smithsonian 14:54-5 (c,2) Ja
        '84
--Farallon Islands, California
    Nat Wildlife 24:50 (c,4) Je '86
--Over lake (Tasmania, Australia)
    Smithsonian 16:130 (c,3) Ag
        '85

--Over mountains (British Columbia)
    Natur Hist 94:34-5 (c,1) D '85
--Scotland
    Nat Geog 166:41 (c,1) Jl '84
--Society Islands
    Sports Illus 64:135 (c,1) F 10
        '86
--Victoria Falls, Zimbabwe
    Trav/Holiday 165:62-3 (c,1) Mr
        '86
RAINWEAR
--Banana leaf cape (Nepal)
    Nat Geog 166:732 (c,4) D '84
--People covered with plastic bag
        (Kentucky)
    Sports Illus 58:35 (c,4) My 16
        '83
--People wrapped in plastic (Georgia)
    Sports Illus 56:18 (c,4) Ap 19
        '82
RAMSES II (EGYPT)
--Statues
    Trav/Holiday 163:78 (c,4) Mr '85
    Trav/Holiday 165:52-4 (c,1) Je
        '86
Ranchers. See
        COWBOYS
RANCHES
--1897 (Montana)
    Am Heritage 33:36-7 (2) Je '82
--1903 (Nebraska)
    Natur Hist 94:48-9 (1) S '85
--Argentina
    Nat Geog 170:234-5 (c,1) Ag '86
--Cattle (Brazil)
    Nat Geog 163:40-1 (c,1) Ja '83
--Horse-breeding ranch (California)
    Nat Geog 165:459 (c,1) Ap '84
--Kansas
    Sports Illus 65:76-7 (c,3) O 6
        '86
--Wyoming
    Life 9:42-8 (c,1) D '86
RANCHING
--Branding cattle (South Dakota)
    Ebony 41:210 (2) N '85
--British Columbia
    Nat Geog 170:64-5 (c,1) Jl '86
--Cattle rustling (Wyoming)
    Life 6:84-90 (c,1) D '83
--Cattle station (Australia)
    Nat Geog 169:30-1 (c,1) Ja '86
--Dude ranch (Wyoming)
    Trav/Holiday 158:46 (c,4) Ag '82
—Georgia
    Sports Illus 59:58-9 (c,1) Jl 25
        '83

RANCHING (cont.)
--Horseback riding on cattle
   ranch (Texas)
   Sports Illus 65:84-5, 96 (c,1)
   S 29 '86
--Killing excess sheep (Australia)
   Nat Geog 165:152 (c,3) F '84
--Mechanical sheep shearer (Aus-
   tralia)
   Nat Geog 161:646-7 (c,1) My
   '82
--Roping calf
   Sports Illus 61:50 (c,3) S 5
   '84
--Roping steer (Paraguay)
   Nat Geog 162:262-3 (c,1) Ag
   '82
--Shearing sheep (Alaska)
   Nat Geog 164:360 (c,4) S '83
--Shearing sheep (Australia)
   Trav/Holiday 162:55 (c,2) Ag
   '84
--Shearing sheep (Idaho)
   Nat Geog 161:800 (c,2) Je '82
--Shearing sheep (Romania)
   Natur Hist 93:48-9 (c,1) Jl '84
--Shearing sheep in 19th cent.
   manner (Massachusetts)
   Am Heritage 33:38-9 (c,4) Ag
   '82
--Sheep (Australia)
   Nat Geog 168:260 (c,1) Ag '85
--Sheep (New Zealand)
   Nat Geog 166:536-7 (c,1) O '84
--Sheep (Scotland)
   Nat Geog 166:64-5 (c,1) Jl '84
--Sheep (Wyoming)
   Life 6:146 (c,2) D '83
--Swinging lariat (Texas)
   Sports Illus 65:58 (c,2) S 8
   '86
--Texas
   Ebony 38:29-34 (c,2) N '82
--Transporting sheep by ship
   (Australia)
   Nat Geog 161:644-5 (c,1) My
   '82
--Western U.S.
   Natur Hist 93:40-1 (c,1) F '84
RAND CORPORATION
--History of the Rand Corporation
   Am Heritage 34:49-63 (1) Je
   '83
RANGOON, BURMA
   Nat Geog 166:96-7 (c,1) Jl '84
RAPHAEL
--"Madonna of the Chair"

Smithsonian 13:68 (painting,c,4)
   N '82
--"Miraculous Draught of Fishes"
   tapestry
   Smithsonian 13:120-1 (c,1) D '82
   Life 5:68 (c,2) D '82
   Nat Geog 168:761 (c,4) D '85
RATS
   Life 9:64 (c,2) Mr '86
--Kangaroo rats
   Natur Hist 93:60-7 (c,1) N '84
--Laboratory rats
   Smithsonian 16:97 (c,2) Ja '86
--Pet rat
   Sports Illus 65:48 (c,4) Jl 7 '86
--Rat playing basketball
   Sports Illus 63:2-3 (c,1) Jl 1 '85
--See also
      PACK RATS
RATTLESNAKES
   Nat Wildlife 20:42 (1) O '82
   Natur Hist 95:66-73 (c,1) N '86
RAYBURN, SAM
   Am Heritage 33:17 (4) F '82
READING
   Ebony 37:58 (4) Ja '82
--1913 painting of man reading
   Am Heritage 36:24-5 (c,1) Ap '85
--Child reading bible (Bahamas)
   Nat Geog 162:393 (c,4) S '82
--High school student studying (New
   York)
   Ebony 38:72 (4) Ag '83
--Man reading book
   Trav/Holiday 164:42 (c,2) Jl '85
--Mother reading to child
   Ebony 39:146 (c,4) S '84
--Mother reading to child (Georgia)
   Nat Geog 164:807 (c,2) D '83
--Newspaper
   Smithsonian 14:105 (drawing,2)
   Je '83
   Ebony 39:104 (4) Mr '84
   Sports Illus 61:64 (c,4) Ag 6 '84
--Newspaper (Brazil)
   Trav/Holiday 159:55 (c,2) Ja '83
--Newspaper (Burma)
   Nat Geog 166:95 (c,1) Jl '84
--Newspaper (Ireland)
   Trav/Holiday 164:63 (c,4) S '85
--Newspaper in bed (South Africa)
   Life 8:112 (c,1) N '85
--Newspapers (19th-20th cents.)
   Am Heritage 33:cov., 16-27
   (painting,c,1) O '82
--Reading Bible to children (1950;
   Missouri)

RECORDS (cont.)
  Life 8:25 (c,4) Ag '85
--Platinum records
  Ebony 41:160 (c,3) My '86
--See also
  VIDEOS
Recreation. See list under
  AMUSEMENTS
  SPORTS
RECREATIONAL VEHICLES
  Trav/Holiday 166:64-5 (c,1)
    Jl '86
--All terrain vehicles
  Trav/Holiday 160:39 (c,4) O
    '83
  Sports Illus 61:96 (c,4) D 10
    '84
--Dune cycling (California)
  Nat Geog 165:456-7 (c,1) Ap
    '84
--Interior of RV
  Sports Illus 65:36 (c,4) D 8 '86
RED CROSS
--Activities of International Com-
    mittee of Red Cross
  Nat Geog 170:646-79 (c,1) N
    '86
--See also
  BARTON, CLARA
REDSTARTS (BIRDS)
  Smithsonian 13:174 (c,4) O '82
RED-WINGED BLACKBIRDS
  Natur Hist 91:63 (c,3) My '82
  Smithsonian 14:83 (c,4) Jl '83
REDWOOD TREES
  Natur Hist 91:54-5 (c,1) O '82
  Nat Wildlife 23:13 (c,4) D '84
REEDS
--Guatemalan Indian cutting reeds
  Natur Hist 92:68 (c,3) F '83
Reefs. See
  CORAL REEFS
REFORMATION
--16th cent. Reformation personal-
    ities
  Nat Geog 164:424-5 (draw-
    ing,c,1) O '83
--Life and works of Martin Luther
  Nat Geog 164:418-63 (c,1) O
    '83
REFUGEE CAMPS
--Afghan (Pakistan)
  Nat Geog 167:778-9 (c,1) Je
    '85
--Cambodian (Thailand)
  Nat Geog 170:662-7 (c,1) N '86
--Haitian (U.S.)

  Ebony 38:132-4 (3) O '83
--Children's drawings of Cambodian
    camps (Thailand)
  Natur Hist 92:64-7 (c,2) Ja '83
--Palestinian (Israel)
  Nat Geog 168:36-7 (c,1) Jl '85
--Somali (Ethiopia)
  Nat Geog 163:634-5 (c,2) My '83
REFUGEES
--Afghan (Pakistan)
  Life 7:16 (c,3) N '84
  Nat Geog 167:cov., 772-97 (c,1)
    Je '85
--Cambodian (Thailand)
  Nat Geog 152:530-1 (c,1) O '82
--Haitians in boats (Florida)
  Nat Geog 162:188-9 (c,1) Ag '82
--Homeless Mexicans after volcanic
    eruption
  Nat Geog 162:678-9 (c,3) N '82
--Nicaraguan (Honduras)
  Nat Geog 164:610-11, 637 (c,1)
    N '83
--See also
  PALESTINIANS
REFUSE DISPOSAL
--Waste treatment facility (Nether-
    lands)
  Nat Geog 163:438-9 (c,1) Ap '83
REINDEER
  Nat Geog 163:216-17 (c,1) F '83
  Natur Hist 92:45 (c,3) Je '83
  Life 8:6 (4) Mr '85
  Sports Illus 62:80-1 (c,1) Ap 29
    '85
--Aerial view of herd (Canada)
  Nat Geog 163:152-3 (c,1) F '83
--Herd
  Natur Hist 95:58-9 (c,1) Mr '86
Religions. See
  BUDDHISM
  CHRISTIANITY
  DEITIES
  HINDUISM
  JUDAISM
  LAMAISM
  MORMONS
  MOSLEMS
  MYTHOLOGY
  RELIGIOUS RITES AND FESTI-
    VALS
  SHAKERS
  SHINTOISM
RELIGIOUS LEADERS
--Bhagwan Shree Rajneesh
  Life 8:87 (4) D '85
--Buddhist Dalai Lama (Tibet)

RENOIR, PIERRE AUGUSTE
   (cont.)
   Life 8:58 (painting,c,4) O '85
REPRODUCTION
--Ants mating
   Nat Geog 165:790-1 (paint-
      ing,c,1) Je '84
--Artificial insemination of boar
   (Minnesota)
   Nat Geog 170:350 (c,2) S '86
--Courtship ritual of flies
   Natur Hist 91:57-9 (c,1) D '82
--Crane flies mating
   Smithsonian 13:67 (c,3) Jl '82
--Cranes mating
   Nat Geog 164:546-51 (c,1) O
      '83
--Frogs fertilizing eggs
   Natur Hist 95:42-3 (c,1) Je '86
--Group mating of frogs
   Natur Hist 95:106-7 (c,1) O
      '86
--Grunion fish
   Nat Wildlife 21:33-6 (c,1) Je
      '83
--Human sperm cells trying to
      penetrate ovum
   Nat Geog 169:730-1 (c,1) Je
      '86
--In vitro fertilization
   Life 5:46-9 (c,1) N '82
   Nat Geog 168:100-1 (c,2) Jl '85
--Katydids mating
   Natur Hist 92:71-5 (c,1) O '83
--Mantids
   Nat Geog 165:274-5 (c,1) F
      '84
--Moths mating
   Natur Hist 92:58 (c,4) F '83
--Mule deer mating
   Natur Hist 91:57 (c,1) Je '82
--Parthenogenesis in aphids
   Nat Wildlife 21:46-7 (c,1) Je
      '83
--Sea lions mating
   Nat Wildlife 23:48 (c,1) Je '85
--Shark embryo
   Nat Wildlife 23:46-7 (c,1) F
      '85
--Slime mold spores
   Nat Wildlife 21:14-15 (c,1) Ap
      '83
--Squid mating
   Natur Hist 91:24-7 (c,1) Ap '82
--Tigers mating
   Nat Geog 166:760-1 (c,1) D '84
--Toads mating

   Natur Hist 93:76-7 (c,3) Mr '84
--Touch-me-not plants
   Natur Hist 91:32-9 (c,1) My '82
--Tree shrews mating
   Natur Hist 91:32 (c,4) Ag '82
--28-week-old human fetus
   Life 9:100-1 (c,1) Fall '86
--Twin calves from embryo splitting
   Nat Geog 166:826 (c,4) D '84
--Wild horses mating
   Natur Hist 95:34-5 (c,1) Ap '86
--X-ray of kiwi with egg inside
   Natur Hist 95:22 (4) N '86
--See also
      CHILDBIRTH
      PREGNANCY
REPTILES
--Ancient reptiles
   Natur Hist 93:54-5 (painting,c,1)
      Je '84
--Anoles
   Nat Wildlife 22:40 (painting,c,4)
      Je '84
   Natur Hist 93:54-5 (c,1) N '84
   Smithsonian 15:125 (c,4) Mr '85
--Basilisk lizard
   Nat Geog 163:50-1 (c,1) Ja '83
--Collared lizard
   Natur Hist 91:76-7 (c,2) Ja '82
--Desert lizards
   Nat Wildlife 24:18-19 (c,4) Ag '86
--Horned lizards
   Trav/Holiday 160:43 (c,4) O '83
--Lizards
   Life 5:49 (c,4) S '82
   Nat Geog 164:375 (c,4) S '83
   Natur Hist 93:34 (c,4) S '84
   Smithsonian 16:51, 55 (c,4) My
      '85
--Skink lizards
   Nat Wildlife 21:14 (c,4) Ap '83
--See also
      ALLIGATORS
      CHAMELEONS
      CHUCKWALLAS
      CROCODILES
      DINOSAURS
      DRAGONS OF KOMODO
      GECKOS
      GILA MONSTERS
      IGUANAS
      SNAKES
      TORTOISES
      TURTLES
RESERVOIRS
--Tenkiller, Oklahoma
   Trav/Holiday 165:54 (c,1) F '86

RESORTS
--Bahamas
Ebony 39:176 (c,4) My '84
--The Cloister, Sea Island,
Georgia
Trav/Holiday 162:44-5 (c,1) Jl
'84
--The Greenbrier, White Sulphur
Springs, West Virginia
Trav/Holiday 162:47 (c,3) Jl
'84
--Las Hadas, Mexico
Trav/Holiday 163:8 (c,3) Ap
'85
--Hot springs (Japan)
Nat Geog 166:243 (c,4) Ag '84
--Kiawah Island, South Carolina
Trav/Holiday 161:55-6 (c,2)
Ja '84
--Mammoth Lake, California
Nat Wildlife 21:40 (2) Ap '83
--Puerto Vallarta, Mexico
Trav/Holiday 164:52-5 (c,2) N
'85
--Sea Pines Plantation, Hilton
Head, South Carolina
Nat Geog 164:817 (c,1) D '83
--Sky Valley, Georgia
Nat Geog 163:466-7 (c,1) Ap
'83
--See also
ATLANTIC CITY, NEW
JERSEY
BEACHES, BATHING
CUERNAVACA, MEXICO
HOTELS
MIAMI BEACH, FLORIDA
RIVIERA, FRANCE
SKI RESORTS
RESTAURANTS
--1890s diner
Smithsonian 17:96 (4) N '86
--20th cent. soda fountains
Smithsonian 17:114-25 (c,1) Jl
'86
--Early 20th cent. Grand Canyon
hotel, Arizona
Natur Hist 91:20 (3) Je '82
--1920s cafe (Iowa)
Smithsonian 16:62 (4) Ag '85
--1930s cafe (Berlin, Germany)
Am Heritage 35:67 (2) Je '84
--1950s style diner (Illinois)
Life 8:78-9 (c,1) Ag '85
--Automats (Northeast)
Smithsonian 16:50-61 (c,2) Ja
'86

--Beer garden (Texas)
Trav/Holiday 159:66 (c,3) Mr '83
--Cafe (Mexico)
Trav/Holiday 160:21 (c,2) D '83
--Coffee shop (Indiana)
Life 8:94 (4) F '85
--Coffee shop (Minnesota)
Smithsonian 16:51 (c,3) D '85
--Demel's Cafe, Vienna, Austria
Nat Geog 166:684-5 (c,1) N '84
--Diner (Florida)
Sports Illus 64:58 (c,3) Ap 7 '86
--Diners
Smithsonian 17:94-103 (c,1) N
'86
--Donut shop
Sports Illus 61:106-7 (c,1) N 12
'84
--Elegant table setting
Trav/Holiday 158:cov. (c,1) D
'82
--Ethiopia
Nat Geog 163:627 (c,2) My '83
--Fast food kitchen
Ebony 38:84 (4) My '83
--Florida
Ebony 39:108 (c,4) Ja '84
--The Four Seasons, New York City,
New York
Smithsonian 13:114 (c,2) F '83
--French (Houston, Texas)
Trav/Holiday 158:46 (c,4) N '82
--Hotel restaurant (Arizona)
Trav/Holiday 160:cov. (c,1) D '83
--Hotel restaurant (Ottawa, Ontario)
Trav/Holiday 157:41 (c,3) My '82
--Ice cream cafe (New York)
Ebony 39:96-8 (c,4) Ap '84
--Interior (Cleveland, Ohio)
Trav/Holiday 164:8 (c,1) Ag '85
--K-Paul's, New Orleans, Louisiana
Life 7:26 (c,4) Mr '84
--Lakeshore restaurant (Switzerland)
Trav/Holiday 160:41 (c,1) Jl '83
--Local diner (New York)
Am Heritage 34:100-1 (paint-
ing,c,1) Ap '83
--Nathan's, Coney Island, Brooklyn,
New York
Trav/Holiday 159:46 (c,4) Ap '83
--New York City, New York
Trav/Holiday 164:60-1 (c,4) Jl
'85
--Outdoor (Taipei, Taiwan)
Trav/Holiday 160:41 (c,3) Ag '83
--Outdoor cafe (Baltimore, Maryland)
Trav/Holiday 163:68 (c,2) Je '85

RESTAURANTS (cont.)

--Outdoor cafe (Cuernavaca, Mexico)
  Trav/Holiday 157:58 (c,3) F '82

--Outdoor cafe (Dallas, Texas)
  Trav/Holiday 166:42 (c,2) Jl '86

--Outdoor cafe (Florence, Italy)
  Trav/Holiday 159:38 (c,4) F '83

--Outdoor cafe (France)
  Trav/Holiday 163:59 (c,3) Ja '85

--Outdoor cafe (Geneva, Switzerland)
  Trav/Holiday 164:30 (c,4) Ag '85

--Outdoor cafe (Innsbruck, Austria)
  Trav/Holiday 157:80 (c,2) Ap '82

--Outdoor cafe (Montreal, Quebec)
  Trav/Holiday 166:67 (c,3) O '86

--Paris, France
  Trav/Holiday 163:81 (c,4) Ap '85

--Plastic food (Japan)
  Smithsonian 14:129-37 (c,1) Mr '84

--Sitting at diner counter
  Life 5:27 (2) My '82

--Snack bar (Miami Beach, Florida)
  Smithsonian 13:66 (c,4) D '82

--Snack bar (Santa Fe, New Mexico)
  Nat Geog 161:334-5 (c,1) Mr '82

--Sushi bar (California)
  Sports Illus 61:57 (c,3) Jl 30 '84

--Sushi bar (Colorado)
  Trav/Holiday 159:34 (c,4) Je '83

--Tableside flambé (Alberta)
  Trav/Holiday 159:53 (c,4) Je '83

--See also
    CHEFS
    COFFEEHOUSES
    COOKING
    DINNERS AND DINING
    KITCHENS
    TAVERNS
    WAITERS
    WAITRESSES

RESTORATION OF ART WORKS

--15th cent. Byzantine embroidery (Romania)
  Nat Geog 164:763 (c,3) D '83

--Acropolis, Athens, Greece
  Smithsonian 12:49-53 (c,1) Mr '82

--Borobudur Temple, Java, Indonesia
  Nat Geog 163:138-41 (c,1) Ja '83

--Cleaning statue (Papua New Guinea)
  Nat Geog 162:147 (c,4) Ag '82

--Delaware studio
  Nat Geog 164:180 (c,4) Ag '83

--Leonardo da Vinci's "Last Supper"
  Nat Geog 164:664-85 (c,1) N '83

--Michelangelo's "Pietà"
  Nat Geog 168:768-9 (c,1) D '85

--Renovating 19th cent. post office (Washington, D.C.)
  Nat Geog 164:412-13 (c,2) S '83

--Salvaging old movie films
  Life 8:68-80 (c,1) Jl '85

--Sistine Chapel, Vatican City
  Nat Geog 168:760 (c,1) D '85

--Statue of Liberty, New York City, New York
  Smithsonian 17:68-75 (c,1) Je '86
  Nat Geog 170:3-9, 12-13 (c,1) Jl '86
  Life 9:67-73 (c,1) Jl '86

--U.S.S.R. restoration of art and architecture
  Smithsonian 13:65-73 (c,1) Mr '83

--Vatican treasures
  Smithsonian 13:120-31 (c,1) D '82
  Life 5:62-70 (c,1) D '82
  Nat Geog 168:760-1 (c,1) D '85

RESURRECTION PLANTS
  Natur Hist 93:38, 40 (c,2) Ja '84

RETRIEVERS (DOGS)
  Life 6:148 (3) Ja '83
  Sports Illus 59:96 (painting,c,4) S 19 '83

--Puppies
  Life 8:48-9 (c,1) D '85

--See also
    GOLDEN RETRIEVERS
    LABRADOR RETRIEVERS

REVERE, PAUL
  Am Heritage 34:21 (painting,c,4) O '83
  Am Heritage 38:29 (painting,c,4) D '86

REVOLUTIONARY WAR
--1778 Battle of Monmouth
    Am Heritage 33:82-3 (paint-
    ing,c,1) F '82
--1781 Battle of Cowpens
    Am Heritage 36:6 (painting,c,1)
    D '84
--American treatment of Tories
    Smithsonian 14:58 (drawing,4)
    S '83
--Fate of fleeing Black Loyalists
    Am Heritage 34:102-9 (c,1) Je
    '83
--Historic Philadelphia buildings,
    Pennsylvania
    Nat Geog 163:326 (c,1) Mr '83
--Louisiana escapades of Bernardo
    de Galvez
    Am Heritage 33:30-9 (c,2) Ap
    '82
--Recreation of 1776 Battle of
    Trenton
    Smithsonian 15:146-7 (c,2) Ap
    '84
--Reenactment of Washington
    crossing the Delaware
    Trav/Holiday 166:32 (c,4) D
    '86
--Siege of Pensacola
    Am Heritage 33:34-5 (engrav-
    ing,1) Ap '82
--See also
    ADAMS, SAMUEL
    BUNKER HILL, BATTLE OF
    DECLARATION OF INDE-
        PENDENCE
    FRANKLIN, BENJAMIN
    JEFFERSON, THOMAS
    JONES, JOHN PAUL
    LIBERTY BELL
    PITCHER, MOLLY
    REVERE, PAUL
    SHERMAN, ROGER
    WASHINGTON, GEORGE
REYKJAVIK, ICELAND
    Trav/Holiday 159:30-2 (4) Ap
    '83
REYNOLDS, SIR JOSHUA
--Portrait of Samuel Johnson
    (1775)
    Smithsonian 15:69 (paint-
    ing,c,1) D '84
RHEAS (BIRDS)
    Natur Hist 92:38 (c,3) S '83
    Smithsonian 16:76 (c,4) O '85
RHINE RIVER, WEST GERMANY
    Trav/Holiday 162:56-9 (c,1)

S '84
RHINOCERI
    Life 5:118 (drawing,c,3) N '82
    Nat Geog 163:347 (c,2) Mr '83
    Nat Wildlife 21:31 (4) Ap '83
    Nat Geog 165:404-22 (map,c,1)
    Mr '84
    Smithsonian 14:169 (c,3) Mr '84
    Sports Illus 61:88 (c,4) Jl 9 '84
    Nat Geog 167:761-3 (c,1) Je '85
--Black rhinos
    Nat Wildlife 24:7 (c,4) D '85
    Nat Geog 169:595 (c,3) My '86
--Rhino horns
    Nat Geog 165:407, 409 (c,1) Mr
    '84
RHODE ISLAND
--Mohegan Bluffs, Block Island
    Trav/Holiday 158:4 (4) Ag '82
--Westerly (1920s)
    Nat Geog 166:793 (4) D '84
--See also
    NEWPORT
    PROVIDENCE
RHODES, GREECE
    Trav/Holiday 160:58-9 (c,1) Ag
    '83
--3rd cent. B.C. Colossus of Rhodes
    Smithsonian 14:59 (drawing,4)
    Mr '84
RHODODENDRONS
    Nat Geog 161:706 (c,4) Je '82
    Nat Wildlife 23:14 (c,3) D '84
    Natur Hist 94:41 (c,1) Ap '85
    Smithsonian 17:cov., 52-63 (c,1)
    My '86
RHONE RIVER, FRANCE
--Arles
    Life 7:118-19 (c,1) O '84
RICE INDUSTRY
--Arkansas
    Ebony 42:100-4 (c,1) D '86
--Burma
    Nat Geog 166:104-5 (c,1) Jl '84
--Cambodia
    Nat Geog 161:590-1 (c,1) My '82
--Flooded rice fields (California)
    Nat Geog 166:564-5 (c,1) N '84
--Flooded rice fields (Indonesia)
    Nat Geog 166:738-9, 744-5 (c,1)
    D '84
--Plowing paddy (Thailand)
    Smithsonian 13:99 (c,4) Ja '83
--Rice farm (Australia)
    Nat Geog 168:262-3 (c,1) Ag '85
--Rice field (India)
    Nat Geog 166:725 (c,4) D '84

RICE INDUSTRY (cont.)
--Rice field (Peru)
    Nat Geog 163:40-1 (c,3) Ja
        '83
--Rice terraces (Philippines)
    Trav/Holiday 159:33 (c,1) Ja
        '83
    Nat Geog 170:94-5 (c,1) Jl '86
--Tasting new rice hybrids
    (Philippines)
    Nat Geog 170:102 (c,4) Jl '86
--Thailand
    Nat Geog 162:524-5 (c,1) O
        '82
RICE INDUSTRY--HARVESTING
--Thailand
    Trav/Holiday 166:65 (c,4) S
        '86
RICHARD I, THE LION-HEARTED
    (GREAT BRITAIN)
    Smithsonian 17:59 (paint-
        ing,c,2) S '86
RICHARD III (GREAT BRITAIN)
    Smithsonian 15:82-93 (paint-
        ing,c,1) Mr '85
--Portrayed by actors
    Smithsonian 15:91 (c,4) Mr '85
--Hong Kong
    Trav/Holiday 161:45 (c,2) Ja
        '84
RIFLES
--19th cent.
    Nat Geog 168:814-15 (c,1) D
        '85
--1876 Henry repeating rifle
    Natur Hist 95:51 (4) Je '86
--1876 Sharp rifle
    Natur Hist 95:52 (4) Je '86
--1876 Springfield rifle
    Natur Hist 95:48 (4) Je '86
--1876 Winchester rifle
    Natur Hist 95:54 (4) Je '86
--1930
    Smithsonian 17:152 (4) N '86
--Used to shoot John F. Kennedy
    (1963)
    Life 6:59, 68-9 (c,4) N '83
Rings. See
    JEWELRY
RIO DE JANEIRO, BRAZIL
    Sports Illus 63:88 (c,2) S 4
        '85
--Copacabana
    Trav/Holiday 161:64 (c,4) F
        '84
RIO GRANDE RIVER, TEXAS
    Life 9:88-95 (c,1) Jl '86

    Life 9:40-7 (map,c,1) Ag '86
RIOTS
--1834 mob burning convent (Massa-
    chusetts)
    Am Heritage 33:100-3 (c,1) F
        '82
--1844 ethnic conflict (Philadelphia,
    Pennsylvania)
    Am Heritage 34:18 (3) F '83
--1849 fight between actors Forrest
    and MacReady (N.Y.)
    Smithsonian 16:168-90 (draw-
        ing,c,2) O '85
--1932 veteran Bonus Marchers
    (Washington, D.C.)
    Am Heritage 33:7 (4) Je '82
--England-Italy soccer game riot
    (Belgium)
    Sports Illus 62:2-3, 20-30 (c,1)
        Je 10 '85
    Life 8:60-1 (1) Jl '85
    Sports Illus 63:68-9 (c,1) D 23
        '85
--Brussels, Belgium
    Life 5:112-13 (1) Ap '82
--New Delhi, India (1984)
    Nat Geog 167:510-11 (c,1) Ap
        '85
Rites and ceremonies. See
    FUNERAL RITES AND CERE-
        MONIES
    HAND SHAKING
    MARRIAGE RITES AND CUS-
        TOMS
    RELIGIOUS RITES AND FESTI-
        VALS
    specific countries--RITES AND
        FESTIVALS
RIVERA, DIEGO
    Smithsonian 16:36, 48 (c,1) F '86
--"Conquest"
    Smithsonian 13:117 (painting,4)
        Mr '83
--Mural of Mexican history (Mexico
    City)
    Trav/Holiday 162:56 (c,2) Jl '84
    Smithsonian 16:40-2 (c,1) F '86
--Mural section depicting Lenin
    (New York)
    Smithsonian 17:18 (4) Ap '86
--Paintings by him
    Smithsonian 16:36-51 (c,1) F '86
--Self-portrait (1949)
    Smithsonian 16:36 (painting,c,1)
        F '86
RIVERBOATS
--19th cent. side-wheeler

RIVERS (cont.)
   Nat Geog 168:514-42 (map,c,1)
      O '85
--Wading River, New Jersey
   Smithsonian 14:82-3 (c,1) Jl '83
--Wong Chu, Bhutan
   Life 5:80-2 (c,1) N '82
--Yamuna, India
   Nat Geog 165:720-1 (c,1) Je
      '84
--Yarra, Melbourne, Australia
   Trav/Holiday 164:67 (c,4) O
      '85
--Yellow, China
   Nat Geog 165:304 (c,2) Mr '84
--See also
      ALLEGHENY
      AMAZON
      AVON
      COLORADO
      CUMBERLAND
      DAMS
      DANUBE
      DELAWARE
      DNIEPER
      DOURO
      EBRO
      FRASER
      GANGES
      HUDSON
      ILLINOIS
      IRRAWADDY
      LIFFEY
      MACKENZIE
      MERRIMACK
      MISSISSIPPI
      MISSOURI
      MONONGAHELA
      MURRAY
      NEVA
      NIGER
      NILE
      OHIO
      ORINOCO
      OZARK NATIONAL SCENIC
         RIVERWAYS
      PARANA
      PLATTE
      POTOMAC
      RHINE
      RHONE
      RIO GRANDE
      ST. LAWRENCE
      SAVANNAH
      SEINE
      SNAKE
      SUSQUEHANNA

      TENNESSEE
      THAMES
      TIGRIS
      TOMBIGBEE
      WATERFALLS
      YELLOWSTONE
RIVIERA, FRANCE
   Trav/Holiday 158:33-7, 60 (c,1)
      Jl '82
--Cannes beach
   Life 9:10-11 (c,1) N '86
--See also
      NICE
ROAD RUNNERS (BIRDS)
   Nat Geog 163:696-702 (c,1) My
      '83
   Natur Hist 94:69 (c,4) O '85
ROADS
--Curved Alpine road (France)
   Sports Illus 65:16-17 (c,1) Ag
      4 '86
--Florida
   Am Heritage 34:40-1 (painting,c,1)
      Je '83
--Mountain road (China)
   Nat Geog 168:302-3 (c,1) S '85
--Roman road (Petra, Jordan)
   Nat Geog 168:512 (c,4) O '85
--Sark, Channel Islands
   Smithsonian 17:92-3 (c,1) My '86
--See also
      HIGHWAYS
ROADS--CONSTRUCTION
--Brazil
   Nat Wildlife 22:17 (c,4) D '83
--China
   Nat Geog 164:65 (c,1) Jl '83
   Nat Geog 165:314 (c,1) Mr '84
   Nat Geog 168:304-5 (c,1) S '85
--Guatemala
   Nat Geog 168:533 (c,2) O '85
--Paving driveway (Ohio)
   Sports Illus 57:38-9 (c,2) Ag 30
      '82
ROBERTS, OWEN
   Am Heritage 38:41 (drawing,4)
      D '86
ROBESON, PAUL
   Ebony 41:256 (4) N '85
   Life 9:302 (4) Fall '86
ROBINS
   Nat Wildlife 21:3 (c,4) O '83
   Nat Wildlife 22:33-6 (c,1) Je '84
--Chicks
   Nat Wildlife 22:34-6 (c,1) Je '84
--Feeding young
   Nat Wildlife 22:56 (c,2) O '84

ROBINSON, EDWARD G.
  Am Heritage 35:32-3, 38 (c,1)
    D '83
ROBINSON, JACKIE
  Sports Illus 58:62-76 (paint-
    ing,c,1) Je 20 '83
  Am Heritage 35:34-9 (3) Ag '84
  Ebony 40:76 (4) Jl '85
  Sports Illus 63:76 (4) O 7 '85
  Ebony 41:75, 250 (4) N '85
--Stamp commemorating him
  Sports Illus 57:99 (c,4) N 1
    '82
ROBINSON, LUTHER (BILL)
  Ebony 41:254 (3) N '85
Robinson Crusoe Island. See
    JUAN FERNANDEZ ARCHI-
      PELAGO
ROBOTS
  Smithsonian 14:60-9 (c,1) N
    '83
  Life 7:168-76 (c,1) D '84
--Austrian factory
  Nat Geog 167:429 (c,4) Ap '85
--Japan
  Smithsonian 16:165 (c,1) Ap
    '85
--Used in automobile plant (Dela-
    ware)
  Nat Geog 162:454-5 (c,1) O
    '82
--Used in automobile plant (Japan)
  Nat Geog 164:11 (c,4) Jl '83
ROCHESTER, NEW YORK
--East Avenue mansion
  Trav/Holiday 165:33 (c,4) Mr
    '86
--Eastman's movie theater (1922)
  Am Heritage 35:19 (4) D '83
ROCK CARVINGS
--Anasazi Indian seasonal calen-
    dar (New Mexico)
  Nat Geog 162:580-1 (c,2) N '82
--Ancient Hawaii
  Nat Geog 164:574-5 (c,1) N '83
--Buddhas carved into cliff
    (Burma)
  Smithsonian 15:107 (c,4) My '84
--Stone Age fish carving (France)
  Natur Hist 95:78 (3) O '86
--See also
    CAVE PAINTINGS
    ROCK PAINTINGS
ROCK CLIMBING
  Sports Illus 58:62 (c,4) F 7
    '83
--Bouldering up man-made

  structures
  Smithsonian 16:80-91 (c,1) Je
    '85
--New Hampshire
  Nat Geog 162:798-9 (c,1) D '82
--North Carolina
  Trav/Holiday 157:61 (c,1) Ap '82
--Tanzania
  Smithsonian 13:45 (c,4) Ag '82
--Texas
  Life 9:92 (c,2) Jl '86
--Yosemite National Park, California
  Life 7:52-64 (c,1) S '84
  Nat Geog 167:66-7 (c,1) Ja '85
  Nat Wildlife 24:42 (c,1) Ap '86
  Sports Illus 64:84-90, 98 (c,1)
    Je 2 '86
Rock musicians. See
    MUSICIANS
ROCK PAINTINGS
--11th cent. (New Mexico)
  Smithsonian 15:143 (c,4) S '84
--Ancient Toldense hand prints
    (Argentina)
  Nat Geog 170:250 (c,3) Ag '86
--Australian aborigines
  Smithsonian 14:45 (c,4) Ap '83
  Nat Geog 169:24-5 (c,1) Ja '86
--Navajo (Arizona)
  Nat Geog 162:72 (c,4) Jl '82
--Nazca Indian lines drawn on the
    pampa (Peru)
  Life 7:169-76 (c,1) N '84
  Trav/Holiday 166:50 (c,3) N '86
--Stone Age (Tanzania)
  Nat Geog 164:84-99 (c,1) Jl '83
--See also
    CAVE PAINTINGS
    ROCK CARVINGS
ROCKEFELLER, JOHN D.
  Am Heritage 37:46 (4) Ag '86
ROCKEFELLER CENTER, NEW
    YORK CITY, NEW YORK
  Am Heritage 33:98-107, 114 (c,1)
    O '82
--1930s architectural renderings
  Am Heritage 33:98-107, 114 (c,1)
    O '82
ROCKETS
--Apollo rocket
  Trav/Holiday 158:42 (c,3) N '82
--History (1920s-1930s)
  Smithsonian 14:248-9 (3) N '83
--History of Soviet rockets (1957-
    present)
  Nat Geog 170:444-5 (drawing,1)
    O '86

ROCKETS (cont.)
--U.S.S.R.
Nat Geog 170:428-9, 444-5
(c,1) O '86
--See also
GODDARD, ROBERT
ROCKNE, KNUTE
Sports Illus 58:67 (4) Ja 10
'83
Smithsonian 16:136, 140 (4) D
'85
Sports Illus 64:34 (painting,c,1)
Ap 21 '86
Sports Illus 64:52 (4) Je 30
'86
ROCKS
--Aerial view of Painted Desert,
Arizona
Nat Wildlife 24:56 (c,2) O '86
--Ancient rocks (Iceland)
Nat Geog 168:173 (c,4) Ag '85
--Ayres Rock, Australia
Life 6:132 (c,2) My '83
Trav/Holiday 166:6-8 (c,2) Jl
'86
--Balancing rocks on one another
(California)
Nat Geog 165:438-9 (c,2) Ap
'84
--Big Bend National Park, Texas
Trav/Holiday 162:30 (c,1) O
'84
--Chimney Rock, Nebraska
Nat Geog 170:162 (c,4) Ag '86
--Hopewell Rocks, New Brunswick
Trav/Holiday 163:85 (c,1) Mr
'85
--Meteora, Greece
Trav/Holiday 162:52-4 (c,1) O
'84
--Percé Rock, Gaspé Peninsula,
Quebec
Trav/Holiday 165:82 (c,2) Mr
'86
--Plume Rocks, Wyoming
Nat Geog 170:150-1 (c,1) Ag
'86
--Rocky Mountains, Colorado
Natur Hist 94:28-9 (c,1) Jl '85
--San Miguel stone, Mexico
Nat Geog 166:431 (c,4) O '84
--Sky Bridge, Kentucky
Natur Hist 95:68-9 (c,1) S '86
--Stone skipping competition
Smithsonian 16:20 (4) O '85
--Yellowstone National Park rock
face

Natur Hist 91:33 (c,1) Mr '82
--See also
DEVILS TOWER NATIONAL
MONUMENT
LIMESTONE
MINERALS
QUARTZITE
ROCKWELL, NORMAN
--1955 Saturday Evening Post cover
showing mermaid
Smithsonian 14:92 (c,4) Je '83
--1959 painting of Boy Scout
Smithsonian 16:cov. (c,1) Jl '85
ROCKY MOUNTAIN GOATS
Nat Wildlife 21:57 (c,2) Ap '83
Natur Hist 93:78-85 (2) Ja '84
Smithsonian 15:cov., 102-9 (c,1)
Ag '84
Nat Wildlife 22:cov., 44-51 (c,1)
Ag '84
Nat Wildlife 23:56-7 (c,1) D '84
--Kid
Nat Wildlife 21:57 (c,2) Ap '83
ROCKY MOUNTAIN NATIONAL PARK,
COLORADO
Smithsonian 13:54 (c,4) F '83
Nat Wildlife 21:3 (c,4) Ap '83
--William Allen White cabin
Smithsonian 17:44 (c,4) O '86
ROCKY MOUNTAINS, BRITISH
COLUMBIA
Sports Illus 56:66 (painting,c,3)
Ja 25 '82
--See also
YOHO NATIONAL PARK
ROCKY MOUNTAINS, CANADA
Natur Hist 93:26-7 (c,1) Jl '84
ROCKY MOUNTAINS, COLORADO
Natur Hist 93:48-53 (c,1) Je '84
Natur Hist 94:28-35 (c,1) Jl '85
--Meadow flowers
Natur Hist 93:28-31 (c,1) Jl '84
--See also
ROCKY MOUNTAIN NATIONAL
PARK
ROCKY MOUNTAINS, IDAHO
Life 9:22 (c,4) N '86
ROCKY MOUNTAINS, MONTANA
Nat Geog 167:686-7 (c,1) My '85
ROCKY MOUNTAINS, WYOMING
--Big Horn Mountains
Trav/Holiday 158:45-7 (map,c,2)
Ag '82
Rodents. See
BEAVERS
CAPYBARAS
CHIPMUNKS

RODENTS (cont.)
    COYPUS
    GOPHERS
    HEDGEHOGS
    MARMOTS
    MICE
    MUSKRATS
    PORCUPINES
    PRAIRIE DOGS
    RATS
    SQUIRRELS
    WHITE-FOOTED MICE
    WOODCHUCKS
    VOLES
RODEOS
    Sports Illus 57:62-74 (c,2) S 6 '82
    Sports Illus 65:110 (c,4) O 20 '86
--Calgary Stampede, Alberta
    Nat Geog 165:385, 398-9 (c,1) Mr '84
    Trav/Holiday 163:66-9, 81 (c,1) My '85
--Man thrown from bull (Texas)
    Nat Geog 165:220-1 (c,1) F '84
--Mechanical bull
    Sports Illus 57:64 (c,4) S 6 '82
--Nevada
    Sports Illus 65:2-3, 78 (c,1) D 15 '86
--Oklahoma City, Oklahoma
    Sports Illus 61:2-3, 30-7 (c,1) D 17 '84
--Riding bull
    Sports Illus 60:34 (c,4) Je 18 '84
    Ebony 40:146-8 (2) Mr '85
RODIN, AUGUSTE
    Smithsonian 16:62 (4) S '85
--Bust of Rodin by Camille Claudel
    Smithsonian 16:57 (4) S '85
--"Faunus"
    Smithsonian 15:153 (sculpture,c,4) N '84
--"Galatée" (1890)
    Smithsonian 16:61 (sculpture,4) S '85
--"The Shade"
    Smithsonian 14:42 (sculpture,c,4) Ja '84
--"The Thinker" (1886)
    Smithsonian 16:59 (sculpture,4) S '85
--"The Thinker" reproduction

Trav/Holiday 157:55 (c,2) Mr '82
ROGERS, GINGER
    Am Heritage 35:45 (1) D '83
    Life 9:171 (c,2) My '86
ROGERS, RANDOLPH
--"Nydia"
    Smithsonian 14:45 (sculpture,c,2) Ja '84
ROGERS, WILL
    Sports Illus 61:143 (4) Jl 18 '84
    Am Heritage 36:110 (4) Ag '85
    Nat Wildlife 24:20 (4) Ap '86
    Am Heritage 37:45 (4) Ag '86
--Depicted on postage stamp
    Am Heritage 34:55 (c,4) D '82
--Farmland portrait (Kansas)
    Nat Geog 168:370-1 (c,1) S '85
ROLLER COASTERS
--Florida
    Ebony 40:78 (4) Ja '85
    Trav/Holiday 166:16 (c,3) D '86
--Immersed in 1937 flood (Cincinnati, Ohio)
    Am Heritage 37:46-7 (2) Je '86
--Ohio
    Life 8:34-5 (c,1) Ag '85
ROLLER SKATES
    Sports Illus 57:34-42 (c,1) S 20 '82
--1877
    Smithsonian 14:121 (c,4) F '84
ROLLER SKATING
    Sports Illus 57:42 (c,4) S 20 '82
    Sports Illus 65:15, 21 (c,2) S 29 '86
--1880s child theater act
    Am Heritage 37:110-11 (2) Ag '86
--California
    Trav/Holiday 160:65 (c,4) N '83
--Children (New Jersey)
    Ebony 42:32 (c,4) D '86
--China
    Nat Geog 164:82-3 (c,1) Jl '83
--Norway
    Nat Geog 163:196-7 (c,1) F '83
--Speed skating
    Sports Illus 57:34 (c,3) S 20 '82
--Wheeling baby stroller (Florida)
    Nat Geog 162:187 (c,3) Ag '82
ROMAN EMPIRE
--5th cent. barbarian Alaric
    Smithsonian 14:146 (etching,4) F '84
--See also
    CONSTANTINE THE GREAT
    HADRIAN
    HERCULANEUM

ROMAN EMPIRE (cont.)
  MYTHOLOGY--GREEK AND
    ROMAN
  NERO
  POMPEII
ROMAN EMPIRE--ARCHITECTURE
--Battlements remains (Formia,
  Italy)
  Sports Illus 58:71 (c,3) My
    23 '83
--Blueprint of villa (Herculaneum)
  Nat Geog 165:596 (c,3) My '84
--Dougga, Tunisia
  Trav/Holiday 158:49 (c,3) O '82
--Hadrian's Wall, Northumbria,
  England
  Smithsonian 16:70-81 (c,1) Ap
    '85
  Nat Geog 169:414-15 (c,2) Mr
    '86
--Herculaneum
  Nat Geog 165:578-85, 596 (c,1)
    My '84
--King Herod's palace (Israel)
  Nat Geog 165:260 (c,2) F '84
--Pozzuoli, Italy
  Nat Geog 162:720-1 (c,1) D
    '82
  Nat Geog 165:616-17 (c,2) My
    '84
--Roman bath (Bath, England)
  Trav/Holiday 158:29 (c,1) Ag
    '82
  Smithsonian 15:126 (c,4) N '84
--Roman Bath (Ostia Antica,
  Italy)
  Nat Geog 170:326 (c,4) S '86
--Roman road (Petra, Jordan)
  Nat Geog 168:512 (c,4) O '85
--Trajan's Forum (Rome, Italy)
  Smithsonian 12:112 (c,1) Ja
    '82
--See also
  COLOSSEUM
  PANTHEON
  ROMAN FORUM
  TEMPLES--ANCIENT
ROMAN EMPIRE--ART
--1st cent. painting (Pompeii)
  Nat Geog 165:557 (c,4) My '84
ROMAN EMPIRE--COSTUME
--15th cent. painting of Roman
  soldiers
  Smithsonian 16:54 (c,3) Ap '85
--Soldier
  Nat Geog 165:573 (drawing,c,1)
    My '84

ROMAN EMPIRE--MAPS
--Vesuvius area
  Nat Geog 165:574-5 (c,1) My '84
ROMAN EMPIRE--POLITICS AND
    GOVERNMENT
--Politics in ancient Rome
  Smithsonian 15:130-8 (draw-
    ing,c,1) O '84
ROMAN EMPIRE--RELICS
--1st cent. (Pompeii)
  Nat Geog 165:607-11 (c,1) My '84
--4th cent. coin depicting Constan-
    tine
  Nat Geog 164:722 (c,4) D '83
--Herculaneum
  Nat Geog 162:686-93 (c,1) D '82
  Nat Geog 165:cov., 556-605 (c,1)
    My '84
Roman empire-sculpture. See
  SCULPTURE--ANCIENT
ROMAN FORUM, ROME, ITALY
  Trav/Holiday 164:48 (c,3) O '85
ROMANCE
--1940s soldier's last embrace at
    station (New York)
  Life 8:94 (3) Spring '85
--Advice to wives on proper way to
    undress (1937)
  Life 9:298 (4) Fall '86
--Couple embracing (France)
  Life 8:64-5 (1) Je '85
--Couple hugging
  Life 5:74-5 (1) S '82
  Sports Illus 63:34 (c,2) Jl 29 '85
--Couple hugging (Puerto Rico)
  Nat Geog 163:517 (c,1) Ap '83
--Couple married 81 years (Alabama)
  Life 9:34 (c,2) Jl '86
--Couple silhouetted in sunset
    (Hawaii)
  Sports Illus 58:52 (c,4) F 14 '83
--Couples
  Ebony 39:134, 138 (4) Je '84
--Depicted on early 20th cent. song
    slides
  Smithsonian 12:cov., 76-83 (c,1)
    Mr '82
--Holding hands
  Ebony 38:48, 50 (3) F '83
--Kangaroos hugging
  Life 6:180 (2) D '83
--Man carrying woman on shoulders
  Sports Illus 56:34-5 (c,2) My 3
    '82
--Pictographic love letter (Siberia,
    U.S.S.R.)
  Natur Hist 94:86 (c,3) Je '85

ROOSTERS (cont.)
    Sports Illus 63:1 (c,4) N 4
        '85
    Nat Geog 168:783 (c,1) D '85
--1861 cast iron stove decoration
        (New York)
    Natur Hist 91:67 (c,4) Ja '82
ROPE JUMPING
    Ebony 37:37 (c,2) F '82
    Sports Illus 58:88 (c,4) Je 27
        '83
    Life 8:88 (c,4) My '85
--Athlete
    Ebony 40:69 (4) Je '85
--Boxer in training
    Sports Illus 59:92 (c,4) N 7
        '83
--Children (Washington, D.C.)
    Nat Geog 163:88-9 (c,1) Ja '83
ROSES
    Nat Wildlife 22:42 (4) O '84
--Pasture rose
    Nat Wildlife 21:22-3 (c,1) F '83
--Rose hips
    Nat Wildlife 21:37 (c,4) O '83
--Wild prairie rose
    Nat Geog 162:77 (c,4) Jl '82
--Wild roses
    Trav/Holiday 158:46 (c,4) Ag
        '82
ROSETTA STONE
    Nat Geog 161:149 (c,4) F '82
ROSSETTI, DANTE GABRIEL
--Paintings by him
    Smithsonian 14:76, 82 (c,4) N
        '83
ROTTERDAM, NETHERLANDS
    Nat Geog 170:500-1 (c,1) O '86
ROTTWEILERS (DOGS)
    Sports Illus 59:44 (c,4) D 26
        '83
    Ebony 39:90 (4) Ja '84
ROUEN, FRANCE
    Nat Geog 161:304-7 (c,1) Ap
        '82
ROUSSEAU, HENRI
--Paintings by him
    Smithsonian 15:80-91 (c,1) F
        '85
--Self-portrait
    Smithsonian 15:80 (paint-
        ing,c,2) F '85
ROWBOATS
    Trav/Holiday 162:8 (c,4) S '84
ROWING
    Sports Illus 56:106 (c,3) My

        24 '82
--Crew team (Florida)
    Trav/Holiday 166:17 (c,3) D '86
--Great Britain
    Nat Geog 163:754-5 (c,1) Je '83
--Oarsmen in traditional costume
        (Great Britain)
    Smithsonian 13:91 (c,4) N '82
--Pennsylvania team
    Nat Geog 163:332, 335 (c,3) Mr
        '83
--Raft (Pakistan)
    Smithsonian 13:49 (c,4) Ap '82
--Ronald Reagan (California)
    Life 6:50-1 (c,1) O '83
--Reenacting voyage of Jason and
        the Argonauts
    Nat Geog 168:406-20 (c,1) S '85
--Synthetic oars
    Sports Illus 61:122 (c,4) N 12
        '84
ROWING--COLLEGE
    Life 5:74-80 (c,1) My '82
    Sports Illus 56:58 (c,4) Je 28
        '82
    Sports Illus 62:64-6 (c,3) Je 24
        '85
    Sports Illus 64:76 (c,3) Je 16
        '86
--Boat at pier
    Sports Illus 59:66-7 (c,1) D 26
        '83
--Royal Regatta (Henley, England)
    Sports Illus 57:26-33 (c,1) Jl 5 '82
--Women
    Nat Geog 161:812-13 (c,1) Je '82
ROWING--COMPETITIONS
    Sports Illus 56:28-9 (c,2) F 22
        '82
    Sports Illus 61:76 (drawing,c,4)
        D 3 '84
    Sports Illus 63:22-3 (c,2) Ag 5
        '85
    Sports Illus 64:102 (painting,c,3)
        Je 2 '86
ROWING--HUMOR
    Sports Illus 58:E3 (drawing,c,4)
        Je 6 '83
ROYCE, JOSIAH
    Am Heritage 34:101 (3) F '83
    Smithsonian 17:142 (4) S '86
RUBBER INDUSTRY
--Making rubber by hand (Malaysia)
    Trav/Holiday 165:68 (c,4) Ap '86
--Tapping latex from tree (Thailand)
    Nat Geog 162:527 (c,4) O '82

RUBENS, PETER PAUL
--Study for Antwerp Cathedral
     altarpiece
     Smithsonian 15:62 (drawing,c,2)
     N '84
RUBIES
     Nat Geog 162:520 (c,4) O '82
RUGBY--COLLEGE
     Sports Illus 64:2-3, 76-9 (c,1)
     My 12 '86
--Women
     Nat Geog 161:813 (c,3) Je '82
RUGS
--Polar bear rug
     Sports Illus 56:70 (c,3) Ja 11
     '82
RUISDAEL, JACOB VAN
--"View of Haarlem" (1670)
     Smithsonian 13:50 (paint-
     ing,c,2) Je '82
RULERS AND MONARCHS
--1932 European rulers
     Am Heritage 37:97 (2) Ag '86
--1963 world rulers at John F.
     Kennedy funeral
     Life 6:66-7 (c,4) N '83
--Idi Amin (Uganda)
     Ebony 39:112 (4) Jl '84
--Corazon Aquino (Philippines)
     Life 9:51-4 (c,2) F '86
     Nat Geog 170:80, 85 (c,3) Jl
     '86
--Ayatollah Khomeini (Iran)
     Nat Geog 168:112, 118 (paint-
     ing,c,1) Jl '85
     Life 8:98 (c,4) S '85
--Beatrix (Netherlands)
     Nat Geog 170:509-11 (c,2) O
     '86
--Caricatures of 1940s world rulers
     Smithsonian 15:178 (c,3) N '84
--Juan Carlos (Spain)
     Life 8:46-54 (c,1) D '85
     Ebony 41:72 (c,4) F '86
     Nat Geog 169:181 (c,1) F '86
--Coronation of Napoleon and
     Josephine
     Nat Geog 161:144-5 (paint-
     ing,c,1) F '82
--Cosimo I (Florence, Italy)
     Smithsonian 13:61 (paint-
     ing,c,4) N '82
--European heirs
     Life 5:72-9 (c,1) Ag '82
--Indira Ghandi (India)
     Life 7:198-200 (2) D '84
--Mikhail Gorbachev (U.S.S.R.)

     Life 9:8-9 (c,1) Ja '86
--Jordan
     Nat Geog 165:252-3 (c,1) F '84
--King Kamehameha (Hawaii)
     Smithsonian 12:164 (painting,c,4)
     Mr '82
     Nat Geog 164:558, 572, 581 (paint-
     ing,c,1) N '83
--Leopold I (Holy Roman Empire)
     Smithsonian 15:60 (painting,c,4)
     Ja '85
--Lord Mayor of London
     Smithsonian 13:90 (c,3) N '82
--Monaco
     Life 6:cov., 4, 22-9 (c,1) Mr '83
     Life 7:56-60 (c,1) Ja '84
--Mongol rulers (India)
     Nat Geog 167:467 (painting,c,4)
     Ap '85
--Netherlands
     Smithsonian 13:44 (4) My '82
--Peru
     Nat Geog 161:290 (c,3) Mr '82
--Rama IV (19th cent.; Thailand)
     Nat Geog 162:491 (4) O '82
--Rulers of black nations
     Ebony 41:78-86 (4) N '85
--Rurik the Rus (Viking)
     Nat Geog 167:279 (sculpture,c,1)
     Mr '85
--Haile Selassie (Ethiopia)
     Ebony 39:56 (4) O '84
--Sudan
     Nat Geog 161:356 (c,4) Mr '82
--Western Samoan chiefs
     Nat Geog 168:464 (c,4) O '85
--See also
     ALEXANDER I
     ALEXANDER THE GREAT
     BREZHNEV, LEONID
     CASTRO, FIDEL
     CHARLEMAGNE
     CHARLES II
     CHIANG KAI-SHEK
     CLEOPATRA
     CONSTANTINE THE GREAT
     CROWNS
     DARIUS
     DE GAULLE, CHARLES
     EDWARD IV
     EDWARD VI
     EDWARD VII
     ELIZABETH I
     ELIZABETH II
     FRANCO, FRANCISCO
     FRANCOIS I
     GENGHIS KHAN

RULERS AND MONARCHS (cont.)
    GEORGE III
    GEORGE VI
    GHANDI, MOHANDAS
    HADRIAN
    HENRY VII
    HENRY VIII
    HITLER, ADOLF
    IVAN IV
    JUSTINIAN THE GREAT
    KHRUSCHEV, NIKITA
    KUBLAI KHAN
    LENIN, NIKOLAI
    LEOPOLD III
    LOUIS XIV
    MAO ZEDONG
    MARCOS, FERDINAND
    MARIE ANTOINETTE
    MARY, QUEEN OF SCOTS
    MARY OF TECK
    MEDICI, COSIMO
    MEDICI, LORENZO
    MEIR, GOLDA
    NAPOLEON
    NAPOLEON III
    NEHRU, JAWAHARIAL
    NERO
    PERON, JUAN
    RAMSES II
    RICHARD I
    RICHARD II
    SADAT, ANWAR
    SALADIN
    SANTA ANNA
    SULEYMAN
    TITO, MARSHAL
    TUTANKHAMUN
    U.S. PRESIDENTS
RUNNING
    Sports Illus 62:72 (c,3) Mr 4
    '85
--6th cent. B.C. Greek vase
    Smithsonian 13:38 (painting,c,4)
    Ap '82
--Australia
    Sports Illus 61:358-9 (c,1) Jl
    18 '84
--California mountains
    Sports Illus 58:32-3 (c,1) Mr
    28 '83
--Runners stretching (Jamaica)
    Sports Illus 58:94-5 (c,1) F
    14 '83
--Running with dog companion
    Sports Illus 65:86 (c,3) Jl 28
    '86
--Sculpture of woman running

    Sports Illus 60:26 (c,4) My 28
    '84
--Slow motion photography
    Sports Illus 62:43 (c,2) Ap 29
    '85
--Wales
    Sports Illus 59:46-7 (c,1) Ag 8
    '83
--West Germany
    Sports Illus 61:76 (c,2) Jl 18 '84
--See also
    CROSS COUNTRY
    JOGGING
    MARATHONS
    RACES
RUSSELL, CHARLES MARION
    Nat Geog 169:60, 74, 84, 92 (4)
    Ja '86
--1926 funeral (Montana)
    Nat Geog 169:93 (3) Ja '86
--"Blackfeet Burning Crow Buffalo
    Range"
    Natur Hist 92:8 (painting,c,2)
    F '83
--Paintings by him
    Nat Geog 169:cov., 63-94 (c,1)
    Ja '86
RUSSELL, LILLIAN
    Smithsonian 16:94 (4) Ja '86
RUTH, GEORGE HERMAN (BABE)
    Am Heritage 33:15 (4) O '82
    Sports Illus 57:53 (4) O 4 '82
    Sports Illus 58:92 (drawing,c,4)
    Ap 4 '83
    Sports Illus 58:92 (4) My 30 '83
    Sports Illus 59:56 (4) O 3 '83
    Sports Illus 63:130 (4) S 4 '85
    Sports Illus 63:76 (4) O 14 '85
    Sports Illus 64:77 (4) Ap 14 '86
    Sports Illus 65:114 (4) N 3 '86
--1927 baseball bat
    Smithsonian 15:176 (c,4) O '84
--Wood carving of him (New York)
    Trav/Holiday 166:28 (c,4) Ag '86
RUTHERFORD, ERNEST
    Natur Hist 93:32 (4) F '84
RWANDA
--Mount Karisimbi
    Natur Hist 91:50-1 (map,c,2) Mr
    '82
--Rain forests
    Natur Hist 91:50-5 (c,1) Mr '82
RYE INDUSTRY--HARVESTING
--Spain
    Natur Hist 94:74-5 (c,2) N '85

-S-

SABER-TOOTHED CATS
Natur Hist 91:50-7 (draw-
ing,c,1) Ap '82
SACCO AND VANZETTI
Am Heritage 37:106-8 (2) Je
'86
--Fake photo of Vanzetti execu-
tion (1927)
Am Heritage 33:54 (3) O '82
SACRAMENTO, CALIFORNIA
Trav/Holiday 158:45-6 (c,1)
Jl '82
Sacrifices. See
RELIGIOUS RITES AND
FESTIVALS
SADAT, ANWAR
Am Heritage 34:55 (4) Ag '83
--Assassination
Ebony 37:33 (4) Ja '82
Life 5:14-16, 26 (c,2) Ja '82
SADDLES
--Camels (Middle East)
Natur Hist 92:52-7 (c,2) Jl '83
SAFARIS
--1930s (Africa)
Smithsonian 17:144-55 (1) N
'86
--Australia by camel
Trav/Holiday 159:53-4, 77 (c,2)
My '83
--Photo safari (Kenya)
Trav/Holiday 160:cov., 46, 49
(c,1) S '83
SAFES
Smithsonian 15:34-45 (c,1) Jl
'84
SAFETY EQUIPMENT
--Auto crash tests
Nat Geog 164:26-7 (c,1) Jl '83
--Life jacket on child (Sweden)
Trav/Holiday 159:76 (4) My '83
SAFFRON INDUSTRY--HARVEST-
ING
--Kashmir
Nat Geog 167:478 (c,4) Ap '85
SAGE
--Made of glass
Smithsonian 13:101 (c,3) O '82
SAGEBRUSH
Natur Hist 93:46-7 (c,1) F '84
Nat Wildlife 24:38-41 (c,1) Ag
'86
SAHARA DESERT, ALGERIA
Natur Hist 92:78 (c,4) F '83

SAHARA DESERT, SUDAN
--Satellite photo
Nat Geog 164:316-17 (c,1) S '83
SAILBOAT RACES
Sports Illus 58:48-58 (c,2) My
23 '83
Life 9:32-8 (c,1) Ap '86
--America's Cup (1893)
Am Heritage 38:61 (painting,c,4)
D '86
--America's Cup 1983 (Newport,
Rhode Island)
Sports Illus 59:2-3, 30-6 (c,1)
S 26 '83
Sports Illus 59:26-35 (c,1) O 3
'83
Sports Illus 59:26-35 (c,2) O 3
'83
Sports Illus 60:141 (c,3) F 8 '84
Sports Illus 60:66-80 (c,1) Mr
12 '84
--America's Cup 1986
Sports Illus 64:30-3 (c,2) F 24
'86
--America's Cup 1986 practice
Life 9:32-8 (c,1) Ap '86
Sports Illus 65:60-5 (c,1) Ag 25
'86
--America's Cup trials
Sports Illus 65:40, 44, 46 (c,2)
N 10 '86
Sports Illus 65:2-3, 22-7 (c,1)
N 24 '86
Sports Illus 65:34 (c,2) D 22 '86
--America's Cup victory celebration
(Australia)
Sports Illus 62:84-100 (c,1) F 11
'85
--California
Sports Illus 62:66, 69 (c,2) Mr
25 '85
--First America's Cup race (1851)
Natur Hist 92:62 (painting,c,4)
My '83
--Maryland
Nat Wildlife 22:14-15 (c,1) Ap '84
--Newport, Rhode Island
Sports Illus 59:46, 48-50 (c,2)
Jl 11 '83
--Practicing for race (Rhode Island)
Trav/Holiday 160:cov., 44 (c,1)
Jl '83
--San Francisco, California
Sports Illus 56:76, 79 (c,3) Je
7 '82
Sports Illus 57:56-7 (c,4) Jl 5
'82

SAILORS (cont.)
    BLIGH, WILLIAM
    SINBAD THE SAILOR
ST. AUGUSTINE, FLORIDA
--Oldest U.S. schoolhouse (18th
    cent.)
    Trav/Holiday 166:16 (c,4) N
    '86
ST. ELIAS RANGE, YUKON
    Nat Geog 168:630-57 (map,c,1)
    N '85
ST. GAUDENS, AUGUSTUS
    Am Heritage 36:42-3 (paint-
    ing,c,1) Je '85
--Late 19th cent. bronze Diana
    weathervane
    Am Heritage 35:44 (c,3) Ag '84
    Am Heritage 36:51 (4) Je '85
--Late 19th cent. marble relief of
    his son
    Smithsonian 14:125 (4) Je '83
--Sculptures by him
    Am Heritage 36:44-52 (c,1) Je
    '85
--Sherman Monument (New York
    City, New York)
    Am Heritage 36:44-5 (1) Je '85
SAINT HELENA
    Nat Geog 161:186-7 (c,2) F '82
SAINT JOHN, NEW BRUNSWICK
--Market Square
    Trav/Holiday 163:84 (c,4) Mr
    '85
ST. JOHN THE DIVINE CATHE-
    DRAL, NEW YORK CITY,
    NEW YORK
--Stained glass
    Am Heritage 35:60-3 (c,1) F
    '84
ST. JOHN'S, NEWFOUNDLAND
    Nat Geog 169:686-7 (c,1) My
    '86
ST. LAWRENCE RIVER, MON-
    TREAL, QUEBEC
    Trav/Holiday 157:41 (c,3) My
    '82
ST. LOUIS, MISSOURI
    Trav/Holiday 157:33-6 (c,1) Je
    '82
    Trav/Holiday 165:60-3 (c,3)
    My '86
--1870s social evil hospital
    Am Heritage 33:54 (4) F '82
--Early 20th cent.
    Am Heritage 33:46-55 (1) Ag
    '82
--Aerial view

    Nat Wildlife 21:4-5 (c,1) Je '83
--See also
    GATEWAY ARCH
St. Maarten. See
    LEEWARD ISLANDS
ST. MARK'S CATHEDRAL, VENICE,
    ITALY
--Bronze horses
    Smithsonian 13:cov., 100-7 (c,1)
    S '82
--Interior
    Smithsonian 15:43 (c,4) S '84
--Mosaics
    Smithsonian 15:42-53 (c,1) S '84
--Pala d'Oro altarpiece
    Nat Geog 164:752-3 (c,1) D '83
ST. MORITZ, SWITZERLAND
    Nat Geog 169:119 (c,4) Ja '86
--Hotel
    Trav/Holiday 164:14 (c,3) N '85
ST. PATRICK'S CATHEDRAL, NEW
    YORK CITY, NEW YORK
    Smithsonian 13:158 (c,1) N '82
ST. PATRICK'S DAY
--Chicago River dyed green (Illinois)
    Life 9:27 (c,4) O '86
--Savannah, Georgia celebration
    Nat Geog 164:804-5 (c,1) D '83
ST. PAUL, MINNESOTA
    Trav/Holiday 158:51-2 (c,3) Jl
    '82
    Sports Illus 58:80-1 (painting,c,1)
    Mr 7 '83
--1872 drawing
    Am Heritage 35:86-7 (1) Je '84
--Capitol Building
    Trav/Holiday 158:51 (c,3) Jl '82
--Winter Carnival
    Life 9:6-7 (c,1) Ap '86
ST. PETER'S BASILICA, VATICAN
    CITY
    Nat Geog 168:720-61 (c,1) D '85
ST. PETERSBURG, FLORIDA
    Nat Geog 162:204-5 (c,1) Ag '82
--Kitchen of Grace Turner House
    Trav/Holiday 157:82 (4) Mr '82
ST. SOPHIA CATHEDRAL, ISTAN-
    BUL, TURKEY
--Interior
    Nat Geog 167:316-17 (c,1) Mr '85
St. Vincent. See
    WINDWARD ISLANDS
SAINTS
--15th cent. icon of St. George
    (U.S.S.R.)
    Smithsonian 13:140 (c,3) F '83
--Coffin of St. John the New

SAINTS (cont.)
    (Romania)
    Nat Geog 164:757 (c,3) D '83
--Dimitry (Greece)
    Nat Geog 164:761 (painting,c,4)
      D '83
--Folk carvings (Puerto Rico)
    Nat Geog 163:525 (c,4) Ap '83
--Joseph (Italy)
    Nat Geog 162:694-5 (sculp-
      ture,c,4) D '82
--Lucy
    Smithsonian 13:111 (painting,c,1)
      Mr '83
--Relics of Spanish saints (Mad-
    rid, Spain)
    Nat Geog 169:179 (c,1) F '86
--St. Peter's tomb (Vatican City)
    Nat Geog 168:745 (c,4) D '85
SAIPAN, MARIANA ISLANDS
--Japanese Suicide Cliff
    Nat Geog 170:468 (c,4) O '86
--World War II battle sites
    Life 8:96-9 (c,1) Spring '85
SALADIN (EGYPT)
    Smithsonian 17:59 (painting,c,4)
      S '86
    Smithsonian 17:157 (paint-
      ing,4) O '86
SALAMANDERS
    Sports Illus 56:82 (4) Mr 15
      '82
    Smithsonian 13:74, 81 (c,1) N
      '82
    Sports Illus 65:98 (c,4) O 20
      '86
SALESMEN
--1885 painting of traveling sales-
    men
    Am Heritage 33:86-7 (c,1) Ap
      '82
    Am Heritage 36:67 (4) D '84
--Avon lady
    Life 9:38 (c,4) D '86
--Fuller Brush men
    Am Heritage 37:26-31 (c,2) Ag
      '86
SALK, JONAS
    Life 5:83 (c,4) O '82
SALMON
    Natur Hist 91:36-7 (c,4) Jl '82
    Nat Geog 163:776-7 (c,2) Je
      '83
    Natur Hist 92:58-63 (c,1) Je '83
    Sports Illus 61:36 (paint-
      ing,c,4) S 17 '84
    Nat Wildlife 23:30-5 (c,1) Je '85

--Being caught by bear
    Nat Wildlife 21:cov. (c,1) Ap '83
--Chinook
    Nat Geog 165:665 (c,2) My '84
--Chinook fry
    Nat Wildlife 23:33 (c,1) Je '85
--Coho
    Nat Geog 170:348-9 (c,1) S '86
--Sockeye
    Nat Wildlife 22:12-13 (c,1) O '84
    Nat Wildlife 24:61 (c,1) Ap '86
--Swimming to spawning grounds
    Natur Hist 94:32 (c,4) N '85
Saloons. See
    TAVERNS
SALT INDUSTRY
--Man-made salt pans (Niger)
    Nat Geog 164:492-3 (c,1) O '83
--Salt evaporation ponds (Utah)
    Nat Geog 167:705 (c,4) Je '85
--Salt farming (Thailand)
    Nat Geog 162:522 (c,3) O '82
--See also
    SALT MINES
SALT LAKE CITY, UTAH
    Trav/Holiday 161:cov., 76, 79
      (c,1) Ap '84
--Capitol Hill
    Nat Geog 167:706-7 (c,1) Je '85
--Flood
    Nat Geog 165:160-1 (c,1) F '84
--Mormon Temple
    Trav/Holiday 165:68 (c,4) Je '86
--See also
    GREAT SALT LAKE
SALT MINES
--Louisiana
    Smithsonian 15:80 (c,4) My '84
SALT MINING
--South Yemen
    Nat Geog 168:494 (c,1) O '85
SALZBURG, AUSTRIA
    Trav/Holiday 162:24 (c,4) D '84
    Nat Geog 167:424-6 (c,1) Ap '85
Samoa. See
    AMERICAN SAMOA
    WESTERN SAMOA
SAMOS, GREECE
--Docks
    Nat Geog 162:708-9 (c,1) D '82
SAMOYEDS (DOGS)
    Ebony 38:144 (c,2) S '83
SAMPANS
--Burma
    Nat Geog 166:98-9 (c,1) Jl '84
SAN ANDREAS FAULT, CALIFORNIA
    Smithsonian 14:48-9 (c,3) Jl '83

Sandstone. See
    QUARTZITE
SANDUSKY, OHIO
--Cedar Point amusement park
    Life 8:33-8 (c,1) Ag '85
SANITATION WORK
--1930 street cleaner (New York
    City)
    Am Heritage 33:44 (3) Je '82
--Hazardous waste sites
    Nat Geog 167:cov., 318-51
    (c,1) Mr '85
--Unloading trash at landfill
    (Illinois)
    Ebony 38:80 (3) Ag '83
SANTA ANNA
    Smithsonian 16:57 (painting,4)
    Mr '86
--Surrendering to Texas (1836)
    Nat Geog 169:323 (painting,c,4)
    Mr '86
SANTA BARBARA, CALIFORNIA
    Nat Geog 165:434-5 (c,2) Ap
    '84
    Smithsonian 15:131 (c,3) My
    '84
SANTA CLARA, CALIFORNIA
--Prefabricated office buildings
    Nat Geog 162:460-1 (c,1) O
    '82
SANTA CLAUS
--Japanese "Shogun Santa"
    California
    Nat Geog 169:539 (c,1) Ap '86
--Man in Santa costume
    Sports Illus 59:16 (c,4) D 26
    '83
--Man in Santa costume (Australia)
    Nat Geog 169:748-9 (c,1) Je
    '86
--Man in Santa costume (Hawaii)
    Trav/Holiday 158:18-19 (c,1)
    D '82
--Man in Santa costume (Truk
    Islands)
    Nat Geog 170:498 (c,4) O '86
--Men in Santa costumes (New
    York)
    Life 8:11, 16 (c,4) D '85
--"Skid Row" Santas (New York
    City, New York)
    Smithsonian 13:87 (3) Je '82
SANTA CRUZ ISLANDS
--Daphne Major crater
    Natur Hist 92:80 (c,4) S '83
SANTA FE, NEW MEXICO
    Nat Geog 161:322-45 (c,1)

    Mr '82
--Early 20th cent. paintings by
    John Sloan
    Am Heritage 33:98-107 (c,1) Ap
    '82
SANTA MONICA, CALIFORNIA
    Smithsonian 13:132-3 (c,1) O '82
--Amusement pier
    Smithsonian 13:66 (c,4) S '82
SANTAYANA, GEORGE
    Smithsonian 17:144 (4) S '86
SAO PAULO, BRAZIL
    Trav/Holiday 159:cov., 55-8
    (c,1) Ja '83
SAPSUCKERS
--Yellow-bellied
    Nat Wildlife 20:14-15 (c,1) O '82
SARAJEVO, YUGOSLAVIA
    Sports Illus 56:50-2 (c,3) Mr 22
    '82
    Sports Illus 58:74-90 (c,1) Mr 14
    '83
    Sports Illus 59:2-3 (c,1) O 24
    '83
    Trav/Holiday 160:56, 59 (c,2) N
    '83
    Sports Illus 60:36-7 (c,2) F 6 '84
SARDINIA, ITALY
--Esporlatu village area
    Natur Hist 92:58 (c,4) Ja '83
SARGENT, JOHN SINGER
    Am Heritage 36:66 (3) D '84
--"Madame X" (1884)
    Am Heritage 37:47 (painting,c,2)
    O '84
--"F. D. Millet House and Garden"
    (1884)
    Smithsonian 13:8 (painting,c,4)
    Je '82
--Paintings by him
    Am Heritage 37:40-7 (c,1) O '86
--Paintings of Venice (1881)
    Am Heritage 35:42-5 (c,1) Je '84
SARK, CHANNEL ISLANDS
    Smithsonian 17:92-105 (map,c,1)
    My '86
SATELLITES
    Nat Geog 164:cov., 280-335 (c,1)
    S '83
--1957-1958
    Smithsonian 13:148-67 (c,2) O '82
--Control center for Intelsat (Wash-
    ington, D.C.)
    Nat Geog 164:296-7 (c,2) S '83
--Earth stations
    Nat Geog 164:294-5 (c,1) S '83
    Nat Geog 169:374 (c,3) Mr '86

SATELLITES (cont.)
--Infrared Astronomical Satellite
Nat Geog 163:727 (diagram,c,4)
Je '83
--Repairing satellites in orbit
Smithsonian 16:96-105 (draw-
ing,c,1) Ag '85
--Rescuing Westar VI satellite
from space
Life 8:14-15 (c,1) Ja '85
--Retrieving wayward satellite
Ebony 40:63 (c,4) Ag '85
--Satellite explosion
Natur Hist 91:12 (painting,3)
Mr '82
--Satellite maps of earth
Nat Geog 164:382-3, 315-25,
334-5 (c,1) S '83
--Sputnik (1957)
Smithsonian 13:148-9 (c,2) O
'82
SATURN (PLANET)
Natur Hist 93:81 (4) F '84
Nat Geog 167:42-5 (c,1) Ja '85
--Moon
Natur Hist 93:92 (c,4) O '84
SAUDI ARABIA
Smithsonian 15:44-52 (c,1) D
'84
Nat Geog 168:485, 508-11
(map,c,1) O '85
--Arabian frankincense areas
Nat Geog 168:474-513 (map,c,1)
O '85
--See also
ARABIAN DESERT
BEDOUINS
MECCA
SAUDI ARABIA--ARCHITECTURE
--Ancient Nabataean mausoleum
Nat Geog 168:480-1 (c,1) O
'85
SAUDI ARABIA--ART
--Bedouin relics
Smithsonian 14:148 (c,4) Ap
'83
SAUDI ARABIA--COSTUME
Life 5:10-21 (c,1) D '82
Nat Geog 168:509-11 (c,1) O
'85
--Bedouins
Smithsonian 15:44-57 (c,1) D
'84
SAUDI ARABIA--MAPS
--Ancient trade routes
Smithsonian 14:46 (c,2) S '83

SAUDI ARABIA--SOCIAL LIFE AND
CUSTOMS
--Bedouin camel race
Smithsonian 15:56-7 (c,1) D '84
SAUDI ARABIA, ANCIENT--RELICS
--Archaeological finds
Smithsonian 14:cov., 42-53 (c,1)
S '83
SAUNAS
--1944 (California)
Life 9:121-2 (4) Fall '86
--Georgia
Sports Illus 64:48 (c,1) F 24 '86
SAVANNAH, GEORGIA
Nat Geog 164:803-13 (map,c,1)
D '83
--1730s engraving of city
Am Heritage 33:6 (4) Je '82
Am Heritage 35:99 (c,2) Ap '84
SAVANNAH RIVER, SOUTH
CAROLINA/GEORGIA
Nat Geog 164:808-9, 812-13 (c,1)
D '83
SAWMILLS
--Laser-assisted saws (Washington)
Nat Geog 165:350 (c,2) Mr '84
SAXOPHONE PLAYING
Sports Illus 57:134 (c,4) Jl 12
'82
SCALES
--1929 bathroom scale advertisement
Am Heritage 36:82 (c,1) Ap '85
--Doctor's scale
Ebony 37:86 (3) O '82
Life 9:371 (2) Fall '86
--Food market (Mexico)
Natur Hist 94:113 (2) O '85
--Large standing scale
Sports Illus 57:66 (c,4) D 13 '82
--Outdoor fruit market (Sri Lanka)
Trav/Holiday 158:42-3 (c,3) S
'82
--Outdoor produce market (New York)
Trav/Holiday 159:51 (c,2) Ja '83
--Professional jockey's scale
Sports Illus 65:43 (c,3) N 17 '86
--Weighing animals (Namibia)
Nat Geog 163:350-1 (c,1) Mr '83
--Weighing baby (1908)
Am Heritage 34:91 (1) D '82
--Weighing baby (Ethiopia)
Nat Geog 163:629 (c,3) My '83
--Weighing boxer
Sports Illus 57:42-3 (c,2) Jl 12
'82
--Weighing fish
Sports Illus 57:42 (c,4) Jl 19 '82

SCALES (cont.)
--Weighing opium (Burma)
    Nat Geog 167:145 (c,1) F '85
SCALPING
--Indians scalping Virginia woman
    (1622)
    Nat Geog 161:52 (painting,c,1)
    Ja '82
SCANDINAVIA--ART
--20th cent. decorative pieces
    Smithsonian 14:127 (c,4) Ag
    '83
Scents. See
    SMELL
SCHLEY, WINFIELD SCOTT
    Am Heritage 34:92 (2) D '82
SCHOLARS
--1400 (France)
    Smithsonian 17:38 (painting,c,4)
    Je '86
--17th cent. Spain (El Greco
    painting)
    Nat Geog 161:744 (painting,c,2)
    Je '82
--1915 (Great Britain)
    Smithsonian 13:34 (4) Ag '82
--See also
    LOWELL, ABBOTT LAW-
        RENCE
SCHOOLS
--18th cent. oldest schoolhouse
    (St. Augustine, Florida)
    Trav/Holiday 166:16 (c,4) N
    '86
--Early 20th cent. American In-
    dian boarding schools
    Natur Hist 93:4-12 (c,1) Ag
    '84
--1955 fifth grader examining
    report card (Washington)
    Life 9:295 (1) Fall '86
--1957 integration of Little Rock
    high school, Arkansas
    Ebony 41:278 (3) N '85
--Avon Old Farms School, Avon,
    Connecticut
    Sports Illus 58:62 (c,4) My
    9 '83
--Boston Latin High School
    Smithsonian 16:122-35 (c,1)
    Ap '85
--Bronx High School of Science,
    New York
    Smithsonian 16:80-8 (1) My '85
--California Institute of the Arts,
    California
    Smithsonian 13:46-55 (c,1) Ja

    '83
--Central High School, Little Rock,
    Arkansas
    Ebony 37:131 (2) Ap '82
--Disabled children using computers
    Smithsonian 14:42-7 (3) F '84
--Faizieh Theological School, Qom,
    Iran
    Nat Geog 168:134 (c,4) Jl '85
--Migrant children (Florida)
    Life 6:147-58 (1) N '83
--One-room schoolhouses (Nebraska)
    Smithsonian 16:118-28 (c,1) O
    '85
--Phillips Exeter Academy, Maine
    Life 8:125 (c,2) O '85
--Professional Children's School,
    New York City
    Smithsonian 13:60-9 (1) My '82
--Yeshiva (Jerusalem, Israel)
    Nat Geog 163:488 (c,4) Ap '83
--See also
    CLASSROOMS
    COLLEGES AND UNIVERSITIES
    EDUCATION
SCIENCE
--Preservation techniques for U.S.
    documents
    Smithsonian 17:134-43 (c,1) O
    '86
--See also
    ANATOMY
    ATOMS
    GENETICS
    LABORATORIES
    MEDICAL RESEARCH
    MEDICINE--PRACTICE
    OPTICAL ILLUSIONS
    SCIENTIFIC EXPERIMENTS
    SCIENTIFIC INSTRUMENTS
    SPACE PROGRAM
SCIENCE--HISTORY
--History of atomic research
    Nat Geog 167:643-8 (c,1) My '85
SCIENCE EDUCATION
--1901 high school physics lab
    Smithsonian 16:128 (4) Ap '85
--Teaching physics with dramatic
    stunts
    Smithsonian 17:112-21 (c,1) O '86
SCIENCE FICTION
--Illustrations of imaginary planet
    Smithsonian 12:86-95 (painting,c,1)
    Mr '82
SCIENTIFIC EXPERIMENTS
--17th-18th cents.
    Natur Hist 93:48-57 (c,1) Ja '84

SCIENTIFIC INSTRUMENTS
(cont.)
Ebony 40:64-6, 92-3 (c,4) Ag
'85
--Plumb line
Nat Geog 165:653 (c,4) My '84
--Radar dome (Great Britain)
Life 8:70-1 (1) N '85
--Remote weather station (Wyoming)
Smithsonian 17:48 (c,4) Ag '86
--Seismograph
Trav/Holiday 159:6 (4) F '83
--Thermogram of shuttle Colum-
bia's touchdown
Nat Geog 162:650-3 (c,1) N '82
--Water monitor measuring acid
in stream
Sports Illus 60:42 (c,4) Ap 23
'84
--See also
BAROMETERS
MAGNETS
MEDICAL INSTRUMENTS
MICROSCOPES
NAVIGATION INSTRUMENTS
RADAR
SCALES
TELESCOPES
TEST TUBES
THERMOMETERS
SCIENTISTS
--18th cent. alchemist (Great
Britain)
Natur Hist 93:48 (painting,c,1)
Ja '84
--History of the Rand Corporation
Am Heritage 34:49-63 (1) Je
'83
--See also
AGASSIZ, LOUIS
BOHR, NIELS
CARVER, GEORGE WASHING-
TON
CRICK, FRANCIS
DARWIN, CHARLES
EINSTEIN, ALBERT
FABRE, JEAN HENRI
FREUD, SIGMUND
GODDARD, ROBERT
HALLEY, EDMUND
HUMBOLDT, ALEXANDER
VON
JUNG, CARL GUSTAV
KELVIN, LORD
LAVOISIER, ANTOINE LAURENT
LEAKEY, LOUIS S. B.
MEAD, MARGARET

MENNINGER, KARL A.
NATURALISTS
OPPENHEIMER, J. ROBERT
PAULING, LINUS
RUTHERFORD, ERNEST
SALK, JONAS
STEINMETZ, CHARLES
TESLA, NIKOLA
VON BRAUN, WERNHER
WATSON, JAMES
SCIENTISTS--HUMOR
--Creating synthetic food flavors
Smithsonian 17:78-88 (draw-
ing,c,1) My '86
SCOREBOARDS
--Baseball
Sports Illus 58:24-5 (c,1) Je 20
'83
Sports Illus 59:48 (c,4) Ag 29
'83
Sports Illus 61:56 (c,4) Jl 9 '84
Sports Illus 62:110-11 (c,1) Ap
15 '85
--Baseball (Japan)
Sports Illus 63:64-5 (c,2) S 9
'85
--Comiskey Park, Chicago, Illinois
Sports Illus 56:28 (c,4) My 31
'82
--Figure skating
Sports Illus 59:34-5 (c,2) N 7
'83
--Football
Sports Illus 65:40, 57 (c,4) D 1
'86
--Golf
Sports Illus 62:62 (c,2) Mr 18
'85
Sports Illus 64:106-7 (c,1) Ap 7
'86
Sports Illus 65:43 (c,3) Jl 28 '86
--High school football
Sports Illus 63:92 (c,4) N 4 '85
--Local baseball scoreboard (Florida)
Sports Illus 62:2-3 (c,1) Mr 18
'85
--Olympic skating events
Sports Illus 60:28 (c,4) F 27 '84
--Softball
Sports Illus 65:82 (c,4) Jl 28 '86
--Swim meet
Sports Illus 57:12 (c,4) Ag 16
'82
SCOTLAND
Nat Geog 166:41-69 (map,c,1)
Jl '84
--Castle of Mey

SENEGAL
    Nat Geog 168:224-49 (map,c,1)
        Ag '85
--See also
    DAKAR
SENEGAL--COSTUME
    Ebony 37:47-50 (3) Jl '82
    Nat Geog 168:224-50 (c,1) Ag
        '85
SENEGAL--SOCIAL LIFE AND
        CUSTOMS
--Diola people manhood rites
    Nat Geog 168:240-1 (c,1) Ag
        '85
SEOUL, SOUTH KOREA
    Sports Illus 61:62-5 (c,1) D
        24 '84
--1953
    Sports Illus 61:62-3 (2) D 24
        '84
--1988 Olympic site
    Sports Illus 60:33 (c,2) My 21
        '84
    Sports Illus 61:64-5 (c,1) D 24
        '84
--Office building
    Sports Illus 65:40 (c,4) S 29
        '86
SEQUOIA NATIONAL PARK,
        CALIFORNIA
    Nat Wildlife 24:64-5 (c,1) D '85
SEQUOIA TREES
--Felling a sequoia (1891)
    Natur Hist 91:88-91 (2) My '82
SEVEN WONDERS OF THE WORLD
--Wonders of the Ancient World
    Smithsonian 14:59 (drawing,4)
        Mr '84
SEWARD, WILLIAM HENRY
--Knife used in 1865 assassination
        attempt
    Am Heritage 34:6 (2) Ap '83
SEWERS
--Mexico City, Mexico
    Nat Geog 166:150 (c,4) Ag '84
--Paris, France
    Life 8:56-7 (1) Jl '85
SEWING
--18th cent. Chinese sewing table
    Natur Hist 93:72 (c,4) F '84
--Early 19th cent. Chinese
        sewing table
    Am Heritage 33:47 (c,3) F '82
--Mending (Portugal)
    Nat Geog 166:480-1 (c,1) O '84
--Stone Age needles (France)
    Natur Hist 95:75 (c,4) O '86

--Using sewing machine
    Sports Illus 59:36 (c,4) D 26 '83
--Using sewing machine (Florida)
    Sports Illus 56:66 (c,4) Ap 26
        '82
--See also
    GARMENT INDUSTRY
    NEEDLEWORK
    QUILTING
SEWING MACHINES
    Ebony 37:121 (4) Ja '82
    Life 9:126 (c,4) My '86
--Late 19th cent. (Japan)
    Smithsonian 13:178 (painting,c,4)
        Mr '83
--India
    Nat Geog 166:cov. (c,1) D '84
--Textile factory (Florida)
    Life 6:38 (c,4) Je '83
SEXTANTS
    Smithsonian 13:85 (c,4) Ja '83
    Nat Geog 170:289 (c,1) S '86
--Ancient Oman
    Nat Geog 162:22 (c,4) Jl '82
SEYCHELLES ISLANDS
    Trav/Holiday 162:49-51 (map,c,3)
        N '84
SHAKERS
--19th cent. room of Shaker furni-
        ture (New Hampshire)
    Am Heritage 34:94-5 (c,1) Ap '83
    Smithsonian 14:103 (c,4) My '83
--New Hampshire
    Nat Geog 162:794-5 (c,1) D '82
--Spinning yarn (Kentucky)
    Trav/Holiday 165:61 (c,3) Ja '86
SHAKESPEARE, WILLIAM
    Smithsonian 13:120-2 (c,4) Ap '82
--Garden at Stratford-Upon-Avon,
        England
    Nat Geog 163:392-3 (c,2) Mr '83
--Items related to him (Folger Li-
        brary, Washington, D.C.)
    Smithsonian 13:118-27 (c,1) Ap
        '82
--Painting of Ophelia drowning
    Smithsonian 14:75 (c,2) N '83
SHALIMAR GARDENS, PAKISTAN
    Nat Geog 167:482-3 (c,1) Ap '85
SHAMANS
--Paper spirit images used in healing
        (Mexico)
    Natur Hist 95:66-73 (c,1) Ja '86
--Texas
    Nat Geog 165:230-1 (c,1) F '84
SHANGHAI, CHINA
    Sports Illus 61:526 (c,3) Jl 18 '84

SHANGHAI, CHINA (cont.)
    Trav/Holiday 162:44-7 (c,3) S
        '84
SHARKS
    Nat Wildlife 20:cov., 4-10 (c,1)
        Ag '82
    Nat Geog 170:680-91 (c,1) N
        '86
--Embryo
    Nat Wildlife 23:46-7 (c,1) F
        '85
--Great white
    Nat Wildlife 20:6-7 (c,1) Ag '82
--Sand sculpture of shark eating
        real boy (Maine)
    Nat Wildlife 25:56 (c,4) D '86
--Shark jawbone
    Sports Illus 65:84 (c,4) Ag 25
        '86
SHAVING
    Ebony 38:142 (c,4) Ag '83
    Ebony 39:28 (c,4) Mr '84
    Life 7:110 (c,2) Ap '84
--Barber shaving man in station
        (Pakistan)
    Nat Geog 165:709 (c,1) Je '84
--Blind man shaving
    Life 9:68 (c,2) O '86
--Man being shaved
    Life 5:44 (2) O '82
--On Arctic expedition
    Nat Geog 170:301 (c,4) S '86
--On balcony (Florida)
    Nat Geog 162:206 (c,3) Ag '82
--Proper shaving technique
        (1955)
    Life 9:235 (4) Fall '86
--With machetes (Pennsylvania)
    Sports Illus 65:12 (c,4) Jl 14
        '86
--Woman shaving husband
    Sports Illus 60:76 (c,3) Ap 16
        '84
SHAW, GEORGE BERNARD
    Smithsonian 13:18 (draw-
        ing,c,4) Ja '83
--1912 poster for "Pygmalion"
    Smithsonian 15:176 (c,4) My '84
SHAWNEE NATIONAL FOREST,
        ILLINOIS
--LaRue-Pine Hills
    Natur Hist 94:86-7 (map,c,1)
        F '85
SHEARWATERS (BIRDS)
    Nat Wildlife 21:9 (c,2) F '83
SHEEP
    Nat Geog 161:286-7 (c,1) Mr

'82
    Am Heritage 33:26 (c,1) Je '82
    Nat Geog 164:63 (c,2) Jl '83
    Trav/Holiday 160:55 (c,4) S '83
    Sports Illus 59:98 (c,3) O 24 '83
    Natur Hist 93:42-9 (c,1) Jl '84
    Trav/Holiday 162:48-9 (c,1) Jl
        '84
    Sports Illus 64:56 (c,4) Ap 7 '86
    Nat Wildlife 24:14-19 (c,1) Je '86
    Trav/Holiday 165:44 (c,1) Je '86
--Attacked by coyotes
    Life 6:88-91 (c,1) Ag '83
--Aoudad
    Sports Illus 65:65 (c,4) S 8 '86
--Bighorn
    Natur Hist 91:38 (c,4) Jl '82
    Nat Wildlife 20:57-63 (c,1) O '82
    Natur Hist 93:18 (c,4) Ja '84
    Trav/Holiday 164:46 (c,4) Jl '85
    Natur Hist 94:26 (4) N '85
    Nat Wildlife 24:18-19 (painting,c,1)
        D '85
    Nat Wildlife 24:4-5 (c,1) Ap '86
--Dall's
    Natur Hist 91:62-9 (c,1) F '82
    Nat Wildlife 20:2 (c,1) Ag '82
    Nat Wildlife 21:8 (c,4) D '82
    Nat Wildlife 23:cov. (c,1) Je '85
    Nat Geog 168:642-3 (c,1) N '85
    Natur Hist 95:82-5 (c,1) Je '86
    Nat Wildlife 24:10-17 (c,1) Ag '86
--Guarded by dogs
    Smithsonian 13:64-73 (c,1) Ap '82
    Nat Wildlife 24:14-19 (c,1) Je '86
--Karakul
    Nat Geog 161:776 (c,3) Je '82
--Lambs
    Natur Hist 95:82-5 (c,1) Je '86
    Nat Wildlife 24:12-17 (c,1) Ag '86
--Merino sheep
    Smithsonian 14:55 (c,1) Ag '83
--Mouflon
    Nat Wildlife 24:10-11 (c,1) D '85
--Ram
    Smithsonian 14:47, 50 (c,4) Ag
        '83
--With artificial heart implant
    Life 6:24 (c,4) F '83
--See also
    RANCHING
SHEEP DOGS
    Smithsonian 13:cov., 64-73 (c,1)
        Ap '82
    Ebony 37:34 (c,4) My '82
    Smithsonian 13:12 (4) Je '82
    Nat Wildlife 24:14-19 (c,1) Je '86

SHIPS (cont.)
--18th cent. navigation book
   Am Heritage 35:45-9 (c,2) F
      '84
--1791 British man-of-war
   Nat Geog 168:422-41 (paint-
      ing,c,1) O '85
--19th-20th cents.
   Am Heritage 36:6, 89-99
      (painting,c,1) F '85
--19th cent. embroideries of ships
      (Great Britain)
   Smithsonian 17:13 (c,4) Ag '86
--1838 sloop-of-war
   Smithsonian 16:60 (painting,c,4)
      N '85
--1872 (Great Britain)
   Natur Hist 95:48 (painting,c,4)
      O '86
--Late 19th cent. cutter
   Smithsonian 13:137 (4) F '83
--Late 19th cent. U.S. Navy
      ships
   Am Heritage 37:81-96 (1) Je
      '86
--1885
   Life 9:50-1 (1) Jl '86
--1885 Navy dispatch boat
   Am Heritage 36:63 (4) D '84
--1888 chart of abandoned ships
   Natur Hist 94:44-5 (1) Je '85
--1888 gunboat (U.S.)
   Am Heritage 37:85 (1) Je '86
--1910 ocean liner
   Am Heritage 34:78-9 (paint-
      ing,c,1) Ap '83
--1926 tall ship (U.S.S.R.)
   Life 8:56-7 (1) S '85
--1930s cruise ship steering wheel
   Am Heritage 35:69 (c,4) D '83
--1936 christening of the U.S.S.
      Enterprise
   Life 8:39 (2) Spring '85
--1940s aircraft carrier the
      U.S.S. Enterprise
   Life 8:39-46 (c,1) Spring '85
--1940s coastal transport (U.S.)
   Am Heritage 36:8 (4) O '85
--Aircraft carrier (U.S.)
   Life 7:76-7 (c,1) F '84
   Life 9:47 (c,2) Je '86
--Antiaircraft cruiser (U.S.)
   Am Heritage 34:10-11 (c,1) Ap
      '83
--Bombed Greenpeace ship (New
      Zealand)
   Sports Illus 63:28-9 (c,2) S

2 '85
--Brigantine
   Trav/Holiday 157:39 (c,1) Je '82
--Bulk-cargo carrier
   Smithsonian 16:88-9 (c,1) O '85
--Damaged aircraft carrier
   Life 8:66-7 (1) Je '85
--Dreadnoughts
   Am Heritage 36:98-9 (painting,c,3)
      F '85
--Floating drydock (Maine)
   Nat Geog 167:224-5 (c,1) F '85
--History of American seafaring
   Am Heritage 34:cov., 10-85 (c,1)
      Ap '83
--Icebreakers
   Smithsonian 15:50-1 (c,3) O '84
   Ebony 40:43-4, 48 (4) F '85
--Icebreakers (U.S.S.R.)
   Nat Geog 163:208-9 (c,1) F '83
--In dry dock (American Samoa)
   Nat Geog 168:459 (c,4) O '85
--Incinerator ship for toxic wastes
   Nat Geog 167:339 (c,2) Mr '85
--Liberty ship from 1940s (U.S.)
   Am Heritage 34:110 (c,4) Ap '83
--Medieval Byzantine naval vessel
      (Turkey)
   Nat Geog 167:286-7 (painting,c,1)
      Mr '85
--Merchant marine vessel (U.S.S.R.)
   Nat Geog 168:414 (c,1) S '85
--Merchant marine vessels (18th-20th
      cents.)
   Am Heritage 34:68-77 (c,3) Ap
      '83
--Model of the "Bounty"
   Nat Geog 164:513 (c,1) O '83
--Nuclear aircraft carriers
   Life 5:22, 56-61 (c,1) N '82
--Paintings of 19th-20th cent. U.S.
      ships
   Am Heritage 34:78-85 (c,1) Ap
      '83
--Pilots guiding incoming ships (New
      York City, New York)
   Smithsonian 17:68-79 (c,1) Jl '86
--Queen Mary
   Sports Illus 64:32 (4) Je 30 '86
--Queen Mary (Long Beach, Califor-
      nia)
   Trav/Holiday 165:74-5 (c,1) Ap
      '86
--Recreation of Columbus' 15th cent.
      Niña
   Nat Geog 170:602-5 (c,1) N '86
--Raising 16th cent. ship (Great

SHOOTING (cont.)
--Cross-country skiing biathlon
Sports Illus 59:104-5 (c,3) N
28 '83
--FBI shooting practice (Virginia)
Ebony 37:48 (4) Ag '82
--Father teaching child to use
gun (California)
Life 7:24 (c,3) My '84
--Police training (Detroit, Michi-
gan)
Ebony 37:126 (4) Ap '82
--Practicing with revolver (Florida)
Nat Geog 162:197 (c,3) Ag '82
--Target
Sports Illus 63:98 (c,4) N 4
'85
--See also
DUELS
GUNS
RIFLES
SHOPPING CARTS
--1940
Am Heritage 36:26 (painting,c,4)
O '85
SHOPPING CENTERS
Smithsonian 17:34-43 (c,1) D
'86
--Caracas mall, Venezuela
Trav/Holiday 163:69 (c,1) F
'85
--Eaton Centre mall, Toronto,
Ontario
Trav/Holiday 157:44 (c,1) My
'82
--Galleria, Dallas, Texas
Nat Geog 166:294-5 (c,1) S '84
Trav/Holiday 166:43 (c,4) Jl
'86
Ebony 42:54 (c,2) D '86
--Galleria, Houston, Texas
Trav/Holiday 158:42 (c,4) N
'82
--Georgetown Park, Washington,
D.C.
Nat Geog 163:102 (c,1) Ja '83
--Lima, Peru
Nat Geog 161:297 (c,2) Mr '82
--Montreal, Quebec
Trav/Holiday 157:38 (c,4) My
'82
--Nicollet Mall, Minneapolis,
Minnesota
Trav/Holiday 158:52 (c,2) Jl
'82
--San Juan mall, Puerto Rico
Nat Geog 163:531 (c,3) Ap '83

--Southdale Mall, Minneapolis, Min-
nesota
Smithsonian 17:39 (c,4) D '86
--Tijuana, Mexico
Nat Geog 167:735 (c,3) Je '85
--West Edmonton Mall, Edmonton,
Alberta
Trav/Holiday 159:53 (c,3) Je '83
Smithsonian 17:34-7, 42-3 (c,1)
D '86
--Woodbridge Center, New Jersey
Smithsonian 17:40-1 (c,2) D '86
SHOT-PUTTING
Sports Illus 58:36-7 (c,2) Je 6
'83
Sports Illus 59:18 (c,1) Jl 4 '83
Sports Illus 59:21 (c,4) S 1 '83
Sports Illus 60:59 (c,4) F 8 '84
Sports Illus 60:25 (c,4) Je 4 '84
Sports Illus 61:195 (c,4) Jl 18 '84
--China
Life 6:54-5 (c,1) D '83
SHREWS
Nat Wildlife 21:22-4 (c,1) Ag '83
Smithsonian 16:147-53 (c,1) O
'85
--See also
TREE SHREWS
SHRIMP INDUSTRY
--Mississippi
Trav/Holiday 159:48 (c,2) My '83
--Weighing shrimp (South Carolina)
Nat Geog 164:818 (c,2) D '83
SHRIMPS
Nat Geog 161:273 (c,4) F '82
Natur Hist 91:64 (c,2) D '82
Nat Geog 164:140-3 (c,1) Jl '83
Nat Geog 165:471 (c,1) Ap '84
Nat Wildlife 25:58-9 (c,1) D '86
--Brine shrimp
Sports Illus 58:80 (c,4) My 30
'83
--Cave shrimp
Smithsonian 13:76 (c,4) N '82
Siamese twins. See
TWINS
SIBERIA, U.S.S.R.
Trav/Holiday 165:51-5 (map,c,2)
My '86
SIBERIAN HUSKIES
Life 5:168 (c,1) D '82
Smithsonian 13:cov., 88-97 (c,1)
Mr '83
Sports Illus 64:2-4, 90-107 (c,1)
F 17 '86
Nat Geog 169:694-5 (c,1) My '86
Trav/Holiday 165:10, 34 (c,4) My

SIBERIAN HUSKIES (cont.)
'86
--Statue of hero dog Balto
Smithsonian 13:89 (c,4) Mr '83
--See also
DOG SLEDS
SICILY, ITALY
--Basilica of Monreale
Life 7:181-8 (c,1) D '84
--Corleone street scene
Life 8:38 (c,3) Mr '85
--Montelepre
Life 8:32 (c,3) Mr '85
--See also
MOUNT ETNA
SIERRA LEONE
--Late 18th cent.
Am Heritage 34:108-9 (drawing,4) Je '83
SIERRA NATIONAL FOREST,
CALIFORNIA
--Nelder Grove
Natur Hist 94:78-81 (map,c,1)
S '85
SIERRA NEVADA MOUNTAINS,
CALIFORNIA
--Donner Lake
Nat Geog 170:172-3 (c,1) Ag
'86
--Mammoth Mountain
Sports Illus 62:58-9 (c,1) F
25 '85
--Mt. Williamson
Nat Wildlife 22:42-3 (1) O '84
--See also
SEQUOIA NATIONAL PARK
SIGNS AND SIGNBOARDS
--19th cent. U.S. trade signs
Am Heritage 33:28-9 (c,1) Ap
'82
--Early 20th cent. neon motel
signs
Smithsonian 16:126-37 (c,1) Mr
'86
--1930s neon motel sign (New
Mexico)
Nat Geog 166:334 (c,3) S '84
--Mid 20th cent. neon signs
Smithsonian 15:128 (c,4) Jl '84
--Bayou water street signs
(Louisiana)
Nat Geog 164:244-5 (c,1) Ag
'83
--Bourbon Street sign, New Orleans, Louisiana
Trav/Holiday 161:63 (c,2) Ap '84
--Frog warning sign (Switzerland)

Nat Wildlife 21:28 (4) Ag '83
--Highway sign warning of fissures
(Arizona)
Nat Wildlife 24:52 (c,4) D '85
--Highway signs (Missouri)
Sports Illus 63:34 (c,4) O 28 '85
--Kosse, Texas city limits sign
Sports Illus 56:40 (c,4) Ap 26
'82
--Lost Springs, Wyoming
Life 7:35 (4) Ja '84
--Motel sign (California)
Smithsonian 17:69 (c,1) D '86
--Neon
Life 6:116-22 (c,1) O '83
--Neon (California)
Trav/Holiday 160:62 (c,4) N '83
--Neon (Florida)
Sports Illus 65:52-3 (c,2) D 22
'86
--Neon (Hong Kong)
Trav/Holiday 161:44 (c,4) Ja '84
--New York City street corner signs
Smithsonian 17:43 (c,3) Ap '86
--Old movie theater sign (New York)
Smithsonian 15:121 (c,2) My '84
--Poisonous gas alert (Wyoming)
Sports Illus 56:86 (4) My 17 '82
--Road work sign (Papua New
Guinea)
Nat Geog 162:144-5 (c,1) Ag '82
--Sign warning of river contamination (Alabama)
Nat Wildlife 22:16 (c,4) Je '84
--Street signs
Ebony 39:70-6 (3) F '84
--Warning for rhino poachers (Kenya)
Nat Geog 165:414 (c,4) Mr '84
--Wyoming night club
Sports Illus 56:80 (c,4) My 17
'82
--Yield sign
Sports Illus 59:48 (c,4) S 1 '83
--See also
POSTERS
SIGNS AND SYMBOLS
--1939 World's Fair Trylon and
Perisphere (New York)
Am Heritage 35:78-9 (c,1) Ap '84
Am Heritage 35:8 (4) Je '84
--1984 Louisiana World Expo logo
Trav/Holiday 161:63 (c,4) Ap '84
--Bald eagle as U.S. symbol
Smithsonian 13:104-13 (c,1) My
'82
--Churchill's "V" for victory hand
sign

SIGNS AND SYMBOLS (cont.)
Life 8:20 (4) Spring '85
--Civil War eagle, "Old Abe"
Smithsonian 13:12 (4) Jl '82
--Deaf sign language
Life 5:75-8 (4) S '82
--Hand-holding unity salute
Ebony 39:162 (2) Mr '84
--Hand over heart for pledge of
allegiance
Life 6:46 (c,4) D '83
--Middle finger gesture (New York)
Life 7:87 (2) Ja '84
--Middle finger gesture by tennis
player
Sports Illus 60:57 (c,4) Mr 5
'84
--Nazi salute (1938)
Am Heritage 35:75 (2) Je '84
--Nazi swastika (1940s)
Life 6:84-8 (c,1) Jl '83
--"O.K." hand sign
Life 5:60-1 (c,1) S '82
--Olympic rings symbol
Sports Illus 61:56 (c,3) Jl 16
'84
--Olympic symbol with broken
ring
Sports Illus 60:cov. (c,1) My
21 '84
--Polish "solidarity" symbol
Smithsonian 13:88-91 (c,4) Ja
'83
--Raised fists at 1968 Olympics
awards (Mexico City)
Ebony 39:148 (4) Je '84
Life 7:106 (c,4) Summer '84
Ebony 41:102 (4) N '85
--Reagan waving hands over ears
Life 7:188 (c,2) Ja '84
--Salute
Life 6:45 (c,2) D '83
--Swastika on Nazi flag
Am Heritage 35:75 (2) Je '84
--Symbolic use of stars
Smithsonian 14:131 (c,4) Jl
'83
--"Thumbs up" signal
Sports Illus 62:60 (c,4) Je 3
'85
Nat Geog 168:284 (c,3) S '85
--"V" for victory hand sign
Ebony 38:177 (3) Ag '83
Ebony 40:146 (2) Ag '85
--"V" for victory sign (Poland)
Life 5:142 (2) O '82
--See also

FLAGS
LIBERTY, STATUE OF
LIBERTY BELL
MEDALS
SEALS AND EMBLEMS
SILHOUETTES
--Early 19th cent. (Great Britain)
Smithsonian 14:184-5 (4) O '83
--Depicting 17th cent. life (Massa-
chusetts)
Am Heritage 35:81-96 (2) D '83
SILK
Nat Geog 165:2-49 (c,1) Ja '84
--Early 19th cent. Chinese silk
Am Heritage 33:46 (c,2) F '82
SILK INDUSTRY
--China
Nat Geog 165:4-31, 34-5 (c,1)
Ja '84
--India
Nat Geog 165:32-3 (c,1) Ja '84
--Japan
Nat Geog 165:44-9 (c,1) Ja '84
SILKWORMS
Nat Geog 165:6-7, 24-7, 35 (c,1)
Ja '84
SILVER
--Silver bars
Nat Geog 163:441 (c,1) Ap '83
SILVER INDUSTRY
--16th cent. remelting activity
(Colombia)
Am Heritage 36:88-9 (drawing,c,1)
Ag '85
SILVER MINES
--Played-out mine (Colorado)
Nat Geog 166:212-13 (c,1) Ag '84
SINATRA, FRANK
Ebony 39:104 (4) Je '84
Life 9:62 (2) Fall '86
Life 9:33 (4) D '86
SINBAD THE SAILOR
--Scenes of legendary voyages
Nat Geog 162:2-41 (map,c,1) Jl
'82
SINGAPORE
Smithsonian 13:131 (c,4) Ap '82
--Tiger Balm Garden
Trav/Holiday 157:111 (4) Ap '82
SINGAPORE--COSTUME
Natur Hist 92:46 (c,4) Je '83
SINGAPORE--HISTORY
--Scenes of its founding (1819)
Smithsonian 13:130, 142 (c,1) Ap
'82
SINGERS
Ebony 38:46, 50, 126 (c,1) D '82

SINGERS (cont.)
Ebony 38:58-9 (4) Mr '83
--Choir (Harlem, New York)
Ebony 37:152 (2) My '82
--Choir (Illinois)
Ebony 38:30 (c,4) Jl '83
--Country
Ebony 39:52-3 (c,2) S '84
Life 8:104-5 (4) N '85
Life 9:43-5 (c,1) F '86
--Duets
Ebony 37:64-5, 68 (4) Ja '82
--Female rock stars
Life 5:100-5 (c,1) Mr '82
Ebony 37:66-7 (c,2) Je '82
--Gospel
Ebony 37:57 (2) S '82
--Groups
Ebony 37:90-8 (3) F '82
Ebony 38:54-5 (c,2) N '82
--Motown celebrities
Life 6:128-9 (c,1) My '83
--Reggae (Jamaica)
Nat Geog 167:124-5 (c,2) Ja
'85
--Rock group
Life 5:163-70 (c,1) N '82
Ebony 38:126-30 (c,1) Jl '83
Life 7:87-96 (c,1) S '84
Life 9:62-3 (c,1) Mr '86
Ebony 42:70-2 (c,3) N '86
--Rock stars
Ebony 40:66-72 (c,1) N '84
Ebony 40:155-61 (c,1) D '84
Life 8:36-48 (c,1) Ap '85
Ebony 40:cov., 76-7 (c,1) My
'85
Ebony 40:cov. (c,1) Je '85
Ebony 40:40 (4) O '85
Ebony 41:126-7 (c,1) Jl '86
--Rock stars at "Live-Aid" concert
Life 8:cov., 39-45 (c,1) S '85
--Rock stars at "We Are the World"
recording session
Life 8:36-48 (c,1) Ap '85
Ebony 40:40 (4) O '85
Ebony 41:350 (3) N '85
Life 9:82-3 (c,1) Ja '86
--Rolling Stones
Life 9:73, 260 (c,2) Fall '86
--The Supremes
Life 9:73 (3) Fall '86
--See also
ANDERSON, MARIAN
BEATLES
CARUSO, ENRICO
CHEVALIER, MAURICE

COLE, NAT KING
DYLAN, BOB
GARLAND, JUDY
HOLIDAY, BILLIE
HORNE, LENA
LENNON, JOHN
PIAF, EDITH
PRESLEY, ELVIS
SINATRA, FRANK
SMITH, KATE
VALLEE, RUDY
WASHINGTON, DINAH
SIOUX INDIANS. See also
CRAZY HORSE
SITTING BULL
SIOUX INDIANS (SOUTH DAKOTA)
--COSTUME
Natur Hist 92:80 (4) Ja '83
--1876
Nat Geog 170:788, 806 (4) D '86
--Beaded sneakers
Natur Hist 95:76 (c,4) Jl '86
SIOUX INDIANS--RELICS
--19th cent. dance shields
Am Heritage 37:18-19, 24 (c,1)
Ag '86
SISTINE CHAPEL, VATICAN CITY
Nat Geog 168:760 (c,1) D '85
SITKA, ALASKA
Nat Geog 165:82-3 (c,1) Ja '84
SITTING BULL
Smithsonian 13:63 (4) Ja '83
Nat Geog 170:788 (4) D '86
SKATEBOARDING
Sports Illus 57:32 (c,4) Jl 26 '82
Sports Illus 63:62 (c,4) N 20 '85
--Boy with no legs (Pennsylvania)
Life 7:70-1 (2) F '84
--California
Sports Illus 65:46-7, 50 (c,1) N
24 '86
--Competition
Sports Illus 65:2-3 (c,2) S 1 '86
SKATING
--19th cent. skates
Sports Illus 63:96 (c,2) D 23 '85
--Children (Connecticut)
Trav/Holiday 160:13 (c,4) D '83
--Children (New Hampshire)
Nat Geog 162:796-7 (c,1) D '82
--China
Life 8:154 (c,3) D '85
--Ivory Coast
Nat Geog 162:115 (c,2) Jl '82
--Netherlands
Nat Geog 170:524-5 (c,1) O '86
--Skating rink at shopping mall

SKATING (cont.)
  (Dallas, Texas)
  Nat Geog 166:294-5 (c,1) S '84
  Trav/Holiday 166:43 (c,4) Jl
    '86
--See also
    ROLLER SKATING
SKATING, FIGURE
  Sports Illus 57:92-106 (c,1) D
    6 '82
  Sports Illus 58:75 (c,4) F 14
    '83
  Sports Illus 58:58-9 (c,4) Mr
    21 '83
  Sports Illus 59:35-43 (c,4) N
    7 '83
  Sports Illus 60:2, 32-4 (c,3)
    Ja 30 '84
  Life 7:78-9 (c,1) F '84
  Sports Illus 60:77, 88-92 (c,1)
    F 6 '84
  Smithsonian 15:116 (c,4) D '84
  Sports Illus 62:28-9 (c,1) F 4
    '85
  Sports Illus 62:74-5 (c,3) F
    11 '85
  Sports Illus 62:64, 67 (c,4)
    Mr 18 '85
  Sports Illus 63:23 (c,4) Ag 5
    '85
  Sports Illus 64:38-46 (c,3) Ja
    20 '86
  Sports Illus 64:22-4 (c,2) F 17
    '86
  Sports Illus 64:55-6 (c,3) Mr
    17 '86
  Sports Illus 64:28-30, 35 (c,2)
    Mr 31 '86
  Ebony 41:147-50 (c,1) My '86
--1924 Olympics (Chamonix)
  Sports Illus 59:102-3 (1) D 26
    '83
--1984 Olympics (Sarajevo)
  Sports Illus 60:26-9 (c,3) F
    20 '84
  Sports Illus 60:23-9 (c,2) F 27
    '84
--Slow motion of 3-revolution jump
  Sports Illus 60:92 (c,3) F 6
    '84
--See also
    HENIE, SONJA
SKATING, SPEED
  Sports Illus 56:38 (c,3) F 22
    '82
  Sports Illus 59:57 (c,2) O 31
    '83

Sports Illus 59:46-8 (c,2) N 21
  '83
Sports Illus 60:68, 72 (c,3) F 6
  '84
--1952 Olympics (Oslo)
  Sports Illus 65:64 (4) Jl 7 '86
--1984 Olympics (Sarajevo)
  Sports Illus 60:27 (c,4) F 27 '84
--Practicing with equipment on land
  Sports Illus 59:2 (c,2) N 21 '83
--Vermont race
  Sports Illus 58:48-9 (c,4) F 28
    '83
SKELETONS
  Nat Geog 164:578-9 (c,1) N '83
--1500 B.C. (Thailand)
  Smithsonian 13:100 (c,4) Ja '83
--1st cent. volcano victims (Her-
    culaneum, Italy)
  Nat Geog 162:686-93 (c,1) D '82
  Nat Geog 165:cov., 556-604 (c,1)
    My '84
--16th cent. sailors (Newfoundland)
  Nat Geog 168:56-7 (c,1) Jl '85
--17th cent. Virginia woman
  Nat Geog 161:75 (c,1) Ja '82
--1876 soldier (Montana)
  Nat Geog 170:802-3 (c,1) D '86
--Ancient Australian man
  Nat Geog 168:269 (c,4) Ag '85
--Ancient man
  Nat Geog 168:cov., 563-629 (c,1)
    N '85
--Ancient Maya (Guatemala)
  Nat Geog 169:444 (c,3) Ap '86
--Animals dead from drought (Aus-
    tralia)
  Nat Geog 165:174-5 (c,2) F '84
--Racehorse
  Natur Hist 92:72 (4) Jl '83
--Ramapithecus jaw
  Natur Hist 93:2 (4) Je '84
--Seals
  Life 8:36 (c,2) F '85
--Trout
  Natur Hist 92:28 (c,4) Ap '83
--Viper skeleton
  Life 9:28-9 (1) Fall '86
--See also
    FOSSILS
    SKULLS
SKI JUMPS
  Sports Illus 59:2 (c,1) D 5 '83
SKI LIFTS
  Sports Illus 56:36 (c,2) Ja 18 '82
  Sports Illus 60:63 (c,4) My 14 '84
  Sports Illus 62:42-3 (c,2) F 25 '85

SKIING--CROSS-COUNTRY
  Sports Illus 56:49 (c,3) Ja
    11 '82
  Sports Illus 60:38-9, 53 (c,1)
    F 6 '84
--1984 Olympics (Sarajevo)
  Sports Illus 60:2-3, 19 (c,1) F
    20 '84
--Grand Canyon, Arizona
  Sports Illus 62:96-7 (c,1) Ap
    8 '85
--Maine
  Sports Illus 62:70 (c,3) Mr 4
    '85
--Montana
  Nat Geog 167:680-1 (c,1) My
    '85
--Shooting in biathlon
  Sports Illus 59:104-5 (c,3) N
    28 '83
--Skiing to North Pole
  Nat Geog 170:318-23 (c,1) S
    '86
--Swiss race
  Sports Illus 56:140-1 (c,1) F
    10 '82
--U.S.S.R.
  Sports Illus 62:88-92 (c,3) Ap
    29 '85
--Vermont
  Trav/Holiday 158:4-6 (c,3) D
    '82
SKIING COMPETITIONS
  Sports Illus 58:40-5 (c,1) F 7
    '83
  Sports Illus 58:151 (c,2) F 16
    '83
  Sports Illus 60:22-7 (c,2) Ja
    23 '84
  Sports Illus 64:44-9 (c,1) F 3
    '86
--Cross-country (U.S.S.R.)
  Sports Illus 62:88-92 (c,3) Ap
    29 '85
--Freestyle
  Sports Illus 64:76-8 (c,3) F 17
    '86
--Ski race (Minnesota)
  Trav/Holiday 166:28 (c,4) D
    '86
--Slalom
  Sports Illus 62:48 (c,2) F 4
    '85
  Sports Illus 62:2-3 (c,1) F 18
    '85
--Switzerland
  Sports Illus 62:34, 38, 45

    (c,2) Ja 28 '85
  Nat Geog 169:102-3 (c,1) Ja '86
--World Alpine championships
  Sports Illus 56:22-5 (c,2) F 15
    '82
  Sports Illus 62:2-3, 12-19 (c,1)
    F 18 '85
--World Cup 1983
  Sports Illus 58:28-37 (c,2) Mr 21
    '83
SKIMMERS (BIRDS)
--Black skimmer
  Nat Wildlife 23:56-7 (c,1) O '85
SKIN
--Animal skin seen through electron
    microscope
  Smithsonian 13:151-4 (3) Mr '83
SKIN DIVING
  Nat Geog 162:390-1 (c,2) S '82
  Sports Illus 57:92 (c,4) N 22 '82
  Nat Geog 162:722 (c,2) D '82
  Nat Geog 165:138 (c,3) Ja '84
  Sports Illus 60:106-9 (c,1) F 13
    '84
  Nat Wildlife 24:43 (c,1) O '86
--Exploring shipwrecks
  Nat Geog 161:233-41 (c,1) F '82
  Smithsonian 14:cov., 78-89 (c,1)
    O '83
--Mexico
  Trav/Holiday 161:cov. (c,1) Ja
    '84
--Police divers (New York City,
    New York)
  Nat Geog 170:38-9 (c,1) Jl '86
--Snorkeling (Cayman Islands)
  Nat Geog 167:800-1 (c,1) Je '85
SKULLS
  Sports Illus 60:4 (c,4) Ap 30 '84
--1940s Japanese soldier
  Life 5:58 (c,4) Ap '82
--Ancient condor skull
  Natur Hist 95:12-13 (c,4) Ap '86
--Ancient hominid skull (Kenya)
  Nat Geog 170:419 (c,4) O '86
--Ancient Paleo-Indian skull (Florida)
  Smithsonian 17:78, 80 (c,4) D '86
--Animal skulls
  Natur Hist 95:20, 22 (drawing,4)
    Jl '86
--Bull moose
  Natur Hist 91:72 (drawing,3) Je
    '82
--Camel skull (Egypt)
  Nat Geog 161:211 (c,3) F '82
--Chimpanzees
  Smithsonian 15:57 (c,1) Ag '84

SKULLS (cont.)
--Eastern Orthodox monks
(Greece)
Nat Geog 164:740-1 (c,1) D '83
--Humpback whale
Life 6:91 (c,2) D '83
--Longhorn cattle
Trav/Holiday 159:66 (c,3) Mr
'83
--Piltdown man forgery (1912)
Life 5:18 (4) F '82
--Prehistoric man
Smithsonian 15:50-6 (c,1) Ag
'84
Nat Geog 168:cov., 563-629
(c,1) N '85
--Victims of Khmer Rouge (Cam-
bodia)
Life 7:14 (c,2) N '84
--Victims of Pol Pot (Cambodia)
Nat Geog 167:575 (c,3) My '85
SKY DIVING
--BASE jumpers
Sports Illus 63:82-92 (c,1) Ag
26 '85
--Montana
Smithsonian 15:170 (c,4) Mr '85
--99 divers linked together (Illi-
nois)
Life 8:104-5 (1) O '85
--South Carolina
Life 5:104 (c,2) S '82
--Stacked parachutists (Great
Britain)
Life 8:98-9 (1) N '85
SLAVERY
--18th cent. slave huts (Bon-
aire, Netherlands Antilles)
Sports Illus 60:116 (c,3) F 13
'84
--19th cent. Wedgwood anti-
slavery medallion (G.B.)
Natur Hist 95:18 (4) Ap '86
SLAVERY--U.S.
Nat Geog 166:cov., 2-37 (c,1)
Jl '84
--Early 19th cent.
Am Heritage 34:85-6 (c,3) D
'82
--1860 plantation funeral (Louisi-
ana)
Am Heritage 34:36-7 (paint-
ing,c,1) Je '83
--Former slaves (1860s)
Ebony 41:138 (2) Ag '86
--Underground Railroad
Nat Geog 166:cov., 2-39

(map,c,1) Jl '84
Ebony 40:52-8 (2) D '84
--See also
ABOLITIONISTS
TUBMAN, HARRIET
SLEDS
--19th cent. sleighs
Am Heritage 33:22-3 (c,4) Ap '82
--Baby riding on sled
Sports Illus 64:76 (c,4) Ap 7 '86
--Child on sled (Italy)
Sports Illus 60:66 (c,4) F 6 '84
--Child on sled (Japan)
Nat Geog 166:252-3 (c,1) Ag '84
--Children sledding (France)
Trav/Holiday 163:60 (c,3) Ja '85
--Father pulling child on sled
Life 9:46 (c,2) Ap '86
--Horse-drawn (French Alps)
Trav/Holiday 163:56-7 (c,1) Ja
'85
--Person pulling sledge (Canada)
Nat Geog 164:468-9 (c,1) O '83
--Reindeer sleigh (Lapland)
Life 8:6 (4) Mr '85
--Skeleton sleds
Sports Illus 56:86 (c,4) F 8 '82
--Sleigh riding (Yugoslavia)
Trav/Holiday 160:56 (c,4) N '83
--See also
BOBSLEDDING
DOG SLEDS
SLEEPING
Life 5:92-3 (1) Ap '82
Life 9:19 (c,4) N '86
--Airport lounge
Sports Illus 58:24 (c,4) F 28 '83
--Child in bed with dolls (West Vir-
ginia)
Life 8:150 (c,4) Je '85
--Depictions of dreams
Smithsonian 13:100-5 (c,2) Ag '82
--Dog sleeping in bed with child
(California)
Life 9:55 (c,3) N '86
--Dream research
Life 9:20 (c,4) N '86
--Man sprawled across bed
Am Heritage 36:97 (painting,4)
Je '85
--Mother awakened by son (1955)
Life 9:153 (2) Fall '86
--On bus
Ebony 38:110 (c,4) Jl '83
--Yawning
Life 6:21 (4) Mr '83
Sports Illus 58:34-5 (c,2) Mr 14 '83

SLEEPING BAGS
  Nat Geog 170:309, 312-13 (c,1)
    S '86
SLIME MOLD
  Nat Wildlife 21:14-15 (c,1) Ap
    '83
SLOAN, JOHN
--Early 20th cent. paintings of
    New Mexico
  Am Heritage 33:98-107 (c,1)
    Ap '82
SLOTHS
  Nat Geog 169:478 (c,4) Ap '86
  Trav/Holiday 166:22 (c,3) Jl
    '86
SLUGS
  Natur Hist 95:104-5 (c,1) N
    '86
--Nudibranches
  Natur Hist 92:52-3 (c,1) Ja
    '83
SLUMS
--1888 (New York City, New York)
  Am Heritage 34:21 (2) F '83
--1910 (New York City, New York)
  Am Heritage 36:100 (4) F '85
--Brooklyn, New York
  Life 6:48-9 (c,1) Ap '83
  Nat Geog 163:602-3 (c,1) My
    '83
--Camden, New Jersey
  Sports Illus 57:40-1 (c,2) Ag
    2 '82
--Ciudad Juarez, Mexico
  Nat Geog 167:740-1 (c,1) Je
    '85
--Delhi, India
  Smithsonian 16:44-5, 49 (c,1)
    Je '85
--Harlem, New York City, New
    York
  Life 8:124, 140 (c,2) O '85
--Honduras
  Nat Geog 164:624-5 (c,1) N '83
--Jamaica
  Nat Geog 167:126-7 (c,1) Ja '85
--Lifestyle of inner-city teenage
    boy (Detroit, Michigan)
  Life 9:51-6 (1) Mr '86
--Manila, Philippines
  Nat Geog 170:108-9, 114 (c,1)
    Jl '86
--Mexico City, Mexico
  Nat Geog 166:151 (c,2) Ag '84
--New York City, New York
  Life 5:26 (c,3) N '82
--Panama City, Panama

  Sports Illus 59:82 (c,4) N 7 '83
--San Juan, Puerto Rico
  Nat Geog 163:532-3 (c,1) Ap '83
--Washington, D.C.
  Nat Geog 163:88-9, 117-19 (c,1)
    Ja '83
SMELL
--Research on smells
  Nat Geog 170:324-61 (c,1) S '86
SMITH, KATE
  Am Heritage 37:47 (4) Ag '86
SMITHSONIAN INSTITUTION,
    WASHINGTON, D.C.
  Smithsonian 13:29 (c,4) N '82
  Smithsonian 13:74-80 (drawing,c,1)
    F '83
  Life 6:98 (c,4) D '83
  Smithsonian 15:79-82 (drawing,c,1)
    S '84
--1900 children's room
  Smithsonian 16:24 (c,4) Ja '86
--Museum Support Center, Suitland,
    Maryland
  Smithsonian 14:20-1 (c,4) My '83
--Smithsonian's heraldic mace
  Smithsonian 15:24 (c,3) Jl '84
--Warehoused collection
  Life 6:91-8 (c,1) D '83
SMOKE
--Canadian hills
  Nat Geog 164:120-1 (c,1) Jl '83
--Forest fire (Montana)
  Smithsonian 17:43 (c,3) Ag '86
--Forest fire (Northwest)
  Smithsonian 16:90 (c,4) Ag '85
--Ontario smokestack
  Life 7:62-3 (c,1) N '84
--Smoke from chimneys (Alaska)
  Nat Wildlife 24:34 (c,4) Ap '86
Smoking. See
    CIGAR SMOKING
    CIGARETTE SMOKING
    MARIJUANA
    PIPE SMOKING
SMOLENSK, U.S.S.R.
  Nat Geog 167:308 (c,1) Mr '85
SNAILS
  Nat Wildlife 20:10 (c,4) O '82
  Natur Hist 91:63 (c,3) D '82
  Smithsonian 15:124 (c,4) Mr '85
  Nat Geog 169:255 (c,1) F '86
  Natur Hist 95:44-9 (c,1) My '86
  Nat Wildlife 24:8 (c,4) O '86
--Shells
  Natur Hist 92:12-16 (3) Ap '83
  Natur Hist 94:18 (drawing,c,3) Ja
    '85

SNAKE CHARMERS
--Morocco
    Trav/Holiday 160:5 (c,2) D
        '83
SNAKE RIVER, NORTHWEST
    Trav/Holiday 164:58-61 (c,1)
        S '85
SNAKES
--Boomslang
    Nat Geog 163:369 (c,1) Mr '83
--Cat-eyed snake
    Nat Geog 163:62 (c,2) Ja '83
--Eastern indigo snake
    Natur Hist 93:60 (c,4) My '84
--Green snake
    Sports Illus 65:90 (c,4) O 20
        '86
--Green snake eating earthworm
    Nat Wildlife 22:50 (c,4) Je '84
--Green vine snake
    Life 5:44-5 (c,1) S '82
--Mangrove snake
    Nat Geog 167:771 (c,3) Je '85
--Rat snake
    Nat Wildlife 22:41 (c,4) Ag '84
--Tree snake
    Nat Geog 168:332 (c,3) S '85
--Water snakes
    Smithsonian 15:125 (c,4) Mr
        '85
--See also
        ADDERS
        BOA CONSTRICTORS
        COBRAS
        FER-DE-LANCE
        GARTER SNAKES
        KING SNAKES
        PYTHONS
        RATTLESNAKES
        VIPERS
SNOW SCENES
    Nat Wildlife 22:4-13 (c,1) D
        '83
--Amman, Jordan
    Nat Geog 165:258-9 (c,2) F '84
--Banff National Park, Alberta
    Trav/Holiday 163:55 (c,1) Ja
        '85
--Child playing in snow
    Nat Wildlife 24:5 (c,1) D '85
--Iowa farmland
    Life 7:30-1 (1) F '84
--Montana wilderness
    Nat Geog 167:680-1 (c,1) My
        '85
--Maine
    Nat Geog 166:798-9 (c,1) D '84

Life 9:278-9 (1) Fall '86
--Midwestern prairie
    Nat Wildlife 25:22-3 (c,1) D '86
--Nepal mountains
    Smithsonian 13:cov., 50-61 (c,1)
        O '82
--New Hampshire mountains
    Nat Geog 162:790-1 (c,1) D '82
--"Snow rollers" (Vermont)
    Nat Wildlife 21:9 (c,3) D '82
--Urban scenes
    Life 5:107 (3) Mr '82
--Wildlife in snow
    Nat Wildlife 21:4-11 (c,1) D '82
--Wisconsin forest
    Nat Wildlife 21:4 (c,3) D '82
--Yellowstone trees covered with
    snow
    Nat Wildlife 20:37-9 (c,1) F '82
--See also
        AVALANCHES
        BLIZZARDS
        SNOW STORMS
SNOW SCULPTURES
--Snowman (Jordan)
    Nat Geog 165:258 (c,4) F '84
--Snowman (Yugoslavia)
    Sports Illus 58:84 (c,4) Mr 14
        '83
SNOW STORMS
--1900 blizzards (Connecticut)
    Am Heritage 37:27 (painting,c,2)
        Je '86
--Alaska
    Nat Geog 165:820-1 (1) Je '84
--Austria
    Nat Geog 167:443 (c,1) Ap '85
--Japan
    Nat Geog 166:248-9 (c,2) Ag '84
--Poland
    Life 9:394-5 (c,1) Fall '86
SNOWFLAKES
    Nat Wildlife 23:42-5 (c,1) D '84
SNOWMOBILING
--Antarctica
    Smithsonian 13:cov., 44-9 (c,1)
        D '82
--Iowa
    Life 7:30 (4) F '84
SNOWSHOES
--Worn on 1909 Arctic expedition
    Ebony 40:114 (4) S '85
SNUFFBOXES
--Early 19th cent. (France)
    Nat Geog 161:169 (c,4) F '82
SOCCER
    Sports Illus 65:62-3 (c,3) O 27 '86

SOCIETY ISLANDS, POLYNESIA
(cont.)
Trav/Holiday 161:59-61 (c,1)
Ja '84
--See also
TAHITI
SOD HOUSES
--Late 19th cent. (Nebraska)
Natur Hist 94:44-51 (1) S '85
SOFAS
--17th cent. (Massachusetts)
Smithsonian 13:111 (c,4) Je
'82
--1764 gilded settee (Great Brit-
ain)
Life 8:36-7 (c,1) N '85
--Red couch
Life 5:14-30 (c,1) N '82
SOFIA, BULGARIA
Trav/Holiday 163:cov., 54-7
(c,1) F '85
SOFTBALL
--Child swinging bat (Bahamas)
Nat Geog 162:387 (c,1) S '82
SOFTBALL--AMATEUR
--Slo-pitch
Sports Illus 65:68-82 (c,1) Jl
28 '86
SOFTBALL--COLLEGE
--Women
Sports Illus 58:83 (c,4) My 23
'83
SOFTBALL TEAMS
Life 5:39 (c,4) Ag '82
SOIL
Nat Wildlife 23:cov., 14-23
(c,1) F '85
--Farm soil problems
Nat Geog 166:350-89 (c,1) S
'84
--Soil erosion
Nat Wildlife 23:14-17 (c,1) F
'85
Solar eclipses. See
ECLIPSES
SOLAR ENERGY
--Model of solar house (Israel)
Nat Geog 168:24 (c,4) Jl '85
--Solar-heated house (New Mexico)
Nat Geog 161:324-5 (c,1) Mr
'82
--Solar panels
Nat Wildlife 22:37 (c,4) Je '84
--Solar-powered vehicle (Aus-
tralia)
Nat Geog 164:600-7 (c,1) N '83
--Solar reflector boiling water

(China)
Nat Geog 165:302 (c,1) Mr '84
--Solar spacecraft
Smithsonian 12:52-61 (c,1) F '82
Soldiers. See
MILITARY COSTUME
WARFARE
SOLE (FISH)
Smithsonian 13:130 (c,4) Mr '83
Solomon Islands. See
GUADALCANAL
SOLZHENITSYN, ALEKSANDR
Life 5:4, 44-8 (c,1) F '82
Life 9:259 (c,3) Fall '86
--Vermont home
Life 5:44 (c,4) F '82
SOMALIA--COSTUME
--Refugees in Ethiopian camp
Nat Geog 163:634-5 (c,2) My '83
SORROW
--Arab woman (Lebanon)
Life 5:27 (2) Ag '82
--Executed man's widow
Life 5:52 (4) Mr '82
--Mother of murdered boy (Georgia)
Life 5:40-1 (1) Ja '82
--Mother weeping for lost son
Life 5:71 (c,2) N '82
--See also
GRIEF
SOUSA, JOHN PHILIP
Am Heritage 33:65 (4) F '82
Am Heritage 37:44 (4) Ag '86
--Tombstone (Washington, D.C.)
Am Heritage 33:67 (c,4) Je '82
SOUTH AFRICA
--Mooi River, Natal Province
Natur Hist 94:40-1 (c,2) Ja '85
--See also
CAPE TOWN
SOUTH AFRICA--COSTUME
--Black South Africans (1948)
Smithsonian 16:164 (4) D '85
--Military
Nat Geog 161:762-3 (c,1) Je '82
--Ndebele people
Nat Geog 169:cov., 261-82 (c,1)
F '86
SOUTH AFRICA--HOUSING
--Ndebele people
Nat Geog 169:262-3, 270-1 (c,1)
F '86
SOUTH AFRICA--MAPS
Nat Geog 169:265 (c,2) F '86
SOUTH AFRICA--POLITICS AND
GOVERNMENT
--Anti apartheid demonstration

SOUTH AFRICA--POLITICS AND
   GOVERNMENT (cont.)
   Ebony 40:94 (3) Ag '85
--Anti apartheid demonstration
   (California)
   Life 8:63 (2) Je '85
--Anti apartheid movement
   Ebony 40:132-44 (c,3) My '85
   Ebony 41:53-62 (3) D '85
--Anti apartheid riot victim
   Life 8:60-1 (1) My '85
--Bishop Tutu
   Life 8:109-14 (c,1) N '85
   Life 9:18 (c,2) Ja '86
--Black lifestyles
   Life 8:101-10 (1) Je '85
--Winnie Mandela
   Life 9:30-6 (c,1) Ag '86
--Murder of black informer
   Life 8:48-9 (1) S '85
--Police beating black woman
   Life 7:198 (2) N '84
SOUTH CAROLINA
--1861 shelling of Fort Sumter
   Am Heritage 37:98 (4) Ap '86
--Chattooga River area
   Nat Geog 163:458-77 (c,1) Ap
   '83
--Cypress Gardens
   Nat Geog 164:800-1 (c,1) D '83
--Daufuskie Island
   Smithsonian 13:88-97 (1) O '82
   Nat Geog 164:814-15 (c,2) D
   '83
--Hilton Head resort
   Nat Geog 164:817 (c,1) D '83
--Kiawah Island
   Trav/Holiday 161:55-6 (c,2) Ja
   '84
--Myrtle Beach
   Trav/Holiday 164:50-1 (c,4) S
   '85
--See also
   CHARLESTON
   COLUMBIA
   SAVANNAH RIVER
SOUTH DAKOTA
   Trav/Holiday 162:cov., 38-43
   (c,1) Jl '84
--Edgemont
   Life 7:106-7 (c,1) Jl '84
--Longhorn Saloon, Scenic
   Smithsonian 15:139 (c,4) N '84
--See also
   MOUNT RUSHMORE
South Korea. See
   KOREA, SOUTH

South Pacific. See
   PACIFIC ISLANDS
SOUTH POLE
--1911 photo
   Smithsonian 13:91 (4) Mr '83
SOUTH YEMEN
   Nat Geog 168:474-7, 485, 488-500
   (map,c,1) O '85
SOUTH YEMEN--COSTUME
   Nat Geog 168:488-500 (c,1) O '85
SOUTHERN U.S.
   Trav/Holiday 157:75-90, 109 (c,4)
   Mr '82
--18th-20th cent. paintings
   Am Heritage 34:29-41 (c,1) Je '83
--19th-20th cent. depictions of
   Southern women
   Am Heritage 34:82-91 (c,1) D '82
--Appalachia
   Nat Geog 163:793-819 (map,c,1)
   Je '83
--Chattooga River area
   Nat Geog 163:458-77 (map,c,1)
   Ap '83
--Scenes of the South
   Trav/Holiday 161:41 (c,2) Mr '84
   Trav/Holiday 163:89-103 (c,2)
   Mr '85
   Trav/Holiday 165:87 (c,2) Mr '86
--See also
   BLUE RIDGE MOUNTAINS
   MISSISSIPPI RIVER
   TENNESSEE RIVER
SOUTHERN U.S.--ART
--Black folk crafts
   Life 6:52-8 (c,1) Ag '83
SOUTHERN U.S.--MAPS
--West Florida (1781)
   Am Heritage 33:37 (3) Ap '82
SOUTHWESTERN U.S.--MAPS
--Colorado River
   Nat Wildlife 23:47 (c,2) O '85
SOUVENIRS
--20th cent. Olympics souvenirs
   Life 7:92-7 (c,1) Summer '84
--1910 Halley's Comet souvenirs
   Life 8:34-5 (c,2) O '85
--1984 Olympics pins
   Life 8:109 (c,3) Ja '85
--Alamo souvenirs
   Am Heritage 37:102-5 (c,2) Je '86
--Football team souvenirs
   Sports Illus 57:162 (c,4) S 1 '82
--Statue of Liberty souvenirs
   Nat Geog 170:14-15 (c,1) Jl '86
   Life 9:76-9 (c,3) Jl '86

SPACECRAFT (cont.)
(Netherlands)
Life 9:12-13 (c,1) Jl '86
--Viking 2 lander
Nat Geog 167:32 (c,3) Ja '85
--See also
ROCKETS
SATELLITES
UNIDENTIFIED FLYING
OBJECTS
SPAIN
--Cantabrian countryside
Natur Hist 92:46-7 (c,1) Ag
'83
--Casares, Andalusia
Trav/Holiday 157:28 (4) My '82
Smithsonian 13:144-5 (c,3) Je
'82
--Catalonia
Nat Geog 165:94-127 (map,c,1)
Ja '84
--La Mancha area
Trav/Holiday 161:73-5 (c,1) Ap
'84
--Northwestern region
Natur Hist 94:68-75 (map,c,1)
N '85
--Pamplona garlic market
Natur Hist 92:86 (4) My '83
--Pedreña
Sports Illus 63:68-9, 74, 76
(c,1) Jl 15 '85
--Picasso murals (Caltojar)
Life 5:100-2 (c,1) Ap '82
--Santillana Del Mar street
Trav/Holiday 159:14 (4) My '83
--See also
BARCELONA
DON QUIXOTE
DOURO RIVER
EBRO RIVER
MADRID
MAJORCA
MONTSERRAT MONASTERY
TOLEDO
SPAIN--COSTUME
Trav/Holiday 161:74-5, 81 (c,1)
Ap '84
Nat Geog 166:483-9 (c,1) O '84
--16th cent. soldiers (Mexico)
Nat Geog 166:420, 442, 459
(painting,c,1) O '84
--Basque costume (Western U.S.)
Trav/Holiday 162:48-51 (c,1)
Jl '84
--Catalonia
Nat Geog 165:94-127 (c,1) Ja '84

--Farmers
Natur Hist 94:68-75 (c,1) N '85
--Flamenco dancers (Seville)
Trav/Holiday 165:48-9 (c,3) Je
'86
--Hunters
Nat Geog 161:172-3 (c,1) F '82
--King Juan Carlos
Life 8:46-54 (c,1) D '85
Nat Geog 169:181 (c,1) F '86
Ebony 41:72 (c,4) F '86
--Madrid
Nat Geog 169:142-81 (c,1) F '86
--Royalty
Life 8:46-54 (c,1) D '85
--Security guards
Sports Illus 56:33 (c,4) Je 21 '82
--Toledo
Nat Geog 161:730-49 (c,1) Je '82
SPAIN--HISTORY
--1783 miniature of Spanish glories
Am Heritage 33:114 (c,2) Ap '82
--Archives at Simancas castle
Nat Geog 166:485 (c,3) O '84
--Picasso's "Guernica" scene of
Spanish Civil War
Nat Geog 169:162-3 (painting,c,2)
F '86
--See also
FRANCO, FRANCISCO
SPANISH-AMERICAN WAR
SPANISH CIVIL WAR
SPAIN--RITES AND FESTIVALS
--Bonfires of St. John (Alicante)
Nat Geog 162:698-9 (c,1) D '82
--Reenactment of battle of Matamoros
(Majorca)
Trav/Holiday 164:26 (c,4) Jl '85
SPANIELS
--Brittany spaniel
Sports Illus 63:96 (painting,c,4)
N 11 '85
--English springer spaniel
Sports Illus 63:4 (c,4) Jl 15 '85
SPANISH-AMERICAN WAR
--1898 cartoon about yellow journal-
ism
Am Heritage 33:50-1 (drawing,1)
O '82
--Yellow fever victim
Am Heritage 35:68-9 (1) O '84
SPANISH CIVIL WAR
--Loyalist being shot (1936)
Life 9:127 (2) Fall '86
SPARROWS
Natur Hist 91:60-1 (c,1) My '82
Smithsonian 13:118 (c,1) Jl '82

SPARROWS (cont.)
  Nat Wildlife 23:12, 14 (c,4)
    Ap '85
--House sparrow's spread across
    America
  Smithsonian 17:174-90 (paint-
    ing,c,1) N '86
SPECTATORS
--1886 America's Cup yacht race
  Natur Hist 92:66-7 (engrav-
    ing,c,1) My '83
--Baseball
  Sports Illus 58:29 (c,2) Ja 24
    '83
  Life 6:8-9 (c,1) Ag '83
  Sports Illus 61:36-50 (paint-
    ing,c,1) O 1 '84
  Sports Illus 65:24-5 (c,4) N
    3 '86
--Baseball (Japan)
  Sports Illus 63:2-3 (c,1) S 9
    '85
  Smithsonian 17:109, 112-13
    (c,2) S '86
  Nat Geog 170:625 (c,4) N '86
--Baseball fans' T-shirts
  Sports Illus 58:22 (c,4) Ap 25
    '83
--Basketball
  Sports Illus 56:56-9 (draw-
    ing,c,4) Mr 1 '82
--Boat race
  Sports Illus 59:2-3 (c,1) S 26
    '83
--Boat race (Bahamas)
  Nat Geog 162:376-7 (c,2) S '82
--Cold football fans
  Sports Illus 56:24 (c,4) Ja 18
    '82
--Destructive football fans
  Sports Illus 57:36 (c,2) D 6
    '82
  Sports Illus 58:62-74 (paint-
    ing,c,1) Ja 31 '83
--Football
  Sports Illus 57:20-1 (c,1) S 1
    '82
  Sports Illus 59:202-11 (c,1) S
    1 '83
  Smithsonian 14:140-1 (c,1) N
    '83
  Sports Illus 63:43 (c,3) O 28
    '85
--Football fans grabbing player
  Sports Illus 65:111 (c,2) D 22
    '86
--Football fans in bar

  Sports Illus 57:170-1 (draw-
    ing,c,1) S 1 '82
--Football team name printed on
    fans' chests
  Sports Illus 64:2-3 (c,1) Ja 6
    '86
--Lone football fan in rain
  Sports Illus 62:2-3 (c,1) Mr 4
    '86
--Football fans toppling goal post
  Sports Illus 59:26-7 (c,1) N 7
    '83
  Sports Illus 59:27 (c,4) N 28 '83
--Golf
  Sports Illus 59:14-17 (c,1) Jl 25
    '83
  Sports Illus 60:54 (c,4) Mr 26
    '84
--Horse racing fans (Florida)
  Sports Illus 62:6-7 (c,1) Ap 8
    '85
--Kentucky Derby
  Sports Illus 58:42-8 (painting,c,1)
    My 2 '83
--Regatta (Great Britain)
  Sports Illus 57:36-49 (c,1) Jl 5
    '82
--Riot at England-Italy soccer match
    (Belgium)
  Sports Illus 62:2-3, 20-30 (c,1)
    Je 10 '85
  Life 8:60-1 (1) Jl '85
--Franklin D. Roosevelt's funeral
    (Washington, D.C.)
  Ebony 41:152 (4) N '85
--Sleeping crew fans (Great Britain)
  Sports Illus 63:2-3 (c,1) Jl 15
    '85
--Soccer game (South Africa)
  Sports Illus 58:78-9 (c,1) My 16
    '83
--Soccer game (Spain)
  Nat Geog 165:94-5 (c,1) Ja '84
--Studying horse racing form (New
    York)
  Sports Illus 65:2-3 (c,1) Ag 11
    '86
--Surfing (California)
  Sports Illus 65:14-15 (c,3) S 8
    '86
--Tennis
  Sports Illus 65:45-8 (c,2) S 1 '86
--Tennis fans (West Germany)
  Sports Illus 63:20-1 (c,2) Jl 22
    '85
--Wrestling
  Sports Illus 57:21 (c,4) Ag 23 '82

SPECTATORS (cont.)
Life 8:30-1 (c,1) S '85
--Young baseball fans at spring
training (Florida)
Sports Illus 62:2-3 (c,1) Mr
18 '85
SPECTATORS--HUMOR
--Baseball
Sports Illus 61:36-50 (paint-
ing,c,1) O 1 '84
--Baseball fans reading box
scores
Sports Illus 58:84-6 (draw-
ing,c,1) Ap 4 '83
--Football fans
Sports Illus 57:120-6 (draw-
ing,c,1) S 1 '82
--Indianapolis 500
Sports Illus 56:42-7 (draw-
ing,c,2) My 31 '82
Speechmaking. See
PUBLIC SPEAKING
SPERM WHALES
Trav/Holiday 160:20 (draw-
ing,4) Ag '83
Nat Geog 166:774-85 (c,1) D
'84
Natur Hist 95:4-9 (c,2) Je '86
--Whale smashing boat (19th cent.)
Natur Hist 95:2 (painting,4)
Ag '86
SPHINX, EGYPT
Smithsonian 17:78-92 (c,1) Ap
'86
--Wind's role in its creation
Nat Geog 161:212-13 (c,1) F
'82
SPICE INDUSTRY
--Grenada
Trav/Holiday 164:55 (c,4) Ag
'85
--History of frankincense trade
(Arabia)
Nat Geog 168:474-513 (map,c,1)
O '85
SPICES
--Frankincense
Nat Geog 168:484, 501 (c,4) O
'85
--Myrrh
Nat Geog 168:500-1 (c,3) O '85
--See also
GINGER
MUSTARD PLANTS
PEPPERS
POPPIES
SAGE

THYME
SPIDERS
Nat Wildlife 20:22 (c,4) Ag '82
Natur Hist 92:44 (c,4) Je '83
Smithsonian 14:100-3 (c,1) O '83
Natur Hist 92:62-9 (c,1) D '83
Nat Wildlife 23:64 (c,1) D '84
Nat Geog 167:768-9 (c,2) Je '85
--Crab spiders
Nat Wildlife 21:68 (c,1) D '82
--Sea spider
Nat Geog 169:510 (c,4) Ap '86
--Webs
Nat Wildlife 21:30 (4) Ap '83
Natur Hist 92:64-7 (c,1) D '83
Nat Wildlife 23:64 (c,1) D '84
--See also
TARANTULAS
SPIDERWORT PLANTS
Nat Geog 163:391 (c,3) Mr '83
Natur Hist 94:83 (c,4) O '85
SPIES
--FBI seizing Soviet spy
Life 9:66-7 (c,1) S '86
--Russians stealing U.S. high tech
secrets
Life 6:28-36 (c,1) Ap '83
--See also
MATA HARI
SPINNING WHEELS
--19th cent.
Nat Geog 166:30 (c,4) Jl '84
--See also
YARN SPINNING
SPIREA PLANTS
Nat Wildlife 22:4, 7 (c,4) O '84
SPOKANE, WASHINGTON
Trav/Holiday 161:54-6 (c,1) Ap
'84
Ebony 39:122 (c,4) Ag '84
SPONGES
Nat Wildlife 21:45-9 (c,1) Ap '83
Sports Illus 60:108 (c,2) F 13 '84
Natur Hist 93:63 (c,3) D '84
Nat Geog 167:801 (c,3) Je '85
--1871 household sponges (Pennsyl-
vania)
Am Heritage 36:38 (2) Ag '85
SPOONBILLS
--Roseate
Natur Hist 92:68 (painting,c,3)
S '83
Smithsonian 15:122 (c,1) Mr '85
Natur Hist 94:69 (c,4) Je '85
Nat Wildlife 24:38-41 (c,1) Je '86
SPORTS
--Athletes training

SPORTSWEAR (cont.)
--Bobsledding shorts
    Sports Illus 65:16 (c,4) D 22
    '86
--Jogging suits
    Ebony 39:72, 78 (c,4) Je '84
--Women's tennis bodysuit
    Sports Illus 63:22 (c,2) Jl 8
    '85
SPORTSWEAR--HUMOR
--Sports clothes worn in cities
    Smithsonian 15:123-37 (draw-
    ing,c,1) Ja '85
SPRING
--Fields of flowers (California)
    Nat Wildlife 22:4-7 (c,1) Je
    '84
--Michigan stream
    Nat Wildlife 22:56-7 (c,2) O '84
SPRINGBOKS
    Nat Geog 163:352-3, 373-7
    (c,1) Mr '83
Springs. See
    HOT SPRINGS
SPRUCE TREES
    Natur Hist 94:58-65 (c,1) Ja
    '85
--Harmed by acid rain
    Natur Hist 92:4 (4) Ag '83
SQUASH PLAYING
    Sports Illus 56:52 (c,4) Je 28
    '82
    Sports Illus 58:55, 58 (c,3) My
    16 '83
    Sports Illus 65:7 (c,4) N 10
    '86
SQUID
    Natur Hist 91:24-7 (c,1) Ap
    '82
    Nat Geog 165:475 (c,4) Ap '84
    Smithsonian 16:48-9 (c,4) Ap
    '85
SQUIRRELS
    Trav/Holiday 158:6 (4) Jl '82
    Nat Geog 163:370 (c,4) Mr '83
    Nat Wildlife 21:2 (c,3) Ap '83
    Nat Wildlife 22:62 (c,4) D '83
    Nat Wildlife 22:31 (4) Ap '84
    Nat Wildlife 22:14-15 (c,1) Ag
    '84
    Nat Wildlife 24:56 (c,4) Ap '86
--Ground squirrels
    Nat Wildlife 24:63 (c,3) D '85
--Red squirrels
    Natur Hist 95:28 (c,4) Mr '86
--Hang gliding
    Life 6:100 (c,2) Mr '83

--See also
    FLYING SQUIRRELS
SRI LANKA
    Trav/Holiday 158:41-3 (c,1) S '82
--Adam's Peak
    Nat Geog 162:20 (c,3) Jl '82
--Tea plantation
    Smithsonian 12:98 (c,1) F '82
--Wildlife
    Nat Geog 164:254-78 (map,c,1)
    Ag '83
SRI LANKA--ART
--Ancient rock painting
    Trav/Holiday 163:46 (c,4) Ap '85
SRI LANKA--COSTUME
    Nat Geog 162:18-19 (c,1) Jl '82
    Trav/Holiday 158:41-3 (c,1) S
    '82
--Farm workers
    Trav/Holiday 165:54 (c,4) Ap '86
STABLES
--Belmont Park, New York
    Sports Illus 57:32-3 (c,3) O 18
    '82
--Breeding barn
    Sports Illus 65:46-7 (c,2) S 15
    '86
--British estate
    Life 8:38 (c,2) N '85
--Horse museum (Chantilly, France)
    Smithsonian 14:62-9 (c,1) My '83
STADIUMS
--19th cent. South End Grounds,
    Boston, Massachusetts
    Am Heritage 34:70-1 (2) Je '83
--1840s Elysian Baseball Field,
    Hoboken, New Jersey
    Sports Illus 64:34 (painting,c,4)
    Je 30 '86
--1903 Huntington Avenue Baseball
    Grounds, Boston, Mass.
    Am Heritage 34:74-5 (1) Je '83
--Aerial view of University of Texas
    stadium interior
    Smithsonian 14:144-5 (c,3) N '83
--Ancient Olympia, Greece
    Natur Hist 93:65 (c,2) Je '84
--Appleton baseball fields, Wisconsin
    Sports Illus 65:37-9 (c,2) Ag 11
    '86
--Arrowhead, Kansas City, Missouri
    Sports Illus 63:42 (c,4) Ag 12
    '85
--Artificial turf
    Sports Illus 63:34-62 (c,1) Ag 12
    '85
--Azteca, Mexico City, Mexico

STAIRCASES (cont.)
Sports Illus 62:50 (c,4) Je 3
'85
--Staircase scene of 74 deaths
during 1913 fire stampede
(Calumet, Michigan)
Am Heritage 37:38-9, 47 (c,1)
Ap '86
Am Heritage 37:9 (c,4) Ag '86
--See also
ESCALATORS
Stalingrad. See
VOLGOGRAD
STAMPS
--Duck stamps
Smithsonian 13:67-72 (paint-
ing,c,1) Je '82
Nat Geog 166:582 (c,4) N '84
Nat Wildlife 24:9 (drawing,4)
Ap '86
--Wildlife stamps
Nat Wildlife 24:16 (c,4) D '85
--See also
POSTAGE STAMPS
STANFORD UNIVERSITY, PALO
ALTO, CALIFORNIA
--Linear acceleration center
Nat Geog 162:477 (c,1) O '82
STARFISH
Nat Wildlife 20:cov., 40-7 (c,1)
F '82
Nat Geog 165:470 (c,2) Ap '84
Nat Wildlife 22:60 (c,4) Ap '84
Nat Wildlife 23:62-3 (c,1) D '84
Smithsonian 16:104-9 (c,1) N
'85
Nat Geog 169:259 (c,4) F '86
Nat Geog 169:503, 510-11 (c,1)
Ap '86
Smithsonian 17:127 (c,4) My '86
--Fossils
Natur Hist 95:64-5 (c,1) My '86
STARS
Nat Geog 163:cov., 707A-733
(c,1) Je '83
--Beta Pictoris
Life 7:191 (c,2) D '84
Nat Geog 167:16 (c,4) Ja '85
--Birth and death of stars
Nat Geog 163:714-17, 728-9
(c,1) Je '83
--Nova
Nat Geog 163:719 (4) Je '83
--Radio photo of R Aquarii
Natur Hist 92:24 (c,4) Je '83
--Supernova eta Carinae
Natur Hist 92:26 (c,4) Jl '83

--Used as symbols
Smithsonian 14:131 (c,4) Jl '83
--See also
CONSTELLATIONS
GALAXIES
Starvation. See
MALNUTRITION
STASSEN, HAROLD
Am Heritage 37:66, 70 (2) F '86
STATESMEN
--1950 state governors
Life 9:106 (3) Fall '86
--See also
ADAMS, SAMUEL
BARUCH, BERNARD
BLAINE, JAMES G.
BOONE, DANIEL
BRECKINRIDGE, JOHN C.
BRYAN, WILLIAM JENNINGS
BUNCHE, RALPH
BURR, AARON
CHURCHILL, WINSTON
CROCKETT, DAVEY
DEWEY, THOMAS
DISRAELI, BENJAMIN
DULLES, JOHN FOSTER
EDEN, SIR ANTHONY
FISH, HAMILTON
FRANKLIN, BENJAMIN
GARIBALDI, GIUSEPPE
GEORGE, HENRY
GERRY, ELBRIDGE
HAMILTON, ALEXANDER
HARRIMAN, W. AVERELL
HOUSTON, SAM
HUGHES, CHARLES EVANS
HUMPHREY, HUBERT H.
JAY, JOHN
KENNAN, GEORGE F.
KENNEDY, JOSEPH P.
KENNEDY, ROBERT
LANDON, ALFRED M.
LEE, ROBERT E.
LIVINGSTON, ROBERT
LONG, HUEY
McCARTHY, JOSEPH
McCORMACK, JOHN
MELLON, ANDREW W.
PENN, WILLIAM
PETAIN, MARSHAL
RAYBURN, SAM
REVERE, PAUL
SANTA ANNA
SEWARD, WILLIAM HENRY
SHERMAN, ROGER
STASSEN, HAROLD
STEVENSON, ADLAI

STATESMEN (cont.)
STEVENS, THADDEUS
TWEED, WILLIAM MARCY
U.S. PRESIDENTS
WALKER, JIMMY
WEBSTER, DANIEL
WILLKIE, WENDELL
Stations. See
RAILROAD STATIONS
Statues. See
LIBERTY, STATUE OF
MONUMENTS
SCULPTURE
STEAMBOATS
--1820s
Am Heritage 38:25 (drawing,4)
D '86
--1865 (West Virginia)
Am Heritage 33:99 (4) Je '82
--Vermont
Am Heritage 33:20-1 (c,4) Ap
'82
Sports Illus 62:78 (c,3) Je 10
'85
STEEL INDUSTRY
--Minimills
Life 7:118-24 (c,1) N '84
STEIN, GERTRUDE
Life 9:167 (4) Fall '86
STEINEM, GLORIA
Smithsonian 13:107 (4) Mr '83
STEINMETZ, CHARLES
Am Heritage 36:71 (1) O '85
Sternwheelers. See
RIVERBOATS
STEVENS, THADDEUS
Am Heritage 34:11 (4) O '83
STEVENSON, ADLAI
Am Heritage 35:49-53, 64 (1)
Ag '84
Smithsonian 15:68 (4) O '84
STEVENSON, ADLAI
--1960 presidential campaign
Am Heritage 36:12 (3) D '84
STEVENSON, ROBERT LOUIS
--Tomb (Western Samoa)
Nat Geog 168:473 (c,1) O '85
STEWART, JAMES
Am Heritage 35:47 (4) D '83
Life 9:182 (c,2) My '86
STIEGLITZ, ALFRED
--"Water Tower and Radio City"
Smithsonian 13:138 (4) N '82
STILT HOUSES
--Cambodia
Nat Geog 161:612-13 (c,1) My
'82

STOCK EXCHANGES
--American (New York)
Life 5:15 (c,4) N '82
--Madrid, Spain
Nat Geog 169:174-5 (c,1) F '86
STOCKHOLM, SWEDEN
Trav/Holiday 161:115 (4) Mr '84
Trav/Holiday 161:58-61 (c,2) My
'84
STONE MOUNTAIN, GEORGIA
--Laser light show on rock
Nat Geog 165:337 (c,1) Mr '84
--Skylift
Ebony 41:80 (c,3) My '86
--Stone Mountain Park
Trav/Holiday 159:93 (4) Mr '83
STORES
--Mid 19th cent. (Atlanta, Georgia)
Nat Geog 166:8-9 (1) Jl '84
--1880 gun store reconstruction
Trav/Holiday 163:85 (4) Ja '85
--1901 cigar store
Am Heritage 34:98 (drawing,c,3)
D '82
--1920s display of radios (New York
City, New York)
Am Heritage 34:66 (2) Ag '83
--Antique shops (Michigan)
Trav/Holiday 163:68, 71, 78 (c,2)
F '85
--Baghdad, Iraq
Nat Geog 167:96-7 (c,2) Ja '85
--Bookstore (Budapest, Hungary)
Smithsonian 17:57 (c,4) N '86
--Bookstores (Paris, France)
Trav/Holiday 158:61-2 (c,4) N '82
--Clothing (Maine)
Sports Illus 63:87 (c,3) D 2 '85
--Convenience store (Rhode Island)
Am Heritage 33:10 (c,4) Je '82
--Cosmetics counter (Paris, France)
Ebony 39:150-6 (c,4) Je '84
--Country convenience store (Mis-
sissippi)
Sports Illus 58:38 (c,3) Je 20 '83
--Country grocery store (Pennsyl-
vania)
Nat Geog 165:512-13 (c,2) Ap '84
--Country store (Georgia)
Trav/Holiday 157:75 (c,4) Mr '82
--Department store exterior (Detroit,
Michigan)
Life 6:156 (c,4) Ja '83
--Florist (Washington)
Natur Hist 94:68-9 (3) Jl '85
--General (South Carolina)
Nat Geog 163:461 (c,4) Ap '83

STORES (cont.)
--General (Yukon, Canada)
Trav/Holiday 157:87 (c,2) Ap
'82
--Greengrocer (Bath, England)
Trav/Holiday 158:30 (c,3) Ag
'82
--Hardware (Brooklyn, New York)
Nat Geog 163:592-3 (c,1) My
'83
--Hilo, Hawaii
Trav/Holiday 166:61 (c,3) Jl
'86
--Ice cream store (New Delhi,
India)
Nat Geog 167:517 (c,2) Ap '85
--Jewelry (Saudi Arabia)
Nat Geog 168:510-11 (c,1) O
'85
--Mandalay, Burma
Nat Geog 166:97 (c,3) Jl '84
--Paraguay
Nat Geog 162:252 (c,4) Ag '82
--Pawnbroker (Illinois)
Life 5:32-3 (c,1) Ap '82
--Reproduction of 19th cent. Ver-
mont general store
Am Heritage 33:25 (c,2) Ap '82
--Selling clothes from van
(California)
Nat Geog 165:436 (c,3) Ap '84
--Shoe (Taiwan)
Nat Geog 161:102-3 (c,2) Ja '82
--Selecting dress in department
store
Ebony 38:70 (3) D '82
--Sportswear (New York)
Sports Illus 63:88 (c,4) Ag 19
'85
--Women's apparel (California)
Ebony 41:53-4 (c,2) Je '86
--See also
BAKERS
BUTCHERS
FLEA MARKETS
FOOD MARKETS
MARKETS
PHARMACIES
RESTAURANTS
SHOPPING CENTERS
STREET VENDORS
STORKS
Nat Geog 169:582, 601 (c,3)
My '86
STORMS
--19th cent. depictions of storm
gods (Japan)

Smithsonian 13:88, 91 (c,1) S '82
--1868 thunderstorm at sea
Am Heritage 37:22-3 (painting,c,1)
Je '86
--1953 ocean storm (Massachusetts)
Life 9:24-5 (1) Fall '86
--At sea
Am Heritage 36:92-3, 96-7 (paint-
ing,c,1) F '85
--At sea (1838 drawing)
Smithsonian 16:52 (3) N '85
--Australia coast
Nat Geog 163:680-1 (c,1) My '83
--California coast
Nat Wildlife 22:48 (c,3) D '83
Nat Geog 165:156-9 (c,1) F '84
--Darkening sky (Niger)
Nat Geog 164:494-5 (c,1) O '83
--Mississippi Delta, Louisiana
Nat Geog 164:226-7 (c,1) Ag '83
--Oregon coast
Trav/Holiday 160:84 (4) N '83
--Radar image of thunderstorm
Smithsonian 13:94 (c,4) Ap '82
--Satellite map of storm
Natur Hist 92:25 (c,4) Jl '83
--Thunderstorm (New Mexico)
Nat Geog 162:582-3 (c,1) N '82
--Thunderstorm (Yellowstone,
Wyoming)
Nat Wildlife 23:58-9 (c,1) D '84
--See also
BLIZZARDS
DUST STORMS
HURRICANES
SNOW STORMS
TYPHOONS
STORMS--DAMAGE
--Wrecked homes (North Carolina)
Nat Wildlife 22:49 (c,4) D '83
STOVES
--19th cent. cast iron stoves (New
York)
Natur Hist 91:67-73 (c,1) Ja '82
--19th cent. wood-burning stove
(Tennessee)
Trav/Holiday 163:24 (c,4) Ap '85
--Mid-19th cent.
Smithsonian 15:84-5 (drawing,c,1)
Ag '84
--1871 (Pennsylvania)
Am Heritage 36:39 (2) Ag '85
--1928 stove advertisement
Am Heritage 36:81 (c,2) Ap '85
--Outdoor stone oven (Caribbean)
Trav/Holiday 164:34 (c,4) N '85

STOWE, HARRIET BEECHER
Smithsonian 13:132 (4) Jl '82
Am Heritage 35:74 (drawing,4)
F '84
--Poster advertising Uncle Tom's
Cabin
Am Heritage 34:111 (c,4) F '83
STRASBERG, LEE
Life 6:144 (4) Ja '83
STRAWBERRIES
--Made of glass
Smithsonian 13:105 (c,4) O '82
STRAWBERRY INDUSTRY
--Israeli desert
Nat Geog 161:452-3 (c,1) Ap
'82
STREAMS
--Michigan stream through the
seasons
Nat Wildlife 22:53-8 (c,4) O
'84
--Mountain stream (Chile)
Smithsonian 16:85 (c,1) O '85
--Stream wildlife
Nat Wildlife 24:30-5 (c,1) Ag
'86
STREET LIGHTS
--19th cent.
Am Heritage 34:54 (paint-
ing,c,3) F '83
--1950s (New York)
Am Heritage 34:54 (painting,c,4)
F '83
--Cast iron lamps on Brooklyn
Bridge, New York City
Smithsonian 14:80-1 (c,2) Ap
'83
--Gas lamp replicas (St. Louis,
Missouri)
Trav/Holiday 157:35 (c,4) Je
'82
--See also
TRAFFIC LIGHTS
Street signs. See
SIGNS AND SIGNBOARDS
STREET VENDORS
--1889 chili stand (Texas)
Am Heritage 37:62-3 (2) F '86
--Balloons (Mexico)
Trav/Holiday 157:57 (c,3) F
'82
--Dishes (Hungary)
Trav/Holiday 163:68 (c,3) Mr
'85
--Eyeglass stand (Italy)
Natur Hist 95:84-5 (2) O '86
--Florence, Italy

Trav/Holiday 159:38 (c,4) F '83
--Flowers (Martinique)
Trav/Holiday 165:23 (c,4) Mr '86
--Grilling sausages (Taiwan)
Nat Geog 161:104 (c,4) Ja '82
--Ice cream (Ecuador)
Trav/Holiday 160:58 (c,4) Jl '83
--Knife peddler (India)
Natur Hist 94:67 (c,3) F '85
--Kvass drinks (U.S.S.R.)
Trav/Holiday 165:54 (c,4) My '86
--Mexican food (Texas)
Smithsonian 16:126-7 (c,1) D '85
--New Delhi, India
Nat Geog 167:514-15 (c,1) Ap '85
--Oranges (China)
Trav/Holiday 158:20 (4) O '82
--Parking lot computer vendors
(New Jersey)
Natur Hist 95:32-4 (4) Ja '86
--Rome, Italy
Natur Hist 91:69 (4) Ap '82
--Snow cones (Ecuador)
Natur Hist 95:42-3 (c,1) F '86
--Soft drink pushcart (Rome, Italy)
Natur Hist 95:68 (4) Je '86
--Tahiti
Sports Illus 64:140-1 (c,2) F 10
'86
Streetcars. See
TROLLEY CARS
STROMBOLI, ITALY
--Volcano
Nat Geog 162:694-5 (c,1) D '82
STUART, GILBERT
--Portrait of John Barry
Am Heritage 34:7 (painting,c,4)
F '83
--Portrait of Thomas Jefferson
Am Heritage 35:6 (painting,c,1)
Je '84
Smithsonian 15:69 (c,4) Jl '84
--Portrait of George Washington
Smithsonian 15:146 (painting,c,4)
Ap '84
--Self-portrait (1787)
Am Heritage 34:20 (painting,c,4)
O '83
STUDIES
--19th cent. house
Sports Illus 57:49 (c,3) O 4 '82
--1850s study of Alexander von Hum-
boldt (Berlin, Germany)
Nat Geog 168:328-9 (drawing,c,1)
S '85
--Washington Irving's home (New
York)

SUNBATHING (cont.)
    Sports Illus 61:124-5 (c,1)
        Jl 18 '84
--In cold weather (Leningrad,
        U.S.S.R.)
    Life 6:126-7 (c,1) My '83
--Lebanon beach
    Nat Geog 163:273 (c,3) F '83
--Nude (West Germany)
    Nat Geog 161:45 (c,3) Ja '82
--Palm Springs, California
    Sports Illus 58:84-7 (c,2) Ap
        25 '83
--Topless
    Life 6:78-9 (c,1) S '83
SUNDEW PLANTS
    Smithsonian 14:85 (c,4) Jl '83
    Nat Geog 167:548 (c,4) Ap
        '85
    Smithsonian 16:153 (c,4) Ap
        '85
    Natur Hist 94:33 (c,4) Je '85
SUNDIALS
--16th cent. pocket sundial
        (Great Britain)
    Nat Geog 163:660 (c,4) My '83
--17th cent. pocket sundial
        (Spain)
    Nat Geog 161:239 (c,4) F '82
SUNFLOWERS
    Natur Hist 93:46-7 (c,1) Je
        '84
    Life 7:126 (c,2) O '84
    Life 9:100-4 (c,1) D '86
SUNRISES
--Brooklyn Bridge, New York
        City, New York
    Smithsonian 14:84 (c,4) Ap '83
--Lake Champlain, New York/
        Vermont
    Sports Illus 62:84 (c,3) Je 10
        '85
--New Hampshire lake
    Nat Geog 162:786-7 (c,1) D
        '82
--Over tepees (Alberta)
    Nat Geog 169:84-5 (c,2) Ja '86
--Thailand city
    Nat Geog 162:534-5 (c,1) O '82
SUNSET CRATER NATIONAL
        MONUMENT, ARIZONA
    Natur Hist 95:42-3 (c,1) D '86
SUNSETS
--1872 painting of sunset over the
        sea
    Smithsonian 16:64-5 (c,1) Jl '85
--Africa

    Life 9:167 (c,4) Fall '86
--Alaska shore
    Nat Wildlife 21:45 (c,4) Ag '83
--California coast
    Nat Wildlife 20:10-11 (c,1) F '82
--Cape Sounion, Greece
    Nat Geog 170:196-7 (c,1) Ag '86
--Couple silhouetted in sunset
        (Hawaii)
    Sports Illus 58:52 (c,4) F 14 '83
--Egyptian beach
    Nat Geog 161:442-3 (c,2) Ap '82
--Fiji Islands
    Trav/Holiday 163:10 (c,4) Mr '85
--Florence, Italy
    Trav/Holiday 59:36-7 (c,1) F '83
--Greek islands
    Trav/Holiday 160:57 (c,1) Ag '83
--Hawaii
    Trav/Holiday 159:58 (c,1) F '83
    Sports Illus 58:82 (c,4) Je 13
        '83
--Huntington Beach, California
    Smithsonian 13:69 (c,1) S '82
--Idaho lake
    Trav/Holiday 165:44 (c,3) My '86
--Iowa lake
    Nat Wildlife 21:7 (c,4) Ap '83
--Leicestershire field, England
    Smithsonian 15:92-3 (c,1) Mr '85
--Montana
    Nat Geog 167:673 (c,3) My '85
--Navajo Lake, Utah
    Natur Hist 95:90 (c,4) My '86
--New York Harbor
    Smithsonian 17:78-9 (c,1) Jl '86
--North Carolina coast
    Trav/Holiday 159:41 (c,4) Je '83
--Ossabaw Island, Georgia
    Sports Illus 65:100 (c,4) O 20 '86
--Over construction site
    Smithsonian 16:53 (c,1) S '85
--Over desert (Dubai)
    Sports Illus 65:94 (c,3) D 1 '86
--Over field of goldenrod
    Nat Wildlife 20:24 (c,4) Ag '82
--Over lake (North Dakota)
    Trav/Holiday 164:57 (c,2) Jl '85
--Over ocean
    Trav/Holiday 164:69 (c,1) O '85
--Platte River, Nebraska
    Nat Geog 170:158-9 (c,1) Ag '86
--Sonoran Desert, Arizona
    Natur Hist 94:36-7 (c,2) F '85
--Southwest
    Life 9:118-19 (c,1) Ja '86
--Tahiti beach

SUNSETS (cont.)
    Sports Illus 64:162 (c,3) F
        10 '86
--Tobago coast
    Trav/Holiday 164:20-1 (c,1) D
        '85
--See also
    TWILIGHT
Supermarkets. See
    FOOD MARKETS
SUPREME COURT JUSTICES
    Life 5:46-7 (c,1) Ja '82
--1954
    Ebony 40:110 (4) My '85
--1958
    Am Heritage 35:102 (4) D '83
--See also
    JAY, JOHN
    MARSHALL, JOHN
    MARSHALL, THURGOOD
    WARREN, EARL
    HOLMES, OLIVER WENDELL
    HUGHES, CHARLES EVANS
    ROBERTS, OWEN
    SUTHERLAND, GEORGE
    TAFT, WILLIAM HOWARD
    TANEY, ROGER
SURFING
    Sports Illus 63:38-47 (c,1) Jl
        8 '85
    Sports Illus 63:92 (c,4) Jl 29
        '85
--Boardsailing
    Sports Illus 56:44-6 (c,1) Mr
        29 '82
    Trav/Holiday 158:56 (4) Ag '82
    Sports Illus 61:444-54 (c,1) Jl
        18 '84
    Sports Illus 63:64 (c,1) O 28
        '85
--Boogie boards
    Sports Illus 56:52 (c,2) My 10
        '82
--California
    Sports Illus 63:24-5 (c,1) O 7
        '85
--Competition (California)
    Sports Illus 65:12-17 (c,1) S 8
        '86
--Hawaii
    Sports Illus 56:cov., 84-101
        (c,1) Mr 8 '82
    Sports Illus 63:66 (c,3) O 28
        '85
--Surfboard scarred from shark
        attack
    Nat Wildlife 20:9 (c,4) Ag '82

--Surfboards
    Sports Illus 65:14 (c,4) N 17 '86
--Windsurfing
    Sports Illus 57:47 (c,4) Ag 9 '82
    Life 6:94-6 (c,1) Ag '83
    Trav/Holiday 163:cov. (c,1) Je
        '85
    Sports Illus 65:24 (c,3) S 29 '86
--Windsurfing (China)
    Life 6:58 (c,2) D '83
--Windsurfing (Hawaii)
    Trav/Holiday 160:43 (c,1) N '83
    Sports Illus 62:2-3, 44, 52 (c,1)
        My 6 '85
--Windsurfing (Italy)
    Nat Geog 162:729 (c,4) D '82
--Windsurfing (Newfoundland)
    Nat Geog 169:698-9 (c,1) My '86
SURGERY
    Ebony 37:158 (4) O '82
    Ebony 38:69 (4) Mr '83
    Ebony 38:42 (4) Ag '83
    Ebony 39:60 (4) Ap '84
--1840s (Massachusetts)
    Am Heritage 35:41 (4) O '84
--1889 (Massachusetts)
    Am Heritage 35:46 (4) O '84
--1894 operating table
    Am Heritage 37:36 (diagram,4)
        Ap '86
--Bone marrow transplants on
        Chernobyl victims (U.S.S.R.)
    Life 9:24 (c,3) Ag '86
--Breast cancer surgery
    Ebony 40:60-1 (c,2) Je '85
--Civil War amputation
    Am Heritage 35:65-7 (1) O '84
--Ethiopia
    Nat Geog 168:392 (c,4) S '85
--Hair transplants
    Ebony 37:44-6 (3) Je '82
--Implanting artificial heart
    Life 8:34 (4) My '85
--Korean War MASH unit
    Am Heritage 35:74-5 (1) O '84
--Laser eye surgery
    Nat Geog 165:344-5 (c,2) Mr '84
--Liver transplants
    Life 5:cov., 24-7 (c,1) S '82
--Neurosurgery
    Ebony 38:72-4 (c,3) S '83
--Open heart (Ivory Coast)
    Nat Geog 162:118 (c,4) Jl '82
--Separating Siamese twins (Canada)
    Life 7:51 (c,3) O '84
--Use of lasers
    Life 5:cov., 129-34 (c,1) My '82

SURGERY (cont.)
   Nat Geog 165:344-7 (c,2) Mr
      '84
--Videotaping surgery
   Nat Geog 164:298-9 (c,3) S '83
--See also
   PLASTIC SURGERY
SURICATES
   Smithsonian 17:54-65 (c,1) Ap
      '86
SURINAM--RITES AND FESTIVALS
--Wedding ceremony (Netherlands)
   Nat Geog 170:504-5 (c,1) O
      '86
SURVIVALISTS
--Camouflaging body in wilderness
   Nat Wildlife 22:42-4 (c,2) Je
      '84
SUSQUEHANNA RIVER, PENN-
      SYLVANIA/NEW YORK
   Smithsonian 15:68 (c,2) Ja '85
   Nat Geog 167:352-83 (map,c,1)
      Mr '85
SUTHERLAND, GEORGE
   Am Heritage 38:38 (drawing,4)
      D '86
SWALLOWS
   Nat Wildlife 20:45, 50 (c,1)
      Ag '82
   Nat Wildlife 22:26 (painting,c,2)
      D '83
--Barn swallows
   Natur Hist 94:36 (c,4) F '85
Swamps. See
   MARSHES
   OKEFENOKEE SWAMP
SWANS
   Nat Geog 163:752-3, 772-3
      (c,1) Je '83
   Nat Wildlife 24:58 (c,2) D '85
--In flight
   Nat Wildlife 24:25 (painting,c,3)
      O '86
--Trumpeter
   Nat Wildlife 21:50-5 (c,1) Je
      '83
   Nat Geog 166:562-3 (c,1) N
      '84
   Nat Geog 168:544-57 (map,c,1)
      O '85
--Trumpeter swans in flight
   Natur Hist 92:72-3 (paint-
      ing,c,1) S '83
SWANSON, GLORIA
   Smithsonian 16:116 (4) N '85
Sweden. See
   STOCKHOLM

   VIKINGS
SWEDEN--RITES AND CEREMONIES
--Changing of the Guard (Stockholm)
   Trav/Holiday 161:60-1 (c,2) My
      '84
SWEDEN--SOCIAL LIFE AND CUS-
      TOMS
--Santa Lucia Day breakfast in bed
   Life 8:55 (3) F '85
SWEEPING
   Natur Hist 93:10 (4) Ag '84
SWEET GUM TREES
--Leaves
   Natur Hist 94:76-7 (c,2) D '85
SWIFTS
   Natur Hist 91:56-61 (c,1) N '82
   Smithsonian 14:69 (c,4) S '83
SWIMMING
   Sports Illus 56:34-5 (c,4) My 31
      '82
--Around Manhattan
   Sports Illus 57:22-3 (c,2) S 27
      '82
   Sports Illus 59:60-1 (c,2) Ag 1
      '83
--Babies playing underwater
   Life 8:11-14 (c,1) Je '85
--Bathing in icy water (China)
   Life 8:153 (c,3) D '85
--Butterfly stroke
   Sports Illus 58:148 (c,3) F 16 '83
--Children playing in pool
   Life 6:86 (4) My '83
--Floating
   Life 7:29-32 (c,1) Ap '84
--Floating in indoor pool (California)
   Life 5:77 (c,1) O '82
--Floating in inner tube (New York)
   Smithsonian 16:146-7 (c,1) N '85
--Floating in pool (Wisconsin)
   Sports Illus 65:53 (c,3) Ag 11
      '86
--Floating on back
   Sports Illus 57:59 (c,3) N 8 '82
   Life 6:81 (c,3) Ag '83
--Floating on inner tube
   Life 5:97 (3) Ap '82
   Sports Illus 57:52-3 (c,2) N 15
      '82
--Playing in pool (California)
   Ebony 37:32 (c,4) My '82
--Playing in pool (New York)
   Life 6:116 (c,1) Jl '83
--Synchronized swimming
   Life 5:48-52 (c,1) Jl '82
   Sports Illus 57:26-7, 30 (c,1) Ag
      2 '82

SWIMMING (cont.)
  Sports Illus 61:2-3 (c,1) Ag
    20 '84
--Woman relaxing in pool (France)
  Life 8:99 (c,2) Mr '85
--See also
    BATHING
    BATHING SUITS
    BEACHES, BATHING
    CRABBE, BUSTER
    DIVING
    LIFEGUARDS
    SWIMMING POOLS
SWIMMING--COMPETITIONS
  Nat Geog 161:23 (c,3) Ja '82
  Sports Illus 56:102-3 (c,4)
    Ja 18 '82
  Sports Illus 56:70, 75 (c,4)
    Ap 19 '82
  Sports Illus 57:20-1 (c,3) Ag
    30 '82
  Sports Illus 58:83-4 (c,4) Ap
    18 '83
  Life 6:65-6 (c,4) Je '83
  Sports Illus 59:34 (c,4) Jl 18
    '83
  Sports Illus 59:50-2 (c,2) Jl 25
    '83
  Sports Illus 59:10-15 (c,1) Ag
    29 '83
  Trav/Holiday 160:61 (c,3) N
    '83
  Sports Illus 60:126-9 (c,1) F
    8 '84
  Sports Illus 60:28-9 (c,2) Mr
    26 '84
  Sports Illus 60:72-85 (c,1) My
    21 '84
  Sports Illus 60:72-4 (c,4) My
    28 '84
  Sports Illus 61:74-5, 97-100
    (c,1) Jl 18 '84
  Sports Illus 62:82-4 (c,4) Ja
    14 '85
  Sports Illus 63:26-7 (c,2) Ag
    19 '85
  Sports Illus 64:2-3, 44 (c,1) Je
    23 '86
  Sports Illus 65:46 (c,4) Jl 7
    '86
  Sports Illus 65:16-19 (c,2) S
    1 '86
  Life 9:244 (c,3) Fall '86
--1910s sporting cards of swimmers
  Sports Illus 63:104-5 (c,1) D
    23 '85
--1984 Olympic trials

  Sports Illus 61:cov., 2-3, 14-21
    (c,1) Jl 9 '84
--1984 Olympics (Los Angeles)
  Sports Illus 61:34-41 (c,2) Ag 6
    '84
  Sports Illus 61:18-36 (c,1) Ag
    13 '84
--Backstroke
  Sports Illus 59:12 (c,3) Ag 15
    '83
--Breaststroke
  Sports Illus 59:10-11 (c,1) Ag 15
    '83
--Butterfly stroke
  Sports Illus 60:32-3 (c,3) Ja 16
    '84
--Goodwill Games 1986 (Moscow)
  Sports Illus 65:54 (c,4) Jl 14 '86
--Ironman triathlon (Hawaii)
  Sports Illus 65:2-3 (c,1) N 3 '86
--NCAA Championships 1982
  Sports Illus 56:22-4 (c,2) Ap 5
    '82
--NCAA Championships 1985
  Sports Illus 62:82-3 (c,4) Ap 8
    '85
--Triathlon (France)
  Sports Illus 59:86-96 (c,1) O 10
    '83
--U.S. National Long Course 1983
    (Fresno, California)
  Sports Illus 59:10-15 (c,1) Ag 15
    '83
--World Aquatic Championships 1982
    (Ecuador)
  Sports Illus 57:10-17 (c,1) Ag 16
    '82
SWIMMING POOLS
--1984 Olympics pool (Los Angeles,
    California)
  Sports Illus 59:50-1 (c,2) Jl 25
    '83
  Sports Illus 60:77 (c,4) Mr 5 '84
--Arizona resort
  Trav/Holiday 161:68 (c,4) Mr '84
--Australia
  Nat Geog 161:650 (c,3) My '82
--Bahamas home
  Ebony 39:50 (c,4) Ja '84
--Bahamas hotel
  Nat Geog 162:379 (c,2) S '82
--Bar in hotel pool (Mauritius)
  Trav/Holiday 162:47 (c,4) N '84
--Bride diving into pool (California)
  Life 5:112 (c,2) F '82
--California home
  Ebony 40:44 (c,3) My '85

SWIMMING POOLS (cont.)
Life 9:142, 171 (c,2) My '86
--Children's pool (Virginia)
Life 7:46 (c,2) N '84
--Child's plastic pool (Colorado)
Sports Illus 57:36 (c,4) Ag
9 '82
--College pool
Sports Illus 56:32-3 (c,1) Mr
29 '82
--Hawaiian resort
Trav/Holiday 161:76-7 (c,2)
My '84
--Hearst castle, San Simeon,
California
Nat Geog 165:452-3 (c,1) Ap
'84
Smithsonian 16:70-1 (c,1) D '85
--Home pool (New Jersey)
Ebony 40:66 (3) O '85
--Hotel (Mexico)
Trav/Holiday 163:65 (c,3) Ja
'85
--Hotel (Miami, Florida)
Ebony 38:122 (c,4) Ja '83
--Hotel roof (Madrid, Spain)
Nat Geog 169:168-9 (c,1) F '86
--Houston home, Texas
Ebony 40:93 (c,4) N '84
--Indoor home pool
Smithsonian 13:60-1 (c,1) Mr
'83
--Indoor home pool (Michigan)
Ebony 38:102 (c,2) D '82
--Lounging at pool
Sports Illus 61:36-7 (c,1) Jl
18 '84
--Nicaragua home
Life 6:24, 27 (c,4) S '83
--Nude bathing (New Mexico)
Nat Geog 161:322 (c,1) Mr '82
--On cruise ship
Trav/Holiday 162:56 (c,4) O
'84
Life 8:150-1 (c,1) Ap '85
--On cruise ship (1930s)
Am Heritage 35:64 (c,4) D '83
--Palm Beach, Florida
Life 6:94, 97 (c,3) Mr '83
--Playing basketball in pool
(Alaska)
Nat Geog 163:168 (c,4) F '83
--Playing volleyball in pool
(California)
Sports Illus 58:66 (c,3) F 7 '83
--Texas
Life 6:104-5 (1) D '83

--Tossing someone in
Sports Illus 56:42 (c,4) Je 14
'82
--West Edmonton Mall, Alberta
Smithsonian 17:43 (c,2) D '86
Swimsuits. See
BATHING SUITS
SWINGS
--Backyard swings
Ebony 39:143 (c,4) S '84
--Child on swing (Florida)
Sports Illus 59:45 (c,3) Ag 29
'83
--Children on swings
Ebony 41:40 (c,4) D '85
Life 9:72 (c,4) Ap '86
Ebony 41:70, 88 (c,2) Ag '86
--Mother and child on swing (New
York)
Sports Illus 65:41 (c,2) Ag 4 '86
--Playground platform swing (Iowa)
Smithsonian 16:114 (c,4) Ag '85
--Rural West Virginia
Nat Geog 163:816-17 (c,1) Je '83
SWITZERLAND
Trav/Holiday 161:80-3, 87, 108
(c,2) Mr '84
Nat Geog 169:96-127 (map,c,1)
Ja '86
--Andermatt
Nat Geog 162:291 (c,1) S '82
--Appenzell
Nat Geog 169:98-9, 120-1 (c,1)
Ja '86
--Baden
Trav/Holiday 161:80 (c,4) Mr '84
--Chateau de Chillon, Montreux
Trav/Holiday 161:69 (c,2) Ap '84
--Countryside
Sports Illus 61:2-3, 50-1 (c,1) S
3 '84
--Gottlieben restaurant
Trav/Holiday 160:41 (c,2) Jl '83
--Great St. Bernard Pass
Nat Geog 161:154-5 (c,1) F '82
--Gstaad
Trav/Holiday 162:cov. (c,1) Ag
'84
--Morcote
Nat Geog 169:116-17 (c,1) Ja '86
--Neuchâtel
Trav/Holiday 161:83 (c,4) Mr '84
--Obernalp Pass
Trav/Holiday 162:34-5 (c,1) Ag
'84
--Wengen, Lauterbrunnen
Nat Geog 162:300-1 (c,1) S '82

SWITZERLAND (cont.)
--See also
    ALPS
    BASEL
    BERN
    GENEVA
    LAKE CONSTANCE
    LAKE GENEVA
    LUCERNE
    MATTERHORN
    ST. MORITZ
    ZURICH
SWITZERLAND--COSTUME
    Trav/Holiday 159:67-8 (c,1)
        Ap '83
    Nat Geog 169:96-127 (c,1) Ja
        '86
SWITZERLAND--HISTORY
--1880 St. Gotthard Tunnel con-
        struction
    Smithsonian 17:69 (engrav-
        ing,4) My '86
--Napoleon crossing Great St.
        Bernard Pass (1800)
    Nat Geog 161:154-5 (c,1) F
        '82
--See also
    CALVIN, JOHN
SWITZERLAND--HOUSING
--Illustrated house facades
    Trav/Holiday 166:38 (c,4) N '86
SWITZERLAND--SOCIAL LIFE
        AND CUSTOMS
--Sechselauten spring fest
        (Zurich)
    Nat Geog 169:96-7 (c,1) Ja '86
SWOPE, HERBERT BAYARD
    Am Heritage 33:66 (4) O '82
SWORDS
--13th cent. (Poland)
    Smithsonian 14:132 (c,4) O '83
--19th cent. ceremonial Asante
        swords (Ghana)
    Natur Hist 93:72 (c,4) O '84
--Great Britain
    Smithsonian 15:83 (c,1) Ag '84
--Japanese samurai sword
    Nat Geog 165:764 (c,4) Je '84
--Japanese sword training (Iaido)
    Ebony 37:48-9 (c,2) S '82
SYDNEY, AUSTRALIA
    Trav/Holiday 158:49-51 (c,2)
        Ag '82
    Nat Geog 164:606-7 (c,1) N '83
SYNAGOGUES
--1270 Altneuschul (Prague,
        Czechoslovakia)

Life 7:90 (c,2) N '84
--Converted into church (Toledo,
        Spain)
    Nat Geog 161:750-1 (c,1) Je '82
--Newport, Rhode Island
    Life 5:22 (c,4) N '82
--St. Thomas Synagogue, Virgin
        Islands
    Trav/Holiday 163:64 (c,4) My '85
--Temple Emanu-El interior, New
        York City, New York
    Smithsonian 13:161 (c,4) N '82
SYRIA, ANCIENT--SCULPTURE
    Smithsonian 16:165 (c,4) Ja '86

-T-

TABLE TENNIS
    Sports Illus 56:146 (c,3) F 10
        '82
    Sports Illus 62:42-4 (c,1) Mr 25
        '85
--Aboard yacht
    Life 8:120 (c,3) N '85
TABLES
--18th cent. Chinese sewing table
    Natur Hist 93:72 (c,4) F '84
--Pizza restaurant (Pennsylvania)
    Life 9:3 (c,3) Mr '86
Tadpoles. See
    FROGS
TAFT, WILLIAM HOWARD
--Depicted on postage stamp
    Am Heritage 34:52 (c,4) D '82
TAHITI
    Sports Illus 64:4, 136-62 (map,c,1)
        F 10 '86
TAHITI--COSTUME
    Sports Illus 64:136-62 (c,1) F 10
        '86
--1791
    Nat Geog 168:422-3 (painting,c,1)
        O '85
--Dancer
    Trav/Holiday 165:61 (c,4) Ap '86
TAHITI--SOCIAL LIFE AND CUSTOMS
--Tiurai festival
    Sports Illus 64:136-62 (c,1) F 10
        '86
TAIPEI, TAIWAN
    Nat Geog 161:96-7, 104-7 (c,1)
        Ja '82
    Trav/Holiday 160:38, 41 (c,3)
        Ag '83
TAIWAN
    Nat Geog 161:92-118 (map,c,1)

TAIWAN (cont.)
    Ja '82
--See also
    TAIPEI
TAIWAN--COSTUME
    Nat Geog 161:94-118 (c,1) Ja
        '82
TAJ MAHAL, AGRA, INDIA
    Nat Geog 167:491-3 (c,1) Ap
        '85
    Trav/Holiday 165:56-7 (c,1) Je
        '86
TAMPA, FLORIDA
    Trav/Holiday 166:16-18
        (map,c,3) D '86
TAMPERE, FINLAND
    Trav/Holiday 161:106 (4) My
        '84
TANAGERS
    Nat Wildlife 22:27, 61 (c,3)
        D '83
    Natur Hist 93:38 (c,3) N '84
--Scarlet
    Natur Hist 93:30 (c,3) Ap '84
--Western
    Nat Wildlife 24:40 (c,4) Ap
        '86
TANEY, ROGER
    Am Heritage 38:26 (4) D '86
TANKERS
    Smithsonian 13:39 (c,2) Jl '82
--1976 supertanker
    Am Heritage 34:75-7 (draw-
        ing,c,4) Ap '83
--Destroyed by explosion
    Life 8:46-7 (1) Jl '85
--Oil (Virginia)
    Nat Geog 168:72-3 (c,1) Jl '85
--Supertankers
    Smithsonian 17:77 (c,3) Jl '86
TANKS
--1943 tanks of mustard gas
        (Great Britain)
    Am Heritage 36:40-1 (2) Ag '85
--Industrial tanks
    Smithsonian 13:140-1 (c,2) N
        '82
TANKS, ARMORED
--1915 armored car (U.S.)
    Smithsonian 15:142 (4) Je '84
--1940s (Germany)
    Smithsonian 16:125 (4) F '86
--1940s (U.S.)
    Life 8:64-5 (2) Spring '85
--1940s Sherman tank (U.S.)
    Trav/Holiday 165:10 (c,4) F '86
--1956 (U.S.S.R.)

Smithsonian 17:54 (4) N '86
--Israel
    Nat Geog 168:35 (c,3) Jl '85
--Nicaragua
    Life 7:10-11 (c,1) N '84
--U.S. amphibious assault vehicle
    Life 6:32 (c,2) Je '83
TANZANIA
--Serengeti National Park
    Nat Geog 169:560-601 (map,c,1)
        My '86
--See also
    KILIMANJARO
    LAKE VICTORIA
TANZANIA--ART
--Stone Age paintings
    Nat Geog 164:84-99 (c,1) Jl '83
TANZANIA--MAPS
--Serengeti National Park
    Natur Hist 92:56 (drawing,c,3)
        Ag '83
TAOS, NEW MEXICO
--Pueblos
    Sports Illus 60:66 (c,2) Mr 26
        '84
TAPE RECORDERS
--1924
    Smithsonian 15:174 (3) Ap '84
--1940
    Am Heritage 33:109-10 (3) O '82
TAPESTRIES
--Raphael's "Miraculous Draught of
        Fishes"
    Smithsonian 13:120-1 (c,1) D '82
    Life 5:68 (c,2) D '82
    Nat Geog 168:761 (c,4) D '85
--Section of "Bayeux Tapestry"
    Life 8:32 (c,4) O '85
    Smithsonian 16:162 (c,3) N '85
--Versailles Palace, France
    Smithsonian 17:112-13 (c,1) N
        '86
--Weaving tapestries (France)
    Smithsonian 17:106-10 (c,1) N '86
TARANTULAS
    Nat Geog 163:56-7 (c,1) Ja '83
TARAWA ATOLL
    Am Heritage 34:2, 26-9 (map,c,1)
        O '83
--1943 battle
    Am Heritage 34:2, 26-35 (c,1) O
        '83
    Smithsonian 14:152 (4) Mr '84
TARBELL, IDA M.
    Am Heritage 34:31 (2) Ag '83
TARPONS (FISH)
    Nat Geog 167:806-7 (c,1) Je '85

TARSIERS
    Smithsonian 12:149 (drawing,4)
        F '82
TARZAN
    Life 6:160-78 (c,1) N '83
    Life 7:82 (4) Summer '84
    Sports Illus 6:151 (4) Jl 18 '84
TASMANIA, AUSTRALIA
--Coat of arms
    Smithsonian 16:121 (c,4) Ag
        '85
--Hobart Harbor
    Trav/Holiday 163:4 (c,3) Ja '85
--Poppy fields
    Nat Geog 167:174-5 (c,1) F '85
--Rainbow over lake
    Smithsonian 16:130 (c,3) Ag
        '85
--Wilderness area
    Nat Geog 163:676-93 (map,c,1)
        My '83
TASMANIAN DEVILS
    Smithsonian 16:128 (c,4) Ag
        '85
TASMANIAN TIGERS
    Smithsonian 16:117-21 (2) Ag
        '85
TATTOOING
--California gang member
    Life 5:56 (c,2) My '82
--Japan
    Nat Geog 170:633 (c,1) N '86
--Tahiti
    Sports Illus 64:152 (c,4) F 10
        '86
--Western Samoa
    Nat Geog 168:465 (c,1) O '85
TATTOOS
--19th cent. (Japan)
    Smithsonian 14:169 (c,4) N '83
--19th cent. Maori facial tattoo
        (New Zealand)
    Natur Hist 94:39 (1) Jl '85
--Alligator tattoo
    Sports Illus 64:62 (c,4) F 3
        '86
--Australian woman
    Nat Geog 169:747 (c,2) Je '86
--Marriage tattoo (Ethiopia)
    Nat Geog 163:640 (c,4) My '83
TAVERNS
--1750 (Annapolis, Maryland)
    Smithsonian 17:28 (c,4) S '86
--19th cent. (London, England)
    Nat Geog 163:757 (c,2) Je '83
--1906 (Missouri)
    Am Heritage 33:50 (2) Ag '82

--Alaska
    Nat Geog 165:81 (c,3) Ja '84
--Arizona
    Sports Illus 64:84-90 (paint-
        ing,c,2) Mr 17 '86
--Bar patrons (California)
    Life 8:88-9 (c,1) My '85
--Drunk Eskimo outside bar (Alaska)
    Nat Geog 163:167 (c,3) F '83
--Edinburgh pub, Scotland
    Nat Geog 166:69 (c,1) Jl '84
--McSorley's bar, New York City,
        New York (1912)
    Am Heritage 34:22-3 (painting,c,1)
        O '83
    Am Heritage 38:57 (painting,c,2)
        D '86
--Missouri
    Sports Illus 64:38 (c,3) Ja 6 '86
--New Jersey
    Sports Illus 57:94 (c,4) D 6 '82
--People sitting at bar
    Sports Illus 65:134 (painting,c,3)
        D 22 '86
--Restaurant bar (New York)
    Smithsonian 15:121 (c,2) My '84
--Rhode Island bar
    Sports Illus 62:50 (c,4) Je 24 '84
--San Antonio, Texas
    Smithsonian 16:124 (c,4) D '85
--Sherlock Holmes Pub exterior,
        London, England
    Trav/Holiday 161:114 (4) Ap '84
--Sitting at table (Scotland)
    Sports Illus 65:62 (painting,c,4)
        Jl 14 '86
--Toledo, Spain
    Nat Geog 161:732-3 (c,1) Je '82
--Virginia
    Nat Geog 168:80 (c,3) Jl '85
--West Virginia
    Nat Geog 163:802-3 (c,1) Je '83
--See also
    BARTENDERS
    DRINKING CUSTOMS
TAXATION
--16th cent. tax gatherer
    Smithsonian 13:44 (painting,c,3)
        Mr '83
TAXATION--HUMOR
--Drawings of tax-deductible ex-
        penses
    Life 7:23, 30 (c,3) Ap '84
TAXICABS
--Cambodia
    Nat Geog 161:608 (c,4) My '82
--Checkers cab (New York)

TAXICABS (cont.)
  Life 6:155 (c,4) Ja '83
--Dispatcher (Toronto, Ontario)
  Natur Hist 91:70 (3) O '82
--India
  Nat Geog 166:722-3 (c,1) D '84
--Jeepneys (Philippines)
  Nat Geog 170:110-11 (c,2) Jl
    '86
--Pedicabs (Bangladesh)
  Nat Geog 165:740-1 (c,2) Je
    '84
--Pedicabs (California)
  Trav/Holiday 165:77 (c,4) Ap
    '86
--Pedicabs (India)
  Nat Geog 167:506-7, 514-15
    (c,1) Ap '85
--Sam-lor cab (Thailand)
  Trav/Holiday 166:62-3 (c,2) S
    '86
TAYLOR, ELIZABETH
  Life 5:cov., 4, 82-90 (c,1) Mr
    '82
  Life 9:66, 176-7 (c,1) Fall '86
--1950 wedding
  Life 9:101 (2) Je '86
TAYLOR, ZACHARY
--1848 Zachary Taylor campaign
    scarf
  Am Heritage 38:28 (c,4) D '86
Tea drinking. See
    DRINKING CUSTOMS
TEA INDUSTRY
  Smithsonian 12:98-107 (c,1) F
    '82
--Early 19th cent. crate of tea
    (China)
  Am Heritage 33:43 (c,4) F '82
--1800 (China)
  Natur Hist 93:66-7 (paint-
    ing,c,1) F '84
--Herbs used in teas
  Nat Geog 163:404-5 (c,2) Mr
    '83
--Tasting
  Smithsonian 12:104 (c,4) F '82
TEA INDUSTRY--HARVESTING
--Sri Lanka
  Smithsonian 12:98 (c,1) F '82
TEACHERS
--1870s professors (Texas)
  Smithsonian 14:143 (2) N '83
TEAKETTLES
  Smithsonian 12:106-7 (c,1) F
    '82
--1851 (Great Britain)

  Smithsonian 12:107 (c,1) F '82
--Early 20th cent. silver service
    (Austria)
  Smithsonian 17:76 (c,4) Ag '86
--Russian samovar
  Smithsonian 12:101 (4) F '82
TEALS
  Nat Wildlife 20:50-1 (c,1) Je '82
  Nat Wildlife 22:19 (c,4) D '83
  Nat Geog 166:580 (c,3) N '84
  Nat Wildlife 23:11 (c,1) Je '85
  Nat Wildlife 24:16D (painting,c,2)
    D '85
--Flock in flight
  Natur Hist 94:68-9 (c,1) Je '85
TEAPOTS
--18th cent. (China)
  Natur Hist 93:76 (c,4) F '84
TEETH
  Life 6:67-86 (c,1) O '83
--Ancient man
  Nat Geog 168:597, 612, 628 (c,3)
    N '85
--Child brushing teeth
  Life 6:86 (c,4) O '83
--Diamonds inlaid in teeth (Yukon)
  Trav/Holiday 164:61 (c,1) Ag '85
--Football player with missing teeth
  Sports Illus 61:cov. (c,1) Jl 30
    '84
  Life 9:297 (c,1) Fall '86
--Lions
  Life 7:144 (c,4) N '84
--See also
    DENTISTRY
TEGUCIGALPA, HONDURAS
  Nat Geog 164:608-9, 612-15, 624-
    5 (c,1) N '83
TEHRAN, IRAN
  Nat Geog 168:128 (c,3) Jl '85
TEL AVIV, ISRAEL
  Nat Geog 168:14-15 (c,1) Jl '85
  Trav/Holiday 165:49-53 (map,c,1)
    Ja '86
TELEPHONE INDUSTRY
--Electronic switching equipment
  Smithsonian 17:66-78 (c,2) N '86
TELEPHONES
  Am Heritage 36:cov., 65-80 (c,1)
    Je '85
--1880
  Am Heritage 36:67 (2) Je '85
--1880s telephone operators
  Am Heritage 36:15 (2) F '85
  Smithsonian 17:72, 74 (3) N '86
--1885
  Am Heritage 36:15 (2) F '85

TELEVISION PROGRAMS (cont.)
   Life 5:96-102 (c,1) My '82
--"Charlie and Company"
   Ebony 40:cov., 69 (c,2) O '85
--"Chotto Kamisama" (Japan)
   Ebony 37:48 (4) S '82
--The Bill Cosby Show"
   Ebony 39:67 (3) S '84
   Ebony 40:cov., 27-30 (c,1) Ap
      '85
   Ebony 40:68 (c,4) O '85
   Ebony 41:cov., 29-34 (c,1) F
      '86
   Ebony 42:27 (c,3) D '86
--"Diff'rent Strokes"
   Ebony 37:82, 86 (2) Mr '82
   Ebony 38:42-4 (4) D '82
   Ebony 38:62 (4) O '83
--"Dynasty"
   Ebony 39:156-8 (c,2) O '84
--"The Facts of Life"
   Ebony 38:62 (4) O '83
--"Fame"
   Ebony 38:78 (2) Mr '83
--"Golden Girls"
   Life 8:175 (c,3) O '85
--"Hell Town"
   Ebony 40:70 (c,4) O '85
--"Hill Street Blues"
   Ebony 37:50-2 (3) Ap '82
--"Howdy Doody"
   Life 9:205-6 (2) Fall '86
--"I Love Lucy" (1950s)
   Life 9:82 (4) O '86
--"The Jeffersons"
   Ebony 37:31 (4) Ap '82
   Ebony 38:62 (4) O '83
--Johnny Carson as "Carnac"
   Sports Illus 59:22 (c,4) D 12
      '83
--"Julia" (1968)
   Ebony 40:122 (4) S '85
--"Late Night with David Letter-
      man"
   Sports Illus 64:42 (c,4) F 10
      '86
--"Mash"
   Life 6:40-8 (c,1) Mr '83
   Smithsonian 14:170-1 (c,4) S
      '83
--"Miami Vice"
   Ebony 40:94-8 (c,2) S '85
   Life 8:59-66 (c,2) D '85
--"The Munsters"
   Sports Illus 62:88 (4) Je 10 '85
--"Roots" (1977)
   Ebony 41:134 (4) Ag '86

--"Route 66"
   Life 6:76 (4) Je '83
--"Saturday Night Live"'s Velvet
      Jones
   Ebony 38:90 (2) Ap '83
--"SCTV" cast
   Life 5:65-72 (c,1) O '82
--"Soap"
   Ebony 39:136 (4) N '83
--Soap opera stars
   Life 5:76-82 (c,1) Ap '82
   Ebony 38:123-8 (c,3) N '82
--"Spitting Image"
   Life 9:84 (c,2) O '86
--"Star Trek"
   Life 9:38 (c,4) D '86
--Starring blacks
   Ebony 38:58-66 (3) O '83
   Ebony 39:67-72 (3) S '84
   Ebony 40:68-73 (c,2) O '85
   Ebony 41:145-54 (c,4) O '86
--"Stir Crazy"
   Ebony 40:69 (c,4) O '85
--"Twenty-One" (1950s)
   Life 9:80 (2) O '86
--"227"
   Ebony 40:68 (c,3) O '85
   Ebony 42:92-4 (2) D '86
--"Webster"
   Ebony 38:58 (4) O '83
   Ebony 39:cov., 35 (c,1) F '84
   Ebony 40:136 (c,3) F '85
TELEVISION WATCHING
   Sports Illus 58:43 (painting,c,4)
      Ap 25 '83
--1951
   Life 9:192 (4) Fall '86
--American Samoa
   Nat Geog 168:456-7 (c,2) O '85
--Australia
   Nat Geog 169:25 (c,3) Ja '86
--Bedouins (Egypt)
   Nat Geog 161:431 (c,1) Ap '82
--Egypt
   Natur Hist 92:52-3 (c,1) Jl '83
--Eskimos (Alaska)
   Nat Geog 165:824-5 (1) Je '84
--Fans watching sports
   Sports Illus 60:50 (c,4) Ja 23 '84
--In car (British Columbia)
   Nat Geog 170:50-1 (c,1) Jl '86
--In family den
   Sports Illus 62:162 (c,4) F 11 '85
--In family den (California)
   Sports Illus 63:92 (c,3) O 28 '85
--In store (China)
   Nat Geog 164:74-5 (c,1) Jl '83

TENNESSEE (cont.)
    KNOXVILLE
    MEMPHIS
    MISSISSIPPI RIVER
    NASHVILLE
TENNESSEE RIVER, SOUTHERN
  U.S.
--Link with Tombigbee River,
    Mississippi
    Nat Geog 169:368-9 (c,1) Mr
      '86
TENNIS
    Trav/Holiday 157:57 (c,3) F
      '82
--18th cent. (France)
    Smithsonian 13:144 (engrav-
      ing,c,4) D '82
--Children playing (Sweden)
    Sports Illus 62:76-7 (c,2) Je
      24 '85
--Original form of "real" tennis
    Smithsonian 13:132-46 (c,1)
      D '82
--"Real" tennis equipment
    Smithsonian 13:139 (c,4) D '82
TENNIS--EDUCATION
--Australia
    Nat Geog 161:650-1 (c,1) My
      '82
TENNIS--PROFESSIONAL
    Sports Illus 56:126-31 (c,1)
      F 10 '82
    Sports Illus 56:25-6 (c,4) Ap
      19 '82
    Sports Illus 56:68, 73 (c,4) My
      17 '82
    Sports Illus 57:30-1 (c,2) D
      27 '82
    Sports Illus 58:126-31 (c,1) F
      16 '83
    Sports Illus 58:40-7 (c,1) My
      16 '83
    Sports Illus 63:28-33 (c,3) Ag
      12 '85
--Celebrating
    Sports Illus 57:16-17, 21 (c,1)
      Jl 12 '82
    Sports Illus 60:120-3 (c,1) F 8
      '84
--Defeated player sulking
    Sports Illus 60:70-1, 80 (c,2)
      Je 25 '84
--Player falling down
    Sports Illus 58:38 (c,4) F 14
      '83
    Sports Illus 60:122 (c,3) F 8
      '84

    Sports Illus 63:28 (c,3) Ag 12
      '85
--Serving
    Sports Illus 60:36 (c,4) Ja 9 '84
    Sports Illus 60:23 (c,2) Ap 30
      '84
--Tennis-playing families
    Sports Illus 57:37-54 (c,4) Ag 23
      '82
TENNIS--PROFESSIONAL--WOMEN
    Sports Illus 56:37 (c,2) Mr 8 '82
    Sports Illus 56:104-5 (c,2) My
      24 '82
    Sports Illus 58:34-41 (c,1) Ap 4
      '83
    Sports Illus 60:50, 52 (c,4) Mr
      12 '84
    Sports Illus 62:48, 52 (c,4) Ap
      1 '85
    Sports Illus 63:46-60 (c,1) S 2
      '85
    Sports Illus 63:40-55 (c,1) S 9
      '85
    Ebony 41:79-80 (c,3) Je '86
TENNIS CLUBS
--West Side Tennis Club, Forest
    Hills, New York
    Sports Illus 63:4 (c,4) S 9 '85
--Wimbledon, England
    Sports Illus 56:64-78 (c,1) Je 21
      '82
    Sports Illus 63:2-3 (c,1) Jl 8 '85
TENNIS COURTS
--1885 (Newport, Rhode Island)
    Am Heritage 36:65 (2) D '84
--Czechoslovakia
    Sports Illus 65:22 (c,2) Ag 4 '86
--Flushing Meadow, New York
    Sports Illus 65:8-9 (c,1) S 15 '86
--Indoor home court (Michigan)
    Ebony 38:102 (c,4) D '82
--Monte Carlo
    Sports Illus 56:24-5 (c,2) Ap 19
      '82
--"Real" tennis courts
    Smithsonian 13:132-44 (c,1) D '82
--Roland Garros, Paris, France
    Ebony 38:38-9 (c,2) N '82
--South Carolina resort
    Nat Geog 164:817 (c,1) D '83
--Wimbledon, England
    Sports Illus 56:66, 78 (c,3) Je
      21 '82
TENNIS PLAYERS
    Life 5:96-7 (c,1) Ag '82
--Early 19th cent.
    Smithsonian 13:140 (4) D '82

TENNIS TOURNAMENTS (cont.)
  Sports Illus 63:26-34 (c,2) S
    16 '85
  Sports Illus 65:45-51 (c,2) S
    1 '86
--U.S. Open 1986 (Flushing
    Meadow, New York)
  Sports Illus 65:cov., 32-9
    (c,1) S 15 '86
--U.S. Open history
  Sports Illus 61:41-52 (c,1) Ag
    27 '84
  Sports Illus 63:5-16 (c,1) Ag
    26 '85
  Sports Illus 65:39-50 (c,2) Ag
    25 '86
TENTS
--1872 U.S. Army encampment
    (California)
  Smithsonian 15:148 (4) F '85
--1930s theater tent (Texas)
  Natur Hist 92:6-7 (1) Mr '83
--Afghan refugee camp (Pakistan)
  Nat Geog 167:778-9 (c,1) Je
    '85
--Antarctic camp
  Nat Geog 166:644 (c,3) N '84
  Nat Geog 169:500 (c,3) Ap '86
--Arctic expedition
  Nat Geog 170:322-3 (c,2) S '86
--Arctic region (U.S.S.R.)
  Nat Geog 163:207 (c,1) F '83
--Camping tents (Japan)
  Nat Geog 166:239 (c,4) Ag '84
--Camping tents (Montana)
  Nat Geog 167:684 (c,1) My '85
--Camping tents (Venezuela)
  Smithsonian 16:59 (c,4) My '85
--Civil War
  Am Heritage 33:68-9 (1) F '82
--Nomads (Pakistan)
  Natur Hist 92:53 (c,4) My '83
--Portable plastic tents (Califor-
    nia)
  Nat Geog 165:440-1 (c,1) Ap
    '84
--Yak-hair (China)
  Nat Geog 161:253 (c,4) F '82
TEPEES
--Alberta
  Nat Geog 169:84-5 (c,1) Ja '86
--Camping trip (Colorado)
  Nat Wildlife 25:52 (c,1) D '86
--Colorado
  Life 6:76-7 (c,1) Ag '83
--Montana
  Natur Hist 94:64-5 (painting,c,1)

  N '85
--South Dakota
  Natur Hist 93:4-5 (1) Ag '84
TERMITES
  Natur Hist 92:40-7 (c,1) My '83
--Preserved in amber
  Natur Hist 91:27 (c,1) Je '82
--Termite mound
  Natur Hist 94:36-7 (c,1) S '85
  Nat Geog 169:580-1 (c,1) My '86
TERNS
  Trav/Holiday 162:cov. (c,1) N
    '84
--Common
  Natur Hist 93:7 (c,3) My '84
--Fairy terns
  Nat Wildlife 21:46-51 (c,1) Ag '83
--Least terns
  Smithsonian 15:68-74 (c,1) Ap '84
--Roseate
  Natur Hist 93:16 (c,3) My '84
TERRIERS
  Smithsonian 15:116 (4) S '84
--See also
    LHASA APSO DOGS
    YORKSHIRE TERRIERS
TERRORISM
--1985 ordeal of hijacked American
    hostage (Lebanon)
  Life 9:50-64 (c,1) Ap '86
--Airport bombing (Frankfurt, West
    Germany)
  Life 8:50-1 (1) Ag '85
--Anti-terrorist protection (Kuwait)
  Life 8:131-6 (c,1) D '85
--Hijacked plane (Algeria)
  Life 8:45-9 (1) Ag '85
--Hostage returning home
  Life 9:6-7 (c,1) Ja '86
--Lebanese hijackers (1985)
  Life 9:51 (c,4) Ap '86
--Libyan diplomat killed by terrorist
    (Rome, Italy)
  Life 8:51 (2) Mr '85
--Shi'ite Muslim terrorist
  Life 8:45 (2) Ag '85
TESLA, NIKOLA
  Smithsonian 17:120, 133 (1) Je
    '86
--Work with electricity
  Smithsonian 17:120-34 (c,1) Je
    '86
TEST TUBES
  Smithsonian 13:77 (c,4) Ap '82
  Smithsonian 15:104 (c,4) Je '84
TETON NATIONAL FOREST, WYOMING
--Wagon train

THEATERS (cont.)
--See also
> COLOSSEUM
> LINCOLN CENTER

THEODORE ROOSEVELT NA-
TIONAL PARK, BAD-
LANDS, NORTH DAKOTA
> Trav/Holiday 164:54-5 (c,1) Jl
> '85

THERAPY
--Acupuncture
> Life 9:72 (c,2) My '86
--Arthritis therapy
> Ebony 38:56 (4) F '83
--Back pain treatments
> Life 8:116-22 (c,1) Ap '85
--Biofeedback
> Life 9:68 (c,2) My '86
--Family therapy session (New
> York)
> Life 5:74-80 (1) Mr '82
--Group session (Minnesota)
> Life 6:62-3 (c,1) Ap '83
--Hypnotherapy
> Ebony 40:68-70 (2) S '85
--Leg strengthening therapy
> Sports Illus 64:97 (c,4) F 10
> '86
--Photographs used in photo-
> therapy
> Life 5:15-22 (c,2) O '82
--Physical therapy
> Life 6:74 (2) Ap '83
--Sensory deprivation tank
> Sports Illus 57:164 (c,4) S 1
> '82
--Shock therapy for child mol-
> esters (Oregon)
> Life 7:50-1 (1) D '84
--Stroke victim learning to walk
> Ebony 41:150 (2) Mr '86
--Therapists working on Hollywood
> stars
> Life 9:63-72 (c,1) My '86
--Treating depression
> Life 5:92-8 (1) Ap '82

THERMOMETERS
--17th cent. (Italy)
> Smithsonian 13:94 (painting,c,4)
> S '82

THISTLES
> Nat Wildlife 20:52 (c,1) Ag '82
> Nat Wildlife 23:61 (c,4) D '84

THOMAS, DYLAN
--Grave marker (Wales)
> Nat Geog 164:57 (c,4) Jl '83
--Home (Laugharne, Wales)

> Nat Geog 164:56 (c,2) Jl '83

THOMPSON, DOROTHY
--Caricature
> Am Heritage 37:54 (4) Je '86

THORPE, JIM
> Sports Illus 57:48-60 (4) O 25
> '82
> Life 7:106 (1) Summer '84
--Birthplace marker (Oklahoma)
> Sports Illus 57:58 (c,4) O 25 '82
--Tombstone (Pennsylvania)
> Sports Illus 57:60 (c,4) O 25 '82

THOUSAND ISLANDS, NEW YORK/
ONTARIO
--International Bridge
> Trav/Holiday 162:10 (4) S '84

THRUSHES
> Smithsonian 13:172, 184 (c,4) O
> '82
--Swainson's thrush
> Smithsonian 13:184 (c,4) O '82

THYME
> Nat Geog 163:398 (c,4) Mr '83

TIBET
> Natur Hist 91:48-57 (c,1) S '82
> Natur Hist 95:56-65 (c,1) Ja '86
--Anyemaqen region
> Nat Geog 161:244-63 (map,c,1)
> F '82
--Himalayas and High Plateau
> Natur Hist 95:56-65 (map,c,1) N
> '86
--Kailas Mountain
> Smithsonian 13:94-8 (c,1) My '82
--Kama Valley
> Ebony 37:67 (c,2) Mr '82
--Labrang area
> Nat Geog 165:306-11 (c,1) Mr '84
--Mythical kingdom of Shambhala
> Natur Hist 92:54-63 (c,1) Ap '83
--Tsaparang citadel
> Natur Hist 95:cov., 34-45
> (map,c,1) Jl '86
--See also
> HIMALAYAN MOUNTAINS

TIBET--ART
--Statues of deities
> Natur Hist 92:cov., 57 (c,1) Ap
> '83

TIBET--COSTUME
> Smithsonian 13:100-1 (c,1) My '82
> Nat Geog 165:306-13, 316-19 (c,1)
> Mr '84
> Natur Hist 95:76 (c,4) Je '86
--Dalai Lama and followers (India)
> Smithsonian 14:82-91 (c,1) Mr '84
--Golog tribe

TOADS
   Nat Geog 161:84-5 (c,1) Ja
      '82
   Nat Wildlife 23:14 (painting,c,4)
      Ap '85
--Golden
   Nat Geog 163:60-1 (c,1) Ja '83
   Natur Hist 93:46-50 (c,1) My
      '84
--Yosemite toads
   Natur Hist 93:72-7 (c,1) Mr
      '84
TOASTERS
--1944
   Am Heritage 35:107 (4) D '83
TOBACCO INDUSTRY
--Binding leaves (Kentucky)
   Nat Geog 161:524 (c,1) Ap '82
--Curing burley tobacco (Ten-
      nessee)
   Nat Geog 169:632 (c,1) My '86
--Florida
   Nat Geog 162:212-13 (c,2) Ag
      '82
--Nicaragua
   Nat Geog 168:794-5 (c,2) D
      '85
--Tobacco ads painted on barns
      (Midwest)
   Smithsonian 13:112-13 (c,3) Ag
      '82
TOBACCO INDUSTRY--PLANTING
--Georgia
   Nat Geog 166:374-5 (c,1) S
      '84
TOCQUEVILLE, ALEXIS DE
   Am Heritage 33:cov., 8 (paint-
      ing,c,1) Je '82
--1830s journey through America
   Am Heritage 33:cov., 8-17
      (map,c,1) Je '82
TOGO
   Trav/Holiday 158:33-6 (map,c,1)
      Ag '82
TOGO--COSTUME
   Trav/Holiday 158:cov., 33-6
      (c,1) Ag '82
TOKYO, JAPAN
   Ebony 37:49 (c,3) S '82
   Nat Geog 170:606-45 (map,c,1)
      N '86
--Early 18th cent.
   Nat Geog 170:616 (painting,c,4)
      N '86
--1923 earthquake
   Nat Geog 170:623 (painting,c,4)
      N '86

TOLEDO, SPAIN
   Nat Geog 161:726-53 (map,c,1)
      Je '82
   Life 5:92-8 (c,1) Jl '82
--1600 El Greco painting "View of
      Toledo"
   Smithsonian 13:54 (c,2) Jl '82
   Life 5:92 (c,4) Jl '82
TOLSTOY, LEO
   Nat Geog 169:759-91 (c,1) Je '86
--Anna Karenina manuscript
   Nat Geog 169:772 (2) Je '86
--Death mask
   Nat Geog 169:790 (c,4) Je '86
--Grave site (U.S.S.R.)
   Nat Geog 169:790-1 (c,1) Je '86
--Home (U.S.S.R.)
   Nat Geog 169:762-91 (c,1) Je '86
--Sites associated with him
      (U.S.S.R.)
   Nat Geog 169:759-91 (map,c,1)
      Je '86
TOMATO INDUSTRY
--Israeli desert
   Nat Geog 161:452-3 (c,4) Ap '82
TOMBIGBEE RIVER, MISSISSIPPI
   Nat Geog 169:364-83 (map,c,1)
      Mr '86
--Link with Tennessee River
   Nat Geog 169:368-9 (c,1) Mr '86
TOMBS
--4th cent. B.C. tomb of Mausolus,
      Halicarnassus
   Smithsonian 14:59 (drawing,4) Mr
      '84
--3rd cent. Roman sarcophagus
   Nat Geog 167:153 (c,4) F '85
--12th cent. Chinese emperor
   Life 8:150-1 (c,1) D '85
--16th cent. (India)
   Nat Geog 167:487 (c,2) Ap '85
--17th cent. cenotaphs (India)
   Nat Geog 167:491 (c,4) Ap '85
--19th cent. cenotaphs (Washington,
      D.C.)
   Am Heritage 33:66 (c,3) Je '82
--19th cent. Vietnamese emperors
      (Hue)
   Smithsonian 17:46-7, 51, 55 (c,1)
      Je '86
--Clover Adams (Washington, D.C.)
   Am Heritage 36:52 (c,2) Je '85
--Ancient Maya tombs (Río Azul re-
      gion, Guatemala)
   Nat Geog 166:137-137B (c,3) Ag
      '84
   Nat Geog 169:434-5, 458-61 (c,1)

TOMBS (cont.)
Ap '86
--Ancient mummy case (Thebes,
Greece)
Smithsonian 14:115 (c,2) S '83
--Ancient stone burial chambers
(Wales)
Nat Geog 164:39 (c,2) Jl '83
--Ancient stone tombs (Saudi
Arabia)
Smithsonian 14:cov., 42-3, 47,
50 (c,1) S '83
--Babur (Kabul, Afghanistan)
Nat Geog 167:498 (c,4) Ap '85
--Daniel Boone (Kentucky and
Missouri)
Nat Geog 168:838-9 (c,1) D '85
--Bronze Age Egyptian (Gaza,
Israel)
Nat Geog 162:738-69 (c,1) D
'82
--Fra Angelico (Rome, Italy)
Smithsonian 17:564 (c,4) D '86
--Francisco Franco (Madrid, Spain)
Nat Geog 169:171 (c,4) F '86
--Inverness, Scotland
Trav/Holiday 159:60 (4) Ja '83
--Abraham Lincoln (Springfield,
Illinois)
Am Heritage 33:76-8, 82 (2)
Ap '82
--Martin Luther (Wittenberg, East
Germany)
Nat Geog 164:456 (c,1) O '83
--Mausoleum (Great Britain)
Nat Geog 168:667 (c,4) N '85
--Mausoleum (Washington, D.C.)
Am Heritage 37:80 (c,4) Ag '86
--Napoleon (Paris, France)
Nat Geog 161:188 (c,4) F '82
--Neanderthal grave (Israel)
Nat Geog 168:612 (c,4) N '85
--Putting human remains in orbit
Life 8:76-7 (c,1) Ap '85
--St. Peter (Vatican City)
Nat Geog 168:745 (c,4) D '85
--South Africa
Sports Illus 59:66 (c,3) Jl 18
'83
--Robert Louis Stevenson (West-
ern Samoa)
Nat Geog 168:473 (c,1) O '85
--Tolstoy's grave (U.S.S.R.)
Nat Geog 169:790-1 (c,1) Je
'86
--Tomb of the Unknown Soldier
(Warsaw, Poland)

Trav/Holiday 165:18 (c,4) F '86
--See also
CEMETERIES
GRANT'S TOMB
TAJ MAHAL
TOMBSTONES
TOMBSTONES
--1681 (New England)
Smithsonian 13:109 (c,2) Je '82
--Jewish cemetery, East Germany
Nat Geog 161:32 (c,4) Ja '82
--Archibald MacLeish (Massachusetts)
Smithsonian 14:64 (c,4) O '83
--Mountaineers (Kenya)
Sports Illus 62:72 (2) My 27 '85
--Peru
Nat Geog 161:303 (c,4) Mr '82
--Edith Piaf (Paris, France)
Trav/Holiday 157:56 (c,4) Mr '82
--Dylan Thomas (Wales)
Nat Geog 164:57 (c,4) Jl '83
--Jim Thorpe (Pennsylvania)
Sports Illus 57:60 (c,4) O 25 '82
--Unsuccessful Arctic explorers
(Canada)
Nat Geog 164:122 (c,4) Jl '83
TONGA ISLANDS
Trav/Holiday 165:16 (c,4) Ja '86
--Tongatapu Island
Natur Hist 92:80-1 (c,1) F '83
TONGA ISLANDS--HOUSING
--Palm-thatched houses
Trav/Holiday 165:16 (c,4) Ja '86
TONGASS NATIONAL FOREST,
ALASKA
Nat Geog 162:334-5 (c,1) S '82
TONGUES
--Lizards
Natur Hist 91:58-67 (c,1) S '82
TONTO NATIONAL FOREST, ARIZ-
ONA
Natur Hist 95:28-32 (map,c,1) D
'86
TOOLS
--Ancient man
Nat Geog 168:602-4, 610-11, 616-
17 (c,1) N '85
Natur Hist 95:24, 26 (drawing,4)
D '86
--Ancient Maya tool craftsmen
(Guatemala)
Nat Geog 169:450-1 (painting,c,1)
Ap '86
--Stone Age needles (France)
Natur Hist 95:75 (c,4) O '86
--Table saw
Sports Illus 58:42 (c,4) Ap 11 '83

TOOLS (cont.)
--Vise
   Sports Illus 57:64-5 (c,1) D
      27 '82
--See also
      AXES
      KNIVES
TOPAZ
   Natur Hist 95:94-5 (c,1) F '86
TORNADOES
   Life 7:84, 88 (c,2) Ag '84
--1895 (North Dakota)
   Am Heritage 37:38-9 (1) Je '86
--Artificially created in lab
   Life 5:172-3 (c,1) D '82
--Midwest farmers running for
      storm cellar (1929)
   Am Heritage 37:28-9 (paint-
      ing,c,1) Je '86
TORNADOES--DAMAGE
   Life 7:84-8 (c,1) Ag '84
--Ruins of house (Texas)
   Life 8:44-5 (1) F '85
--Tionesta Forest, Pennsylvania
   Natur Hist 95:74-8 (c,2) N '86
TORONTO, ONTARIO
   Trav/Holiday 157:38, 44 (c,1)
      My '82
--CN building
   Sports Illus 59:19 (c,2) Jl 18
      '83
--Eaton Centre mall
   Trav/Holiday 157:44 (c,1) My
      '82
TORTOISES
   Sports Illus 59:46 (c,4) Jl 18
      '83
   Nat Geog 164:271 (c,4) Ag '83
   Nat Geog 165:142 (c,2) Ja '84
   Nat Wildlife 22:22-8 (c,1) F '84
   Trav/Holiday 161:79 (c,3) Mr
      '84
   Trav/Holiday 162:50 (c,3) N '84
--Baby Galapagos tortoise
   Life 5:44-5 (c,1) Je '82
--Great tortoise
   Smithsonian 16:150 (4) Je '85
TOSCANINI, ARTURO
   Life 9:355 (2) Fall '86
TOTEM POLES
--Alaska
   Trav/Holiday 157:48 (c,4) My
      '82
   Nat Geog 165:71 (c,4) Ja '84
   Trav/Holiday 161:58 (c,4) F
      '84
   Trav/Holiday 163:50 (c,4) F '85

--Vancouver, British Columbia
   Ebony 38:157 (c,4) My '83
TOUCANS
--Toucanets
   Nat Wildlife 21:45 (painting,c,3)
      F '83
TOUCH-ME-NOT PLANTS
   Natur Hist 91:32-9 (c,1) My '82
TOULOUSE-LAUTREC, HENRI DE
   Smithsonian 16:66-7 (c,4) N '85
--Paintings by him
   Smithsonian 16:64-73 (c,1) N '85
--Self-portrait (1880)
   Smithsonian 16:67 (painting,c,4)
      N '85
TOURISTS
--Airboat tour (Everglades, Florida)
   Trav/Holiday 165:44-5 (c,1) Ja
      '86
--Arctic sightseeing bus (Manitoba)
   Smithsonian 16:41 (c,4) Mr '86
--Hawaii
   Life 7:16 (c,3) Ag '84
--Japanese (Saipan, Mariana Islands)
   Nat Geog 170:469 (c,1) O '86
--Michelin guidebooks
   Smithsonian 17:57-8, 62-4 (c,3)
      Je '86
--National parks (early 20th cent.)
   Natur Hist 91:16-20 (3) Je '82
--New Hampshire
   Nat Geog 162:775 (c,3) D '82
--Oceania
   Trav/Holiday 158:56 (c,2) N '82
--Satirical portrayal of tourists
      (Spain)
   Nat Geog 162:698-9 (c,1) D '82
--Sightseeing in glass-bottom boat
      (Australia)
   Trav/Holiday 165:40 (c,4) F '86
--Wearing turbans (India)
   Trav/Holiday 165:61 (c,4) Je '86
--World Trade Center Observation
      Deck, New York (1976)
   Life 5:18 (c,4) Ap '82
--Yosemite National Park, California
   Nat Geog 167:62-3 (c,1) Ja '85
TOWER OF LONDON, ENGLAND
--White Tower
   Smithsonian 13:66-7 (c,3) O '82
Town halls. See
      CITY HALLS
TOY INDUSTRY
--Chinese plant
   Nat Geog 164:72-3 (c,1) Jl '83
TOYS
   Ebony 38:63-6 (2) N '82

TRACK AND FIELD--MEETS
(cont.)
Sports Illus 63:28 (c,3) Jl 15
'85
--Switzerland
Sports Illus 61:16-19 (c,3) S
3 '84
--World Championships 1983 (Hel-
sinki, Finland)
Sports Illus 59:cov., 16-29
(c,1) Ag 22 '83
--See also
DISCUS THROWING
HIGH JUMPING
HURDLING
JAVELIN THROWING
JUMPING
POLE VAULTING
SHOT-PUTTING
TRACK
TRACTORS
Ebony 38:116 (3) Ag '83
Ebony 41:46-7 (c,2) Je '86
Sports Illus 65:53 (c,3) Ag 11
'86
--Kenya
Sports Illus 62:72 (c,4) My 27
'85
TRADING CARDS
--1910s sporting cards of swim-
mers
Sports Illus 63:104-5 (c,1) D
23 '85
Traffic. See
AUTOMOBILES--TRAFFIC
TRAFFIC LIGHTS
--Minnesota
Smithsonian 16:48-9 (c,3) D
'85
TRAILERS
Smithsonian 16:74-83 (c,1) D
'85
--1930s trailer camps
Am Heritage 37:99-103 (c,3)
D '85
--Trailer home
Sports Illus 65:118 (c,3) S 3
'86
--Virginia
Nat Geog 163:810-11 (c,1) Je
'83
--See also
MOBILE HOMES
Train stations. See
RAILROAD STATIONS
TRAINS
Trav/Holiday 158:56 (c,4) O '82

Ebony 40:78 (4) Ja '85
--1880s passenger car interior
Am Heritage 36:54 (drawing,4)
Je '85
--1885 interior
Am Heritage 33:86-7 (painting,c,1)
Ap '82
--1890s caboose
Smithsonian 16:101 (4) F '86
--1930s hoboes on boxcars (Utah)
Am Heritage 36:62-3 (paint-
ing, c,1) Ag '85
--1934 Union Pacific streamliner
Am Heritage 35:16 (4) O '84
--Abandoned 1910s train (Saudi
Arabia)
Nat Geog 168:506-7 (c,1) O '85
--Australian outback
Nat Geog 169:738-49 (c,1) Je '86
Smithsonian 17:100-13 (c,1) Je
'86
--Cabooses
Smithsonian 16:100-11 (c,1) F '86
--Canada
Trav/Holiday 166:65-6 (c,2) O '86
--Great Britain
Nat Geog 169:392-3 (c,1) Mr '86
--History of the Orient Express
Smithsonian 14:58-69 (c,1) D '83
--India
Nat Geog 165:cov., 696-748 (c,1)
Je '84
--Magnetically levitated train (Japan)
Smithsonian 15:89 (c,1) Jl '84
--Night scene of train
Trav/Holiday 165:66-7 (c,1) Je
'86
--Pullman cars
Am Heritage 36:55-7, 114 (c,2)
Je '85
--Royal train interior (India)
Trav/Holiday 160:46 (c,1) N '83
--Steam trains (Mali)
Trav/Holiday 159:30, 32 (c,3) Mr
'83
--Taiwa
Trav/Holiday 166:80 (4) O '86
--See also
LOCOMOTIVES
RAILROADS
SUBWAYS
TRANSIT WORKERS
--Bus drivers (Chicago, Illinois)
Ebony 38:60 (2) Ag '83
TRANSPORTATION
--All-terrain vehicles (Canada)
Nat Geog 161:389 (c,4) Mr '82

TREES (cont.)
--Research on water-conducting
    vessels
    Natur Hist 91:10-11 (c,4) Jl
    '82
--Roots (Brazil)
    Nat Geog 163:42-3 (c,2) Ja '83
--Sloanea
    Smithsonian 13:40 (c,4) Ja '83
--Straw coats on plants for win-
    ter protection (Japan)
    Smithsonian 15:94-101 (c,1)
    F '85
--Stripped by moths (Maryland)
    Smithsonian 15:47, 50 (c,4)
    My '84
--Traveler tree
    Nat Wildlife 22:57 (c,2) D '83
--Tree line spruces
    Natur Hist 94:58-65 (c,1) Ja
    '85
--Triple Twist Tree, Idaho
    Trav/Holiday 158:4 (3) Jl '82
--Twisted trunk (Arkansas)
    Natur Hist 94:82 (c,1) O '85
--Wildlife living in trees
    Nat Wildlife 23:34-5 (draw-
    ing,c,2) Ag '85
--See also
        ACACIAS
        AILANTHUS
        ALMOND
        AMBER
        APPLE
        ASPEN
        AUTUMN
        BIRCH
        BLACK TUPELO
        BREADFRUIT
        BRISTLECONE PINE
        CHERRY
        CHESTNUT
        CHRISTMAS TREES
        COTTONWOOD
        CYPRESS
        DOGWOOD
        DOUGLAS FIR
        ELDER
        ELM
        EVERGREEN
        FIG
        FIR
        FORESTS
        LARCH
        LAUREL
        LEAVES
        LINDEN

        MAGNOLIA
        MANGROVE
        MAPLE
        MOUNTAIN ASH
        MULBERRY
        OAK
        OLIVE
        PALM
        PEAR
        PINE
        PLUM
        POPLAR
        RAIN FORESTS
        REDWOOD
        SEQUOIA
        SPRUCE
        SWEET GUM
        TREE PLANTING
        TULIP
        WILLOW
Trials. See
        COURTROOMS
        JUSTICE, ADMINISTRATION
        OF
TRILOBITES
--Fossils
    Smithsonian 15:70, 72 (c,3) Ja
    '85
    Nat Geog 168:184 (c,1) Ag '85
    Natur Hist 94:37 (c,4) D '85
TRINIDAD AND TOBAGO
    Ebony 40:102-8 (c,2) N '84
    Trav/Holiday 164:20-4 (map,c,1)
    D '85
--See also
        PORT-OF-SPAIN
TRINIDAD AND TOBAGO--COSTUME
    Ebony 40:102-8 (c,2) N '84
--Mardi Gras
    Trav/Holiday 157:56 (c,4) Ja '82
TROGONS (BIRDS)
    Natur Hist 93:102-3 (c,1) My '84
    Natur Hist 93:90 (c,4) N '84
TROLLEY CARS
--19th cent. cable car system dia-
    gram
    Am Heritage 36:95, 114 (2) Ap
    '85
--1870s San Francisco cable cars
    Am Heritage 36:90-3 (1) Ap '85
--1872
    Smithsonian 13:42-3 (2) S '82
--1880s ads for cable cars
    Am Heritage 36:95, 114 (c,2) Ap
    '85
--1880s cable cars (Portland, Oregon)
    Am Heritage 36:96 (2) Ap '85

TROLLEY CARS (cont.)
--Early 20th cent. (Boston,
    Massachusetts)
  Am Heritage 35:30 (3) F '84
--Early 20th cent. (St. Louis,
    Missouri)
  Am Heritage 33:46 (1) Ag '82
--Budapest, Hungary
  Nat Geog 163:234-5 (c,1) F
    '83
--Cable cars on Brooklyn Bridge,
    New York City (1880s)
  Nat Geog 163:574-5 (c,1) My
    '83
--Chattanooga, Tennessee
  Trav/Holiday 157:75 (c,4) Mr
    '82
--History of cable cars
  Am Heritage 36:90-3, 99-101
    (c,1) Ap '85
--Mexico City, Mexico
  Nat Geog 166:154-5 (c,1) Ag
    '84
--Replica of 1901 trolley (Lowell,
    Massachusetts)
  Trav/Holiday 164:12 (c,4) O
    '85
--San Francisco cable cars
  Am Heritage 36:90-3, 99-101
    (c,1) Ap '85
  Sports Illus 64:38 (c,2) Je 9
    '86
--Streetcars (New Orleans,
    Louisiana)
  Ebony 41:120 (c,4) Jl '86
--Trams (Melbourne, Australia)
  Trav/Holiday 164:65 (c,3) O
    '85
--Trams (Sacramento, California)
  Trav/Holiday 158:46 (c,4) Jl
    '82
TROLLOPE, ANTHONY
--1873 caricature
  Smithsonian 13:214 (4) N '82
TROPHIES
--1904 Olympics (St. Louis)
  Life 7:29 (4) Summer '84
--America's Cup
  Life 7:18-19 (c,1) Ja '84
  Sports Illus 60:66 (c,4) Mr 12
    '84
  Sports Illus 62:85 (c,4) F 11
    '85
  Sports Illus 65:15 (c,2) S 22
    '86
--Auto racing
  Sports Illus 56:81 (3) Ja 11 '82

Sports Illus 56:44 (c,4) F 22 '82
Sports Illus 64:20 (c,1) Je 9 '86
--Baseball (1954)
  Sports Illus 58:116 (4) Ap 4 '83
--Basketball
  Sports Illus 56:47 (c,2) Je 21 '82
  Sports Illus 57:79 (4) Ag 9 '82
  Sports Illus 58:cov. (c,1) Ap 11
    '83
  Ebony 38:126 (4) S '83
  Sports Illus 64:92 (4) Mr 10 '86
--Bowling
  Ebony 41:157 (3) F '86
--Boxing
  Ebony 41:48 (2) Jl '86
--Boxing title belts
  Sports Illus 57:41 (c,4) Ag 2 '82
  Sports Illus 58:20-1 (c,2) Mr 28
    '83
  Sports Illus 58:53 (c,4) Je 6 '83
  Sports Illus 60:32 (c,4) F 18 '85
  Ebony 39:27 (c,2) Mr '84
  Sports Illus 62:32 (c,4) F 18 '85
  Sports Illus 62:80 (c,2) My 20
    '85
  Sports Illus 63:25 (c,4) Ag 19 '85
  Sports Illus 63:66 (c,4) D 23 '85
--Breeder's Cup
  Sports Illus 63:11 (c,4) O 21 '85
--Bridge
  Ebony 40:146 (3) O '85
--Chess
  Life 8:150 (c,3) Je '85
--Figure skating
  Sports Illus 58:76 (c,4) F 14 '83
--Flying
  Sports Illus 60:96 (c,2) Ja 16 '84
--Football
  Sports Illus 59:44-5 (c,1) N 7
    '83
  Sports Illus 63:39 (c,4) Jl 1 '85
  Sports Illus 64:40 (c,2) Mr 24
    '86
--Golf
  Ebony 37:72 (2) Ja '82
  Sports Illus 56:45 (c,4) F 8 '82
  Ebony 37:102 (3) O '82
  Ebony 38:96 (4) N '82
  Sports Illus 58:42 (c,2) Je 20 '83
  Sports Illus 59:cov. (c,1) Jl 25
    '83
  Sports Illus 59:17 (c,4) Ag 15
    '83
  Sports Illus 59:39 (c,4) O 24 '83
  Sports Illus 61:13 (c,4) Jl 30 '84
  Sports Illus 63:23 (c,2) Jl 29 '85
  Sports Illus 64:cov. (c,2) Je 23

TRUCKS (cont.)
Smithsonian 15:53 (c,2) Ap '84
--Red Cross trucks (El Salvador)
Nat Geog 170:677 (c,3) N '86
--Scouting for oil and gas (Montana)
Life 6:111 (c,4) Jl '83
--Tow trucks
Sports Illus 60:22 (c,4) Je 4 '84
--Van
Life 7:10 (c,4) S '84
TRUFFLES
--Hunting for truffles (Oregon)
Nat Geog 170:338-9 (c,1) S '86
TRUK ISLANDS
Nat Geog 170:484-7 (c,1) O '86
--Underwater wreckage of Japanese World War II fleet
Life 5:54-8 (c,1) Ap '82
TRUK ISLANDS--COSTUME
Nat Geog 170:484-5 (c,1) O '86
TRUMAN, HARRY S
Ebony 37:60-2 (2) O '82
Smithsonian 14:105 (4) N '83
Am Heritage 35:105-8 (3) D '83
Life 7:107-12 (c,4) My '84
Ebony 41:249 (4) N '85
Am Heritage 37:62 (1) D '85
Life 9:211, 214-15, 267 (1) Fall '86
--Bess Truman
Am Heritage 34:100 (4) Ag '83
--Depicted on postage stamp
Am Heritage 34:56 (c,4) D '82
--Home and library (Independence, Missouri)
Trav/Holiday 159:6 (4) Mr '83
Life 7:107-14 (c,1) My '84
TRUMPET PLAYING
Ebony 38:29-30 (2) Mr '83
Sports Illus 59:58-9 (c,4) N 21 '83
Life 6:153-60 (1) D '83
Ebony 39:78 (3) F '84
Smithsonian 15:162 (3) My '84
Ebony 41:50-6 (c,2) S '86
--Boy Scout playing reveille
Smithsonian 16:32 (c,1) Jl '85
TRUTH, SOJOURNER
Ebony 40:28 (drawing,4) F '85
Ebony 41:240 (drawing,4) N '85
TSETSE FLIES
Nat Geog 170:814, 820, 824-5 (map,c,2) D '86

--Fighting tsetse fly menace (Africa)
Nat Geog 170:814-33 (c,1) D '86
--Tsetse fly fossil
Nat Geog 170:825 (c,4) D '86
TUAMOTU ISLANDS, FRENCH POLYNESIA
--Pearl industry (Marutea)
Nat Geog 168:194-7 (c,1) Ag '85
TUBA PLAYING
Sports Illus 63:146 (c,4) D 23 '85
TUBAS
Sports Illus 59:202 (c,3) S 1 '83
TUBMAN, HARRIET
Nat Geog 166:cov., 2 (c,1) Jl '84
Ebony 40:52-8 (2) D '84
Ebony 41:240 (4) N '85
TUCSON, ARIZONA
Trav/Holiday 159:cov., 51-5 (c,1) F '83
--Fort Lowell storehouse
Am Heritage 33:84-5 (c,2) Ap '82
TUGBOATS
Life 8:72-3 (1) Mr '85
--Early 20th cent.
Am Heritage 34:83 (painting,c,4) Ap '83
TULIP TREES
Nat Wildlife 22:10 (c,3) Ag '84
TULIPS
--X-ray photo
Smithsonian 17:90 (4) O '86
TULSA, OKLAHOMA
Nat Geog 164:378-403 (map,c,1) S '83
--Boston Avenue Methodist Church interior
Trav/Holiday 163:8 (c,4) Mr '85
TUNA
--Bluefin
Nat Geog 162:220-39 (c,1) Ag '82
TUNISIA
Trav/Holiday 158:49-50 (c,2) O '82
TUNNELS
--19th cent. construction of Hudson River tunnels
Smithsonian 17:74-6 (2) My '86
--19th cent. tunnel construction
Smithsonian 17:66-76 (1) My '86
--1827 near-disaster in Thames tunnel, England
Smithsonian 17:68 (cartoon,c,3) My '86
--1880 St. Gotthard Tunnel construction

TURTLES (cont.)
Nat Geog 168:802 (c,3) D '85
--Green sea turtles with barnacles
Nat Wildlife 22:22-3 (c,1) Ag
'84
--Painted
Nat Wildlife 20:44 (c,4) Je '82
--Ridley turtles
Natur Hist 95:90, 92 (c,3) N
'86
--Snapping turtles
Nat Geog 169:44-9 (c,1) Ja '86
--Turtle varieties
Nat Wildlife 24:42-3 (draw-
ing,c,4) Je '86
--See also
TORTOISES
TUTANKHAMUN
--Reconstruction of facial features
Life 6:131-4 (c,1) Je '83
--Tomb artifacts
Trav/Holiday 163:35 (4) Ja '85
TWAIN, MARK
Sports Illus 58:90 (4) My 30
'83
Am Heritage 35:68 (drawing,4)
F '84
Am Heritage 35:82 (4) Je '84
Am Heritage 36:cov., 3, 102-6
(c,1) F '85
Life 8:155-62 (c,2) N '85
Life 9:333 (4) Fall '86
--1981 medal depicting him
Nat Geog 162:75 (c,4) Jl '82
--Caricatures of him
Nat Wildlife 23:6-10 (c,4) Je
'85
--Children dressed as Tom Sawyer
characters (Missouri)
Life 8:156-7 (c,1) N '85
--Home (Hartford, Connecticut)
Life 8:160 (c,3) N '85
--Illustrations from Huckleberry
Finn
Am Heritage 35:81-5 (draw-
ing,4) Je '84
Am Heritage 36:10 (drawing,4)
D '84
Nat Wildlife 23:5 (drawing,4)
Je '85
--Statue (California)
Life 8:155 (c,3) N '85
TWEED, WILLIAM MARCY (BOSS)
--19th cent. rule of Boss Tweed
(New York City)
Am Heritage 38:81-96 (draw-
ing,2) D '86

TWILIGHT
--Dusk over Brooklyn Bridge, New
York City
Smithsonian 14:84 (c,4) Ap '83
--Ireland
Sports Illus 60:68-9 (c,1) Je 4
'84
TWINS
--19th cent. Siamese twins
Natur Hist 91:20 (4) N '82
--Adult women
Ebony 39:41 (c,3) Jl '84
--Interracial twins (Great Britain)
Ebony 39:42-8 (3) Ap '84
--Siamese twins
Life 7:48-52 (c,1) O '84
TYPEWRITERS
--1867 invention
Am Heritage 33:79 (painting,3)
Ag '82
--Early 20th cent.
Nat Geog 162:356 (c,1) S '82
--Antique
Smithsonian 13:168 (c,4) Mr '83
--William Faulkner's typewriter
Trav/Holiday 166:56 (c,2) Jl '86
--Old model
Nat Geog 162:199 (c,4) Ag '82
--Portable
Life 5:74-5 (c,1) D '82
--Writer working at typewriter
Sports Illus 63:94 (c,4) N 4 '85
TYPHOONS
Smithsonian 13:98-9 (c,1) S '82
--Photo of vortex
Smithsonian 13:94-5 (c,2) Ap '82
TYPING
Life 6:92 (4) My '83

-U-

UCCELLO, PAOLO
--"Battle of San Romano"
Smithsonian 13:65-7 (painting,c,1)
N '82
UFFIZI GALLERY, FLORENCE, ITALY
Smithsonian 13:cov., 58-71 (c,1)
N '82
UFOs. See
UNIDENTIFIED FLYING OB-
JECTS
UGANDA
Nat Geog 167:586-9, 622-33
(map,c,1) My '85
--Ruwenzori Range
Nat Geog 167:633 (c,4) My '85

UGANDA (cont.)
--See also
    LAKE VICTORIA
    NILE RIVER
UGANDA--COSTUME
    Nat Geog 167:622-3 (c,1) My
        '85
--Idi Amin
    Ebony 39:112 (4) Jl '84
UKULELES
    Smithsonian 12:164 (c,4) Mr '82
ULAN BATOR, MONGOLIA
    Nat Geog 167:244-5 (c,4) F '85
ULYSSES
--1909 painting of Ulysses and
        mermaids
    Smithsonian 14:86-7 (c,2) Je
        '83
--Retracing route of Ulysses
        (Greece)
    Nat Geog 170:196-225 (map,c,1)
        Ag '86
UMBRELLAS
    Life 5:114-15 (c,1) Ja '82
    Life 5:32-3 (c,1) Mr '82
    Trav/Holiday 158:64 (c,1) N
        '82
    Sports Illus 58:35 (c,4) Ap 18
        '83
    Smithsonian 14:111 (c,4) O '83
    Nat Geog 165:738-9 (c,1) Je '84
--Aerial view of many umbrellas
        during snow storm (Poland)
    Life 9:394-5 (c,1) Fall '86
--Beach umbrella (France)
    Sports Illus 61:124-5 (c,1) Jl
        18 '84
--Golf umbrellas
    Sports Illus 56:73 (c,4) Je 7
        '82
--India
    Nat Geog 166:712-13 (c,1) D
        '84
--Papua New Guinea
    Nat Geog 162:142 (c,1) Ag '82
--Thailand
    Nat Geog 162:513 (c,1) O '82
--Umbrella making (Thailand)
    Trav/Holiday 166:64-5 (c,2) S
        '86
--Woven straw umbrellas (Nepal)
    Nat Geog 166:733 (c,1) D '84
UMIAKS (BOATS)
--Arctic
    Nat Geog 164:100-3, 106, 109
        (c,1) Jl '83

UNCLE SAM
    Nat Wildlife 21:31 (drawing,c,4)
        Ag '83
--1918 U.S. poster asking children
        to plant gardens
    Am Heritage 37:6 (drawing,c,2)
        Ap '86
--1936 costume (New York)
    Smithsonian 13:114 (c,4) S '82
UNICORNS
    Life 6:10-18 (c,1) O '83
    Life 6:23 (4) D '83
UNIDENTIFIED FLYING OBJECTS
    Sports Illus 64:52 (painting,c,4)
        Je 2 '86
Unions. See
    LABOR UNIONS
UNITED NATIONS
--New York City headquarters lit up
        for 40th anniversary
    Life 8:80-1 (1) D '85
--See also
    BUNCHE, RALPH
U.S.S.R.
--Arctic region
    Nat Geog 163:207-23 (c,1) F '83
--Murmansk area
    Sports Illus 62:80-92 (c,1) Ap 29
        '85
--Pik Pobedy Mountain
    Nat Geog 170:256-71 (map,c,1)
        Ag '86
--Rioni River, Georgia
    Nat Geog 168:418-19 (c,1) S '85
--Suzdal Cathedral
    Nat Geog 169:778-9 (c,2) Je '86
--Victims of Chernobyl nuclear dis-
        aster, U.S.S.R.
    Life 9;cov., 20-6 (c,1) Ag '86
--Yukagir people pictographic love
        letter (Siberia)
    Natur Hist 94:86 (c,3) Je '85
--Zagorsk
    Nat Geog 164:758-9 (c,1) D '83
--See also
    DNIEPER RIVER
    KIEV
    LENINGRAD
    MOSCOW
    NEVA RIVER
    SIBERIA
    SMOLENSK
    VOLGOGRAD
U.S.S.R.--ART
--15th cent. icon of St. George
    Smithsonian 13:140 (c,3) F '83
--16th cent. Russian icon

U.S.S.R.--ART (cont.)
Nat Geog 168:192 (c,1) Ag '85
--Late 19th cent. imperial Fabergé
eggs
Smithsonian 14:cov., 46-53
(c,1) Ap '83
Smithsonian 14:12 (c,4) Je '83
U.S.S.R.--COSTUME
Nat Geog 167:276-301, 314-15
(c,1) Mr '85
--Arctic region
Nat Geog 163:207-21 (c,1) F
'83
--Army deserters (Afghanistan)
Life 7:22-8 (c,1) F '84
--Centenarians
Nat Wildlife 22:44 (c,4) D '83
--Mikhail Gorbachev
Life 9:8-9 (c,1) Ja '86
--Kirghiz people
Nat Geog 170:258-9 (c,3) Ag
'86
--Sunbathing in cold weather
(Leningrad)
Life 6:126-7 (c,1) My '83
--Young Pioneers
Life 9:8-9 (c,1) Ja '86
U.S.S.R.--HISTORY
--1807-1808 summits between Napo-
leon and Alexander I
Smithsonian 17:62, 67 (paint-
ing,c,2) S '86
--1812 retreat of Napoleon's army
Nat Geog 161:176-7 (paint-
ing,c,1) F '82
--Medieval invasions by Vikings
Nat Geog 167:278-317 (map,c,1)
Mr '85
--See also
ALEXANDER I
BREZHNEV, LEONID
IVAN IV, THE TERRIBLE
KHRUSHCHEV, NIKITA
LENIN, NIKOLAI
SOLZHENITSYN, ALEKSANDR
TOLSTOY, LEO
U.S.S.R.--HOUSING
--9th cent.
Nat Geog 167:280-1 (paint-
ing,c,1) Mr '85
--Medieval wooden window frame
(Novgorod)
Nat Geog 167:302 (c,1) Mr '85
U.S.S.R.--MAPS
--Middle Ages
Nat Geog 167:288-9 (c,1) Mr
'85

U.S.S.R.--POLITICS AND GOVERN-
MENT
--Photos retouched for political rea-
sons
Life 9:67-8 (4) D '86
--War with Afghanistan
Life 7:22-8 (c,1) F '84
U.S.S.R.--SHRINES AND SYMBOLS
--Soviet hammer and sickle
Am Heritage 38:30 (c,4) D '86
UNITED STATES
--Aerial photographs of landscape
Natur Hist 91:cov., 74-7 (c,1)
O '82
Life 5:118-25 (c,1) O '82
Nat Wildlife 24:53-9 (c,1) O '86
--Bald eagle as U.S. symbol
Smithsonian 13:104-13 (c,1) My
'82
--Geographic center of the U.S.
(Lebanon, Kansas)
Trav/Holiday 159:40 (4) My '83
--Population center of the U.S.
(Missouri)
Life 9:32 (c,4) Jl '86
--See also
APPALACHIAN TRAIL
EASTERN U.S.
LIBERTY BELL
MISSISSIPPI RIVER
ROCKY MOUNTAINS
SOUTHERN U.S.
UNCLE SAM
WESTERN U.S.
individual states
U.S.--COSTUME. See also
MILITARY COSTUME
list under OCCUPATIONS
U.S.--COSTUME--17TH CENT.
--Recreation of 17th cent. costume
(Massachusetts)
Natur Hist 91:38-49 (c,1) O '82
--Wealthy child
Smithsonian 13:113 (painting,c,1)
Je '82
U.S.--COSTUME--18TH CENT.
--1750 Virginia gentleman
Am Heritage 34:29 (painting,c,2)
Je '83
--Late 18th cent. gentleman
Natur Hist 93:65 (painting,c,1)
F '84
--1775 apparel on mannequins
Smithsonian 16:24 (c,4) F '86
--1780s
Smithsonian 14:56-9 (painting,c,3)
S '83

U.S.--HISTORY--COLONIAL
    PERIOD (cont.)
--1628 Thomas Morton and Merry
    Mount (Massachusetts)
    Am Heritage 37:82-6 (paint-
    ing,c,1) O '86
--1670s King Philip's War with
    Indians (New England)
    Natur Hist 94:50-7 (c,1) D '85
--1686 New England governor Ed-
    mund Andros
    Am Heritage 38:104 (drawing,4)
    D '86
--1692 Salem witch trial
    Am Heritage 35:83 (paint-
    ing,c,2) Ag '84
--18th cent. travels of Daniel
    Boone
    Nat Geog 168:812-41 (map,c,1)
    D '85
--Early 18th cent. meeting of
    French and Louisiana In-
    dians
    Natur Hist 95:8 (drawing,2) S
    '86
--1733 plan of Savannah, Georgia
    Am Heritage 33:6 (engrav-
    ing,4) Je '82
--1778 Indian siege of Boones-
    borough, Kentucky
    Nat Geog 168:828-9 (draw-
    ing,c,1) D '85
--British emigrants on ship to the
    New World
    Am Heritage 37:25 (paint-
    ing,c,1) F '86
--Methods of food preservation
    (New England)
    Natur Hist 91:38-49 (c,1) O
    '82
--Recreation of 1627 life (Plimouth
    Plantation, Mass.)
    Trav/Holiday 158:6, 10 (4) N
    '82
--Scenes of colonial life
    Am Heritage 35:40-1 (4) Ag '84
--Silhouettes depicting 17th cent.
    life (Massachusetts)
    Am Heritage 35:81-96 (2) D '83
--Wolstenholme Towne, Virginia
    Nat Geog 161:62-76 (map,c,1)
    Ja '82
--See also
    PENN, WILLIAM
    WILLIAMSBURG, VIRGINIA
U.S. History--Revolutionary
    War. See
    REVOLUTIONARY WAR
U.S.--HISTORY--1783-1861
--1783 events surrounding indepen-
    dence treaty
    Smithsonian 14:56-63 (paint-
    ing,c,2) S '83
--1786 Shay's Rebellion (Massachu-
    setts)
    Am Heritage 37:106 (drawing,3)
    Ag '86
--1787 Constitutional Convention
    (Philadelphia, Pa.)
    Am Heritage 34:7 (drawing,3) Ag
    '83
--1830s Indian Stream Republic, New
    Hampshire
    Smithsonian 14:87-95 (paint-
    ing,c,1) My '83
--1831 de Tocqueville journey
    through America
    Am Heritage 33:cov., 8-17
    (map,c,1) Je '82
--1833 cartoon about Nullification
    Am Heritage 33:14 (drawing,4)
    O '82
--1840s Fruitlands Utopian community
    (Massachusetts)
    Am Heritage 37:72-5 (3) F '86
--Artifacts from Texas steps to
    statehood
    Am Heritage 37:43-7 (c,2) F '86
--Reconstruction of typical 1830 town
    (Old Sturbridge Village, Mas-
    sachusetts)
    Am Heritage 33:33-43 (c,1) Ag
    '82
--Recreation of Sutter's 1848 mill
    (California)
    Smithsonian 13:97 (c,1) D '82
--Scenes of 1835-36 Texas fight
    against Mexico
    Nat Geog 169:316-23 (map,c,1)
    Mr '86
--See also
    GOLD RUSH
    WAR OF 1812
    WESTERN FRONTIER LIFE
U.S. History--Civil War. See
    CIVIL WAR
U.S.--HISTORY--1865-1898
--19th-20th cent. household artifacts
    Am Heritage 37:34-43 (c,1) Ag
    '86
--1866 laying of Atlantic Cable
    Smithsonian 14:178 (lithograph,c,4)
    Mr '84
--1869 Golden Spike railroad ceremony

U.S.--HISTORY--1865-1898
    (cont.)
    (Utah)
    Am Heritage 36:24 (1) D '84
--Late 19th cent. "Robber Barons"
    Am Heritage 38:28 (drawing,c,4)
        D '86
--1885 events
    Am Heritage 36:61-7 (2) D '84
--Hatfield clan (Kentucky)
    Am Heritage 33:107 (4) Ag '82
--New York City's Boss Tweed
        scandals
    Am Heritage 38:81-96 (draw-
        ing,2) D '86
--Relics from the Gilded Age
    Am Heritage 35:42-8, 114 (c,1)
        Ag '84
--See also
        GOLD RUSH
        INDIAN WARS
        RECONSTRUCTION
        SPANISH-AMERICAN WAR
        WESTERN FRONTIER LIFE
U.S.--HISTORY--1898-1919
--1899 views of cities
    Am Heritage 34:110-11 (4) O
        '83
--Early 20th cent. immigrants to
        U.S.
    Trav/Holiday 164:34-9 (4) Jl
        '85
--1912 events shown in lantern
        slides
    Am Heritage 36:48-53 (c,1) F
        '85
--Current scenes of Ellis Island,
        New York City, New York
    Life 6:44-9 (c,1) Jl '83
    Trav/Holiday 164:34-9 (c,1) Jl
        '85
--See also
        WORLD WAR I
U.S.--HISTORY--1919-1933
--1920s flappers depicted by
        John Held, Jr.
    Smithsonian 17:cov., 95-8 (c,1)
        S '86
--1932 Bonus Marchers (Washing-
        ton, D.C.)
    Am Heritage 33:7 (4) Je '82
--See also
        DEPRESSION
U.S.--HISTORY--1933-1945
--1930s WPA poster
    Am Heritage 34:84 (c,4) Ag '83
--1936 events as depicted in Life

    magazine
    Life 9:50-6 (4) Fall '86
--NRA eagle emblem
    Am Heritage 34:107 (c,4) Ag '83
--Okies traveling West (1930s)
    Nat Geog 166:322-49 (map,c,1)
        S '84
--Scenes of early 20th cent. life
    Am Heritage 35:19-25 (draw-
        ing,c,1) Ap '84
--World War II homefront activities
        and artifacts
    Life 8:20-4, 85-94 (c,2) Spring
        '85
--See also
        DEPRESSION
        WORLD WAR II
U.S.--HISTORY--1945-1953
--1948 events
    Life 9:266-7 (4) Fall '86
--See also
        KOREAN WAR
U.S.--HISTORY--1953-1961
--1950s cartoons about Eisenhower
    Am Heritage 37:50-61 (4) D '85
--1954 cartoon about Joseph Mc-
        Carthy
    Am Heritage 37:50 (4) D '85
--See also
        CIVIL RIGHTS
U.S.--HISTORY--1961-
--1970s Watergate hearings
    Am Heritage 35:22-35, 114 (c,1)
        Je '84
    Life 9:346-7 (c,1) Fall '86
--1984 events
    Life 8:entire issue (c,1) Ja '85
    Ebony 40:64-71 (4) Ja '85
--1985 events
    Life 9:entire issue (c,1) Ja '86
--Freed Iranian hostages (1981)
    Life 5:36-7, 73-8 (c,1) Ja '82
    Nat Wildlife 21:32 (4) D '82
--See also
        CIVIL RIGHTS
        VIETNAM WAR
        WOMEN'S LIBERATION MOVE-
            MENT
U.S.--MAPS
--1585 Roanoke Island
    Am Heritage 34:34 (c,4) Ag '83
--1651 Virginia
    Am Heritage 34:18 (2) O '83
--1656 French map
    Smithsonian 15:126 (c,3) My '84
--1783 U.S.
    Smithsonian 14:60-1 (c,2) S '83

U.S.--MAPS
--1860 map of Underground Railroad routes
  Nat Geog 166:6-7 (c,1) Jl '84
--1930s map of Okies' westward migration
  Nat Geog 166:326-7 (c,1) S '84
--Acid rain sensitivity
  Nat Wildlife 21:9 (c,3) Je '83
--Federal lands
  Nat Wildlife 21:6-7 (c,1) Ap '83
  Sports Illus 59:70 (c,3) S 26 '83
--Map drawn with tape
  Life 9:106 (3) Fall '86
--Physical map of Eastern U.S.
  Natur Hist 92:50-1 (c,1) Mr '83
U.S.--POLITICS AND GOVERNMENT
--1777 Congressional prayer session
  Am Heritage 35:77 (painting,4) Ag '84
--19th cent. rule of Boss Tweed (New York City)
  Am Heritage 38:81-96 (drawing,2) D '86
--1885 Cleveland inauguration
  Am Heritage 36:62 (2) D '84
--1954 cabinet meeting
  Am Heritage 37:60 (3) D '85
--1970s Watergate hearings
  Am Heritage 35:22-35, 114 (c,1) Je '84
  Life 9:346-7 (c,1) Fall '86
--Cartoons about 20th cent. presidential races
  Am Heritage 35:81-9, 114 (c,1) O '84
--Congressman taking oath of office (Michigan)
  Ebony 37:80 (4) F '82
--Swearing in Lyndon Johnson as President (1963)
  Life 6:59 (4) N '83
--Swearing in lieutenant governor (1970s)
  Ebony 37:96-8 (4) O '82
--Swearing in lieutenant governor (Virginia)
  Ebony 41:67-8 (c,2) Ap '86
--Swearing in lieutenant governors
  Ebony 42:120 (4) N '86
--Swearing in mayor (Atlantic City, New Jersey)

  Ebony 40:65 (4) Ja '85
--Swearing in mayor (Chicago, Illinois)
  Ebony 38:27 (c,2) Jl '83
--Swearing in mayor (New Orleans, Louisiana)
  Ebony 41:122 (2) Jl '86
--Swearing in mayor (Philadelphia, Pennsylvania)
  Ebony 39:49 (c,4) My '84
--Teenage pages at the Capitol
  Life 7:58-64 (1) Je '84
--See also
    CAPITOL BUILDINGS
    ELECTIONS
    ENVIRONMENTAL PROTECTION AGENCY
    FEDERAL BUREAU OF INVESTIGATION
    GOVERNMENT--LEGISLATURES
    GOVERNMENT BUILDINGS
    INTERIOR, DEPARTMENT OF
    POLITICAL CAMPAIGNS
    U.S. PRESIDENTS
U.S.--RITES AND CEREMONIES
--20th cent. patriotic events and activities
  Life 9:115-20 (c,2) Jl '86
--Pledging allegiance to the flag
  Nat Geog 163:123 (c,4) Ja '83
  Life 6:46 (c,4) D '83
--Pledging allegiance to the flag in school (Texas)
  Life 5:36-7 (1) D '82
  Nat Geog 167:738 (c,4) Je '85
U.S.--SOCIAL LIFE AND CUSTOMS
--20th cent. patriotic events and activities
  Life 9:115-20 (c,2) Jl '86
--Early 20th cent. (Texas)
  Am Heritage 37:49-64 (2) F '86
--Early 20th cent. illustrated song slides
  Smithsonian 12:cov., 76-83 (c,1) Mr '82
--1920s-1930s advertisements
  Am Heritage 36:cov., 75-89 (c,1) Ap '85
--1933 men's grooming rituals aboard train
  Am Heritage 36:57 (drawing,4) Je '85
--1949 chart of hi-, middle-, and low-brow lifestyles
  Am Heritage 34:44-5 (1) Je '83
--1950s
  Life 8:cov., 77-84 (c,1) Ag '85

U.S. NAVY (cont.)
  LAWRENCE, JAMES
  MAURY, MATTHEW FON-
    TAINE
  MILITARY COSTUME
  SAILORS
  SCHLEY, WINFIELD SCOTT
  U.S. NAVAL ACADEMY
U.S. PRESIDENTS
  Am Heritage 35:14-19 (4) F '84
--1936-1986
  Life 9:211-29 (c,1) Fall '86
--Children of Presidents
  Life 7:cov., 2, 32-50 (c,1) N
    '84
--Depicted on postage stamps
  Am Heritage 34:52-9 (c,4) D
    '82
--First ladies
  Am Heritage 34:99 (4) Ag '83
--Group photo of recent presi-
    dents
  Life 5:147 (c,2) Ja '82
--See also
  WASHINGTON, GEORGE
  ADAMS, JOHN
  JEFFERSON, THOMAS
  ADAMS, JOHN QUINCY
  JACKSON, ANDREW
  TAYLOR, ZACHARY
  PIERCE, FRANKLIN
  LINCOLN, ABRAHAM
  JOHNSON, ANDREW
  GRANT, ULYSSES S.
  CLEVELAND, GROVER
  McKINLEY, WILLIAM
  ROOSEVELT, THEODORE
  TAFT, WILLIAM HOWARD
  WILSON, WOODROW
  HARDING, WARREN GAMA-
    LIEL
  COOLIDGE, CALVIN
  HOOVER, HERBERT
  ROOSEVELT, FRANKLIN
    DELANO
  TRUMAN, HARRY S
  EISENHOWER, DWIGHT
    DAVID
  KENNEDY, JOHN FITZ-
    GERALD
  JOHNSON, LYNDON BAINES
  NIXON, RICHARD M.
  FORD, GERALD
  CARTER, JIMMY
  REAGAN, RONALD
  POLITICAL CAMPAIGNS
  WHITE HOUSE

UNIVERSAL PRODUCT CODE
--Technology
  Nat Geog 165:374-5 (c,1) Mr '84
UNIVERSE
  Nat Geog 163:cov., 707-49 (c,1)
    Je '83
--Black holes
  Nat Geog 163:737 (drawing,c,1)
    Je '83
  Natur Hist 94:94 (painting,c,4)
    O '85
--Diagram of planet positions
  Natur Hist 91:82 (3) Mr '82
--Diagram of stellar universe (1903)
  Natur Hist 92:38 (3) My '83
--Illustration of Big Bang theory
  Nat Geog 163:710-17, 740 (c,1)
    Je '83
  Life 8:32-3 (painting,c,1) D '85
--Solar system
  Nat Geog 167:4-50 (c,1) Ja '85
--Theories of birth of the universe
  Smithsonian 14:cov., 32-51 (draw-
    ing,c,1) My '83
--Theories of end of the universe
  Smithsonian 14:72-83 (paint-
    ing,c,1) Je '83
--See also
  ASTEROIDS
  EARTH
  ECLIPSES
  GALAXIES
  HALLEY'S COMET
  JUPITER
  MARS
  MERCURY
  METEORITES
  MOON
  NEBULAE
  NEPTUNE
  PLANETARIUMS
  PLUTO
  SATURN
  SCIENCE FICTION
  SPACE PROGRAM
  SPACECRAFT
  STARS
  SUN
  URANUS
  VENUS
URANUS (PLANET)
  Nat Geog 167:49 (c,4) Ja '85
  Nat Geog 170:178-93 (c,1) Ag '86
--Moon Miranda
  Natur Hist 95:14 (c,4) Je '86
  Nat Geog 170:186-91 (c,1) Ag '86
  Smithsonian 17:38 (painting,c,4)

URANUS (PLANET) (cont.)
S '86
--Moons
Nat Geog 170:186-93 (c,1) Ag
'86
URBAN SCENES
--19th cent.
Am Heritage 34:17-21 (c,2) F
'83
--Late 19th cent. book on the
horrors of the big city
Am Heritage 35:111 (4) Ag '84
--Early 20th cent. street children
Natur Hist 94:86-91 (2) O
'85
--See also
AUTOMOBILES--TRAFFIC
COMMUTERS
CROWDS
SLUMS
SUBURBAN SCENES
Uruguay. See
MONTEVIDEO
UTAH
Nat Geog 167:694-719 (map,c,1)
Je '85
--Early 20th cent. paintings by
LeConte Stewart
Am Heritage 36:62-9 (c,1) Ag
'85
--1980s floods
Nat Geog 167:694-717 (map,c,1)
Je '85
--Bonneville Salt Flats
Nat Geog 167:712-13 (c,1) Je
'85
--Navajo Lake
Natur Hist 95:90 (c,4) My '86
--Navajo Mountain
Life 5:120-1 (c,1) O '82
--Ogden Valley (1929)
Am Heritage 36:64-5 (paint-
ing,c,2) Ag '85
--Pink Cliffs, Dixie National
Forest
Natur Hist 95:90-2 (map,c,1)
My '86
--See also
BRYCE CANYON NATIONAL
PARK
DIXIE NATIONAL FOREST
GREAT SALT LAKE
MONUMENT VALLEY NAVAJO
TRIBAL PARK
SALT LAKE CITY
WASATCH RANGE

UTE INDIANS (COLORADO)
--Cemetery
Am Heritage 33:112 (4) Ap '82
UTE INDIANS (COLORADO)--
COSTUME
--19th cent.
Am Heritage 33:112 (4) Ap '82
UTRECHT, NETHERLANDS
--Street scene
Life 9:12-13 (c,1) Jl '86

-V-

VACCINATIONS
Smithsonian 13:40 (c,4) Jl '82
VACUUMING
Life 5:126 (2) Je '82
--Nuclear power plant
Life 5:42 (c,3) My '82
--Official red carpet (Washington,
D.C.)
Nat Geog 163:114 (c,4) Ja '83
VALENTINES DAY
--19th cent. valentines cards
Am Heritage 33:25-9 (c,2) F '82
VALLEE, RUDY
Am Heritage 37:45 (4) Ag '86
VAN GOGH, VINCENT
--Paintings at Arles, France
Life 7:118-26 (c,1) O '84
--Paintings by him
Smithsonian 15:76-89 (c,1) O '84
--Self-portrait
Life 7:118 (painting,c,4) O '84
Smithsonian 15:76 (painting,c,4)
O '84
--"Vase with Five Sunflowers"
Life 9:100 (painting,c,4) D '86
VANCOUVER, BRITISH COLUMBIA
Trav/Holiday 157:38, 42-3 (c,2)
My '82
Trav/Holiday 160:42-4 (c,2) Ag
'83
Trav/Holiday 165:46-7 (c,1) F
'86
Nat Geog 170:52-3, 74 (c,1) Jl
'86
--Expo 86 Canada pavilion
Nat Geog 170:74-5 (c,1) Jl '86
--Expo 86 exhibits
Trav/Holiday 166:16 (c,4) S '86
--Expo 86 site
Trav/Holiday 165:46-7 (c,1) F '86
--Stadium at British Columbia Place
Sports Illus 59:56-7 (c,2) Jl 18
'83

VANCOUVER, BRITISH
    COLUMBIA (cont.)
--See also
    FRASER RIVER
VANDERBILT, WILLIAM H.
    Am Heritage 36:67 (painting,2)
        D '84
    Am Heritage 37:106 (paint-
        ing,4) D '85
--1885 cartoon about railroads
    Am Heritage 33:15 (drawing,c,4)
        O '82
--Newport, Rhode Island mansion
    Am Heritage 35:42-3, 48 (c,1)
        Ag '84
Vanzetti, Bartolomeo. See
    SACCO AND VANZETTI
VATICAN CITY
    Nat Geog 165:188-9 (c,1) F
        '84
    Nat Geog 168:720-75 (map,c,1)
        D '85
--1482 Perugino fresco of Jesus
    and St. Peter
    Smithsonian 15:42 (c,3) F '85
--Art works of the Vatican Palace
    Smithsonian 13:120-31 (c,1)
        D '82
    Life 5:58-70 (c,1) D '82
    Nat Geog 168:764-77 (c,1) D
        '85
--Garden behind St. Peter's
    Life 5:58-9 (c,1) D '82
--St. Peter's Square
    Trav/Holiday 164:50 (c,2) O
        '85
--See also
    POPES
    ST. PETER'S BASILICA
    SISTINE CHAPEL
VATICAN--COSTUME
--Swiss guard
    Trav/Holiday 164:49 (c,4) O
        '85
    Nat Geog 168:738-41 (c,1) D
        '85
VEGETABLES
--Exotic vegetables
    Smithsonian 16:34-42 (c,1) D
        '85
--Served on platter (France)
    Life 5:64-5 (c,1) Ap '82
--See also
    CARROTS
    CHIVES
    CORN
    CUCUMBERS

GARLIC
PEPPERS
POTATOES
PUMPKINS
RADISHES
SUGAR BEETS
YAMS
VELASQUEZ, DIEGO
--"Las Meninas"
    Nat Geog 169:163 (painting,c,2)
        F '86
VENDING MACHINES
--1939 Keydoozle store
    Am Heritage 36:25 (2) O '85
--Automats (Northeast)
    Smithsonian 16:50-61 (c,2) Ja '86
VENEZUELA
--Cloud forest
    Nat Geog 168:333 (c,1) S '85
--Neblina Mountain
    Natur Hist 93:89 (c,3) S '84
    Natur Hist 93:16 (c,4) D '84
    Smithsonian 16:50-63 (c,1) My
        '85
--Rain forests
    Natur Hist 92:70-8 (c,1) Ap '83
--Ranchland
    Trav/Holiday 157:62 (c,3) Mr '82
--See also
    CARACAS
    ORINOCO RIVER
VENEZUELA--COSTUME
--Makiritare woman
    Nat Geog 168:334-5 (c,1) S '85
VENICE, ITALY
    Nat Geog 164:750-3 (c,1) D '83
    Trav/Holiday 164:40-1 (c,1) S
        '85
--Late 19th cent. paintings
    Am Heritage 35:36-47 (c,1) Je '84
--Doge's Palace gateway
    Smithsonian 13:140-1 (4) S '82
--Flooded St. Mark's Square
    Nat Geog 162:696-7 (c,1) D '82
--Peggy Guggenheim Museum
    Smithsonian 17:58-64 (c,1) Jl '86
--Horses of San Marco
    Smithsonian 13:cov., 100-7 (c,1)
        S '82
--St. Mark's Square (late 19th cent.)
    Am Heritage 35:39, 46 (paint-
        ing,c,2) Je '84
--See also
    ST. MARK'S CATHEDRAL
VENUS
--Ancient Roman sculpture
    Nat Geog 165:590 (c,1) My '84

VIENNA, AUSTRIA (cont.)
  Trav/Holiday 164:53 (c,4) Ag
    '85
VIETNAM
--Hue
  Smithsonian 17:44-55 (map,c,1)
    Je '86
--See also
  HANOI
VIETNAM--ARCHITECTURE
--19th cent. tombs of emperors
    (Hue)
  Smithsonian 17:46-7, 51, 55
    (c,1) Je '86
VIETNAM--COSTUME
  Life 8:88-9 (1) Je '85
--19th cent. emperors
  Smithsonian 17:48 (c,4) Je '86
--Amerasians
  Life 8:98-103 (c,1) Ag '85
--Hue
  Smithsonian 17:45-53 (c,2) Je
    '86
VIETNAM WAR
--1962 photos
  Life 5:7 (2) Mr '82
--1964 cartoon of U.S. involve-
    ment
  Am Heritage 35:16 (4) Ag '84
--1965 battle of the La Drang
    valley
  Am Heritage 35:50-9 (1) F '84
--1965 helicopter rescue of
    marines
  Life 9:132-4 (1) Fall '86
--1968 battle at Hue
  Smithsonian 17:44, 46 (map,3)
    Je '86
--1968 demonstration at Demo-
    cratic Convention (Chicago)
  Life 9:342 (2) Fall '86
--1969 U.S. war dead
  Life 9:136 (4) Fall '86
--1985 parade for Vietnam veterans
    (New York City)
  Life 8:38-9 (1) Jl '85
--Airlifting wounded soldiers
  Am Heritage 35:76-7 (c,1) O
    '84
--Coffins of U.S. soldiers
  Life 9:39-40 (c,2) Jl '86
--Marines in combat (1966)
  Life 9:18-19 (c,1) Fall '86
--Memorial to U.S. dead (Wash-
    ington, D.C.)
  Life 6:55-8 (c,1) Ja '83
  Nat Geog 167:cov., 551-72

  (c,1) My '85
  Life 8:56-7 (1) My '85
  Ebony 41:122-3 (c,1) Ap '86
--Napalm victim
  Smithsonian 12:122 (4) Ja '82
--North Vietnamese veterans
  Life 9:41 (c,4) Ja '86
--Plane wreckage (Laos)
  Nat Geog 170:692-6 (c,1) N '86
--Tunnel warfare
  Life 8:98-112 (c,1) Ap '85
--U.S. flag upside-down in 1969
    Vietnam War protest
  Am Heritage 37:79 (4) Ap '86
--U.S. soldier's funeral
  Ebony 38:42 (3) Ag '83
--U.S. veterans embracing (Washing-
    ton, D.C.)
  Life 8:56-7 (1) My '85
--Vietnam veterans memorial (New
    York City, New York)
  Life 9:44-5 (c,1) Ja '86
VIKINGS
--Medieval travels into Russia
  Nat Geog 167:278-317 (map,c,1)
    Mr '85
--Reconstructed Viking farm (Ice-
    land)
  Smithsonian 16:118-19 (c,3) Ja
    '86
VIKINGS--COSTUME
--Rurik the Rus, Prince of Novgorod
  Nat Geog 167:279 (sculpture,c,1)
    Mr '85
VIKINGS--HOUSING
--Sod houses (Newfoundland)
  Trav/Holiday 162:41 (c,4) S '84
VIKINGS--RELICS
--11th cent. rune stones (Sweden)
  Nat Geog 167:291 (c,4) Mr '85
--U.S.S.R.
  Nat Geog 167:310-11 (c,4) Mr '85
VILLAGES
--Aerial view of Ivory Coast village
  Nat Geog 162:98-9 (c,1) Jl '82
--Casares, Spain
  Trav/Holiday 157:28 (4) My '82
  Smithsonian 13:144-5 (c,3) Je '82
--Cotswald Hills, England
  Natur Hist 92:104 (c,3) O '83
--Eskimo Point, Canada
  Nat Geog 161:386-7 (c,1) Mr '82
--Fengxiang, China
  Nat Geog 165:326-7 (c,1) Mr '84
--Pedhoulas, Cyprus
  Trav/Holiday 157:72 (c,3) Mr '82
--Siberia, U.S.S.R.

VIRGINIA (cont.)
    CHESAPEAKE BAY
    CUMBERLAND MOUNTAINS
    GEORGE WASHINGTON
        NATIONAL FOREST
    HAMPTON ROADS
    NORFOLK
    POTOMAC RIVER
    WILLIAMSBURG
VIRGINIA CITY, NEVADA
    Trav/Holiday 157:42-3 (3) Je
        '82
VIRUSES
    Smithsonian 14:50 (4) D '83
Vision. See
    BLINDNESS
    EYES
    OPTICAL ILLUSIONS
VOLCANIC ERUPTIONS
--El Chichón, Mexico (1982)
    Nat Geog 162:654-65 (c,1) N
        '82
    Natur Hist 94:46-55 (c,1) Jl
        '85
--Kilauea, Hawaii
    Natur Hist 91:68-9 (c,2) D '82
    Nat Geog 164:583 (c,1) N '83
    Trav/Holiday 162:34-5 (c,1)
        O '84
    Nat Geog 168:144-5 (c,1) Ag
        '85
--Krafla, Iceland
    Smithsonian 12:52-61 (c,1) Ja
        '82
--Krakatoa (1883)
    Smithsonian 14:32 (4) O '83
--Krakatoa (1981)
    Nat Geog 167:752-7 (c,1) Je '85
--Mount Etna, Sicily, Italy
    Life 6:128-9 (c,1) Jl '83
    Life 7:184-5 (c,1) Ja '84
--Mount St. Helens, Washington
        (1980)
    Sports Illus 62:63 (c,4) F 25
        '85
    Life 8:21 (c,4) S '85
--Mount Soufrière, St. Vincent
    Natur Hist 91:64-5 (c,1) Mr
        '82
--Pu'u O'o, Hawaii
    Natur Hist 95:81 (c,4) D '86
--Sequence of 79 A.D. Vesuvius
        eruption
    Nat Geog 165:577 (drawing,c,1)
        My '84
VOLCANOES
--Chimborazo, Ecuador

    Natur Hist 95:40-1 (c,1) F '86
--Damage prevention tactics (Japan)
    Nat Geog 169:650 (c,3) My '86
--Diagram of steps to eruption
    Nat Wildlife 21:43 (4) Ap '83
--El Chichón, Mexico
    Natur Hist 94:46-55 (c,1) Jl '85
--Galway's Soufrière, Montserrat,
        Leeward Islands
    Trav/Holiday 162:47 (c,3) O '84
--Haleakala Crater, Maui, Hawaii
    Natur Hist 91:39 (c,1) D '82
--La Solfatara, Italy
    Nat Geog 165:619 (c,3) My '84
--Mars
    Nat Geog 167:30-1 (c,2) Ja '85
--Mount Soufrière, St. Vincent
    Natur Hist 91:60-8 (c,1) Mr '82
--Mount Veniaminof, Alaska
    Smithsonian 14:161 (c,2) Mr '84
--Mud volcanoes (Colombia)
    Nat Geog 168:338-9 (c,1) S '85
--Observatories atop Mauna Kea,
        Hawaii
    Nat Geog 163:724-5 (c,1) Je '83
--Pacifying Hawaiian volcano with
        gift (1801)
    Nat Geog 164:580-1 (painting,c,1)
        N '83
--Research in Iceland
    Smithsonian 12:59 (c,4) Ja '82
--St. Lucia
    Trav/Holiday 160:27 (c,4) D '83
--Stromboli, Italy
    Nat Geog 162:694-5 (c,1) D '82
--See also
    DIAMOND HEAD
    KILAUEA
    KILIMANJARO
    KRAKATOA
    LAVA
    MOUNT ETNA
    MOUNT HOOD
    MOUNT ST. HELENS
    MOUNT SHASTA
    POPOCATEPETL
    VESUVIUS
VOLCANOES--DAMAGE
--1st cent. relics from Herculaneum,
        Italy
    Nat Geog 162:686-93 (c,1) D '82
    Nat Geog 165:cov., 556-611 (c,1)
        My '84
--79 A.D. and 1980 victims of Mount
        Vesuvius (Italy)
    Nat Geog 162:716-17 (c,1) D '82
--1883 Krakatoa eruption

VOLCANOES--DAMAGE (cont.)
    Nat Geog 167:754 (4) Je '85
--Ash-covered bull (Mexico)
    Life 5:119 (c,2) Je '82
--Colombia (1985)
    Life 9:12-13, 139 (c,1) Ja '86
    Nat Geog 169:640-9, 652-3
        (map,c,1) My '86
--El Chichón, Mexico (1982)
    Nat Geog 162:654-84 (c,1) N
        '82
    Natur Hist 94:50-5 (c,1) Jl '85
--Mount Etna lava on railroad
        track (Italy)
    Nat Geog 162:714 (c,4) D '82
--Plaster cast of 1st cent. vol-
        cano victim (Italy)
    Nat Geog 162:716-17 (c,1) D
        '82
VOLCANOES--MAPS
--Map of Hawaiian chains
    Natur Hist 91:70-1 (c,2) D '82
--Map of West Coast volcanoes
    Nat Wildlife 21:42 (3) Ap '83
    Nat Geog 169:638-9 (c,1) My
        '86
--Volcanic risk areas in U.S.
    Nat Geog 168:153 (c,1) Ag '85
VOLES
    Natur Hist 93:3, 9 (c,1) My
        '84
VOLGOGRAD, U.S.S.R.
    Life 8:48-9 (c,1) Spring '85
VOLLEYBALL
    Sports Illus 63:19 (c,3) Ag 26
        '85
    Sports Illus 64:71, 74 (c,3) Je
        2 '86
--California
    Sports Illus 57:26-31 (c,1) Ag
        23 '82
--Community street game (Wiscon-
        sin)
    Sports Illus 65:48 (c,3) Ag 11
        '86
--In swimming pool (California)
    Sports Illus 58:66 (c,3) F 7
        '83
--Women
    Sports Illus 65:28 (c,2) S 22
        '86
VOLLEYBALL--AMATEUR
    Sports Illus 61:46-50 (c,4) Jl
        23 '84
--1984 Olympics (Los Angeles)
    Sports Illus 61:84-6 (c,2) Ag
        20 '84

VOLLEYBALL--COLLEGE
--NCAA Championships 1985
    Sports Illus 62:78, 81 (c,3) My
        13 '85
VON BRAUN, WERNHER
    Smithsonian 13:154, 158-9 (4) O
        '82
VON STROHEIM, ERICH
    Smithsonian 13:106 (4) Mr '83
VOODOO
--Voodoo festival (Haiti)
    Nat Geog 167:394-408 (c,1) Mr
        '85
VULTURES
    Natur Hist 91:54-5 (c,2) My '82
    Smithsonian 13:138 (painting,c,4)
        Je '82
    Nat Geog 163:358-9 (c,1) Mr '83
--Silhouettes of black vultures
    Natur Hist 94:36-7 (c,2) F '85

-W-

WAGNER, RICHARD
    Smithsonian 17:122 (4) Ag '86
--Scene from "Tannheuser" (1864)
    Smithsonian 14:74 (painting,c,3)
        Jl '83
Wagons. See
    COVERED WAGONS
WAILING WALL, JERUSALEM, ISRAEL
    Nat Geog 163:502-3, 505 (c,1)
        Ap '83
    Nat Geog 168:4-5 (c,1) Jl '85
WAITERS
--On train (India)
    Nat Geog 165:697, 714-15 (c,1)
        Je '84
--Robot (California)
    Smithsonian 14:67 (c,4) N '83
WAITRESSES
--1950s style (Illinois)
    Life 8:78-9 (c,1) Ag '85
--Anchorage, Alaska
    Trav/Holiday 160:53 (c,2) Jl '83
--Carrying beer mugs (Austria)
    Trav/Holiday 164:cov. (c,1) Ag
        '85
--Mexico
    Trav/Holiday 163:66 (c,3) Ja '85
WALES
    Nat Geog 164:36-63 (map,c,1) Jl
        '83
--Blanket bogs
    Natur Hist 91:48-51 (c,1) N '82
--Coastal area

WALES (cont.)
   Trav/Holiday 166:60-1
     (map,c,1) O '86
--Countryside
   Trav/Holiday 159:63 (c,4) My
     '83
--Milford Haven
   Am Heritage 36:38-41 (c,1) Je
     '85
--Narrow gauge railway
   Trav/Holiday 166:58-60 (map,c,2)
     O '86
--Powis Castle
   Nat Geog 168:680-1 (c,1) N '85
   Life 8:34-5 (c,1) N '85
--St. David's Cathedral
   Trav/Holiday 159:64 (c,2) My
     '83
WALES--COSTUME
   Nat Geog 164:40-61 (c,1) Jl '83
WALKER, JIMMY
--1920s mayoral campaign artifact
   (New York City)
   Am Heritage 33:107 (4) Ag '82
WALKING
--Computer analysis of race walk-
   ing
   Nat Geog 162:424 (c,1) O '82
--Long-distance walking
   Sports Illus 60:58-62, 72 (c,1)
     Mr 26 '84
WALKING STICKS
--19th cent. canes concealing
   weapons and toys
   Smithsonian 14:156 (c,4) My
     '83
WALLETS
   Sports Illus 56:80 (c,4) Ja 11
     '82
--Gold money clip
   Sports Illus 60:33 (c,4) Mr 5
     '84
WALLPAPER
--1930s newspaper wall coverings
   Natur Hist 91:4-14 (2) F '82
--1770 Chinese design (Delaware
   mansion)
   Am Heritage 34:93 (c,4) Ap '83
   Smithsonian 14:102 (c,2) My '83
--Putting up wallpaper (Great
   Britain)
   Life 7:49-52 (c,1) Jl '84
WALLS
--Stone (Great Britain)
   Smithsonian 14:122 (c,2) N '83
--Surrounding ancient capital
   Taima, Saudi Arabia

   Smithsonian 14:44-5 (c,3) S '83
--See also
   GREAT WALL OF CHINA
WALRUSES
   Nat Wildlife 21:62-3 (c,1) D '82
   Smithsonian 14:68-75 (c,1) O '83
   Nat Wildlife 24:6 (c,4) Ap '86
   Nat Wildlife 25:15 (c,3) D '86
--Tusks
   Nat Geog 165:827 (2) Je '84
WAR OF 1812
--Battle scene
   Nat Geog 169:314 (woodcut,2) Mr
     '86
--Naval battles of the "U.S.S. Con-
   stitution"
   Am Heritage 34:cov., 65-7
     (painting,c,1) Ap '83
--Sunken U.S. ships
   Nat Geog 163:cov., 288-313 (c,1)
     Mr '83
--See also
   LAWRENCE, JAMES
WARBLERS
   Natur Hist 91:64-5 (c,1) My '82
   Natur Hist 91:46-7 (c,1) S '82
   Smithsonian 13:169-186 (c,2) O
     '82
   Nat Wildlife 21:61 (c,2) D '82
   Natur Hist 92:24, 84-8 (c,4) S
     '83
   Natur Hist 94:89 (painting,c,1)
     Ap '85
   Nat Geog 168:646 (c,4) N '85
--Kirtland's warbler
   Nat Wildlife 23:13, 30 (c,4) Ap
     '85
--See also
   OVENBIRDS
   REDSTARTS
   YELLOWTHROATS
WAREHOUSES
--Mail order distribution center
   (Maine)
   Sports Illus 63:94 (c,2) D 2 '85
WARFARE
--9th cent. Viking-Petcheneg battle
   (Russia)
   Nat Geog 167:282-3 (painting,c,1)
     Mr '85
--1066 Battle of Hastings, England
   Smithsonian 17:84 (painting,c,3)
     Jl '86
--13th cent. Byzantines fighting with
   fire
   Nat Geog 164:747 (painting,c,3)
     D '83

WARFARE (cont.)
--13th cent. Mongolian invasions
    of Japan
    Nat Geog 162:634-49 (paint-
        ing,c,1) N '82
--15th cent. battle between
    Florence and Siena
    Smithsonian 13:65-7 (paint-
        ing,c,1) N '82
--1453 fall of Constantinople to
    Turks
    Nat Geog 164:764-5 (fresco,c,1)
        D '83
--1519 battle between Cortés and
    Indians (Mexico)
    Nat Geog 166:442-3 (paint-
        ing,c,1) O '84
--1526 battle between Mongols and
    Indians (Panipat)
    Nat Geog 167:462 (painting,c,1)
        Ap '85
--1545 French attack on Ports-
    mouth, England
    Nat Geog 163:648-51 (paint-
        ing,c,1) My '83
--1683 Turkish siege of Vienna
    Smithsonian 15:56-7 (paint-
        ing,c,1) Ja '85
--18th cent. (Hawaii)
    Nat Geog 164:560-77 (paint-
        ing,c,1) N '83
--18th cent. Mediterranean Sea
    battle
    Smithsonian 12:120 (paint-
        ing,c,4) Ja '82
--1803 engraving of possible
    French attack on England
    Smithsonian 17:66-7 (1) My '86
--1836 battle of the Alamo, Texas
    Smithsonian 16:54-67 (c,1) Mr
        '86
--1940s proposed Mickey Mouse
    gas mask for children
    Am Heritage 36:6 (drawing,c,2)
        Ag '85
--1943 tanks of mustard gas
    (Great Britain)
    Am Heritage 36:40-1 (2) Ag '85
--1950s simulated war game
    Am Heritage 34:58 (2) Je '83
--1980s civilian victims of wars
    Life 7:10-16 (c,1) N '84
--Ethiopia vs. Eritrean rebels
    Nat Geog 168:384-99 (c,1) S
        '85
--Impact of Iran-Iraq war on
    Iranians

    Nat Geog 168:108-35 (c,1) Jl '85
--Medical practices during wars
    Am Heritage 35:66-77 (c,1) O '84
--National Survival Game (New
    Hampshire)
    Life 6:68-72 (c,1) My '83
--Nicaragua
    Nat Geog 168:806-11 (c,1) D '85
--U.S.S.R.-Afghanistan war
    Life 7:22-8 (c,1) F '84
--U.S. invasion of Grenada (1983)
    Life 6:34-7 (c,1) D '83
--Use of lasers in warfare
    Nat Geog 165:358-61 (painting,c,1)
        Mr '84
--See also
    ARMS
    AUSTERLITZ, BATTLE OF
    BUNKER HILL, BATTLE OF
    DUELS
    SPIES
    WARS
    WATERLOO, BATTLE OF
WARHOL, ANDY
--Robot in his image
    Smithsonian 14:60 (c,1) N '83
WARNER, JACK
    Am Heritage 35:33 (drawing,c,1)
        D '83
WARREN, EARL
    Ebony 41:75, 268 (4) N '85
WARS
--1840 Opium War (China)
    Nat Geog 167:152-3 (painting,c,1)
        F '85
--Falkland Islands (1982)
    Life 5:31-5 (c,1) S '82
    Life 6:10-11 (1) Ja '83
--Iraq vs. Iran (1982)
    Life 6:14-15 (c,1) Ja '83
--Napoleonic battles
    Nat Geog 161:147-85 (c,1) F '82
--See also
    ARMS
    CIVIL WAR
    INDIAN WARS
    KOREAN WAR
    REVOLUTIONARY WAR
    SPANISH-AMERICAN WAR
    SPANISH CIVIL WAR
    VIETNAM WAR
    WAR OF 1812
    WARFARE
    WORLD WAR I
    WORLD WAR II
WARSAW, POLAND
--Street demonstration

WARSAW, POLAND (cont.)
Life 5:106-7 (1) F '82
--Tomb of the Unknown Soldier
Trav/Holiday 165:18 (c,4) F
'86
WASATCH RANGE, UTAH
Life 5:60-1 (c,1) Mr '82
Nat Geog 167:696-9, 718-19
(c,1) Je '85
--Wasatch fault
Natur Hist 95:34-5 (1) Je '86
WASHINGTON, BOOKER T.
Ebony 37:29 (4) S '82
Ebony 40:30 (4) F '85
--Statue (Tuskegee, Alabama)
Ebony 37:53 (4) Jl '82
--Wives
Ebony 37:29 (4) S '82
WASHINGTON, DINAH
Ebony 40:146A (4) Ap '85
WASHINGTON, GEORGE
Smithsonian 12:75 (sculp-
ture,c,4) F '82
Am Heritage 34:105 (engrav-
ing,3) F '83
--1783 farewell to troops
Am Heritage 35:14 (litho-
graph,4) D '83
--19th cent. painting on glass
Am Heritage 35:4 (c,1) F '84
--At Battle of Monmouth (1778)
Am Heritage 33:82-3 (paint-
ing,c,1) F '82
--China export porcelain owned
by him
Natur Hist 93:70 (c,4) F '84
--Depicted on 1892 Pennsylvania-
German tile
Am Heritage 34:114 (c,2) F '83
--Family coat of arms
Smithsonian 15:94 (drawing,4)
My '84
--Humorous sculpture of him
Life 5:46-8 (c,1) Ag '82
--Son George Washington Parke
Custis
Smithsonian 16:156-62 (paint-
ing,c,2) O '85
--Mount Vernon, Virginia
Trav/Holiday 164:10 (c,3) Jl
'85
--Mount Vernon in run down con-
dition (1850s)
Am Heritage 34:109 (4) F '83
--Portrait by Gilbert Stuart
Smithsonian 15:146 (paint-
ing,c,4) Ap '84

--Reenactment of Washington crossing
the Delaware
Trav/Holiday 166:32 (c,4) D '86
--Symbolic representations of him
Smithsonian 12:74-81 (c,1) F '82
--Washington's life depicted in TV
movie
Smithsonian 15:144-50 (c,1) Ap
'84
--Writing case and camp cup
Am Heritage 33:81 (c,3) F '82
WASHINGTON
--1880s buildings (Jefferson County)
Trav/Holiday 159:20-3 (drawing,4)
Ja '83
--Chateau Ste. Michelle Winery,
Woodinville
Trav/Holiday 158:14 (c,4) Jl '82
Trav/Holiday 164:34-5 (c,2) S
'85
--Olympic Peninsula
Trav/Holiday 159:cov., 42-7 (c,1)
My '83
Nat Geog 165:644-73 (map,c,1)
My '84
--Palouse country
Nat Geog 161:798-819 (map,c,1)
Je '83
--See also
BREMERTON
CASCADE RANGE
GRAND COULEE DAM
MOUNT RAINIER
MOUNT RAINIER NATIONAL
PARK
MOUNT ST. HELENS
OLYMPIC MOUNTAINS
OLYMPIC NATIONAL PARK
SAN JUAN ISLANDS
SEATTLE
SNAKE RIVER
SPOKANE
WASHINGTON, D.C.
Nat Geog 163:85-125 (map,c,1)
Ja '83
Nat Geog 64:410-11 (c,1) S '83
Trav/Holiday 161:cov., 24, 62-7
(c,1) Mr '84
Am Heritage 37:cov., 22-31 (c,1)
Ap '86
--18th cent. Treasury Dept. Build-
ing
Am Heritage 37:74 (drawing,c,3)
Ag '86
--Blair House
Am Heritage 37:24-5 (c,2) Ap '86
--British embassy interior

WATER (cont.)
--Leon Sinks, Florida
  Natur Hist 94:78 (map,c,4) D
    '85
--Pumping water (Alabama)
  Nat Geog 169:385 (c,1) Mr '86
--Sinkholes (Australia)
  Nat Geog 165:128-42 (c,1) Ja
    '84
--Storm-surge barrier across
    Oosterschelde, Netherlands
  Smithsonian 15:94-101 (c,1) Ag
    '84
--Tennessee-Tombigbee Waterway,
    Mississippi
  Nat Geog 169:364-83 (map,c,1)
    Mr '86
--Testing for poisons in water
  Nat Wildlife 22:16-17 (c,3) F
    '84
--Tides (Leigh on Sea, England)
  Nat Geog 163:790 (c,4) Je '83
--U.S. water problems
  Nat Wildlife 22:cov., 7-21 (c,1)
    F '84
--U.S. wetlands
  Nat Wildlife 20:43-51 (c,1) Je
    '82
  Nat Geog 166:568-85 (c,1) N
    '84
--Winter Park sinkhole, Florida
  Nat Geog 162:214-15 (c,1) Ag
    '82
  Smithsonian 13:56 (c,4) Mr '83
--See also
    ARTESIAN WELLS
    FOUNTAINS
    GROUND WATER
    IRRIGATION
    WELLS
    list under WATER FORMA-
      TIONS
WATER BUFFALOES
  Nat Geog 164:270-1 (c,1) Ag
    '83
  Life 7:10-11 (c,1) S '84
  Sports Illus 61:110-21 (c,1) D
    24 '84
  Nat Geog 166:720-1 (c,1) D '84
WATER BUGS
  Smithsonian 13:62 (c,1) Jl '82
Water formations. See
    ARTESIAN WELLS
    ATLANTIC OCEAN
    BERING SEA
    CANALS
    CHESAPEAKE BAY

    CREEKS
    DAMS
    DEAD SEA
    DELAWARE BAY
    ENGLISH CHANNEL
    FLOODS
    FOUNTAINS
    GROUND WATER
    GULF OF MEXICO
    HARBORS
    HOT SPRINGS
    HUDSON BAY
    IRRIGATION
    LAKES
    LEVEES
    MEDITERRANEAN SEA
    OCEANS
    PACIFIC OCEAN
    PONDS
    RESERVOIRS
    RIVERS
    STREAMS
    WATERFALLS
    WAVES
    WELLS
    list under LAKES; RIVERS
Water fountains. See
    FOUNTAINS
WATER HYACINTHS
  Nat Wildlife 22:21 (c,4) D '83
--Made of glass
  Smithsonian 13:102 (c,4) O '82
WATER LILIES
  Natur Hist 91:34 (c,4) Jl '82
  Natur Hist 93:48-9 (c,1) N '84
  Trav/Holiday 166:62 (c,4) Jl '86
WATER OUZELS
--Chicks
  Nat Wildlife 21:50-1 (c,1) Ap '83
WATER POLLUTION
--Acid rain
  Life 7:60-4 (c,1) N '84
--Collecting rain samples to test for
    acid rain (N.Y.)
  Smithsonian 14:26 (c,4) My '83
--Damage caused by acid rain
  Nat Wildlife 21:4-11 (map,c,1) Je
    '83
--Dropping lime on acid rain-polluted
    lake (New York)
  Nat Wildlife 21:10 (c,4) Je '83
--Effect of acid rain on trees (Ver-
    mont)
  Natur Hist 91:10-14 (c,3) N '82
--Pollution sign (California)
  Nat Geog 167:736 (c,4) Je '85
--Stream containing sulfuric acid

WAVES (cont.)
--Pacific coast (Washington)
    Nat Geog 165:644-5 (c,1) My
        '84
WAXWINGS
--Cedar waxwings
    Natur Hist 93:45 (c,4) Ag '84
WAYNE, JOHN
    Smithsonian 13:105 (4) F '83
    Smithsonian 15:112 (4) D '84
--Statue
    Life 7:40-6 (c,1) Jl '84
WEASELS
    Nat Wildlife 21:8 (c,4) D '82
    Nat Wildlife 21:52 (c,1) F '83
--See also
    BADGERS
    FERRETS
    MINKS
WEATHER
--1930 weather control instru-
        ments
    Am Heritage 37:45 (4) Je '86
--Devastation of El Niño
    Nat Geog 165:144-83 (map,c,1)
        F '84
--Historic U.S. weather events
    Am Heritage 37:36-7 (c,1) Je
        '86
--Mediterranean problems
    Nat Geog 162:694-737 (c,1) D
        '82
--Recreation of weather phenomena
        in lab
    Life 5:170-6 (c,1) D '82
--Remote weather station
        (Wyoming)
    Smithsonian 17:48 (c,4) Ag '86
--Scenes of different weather
        conditions
    Am Heritage 37:22-48 (c,1) Je
        '86
--Weather maps tracking pollution
        paths
    Natur Hist 95:64-5 (c,3) Jl '86
--Weather research
    Smithsonian 13:88-97 (c,1) Ap
        '82
--Weather station (Yugoslavia)
    Sports Illus 58:86 (c,4) Mr 14
        '83
--See also
    AURORA BOREALIS
    AVALANCHES
    BAROMETERS
    BLIZZARDS
    CLIMATE

CLOUDS
CYCLONES
DROUGHT
DUST STORMS
FLOODS
FOG
HURRICANES
ICE
LIGHTNING
MONSOONS
RAIN
RAINBOWS
SEASONS
SNOW SCENES
SNOW STORMS
STORMS
TORNADOES
TYPHOONS
WEATHERVANES
WIND
WEATHERVANES
--Late 19th cent. bronze Diana
        weathervane (New York)
    Am Heritage 35:44 (c,3) Ag '84
--Nevis, Leeward Islands
    Trav/Holiday 163:74 (c,4) F '85
WEAVERBIRDS
    Nat Geog 163:368-9 (c,1) Mr '83
--Social weavers
    Natur Hist 91:82 (4) S '82
WEAVING
--Baskets (Haida Indians; Northwest)
    Natur Hist 91:40-7 (c,1) My '82
--Blankets (Nepal)
    Smithsonian 16:134-5 (c,2) N '85
--Carpet (Pakistan)
    Nat Geog 167:783 (c,3) Je '85
--Dyeing wool (Mexico)
    Natur Hist 95:66-71 (c,1) Mr '86
--Japan
    Trav/Holiday 159:82-3 (3) Mr '83
--Leaves (Seychelles)
    Trav/Holiday 162:49 (c,3) N '84
--Making fans from palm leaves
        (Brazil)
    Natur Hist 94:45 (c,4) D '85
--Mats (Western Samoa)
    Nat Geog 168:470 (c,1) O '85
--Mexico
    Trav/Holiday 159:65 (c,4) Mr '83
    Natur Hist 95:70-1 (c,1) Mr '86
--Philippines
    Trav/Holiday 159:35 (c,1) Ja '83
--Silk (China)
    Nat Geog 165:8-9, 31 (c,1) Ja '84
--Silk (Japan)
    Nat Geog 165:44 (c,1) Ja '84

WHALES (cont.)
Ag '83
--1850s whale chart for hunters
Smithsonian 14:174-5 (drawing,4)
Mr '84
--Beached whales (Australia)
Life 8:68-9 (1) Ag '85
--Blue whales
Nat Geog 166:786-9 (c,1) D '84
--Gray
Trav/Holiday 160:20 (drawing,4)
Ag '83
--Humpback
Nat Geog 161:462-77 (c,1) Ap
'82
Nat Wildlife 21:64 (c,2) D '82
Natur Hist 92:44 (c,3) Je '83
Trav/Holiday 160:22 (drawing,4)
Ag '83
Nat Geog 165:cov., 50-2, 88-
93 (c,1) Ja '84
Natur Hist 94:97-9 (c,1) Ja
'85
Nat Wildlife 23:23-7 (c,1) Ap
'85
Natur Hist 94:52-61 (c,1) O
'85
Nat Wildlife 24:54-5 (c,1) Ap
'86
Nat Geog 169:698-9 (c,1) My
'86
Trav/Holiday 166:50 (c,4) Jl '86
--Humpback caught in fishing net
Life 6:60-3 (c,1) O '83
--Humpback skull
Life 6:91 (c,2) D '83
--Right
Natur Hist 92:40-5 (c,1) Ap '83
Trav/Holiday 160:20 (drawing,4)
Ag '83
--Slaughtered pilot whales (Faeroe
Islands)
Life 9:8-9 (c,1) O '86
--Whale smashing boat (19th cent.)
Natur Hist 95:2 (painting,4)
Ag '86
--White whales
Natur Hist 95:40-9 (c,1) Ja '86
--See also
BELUGAS
KILLER WHALES
NARWHALS
SPERM WHALES
WHALING SHIP
Am Heritage 36:6 (painting,c,2)
F '85
--16th cent. Basque galleons

(Newfoundland)
Nat Geog 168:cov., 40-68 (c,1)
Jl '85
--19th cent. (Canada)
Natur Hist 94:72 (4) Ja '85
--Early 19th cent.
Am Heritage 34:50-63 (painting,1)
Ap '83
--Whale smashing boat (19th cent.)
Natur Hist 95:2 (painting,4) Ag
'86
WHARTON, EDITH
Am Heritage 35:91 (painting,c,4)
O '84
WHEAT
Natur Hist 91:26 (woodcut,3) N
'82
WHEAT FIELDS
--1908 (Wyoming)
Am Heritage 36:cov. (2) O '85
--Aerial view (Washington)
Nat Wildlife 24:54-5 (c,1) O '86
--Colorado
Nat Geog 166:188-9 (c,1) Ag '84
--France
Life 7:120-1 (c,1) O '84
--Kansas
Nat Geog 168:352-3 (c,1) S '85
--North Dakota
Life 5:152-3 (1) N '82
--Oregon
Nat Wildlife 24:38-9 (c,1) Ag '86
--Washington
Life 5:122-3 (c,1) O '82
Nat Geog 166:378-9 (c,2) S '84
WHEAT INDUSTRY--HARVESTING
--Mykonos, Greece
Trav/Holiday 165:86 (c,4) Mr '86
--Pennsylvania
Nat Geog 165:508-10 (c,1) Ap '84
--Threshing wheat (Utah)
Am Heritage 36:68 (painting,c,4)
Ag '85
--Washington
Nat Geog 161:804-5 (c,2) Je '82
--West Germany
Nat Geog 161:44 (c,4) Ja '82
WHEAT INDUSTRY--TRANSPORTA-
TION
--Australia
Nat Geog 161:658 (c,1) My '82
WHEELCHAIRS
Ebony 37:70 (2) S '82
Sports Illus 57:45 (c,4) S 6 '82
Nat Geog 163:237 (c,4) F '83
Life 6:122 (c,4) Jl '83
Ebony 38:45 (c,2) S '83

WHEELCHAIRS
Life 7:47-51 (c,2) Je '84
Nat Geog 167:388 (c,4) Mr '85
Life 8:150 (4) N '85
Nat Geog 169:635 (c,4) My '86
Life 9:50-5 (c,1) N '86
--Early 20th cent. (France)
Life 8:54 (c,2) O '85
--Antique wheelchair (Pennsyl-
vania)
Trav/Holiday 165:76 (c,4) My
'86
WHIPPETS (DOGS)
Life 9:251 (c,4) Fall '86
WHISTLER, JAMES McNEILL
--Paintings by him
Smithsonian 15:cov., 57-65
(c,1) Ap '84
--Self-portrait (1850s)
Smithsonian 15:57 (painting,c,2)
Ap '84
--"Venetian Scene" (1880)
Am Heritage 35:38 (paint-
ing,c,4) Je '84
WHISTLES
--17th cent. gold boatswain's
whistle (Spain)
Nat Geog 161:237 (c,3) F '82
--Mayan civilization (Belize)
Nat Geog 162:140 (c,4) Jl '82
--Early 20th cent. professional
whistlers
Am Heritage 33:58-63 (2) Ag
'82
Smithsonian 16:94 (4) F '86
--Whistling competition (Nevada)
Smithsonian 16:90-9 (c,1) F
'86
WHITE, E. B.
Smithsonian 15:179 (4) Ap '84
WHITE-FOOTED MICE
Nat Wildlife 20:6 (c,4) O '82
Natur Hist 95:44-9 (c,1) S '86
--Baby
Nat Wildlife 21:54-5 (c,4) Ap
'83
WHITE HOUSE, WASHINGTON,
D.C.
Life 5:31 (painting,c,4) Ja '82
Nat Geog 163:110-11 (c,1) Ja
'83
Trav/Holiday 161:24 (4) Mr '84
Am Heritage 35:32 (c,4) Je '84
Life 7:125 (2) Je '84
--1931
Am Heritage 34:110 (3) F '83
--Cabinet Room

Life 7:4 (c,4) Ap '84
Life 9:224-5 (1) Fall '86
--Interior
Life 5:148-53 (c,1) Ja '82
--Kitchen supply room (1958)
Life 9:216-17 (c,1) Fall '86
--Oval office
Ebony 37:40 (2) Ap '82
Life 6:42 (c,2) N '83
--Oval Office desk
Am Heritage 33:8 (1) F '82
--Red Room
Life 9:106-7 (c,1) Jl '86
WHITE MOUNTAIN NATIONAL
FOREST, NEW HAMPSHIRE
Nat Geog 162:306-7 (c,1) S '82
--Alpine Garden
Natur Hist 94:22-7 (c,1) Jl '85
WHITE MOUNTAINS, NEW HAMP-
SHIRE
Life 9:40 (c,4) O '86
--Old Man of the Mountain
Nat Geog 162:798 (c,1) D '82
--See also
MOUNT WASHINGTON
WHITE MOUNTAIN NATIONAL
FOREST
WHITE RIVER NATIONAL FOREST,
COLORADO
Nat Geog 162:336-7 (c,1) S '82
WHITMAN, WALT
Smithsonian 13:133 (4) Jl '82
Am Heritage 34:21 (painting,c,4)
O '83
WHITNEY, ELI
--1794 patent for cotton gin
Am Heritage 35:93 (c,2) Ag '84
WHITTIER, JOHN GREENLEAF
Nat Geog 166:13 (painting,c,4)
Jl '84
WHOOPING CRANES
Natur Hist 91:70-2 (c,1) F '82
Nat Wildlife 20:7 (c,2) Ap '82
Nat Wildlife 21:35 (4) D '82
Nat Wildlife 21:33 (c,4) Ap '83
Nat Wildlife 22:31 (4) Ap '84
Nat Wildlife 23:10-11 (c,2) Ap '85
WICHITA, KANSAS
Trav/Holiday 166:62-5 (c,1) Ag
'86
--Office building lobby
Nat Geog 168:372-3 (c,1) S '85
WIDGEONS (DUCKS)
Sports Illus 60:82 (painting,c,4)
Je 18 '84
WIGS
--Judges (Great Britain)

WIGS (cont.)
    Nat Geog 170:735, 749 (c,3)
        D '86
--Wig making (Great Britain)
    Trav/Holiday 166:84 (4) S '86
WILBERFORCE, SAMUEL
    Natur Hist 95:24 (drawing,3)
        Ap '86
WILDEBEESTS
    Nat Geog 162:806-7 (c,1) D '82
    Nat Geog 163:350-1 (c,1) Mr
        '83
    Life 7:16 (c,2) S '84
    Nat Geog 169:560-77 (c,1) My
        '86
    Nat Geog 170:347 (c,3) S '86
WILDER, THORNTON
    Smithsonian 14:190 (4) O '83
WILDLIFE REFUGES
--Blackwater National Wildlife
        Refuge, Maryland
    Nat Wildlife 22:10-11 (c,1) Ap
        '84
--Bob Marshall Wilderness, Mon-
        tana
    Nat Geog 167:664-92 (map,c,1)
        My '85
--Bosque del Apache, New Mexico
    Nat Wildlife 24:46-51 (c,1) F
        '86
--Colusa, California
    Nat Geog 166:564-5 (c,1) N
        '84
--Costa Rica
    Nat Geog 163:48-65 (c,1) Ja '83
--Keoladeo Ghana, India
    Trav/Holiday 158:44 (c,2) O '82
--Klamath Basion, Pacific coast
    Nat Wildlife 21:24-31 (map,c,2)
        D '82
--Pelican Island, Florida
    Nat Geog 162:353 (c,1) S '82
WILKES, CHARLES
    Am Heritage 37:106 (4) O '86
WILKINS, ROY
    Ebony 37:72 (4) Jl '82
    Ebony 39:114 (2) F '84
WILLIAMS, TED
    Smithsonian 15:163 (4) O '84
    Life 9:65 (4) Fall '86
WILLIAMS, TENNESSEE
    Life 7:171 (3) Ja '84
    Life 9:266 (4) Fall '86
--Scenes from "A Streetcar Named
        Desire"
    Life 7:73-6 (c,1) Mr '84

WILLIAMSBURG, VIRGINIA
--Governor's Palace at Christmas
    Am Heritage 38:20 (c,4) D '86
WILLKIE, WENDELL
    Am Heritage 33:22 (4) F '82
WILLOW TREES
    Natur Hist 94:70-1 (c,1) Je '85
--Black willow
    Smithsonian 15:111 (c,1) S '84
WILLS, HELEN
    Sports Illus 57:64 (c,4) S 13 '82
    Sports Illus 63:23 (4) Jl 8 '85
WILMINGTON, DELAWARE
    Nat Geog 164:178-9 (c,2) Ag '83
--Rooney Square
    Trav/Holiday 157:56 (c,2) Je '82
WILSON, EDMUND
    Smithsonian 13:130 (4) Jl '82
WILSON, WOODROW
--Depicted on postage stamp
    Am Heritage 34:53 (4) D '82
--Edith Wilson
    Am Heritage 34:100 (4) Ag '83
--Study in his home (Washington,
        D.C.)
    Trav/Holiday 157:42 (c,2) F '82
WIND
--Diagram of wind shear
    Natur Hist 95:49 (c,2) Mr '86
--See also
        MONSOONS
        STORMS
        TYPHOONS
WINDHOEK, NAMIBIA
    Nat Geog 16:766-7 (c,2) Je '82
WINDMILLS
--19th cent.
    Smithsonian 16:194-6 (drawing,4)
        O '85
--California
    Nat Wildlife 24:32-3 (c,1) Ap '86
--Modern wind generator
    Natur Hist 91:49 (drawing,2) F '82
--Modern windmills used for energy
    Life 6:84-8 (c,1) N '83
--Portugal
    Trav/Holiday 160:53 (c,2) Ag '83
--Spain
    Nat Geog 161:752-3 (c,1) Je '82
    Trav/Holiday 161:73-5 (c,1) Ap
        '84
--Texas
    Life 9:50 (c,4) Ag '86
--Wind turbines (California)
    Smithsonian 13:122-7 (c,1) N '82
WINDOWS
--Art deco style (Miami Beach,

WINDOWS (cont.)
Florida)
Nat Geog 162:206 (c,4) Ag '82
--Man on ledge threatening sui-
cide (Missouri)
Life 7:88 (2) Mr '84
--Medieval wooden window frame
(Novgorod, U.S.S.R.)
Nat Geog 167:302 (c,1) Mr '85
--Window seat (Maine)
Sports Illus 62:76 (c,3) Mr 4
'85
WINDWARD ISLANDS
--St. Lucia
Trav/Holiday 160:26-9 (c,4)
D '83
--St. Vincent
Trav/Holiday 159:47-8 (c,2) F
'83
--See also
GRENADA
WINDWARD ISLANDS--COSTUME
--St. Vincent
Trav/Holiday 159:47-8 (c,2)
F '83
WINE
--California wine labels
Trav/Holiday 159:81 (c,4) Mr
'83
--Champagne labels (France)
Trav/Holiday 158:62-5 (4) S
'82
--Home wine cellar (New York)
Natur Hist 92:59 (c,3) Ja '83
--Pouring champagne over sports
winners
Sports Illus 63:64-5 (c,2) D
23 '85
--Wine bottles
Trav/Holiday 159:78 (c,2) Mr
'83
--Wine cellars (French cave)
Smithsonian 14:54 (c,4) Je '83
--Wine cellar (Hungary)
Nat Geog 163:251 (c,4) F '83
--Wine cellar (Meursault, France)
Nat Geog 170:342 (c,1) S '86
--See also
DRINKING CUSTOMS
WINE INDUSTRY
--Blending port (Portugal)
Nat Geog 166:462 (c,1) O '84
--Chateau Ste. Michelle Winery,
Woodinville, Washington
Trav/Holiday 158:14 (c,4) Jl
'82
Trav/Holiday 164:34-5 (c,2) S

'85
--Crushing grapes by foot (Greece)
Nat Geog 170:208-9 (c,1) Ag '86
--New England
Trav/Holiday 160:48, 71 (c,4) Ag
'83
--Working with cask (France)
Trav/Holiday 165:45 (c,4) Je '86
--See also
GRAPE INDUSTRY
VINEYARDS
WINNIPEG, MANITOBA
Trav/Holiday 157:38 (c,4) My '82
--Skyline during eclipse
Life 9:388-9 (c,1) Fall '86
WINTER
Nat Wildlife 21:48-51 (c,1) F '83
--1982 urban snow scenes
Life 5:107 (3) Mr '82
--Frost on trees (China)
Life 8:152 (c,3) D '85
--Michigan
Nat Wildlife 22:54-5 (c,2) O '84
--Rural scene (Connecticut)
Trav/Holiday 160:12-13 (c,1) D
'83
--See also
SNOW SCENES
WINTER PARK, FLORIDA
--Sinkhole
Nat Geog 162:214-15 (c,1) Ag '82
Smithsonian 13:56 (c,4) Mr '83
WINTERBERRIES
Nat Wildlife 22:6 (c,4) D '83
WIRES
--Telephone switching equipment
Smithsonian 17:66-78 (c,2) N '86
WISCONSIN
--Appleton
Sports Illus 65:32-65 (c,1) Ag 11
'86
--Appleton lifestyles
Sports Illus 65:32-65 (c,1) Ag 11
'86
--Door County
Trav/Holiday 159:57-60 (c,1) My
'83
--Little Rock Lake
Life 7:64 (c,2) N '84
--Monroe
Trav/Holiday 164:62-3 (c,2) O '85
--Southwestern Wisconsin
Trav/Holiday 164:60-3 (c,1) O '85
WITCHCRAFT
--16th cent. French witch trials
Natur Hist 95:11, 15 (2) O '86
--1612 depiction of witch Sabbath

WITCHCRAFT (cont.)
    (France)
      Natur Hist 95:6 (2) O '86
--1692 Salem witch trial
    Am Heritage 35:83 (paint-
      ing,c,2) Ag '84
--18th cent. depiction of witch
    not sinking in water
    Natur Hist 95:8 (2) O '86
--1787 witch-hunt (Pennsylvania)
    Am Heritage 34:6-11 (draw-
      ing,3) Ag '83
WOLF FISH
    Nat Wildlife 24:cov. (c,1) Ag
      '86
WOLVERINES
    Nat Wildlife 21:32-9 (c,1) Ag
      '83
WOLVES
    Life 5:108 (c,4) D '82
    Nat Geog 164:468 (c,4) O '83
    Smithsonian 15:78-87 (c,1) Ja
      '85
    Nat Wildlife 23:54-9 (c,1) F '85
    Nat Wildlife 24:52 (c,1) F '86
    Nat Wildlife 24:62 (c,4) Ap '86
    Natur Hist 95:cov., 6, 10
      (c,1) My '86
    Natur Hist 95:24-8 (2) Ag '86
--Gray
    Natur Hist 95:80 (c,4) Je '86
--Red
    Nat Wildlife 20:5 (c,2) Ap '82
    Nat Wildlife 23:14 (painting,c,4)
      Ap '85
WOMEN
--Female newscasters
    Ebony 37:100-6 (c,1) Je '82
--World Conference on Women
    (Nairobi, Kenya)
    Ebony 40:156-62 (c,3) O '85
--See also
      PREGNANCY
      different occupations
WOMEN IN HISTORY
--20th cent. female Olympic ath-
    letes
    Life 7:38-45 (c,1) Summer '84
--1910 Women's League convention
    (Missouri)
    Am Heritage 35:70-2 (1) Ag
      '84
--1940s women in defense plants
    (U.S.)
    Am Heritage 35:99-103 (4) F
      '84
--Black women writers

    Ebony 40:59-64 (4) N '84
--Depictions of Southern women
    Am Heritage 34:82-91 (c,1) D '82
--U.S. women depicted on postage
    stamps
    Am Heritage 34:59 (c,4) D '82
--See also
      ADAMS, MAUDE
      ALCOTT, LOUISA MAY
      ANDERSON, MARIAN
      ANTHONY, SUSAN B.
      BARTON, CLARA
      BERGMAN, INGRID
      BETHUNE, MARY McLEOD
      BOURKE-WHITE, MARGARET
      BOW, CLARA
      CARSON, RACHEL
      CASSATT, MARY
      CATHER, WILLA
      DAVIS, BETTE
      DIDRIKSON, BABE
      DIETRICH, MARLENE
      DUSE, ELEONORA
      EARHART, AMELIA
      EDDY, MARY BAKER
      FRANK, ANNE
      FRIEDAN, BETTY
      GARBO, GRETA
      GARLAND, JUDY
      GISH, LILLIAN
      GOLDMAN, EMMA
      GRABLE, BETTY
      HARLOW, JEAN
      HAYES, HELEN
      HELLMAN, LILLIAN
      HENIE, SONJA
      HEPBURN, KATHERINE
      HOLIDAY, BILLIE
      HORNE, LENA
      JOSEPHINE
      KELLER, HELEN
      LAZARUS, EMMA
      LOMBARD, CAROLE
      LOW, JULIETTE
      MATA HARI
      McPHERSON, AIMEE SEMPLE
      MEAD, MARGARET
      MEIR, GOLDA
      MONROE, MARILYN
      MOTT, LUCRETIA
      OAKLEY, ANNIE
      PARKER, DOROTHY
      PIAF, EDITH
      PICKFORD, MARY
      PITCHER, MOLLY
      POMPADOUR, MARQUISE DE
      POST, EMILY

WOMEN IN HISTORY (cont.)
        ROGERS, GINGER
        ROOSEVELT, ELEANOR
        RUSSELL, LILLIAN
        SAND, GEORGE
        SMITH, KATE
        STEIN, GERTRUDE
        STEINEM, GLORIA
        STOWE, HARRIET BEECHER
        SWANSON, GLORIA
        TARBELL, IDA M.
        TAYLOR, ELIZABETH
        TEMPLE, SHIRLEY
        THOMPSON, DOROTHY
        TRUTH, SOJOURNER
        TUBMAN, HARRIET
        WASHINGTON, DINAH
        WHARTON, EDITH
        WILLS, HELEN
WOMEN'S LIBERATION MOVEMENT
--Ethiopian parade
    Nat Geog 163:630-1 (c,1) My
        '83
--Pro-ERA sit-in (Illinois)
    Life 6:40-1 (c,1) Ja '83
--See also
        FRIEDAN, BETTY
        STEINEM, GLORIA
WOMEN'S SUFFRAGE MOVEMENT
--Susan B. Anthony trying to
        vote (1872)
    Am Heritage 37:24, 29 (paint-
        ing,c,1) D '85
--See also
        ANTHONY, SUSAN B.
        MOTT, LUCRETIA
WOOD
--Sawing firewood (Vermont)
    Life 5:46 (c,4) F '82
--Stacking firewood (Wisconsin)
    Nat Wildlife 20:23 (4) O '82
--Woodpile (New Mexico)
    Life 6:25 (3) D '83
--See also
        DRIFTWOOD
        LUMBERING
WOOD, GRANT
--"American Gothic" (1930)
    Life 6:57 (painting,c,4) S '83
    Am Heritage 38:29 (paint-
        ing,c,4) D '86
--Paintings by him
    Life 6:57-64 (c,3) S '83
--Parodies of "American Gothic"
    Life 6:58-9 (c,2) S '83
--"Parson Weem's Fable" (1939)
    Smithsonian 12:80 (painting,c,4)

        F '82
--Self-portrait (1932)
    Life 6:63 (painting,c,4) S '83
WOOD CARVING
--Palau
    Nat Geog 170:495 (c,3) O '86
--Togo
    Trav/Holiday 158:35 (c,4) Ag '82
WOOD CARVINGS
--Early 20th cent. carving of baker
    Am Heritage 37:40-1 (c,1) Ag '86
--Tulipwood bowl
    Life 9:85 (c,2) Jl '86
--Turned wood bowls
    Smithsonian 17:156 (c,4) Jl '86
WOOD DUCKS
    Nat Wildlife 20:32-3 (drawing,c,1)
        O '82
    Nat Wildlife 22:21 (c,4) F '84
    Nat Wildlife 22:cov. (c,1) O '84
    Nat Geog 166:581 (c,3) N '84
--Chick
    Nat Wildlife 24:cov. (c,1) Je '86
WOOD PEWEES
    Natur Hist 91:42 (c,4) S '82
Wood rats. See
        PACK RATS
WOOD WORKING
--Alabama shop class
    Ebony 38:116 (3) Ag '83
WOODCHUCKS
    Smithsonian 15:60-9 (c,1) F '85
--Groundhog Day (Punxsutawney,
        Pennsylvania)
    Smithsonian 15:61 (4) F '85
WOODCOCKS
    Nat Wildlife 22:40 (painting,c,4)
        Je '84
    Sports Illus 63:108-22 (paint-
        ing,c,1) O 14 '85
    Sports Illus 64:47 (c,4) Je 30 '86
WOODPECKERS
    Nat Geog 169:294 (c,4) Mr '86
--Downy
    Nat Wildlife 21:43 (drawing,4) Je
        '83
    Nat Wildlife 21:42 (painting,c,2)
        O '83
--Ivory-billed
    Nat Wildlife 22:4 (c,4) Ag '84
    Natur Hist 94:67 (drawing,c,4)
        Ag '85
    Nat Wildlife 24:4 (c,4) Ap '86
    Natur Hist 95:26 (drawing,c,4)
        Jl '86
--Pileated
    Nat Wildlife 22:4-5 (c,1) Ag '84

WORLD WAR II (cont.)
  Life 8:14 (4) Spring '85
--1945 battle at Iwo Jima
  Life 8:12-13 (1) Spring '85
--1945 German surrender cere-
    mony
  Am Heritage 36:66-73 (1) Ap
    '85
--1945 U.S. return to Philippines
  Life 8:168 (3) O '85
  Life 9:240 (3) Fall '86
--1945 V-J Day celebration (New
    York)
  Life 9:116 (4) Jl '86
--Aleutian Islands battles, Alaska
  Nat Geog 164:342-5 (c,1) S
    '83
--Allied air missions over the
    Himalayas
  Am Heritage 37:66-73 (c,1) Ag
    '86
--American camouflage and decep-
    tion activities (France)
  Smithsonian 16;138-47 (paint-
    ing,c,1) Ap '85
--Anti-Nazi propaganda in Latin
    America
  Am Heritage 35:105-9 (c,4) Ap
    '84
--Artifacts from crashed allied
    planes (Netherlands)
  Smithsonian 17:106-15 (c,1) Ap
    '86
--Camouflaged defense plant
    (California)
  Smithsonian 14:154-5 (2) Mr
    '84
--Child driven mad by war (Poland)
  Life 9:96 (1) Fall '86
--Churchill's Cabinet War Rooms
    (Lond, England)
  Trav/Holiday 165:86 (4) Ja '86
--Civilian victims
  Life 8:76-83 (1) Spring '85
--Corregidor
  Nat Geog 170:118-29 (c,1) Jl
    '86
--Depicted on U.S. postage stamps
  Am Heritage 34:57 (paint-
    ing,c,4) D '82
--Escape attempts by Allied POWs
    (Germany)
  Life 6:8-14 (1) Ap '83
--German bunker (Sicily, Italy)
  Life 8:36 (c,3) Mr '85
--German defenses (Normandy)
  Smithsonian 14:152 (4) Mr '84

--Giving plasma to wounded Ameri-
    can soldier (Italy)
  Am Heritage 35:72-3 (1) O '84
--Japanese attacks on U.S. by bal-
    loon
  Am Heritage 33:88-92 (painting,c,1)
    Ap '82
--Japanese caves (Papua New Guinea)
  Nat Geog 162:164 (c,3) Ag '82
--Japanese caves (Saipan)
  Life 8:99 (c,3) Spring '85
--Japanese gun emplacement (Palau)
  Smithsonian 17:55 (c,1) S '86
--Japanese Suicide Cliff, Saipan,
    Mariana Islands
  Nat Geog 170:468 (c,4) O '86
--Jewish deportations from Prague
  Life 7:84, 89 (3) N '84
--K rations for U.S. servicemen
  Life 8:24 (c,4) Spring '85
--MacArthur returning to the
    Philippines (1945)
  Life 9:240 (3) Fall '86
--Paintings by Albert K. Murray
  Am Heritage 33:30-9 (c,1) F '82
--Peleliu ruins, Palau
  Nat Geog 170:496-7 (c,1) O '86
--Philippine World War II memorial
    (Corregidor)
  Nat Geog 170:129 (c,3) Jl '86
--Planned U.S. bat attacks on Japan
  Am Heritage 33:93-5 (painting,c,1)
    Ap '82
--Plans for U.S. invasion of Japan
  Life 8:105-8 (c,1) Spring '85
--Post-war German graffiti (Munich)
  Am Heritage 34:6 (4) D '82
--Punishing Italian Nazi collaborator
    (1945)
  Life 8:81 (4) Spring '85
--Russian front
  Life 8:139-47 (1) Ap '85
  Life 8:48-55 (c,1) Spring '85
--Sinking of the "Indianapolis"
    (1945)
  Am Heritage 33:81-96 (painting,1)
    Ag '82
--U.S. airplanes over the "Nimitz"
  Am Heritage 37:cov., 114 (c,1)
    O '86
--U.S. homefront activities and arti-
    facts
  Life 8:20-4, 85-94 (c,2) Spring
    '85
--U.S. internment camps for Japanese-
    Americans
  Nat Geog 169:520-7 (c,1) Ap '86

WYETH, ANDREW (cont.)
   Smithsonian 15:150-1 (c,1) Mr
   '85
--"The Patriot"
   Life 9:201 (painting,c,4) Fall
   '86
--"Weather Side"
   Trav/Holiday 160:20 (paint-
   ing,4) O '83
WYOMING
--Early 20th cent.
   Am Heritage 36:cov., 34-41
   (1) O '85
--Big Horn Mountains
   Trav/Holiday 158:45-7 (map,c,2)
   Ag '82
--Countryside
   Life 6:88 (c,2) D '83
   Smithsonian 16:64-5 (1) Ag '85
--Diamondville (1903)
   Am Heritage 36:36-7 (1) O '85
   Am Heritage 37:10 (3) F '86
--Jackson Lake
   Nat Geog 170:416-17 (c,1) S
   '86
--Landmarks from 19th cent.
   Oregon Trail
   Nat Geog 170:150-1, 164-6
   (c,1) Ag '86
--Lost Springs
   Life 6:122-8 (c,1) N '83
--Plume Rocks
   Nat Geog 170:150-1 (c,1) Ag
   '86
--Sweetwater River area
   Nat Geog 170:164-5 (c,1) Ag
   '86
--Western area
   Sports Illus 56:74-88 (map,c,1)
   My 17 '82
--Wind River (1870 painting)
   Natur Hist 94:58-9 (c,1) N '85
--See also
      DEVILS TOWER NATIONAL
         MONUMENT
      GRAND TETON NATIONAL
         PARK
      TETON NATIONAL FOREST
      TETON RANGE
      YELLOWSTONE NATIONAL
         PARK
      YELLOWSTONE RIVER

-X-

X-RAYS
   Ebony 37:98 (3) Ja '82

   Ebony 38:36 (4) D '82
   Ebony 38:70 (3) Mr '83
   Life 6:42-3 (c,1) Ap '83
   Life 7:78-81 (c,1) Mr '84
   Ebony 39:52 (3) Mr '84
   Sports Illus 63:41 (c,3) Jl 29 '85
--Brain
   Sports Illus 58:60 (c,4) Ap 11 '83
--Taking X-ray (Illinois)
   Ebony 37:155 (4) O '82
--X-ray equipment
   Life 6:43 (c,4) Ap '83
--X-ray pictures of flowers
   Smithsonian 17:cov., 88-91 (1)
   O '86
   Smithsonian 17:16 (4) D '86
XYLOPHONE PLAYING
   Ebony 41:56 (4) Je '86
XYLOPHONES
--Marimbas (Guatemala)
   Trav/Holiday 166:25 (c,4) D '86

-Y-

YACHTS
   Sports Illus 59:38-9 (c,1) Ag 29
   '83
   Ebony 39:100-4 (c,2) S '84
   Trav/Holiday 165:69 (c,2) Mr '86
--Australia
   Trav/Holiday 166:45 (c,4) Ag '86
--Design for fast yacht (Australia)
   Sports Illus 59:36-7 (diagram,c,3)
   Ag 29 '83
--Yacht races
   Natur Hist 92:cov., 60-74 (c,1)
   My '83
   Sports Illus 59:22-3 (c,1) S 12
   '83
YAKS
   Nat Geog 161:260-1 (c,1) F '82
   Nat Geog 161:718-19 (c,1) Je '82
   Natur Hist 91:48-57 (c,1) S '82
   Smithsonian 13:cov., 50-61 (c,1)
   O '82
   Natur Hist 95:56-65 (c,1) Ja '86
--Performing in circus (Mongolia)
   Nat Geog 167:254 (c,3) F '85
YALE UNIVERSITY, NEW HAVEN,
   CONNECTICUT
--1895 design for Phelps Hall
   Am Heritage 35:70 (c,2) Ap '84
--Branford College
   Smithsonian 15:174 (4) My '84
--Sterling Library fountain
   Am Heritage 37:77 (drawing,c,3)
   Je '86

YAMS (cont.)
  Natur Hist 95:96 (c,4) Mr '86
YAP--COSTUME
  Nat Geog 170:461, 476, 488-91
      (c,1) O '86
YAP--SOCIAL LIFE AND CUSTOMS
--Male dancers
  Nat Geog 170:488-9 (c,1) O '86
YARN
--Dyeing wool (Pakistan)
  Nat Geog 167:782 (c,3) Je '85
YARN SPINNING
--13th cent. B.C. fiber spinning
      (Egypt)
  Nat Geog 162:762 (drawing,4)
      D '82
--19th cent. carding mill (Massa-
      chusetts)
  Am Heritage 33:39 (c,4) Ag
      '82
--Alaska
  Nat Geog 164:360 (c,4) S '83
--Colonial style (North Carolina)
  Trav/Holiday 157:53 (c,4) My
      '82
--India
  Nat Geog 169:238 (c,3) F '86
--Kentucky
  Trav/Holiday 165:61 (c,3) Ja
      '86
--Nepal
  Smithsonian 16:134, 140 (c,3)
      N '85
--Scotland
  Nat Geog 166:62 (c,2) Jl '84
--Spinning cotton (French Guiana
      Indian)
  Nat Geog 163:76 (c,1) Ja '83
--See also
      SPINNING WHEELS
YEATS, WILLIAM BUTLER
  Smithsonian 16:162 (4) My '85
YELLOW JACKETS
  Nat Wildlife 20:7 (c,1) O '82
YELLOWLEGS (BIRDS)
  Nat Wildlife 22:41 (painting,c,4)
      Je '84
YELLOWSTONE NATIONAL PARK,
      WYOMING
--1886 painting
  Natur Hist 94:61 (c,2) N '85
--Early 20th cent.
  Natur Hist 91:16 (4) Je '82
--Hot spring pool
  Nat Geog 162:363 (c,1) S '82
--Old Faithful
  Nat Wildlife 21:6 (c,4) Ap '83

  Trav/Holiday 165:18 (c,4) Ja '86
--Winter scenes
  Nat Wildlife 20:37-9 (c,1) F '82
  Nat Geog 168:162-3 (c,1) Ag '85
YELLOWSTONE RIVER, WYOMING
  Nat Wildlife 24:36-7 (c,1) Ap '86
YELLOWTHROATS (BIRDS)
  Smithsonian 13:169 (c,2) O '82
Yemen. See
      NORTH YEMEN
      SOUTH YEMEN
YOGA
  Ebony 37:82 (4) F '82
  Ebony 37:32 (c,4) My '82
  Life 9:66 (c,2) My '86
--Headstand
  Life 5:106 (c,4) Jl '82
--India's Nehru doing headstand
      (1948)
  Life 8:10 (2) My '85
--Lotus position (Malaysia)
  Trav/Holiday 165:67 (c,4) Ap '86
--Plow position
  Sports Illus 58:69 (c,4) F 14 '83
YOHO NATIONAL PARK, BRITISH
      COLUMBIA
--Mt. Stephen
  Nat Geog 162:296 (c,2) S '82
YOKOHAMA, JAPAN
--1945 ruins of city
  Am Heritage 36:31 (4) Ag '85
YORKSHIRE TERRIERS
  Sports Illus 57:214 (c,2) S 1 '82
  Sports Illus 58:44 (c,4) My 9 '83
YOSEMITE FALLS, YOSEMITE NA-
      TIONAL PARK, CALIFORNIA
  Sports Illus 64:86 (c,2) Je 2 '86
YOSEMITE NATIONAL PARK,
      CALIFORNIA
  Trav/Holiday 160:37 (c,1) Ag '83
  Natur Hist 93:72-3 (c,1) Mr '84
  Life 7:52-3 (c,1) S '84
  Nat Wildlife 22:44-5 (1) O '84
  Nat Geog 167:52-79 (map,c,1) Ja
      '85
--1903
  Nat Geog 16:345 (2) S '82
--Rock climbing
  Sports Illus 64:84-90, 98 (c,1)
      Je 2 '86
--See also
      YOSEMITE FALLS
YOUNG, BRIGHAM
--His telescope and tool chest
  Nat Geog 170:163 (c,2) Ag '86
--Statue (Provo, Utah)
  Sports Illus 59:65 (c,4) N 14 '83

YOUTH
--1916 gang (Massachusetts)
  Natur Hist 94:88 (4) O '85
--1948 Harlem gang leader, New
  York
  Life 9:256 (4) Fall '86
--1954 teenage dance party
  (Colorado)
  Life 9:291 (1) Fall '86
--1961 "Happening" (Florida)
  Am Heritage 37:103 (4) Ap '86
--1969 Woodstock concert, New
  York
  Life 9:344-5 (c,1) Fall '86
--1986 youth fads
  Life 9:46-7 (drawing,c,1)
  Mr '86
--Cruising in car (California)
  Nat Geog 164:2-3 (c,1) Jl '83
--High school students on bus
  (Minnesota)
  Sports Illus 63:92 (c,3) N 4
  '85
--Lifestyle of affluent teenage
  girl (Texas)
  Life 9:38-42 (c,1) Mr '86
--Lifestyle of inner-city teenage
  boy (Detroit, Michigan)
  Life 9:51-6 (1) Mr '86
--Motorcycle gang (Japan)
  Nat Geog 170:628-9 (c,1) N
  '86
--Motorcycle gang (Texas)
  Nat Geog 166:296-7 (c,1) S '84
--Motorcycle gang (West Germany)
  Life 5:24-5 (c,1) Mr '82
--Punk rockers (Great Britain)
  Nat Geog 163:781 (c,4) Je '83
--Rock concert audience (Hun-
  gary)
  Nat Geog 163:232-3 (c,1) F '83
--Street life of runaway teens
  (Washington)
  Life 6:34-42 (1) Jl '83
--Teenager's lifestyle (Harlem,
  New York)
  Ebony 38:68-76 (2) Ag '83
--Teenagers' Saturday night activ-
  ities
  Life 9:3, 28-35 (c,1) Mr '86
--Unemployed youths (Scotland)
  Nat Geog 166:56-7 (c,1) Jl '84
--Youth gang rockers (Japan)
  Natur Hist 94:48-57, 70 (c,1)
  Ag '85
--Youth gang violence (Los Ange-
  les, California)

Life 5:54-8 (c,1) My '82
--See also
  BOY SCOUTS
  CHILDREN
  COLLEGE LIFE
  GIRL SCOUTS
YUGOSLAVIA
  Sports Illus 59:2-3, 86-106
  (map,c,1) O 24 '83
--Dubrovnik
  Trav/Holiday 159:42-7 (c,1) Je
  '83
  Sports Illus 59:87, 100 (c,1) O
  24 '83
  Trav/Holiday 161:118 (4) Mr '84
  Trav/Holiday 164:42 (c,4) S '85
--See also
  SARAJEVO
  TITO, MARSHAL
YUGOSLAVIA--COSTUME
  Trav/Holiday 159:cov., 43, 47
  (c,1) Je '83
  Sports Illus 59:86-100 (c,1) O 24
  '83
--Peasant family
  Trav/Holiday 164:42 (c,2) S '85
--Traditional
  Trav/Holiday 159:58 (4) Mr '83
YUKON, CANADA
  Trav/Holiday 157:84, 87 (c,2)
  Ap '82
  Trav/Holiday 164:59-63 (c,1) Ag
  '85
--Alsek River
  Nat Geog 168:630-1 (c,1) N '85
--Lowell Glacier
  Nat Geog 168:630-1, 636-7 (c,1)
  N '85
--See also
  KLUANE NATIONAL PARK
  RESERVE
  ST. ELIAS RANGE
YURTS
--China
  Nat Geog 165:296-7 (c,3) Mr '84
--Gers (Mongolia)
  Nat Geog 167:258-9, 262-5 (c,1)
  F '85

-Z-

ZAIRE
--Rain forests
  Nat Geog 163:25, 39, 46-7 (c,1)
  Ja '83
--Ruwenzori Range